KU-635-599

JACK SHENKER

The Egyptians

A Radical Story

ALLEN LANE
an imprint of
PENGUIN BOOKS

ALLEN LANE

UK | USA | Canada | Ireland | Australia
India | New Zealand | South Africa

Allen Lane is part of the Penguin Random House group of companies
whose addresses can be found at global.penguinrandomhouse.com

First published 2016
001

Copyright © Jack Shenker, 2016

The moral right of the author has been asserted

Set in 10.5/14 pt Sabon LT Std
Typeset by Jouve (UK), Milton Keynes
Printed in Great Britain by Clays Ltd, St Ives plc

A CIP catalogue record for this book is available from the British Library

ISBN: 978-1-846-14632-9

www.greenpenguin.co.uk

MIX
Paper from
responsible sources
FSC® C018179

Penguin Random House is committed to a
sustainable future for our business, our readers
and our planet. This book is made from Forest
Stewardship Council® certified paper.

THE EGYPTIANS

This uncorrected advance proof is made available on a confidential basis and may not be sold or otherwise circulated. The appearance and contents of this proof may not resemble the finished book and under no circumstances may it or any of its contents be reproduced before publication of the finished book without the publisher's consent.

Dedicated to the Egyptians of Revolution Country
and for Mary

هما مين و إ حنا مين ؟
'Who are they and who are we?'
Ahmed Fouad Negm, Egyptian poet 1929–2013

Contents

Maps

List of Maps

List of Maps

List of Maps

Note on Transliteration

The transliteration of Arabic words into English is notoriously tricky; any standardized system must inevitably sacrifice at least one of accuracy, simplicity or complete consistency. In this book, Arabic words have been transliterated according to a system that aims to render them familiar to Arabic speakers and pronounceable for non-Arabic readers.

Nearly all Arabic vocabulary is transliterated from Egyptian Colloquial Arabic, rather than the more formal Modern Standard Arabic. Where an Arabic word is already commonly known in English, the familiar English spelling has been used even when it conflicts with the transliteration system. The same applies when a person or institution has already adopted a particular English spelling of their own name.

Prologue: the people want . . .

The video is shot from a balcony, and its style is familiar. A shaky, handheld camera, tracking the action back and forth. Figures below, mustering on some unspecified stretch of tarmac and urging one another forward. The chants of the crowd, and eventually their screams. '*El-sha'ab, yureed, isqat el-musheer! El-sha'ab, yureed, isqat el-musheer*,' they bellow, again and again. '*El-sha'ab, yureed, isqat el-musheer! El-sha'ab, yureed, isqat el-musheer!*'

The rhythm of the words is like a mounting drumbeat, steeling the children – and they are children, some almost in their early teens but most no more than nine or ten years old – for the battle ahead. In Arabic, *el-sha'ab, yureed, isqat* . . . means 'The people want the downfall of . . .' and *el-musheer* is 'the field marshal'. Because this is Egypt in early 2012, a year on from the toppling of former president Hosni Mubarak, the field marshal being referred to must be General Mohamed Hussein Tantawi, the head of a junta under whose watch more than a hundred revolutionary demonstrators have been killed and thousands more have been dragged before military tribunals. Calling for his downfall is a brave and dangerous thing to do. Yet still, the children chant. And now they have gathered strength in numbers, and are staring defiantly at something, or someone, which stands unseen beyond the left-hand edge of the screen. There are more and more children in the shot, clapping and chanting and feeding off each other's energy, and suddenly – imperceptibly, without a signal from any leader – the air distornts a little, something intangible cracks, and for a moment the whole world seems to tip on its head and bevel with possibility. You can feel this shift in the blurry pixels, you can feel it surging through the children like a rustle of volts through the bones, you can feel something ineffable is building and building . . . and now there, it's started! The march begins and they are advancing, their eyes trained on the prize; off to the left towards that invisible adversary, arms in the air and chests puffed forward, and the jittery camera is following their progress, and that off-screen enemy is silent, and watching, and waiting.

And then there is a noise.

And now there is choking and spluttering and shouts and confusion and everyone begins to turn and run back the way they came. Everyone, that is, but the smattering of children who have dropped to the floor in a heap of clothes and flesh, everyone but the children now lying completely still amid the madness.

And yet, despite all this terror, the fleeing survivors quickly rally themselves and gather in a group once more. The injured and lifeless are retrieved, that melodic drumbeat thuds again in the roofs of the children's mouths, and within moments the crowd has returned to its starting position, unbowed and eyes blazing off to the left, everyone readying themselves for another reckless push into the unknown. *'El-sha'ab, yureed, isqat el-musheer!'* they roar. *'El-sha'ab, yureed, isqat el-musheer!'*

This is Zawyet el-Dahshour school, twenty miles south of Cairo city centre, and what you're watching on screen is playtime.

Egypt's revolution has been misunderstood, and a great deal of that misunderstanding has been deliberate. A process that began on 25 January 2011, and which will continue yet for many more years to come, has been framed deceptively by elites both within Egypt's borders and beyond. The aim of this deception has been to sanitize the revolution and divest it of its radical potential. Over the past half-decade the Arab World's most populous nation has been engulfed by unprecedented turmoil, the result of millions of ordinary people choosing to reject the political and economic status quo and trying instead to build better alternatives. Their struggle has pitted them against a violent and exclusionary state, an entity not confined within neat territorial limits but rather something enmeshed with global capital and thus linked inextricably to systems of governance that structure all our lives. By distorting the lens through which most of us view and interpret that struggle, those who benefit most from the way things are hope to prevent us from thinking too seriously about the way things could be.

Since the revolution started – and with it, the counter-revolution – the media presentation of Egypt's headline moments has been laden with insta-emotion: awe at an uprising against one of the Middle East's longest-reigning and best-armed dictators, joy at its success, confusion in its aftermath, sadness that the young protesters were seemingly defeated in the end, that elections were overturned, and that the autocrats rose to the summit once again. At times, far from being a political inspiration, events in Egypt have felt like a textbook example of why mass resistance is doomed to failure; a study in how 'business as usual' always wins out in the end. But this book argues that such a narrative is too simplistic, and profoundly misleading. The revolution has never been just about Mubarak, or his successors, or elections. It is not merely a civil war between Islamists and secularists, nor a fight between oriental backwardness and Western liberal modernity, nor an 'event' that can be fixed and constrained in place or time. In reality, the revolution is about marginalized citizens muscling their way on to the political stage and practising collective sovereignty over domains that were previously closed to them. The national presidency is one such domain, but there are many others: factories, fields and urban streets, the mineral resources that lie under the desert sand and beneath the seabed, the houses people live in, the food they eat and the water they drink.

Over the previous few decades, all of these domains had been sealed off and commodified for the purpose of private gain. This act of enclosure was made possible not only by the authoritarian nature of the Egyptian state, but also by an economic orthodoxy that today spans the planet – from Chicago to London, Cairo to Cape Town, and virtually everywhere in between. The outcomes of that economic orthodoxy are neither regrettable aberrations nor dastardly conspiracies: they are a condition of this particular system of thought. In our neoliberal age, we are told that politics is something separate from economics, that the management and distribution of goods and services are best supervised by the market, and that governments should get out of the way. But as the progress of Egypt's revolution makes clear, neoliberal capitalism is not antithetical to the state, in Egypt or anywhere else. It is at the very core of it. Despite many setbacks, Egyptian revolutionaries have exposed and resisted deep-rooted, international patterns of privileged accumulation and mass dispossession, and the brutal force needed to sustain them; they have demanded meaningful democratic power over the things which affect their lives. Put simply, they have battled to replace a 'me first' system with an 'all of us' system. In doing so, they have connected the dots of political and economic injustice – at a time in which rampant inequality is compelling many others, in the global north and the global south, to try and do the same. Therein lies the revolution's threat, and its living, giddying possibilities.

This book is the story of those Egyptians. It explores the revolution not through the eyes of political leaders such as Mubarak, Field Marshal Tantawi, the Muslim Brotherhood's short-lived president Mohamed Morsi or the military general who overthrew him, Abdelfattah el-Sisi – elites and counter-elites jockeying for supremacy amid the chaos – but rather through the eyes of the people who are fighting to dismantle the constellation of power which enables such supremacy in the first place. Its characters are women and men who look very different from many of the protesters who appeared in front of international television cameras during the original anti-Mubarak uprising, women and men who for the most part live a long way from Tahrir Square. They are the farmers revolting against the privatization of their fields, the DJs creating illicit new music in backstreet garages, the ceramics plant workers kidnapping their boss and seizing control of their factory, the Bedouins storming a government nuclear site to reclaim stolen land, the schoolchildren who spend their lunch breaks playing games of revolution in Zawyet el-Dahshour. Their circumstances vary, but the revolution has enabled all of them to mobilize in some way against the specific conjunction of political arrangements and money through which the Egyptian state has long exercised its authority. Likewise, the rise in protest movements around the world in recent years can be attributed to many diverse sources; the common thread that runs through nearly all of them, though, is a relationship between the expansion of financial markets and a diminishment of the autonomy afforded to citizens as individuals and as collectives – be they living under dictatorships or long-established formal democracies. The attempt to break this relationship and democratize our societies beyond their electoral systems is the principal battle of our generation, and revolutionary Egyptians are on the frontline. Contained within their struggles, and the counter-revolutionary fight-back ranged against them, are hopes and warnings for us all.

Zawyet el-Dahshour lies on the edge of the Sahara just south of the Memphis ruins – all that remains of one of Pharaonic Egypt's most important capitals – and across the Nile from Helwan. As in many corners of Egypt, the physical environment here is scored with competing visions of power and development. Today's playground clashes between the area's youngest residents and imaginary security forces reveal much about the dynamics of Egypt's revolutionary era, but to understand where they came from we must first cross some other faultlines, and journey back into Helwan's history. In the late nineteenth century this region's sulphurous springs and luxury bathing houses were a magnet for Cairo's well-heeled gentry. By the 1960s though, under the presidency of Gamal Abdel Nasser, the modern capital's spa retreat had become a smokestack suburb; Helwan was transformed into a hive of industrial activity, and the chimneys of its iron and steel mills have belched black smoke into the sky ever since. Nasser saw Helwan as the engine of a new, pos colonial nation in command of its own destiny; from within the foundries and the furnaces, Egypt's long history of imperial conquest and feudal oppression would be overcome at last. The Nasserite state succeeded in delivering material security to much of its population, but it was based on a strictly paternal model of authority: the highest ranks of the military would rule in the interests of everybody, and everybody would be grateful for their munificence. There was no room for popular participation, active citizenship or dissent. Over the following decades, as Nasser passed away and others succeeded him, that fundamental exclusion of most Egyptians from the political arena remained in place. One could plead for concessions, as a child might petition a father, but never intrude on to the state's private fiefdoms, never exist as an equal.

By the time Hosni Mubarak took office, in the early 1980s, the

Egyptian state was geared less towards delivering material security to its population and concerned more with carving up social assets for the financial benefit of its custodians. In 1991, the Mubarak regime signed Egypt up to a structural adjustment programme administered by international financial institutions tasked with enforcing the free market mantra – 'stabilize, privatize, liberalize' – wherever they wielded influence. Throughout the 1990s and 2000s, Egypt's government sold off hundreds of public institutions, usually at below-market prices, to private investment consortiums that were often partnered with cabinet ministers or close Mubarak allies; social safety nets were scaled back, workers' rights curtailed, and ordinary living standards decimated. One of the many collectively held resources affected was the mammoth Helwan Cement Company, founded in 1929 by royal decree and located on the fringes of Helwan's town centre. In 2001 it was part-purchased by a Swiss management and consultancy venture that was later taken over by the region's largest private equity firm, before being bought out by the French subsidiary of an Italian multinational, which continues to run the plant today.[1] The new owners took advantage of Egypt's reformed labour laws, pushed through under pressure from the International Monetary Fund (IMF) and World Bank, which enabled bosses to place workers on temporary contracts with virtually no benefits or protections – contracts that could be indefinitely renewed.[2] In 2007 nearly a hundred workers who had been employed continuously for more than five years on such temporary contracts were sacked without notice; their request to speak to the company's directors was denied, and they were locked outside of the factory gates. In protest, several went on hunger strike.[3] A local labour leader said the decision would 'deprive dozens of families of their source of living'. That year Helwan Cement's parent company, headquartered 1,600 miles away in Bergamo, made a net profit of €613 million.[4]

The neoliberal restructuring of Egypt involved a mass transfer of wealth from the poor and middle classes to the rich, and impoverished vast swathes of its citizenry. But it was justified with terms like 'progress', 'innovation' and 'efficiency'. Egyptians were told that the complex financial instruments that now dictated economic production would promote growth, and be managed responsibly by experts who understood the language of money far better than ordinary citizens. In many ways, an aggressive embrace of market fundamentalism dovetailed neatly with the philosophy of the Egyptian state; both were predicated on the notion of governance being left to authorities that existed beyond the realm of popular oversight, technocrats and elders for whom democracy did not apply but who could be trusted to rule in the interests of the greater good. In his book *How to Speak Money*, John Lanchester compares the priesthoods of ancient Egypt with the supervisors of our contemporary financial system: both, he claims, have been adept at making self-interested calculations in private and then using elaborate ritual and language to bamboozle and obscure the reality of their operations in public.[5] Historically, the priests and the ruling class they served drew power from their ability to predict the rise and fall of the Nile's seasonal floods, on which all life depended. A whole series of myths and symbols was constructed to shroud this process in secrecy; the truth was that the priests had installed Nilometers – devices which provided measurements of the river level – in hidden chambers of the temples, to which only they and the monarchs had access, and the accumulated data provided by those Nilometers made predictions relatively easy. When General Amr Ibn 'As conquered Egypt for the Arabs in AD 641, one of his first acts was to build a Nilometer at Helwan.* The military rulers who followed him, as well as the global financiers who eventually partnered with them and helped construct a system in which the Helwan Cement Company could be diced, spliced and passed around a bewildering array of multinational investment vehicles while its workers lost their jobs, have been relying on metaphorical Nilometers ever since. In Egypt, as elsewhere under neoliberalism, those already at the commanding heights of capital and influence tend to win at their own games.

There was another reason too that structural adjustment intersected smoothly with the exclusionary model of the Egyptian state. The latter required a far-reaching security apparatus to protect the military's reserved bastions of control from being trespassed by

---

* The Helwan Nilometer fell into disrepair in the eighth century; a new one was built downstream at Roda Island, where it remains today.

outsiders, and to discipline anyone who overstepped the mark. Egypt's government spends more on its ministry of interior, the main element of its policing system, than on health and education combined.*⁶ As economic reforms fuelled disentitlement and poverty among the Egyptian population, that security apparatus was vital in facilitating the opening up of new terrains upon which the wealthy could speculate and profit, and in repressing opposition from below. In 2003, for example, a powerful businessman in Helwan attempted to evict a woman named Zeinab – a local street vendor who sold vegetables outside the Helwan metro station – from her apartment. When Zeinab and her family stood firm and refused to move, the businessman called on the services of the local police station, where a young and ambitious intelligence officer named Mohamed al-Sharkawy was based. Zeinab later met with el-Nadim, an organization which provides support for victims of police abuse, and made a series of claims. 'On the night of mid-Shaaban [an Islamic religious festival] we were busy making preparations for a wedding,' she explained. 'After midnight the house was surrounded by more than forty armed men, who tried to break into our apartment.' According to Zeinab, the family was herded into minibuses like sheep and taken to Helwan police station, where informants were made to urinate in front of them on the floor and a whip was used to prevent Zeinab from looking away.

> I had three sleepless days and nights. Twice or three times a day they would strip me naked. Mohamed al-Sharkawy said to me, 'You are only good enough for*******and I'm specialized in*******.' I pleaded with them: 'Kill me, remove my nails, torture me the way you wish, but don't strip me of my *gallabeya* [clothing]. Even my husband has never seen me fully naked.' He tied my legs with a thick rope at the ankles and turned me upside down and whipped my soles. In another torture session they stripped me naked again and al-Sharkawy made one of his men lie on top of me. I lost consciousness. They stripped me several times and lay on top of me.

* By comparison, in the UK in 2012 the budget for the Home Office was £10.1 billion, of which £5.1 billion was for policing; the education and health budgets were £56.27 billion and £106.66 billion respectively.

Al-Sharkawy tole me: 'I'm going to file a case of prostitution against you. I'll prove I picked you up from a place of ill repute.' And he threatened he would send me down to the prisoners to rape me. He grabbed my breasts and my private parts with his hands. I was naked, while my brother was hanging upside down and his wife lay there naked with a man on top of her. I was dying. And I was pulling at my body, at my hair, and wanted to die . . .

Eleven members of the family have been tortured and scandalized. We can't forgo our rights: reconciliation and compensation are out of the question. It's either they die or we die.[7]

After a long campaign by human rights activists, Mohamed al-Sharkawy – who was accused of multiple atrocities against Egyptian citizens – was finally brought before a court in 2005. He was found innocent of all charges. In Mubarak's Egypt, there were thousands of Mohamed al-Sharkawys, and too many Zeinabs to count. Many of el-Sharkawy's security service colleagues had packed out the courthouse for his trial; before the verdict had even been announced, they were already handing out sweets among themselves.

The Egyptian state that Nasser claimed would offer an escape from feudal violence and imperialism had, by Mubarak's era, become a transmission line for neo-colonial appropriation and brutality. International power-brokers queued up to applaud the transformation. In the run-up to revolution, the IMF hailed Egypt's economic policies as 'prudent', 'impressive' and 'bold', and the World Bank labelled the country its 'top Middle East reformer' three years in a row.[8] The United States government, which made Egypt a key partner in its 'War on Terror' and used the country as a central base in the CIA's extraordinary rendition programme, transferred more annual aid to the Mubarak regime than to any other nation on earth bar Israel. 'I really consider President and Mrs Mubarak to be friends of my family,' said then Secretary of State Hilary Clinton in 2009. A few months later Barack Obama described Mubarak as 'a leader and a counsellor and a friend to the United States', and the American ambassador in Cairo, Margaret Scobey, concluded that Egyptian democracy was 'going well'.[9] The following year, a young man was beaten to death by police officers outside an internet café in broad daylight, one of several high-profile incidents of state torture, and Mubarak's ruling National Democratic Party awarded itself 96 per cent of the vote in the first round of parliamentary elections.[10]

But in Helwan, as in every other part of Egypt, Egyptians fought back. People like Zeinab, the vegetable vendor, risked everything to share their stories and identify their tormentors. Communities deprived of basic services because of corruption and marketization came together to cut off major roads and hold protests. At the colossal iron and steel works that dominate the Helwan skyline, strike after strike brought citizens into direct confrontation with the state. 'Seventeen thousand of us had laid down tools, and most were holed up inside the plant,' remembers Kamal Abbas, the leader of a famous 1989 labour stoppage who was later imprisoned for his agitation and went on to found one of the country's main trade union organizations.[11] 'When the central security forces arrived, we knew they didn't just want to break the strike but also send a message. First came the tear gas, then the rubber bullets and then the live ammunition. But the strike held and we won our demands. We helped show people that an alternative was possible.' When the revolution erupted, it built on this proud and stubborn heritage of resistance. Through their battles with the existing state, some Egyptians began to imagine a different one altogether.

The taxi was purple. Amid an ocean of identikit black and white cabs crawling along the roads around Helwan station, this one stood out like an evolutionary accident – a rich violet emulsion from roof to bumper, complete with interior blue trim and metallic footmats. The driver, a young man in a brown hoodie with a Cleopatra cigarette drooping from his lips, stared languorously at us through the window as we explained our request, then absent-mindedly stroked a Spongebob Squarepants figurine dangling from the rear-view mirror. 'Zawyet el-Dahshour is across the bridge and there's a lot of traffic,' he shrugged, jerking his thumb towards the road and tracing an arc with his right hand that seemed to encompass most of the known universe. He lapsed back into a contemplative silence, as if the weight of all the traffic on earth was bearing down upon his soul – a common existential crisis in Egypt – before eventually breaking into a

smile and lifting his eyes to meet ours. 'Traffic everywhere,' he
grunted once more, 'still, we'll give it a try though.' My colleague
Ghamrawi and I climbed in gratefully. 'Why did you paint the taxi
purple?' ventured Ghamrawi, as we began threading our way through
Helwan's backstreets towards the Nile. The driver threw a contemptuous look back in his direction. 'It's the revolution,' came the reply.
'Why not?'

What defines a revolution – where it can be located on a calendar
and a map, what it includes, who speaks for it, the things it seeks to
change – is never a neutral question. On 25 January 2011, I marched
alongside a group of anti-Mubarak protesters down the corniche in
central Cairo, and felt that weird distortion of the air as a line of
armed *amn el-markazi* ('central security forces') fanned across the
road with their shields up, blocking the path ahead. Prior to that day
I had attended countless demonstrations consisting of a few dozen
Egyptians shunted to some inconspicuous corner of the street, a tight
bristle of political energy marooned in an ocean of black-clad troops.
The deployment of the police across the road in front of us was a signal that the next section of this script was due to commence; we
would come to a stop, engage in some minor scuffling, and then be
herded into a harmless protest pen so that the capital could get on
with its day. But on this occasion, with reports of mass unrest spreading throughout the city, something was different. Nobody among the
marchers slowed, nobody broke ranks, and instead they just kept on
going, right towards those shields, chanting and glaring mutinously
into the eyes of those that held them – who glanced uneasily around
at one another and wondered nervously how to respond. In the end,
the troops simply gave way. And as we pushed past them and onto the
empty street behind, several protesters broke into a run – or more
accurately a skip, a dance, a hodgepodge of jumps and hops – and
many began whooping and hollering and even kissing the ground.

Doubtless more important things were happening elsewhere at that
moment, beyond that tiny carpet of liberated asphalt. Certainly episodes of much greater drama would unfold afterwards, both later
that evening, as security forces broke the occupation of Tahrir with
volleys of tear gas, and three days on, when more than a hundred
police stations were burnt to a cinder and Egypt's people finally

forced Mubarak's security forces to flee into the night. But for me, that single moment in time – when those around me spontaneously decided to break through the police line and rewrite a moth-eaten playbook from the bottom up, that nano-second when the globe spun dizzyingly, a street was reclaimed and everything in the old world tumbled forward into infinite opportunity – that was revolution, distilled to its purest form. It felt like a tiresome step dance had just gone freestyle as the performers reimagined their collective horizons and careened wildly into a space they had always been told was not for them. That newfound sense of agency, of an ability to shape things around you in ways you never knew existed – that gave me my definition of revolution: not a time-bound occurrence, nor a shuffle of rules and faces up top, but rather a state of mind. It felt as if nothing could be the same again.

Egypt's revolution has pitted citizens in that same state of mind – people who are no longer willing to let self-appointed patriarchs make decisions on their behalf, wherever those patriarchs may be – against those who wish to preserve the existing model of authority, and thus the existing structure of the state. There are Egyptian men and women of every age, religious persuasion and social background on both sides of this divide. It is an unresolved struggle between the old ways and the new, and it is playing out in the form of millions of skirmishes in millions of different arenas, from family dining tables to office corridors, village councils to city squares, right across the country. Some of these skirmishes have already come to an end, with victories and losses on both sides. Some are still ongoing, and many more are yet to come.

Of course these two camps have never been static, and nor are the borders between them neatly drawn. Not all Egyptians who have participated in the revolution would describe themselves as adversaries of the paternalistic state, even though many of their demands – social justice, an end to corruption, the elimination of state violence – cannot be delivered by the state as it currently exists. Among those who joined the uprising against Hosni Mubarak were citizens angry that the state was no longer carrying out its paternal duties effectively enough, and defenders of the old ways have proved to be skilled at harnessing revolutionary rhetoric to present a strong, reactionary regime as the fulfilment of revolutionary aspirations, winning many over in the process. The trajectory of Egypt's past half-decade has been complicated, bringing many rival political actors to the fore who have tried to exploit the country's unrest to serve their own interests; amid the fluidity of street mobilizations and elite machinations, some Egyptians have found themselves undermining state authority one minute and defending it the next. But although the specific moment of political change that accompanied the downfall of Mubarak in 2011 has since been subdued, this book makes the case that a deeper chasm – one marked by fundamentally incompatible notions of power and sovereignty – still persists. The privileged have succeeded in winning short-term popular support for their counter-revolutionary project, but they cannot resolve this elemental contradiction. For that reason, in an effort to protect themselves, they have done everything they can to render it invisible.

Presenting the revolution predominantly as a tug of war between Islamists – and more particularly the Muslim Brotherhood – on the one hand, and enlightened, secular forces on the other, as President Sisi and his international supporters, such as former British prime minister Tony Blair, have done, is one way of doing exactly that. By bifurcating the future into a false choice between military authoritarianism and religious extremism, and by warning that terrorism and chaos will triumph unless the right option is selected, elites hope to shut down any space for alternatives; instead of fighting the state and unravelling its many cross-border mechanisms of political and economic exclusion, it obliges Egyptians to embrace both the ruling class and their own subordinate role as dependents. The same is true of another, related misconception: that Egypt's revolution is a quest for liberal modernity, procedural democracy, free markets and individual rights. Rather than imagining new forms of sovereignty over social resources and new ideas for making states work in the interest of everybody, the revolution becomes a struggle to push Egypt a little bit further along its existing route of travel – at the end of which lie the model institutions of the West. This keeps the focus of the revolution local; rather than challenge modes of injustice that operate worldwide, it affirms those modes and reduces revolutionaries to the status of aspirational consumers seeking only to upgrade their lot.

Under this reading of the revolution, Egyptians will ultimately get to congregate once every few years in order to cast ballots for a figurehead, before traipsing dutifully back to the political hinterlands; after some cosmetic changes to the state's perimeter fences, those inside it will be able to continue as before. The reality is that post-Mubarak Egypt has staged election after election after election, a process that has delivered less and less meaningful democracy.

Outside of Egypt too, including in many august procedural democracies, citizens living in states structured by neoliberal doctrine are wondering how strong the connection is between regular elections and real popular political agency; the Egyptian revolution has helped to force this vital question open. Reorientating its faultlines in a more harmless direction is another way of imposing political choicelessness on the Egyptian people, and of shielding the deeper workings of the state from broader scrutiny. Tony Blair, a dependable friend of autocracy in Egypt, has particularly relished entwining both the 'religious war' prism and the 'Western modernity' prism to try to stamp out the revolution's radicalism:

> [U]nderneath the turmoil and revolution of the past years is one very clear and unambiguous struggle: between those with a modern view of the Middle East, one of pluralistic societies and open economies, where the attitudes and patterns of globalisation are embraced; and, on the other side, those who want to impose an ideology born out of a belief that there is one proper religion and one proper view of it, and that this view should, exclusively, determine the nature of society and the political economy.

[W]herever you look – from Iraq to Libya to Egypt to Yemen to Lebanon to Syria and then further afield to Iran, Pakistan and Afghanistan – this is the essential battle . . . [T]here is something frankly odd about the reluctance to accept what is so utterly plain: that they have in common a struggle around the issue of the rightful place of religion, and in particular Islam, in politics.[12]

Blair's narrative, like those – commonly found in mainstream media coverage of Egypt – that depict the revolution as having come 'full circle'[13] and now being 'dead'[14], 'failed'[15] and 'officially over',[16] as if it were a computer game character that reached the final boss level before being dumped back to the start again, lies at the heart of Egypt's most important conflict today. It is a conflict over how the revolution is framed and over the ownership of its historical memory, and it is very far from settled. Part of the uncertainty comes from the fact that Egyptian revolutionaries' own visions of change have not, for the most part, involved the capturing or replication of state power. Unlike in many other notable revolutions, Egypt's corridors of government have not been stormed, nor have charismatic leadership figures or mass political parties been established in parallel to the existing hierarchy of regime control. In common with many radical social movements around the world in recent years, from the Occupy movement to mass mobilizations in Turkey, Chile and Brazil, the revolution's targets have been more diffuse and its organization more horizontal; rather than working off ideological blueprints, revolutionaries have attempted to make space for the autonomy of many different individuals and communities as part of their struggle. This strategy has proved sensationally effective in plunging elites into crisis after crisis, forcing them to sacrifice front-men and scramble their decks in a desperate bid to cling on amid the revolution's storms.

Until 2011, most Egyptians had lived their entire lives under a single head of state; in the half-decade since then, there have been four more. And yet, as things stand, despite all the tumult, at a formal level the old ways still hold sway. None of this is occurring in isolation. Both the revolution and counter-revolution have been globalized; just as revolutionaries in Cairo, Alexandria and Suez have borrowed tactics and imagery from protests abroad, so their own symbols, words and demonstrations have inspired others elsewhere, at a moment in which the international financial crisis has dealt a blow to all sorts of establishments and left many societies ripe for revolt. In London, anti-austerity campaigners have attempted to turn Trafalgar Square into Tahrir; in Madison, Wisconsin, protesters mobilizing for trade union rights plastered the walls of the town with photos from Egypt and taped up solidarity statements made by Egyptian labour activists.[17] Meanwhile Egypt's 1 per cent digs in with the support of regional and global superpowers, forms alliances with corporate giants, and secures political cover from Western politicians. The present situation is completely unsustainable, because a profound gulf now exists between a ruling class intent on governinng as if nothing has changed and large swathes of a democratic citizenry for whom something fundamental has altered.

The revolution defies easy categorization; it has already confronted stubborn inequalities, but its gales have also helped to crystallze an authoritarian order and its energies have been at risk of getting lost within the safe grooves of neoliberal gradualism – where 'legitimate' protest can occur only within the boundaries of the system, political struggles can only be waged via civil society pressure groups and reformist electoral blocs, the extent of change is limited to the construction of better regulatory frameworks, and no one ever indulges in grand visions of something bigger, something else. Whether or not revolutionaries can go further next time round and do more than produce moments of transitory destabilization at the top of the state, whether or not they can transform an emancipated state of mind into a more concrete and equitable architecture of governance – that remains an open question. It is inside that question, within Egypt's ongoing moment of flux, that the revolution continues.

Outside the purple taxi's windows, a sandstorm was blowing. Pudgy dust eddies swirled through the air, making everything feel brown and granular. We looped around the university district, where protests against Sisi have persisted since his ascension to the presidency, and past the steel and cement plants where thousands of workers have maintained a series of rolling strikes and sit-ins, often in solidarity with striking workers in other factories and cities – one of many signs that the latest leader's grip on this restless landscape may be weaker than it first appears. Just before the river, on Omar Ibn Abd el-Aziz Street, we passed the old rest house of King Farouk, Egypt's last monarch, now supposedly open to the public as a museum. In fact, soldiers have been occupying the building since 2011, and as in many of Egypt's heritage sites more efforts are deplayed to keep people out than to encourage them in. I've never managed to enter the house, but according to reports it is crammed with precious memorabilia; the smoking room features gem-studded furniture and boxes of inlaid pearl, part of an exact recreation of the treasures discovered in Tutankhamen's tomb which Farouk ordered made for himself when he took the throne. More than 3,000 years separate the reigns of these two Egyptian rulers, but both clearly shared a taste for exclusivity: they amassed fabulous wealth and locked it away in private sanctums, and viewed most of their subjects as little more than inanimate pieces, with no active role to play in the governance of their nation. From colonial governors to the post-1952 military leadership, through the rule of the Muslim Brotherhood and Sisi's totalitarianism today, that conception of the basic relationship between state and society has held firm. The revolution seeks to shatter it.

I first came to Egypt at the beginning of 2008, after making a long journey overland from London – trains down through Hungary, Serbia and Bulgaria, coaches across Turkey, motorbikes in Syria and a ferry from Jordan over the Red Sea. I finally reached Cairo in the middle of a winter's night, dropped off at a suburban bus station with no one to call upon, nowhere to stay, and no Arabic to help me find my way around. I'd never been more excited. Back then I was determined to make a life in Egypt that avoided the comfortable rhythms of expat existence. I was going to report instead on what was really out there, offer readers of my articles an unmediated window on to a dictatorship in terminal decline. Of course as I built up a career as a journalist, I realized that gaining deeper understanding of a place doesn't mean escaping subjectivity: we all live in green zones of our own creation, with our own biases and our own skewed viewfinder on the world around us.[18] The key is to interrogate and acknowledge those biases, rather than putting up a pretence that they don't exist at all. Unfortunately a great deal of mainstream media coverage of the Middle East, as well as academic analysis of the region, maintains exactly that pretence. In the years leading up to the revolution, 'objective' accounts of events in Egypt – elite-level infighting within Mubarak's clique, cultural clashes between Islamists and liberals, shenanigans at the pyramids and shark attacks in the sea – were abundant, but few of them picked up on the rumbles below the surface: strike waves that were bringing huge sectors of the economy to a standstill, urban insurgents who were setting fire to Mubarak posters in the streets, a widening gap between rich and poor that saw new corporate towers claw at the skies while the most vulnerable sold their organs for cash. By passively accepting the optics of those in power, much of the revolution's backstory was missed. Now, as the revolution's obituaries are written prematurely and homilies are penned on the lost cause of the 'Arab Spring',* there is a risk of the same mistake being made all over again.

This book aims at going some way to redressing the balance, but it is of course as personal, dishevelled and incomplete as any other that has come before it. It makes no claim to be a definitive portrait of contemporary Egypt, or of revolutionary Egyptians themselves. While peeling back the skin of events in recent years I have tried to be as honest as possible about what I've found there, but the places I've looked at have been of my own selection; the stories that emerged from them are shot through with gaps and uncertainties, and they are refracted through my own hopes and dreams of what the revolution could yet achieve. The very language of 'revolution' is a political choice; within Egypt it is a vocabulary that millions have adopted, rightly or wrongly, to enable the creation of new political imaginations, and to challenge different forms of authority in unprecedented ways.[19] I make that choice too, partly because it reflects what I see on the ground in Egypt but also because I want to support that challenge, and I believe that one way of doing so is to attempt a richer understanding of how the revolution's battles have played out so far – for better and for worse – so that it is in a better position to succeed when the next round of battles arises. As George Orwell noted in *Homage to Catalonia*, 'Consciously or unconsciously everyone writes as a partisan . . . beware my partisanship, my mistakes of fact and the distortion inevitably caused by my having seen only one corner of events. And beware of exactly the same things when you read any other book.'[20] Which is another way of saying, unapologetically, that this book, like all books, takes sides.[21]

The chapters that follow are split into three sections; together they attempt to illuminate the shape and substance of the neoliberal state,

* In this book I try to avoid the term 'Arab Spring' as far as possible; no term better exemplifies the unfortunate habit of attempting to frame the uprisings and turmoil in the region over the past half-decade through a rigid and Western world-historical lens.

and explore the different realms in which revolutionary struggles continue to rage against it. The first section, 'Mubarak Country', unpacks the infrastructure of political and economic exclusion in modern Egypt. The second, 'Resistance Country', looks at the ways in which that infrastructure was exposed and undermined during the latter years of Mubarak's rule, and ends with an account of the eighteen-day anti-Mubarak uprising with which the revolution started. The longest and final section, 'Revolution Country', interrogates both revolution and counter-revolution since 2011, and presents Egypt as a country caught between two models of power: one broken, but not yet fully defeated, the other full of life, but not yet fully emerged.

By the time we reached el-Maraziki bridge, which links Helwan to the west bank of the Nile, the sun had disappeared and the bridge's giant metal girders were dimming with the last of the day's light. On the other bank of the river, everything was onyx green. The driver lit another cigarette and wound down the window; the duststorm seemed to have eased off, and through the growing shadows we could make out clumps of palms and reed-strewn lagoons. Cairo is one of the few major metropolises in the world where, as urban geographer David Sims puts it, 'one can still walk from the centre of town and in less than two hours find oneself in the midst of verdant fields.'[22] The metamorphosis of city into countryside was absolute; even the trucks had melted away down the Nile corridor, leaving us with the road to ourselves and a starry night rapidly unfurling through the trees. We were in the last band of foliage before the start of the desert. Ghamrawi nudged me and pointed at a shimmer of lights to the south, beyond a large expanse of open land. It had to be Zawyet el-Dahshour. We turned off the main track and motored softly towards the village.

I recognized the school straight away from the video: tidy red-brick blocks with wraparound external walkways, a bare set of goalposts on the ground below. It was dark and late, but a few lights were on. Past the open gate, some children were playing football in the playground – the same playground in which they had re-enacted revolutionary clashes against the security forces during their lunch break. It was only by the merest chance that a visiting medic, Abdel Rahman Seyam, had been up on a balcony that day and, unbeknownst to the students, recorded a fuzzy minute of footage on his mobile phone. The film later went viral on YouTube.[23] 'Egypt's next president will come from this generation,' wrote Seyam in his online caption for the video. Hundreds of people commented below the line. 'What a tribute to the Egyptian people,' said one viewer. Another wrote: 'This means there will be a lifetime of revolution.'

A man emerged from a door on the edge of the playground and walked across to ask me and Ghamrawi what we were doing there. He was a young maths teacher named Reda Islam, and after we explained that we wanted to see the school where the YouTube video had been shot, he invited us back into the staffroom for tea. 'You have no idea how obsessively the children throw themselves into it,' he confided. 'That video became a bit famous but it was just one minute of footage – they've been playing like that since the revolution started, during every break time and again when classes finish at the end of the day. Sometimes they do it twenty times in a row, pretending to attack the police, miming being shot and gassed, then picking themselves up again to carry on fighting.' I said that it was brave of them to chant so openly against the army, and Reda shook his head and laughed.

'They're braver than that,' he replied. 'The sound on the video is very crackly so people didn't realize; everyone who watched it thought the children were calling for the downfall of the *musheer* ['field marshal'], but actually they were yelling *'el-sha'ab, yureed, isqat el-mudeer'* – 'The people want the downfall of the headmaster.' They weren't just copying what they saw on television coverage of the protests, they were changing it to carry out their own mini-revolution right here at the school!' He poured out more tea and shovelled a small mountain of sugar into each glass. 'The children are completely different now. Within two minutes of the revolution starting they had begun speaking out in class, challenging things the teachers said, asking us about what was happening on the streets and what it all meant. Some of the staff, including me, had participated in the protests in Tahrir, and the students wanted to know everything, they wanted to know how it felt to have a voice at last. We changed, and they changed with us.'

Outside, the football game had come to an end. As we emerged from the staffroom into the playground the children flocked around us, clambering over each other's shoulders in an effort to be in one of Ghamrawi's photos. 'We hated him!' shouted one, when I asked why they had been trying to bring down the headmaster – who has, sure enough, now departed from the school. 'I don't want to be rude,' added another sternly, 'but he was a thief. We've had enough of cor-ruption. Also he wouldn't let us have a football tournament, even though he had promised us one the year before.' Several heads nod-ded vigorously in agreement. 'We saw the revolution on the television and we learned that if you want to change something in your life, this is what you do,' interjected one small boy named Ahmed, who ran the zip of his tracksuit top up and down as he spoke. 'I'm sorry, but the football tournament is a red line.'

Since the revolution began, the term 'red line' has often been used by state officials and military generals to denote the elite-sanctioned border between acceptable and non-acceptable forms of public dis-sent. Revolutionaries have appropriated the term for themselves, declaring that 'the people are the red line'. Ahmed's words, delivered with an almost comical gravity, reminded me of a moment on 11 Feb-ruary, soon after Mubarak's resignation had been announced on TV. Standing outside the presidential palace with hundreds of thousands of protesters, I was convulsed in a wild, directionless sea of noise and colour that seemed as if it would never end. Slowly though, the crowd resolidified, and we began a triumphant victory parade back towards Tahrir. Amid exploding fireworks and wistful songs for the martyrs, our march passed the high-walled Ministry of Defence, the occu-pants of which had now assumed formal control of the country. The soldiers on guard outside were friendly and flashed peace salutes at the crowd, but behind them there were expressionless faces watching us through darkened windows. We came to a stop and stared up towards them, the festive mood temporarily suspended, and from the mouths of all those around me came a spine-tingling assertion of where authority now lay, where Egypt's revolution would always be found. '*Ahum, ahum, ahum, el-masryeen ahum,*' the people around me thundered, a thousand fingers pointing down at the street below our feet – 'Here, here, here, the Egyptians are here.' My friend Karim

Mehdat Ennarah turned to me and he had tears in his eyes. 'You know my late father was part of a sit-in at the faculty of engineering in Cairo University in 1968 – the first protests seen in Egypt since Nasser took over in 1952,' he said, as we turned away from the ministry of defence and began to walk on. 'His generation tell me that they were not as brave as us, but they started something and played their part. Today, we finished the job for them.'

Karim knew that the job was never really finished; that it would take more than the overthrow of Mubarak, or his successor, or the ones after that, to redraw the relationship between Egypt's society and its rulers. But he was trying to lay his finger on the durability of hope and imagination in the face of the old ways, the belief that each generation needs to place in the next in order to summon the strength to keep fighting. It was Karim that first sent me the video of the Zawyet el-Dahshour schoolchildren: his evidence that even at its bleakest moments, the revolution really does continue. Today many revolutionaries are locked behind bars, but the children's understanding of revolution – not just the toppling of a figurehead, like the *musheer*, but a rearrangement of power and sovereignty, one that would sweep away the *mudeer* and many others like him in its wake – is proving far harder for the state to vanquish. Back at the school the kids were reeling off a list of ways in which their lives had been transformed in recent months: the school bullies, which the other children called the playground *shurta* ('police'), had been chased away; in classes students refused to be yelled at any more by teachers, and regularly walked out if they felt disrespected. I asked one of the quieter children if he thought that his generation of Egyptians was ready to shout back against injustice, and he pondered silently for a moment, shyly biting his finger. 'The Egyptian people are lions,' he concluded at last, looking up at me. 'We always shouted, but now we roar.'

PART I

Mubarak Country

I

'This is our Egypt'

Shahenda Maklad had run away from her village once before; now she was at it again. Out in the early hours past the snoozing doorman, through a mist turned silver by the rising sun. Out past the squat concrete post office – quickly now before the old Greek grocer starts to pile up his wares or the barber's first customers of the day begin traipsing in for a haircut, shave or minor piece of surgery. Out along the path where bundles of bamboo lie waiting to be whittled and thrashed together into rooftops, out across the sloughy canal-bank where sedentary water buffaloes watch on with impassive, sleepy eyes. Out to the Tala road where the dawn rattle of trucks and horse-carts is slowly building, out on a hitched ride to the industrial city of Shibin el-Kom and then beyond – to the wide expanse of the Nile Delta, to the Mediterranean coastline, to the elegant boulevards and seafront of Alexandria. Shahenda was going to stop at nothing. She was nineteen, and in love.

At the other end of this journey stood Shahenda's older cousin, Salah Hussein, who had entranced her for as long as she could remember. As a little girl, she often heard her father and other villagers swap tales of Salah's heroics while fighting alongside the Palestinian *fedayeen* ('resistance') units who battled the fledgling state of Israel in the late 1940s.* By the time Shahenda became a teenager, Salah was back in Egypt and brimming with radical ideas. It was the early 1950s, the nation's corrupt, imperial-backed monarchy was faltering, and groups of dissident students were starting to arm themselves and

---

* Local rumour has it that Salah sold a gold-plated Quran to fund his journey to Palestine.

launch guerrilla attacks against British colonial forces. Salah had joined their struggle, and it wasn't long before he returned to his home village of Kamshish, a small farming community in Munifaya, north-west of the capital, to agitate for revolution. 'At the time we lived under a feudal system; the lords owned the land and protected it by force, and the *fellaheen* ['farmers' or 'peasants'] were enslaved. It was a scene from the Middle Ages,' remembers Shahenda. Now she is much older, her face pinched and lined; she probes her way through these memories with care. 'Salah told us that he had learned many things on his travels, and that the war for liberation lay not just in Jerusalem or Cairo, but here in Kamshish as well.'

Salah's seditious rhetoric was in keeping with the times. Within a few months of his reappearance in Kamshish, breathless news reports and patriotic songs crackled out of the village radio announcing the toppling of the royal family, and the ascension to power of a group of nationalist military generals, the Free Officers, with Gamal Abdel Nasser at their helm. One of the core pillars of Nasser's coup was a modernization programme that promised to transform Egypt's stagnant rural economy and address a burning injustice: the massive concentration of fertile land in the hands of a tiny elite. On the eve of what became known as the 1952 revolution, 20 per cent of the nation's cultivated fields were owned by 0.1 per cent of the population,[1] including the ever-bloating,* wild-womanizing King Farouk, who was able to claim 250,000 *feddans* (one *feddan* is just over an acre) in the monarch's name.[2] Meanwhile 90 per cent of the *fellaheen* officially classified as 'landowners' owned less than the minimum required to sustain a family; 3 million of them had under a single *feddan* to call their own, and millions more were completely landless.[3] By the time soldiers kicked in the door of Farouk's palace, the average Egyptian was worse off than she had been at the start of the First World War.

Nasser's land reforms saw fields seized from the largest landowners and distributed to the landless and near-landless, and new controls

---

* Farouk's considerable weight, most of which developed while he was on the throne, was legendary. A CIA plot to overthrow him was codenamed 'Project FF' – short for 'Fat Fucker'.

placed on rents and foreign ownership. Law number 178, which was followed by a series of further reforms throughout the 1950s and 60s, was promoted by its drafters as the most important decree in modern Egyptian history, vitally reaffirming the link between ordinary Egyptians and their land. But beyond the capital, those targeted directly by the new measures – like the grand al-Fiqi family of Kamshish – saw Law 178 as an existential threat to their power and privilege, and they weren't about to give up without a fight. The al-Fiqis owned nearly 1,500 *feddans* in the area, and as leaders of the local agricultural cooperative the family also maintained almost complete control over other farmers' access to credit, seed and fertilizer. They ruthlessly exploited their dominance of the village council to dictate all manner of land transactions and agricultural activity; labour for their own fields could be demanded from villagers at a whim.[4] On one occasion, according to the *fellaheen*, when a nearby linen factory began recruiting workers – which drove up wages and threatened to deplete the pool of agricultural labourers that the al-Fiqis relied upon in the cotton-harvesting season – the family arranged for the whole plant to be burned down. With relatives holding key positions in the provincial government, the al-Fiqis had little to fear in terms of retribution from the law.[5] In Kamshish, as in the rest of the Egyptian countryside, local flows of power and money beat to the rhythm of the land-owning clan. That was the way it always had been – and to the al-Fiqis, that was the way it always must be.

For Salah, on the other hand, land reform was only the start. He knew that it wasn't just soil and crops the al-Fiqis depended on for their wealth and status – it was a whole way of life, codified and normalized by everyone in the village. Up the length of the Nile Valley and across the lotus-shaped Delta that fans north out of Cairo, relationships in the countryside were built upon centuries of class oppression. Henry Habib Ayrout, a Syrian Christian and contemporary observer of rural Egypt who wrote up his experiences in French as *Moeurs et coutumes des fellahs*, recounts a rich landowner telling him, 'The *fellah* can only be driven by the lash.'[6] A police officer, whose beating of a local farmer was accidentally interrupted by the writer, explained: 'You have to treat the peasants like that. They are only brutes.' Over time, the subordinate position of ordinary farmers was reinforced by colonial violence. On a sunny June afternoon in 1906, five British officers strolled into the village of Denshawai – which lies a few miles to the east of Kamshish – for a spot of pigeon shooting; after killing several birds kept by residents as domestic animals and wounding the wife of the *muezzin* at the village mosque, the officers were set upon by an angry mob. In response, they murdered one Egyptian on the spot (who was tending to an injured British soldier at the time), hanged four more in the village square, and handed down twenty-eight other punishments ranging from a life sentence of penal servitude to hard labour and flogging. The social filter that sifted Kamshish's population into its right and proper order was therefore deeply entrenched. Whenever the head of the al-Fiqis, known locally as 'the lord', deigned to ride through the village, formal respect was demanded of all those he passed – which meant that radios had to be switched off and *tawla* ('backgammon') boards snapped shut. At the call to prayer, kneeling arrangements in the village mosque consisted of al-Fiqi on his own at the front and everyone else crammed together at the back. A popular song at the time called on the overhanging branches of trees to raise themselves magically and enable al-Fiqi to pass unhindered, and the young people who hummed it were required to wear special hats in public marking their deference to the lord.

Salah knew that real liberation was going to take more than a few redrawn field maps handed down from on high in Cairo. What Kamshish needed was a psychological revolution – a reimagining of what ordinary citizens could achieve in the face of sustained exploitation – and there was plenty of historical inspiration for him to draw on. As recently as 1951, hundreds of farmers had risen up in rebellion in the northern province of Behout and destroyed properties belonging to the land-owning al-Badrawi family (some of whom would later become leading lights of Mubarak's ruling National Democratic Party). In his book, Ayrout offered many examples of 'entire populations' revolting against both landlords and the state that protected them, often holding out against security forces for several days. 'The women stood in the front line to urge on the men, the children gathered fresh supplies of missiles, and regular strategy was improvised,' he noted. Sometimes retribution against oppressors was stealthy, and swift: Ayrout observed that 'when a usurer, landowner or *nazir* [the landlord's 'overseer'] has carried out his exactions too far, and is murdered with public approval, the finest sleuth cannot discover the murderer, so close is the conspiracy of silence'.[7] On other occasions, revenge took longer. Following the bloodshed at Denshawai, any hope of reconciliation between Egypt's growing independence movement and London was dashed; by 1919, a mass Egyptian revolt against the British was sending tremors through the realm.* Almost half a century later, when Britain and its allies were defeated by Egypt in the Suez War, Egyptian journalist Mohamed Hassanein Heikal said simply, 'The pigeons of Denshawai have come home to roost.'[8]

Salah started with those demeaning hats. 'His slogan was "live free" over the land, and he began to educate the villagers,' explains Shahenda. 'He encouraged the youth to refuse to wear the hats, to deliberately break that tradition in an act of passive resistance.' Soon Salah was using local religious gatherings, wedding ceremonies and funerals to agitate for change, calling on the *fellaheen* to withdraw their *corvée* (unpaid) labour and to start questioning the status quo.[9] It didn't take long for a group of youths known as the *tullab* ('students') to gather around Salah and commit themselves to anti-feudal activism. For the al-Fiqis, Salah was fast becoming an ugly headache; government legislation was something that could be resisted in the courts, but there were no state institutions that could be depended upon to halt the tide of Salah's speeches. These were thrilling, slippery days; all the old certainties of Kamshish were undergoing profound disruption, but no one could quite put their finger on the whats, whens or hows emerging in their place. Then came the attack on the dam.

For months, farmers had been troubled by an irrigation canal dug by al-Fiqi which ensured that the best water supply reached his own fields at the expense of the ordinary *fellaheen*, whose personal plots

---

* British playwright George Bernard Shaw wrote in response to Denshawai: 'If [England's] Empire means ruling the world as Denshawai has been ruled in 1906 – and that, I am afraid, is what the Empire does mean to the main body of our aristocratic-military caste and to our Jingo plutocrats – then there can be no more sacred and urgent political duty on earth than the disruption, defeat, and suppression of the Empire, and, incidentally, the humanisation of its supporters.'

were bisected by the new waterway. 'Only when the al-Fiqis were done irrigating their own land would they open it to allow the left-over water to reach the farmers, so we got the very last drops,' remembers Shahenda. For Salah, the dam embodied everything that was wrong about the state of affairs in Kamshish, a daily reminder, both logistical and symbolic, of the lord's distorted ascendancy over Kamshish's poorer farmers. In secret, *the tullab* hatched their plans. But a man of al-Fiqi's clout had informants everywhere. On the rebels' first raid they were met on the pathway by hired muscle who opened fire, injuring seventeen *fellaheen*, male and female. Salah was shaken but undeterred; he knew that failure here would be a huge blow and allow al-Fiqi to shore up his crumbling authority through renewed violence and fear. A few nights later, the militants tried to reach the dam again. This time, they succeeded; a dynamite pop echoed through the dark sky and was followed by the sound of water gurgling rapidly into the farmers' undernourished fields.

Shahenda was fourteen years old, and the following day she joined the festive celebrations as news spread of *the tullab*'s audacious assault. 'I had already been proud of the fact that my cousin had gone off to Palestine and then returned to try and liberate Egypt from injustice as well,' she says. We are sitting in Groppis cake shop, a slice of faded Cairene grandeur off Talaat Harb Square, as Shahenda unpacks her story. 'I was so happy when I found out about the dam, because even as a fourteen-year-old I felt a sensation that justice was on our side.' Her diminutive frame rises and falls with a deep breath. 'Salah was leading us to victory. And I was . . . I was fond of him.'

Shahenda's father was the chief of police in a nearby town, though in these turbulent times of fast-shifting loyalties, that didn't mean he was against the rebels. In fact, he had been arming them secretly, as had the Muslim Brotherhood, a movement Salah had been a member of in the 1940s. But the dam explosion was serious business, and above the pay grade of a district lawman. In its aftermath, official security forces flooded the area and a curfew was imposed on the village; the village mayor was suspended and Anwar Sadat – one of Nasser's Free Officers, future president of Egypt and child of the nearby town of Mit Kom – was drafted in from Cairo to investigate Kamshish's disturbances. The Free Officers may have publicly espoused a progressive agenda, but the prospect of an independent agrarian resistance movement outside of their control, of the type being pieced together by Salah, was considered more of a mortal threat than the landowners. Sadat sided with the latter, as did the Brotherhood, who were persuaded to withdraw their support from *the tullab* – prompting a disgusted Salah to break his final ties with the Islamists. He was imprisoned for a year and exiled to Shibin el-Kom, the provincial capital. In the years that followed, skirmishes between al-Fiqi and the farmers continued in Kamshish, and so did the village curfew.

Shahenda, now a confident and politically conscious nineteen-year-old, had her own repressive edicts to contend with. The previous year she had been married off to a local police officer, but it proved to be a joyless union. 'I fought with all my strength to get away from him,' she grins. 'I even fled the house and told my family "I won't come back until I get a divorce." ' This was 1956, when divorces were scarce and the idea of women initiating them even scarcer. But Shahenda was defiant, and eventually her parents had little choice but to help facilitate the separation. Shahenda returned to Kamshish and waited for Salah, whose passion and politics filled her with a fire she hadn't known before. She didn't have to wait long. Salah saw in her a kindred spirit of rebellion, and asked for her hand in marriage. Her parents were aghast. 'I would rather see my daughter hacked to pieces and fed to the dogs,' Shahenda's mother confided to Salah's mother, who couldn't help but sympathize. Salah may have been extraordinarily popular in Kamshish, but a renegade at war with authority didn't meet most people's definition of an ideal husband. Sensing that the obstacles to this marriage in Kamshish might be too big to circumvent, Shahenda packed her bags once again – this time with her fugitive lover in tow – and escaped to the coast.

When Salah and Shahenda arrived in Alexandria to seal their matrimony, they found a metropolis locked in steep decline, its grand hotels and seafront coffee houses looking as dishevelled as the pair of outcasts who had just blown in from the Delta. Following the Suez War and a government-led crackdown on 'foreign' interests, most of the city's multicultural populations – Jewish, Greek, Armenian – were heading to the harbour and exiting in droves; many churches, cafés and pensions now stood abandoned. Amid the turmoil, Salah had managed to secure a tiny room near the train station and find a job at a trade company paying 12 Egyptian pounds a month*; Shahenda moved in and together they gathered all the paperwork they needed to become husband and wife legally. 'When we finally presented ourselves to the *maz'oon* [a religious functionary who carries out weddings] we had Salah's two cousins with us plus one of his friends, to act as witnesses,' says Shahenda. 'The *maz'oon* saw this little teenage girl with four big men and assumed I must have been kidnapped; he refused outright to perform the marriage.' Even when the party produced all the requisite paperwork and showed that Shahenda was of legal age to marry without her parents' consent, the *maz'oon* remained jumpy. 'He kept trying to find excuses not to do it, first claiming that the date on one of the documents was wrong, then saying that his official stamp wasn't working!' Eventually the official's intransigence crumbled, and Shahenda and Salah walked out of the building and into the fresh sea air as a married couple. Now they were legally wedded, they could return to Kamshish. On the journey home, Shahenda felt sick with fear over how the community would react to their flight. She needn't have worried. 'The whole village had been following the soap opera of our relationship and they were delighted that we'd succeeded,' she smiles. 'I was stunned at how welcoming everyone was.'

The years that followed were happy ones for Shahenda and Salah, the happiest they'd ever been. For those fighting to change society, Nasser's erratic programme of political reform threw up both risks and opportunities; those smart enough to navigate the contradictions were often rewarded with success. In 1958, a new law allowed women to become elected officials for the first time in Egyptian history and Shahenda – the bantam teen from Kamshish who had twice run away – amazed everyone by winning a seat on the new national

---

* The Egyptian unit of currency is the Egyptian pound, referred to in Arabic as a *gineih* (from the British currency unit 'guinea'). When expressed as a written amount, both the French abbreviation LE (for *livre égyptienne*) and the international currency code EGP are widely used. In this book, EGP and *gineih* are used to indicate Egyptian pounds; other references to pounds or £ indicate the British pound sterling.

council of villages, representing the whole of Munifaya governorate. 'I always saw myself more as a soldier than a leader, but now I was at the front,' she recalls. Salah had also been continuing with his political activism and the pair refocused their sights on the al-Fiqi family who, through a technical sleight of hand, had managed to exempt most of their sprawling estate from the land redistribution programme. It took a blizzard of legal manoeuvres and grassroots protests to eventually defeat the old lord, but they did it; in 1961 the majority of al-Fiqi's fields were formally appropriated by the government and shared out between 190 local farmers. Salah and Shahenda were delirious. A decade earlier the farmers of Kamshish had to resort to nocturnal guerrilla attacks to blow up a dam and divert water from the feudalist's land; now those same crops belonged to them.

Al-Fiqi fought with all his might to turn back the clock, launching lawsuit after lawsuit and accusing Salah and his comrades of thuggery – a charge that continues to be levelled against political agitators today – but to no avail. Listed variously by the authorities as a communist, an Islamist and an incendiary anarchist, Salah was eventually arrested again in 1965, though popular protests in the district quickly forced his release. His and Shahenda's brand of social revolution was seemingly irrepressible, their popularity spreading beyond the village and into neighbouring regions, their fame skipping borders and attracting interest from revolutionaries around the globe. Soon after Salah's brief imprisonment, Che Guevara himself made a pilgrimage to this growing oasis of peasant resistance. Salah was even invited to meet President Nasser in Cairo after sending the president a report on Egypt's educational deficiencies, parts of which recommended the government seizure of feudal palaces for the purposes of turning them into public clinics and schools. He and Shahenda were never more excited – for their politics, for their village, for each other.

It was at that point, on 30 April 1966, that a group of men lured Salah into a building on the edge of Kamshish and shot him dead.

To reach Kamshish today, follow the Nile downstream out of Cairo and along the old agricultural road, up past the furthest reaches of Shubra – the capital's northernmost quarter – and stay parallel to the railway line, where apartment blocks bleed into factories, factories bleed into fields, and fields bleed back into apartment blocks. Soviet-style and squat, these massive housing units recede perpendicularly from the road into palm-studded greenery, their long grey façades flecked with colourful splashes of drying laundry. This is the Delta. Writers once venerated its wild marshlands. Now you'll find it hard to pinpoint where the city ends and the countryside begins; the lushness of the Nile's arteries is stippled with apartment blocks and spliced with roads in every direction, and any clear-cut divisions have been long buried under layer of rebars and asphalt. Here, the urban and rural get lost in one another, with livestock living in doorways and workers camping out in fields.

Something of the Delta's centrality to Egypt can be found in the statistics: two-thirds of the country's population live within these 10,000 square miles of farmland fed by the Nile's branches, and the fields it contains – some of the most fertile on the planet – are responsible for more than 60 per cent of the nation's food supply. But numbers and percentages can't explain the hold this region has over Egypt's popular imagination; better instead to search out Youssef Chahine's 1969 cinematic masterpiece el-'Ard ('The Land'), based on a novel by Abdelrahman al-Sharkawi, which brought the cadence of daily rural life to the big screen and explored the almost sacred historical attachment of Egyptians to the soil. The film's final scene features an ageing villager who has stood up to feudal oppression and is now being punished by the overlord; his feet are bound and his body tied to the legs of a horse ridden by the village sheriff, his clothes torn and skin wounded with each bump in the ground. Tarek Osman, who has written elegantly on the historical iterations of Egyptian popular identity, describes the final shots of the reel: 'Yet as he is dragged along, his hand clutches at the mud, the soil. He refuses to let go, to abandon his land, his home, his life. The audience – millions of whom wept while watching this scene – almost questioned whether [actor] Mahmoud al-Meligui's hands were clutching the earth, or the earth clutching him.'[10]

By the mid-1960s, word began to circulate in Kamshish that the al-Fiqi family were trying to find someone who could be paid to kill Salah. Shahenda heard the rumours too, and they petrified her. 'It made sense because nothing else had worked; they tried arrests, jailing, intimidation but the revolutionaries of Kamshish just got stronger,' she explains. She orders another coffee and takes a minute to compose herself; this is the hardest part of the tale. By 1966, the tight-knit village community already knew who had been picked for the hit job: a young man by the name of Mahmoud, widely believed to be in al-Figi's pay. Shahenda knew the boy's family and even called on Mahmoud's brother in the hope he could dissuade his sibling from carrying out the murder. But Salah seemed largely unconcerned. 'I warned him again and again and begged him to take care of himself, but he just told me not to worry and that Mahmoud was a coward,' says Shahenda quietly. 'He said the people's will was stronger than any bullets.'

Shahenda wasn't moved by Salah's assurances and felt a wave of relief when he agreed to spend *sham el-nisseem*, a national holiday marking the start of spring, together with her and away from the village, up on the north coast in the resort town of Agami. Towards the end of the romantic break Salah received word that he needed to meet with some members of a *fellaheen* union back home; he resolved to pop over to Kamshish quickly and then return that same evening to Agami via a train from the capital. 'Whenever he told me he was coming, he would always come,' says Shahenda, her eyes wet. 'The last train of the day from Cairo arrived and he wasn't on it. I curled up on the couch next to the front door, ready to open it for him as soon as he arrived. At 2 a.m. the doorbell rang and I jumped up to open the door. But it wasn't Salah. It was my cousin, and I knew. Before he could say anything, I knew.'

Salah's body lay in the hospital at Shibin el-Kom. The local head of state security – mindful of how potent Salah's status as a revolutionary martyr was in the region – ordered that the corpse should not be buried in Kamshish. But he hadn't reckoned on Shahenda, who had arrived straight from Agami. 'I turned to him and said: "Salah was born in Kamshish, he fought for Kamshish, he died in Kamshish, and he will definitely be buried in Kamshish. There is no force on earth that will ever stop me from burying him there."' At the entrance to the village, Shahenda found the entire local community congregating in wait for the body. One of Salah's closest friends was crying, and Shahenda slapped him on the face. 'I said, "No one will cry for Salah, we will fight for him instead." When the body arrived I carried it aloft with the men and we started chanting, "Salah has left the revolutionaries but the revolutionaries will continue his struggle." ' She dabs at her face with a tissue. 'It's been forty-six years since he died, but I'll never forget. They killed him to spread fear to the heart of the people, but we had to spread hope instead and show them the revolt would continue. Over four decades later I found myself shouting exactly the same thing in Tahrir – we must stay and continue the revolution, we must never leave the square.'

Almost half a century on from Salah's murder, two rangy palm trees now stand watch over the old al-Fiqi family house in Kamshish. The villa is abandoned and succumbing, brick by brick, to the elements; a few sheets of corrugated iron hem the whole building in on itself and out of sight from the rest of the village, as if the farmers want to consign to the past everything the al-Fiqis represented Beyond the house lies the beginning of open fields and the infamous dam that Salah successfully dynamited in 1952. The night before my visit a rainstorm had flashed across the Delta, leaving communities without proper drainage systems – like Kamshish – beating back peewee-tides of dislodged soil and slush. My car churned up eddies of mud as I slipped off the main village road and on to the agricultural path that led down to the dam; it was getting late, and I knew Abdel Meguid, president of Egypt's independent farmers union, would be waiting.

Abdel Meguid el-Khouli was only a small child when Salah made his first, thwarted attempt to destroy al-Fiqi's dam, but he remembers only too well the firefight and the bullets and the procession of the injured back to the village. 'Al-Fiqi himself was almost gunned down in that clash,' recalled the 61-year-old, as he led me past herds of goats and donkey-drawn carts sagging with fresh greens. 'His guards saved his life by throwing him to the floor to protect him, and they shot plenty of farmers in the process. But you know we have a saying here: "A hit that doesn't kill you makes you stronger." The history of Kamshish demonstrates this perfectly; each struggle has made us more aware of what we're capable of, of what we can achieve.' He also remembers Salah's murder, as does everyone in the village who was alive at the time. 'It was a turning point for us all,' he sighed. 'Especially Shahenda.'

In the aftermath of the shooting, Kamshish became a national and even global icon of peasant resistance, and began staging an annual conference on the anniversary of Salah's death. Back in Shahenda's house on the main village square, Abdel Meguid served up a selection of fizzy pop as he explained the conference's growing fame throughout the 1960s and 70s, drawing everyone from subversive Egyptian poets such as Ahmed Fouad Negm to French philosophers Jean-Paul Sartre and Simone de Beauvoir. 'The governor had planned to receive them as guests of the state but the force of the people overcame these official plans,' he chuckled. 'We gave Sartre a *gallabeya* [a traditional Egyptian garment] and sat him down in a *fellaheen* house, talking with him about our situation.' As a young boy Abdel Meguid attended the night classes run by Salah to improve the education of *fellaheen* families; it was called 'the school of thoughts and awareness' and it was there that many of today's older Kamshish residents first developed their views on state, society and political radicalism. 'We debated everything from minor concerns in the village to the impact of the Balfour Declaration and revolution in Latin America,' said Abdel Meguid proudly. 'Sometimes it felt as if our village was at the centre of an entire world on the cusp of change.' In many ways, it was. During the coming years, Kamshish bore witness to a series of pivotal struggles over the relationship between the Egyptian state and its citizenry, struggles that had echoes in many other communities and countries right around the world. At the heart of this conflict lay the question of whether or not Egypt's people were able to project their own autonomous political voices, moulding the state into a vehicle for defending and expanding their collective interests – or whether the state would instead stand apart from the people, becoming an instrument through which elites both at home and abroad might exclude citizens from politics and plunder the nation's resources for themselves. It is the same question that provoked revolution in 2011, and which continues to animate Egypt's turmoil today.

When he seized power, Gamal Abdel Nasser presented the Egyptian people with a contract: stay out of politics, and decolonization – under my leadership – will bring a series of concrete improvements to your life in return. The Free Officers framed Egypt's rulers and ruled as partners in a joint battle to defeat feudalism and imperialism; the sort of power wielded by the al-Fiqis in Kamshish or British soldiers in Denshawai would be curbed, and a new, nationalist government would ensure healthcare, education and employment was available to all. But the mechanisms through which these material gains were delivered would be controlled by the state: a muscular, patriarchal and domineering state, off-limits to ordinary Egyptians. Under this sort of polity, there was no room for anti-regime protest or democratic participation by the masses; those who tried to intrude upon the realm of governance would be cast out from the national family as unpatriotic and dangerous – and face punishment. Nor could the state countenance political organization on the ground by individuals or communities that lay outside of its control – who could tell where that sort of grassroots momentum might lead? And so alongside the preaching of radical change from above, Nasser's regime fought to appropriate and blunt any shoots of radical change from below. His flagship land reform programme, for example, was in part intended as a prophylactic against a much deeper agrarian revolution which had been threatening to erupt for years; without it, citizens might have begun transforming the countryside for themselves.

In the aftermath of Salah's murder, as rural fury against the landed elite surged once more, Nasser's government again moved quickly to ensure that any talk of revenge, or rebellion, was crafted and restrained by bureaucratic power at the centre rather than emerging from local communities like Kamshish. Hence, while Abdel Meguid and his fellow night-school students were entertaining Sartre and swotting up on Bolivarian insurgencies, Nasser ordered the formation of a new state-controlled body, the Higher Committee for the Liquidation of Feudalism (HCLF), supposedly tasked with investigating and wiping out all forms of peasant exploitation in the countryside. The HCLF went on to produce reports on more than 300 land-owning families, and its tactics were brutal; there are reports of soldiers attacking and torturing members of the rural upper class, sometimes in front of watching *fellaheen*.[11] But the HCLF's remit was kept deliberately narrow. Social injustice in Egypt's fields had complex historical roots and, despite a decade and a half of land reform, Nasser had made little progress in unpicking them. The persistent influence of land-owning interests was to some degree a product of the post-1952 Egyptian state itself: Nasser's determination to silence dissent and lock citizens out of political participation necessitated the creation of a security apparatus that spanned the country and, at ground level, inevitably relied on alliances with local power-brokers like the al-Fiqis. In fact, the first 'revolutionary' political organization created by Nasser following his coup installed the al-Fiqis as official representatives of the Kamshish area; after Salah's shooting, Shahenda produced many documents which indicated close collaboration between the al-Fiqis on the one hand and both government security agents and high-ranking members of the Arab Socialist Union, Nasser's ruling political party (all others were banned), on the other. The authoritarian instincts of the Free Officers – who chose to harness the age-old authority of families such as the al-Fiqis, rather than undo it – were the reason that Shahenda described independent Egypt's revolutionary political organizations as having been 'stillborn'. Naturally, the HCLF glossed over all of this, concluding that there were no systemic problems in Egypt's countryside and that incidents of peasant exploitation and landlord violence were caused by a few isolated remnants of the pre-1952 aristocracy – bogeymen like the al-Fiqis. The HCLF was designed to show that state bureaucracy could be used as a revolutionary instrument; in reality it demonstrated the opposite.[12] Less than two years after it was established in a blaze of publicity, the HCLF was quietly scaled back and many of its rulings reversed. Members of the al-Fiqi family who had been temporarily imprisoned for their connection to Salah's death following HCLF investigations were acquitted at trial owing to lack of evidence. Not for the first time, or the last, popular anger that threatened to fundamentally alter asymmetries of political and economic power in Egypt was instead diverted into safe channels that posed little danger to the structure of the state.

Nasser's determination to ensure that the contours of state power were never breached by the people amounted to the biggest failure of his 'revolutionary' project. The pact struck under Nasserism succeeded in substantially improving millions of Egyptian lives, but the political quietude it demanded from most of the population concentrated decision-making in the hands of a crony military and economic elite, leaving social gains vulnerable to any change in personnel at the top. Exclusionary politics necessitated the expansion of a police state in which free expression was neutered, privacy impossible and official violence normalized in the name of security. It also meant that anyone who succeeded Nasser would be able to deploy that same rigid and impenetrable state architecture to institute policies geared towards private enrichment rather than any broader notion of the common good. And that, after Nasser's demise, is exactly what transpired. Over the decades that followed, the state that Nasser created became a tool – not, as Shahenda Maklad had imagined it, by which citizens could come together and pool their sovereignty in order to benefit society as a whole, but rather as a means of reimposing feudal and colonial divisions. Old foes would soon be arriving in the Delta, in very modern forms.

In September 1970, just hours after closing a major Arab League summit, Nasser – the man who once declared that he was every Egyptian and that every Egyptian was him* – suffered a massive heart attack, and died. His passing brought more than 5 million Egyptians on to the streets and one of them, fellow Free Officer Anwar Sadat, into power. Sadat had come a long way from the days when he was tasked with investigating local village disturbances, like the one provoked by Salah when the young rebel dynamited the al-Fiqi dam in Kamshish all those years ago. Now Sadat, the son of an impoverished Upper Egyptian hospital clerk who succeeded in climbing to the very top of his country's military elite, was leader of the most populous nation in the Arab World.

The new president did not share Nasser's faith in broad economic redistribution. His priorities were to open up the Egyptian market and generate more opportunities for private wealth creation at the top; to do so, many Nasserite policies designed to reduce inequality and promote social justice would have to be scaled back, or dismantled altogether. Sadat's liberalizing reforms were a major break with

---

* If Gamal Abdel Nasser should die, each of you shall be Gamal Abdel Nasser . . . Gamal Abdel Nasser is of you and from you and he is willing to sacrifice his life for the nation.[13]

the Nasser era, but they fitted neatly with a global trend away from state oversight of the economy and towards a model in which capital would be free to move without regulation. Since the Second World War, capital accumulation – the driving force behind capitalism as an economic system – had been grounded in a compromise between capital and labour; states generally enabled some economic growth through the markets but also guarded against over-speculation or rampant profiteering. This set of arrangements came to be known as 'embedded liberalism', because unlike in the pre-war era the 'liberalism' of free markets was now 'embedded' in a web of social and political constraints. By the time Sadat assumed office though, global capital accumulation had slowed and embedded liberalism was entering a period of crisis. Two distinct alternatives were vying for prominence: socialism, which was gaining ground across pockets of Western Europe such as Italy's 'Red Bologna', and a form of 'market fundamentalism' aimed at 'disembedding' the private exchange of goods and services from government control. The intellectual ideas behind market fundamentalism were radical, and had been developing in the shadows for many years via organizations such as the Mont Pelerin Society, a group of economists and academics named after the Swiss spa at which they first met in the late 1940s. The society counted among its members some of the founding fathers of modern right-wing economic thought, including Austrian philosopher Friedrich von Hayek and American economist Milton Friedman, who would later go on to put many of the group's ideas into practice in Latin America, to devastating effect.

The society's aim wasn't just to produce theoretical blueprints. Members wanted to find ways in which their theories could actually be implemented across the Western world, and beyond. They knew that it would be difficult to secure popular consent for an economic system that rolled back protections for ordinary people and concentrated resources in the hands of the few, and so they sought out ways to repackage economic liberalization: not a sectional power-grab by privileged segments of the population, but rather a way of thinking about the world that appeared to be suffused with common sense, and inevitable. Over the coming decades, at a time when young people all over the political spectrum, right across the planet, were struggling to free themselves from various forms of state tyranny – from peace activists on US college campuses to anti-Soviet revolutionaries behind the Iron Curtain – the Mont Pelerin Society sought to redefine fundamental liberty not as freedom for citizens from poverty, exploitation or ignorance, but as freedom to do anything with one's own property, constrained only by contracts drawn up by consenting individuals. In practice that meant freedom for markets and for the entrepreneurs operating within them; freedom for capital to zip through people, places and solidarities without interruption or consideration for the social wreckage that trailed in its wake. 'The central values of civilization are in danger,' began the group's founding statement. 'Over large stretches of the world's surface the essential conditions of human dignity and freedom have already disappeared.' These developments, it went on to explain, had been 'fostered by a decline in belief in private property and the competitive market; for without the diffuse power and initiative associated with these institutions it is difficult to imagine a society in which freedom may be effectively preserved'.[14] As the sceptical economist and philosopher Karl Polanyi pointed out, the 'freedom' being advocated here was freedom for a certain social class to divorce itself from any sense of obligation towards a broader collective good; among the writings of Mont Pelerin Society members, the freedom and dignity afforded to ordinary people by a tax-funded welfare state or school system, for example, was nowhere to be found. Under this interpretation, Polanyi argued, 'the freedom that regulation creates is denounced as unfreedom; the justice, liberty and welfare it offers decried as the camouflage of slavery'.[15]

It was against the backdrop of this debate that Sadat arrived in the presidential palace, and he moved quickly to align Egypt with the sort of economic vision that members of the Mont Pelerin Society had been championing so fiercely. Those who believed they had lost out under Nasserism – rural plutocrats, like the al-Fiqis, among them – saw in this shift an opportunity to claw back wealth and influence. The government's language surrounding power and liberty now revolved around personal property rights rather than collective welfare; the old mantra of Arab nationalism was replaced by a wholesale diplomatic repositioning of Egypt into Washington's orbit. The result was that Egypt wasn't left to make its forthcoming economic adjustments alone. The Sadat era began with the arrival of a new army on the Nile – shock troops sporting not guns, but Samsonite suitcases and bulging portfolios, men who were ready 'to instruct the Egyptian government how to run its economy on sensible Western lines . . . and bring Harvard Business School methods to dark, insanitary Cairo shopfloors'.[16] For Abdel Meguid and the *fellaheen* of Kamshish, subjugation at the hands of the al-Fiqis was about to be rebooted, this time with more help than ever from the global market.

Within six months of Sadat taking power, left-leaning rivals in the higher reaches of the state were ousted. Many had been members of the controversial Higher Committee for the Liquidation of Feudalism that was established by Nasser in the aftermath of Salah's murder and tasked with enforcing land redistribution to the poor. On government orders, Salah's most prominent supporters were ordered out of Kamshish; Shahenda spent the following years being batted between exile and prison. The al-Fiqi palace, which had previously been seized by the state, was swiftly returned to the family, along with 100 *feddans* of prime orchards. HCLF personnel who had interrogated the al-Fiqis over Salah's death were now themselves arrested and brought to court. Just as Nasser had appropriated events in Kamshish to bolster his own ideology, so Sadat did the same: villains became victims, and one-time heroes were recast as misguided or malicious peasants, consumed by class hatred and standing in the way of Egypt's unstoppable march towards modernity.[17] The HCLF trial lasted two years and summoned 120 government officials and police officers to give evidence on the stand. Witness after witness lamented the tragedy of Nasser-era land reform; Shahenda, who appeared for the defence, was humiliated by prosecutors and accused of being a communist agent, a national saboteur and an immoral seductress hell-bent on corrupting members of the political elite.* In the courtroom, lawyers for the al-Fiqi family suggested that the prison where their clients had been temporarily detained following

---

* When Shahenda was brought to the stand she faced a hostile reception and repeated innuendo about an alleged relationship with Nasser's brother, something which she consistently denied.[18]

Salah's assassination should be torn down to make way for a monument commemorating the injustices of socialism. When the judge finally ruled in favour of the prosecution, his closing statement made it clear that it was not only the individual defendants that stood in the dock, but Nasserite history. Throughout the 1950s and 60s, according to the verdict, human dignity in Egypt had been 'trampled upon'. In words that might have been lifted straight from the pages of a Mont Pelerin Society manifesto, the judge declared that his court was 'overcome by sorrow for what the Egyptian man had to endure: the loss of his liberty and humanity, the stifling of his potentialities and loss of his security, property and honour'.[19]

Sadat's ambitious package of economic reforms, announced formally in 1974 and collectively known as *the infitah* ('opening'), was pitched as a means of liberating all those potentialities that had been stifled under Nasser, and of delivering prosperity to all Egyptians. The reality was different. A *meeri* ('government') job had once been the gold standard of employment for aspirational Egyptians; now, although the size of the public sector tripled under Sadat's watch, money and stature became the preserve of private industry instead. Well-connected companies skimmed off the best of each year's university graduates, while the living conditions of state employees tumbled. Large numbers of Egyptians travelled abroad to work in the Gulf, sending remittances home that fuelled inflation and decimated the purchasing power wielded by the majority of the population. Great swathes of the countryside that had been nationalized under Nasser were returned to their original owners; rent freezes were cancelled, peasant-run agrarian reform cooperatives were crushed, and compensation was doled out by the state to the previous era's rural gentry. Aristocratic families like the al-Fiqis, who entered the national parliament under the new regime and formed an effective lobby group for their interests, were able to re-establish their estates after winning exemptions from national land-ownership limits. Meanwhile, the landless and near-landless were disregarded once again. Gross investment in agriculture declined, while local corruption grew. Once one of the world's largest exporters of grain, Egypt became its third biggest importer, and national shortages of cereals quadrupled. An agricultural trade surplus of $300 million in 1970 turned into a deficit of $800 million by 1977.[20] Food poverty expanded. For a narrow band that reaped the benefits of social mobility, new refrigerators, televisions and telephones became the norm; for everyone else, as Nasser-era social safety nets were broken, life became wracked by insecurity. Within three years of the start of *infitah*, up to 80 per cent of Egyptians were worse off than before it began.[21] In the cities, there were bread riots. In Kamshish, the *fellaheen* declared simply that the age of feudalism had returned.[22]

Infitah had a profoundly political goal. Sadat's reforms not only provided succour to the *ancien régime*, they also created a new capitalist class whose profits were derived directly from links to Sadat's rule and whose loyalties flowed the other way.[23] High-ranking security figures landed plum government contracts and investment opportunities; merchants, brokers, lawyers and middlemen thrived parasitically off the new unabashed alliance between power and money.[24] Those best placed to flourish within a new Egypt which venerated private enrichment were co-opted into the governing status quo. Beyond them, the state remained as closed to and removed from the Egyptian people as it had been under Nasser. For all the Mont Pelerin Society's rhetoric about market freedoms acting as a bulwark against arbitrary state power, its members had a deep suspicion of democracy: anything which allowed majority interests to place limits on the ability of capital to move and accumulate was an aberration. Sadat shared that suspicion, though out of self-interest rather than any ideological affinity to economic liberalism. In public he claimed that the *infitah* contained within it the seeds of a politically pluralistic Egypt; in private, he used the hard outlines of Nasser's exclusionary state to build a support base which owed its allegiance not to free markets or entrepreneurship, and certainly not to democracy, but rather to the leader himself. *Al-Ahram* editor-in-chief Bahaa el-Din interviewed the president at the height of the *infitah* programme. 'Nasser and I are the last pharaohs,' Sadat told him.[25] In Egypt, economic liberalization and political authoritarianism marched firmly hand in hand.

Three revelations emerged from Sadat's *infitah* programme; between them, they shaped the entire reign of Sadat's successor, and helped force the revolution which eventually overthrew him. The first was that, contrary to Mont Pelerin ideology, the promotion of free markets did not entail the withdrawal of the state from the market but rather a transformation of the state's role – away from being an aggregator of the common good and towards that of being an active facilitator for the accumulation of private capital. The second was that state policies aimed at privatization and the enrichment of the few at the expense of the many ate away at the core of Nasser's social contract; with material security no longer guaranteed by the government, Egypt's citizens had little reason to accept their expulsion from the political arena. The third was that as a result of the slow unravelling of that contract, the authoritarian state came under pressure like never before. In January 1977, with basic commodity prices already spiralling due to his disastrous agricultural reforms, Sadat – at the behest of the World Bank – cut hundreds of millions of Egyptian pounds' worth of food subsidies at a stroke. Almost immediately, mass strikes erupted in Cairo's industrial districts of Helwan and Shubra al-Khayma, followed by widespread violence in which railway lines were cut, upmarket hotels, shops and casinos attacked, and the ruling party headquarters set on fire. Egypt's urban centres shook with the chant 'el-ra'ees el-deemuqrati, 'ayiz kull el-sha'ab yitati!' ('The democratic president wants the people to bow low!'). Sadat called it an 'uprising of thieves' and sent in the army to restore order; seventy-nine were killed and hundreds left injured.

The machinery of official regime violence succeeded in quelling unrest, but at a price. Sadat was forced to cancel his own economic decrees less than forty-eight hours after announcing them, and – more importantly – tens of thousands of Egyptians now had their first taste of direct confrontation with the state. With it invariably came the questioning of old political assumptions, acquired knowledge about how to do battle with security forces in the streets, and deep-seated anger against a government that shoots one's friends. In the years to come, the willingness of Egyptian citizens to fight for the social rights they believed they were entitled to ensured that the expansion of market fundamentalism in Egypt could never be entirely scripted from above, however disinterested its ruling class was in the political perspective of the wider population. The lesson was that each time the government overstepped another line and provoked popular anger, the resistance that followed left the state's repressive toolkit a little rustier, and the self-confidence of many citizens a little more assured. When Sadat was shot dead by his own soldiers during a public military parade on the streets of Cairo in October 1981, the man sitting next to him – Vice President Mohamed Hosni el-Sayed Mubarak – would have been wise to take note.

Like the president he succeeded, Mubarak – a career air force pilot known for little more than his early starts and abstemious lifestyle – was born only a few miles away from Kamshish, in the village of Kafr el-Musalha. And, also like his predecessor, Mubarak's swearing-in ceremony in October 1981 took place at a critical moment on the world stage. The project to dismantle all restraints on global capital had been boosted by the rise to power in Britain and the US of committed market fundamentalists Margaret Thatcher and Ronald Reagan, the liberalizing of China's economy by Deng Xiaoping, and the gradual takeover of key financial institutions – such as the American Federal Reserve and the economics faculty at the University of Chicago – by ardent believers in the Mont Pelerin economic model. From different epicentres, a coherent new orthodoxy was taking shape: one that would come to restructure many corners of the planet, possibly nowhere more so than in Egypt.

Neoliberalism built on the intellectual ideas of the Mont Pelerin theorists, but went further. Capital regulation was not only to be curbed; for economies to grow and capital accumulation to function effectively, whole new areas of human activity needed to be brought under the domain of transactional exchange and made subject to market relations. Social goods, long held in common, were to be parcelled up and privatized. According to neoliberal doctrine, politics and the economy should be considered as entirely separate realms – the latter managed by technocratic experts schooled in the tenets of economic liberalization, the former hollowed out so as to minimize the chances of states, governments or populations attempting to bring markets under democratic control. The more a neoliberal state ceded its sovereignty to the 'hidden hand' of global capital flows, the more efficient an economy would become, the more resources would be amassed at the top, and the more wealth would eventually trickle down to those below them. In theory, the advance of neoliberalism would involve a withdrawal of states from the economy; in reality, as Sadat's *el-infitah* programme in Egypt had illustrated, market fundamentalism required strong states to facilitate wealth appropriation by elites and to discipline citizens who attempted to fight back. Three decades on since its inception, the outcome of neoliberalism as a political project to redistribute resources from the many to the few is crystal clear. Since the late 1970s, the share of national income held by the richest 1 per cent of the population has tripled in most advanced economies, including Britain and the US; the share of the top 0.1 per cent has quadrupled. On a global scale, the wealthiest 1 per cent now own more than the rest of the world put together, and the richest eighty-five individuals among that 1 per cent control more money than the poorer half of the planet – that's 3.5 billion people – combined.

Although neoliberalism is often characterized as a creature of the West, it was on the periphery of the global economic order, not at the core, that its dictums were first trialled in earnest and have continued to be implemented most conclusively since. When democratically elected Chilean president Salvador Allende was overthrown by General Pinochet in 1973 in a coup backed by local business elites, American corporations and the US state, it was to the 'Chicago Boys' – Chilean economists who had trained at the University of Chicago under Milton Friedman – that the new regime turned for economic guidance. The reforms that followed came at the cost of more than 3,000 lives: Chileans who were killed or disappeared in an effort to stifle popular resistance to liberalization. Although the country was mired in economic crisis within a decade, Chile's experiment demonstrated that, with sufficient state violence to support it, neoliberal ideology could work as a successful cover for the restoration of domestic upper-class power and provide a rich profit stream for investors abroad. As the petrodollar boom in the mid-1970s flooded Western financial institutions with money and the wealthy went searching for new markets on which to speculate, the appeal of replicating Chile's trajectory in other countries across the global south expanded. And it was to the international regulators of the global economic system – the IMF and the World Bank – that capital turned to make this happen.

In the aftermath of the Second World War, at the famous Bretton

Woods conference, these transnational bodies had been created to provide investment and manage a system of fixed-price exchange rates under the old model of embedded economic liberalism. By the 1980s though, the collapse of that system had stripped the IMF and World Bank of much of their relevance and left them searching for a purpose. Neoliberalism provided it. Their new mission was to serve as financial police officers on a global scale, dedicated to enforcing market fundamentalism; whenever countries needed financial help from the international system, the Bretton Woods institutions would ensure they got it only in return for a commitment to neoliberal dogma – a one-size-fits-all reform model based around the mantra: 'stabilize, liberalize, privatize'.[26] The agreements governing this relationship are euphemistically title Economic Reconstruction and Structural Adjustment Programmes (ERSAP), and in the past thirty years, from Azerbaijan to Zambia, they have proliferated with astonishing speed. By the end of Mubarak's first decade in power, Egypt had secured an ERSAP of its own.

Egypt's economic problems in the 1980s – rising unemployment, inflation and budget deficits, alongside falling growth – brought the country to the brink of a default on government debt and saw technocrats from international financial institutions (IFIs) flooding back in to the arrivals lounge at Cairo airport once again with privatization strategies tucked under their arms. Their diagnosis of where Egypt had gone wrong was lifted straight from the neoliberal playbook: the state was attempting to support too many loss-making public sector institutions, government spending was profligate, and Egypt's currency was overvalued. These explanations were mostly wrong. Public sector enterprises were, by and large, profitable; at the time of the bailout negotiations, more than 80 per cent of non-financial, state-owned outfits were turning a profit, and the public sector as a whole was banking $440 million a year after tax.[27] The government's most 'profligate' area of spending was not the welfare state or public services but rather the purchase of military equipment, overwhelmingly from the United States (an arrangement which was slated to continue under liberalization reforms). Rather than Egypt's economic crisis being the fault of 'Nasser-era socialism', the budget deficit in the late 1980s was largely a consequence of falling global oil prices – a factor Egypt had little control over – and the turmoil was intensified by a private banking sector crisis fuelled by the machinations of super-rich financiers and businessmen: by 1989, a quarter of private and investment loans were in default, most of them held by a tiny minority of speculators.[28] But such facts didn't suit the narrative thrust of structural adjustment, so they were forgotten, reframed or morphed into their opposite to make neoliberal solutions look like an inevitability. Beyond the country's borders, argued neoliberalism's supporters, the world was being reordered: by 1991 the Berlin Wall had crumbled and political theorist Francis Fukuyama had published his seminal essay proclaiming 'The End of History' and the final, immutable triumph of Western-style economic liberalism and democracy. If Egypt pushed back against the tide, it risked being left behind. Throughout that year, the Egyptian government and a series of IFIs concluded loan agreements which bound the country to a rigid ERSAP blueprint: deals were struck with the IMF in May, the African Development Bank in September, and the World Bank in November. The following month, as the year drew to a close, the Soviet Union was formally dissolved.

The gritty details of Egypt's structural adjustment programme will look familiar to anyone with a passing interest in Jamaica, Jordan, Bolivia or any one of the dozens of countries which have embraced IFI-sponsored neoliberal reform packages in the global south. Through a series of laws passed throughout the 1990s and early 2000s, Egypt's public sector was divided into dozens of 'holding companies' which could then dispose of their assets on the open market. No longer were state institutions to be thought of as economic development projects, the success of which would be judged by whether or not they met the social and political goals of the state. Now, they were merely an epic estate agent's inventory.[29] Huge corporate tax exemptions were established, and Egypt's richest were eventually granted a flat-rate income tax of 20 per cent; by the mid-2000s, the average tax liability of many of Egypt's biggest and most profitable companies was just 8 per cent.[30] New labour laws established fixed-term hiring as a norm and allowed employers to renew the temporary contracts of their staff indefinitely without offering them any longer-term employment rights; workers also faced new limits on their right to strike. Egypt's rulers were so enthused by structural adjustment that they went further and faster in implementing it than even the IMF had expected. Soon after ERSAP began, the government promised technocrats it would sell off 'a company a week'[31] and they came darn close to succeeding – by the end of Mubarak's reign no fewer than 336 previously public entities had been privatized.[32]

Those supervising the firesale of Egypt's assets quickly amassed a host of statistics to justify structural adjustment. Inflation fell from around 20 per cent in the late 1980s to just 5 per cent a decade later. The budget deficit tumbled from 15 per cent of GDP to under 3 per cent.[33] The private sector's contribution to GDP soared from 30 per cent to 80 per cent, and in some sectors – such as agricultural production or the provision of services such as health and education – virtually pushed out the state altogether.[34] Annual GDP growth rose up to 7 per cent a year, every year.[35] It was, according to the headline figures, one of the most stunning economic turnarounds in contemporary history. As with the 'tiger economies' of South East Asia, foreign politicians and capitalists alike scrambled to bestow ever-higher accolades on the Mubarak regime, and urged it to push on with neoliberal reforms. 'You know what you have to do,' Washington's ambassador to Egypt told an audience in Cairo in 2004. 'Just do it, and you'll truly see a tiger on the Nile.'[36] From its headquarters in central Washington DC, the World Bank heralded Egypt's neoliberal turn as a 'major achievement' and congratulated the regime on 'undertaking these reforms without significant social unrest'.[37]

Back in the fields of the Nile Delta, meanwhile, ERSAP's record read very differently.

Sarandu proved hard to find. The little hamlet is tucked away within a dense tapestry of farmland around Damanhour, provincial capital of Beheira governorate – one of the Delta's most fertile regions – and reaching it involved two hours of near-blind navigation through a gathering dusk: criss-crossing agricultural roads, skirting irrigation canals, careering around hairpin bends into milk-yellow truck headlights and Lilliputian *tuk-tuk* carts (automated rickshaws) honking their way through the gloom. My research colleague, Effat – a thoroughly urban soul, who refuses point-blank to drive anything larger than a Vespa – ploughed through two full packs of cigarettes along the journey, while offering me vague noises of encouragement from the passenger seat. We sourced help from everyone we came across: a riotous wedding party; a bunch of wary teenagers who had gathered below a clump of palms to watch porn on their mobile phones and smoke *bango**; a small army of loquacious male elders who interrupted their shisha-smoking to gather around our creaking Honda and sent limbs and spittle flying through the windows as they argued among themselves over the optimum route. Each set of fresh directions entirely contradicted the last. By the time we finally rolled up to Sarandu's central square, darkness had truly fallen. A stream of people was heading towards the mosque for prayers; on a dusty patch of ground beyond, kids were kicking a football around under the glow of orange lamplight and managing, somehow, to keep a game going despite the keen involvement of several scampering dogs. As we got out of the car, a passing youth waved hello. Despite its remote location, the place felt welcoming, and lively. It didn't look like the frontline of a war. That, however, is exactly what Sarandu has become.

From the moment all those international loan agreements were signed in 1991, structural adjustment had rural Egypt in its sights. The World Bank believes there is only one credible strategy for rural development anywhere in the world, and it has spelled out that strategy explicitly in multiple and lengthy policy documents over the past three decades: the removal of state controls on land, an expansion in exchangeable private ownership, a shift away from local needs and towards agricultural production geared at the demands of the global market.[38] In Egypt, this meant that Nasser's limited land reforms in favour of redistribution to the poor – already chipped away at under Sadat's presidency and undermined still further by a succession of reforms overseen by USAID (the American federal government agency responsible for administering civilian foreign aid) in the 1980s – were now to be rolled back in their entirety. Starting with Law 96 of 1992, which increased land rents more than threefold at a

* Local low-grade cannabis

stroke, ordinary farmers entered a five-year 'transition period' in which fields under *fellaheen* control were gradually removed from them by force and placed back in the hands of their original, pre-1952 owners, or their descendants. By 1997, 'returning' land-lords, or whomever they had chosen to sell their fields on to, were free to charge peasants any rent they pleased, fuelling further hikes of up to 400 per cent. Under new legislation, landowners could refuse to renew long-term contracts and were permitted to dispose of tenancies at will. Farmers who had spent their entire lives working a plot but could not afford the new rents received no protection from the state. Nor did anyone who was able to pay, but to whom the landlord took a personal disliking; female-headed tenant households were particularly vulnerable to eviction on a whim. The first that many *fellaheen* knew of these changes was when landowners drove up to the fields accompanied by government security forces and a sheaf of paperwork, before ordering farmers to put down their tools.

Egypt's counter-revolution in the countryside strengthened Mubarak's connection with two key constituencies his regime depended upon for survival: landed domestic elites and the representatives of international capital, whose seal of approval for the government's structural adjustment reforms was constantly being sought. Following the land privatization programme, such approval was delivered in spades. Law 96, claimed USAID in 2000, had done away "with more than 40 years of an imbalanced relationship between landlords and tenants'.[39] The World Bank went further. '[Egypt's] agricultural sector is now a fully private sector,' it concluded admiringly in 2001, 'operating in a market and export-orientated economy.' In the five-star Cairo hotels where IFI consultants set up shop, occasional misgivings were expressed regarding a mammoth petition against land privatization, signed by 350,000 Egyptian citizens in a country where open opposition to the regime could get you killed. And yet officials at the ministry of agriculture assured their partners that the petition numbers must be skewed; it was simply impossible, they explained, for popular feeling against government policy to be so widespread. Experts from the American government, who co-published a report with their Egyptian counterparts on public reaction to the land reforms, seemingly concurred. The report heralded the 'good relations' between landlords and tenants as a result of structural adjustment; anti-reform protest, it assured readers, remained 'minimal'.[40]

Sarandu, and hundreds of other small villages like it, are living refutations of that report. Most have paid a heavy price for their honesty.

Dawn had not yet broken on 4 March 2005, when police trucks rumbled into Sarandu's tiny streets and roused seven men from their beds, locking them up for stealing crops and illegally occupying land.[41] The figure behind these allegations, hereditary landlord Salah Nawar, arrived himself a few hours later along with dozens of supporters bussed in from other parts of the country. Many came driving tractors, and most were armed. He had tried this once before, but without the backup of the state's security apparatus the local peasants were too strong to be forced off the fields and Nawar's private militia had merely dallied on the edge of the village before turning back. This time, with the police watching on, things were different. Nawar's men moved in, and were met with fierce resistance. By 9 a.m., it looked as if the locals had successfully repelled the attack: Nawar's tractors were in flames, and one of his drivers dead. Then, relentlessly, came the police. By 10 a.m. fifty villagers had been arrested, among them thirteen women and five young children aged between two and nine years old. A Human Rights Watch report, based on an investigation by Egyptian human rights organizations, later recounted testimony from villagers detailing how officers broke into homes, 'stealing food and valuables and destroying furnishings, beating women who attempted to protect their husbands and sons . . . police reportedly humiliated women and girls, cursing them, binding the detained women and girls together by their braided hair in addition to handcuffs, and in some cases beating them in the face with shoes'.[42] Truck-loads of armed central security forces, visors down and shields up, encircled the hamlet. The six-month siege of Sarandu was underway.*

'The whole village was surrounded, and no one was allowed in or out without checks,' Taher Badr, a 57-year-old Sarandu *fellah*, explained to me and Effat over a warm meal of rice and meat, washed

---

* Contemporary news reports likened it to a modern-day version of *el-'Ard* ('The Land'), the classic Youssef Chahine film on peasant exploitation in the 1930s.

down with Fanta from the finest family cups. 'If people left for work, they were afraid they wouldn't be able to get back in. Of course many of the men had simply fled through the fields when the siege began. Those of us that were left, we lived in handcuffs. We all lived with the knowledge that they could break into our homes at any time of the night, plant a bit of hashish or a weapon on us, and then destroy us just like that.' A ginger cat skittered beneath the table in search of scraps and was forced out by a succession of prods and hisses. 'The thing is, Nawar's boot came down upon us and our land just as the crops were ready for harvest, so we had nothing,' added Taher, smoothing down his white skullcap and contracting his trim moustache into a frown. 'We couldn't stay silent. We had to fight back.'

The following weeks were surreal. Raids on houses after dark were common, as was the ritual beating and humiliation of villagers by the security forces. Phone lines into Sarandu and the neighbouring hamlet of Ezbit Bahariyya were cut by the police to intensify the villagers' isolation, and most farmers were barred from access to their land and livestock, leaving valuable animals to die from lack of care. With many men having fled following the initial violence to avoid arrest, it was often women who bore the brunt of arbitrary detention during the siege. 'One woman described being part of a group of fourteen women, including three elderly women, whom police blindfolded and moved from police checkpoint to police checkpoint for five days, sleeping on bare tile floors without blankets, food, or water,' detailed the Human Rights Watch report. 'Another woman described being detained outdoors with her three young children for three days without food or blankets in an effort to force her to falsely testify that her husband had participated in burning a tractor.' Just over a week into the siege, a 38-year-old woman named Nafisa Zakaria al-Marakbi was taken from her home by police and into a private house in the village that had been commandeered as a makeshift prison. According to other women being detained there at the time, 'police terrorised and humiliated al-Marakbi by removing her *niqab* and grabbing her breasts and belly while making sexual threats'. They then took her out of the house on her own, out of sight of the others; when she was finally released at 3 a.m. eyewitnesses described her physical and psychological state as 'extremely bad'. With her condition deteriorating, family members managed to get her past police lines later that day and send her towards Damanhour general hospital. By the time she arrived at 9 p.m., al-Marakbi was in a coma; the following morning, she was pronounced dead.

After dinner, Taher pulled out a carefully folded plastic bag and, with fierce pride, arranged its contents on the red mat where we sat. They were old land records, all he had left of the two and a half *feddans* of soil he had spent most of his life cultivating. Next to them were records of a different kind: news reports of the siege, correspondence with lawyers, details of failed legal appeals. I've seen so many bags and folders like this over the years, stuffed to the brim with foolscaps of bureaucracy – dog-eared photocopies of official letters, neon-highlighted newspaper cuttings, ink-smudged stamps of lower court officialdom – and unfurled on the floor of family houses. For many Egyptians marginalized by the state, these papers are a form of reclaiming presence. They serve as tangible proof of some recognition by authority, as a reminder of a time when one's family was placed on a map, any sort of map, and the feelings of worth and legitimacy that entails. Perhaps most importantly, they are a crumpled, institutional memory of individual and community struggle. 'Before our fight in Sarandu began, we had in mind that the government was just, a fair arbiter between different interests,' said Taher, sifting painstakingly through his bundle. 'And we had no idea how wrong this sentiment was.' He pulled out an *al-Masry al-Youm* front page from the time, with the headline: 'Sarandu: Land of Terror'. 'Why do you have a government?' Taher demanded. 'Surely it's above all to represent the collective will of the people and decide fairly between competing forces, not to side overwhelmingly with one side, the rich, in an effort to crush another, the poor.'

Sarandu was among the last of a long line of villages that attempted to stand firm against the combined might of Egypt's wealthiest landowners and the government's security apparatus, girded by a global web of neoliberal legitimacy. Initial protests began as early as 1996 in Beni Suef, just south of Cairo, where over 3,000 demonstrators took to the streets. Within the first nine months of land rents becoming fully marketized in 1997, the Land Center for Human Rights (LCHR) recorded seventeen deaths, over 500 wounded and more than 1,500 arrested in battles between landowners and *fellaheen*. In the years that followed, black flags fluttered at the entrances of thousands of villages to signify that the inhabitants were openly defying the regime's efforts to sever their link with the land. Even as government officials and their American counterparts continued to maintain that there was no sustained opposition to the land reform programme, Egypt's security forces responded to just such an opposition with a wave of rural repression that was modelled on the tried and tested strategy they had used against Islamist groups in Upper Egypt, the most militant of which had mounted an insurgency against the state throughout the early and mid-1990s and claimed hundreds of casualties.[43] Mubarak had reinstituted Emergency Law upon his arrival in office and maintained it throughout his entire reign with the justification that it was needed to fight terrorism; this legalized suspension of constitutional rights enabled the security forces to engage in arbitrary detention, collective punishment and extensive state torture, and all were brought down to bear upon recalcitrant *fellaheen*. Despite the crackdown, resistance flashpoints continued to appear in many unexpected places. In Minya, far south on the Nile, several thousand tenant farmers gathered in two villages and set fire to the houses of landowners before blocking main roads and torching a railway line. In the Delta village of el-Attaf, hundreds attacked the local office of the agricultural ministry in an attempt to destroy official records. In Qamaruna, north-east of Cairo, a seventy-year-old farmer and his wife were beaten to death by a landlord and his son after refusing to pay a rent increase.[44] As evictions mounted and rural poverty spiralled, far from tail off, the level of protest intensified; in 2004, the year leading up to the Sarandu siege, forty-nine were killed in landowner–farmer disputes, many involving the police.

In Kamshish, thirty years after Shahenda and her lover first managed to beat back the al-Fiqis, the old family reasserted its full rights to the land, leaving 500 local farmers facing eviction. 'Where should I go? I do not have anything else besides this half *feddan* of land, and all these years I have not saved a penny,' Abd al-Rasul, one of the threatened tenants, told a journalist.[45] 'Should I send my children to steal?' Having lived through the days when a single feudal family could determine the fate of an entire village – and where those who refused to submit ended up in the private prison of the patron – many older Kamshish residents simply could not believe what was happening. 'Something like this, after all those years I burned my skin out in my field,' said one elderly farmer incredulously. 'We simply could not imagine that water would flow upriver,' added another. Their words fell on deaf ears. Salah Nawar, the Sarandu landowner, summed up the sentiment of much of Egypt's political class when he attempted to justify the violence meted out against *fellaheen* trying to resist the neo-colonial usurpation of their livelihoods. 'If the peasants get away with this, such things will spread all over,' Nawar argued. 'The farmers will revolt and attack all the owners.'

Egypt's farmers did revolt, though they didn't win. In Sarandu, under the intolerable pressure of the police siege, Taher eventually surrendered his *feddans*. 'It was a choice between that or prison,' he told us. At the time of the siege Taher was just out of surgery, and feared for his health if he was thrown in jail. The last straw came when he went to visit a police officer to enquire about a detained relative, and was told that he too would end up behind bars if the resistance didn't end. 'We have 700 cases [against *fellaheen*] on the go, and you know how easily we could add you,' smirked the officer. Taher wasn't the only one who gave in. Sarandu's barricades gradually buckled and Nawar got its fields. He sold them two years later and cashed in; he now lives in Alexandria, and steers well clear of the village. The hereditary landowner continues to insist that the *fellaheen* had no reason to feel hard done by, arguing that resistance had been whipped up artificially by external forces. 'People come from Cairo and tell them they can have all the land,' he told reporters. 'The peasants never acted like this before ... What you have to understand is that the peasants aren't educated, they're very simple and it's been easy for the activists to brainwash them.'[46]

The IFI-sponsored 'modernization' of the Egyptian countryside throughout the 1990s and 2000s and the shift towards an agricultural production model based around exports rather than domestic demand have enabled major multinational food and agribusiness groups – including Heinz, Unilever, Cadbury, Danone and Coca-Cola, as well as Gulf-based conglomerates such as Dina Farms, Juhayna and Wataniya Poultry – to extract large profits from the fields of the

Nile Delta, while decimating the prosperity of those who lived there.[47] In total, evictions enabled by the passing of Law 96 left 1 million families – one-third of Egypt's rural population – without land. The removal of most families' primary source of income sparked a rash of 'abrupt impoverishment', devastating the most vulnerable social groups.[48] Research carried out in rural areas in the years following the 'transition' has exposed the many hidden catastrophes of land-lessness: children taken out of school, especially girls, to cut down on household expenditure, severe food shortages (the Land Centre for Human Rights listed 'sleeping early to avoid feeling hungry' as a common coping strategy deployed by peasants), a dramatic expansion of child labour, and the selling off of household assets from livestock to furniture, kitchen appliances to women's jewellery. There were other less tangible sacrifices too; in tight-knit villages, great weight is placed on the fulfilment of communal obligations but sudden poverty forced many to choose physical endurance over social survival. Tribal elders whose traditional job it was to buy and slaughter a lamb or goat at the time of harvest could no longer afford to do so and saw their local standing evaporate as a result; wives walked out on husbands who weren't able to pay the customary *nuqta* ('monetary gift') to family members on the occasion of their wedding.[49] And, perhaps most critically, rural Egypt's young men broke with generations of their ancestors who had farmed the land and instead joined an exodus: to the outskirts of the country's urban sprawls, to the Gulf via agency work programmes, or to more exotic climes such as Malta, Greece or Lampedusa, passage to which consisted of cramming oneself in with dozens of others beneath the hull of a Mediterranean fishing boat and praying that you would arrive on Europe's doorstep alive.

Mohamed Radi knows those boats. He was one of the many young people who fled Sarandu during the siege, in his case after being arrested in the aftermath of the battle with Nawar's men. Police were on the hunt for one of his relatives, and regularly used the tactic of detaining family members to force their suspect to give himself up. Mohamed was en route to school when he was pointed out to officers by a local informant; within moments he had been snatched from the roadside. 'They asked me where my relative was and I said I didn't know,' he recalls. 'Then they got threatening, and asked whether I was going to cooperate with them or whether they would have to file a case against me as well. I was young then and I have to admit I had strong words for them in my reply. I was ... upfront. And angry.' Mohamed leaned forward when he spoke, holding eye contact throughout and rocking slowly, as if the intensity of what he had to say was propelling his body into motion. The land seizures and accompanying violence politicized him, like many across the Delta and Upper Egypt, in a way he would barely have thought possible. Before the siege of Sarandu he had failed to draw a connection between local grievances and the broader corruption of the Egyptian state; back then, he still imagined that Mubarak and his ministers were essentially good people, constantly let down by the avarice and violence of ground-level functionaries. 'At the beginning of our strug- gle, we felt that if only a responsible official from the government would come and listen, then everything would change. But as I saw police attacking the village, as I went through prison, I sensed that feeling alter. It was as if the truth was unfolding bit by bit, and once it was fully stretched out before us we could see that this was a gov- ernment of nothing more than injustice.'

Mohamed was among twenty-six locals formally charged in Sarandu; when most were declared innocent, President Mubarak ordered a retrial to be held in a supreme state security emergency court, where defendants are denied many of the rights they theoretically enjoy in an ordinary court.[50] This time around, Mohamed was found guilty. 'I was here at home when the lawyers called to say that the verdict had come through, and as soon as I heard it I knew what I had to do. I knew prison, and I knew its humiliations. I knew I had to get out.' Hiding in the village was impossible; the local network of police spies would have flushed him out in no time. So, as Shahenda Maklad had once done herself under very different circumstances, Mohamed fled the Delta for the north coast. Twice he attempted to escape across the ocean as an irregular migrant: one boat was heading to the Greek islands, another to the Levant, but due to various pieces of bad luck neither succeeded and Mohamed found himself holed up as a fugitive in Alexandria, bereft of money and contacts.[51] He earned bits and pieces as a doorman and a garage attendant, but never risked trying to return home. 'He never came back all this time, he couldn't,' said his mother Sabri softly. Sabri's burden in those years was heavy; her other sons had also disappeared, fearing similar targeting by the police. 'I had to face everything alone in the village,' she told us tearfully. 'All the trials. I was sick. And alone.'

Mubarak's assault on the rural poor was in part a test of how uncompromisingly his regime could push through socially destructive policy reforms in the face of widespread opposition. For the IFIs, it was a preview of the financial opportunities a more neoliberal Egyptian state, fully integrated into the international financial markets (and thus far less capable of taking sovereign economic decisions of its own) could potentially provide. Over the following two decades, Western states and the multilateral financial and development institutions they dominated – not just the World Bank and IMF, but also USAID, the African Development Bank and the various investment and development organs of the European Union – blitzed Egypt with progress reports, policy guidance and multilateral treaties that cemented the country within a global economic orthodoxy: membership of both the Euro – Mediterranean Partnership (EUROMED) and the World Trade Organization in 1995, a US–Egypt Trade and Investment Framework Agreement in 1999, accession to the planned US–Middle East Free Trade Area in 2003 and the EU's European Neighbourhood Policy in 2004, to name only a few. The final resolution of a Middle East and North African economic summit, held in Cairo in 1996, noted, 'The region's economic, commercial and trade potential . . . is being greatly enhanced by important economic reform programs currently being undertaken.' These reforms, it concluded, 'have provided for a more business-friendly economic climate throughout the region'. US Secretary of State Warren Christopher declared breezily that the Middle East was finally 'open for business'.[52]

Structural adjustment – not just in terms of agricultural land privatization, but as a way of reworking Egypt's towns, cities, workforce, welfare state, factories, industry and infrastructure – served to tether Mubarak's closed political circle to foreign investors and a privileged domestic support base, thanks to the new avenues of capital accumulation it made available to both. And crucially, it was the very nature of the Egyptian state – stretching right back to the dictatorship established by Nasser, itself built upon colonial and feudal foundations – that made it such an ideal vehicle for the expansion of markets, upon which all those parties came to rely. Neoliberal logic demands that economic decision-making be walled off from broader political influence; the exclusionary Egyptian state was already well configured for exactly that purpose, and throughout the 1990s and 2000s the sequestration of those who would draw up and implement economic reform policies intensified even further. In 1992, with the help of a $10 million endowment from USAID, a new think-tank named The Egyptian Center for Economic Studies (ECES) was formed.[53] It brought together members of the president's inner circle, like his son Gamal Mubarak, with the country's wealthiest businessmen, many of whom already had strong links to IFIs (the organization's first director, Ahmed Galal, was a former World Bank economist). Over time, the ECES became a key conduit through which neoliberal reform strategies, developed on a global scale by IFI consultants and assuming concrete form in all those international treaties, could be funnelled straight into the heart of the Egyptian government. By the early 2000s, the ruling National Democratic Party had been reorganized by Gamal Mubarak around a new 'central policy committee', which heavily liaised with and overlapped the ECES. In 2004, following pressure from USAID, a whole new national government was appointed consisting almost entirely of ECES tycoons.

One of neoliberalism's great strengths is to appear as if it is the irresistible outcome of decentralized, common-sense management decisions, the origins of which are so diffuse that they are impossible to identify accurately and resist. In reality, the opposite is often true. The trajectory of Egyptian neoliberalism was engineered by a highly centralized and undemocratic system of governance with the aid of the global financial community, whose operators hid behind layers of acronyms and escaped any public accountability. The ring of Mubarak Country's economic authority was bound so tight that even other elements of the regime's bureaucracy were scarcely able to mount opposition; potential trouble-makers, such as the country's top military generals, were assimilated into the new status quo by being offered a slice of the plunder to follow. Resistance elsewhere, meanwhile, among the likes of Mohamed and his mother Sabri in Sarandu, was dealt with by the state's formidable security apparatus.

Mohamed and Sabri's experiences represent the flipside of structural adjustment's official scorecard. Despite inflation initially falling, ERSAP eventually sent it spiralling upwards, just as had happened under Sadat's *infitah*. With foreign investment booming, corporate profits soaring and GDP rises supposedly shooting off the scale, the vast majority of Egyptians – stuck in fixed low-wage government work or scrambling for odd jobs on the fringes of the formal economy to make ends meet – saw their purchasing power decimated. Mubarak presided over the highest inflationary period in Egyptian history;[54] in 1970 the monthly salary of a new government employee was enough to buy sixty-eight kilos of meat, yet by 2008 an Egyptian in exactly the same position could purchase only six kilos – a drop of over 90 per cent.[55] The result was that, under Egypt's 'business-friendly' makeover, 95 per cent of state employees fell into poverty.[56] Industrial workers, forced by their newly private employers to work harder, longer and with fewer rights than ever before,[57] delivered increasingly higher productivity rates for their bosses – and were rewarded with a constant reduction in salaries.[58] As tax rates for the super-rich tumbled, and private wealth in the top decile exploded, the national minimum wage remained at 34 Egyptian pounds (£3.50 GBP) a month – an amount unchanged since 1984. For many, even that paltry figure was out of reach. By the late 2000s unemployment had risen so sharply that one in four Egyptians was out of work; among the millions who had been born since 1981 and knew no other president than Mubarak, the jobless figure was estimated at over 75 per cent.[59] At the same time, subsidies for foodstuffs such as sugar, cooking oil and dairy products were slashed, just as the introduction of 'cost-recovery mechanisms' in the healthcare and education sectors forced ordinary Egyptians to pay a whole raft of fees for state services that had previously been free.[60] In a stark example of how skewed the neoliberal fixation on economic growth is, the percentage of Egypt's citizens who rated their overall wellbeing as 'thriving' fell year after year in the run-up to the revolution, even as GDP-per-capita figures continued to increase.[61] The cumulative effect of Egypt's 'major achievement' under neoliberalism was that the number of

Egyptians living below $2 a day – the international poverty line – more than doubled, from 20 to 44 per cent. Those living in absolute poverty, unable to meet their most basic daily needs, swelled to 15 million – one in five of Mubarak's citizens.[62]

In 2007, a prominent Egyptian state official and economist asserted on television that although Mubarak may not have studied economics, he was clearly gifted with 'economic inspiration': this enabled him to have brilliant economic ideas that had eluded even academic economists themselves.[63] That year, as GDP growth rates topped 7 per cent, the United Nations Human Poverty Index relegated Egypt to the bottom third of all developing countries,[64] and child malnutrition climbed to such a level that almost one in three babies did not have enough to eat and suffered from stunted growth.[65] As with the obsequious state official, none of this was enough to dent the unbridled enthusiasm of international finance. In 2010, less than twelve months before the revolution began, the IMF called Egypt a 'top performer' and issued a report looking back at twenty years of structural adjustment in Egypt, with glowing conclusions. 'Economic performance was better than expected,' declared the report's authors. They went on to praise the regime's 'careful fiscal management' and observed with approval that 'sustained and wide-ranging reforms [have] improved the investment climate'.[66]

Why did seemingly unstoppable economic growth translate into such deep immiseration for the majority of Egypt's citizens? The answer lies in the details of what sort of wealth was created in neoliberal Egypt, and which forces were in the best position to capture it. The privatization programme, for example, which saw everything from textile mills to wastewater services being transferred out of collective social ownership and sold into corporate hands, did not produce a buoyant private sector; instead, it enriched nepotistic clusters of politically powerful individuals and families, either closely connected to the regime or positioned at a senior level within it. The main economic institution inside Egypt was never the market but rather a web of personal ties that spanned businesses, state institutions, the banking sector, the armed forces and the local franchises of transnational corporations.[67] Within that web, key players, nurtured by prized government contracts (civilian and military) and often by USAID money as well, established vast high-end goods and services consortiums out of the flotsam discarded by the state. Their names became internationally synonymous with Egypt's wafer-thin glitzy exterior: the Seoudis, the Bahgats, the Metwallis, the Mohamed Mahmouds, the Mansours, the Sawirises and the Lakahs. All maintained close links with the state, and some, like steel magnate Ahmed Ezz (senior official within the ruling NDP, member of parliament and chairman of the People's Assembly budget committee), property developer Hisham Talaat Moustafa (Shura Council representative and member of the NDP central policy committee), or bottled water tycoon Sayed Meshaal (army general, minister of military production and head of the armed forces' military production consortium) were critical elements within it. Given their position and the economic muscle afforded to them by $1.3 billion worth of American aid each year, members of the military's top brass like Meshaal were particularly well placed to navigate to their personal advantage the growing points of connection between the state and private capital. As the land privatization programme gathered pace, for example, the Food Security Division of Egypt's army grew its empire; by the late 1990s, it had become the largest agro-industrial complex in the country.[68] Strategic assets acquired by the military, such as the Alexandria shipyards, were then expanded and developed in partnership with multinational corporations and financiers. On the management board of virtually every new 'holding company' conjured out of once-public entities, a retired army general was always to be found.

As sizeable chunks of the state were flogged off one by one, evidence of staggering malfeasance mounted. Egypt's state-owned bottling company was sold to private Egyptian buyers for 158 million EGP in 1994, then sold on a few years later to Pepsi Co. for eleven times that amount. The state-run el-Nasr Boilers Company sat on land which alone was worth $100 million; despite sustained protests by company workers, the whole enterprise was sold to the private sector for just $750,000. The state-owned Egyptian American Bank, one of the country's few financial institutions that appeared to be sustainably run and reliably profitable, was trading on the stock exchange at 56 EGP a share ahead of its privatization in the mid-2000s, and yet was sold at an effective share price of 40 EGP. Small investors lost heavily and the state sacrificed over 300 million EGP in potential revenue; meanwhile the buyers – the French firm Crédit Agricole CIB and two of Mubarak's cabinet ministers (housing minister Ahmed el-Maghraby and transport minister Mohamed Mansour) – cashed in. Under Egyptian law it is mandatory for an extraordinary general meeting to be held whenever a publicly traded company is being sold en masse so that all shareholders can have their say; in this instance, and in many others, no such meeting was ever called.[69] After the government rejected a 400 million EGP bid for the al-Ahram Beverage Company (ABC) for being too low, it went on to sell the firm in 1997 to an investment consortium led by Ahmed Zeyat, a racehorse-breeder and close friend of Gamal Mubarak, who offered half that amount. Five years later Zeyat sold the firm to Heineken for 1.3 billion EGP, the most profitable corporate turnover in Egypt's modern history.[70] The Egyptian newspaper *al-Shaab* declared the ABC episode to be among the 'worst privatization sales ever'.[71] The verdict of the local business press, Wall Street and international financial consultants, on the other hand, was quite different. Egypt's English-language *Business Today* called the ABC privatization an unqualified success story; a Credit Suisse First Boston analyst deemed it 'one of the most obvious examples of a successful privatization in Egypt'; a USAID-commissioned report repeated exactly the same words.

All these under-priced privatizations meant that within five years of the appointment of Mubarak's ultra-reformist government in 2004, Egypt's public debt had more than doubled. And it was the poor – despite being the social group most harmed by the 'accumulation by dispossession' strategy that privatization amounted to at the top – who were left to service it. National debt repayments cost the taxpayer twenty-three times what the government was spending on education, and 3,000 times what it spent on housing. But still, it was never enough. The IMF and the World Bank maintained almost constant pressure on the Egyptian government to both continue and extend the privatization programme, threatening to withhold debt relief if sales were not sped up, and using each new round of loan negotiations to ensure that areas of the economy previously exempted from privatization were now opened up to private competition.[72] At every opportunity, new austerity measures to help break down what remained of the public sector were encouraged; in 2004, for example, a World Bank report on government employment recommended 'lowering remuneration for new entrants' and 'focusing on non-wage benefits that distort labour decisions, such as generous pension systems and family allowances that add to the allure of employment in the public sector'.[73]

Internationally, those who spent their lives manipulating financial flows and making money from money eyed Egypt with rising glee. 'The daily 747 from London's Heathrow to Cairo is packed, but not with tourists en route to see the Pyramids. Businessmen fill the seats,' gushed *Forbes* magazine in 1999.

> They are looking for ways to deploy capital in what was, until very recently, a socialist basket case: Egypt. The collapse of stock markets in Latin America, Southeast Asia and Russia has made a joke out of Third World investing. Yet Egypt is proving that a poor, belligerently anticapitalist nation can adopt capitalism. The process hasn't been fast or seamless, but then if it had been you wouldn't be finding bargains on the Cairo Stock Exchange.[74]

The report went on to hail the absence of kleptocracy in contemporary Egypt.

Across the twenty-year privatization programme implemented between the dawn of structural adjustment and the outbreak of revolution two decades later, the total market value of all the assets sold by the Egyptian government to the private sector was estimated by experts at $104 billion. The actual amount received by the state was $9.4 billion, less than a tenth of what the Egyptian people were owed.[75]

When the US ambassador to Egypt engaged in all that 'Tiger on the Nile' fist-pumping back in 2004, what was really being sold was a highly selective story, each chapter of which was written to mask a remarkable act of larceny. The tale of Egypt's 'growing' private sector was actually a tale of direct wealth distribution from the bottom upwards, and of an intense concentration of economic power in the hands of those most invested in Mubarak's regime. In reality, public monopolization was simply replaced by private monopolization on the part of figures occupying the highest reaches of the state. By the eve of revolution, for example, 90 per cent of Egypt's cement market consisted of just four companies. Almost the entire production and retailing of steel, meanwhile, was comprised of just three companies, and one of them – Ezz Steel, owned by senior NDP official Ahmed Ezz – was responsible for more than half of the industry on its own.[76] The flood of foreign investment that came pouring into the country as a result of neoliberal reforms, particularly the dismantling of capital restrictions – another chapter in the Egyptian structural adjustment success story – did little to boost the livelihoods of most Egyptians. By and large, incoming funds didn't flow into sustainable industries that might generate local prosperity or employment for the long-term; instead they were insta-profit gambles by international speculators betting on sectors that looked set for a temporary surge. Most of Egypt's overall GDP growth took place inside two relatively small areas of economic activity – tourism and construction – which grew frenetically as the beneficiaries of so-called 'hot money', amassed in the Gulf as a result of rising oil prices in the mid-2000s, searched for a quick new outlet for capital accumulation. By selling off undervalued public desert land to themselves and building vast (and empty) developments upon it, Egypt's ruling class provided just such an outlet. The expansion of these sectors was built on little more than an inflated capital bubble, liable to burst as soon as there was a downturn in global financial confidence or more lucrative speculation opportunities arose elsewhere. That's exactly what happened in 2008, when the Cairo stock market lost 40 per cent of its value overnight and food prices rose by a third, causing bread lines to form across the country.[77] While standing in these queues for basic sustenance, eleven citizens died – some from fighting, others from exhaustion.[78]

Mubarak's Egypt is sometimes described as an example of 'crony capitalism', as if the imbalances in the economy that arose out of structural adjustment were somehow an aberration from the norm. But as the international adulation for Mubarak's economic policies throughout his reign demonstrates, nothing could be further from the truth. Neoliberalism is a political project, and its implementation always involves a mass transfer of resources from the poor to the rich. The meshing of Egypt's insulated and patrician state on the one hand and the power-brokers of private capital on the other, was an absolute necessity if the reforms were to work, not a glitch in the system. Without the state intervening to open up new markets and repress dissent among the citizenry, liberalization policies could never have been pushed through; without Mubarak's patronage of Egypt's domestic business elites and the profit-streams he supplied to his closest allies, his increasingly hated regime would not have survived its collapse in popular legitimacy for long, and foreign investors would never have had anybody to partner with. Public assets may have been privatized away, but as political scientist Timothy Mitchell observes, the Egyptian state didn't shrink under neoliberalism – it fortified itself and adjusted its priorities, subsidizing financiers instead of factories, cement kilns instead of bakeries, and speculators instead of schools. 'The reform program did not remove the state from the market or eliminate profligate public subsidies,' he observed. 'Its main impact was to concentrate public funds into different hands, and many fewer.'[79]

The result was that, under neoliberalism, Mubarak Country became a land of minority accumulation and majority degradation; Nader Fergany, lead author of the UN's Arab Human Development Report, described the last decade of Mubarak's rule as the one that boasted the starkest inequality witnessed since colonial times, a return to a society where 'one per cent controls almost all the wealth in the country'.[80] From 1991 onwards, Egypt's richest 10 per cent got richer, and its poorest 10 per cent got poorer; before ERSAP the nation's wage-earners acquired about half of the national GDP, yet by 2007 their share had fallen to less than a fifth.[81] The statistics are incredible, but what they can't relate was the pervasive aura of disenfranchisement that touched upon every aspect of most Egyptians' daily lives, the constant, visible reminders – with every imported luxury car passed on the highway, every new billboard envisioning an airbrushed escape from the city – that this nation, in these times, with these celebrated economic triumphs, was not designed for the likes of them. Increasingly economic energy was directed towards the tiny band of Egyptians who could afford to buy into Mubarak's model of modernity: a 'Value Meal' at McDonald's cost more than an average day's wages; a trip to a new desert entertainment complex would consume a whole fortnight's worth of a normal family income; a pair of children's shoes at a boutique fashion retailer exceeded the monthly salary of a schoolteacher.[82] Meanwhile, soup kitchens returned to the streets of Cairo. One national newspaper celebrated their appearance by arguing that it was a welcome return to the sort of private benevolence not seen since the days of the monarchy.[83]

The state's empowerment of its 'whales' and 'sharks' – as the big-business beasts who amassed fortunes out of market fundamentalism were often referred to in Egypt – and its parallel abandonment of ordinary Egyptians, were brazen acts of betrayal and corruption that took countless, nuanced forms.[84] Some made the headlines in a flash of momentary outrage; others ground silently below the surface, far beyond the national gaze. On 3 February 2006, a Red Sea ferry carrying 1,400 Egyptians returning home from Saudi Arabia developed a small fire. The ship was only an hour out of port and passengers assumed it would turn back. Instead it continued, and the fire spread. By the time the ship sank, it was clear that there were not enough lifeboats or lifejackets for those on board; more than 1,000 Egyptians perished in the water. 'This is a dirty government, may God burn their hearts as they burned mine,' said one woman who lost her brother.[85] The boat's owner was Mamdouh Ismail, a senior NDP lawmaker. An investigation later concluded that the vessel had not met minimum safety standards and that Ismail and his son had collaborated with maritime authorities to ensure it sailed anyway. Ismail, who was charged with manslaughter, was allowed by the authorities to leave the country before his trial, and promptly escaped to Britain. In absentia, he was acquitted.* 'It is a black comedy,' said dissident judge Ibrahim Darwish in response to the verdict, 'when critics and opponents of the government face trial before military courts while wealthy NDP members such as Mamdouh Ismail are allowed to flee the country.' When the head of the investigation into the fire questioned military officers as to why Egypt's navy didn't

---

* Two years later Ismail's acquittal was overturned and he was sentenced to seven years in prison. He has never returned to Egypt to serve his sentence.

come to the aid of drowning passengers once the ferry started sinking, he was allegedly told by Field Marshal Mohamed Hussein Tantawi, Mubarak's defence minister, that 'The Armed Forces is not to be questioned and should never be investigated. They are above questioning or investigation.'[86] One credible theory put forward by insiders is that, as part of the regime's intricate mechanisms of self-preservation, no military action – even a search and rescue mission – was able to take place without the express authorization of the commander-in-chief. The commander-in-chief at that time was Tantawi. Because the accident occurred after midnight, Tantawi was sleeping, and no one dared to wake him up.[87]

I thought about the connection between fire, tragedy and economic violence again one summer's morning in 2010, when I heard news that a car had crashed on Cairo's el-Tinsi bridge, sending flaming debris down into Souq el-Gum'a – the capital's Friday Market – which sprawled out from the pillars below. I'd first visited Souq el-Gum'a in 2008, the year the World Bank labelled Egypt its 'top reformer'. The market started half a century earlier as a ragged assortment of faded silverware and broken antiques, laid out underneath the road to Suez. Those were the days when each corner of the capital boasted its own daily street-stall extravaganza – Munib on a Tuesday, Matariya on a Thursday, and now this patch of dusty land below the Mokattam cliffs on a Friday. Over the years the other markets faded, driven out by overzealous officialdom or a dwindling customer base, and slowly but surely the vendors – of pigeons and puppies, carpets and sinks, telephones with no handles and shoes with no soles – made their way to Souq el-Gum 'a instead, which began spilling out from the underpass across disused train tracks to the east and into the narrow alleys of a huge cemetery to the west. No one could quite pin down its edges, but by the late 2000s it was widely believed to be the largest street market in the Middle East, the place where anything from camel hooves to second-hand toilet lids could be obtained for the right price. The *souq* offered something else as well: a dirt-streaked microcosm of Mubarak's Egypt. Structural adjustment consigned millions of Egyptians to the economic margins, and Souq el-Gum'a, a frenzied city within a city itself on the margins of the metropolis, welcomed them all.

My guide through the *souq* was a man named Ayman Mohammed Rafat Hashush. During the week Ayman worked as a contractor for a firm doing restoration jobs on old houses, but with so much capital flowing out to new-build compounds in the desert and rising poverty among the country's middle classes, demand for those sort of services had largely dried up. The fifty-year-old and his wife were still waiting for God to send them children; until then, he told me, he was throwing all his energies into the *souq*. He'd first started coming here in the 1980s and eleven years previously had made the transition from customer to stall-holder, paying an old woman ten *gineih* a week for the sandy ground in front of her home and another 150 *gineih* a month to store his wares in her building. Back then Ayman's trestle table of vintage film posters, out-of-date calendars and broken games consoles stood on the market's fringes; by the time we met, though, it had long been enveloped by Souq el-Gum'a's unstoppable expansion. Ayman couldn't really say whether the stall was near the centre of the market any more, or where the centre was. He just knew that hundreds or thousands of other stalls now stretched out in every direction from where he sat, all the way into the 'City of the Dead' where some Egyptians had made their homes and set up shop amid several square miles of Cairo's oldest tombs. Ayman said that the mushrooming of Souq el-Gum'a was a direct result of Mubarak's economic reforms. "Half the sellers here are respectable government employees who are forced to supplement their salaries with work at the market," he told me. "Many more are downtown shopkeepers whose goods won't sell in the economic climate. They come to get rid of their stuff here, hoping to earn a few extra *gineih* for their families." He took me down past the metalwork stalls, through the lizard and snake cages, and across a parade of computer parts and leaking fridges to reach the newest area of the market; here people laid out used batteries, plastic trinkets from China and the Emirates, and family photos from their apartments side-by-side on rugs rolled out in the sun. I asked one vendor what he thought about the *souq*. "This is our Egypt," he shrugged. "It's the bread we eat.'

When the car crashed up on the bridge and fire spread through the market, emergency services took three hours to respond. By the time the flames subsided, most of Souq el-Gum'a was in ruins. "We don't know how many people died," a resident called Hanan told local news sources, adding that one of the destroyed buildings had been home to three orphans.[88] Another witness said locals had appealed to the district authority for financial help, pointing out that thousands of livelihoods were now destroyed, but that uninterested officials had turned them away. The only formal response from the Egyptian government to the incident was to reiterate that it considered the market illegal in the first place, and that all stallholders should be vacating the area anyway. "Everything inside is totally destroyed, it looks like the 6th of October War," concluded Sayed Tawfik, a *souq* veteran who operated an *'ahwa* ('coffee shop') in the market. 'If the government had been harmed in any way ... [But] they sit in their offices and give eviction orders. That's all they do.'[89]

Structural adjustment could only ever be implemented by state violence – the direct violence ranged against the citizens of Sarandu, the violence of neglect that condemned a thousand Egyptians on the Red Sea ferry, the economic violence that turned so many Egyptian workers into stall-holders at the Friday Market. Of course, Egypt's international partners, like the US and the EU, publicly condemned examples of regime authoritarianism that the press brought to their attention. In November 2003, President George Bush called on Egypt to 'show the way toward democracy in the region'; when the Egyptian government cracked down on pro-democracy protesters in the mid-2000s and imprisoned a prominent critic of Mubarak, Ayman Nour, European Union representatives issued statements lamenting state coercion. Their ongoing support for an economic system which denied most Egyptians any democratic input over their economic fate and necessitated such coercion was never acknowledged. Throughout the 1990s and 2000s, USAID disbursed hundreds of millions of dollars a year to promote tariff reductions, privatization schemes, the taxing of basic food staples, the elimination of subsidies, and the development of 'commodity import programmes' designed to encourage Egyptians to buy American goods (thus undercutting local manufacturers).[90] In 2008, just as residents of the industrial Delta city of el-Mahalla el-Kubra (commonly known as 'Malhalla') came out in an insurrection against Mubarak's neoliberalism, the United States government – through its Economic Support Fund, which aims to promote 'economic stability' in 'strategically important regions' (Egypt, thanks to its geopolitical influence, large population, peace treaty with Israel and vital geographical location in a prime candidate) – handed over more money to the Mubarak regime than it did to the whole of sub-Saharan Africa combined. At the same time, it was reflecting contentedly on a decade's worth of intimate links between the American and Egyptian security establishments – the latter being a key member of the subcontracted torturers' network operated by the CIA during the agency's extraordinary rendition programme. American weapons, training, intelligence expertise and political cover were all used by Mubarak to help break protest movements generated by USAID-sponsored neoliberalism; in Washington's eyes, the Egyptian state's competence here was a credit, not a concern. 'Egypt, as all of us know, is really ahead of us on this issue . . . we have much to learn from them and there is much we can do together,' declared US Secretary of state Colin Powell in 2001.[91]

When the EU spoke out against the detention of Ayman Nour, its trade commissioner at the time was Peter Mandelson, a former New Labour cabinet minister, who, like his previous boss, Tony Blair, went on to develop a lucrative career offering lobbying and consultancy services to international corporations and authoritarian regimes like Mubarak's.[92] On 4 February 2011, as millions took to the streets to demand an end to repression, Lord Mandelson issued a public plea for Gamal Mubarak, the one figure most associated with the imposition of neoliberal strictures, to be spared from opprobrium. 'Gamal Mubarak . . . has been the leading voice in favour of change within the government and the ruling party,' he wrote in a letter to the *Financial Times*. 'Of course, it is easy to cast him as a putative beneficiary of a nepotistic transfer of family power, the continuation of "tyranny" with a change of face at the top. This analysis, in my view, is too simplistic.'[93]

Placing 'tyranny' in quotation marks doubtless made perfect sense to Mandelson and the many others who helped construct and defend Mubarak's Egypt. For them, as for the Mont Pelerin intellectuals who began theorizing free market utopias half a century earlier, real 'tyranny' was anything that threatened the march of neoliberal reform. Just like in Kamshish in the 1970s, when peasants resisting feudalism were transformed into villains and the feudal lords recast as heroes, members of the Mubarak regime were in Mandelson's eyes defenders of the freedom that really mattered, the freedom of capital and markets, and it was those who opposed them that really stood in the way of liberty. In the 1970s and the decades that followed, that was the story told time and again by elites. But not for ever. Shahenda finishes up her coffee, and rises to leave the café. 'Today we feel our power,' smiles the 76-year-old. In Egypt, the excluded fought back with a story of their own.

2

Palace Ghosts and Desert Dreams

Mohamed Lipton's coffee shop opened in the 1960s. No one can remember the exact year, but most people recall that it followed the departure of *khawaga* ('foreigner') Mano, a Greek, who packed up his things unexpectedly one morning and disappeared to Alexandria. Mano's workshop, a hole in the wall on the alleyway that runs off Cairo's Champollion Street at the back of the old palace, was left empty, so Mohamed took it over and began transforming it into an *ahwa*. This was around the time that the tea brand Lipton emerged on to the Egyptian market, and as an aspiring purveyor of caffeinated goods, Mohamed naturally acquired the name. Today some people still call the café 'Lipton', though it's better known as *tak'eeyba* – a description of the shaded canopy that Mohamed cultivated along the alleyway to provide his loyal band of drinkers and shisha smokers with some relief from the sun. Over the years the coffee shop expanded as Mohamed bought up the adjacent restaurant and toilets, and it became a hub for the local mechanics who spent their days clanking away at motor engines in small garages dotted throughout the neighbourhood. Lipton had a reputation for serving the best hot honeyed hibiscus in town, and customers who came to sit under the natural pergola could also listen to cassettes of singing legends Umm Kulthum and Abdel Halim Hafez through a pair of speakers that Mohamed propped up against the palace wall. The pergola was entwined with grape vines that he had planted himself; local legend has it that the day after Mohamed passed away, in his customary chair next to the coal scuttle, the whole edifice inexplicably collapsed to the ground. Less romantic souls demur, insisting that it was the police who tore down the *tak'eeba* following a long-running

dispute with Mohamed. But the legend lives on. 'He was buried at
11 a.m., and at 1 p.m. the *tak 'eeba* was falling down,' remembers
one long-running employee. 'Even the things were mourning his
death.'[1]

Although Mohamed was gone, the coffee shop survived. It was the
shisha of *tak'eeba* that first attracted me to Marouf, the little quarter
just north of Mahmoud Bassyuni Street and to the west of the Tal'at
Harb thoroughfare – downtown Cairo's noisy, commercial spine.
Compared to Tal'at Harb, tree-lined Marouf felt serene and hushed.
Once I'd found an apartment though, just across the road from Lipton's alleyway, previously unheard peals and patters began floating
up to my fourth-floor balcony and I realized that, in its own way,
Marouf was as deafening as any other corner of the city. There were
the metallic twangs of mechanics working late into the night on
the street below, each one illuminated by a small boy holding aloft
a naked lightbulb over the bonnet.* There were the car alarms,
which performed a regular klaxon sonata thanks to the efforts of
the *minadis* – informal parking managers who, through an incessant
vehicular jive, managed to fold four rows of stationary cars into
a residential road barely wide enough to shoulder a single lane of
traffic – and the disgruntled beeps of those trying to navigate through
the muddle. There were the gas canister vendors on their bicycles and
the *bikya* ('clutter') collectors on their carts and the donkey-drawn
watermelon merchants on their wagons, all with their own repertoire
of bellows, plus a regular rotation of seasonal supplements like the
trucks full of bleating goats that would be shepherded into the ground
floor of the building during *eid* in preparation for a ritual slaughter,
or the *misahharateya* – self-appointed human alarm clocks who (with
the help of drums) roused the faithful from their sleep in the early
hours of *ramadan* mornings, often standing beneath windows and
summoning families to prayer by their names.

As I began to explore the neighbourhood, I realized that just as
Marouf's soundscape was knitted together from many different
sources, so too were its buildings and their overlapping histories.

---

* The mechanics survived a government-led crackdown on downtown car repair
workshops in the 1980s.

There was no definitive record of each house or apartment block, at least not among the people who lived and worked in them – just dozens of competing memories, each cheerfully recounted, disputed and defended by different locals. On the far side of Lipton's *tak'ayba*, a handsome early twentieth-century townhouse boasted multiple past lives: home to a deposed monarch's doctor, a Jewish synagogue, a short-lived Hindu prayer circle that some say was shut down by the police, and a dramatic showdown in the 1980s between residents and speculators that ended in victory for those resisting eviction. There were secrets there too: supposedly when maintenance work was carried out on the building several years back, four corpses were found cemented into the walls, though no one can explain how they got there. A nearby villa used to be owned by the minister of electricity, or maybe the electricity company's chief technician, and could have once housed the main substation for the whole of central and southern Cairo, or possibly just a bunch of electrical tools. Either way it was from here that George, the engineer, would appear whenever a power blackout afflicted a certain part of town; he never used a map, people say, but knew off the top of his head where every cable in Cairo intersected and could drive straight to the right manhole and sort the problem out – until one day an electricity box in nearby Sayida Zainab exploded in the poor man's face.

The apartment building on the corner of Champollion and Sheikh Marouf was owned by legendary acting diva Sherihan, and used to host parties that the gossip magazines salivated over. This may or may not be the same building where Sarandino and his father – electricians to King Farouk – plied their trade. Or maybe Sarandino lived where Abu Tarek stands today – a three-storey *kushari* (a rice, lentils, pasta and dried onion-based carnival of carbohydrates) emporium. The place was known by every taxi driver and *kushari* connoisseur in town: part restaurant, part cult-of-personality tribute to Mr Abu Tarek himself, whose airbrushed face is framed upstairs by gurgling fountains and smiles down approvingly from every wall. Opposite my own balcony was an industrial bank, built on the site of an ornate workers' syndicate headquarters and sandwiched next to a French school for nuns. 'This whole area was the engine of Egypt,' Mohamed Ali – a grizzled mechanic in his sixties who worked on my street – once told me. 'Everywhere you looked there were workshops: carpenters, blacksmiths, electricians, mechanics. People learned their trade here and then took those skills out to the rest of the country. I'm proud to say I was born here.' Mohamed was now living down in Helwan – a good seventeen miles south of Marouf – but he still travelled all the way here each morning, even on his days off, just to sit on his rickety wooden chair by the garage and watch the world go by, 'A lot of the changes – and it has changed a lot – have saddened me,' he said. 'But I still love it. You can't get your birthplace out of your blood.'

And then, most captivating of all, there was the *qasr*: Said Halim Pasha's wondrous Italianate palace which rose from the ground like an ageing beauty queen, blemished but still refined, staring down haughtily at the slipshod modernity all around her which had swollen over the decades from every direction to reach the brink of the royal walls. Its fate provides a useful insight into Cairo's development trajectory. Halim, the grandson of Mohamed Ali (Egypt's nineteenth-century ruler, and namesake of my local car mechanic) built the palace for his Turkish wife. Once it was completed in 1897, she reportedly took one look at the building and its *shaabi* ('popular') surroundings, its parking spaces for horses and its general air of bawdiness, and declared: 'This literally looks like a stable.' Mrs Ali found the environs so repellent that she refused to live there, an early sign of the bad luck that would continue to come the pasha's way. After the young aristocrat made the mistake of putting his name on the Ottoman – German alliance of 1914, the British expelled him from Egypt; he was exiled to Malta and eventually ended up in Sicily, where he was assassinated at the hands of American agents. Halim's resplendent, disused homestead outlasted its owner, passing through the hands of an Italian noble before winding up as a public school – the students of which would throw coins over the wall to Mohamed Lipton as payment for the hot milky drinks he then delivered on trays to the playground.

By the time I arrived, the palace had been long abandoned. The windows were broken, the ornate statues weather-cowed and chipped; even the grand ballroom entrance was tumbledown, its central staircase carpeted with a thick layer of dust. All that was left was a dozing watchman, unless you counted the genitalia-graffiti of several decades of schoolchildren which remained etched on the corridor walls, or the countless ghosts of forgotten occupants – most notably, according to locals, the beloved sweetheart of a visiting count who drowned in one of the many bathrooms and whose spirit continues to stalk the hallways at night, wearing different garments from Egyptian history. Whether or not she ever frequents the tunnels which run below the palace grounds all the way out to the Nile is unknown; built to allow the lord and lady of the house to walk to the river unmolested by commoners, they were flooded with water when construction on the metro network began in the 1990s. There are rumours of subterranean aquariums down in the passageways, grand pianos hidden away in locked chambers and an underground single-track railroad built to hastily convey hot food from the palace scullery to the corniche. True or not, the era of such fantastical legends is long past. Of all the living things that have stared out from the *qasr* rooftop over the decades, only falcons still have the run of the place now.

The reality is that since it began its spiral of decline in the final decade of Mubarak's reign, Marouf's *qasr* has faded from popular memory. Once it was the mental centrepiece of the entire neighbourhood; now many locals say they have forgotten it is even there. The diminishing status of the palace reflects a broader trend: once the heart of the Arab World's largest metropolis, Marouf and the downtown district that surrounds it are today no longer the main geographical reference point for Cairenes. The neighbourhoods of 'historic' Cairo – places that have existed since the French invasion of Egypt in 1798 – are now home to only 2 per cent of the city's population, and the capital's modern nucleus instead lies far away, out towards the ring road.[2] To reach it, you have to turn right out of the palace gates, jump in a car, drive north up Champollion (a violation of the one-way rule, but you'll have plenty of company) and mount the mammoth 26th July overpass which begins climbing into the sky at the edge of Marouf before plunging westwards across the Nile.

At the end of this motorway stand two interlocking faces of urban Egypt under neoliberalism: informal neighbourhoods, born of necessity and constraint, and the gated compounds of Cairo's satellite cities, the sprawling product of excess and exclusion. Their story tells us a great deal about how money, power and poverty became entwined in the name of Egypt's economic progress, and about who stands to gain from the free market remodelling of our cities. They tell us something too about neoliberalism's weaknesses, and the spaces it gives rise to in which opposition and resistance can develop.

The first face is made up of soaring redbrick apartment blocks, mile upon mile of them, many close enough to the highway for passing drivers to peer right into each family living room. These buildings jostle for space on impossibly thin parcels of what was once agricultural land, often permanently half-finished and with clumps of steel rebars sprouting from their rooftops in preparation for the next storey. There are few exits on this section of the highway. By and large the settlements below – known as 'ashwa'iyat, an Arabic word meaning 'random' or 'haphazard' – don't appear on official maps; what's more, most of their inhabitants don't have cars, and the Egyptians who do drive would rarely have cause to visit. Beyond the 'ashwa'iyat, once the overpass has ploughed through acres of barren desert and left the 4,000-year-old Giza pyramids behind it, the second face of neoliberal Cairo begins to come into view. A first-time traveller could be forgiven for asking themselves what anybody could possibly be driving towards out here, a place far beyond the old city perimeter where addresses can only be expressed in motorway distance markers, the history-laden palaces of downtown are a universe away, and the monotony of sand is broken up by nothing more than an occasional pile of rubble.

The answer lies scrawled on the advertising billboards above. 'Welcome to the future of Cairo,' they read. 'Where life is more complete.'

Ahmed Seif is trying to manoeuvre a full-sized speedboat through a single pair of doors, and sweat is dripping from his brow. His eight exhausted assistants have been unsuccessfully experimenting with different angles for thirty minutes now. 'Right, let's try one more time with the boat on its side,' demands Ahmed, ignoring the contemptuous looks being thrown in his direction by the rest of the team. After some fairly frantic shouting and a painful scraping of metal the boat is finally propelled inside, immediately knocking over a pyramid of salmon canapés. Ahmed shakes his head disbelievingly. 'Let's get this over and done with,' he sighs.

It's a hot spring day in April 2010, and Ahmed's speedboat is being installed as the centrepiece of a sales stand for the Wadi Degla Real Estate company at the annual Next Move conference, the biggest property expo in Egypt. Wadi Degla is one of forty firms who have set up shop at Cairo's International Convention Centre, and competition is fierce. Most companies are spending the opening morning sprucing up their displays with something a little bit special in the hope of attracting the attention of visitors, 27,000 of whom will pass through the conference centre over the next three days. Palm Hills has created a lavishly landscaped fake lawn replete with a built-in Starbucks; further along the Porto Cairo display is being attended to by a full travelling circus comprising a juggler, two trumpeters and one furry mascot of unidentified origin that may or may not be a rat. Not content with offering a speedboat for visitors to admire as they leaf through the company's glossy brochures, Wadi Degla has also ordered in a Ferrari to sit next to it. Next door a rival set of staff at La Vista are throwing envious looks towards the car and grimacing at their own marketing ruse – a somewhat lacklustre string quartet.

Cellists, cars and speedboats don't come cheap, but for the companies involved in Next Move back in 2010 the cost of such gimmicks was a small price to pay when set against the prize at hand: a share of the mammoth Egyptian real estate market, which in the twilight days of the Mubarak regime was responsible for up to $14 billion of the country's annual GDP, and growing by more than 20 per cent a year. Printed on the centrespread of the conference brochure was a map indicating where all that growth was coming from: out of sixty-seven 'Cairo'-based construction projects undertaken by companies represented at Next Move on the eve of revolution, only three were actually located in the capital, while sixty-four others lay deep in the desert sand beyond. Some of these desert developments featured the names of internationally renowned architects like Zaha Hadid; others were colossal enough to be considered fully-fledged cities in their own right, such as the $3 billion Madinaty complex which promised 80,000 new villas and townhouses as well as hotels, hospitals and schools. These ambitious construction projects weren't merely the brainchild of the private sector; they were a commercial response to a distinctly state-led vision of massive desert development – one that aimed to turn Cairo inside out, transforming the capital's historic margins into its core and consigning its historic core to the periphery. According to official plans, the two biggest desert building hubs – 6th October to the west of the capital and New Cairo to the east – would soon house up to 5 million people each, creating an urban centre double the size of Paris on either side of the old city. Government estimates suggested that by 2030, when Greater Cairo's population is predicted to top 30 million, half its residents will be living not in Cairo itself, but in a satellite city.

For the first thousand years or so following its creation, Cairo's urban sprawl was bound by rigid natural contours. Armies conquered and were conquered in turn, slaves became sultans then fell back into penury, merchants, spies and storytellers washed in and out with the capital's endless waves of prosperity and plague, and throughout it all two stony titans – the Mokattam clifftops to the east and the Sphinx, marking the start of the Sahara, to the west – bookended the city's expansion. By the late twentieth century though, the city had burst its banks. The genesis of Cairo's extension into the desert can be traced back to the Nasser era, when the idea was touted in a series of masterplans. To the governments of the 1950s and 60s, desert construction was infused with revolutionary legitimacy: industrial zones and workers' compounds would emerge from the sand, expanding the country's habitable space and taming the wilderness into newly green pastures to serve a newly independent Egypt. But it wasn't until the 1970s, under President Sadat's liberalizing economic reforms, that serious desert building work began. The creation of new cities out of nothing in the desert dovetailed nicely with the Sadat-era embrace of private capital and its selective championing of 'Western' modernity. Virginal sand was a *tabula rasa* on which Sadat's notion of progress – one that depended on an alliance between big business and the state (no individual or small community could ever hope to build a desert city from scratch) – would be firmly inscribed. For urban planners, the desert was a dream playground; one that offered a chance, finally, for their visions to trascend the crowded realities of Egypt's existing cities.[3] Initial efforts were directed at drawing heavy industry to the dunes, and they worked; a package of generous government incentives ensured that brand-new towns like 10th Ramadan – situated halfway down the desert highway between Cairo and Suez – quickly filled up with factories.

But the government's success at establishing manufacturing bases in the desert wasn't matched on the residential front. By the early 1990s, few of the settlements boasted more than a few thousand inhabitants and some barely managed more than a few hundred. The failure of the new towns to attract even a fraction of their target populations shouldn't have been a surprise: strict building regulations, astronomical travelling distances, restrictions on all manner of organic informal enterprise and an almost complete lack of sustainable transport options meant that, despite the glitzy presentations of their backers, these desert 'communities' were incapable of offering housing that genuinely responded to the needs of most Cairenes. Meanwhile, residents of the capital were addressing the shortage of housing stock in the old city themselves, by creating new informal neighbourhoods in any pockets of vacant space they could find, and by colonizing fields on the edge of town. The existence of these 'ashwa'iyat was rarely acknowledged by the state, but by the time Egypt signed up to ERSAP, its internationally sponsored structural adjustment programme, in 1991, such districts were rapidly absorbing the majority of the capital's people, accommodation and economic activity. In total defiance of government planning, Cairo had quietly become a city where informality reigned supreme.[4]

That might have been the end of the urban desert chimera. Officials could have concluded that although empty stretches of sand made for good industrial zones, they were less suited to major population centres; instead, the state could have turned its attention – and resources – to the 'ashwa'iyat that millions of Egyptians now called home. Under the neoliberal policy reforms though, the government's agenda had little in common with the needs and aspirations of ordinary Egyptians. Egypt's nexus of elite interests – politicians, tycoons and financial investors – decided that the construction of satellite cities presented lucrative opportunities, even though virtually no one wanted to live in them. Because the state owned all desert land by default, the Mubarak regime was able to convert sand into patronage – handing over vast tracts of dunes to influential businessmen for below-market prices, and rewarding political allies for their loyalty. As with the corrupt privatization programme, many of those who benefited directly from the government's satellite cities vision were members of the government themselves.[5] As plots were snapped up and the land bubble inflated, foreign investors looking to find a home for surplus capital piled in, especially from the Gulf, and the desert development free-for-all intensified further.

Walking around the outer fringes of Cairo's desert developments in those final days of Mubarak's rule was a disorientating experience; no matter which direction you gazed in, the pace of construction was breathtaking. 'If you leave the area for two months and then come back, the whole place is unrecognizable,' one project manager, employed at a major New Cairo development, told me when I visited his construction site. 'This is probably the fastest growing urban area you'll ever see in your life.' Although the housing going up was private, the pipes, roads, electricity, gas and water supplies that made construction in this wilderness a possibility had all been provided by the Egyptian state, the same state, of course, that had sold the land in the first place for a pittance. If you knew the right people, the bargains to be had were astonishing. One huge 893-hectare parcel of sand to the west of Cairo – which would later be appropriately unveiled as 'Dreamland', one of the capital's most famous high-end compounds – was handed over to a prominent businessman for 90,000 EGP (£10,000), or about one-third of a piaster per square metre (which equates to three one-thousandths of a penny). Meanwhile, the infrastructure needs of the millions of Egyptians living in *'ashwa'iyat* neighbourhoods were ignored.

Cairo's lopsided development are was hardly unprecedented. Mammoth, top-down development schemes have often materialized due largely to the desire of investors to establish fresh speculative frontiers, rather than in response to the needs of residents. Examples include Hausmann's Paris in the nineteenth century, American suburbanization in the 1960s and the petro-enclaves of Dubai and Abu Dhabi today. But in Mubarak's Egypt, at a time when the majority of the population was facing severe economic hardship due to ERSAP's erosion of living standards, the scale of national resources pumped into the near-empty satellite cities felt uniquely obscene. Mubarak once described the 'conquest' of the desert as 'no longer a slogan or dream, but a necessity'.[6] In reality it was a conjuring trick of vast and expensive proportions, performed in the service of private capital and regime survival. In Mubarak Country, more upmarket residential developments were launched in the desert than could ever be lived in, and more upscale luxury shopping malls were built in the dunes than could ever be shopped at. According to Egypt's 2006 census, 63 per cent of homes in the satellite cities were unoccupied; since then, new developments have added to this empty stock by the tens of thousands, while the shortage of affordable housing means that more than 1.5 million Egyptians every year are unable to find a home.[7] And although the CityStars mega-mall in the east of Cairo and Dandy Mall to the west already pretty much cover all of Cairo's current demand for high-end mega-mall retailing, given that the vast majority of the population could never afford the sort of products on offer there, on the eve of revolution there were no fewer than eight new luxury mega-malls planned in New Cairo alone, one of which – Park Avenue – was being advertised as the 'biggest retail destination in the Middle East'.[8] Through the rural land privatization programme, neoliberalism had already inflicted vast inequalities on the countryside. Now it was transforming Egypt's cities as well.

From Saladin's twelfth-century Citadel, built high to the east of the metropolis to protect the sultan's empire from crusaders, you can gaze out on to a visual tableau of Mubarak's Cairo and get a sense of what a metropolis looks like when its development trajectory has been hijacked and re-engineered as a vehicle for private enrichment. Directly below you is the 'City of the Dead', where the corpses now share their homes with the living; thousands of Cairenes have squeezed in here alongside the coffins, rigging up the resting places of the departed with satellite television and turning grave markers into desks and shelving.[9] Behind lie the assorted poor neighbourhoods of Manshiyet Nasr, improbably packed coils of informal housing at the base of the Mokattam cliffs – a rockslide from which killed over a hundred people at Duweiqa in 2008.* And just above the Citadel, up on the

---

* Accusations have been levelled at Emaar Misr claiming that the company's development works on the clifftop caused the landslide, something the company denies; an official investigation deemed the cause of the tragedy to be 'fate'.

clifftop, a new fortress is taking shape. Like its medieval predecessor, this one stands apart from the city scrimmage. It is being built by the Egyptian arm of Emmar, a Dubai-based company responsible for the Burj Khalifa, the tallest building in the world. Their project here is called Uptown and the long approach to its sales centre is lined by giant pictures of light-skinned families frolicking on the grass, serving up barbecues and parking their Mercedes in the garage. Each photo is emblazoned with a single English word: 'Upscale', 'Upmarket', 'Upbeat'. Behind the billboards, emptiness stretches to the horizon.

As the speculative property bubble continued to drive land and property prices up, and mass migration to the satellite cities failed to materialize, desert developers sought to target their compounds at more elite social constituencies in an effort to recoup costs. Gone was the heroic everyman pioneer of the dunes once envisaged by Nasser; now those breaking the boundaries of the old city were entering a world of Greg Norman signature golf courses and fourteen different configurations of underfloor heating. At places such as Katameya Heights – once a ragtag settlement of people whose homes had been destroyed in a 1992 earthquake, now one of Egypt's most prestigious high-end gated compounds and home to members of the Mubarak family[10] – membership packages for the cigar-scented clubhouse began at $22,000 and in-house magazines distributed around the pool terrace featured Nina Ricci dresses and Bulgari jewellery on the front page. Despite the extremely limited size of Egypt's upper class, other satellite city developers have tried to follow in Katameya's footsteps by transforming their desert plots into walled-off bastions of security and sophistication, complete with landscaped shrubbery, toy-town driveways and palatial villas.

But the desert is a place of feverish heat and choking dust; this is the land of lost legends, where the ancient god of chaos, Seth, was sent into exile, and where 50,000 hardened soldiers of the Persian king Cambyses were swallowed up by a sandstorm, never to be seen again. Rebranding such terrain into the apex of privatized luxury was never going to be easy. To pull it off, developers needed to draw a powerful link between life in the desert and urbane modernity – and simultaneously cast the old city and its inhabitants as something not only very different, but also dangerous.

You can get a sense of what the modernity is supposed to feel like in the 'mood rooms' of the Emaar Misr sales centre in Uptown, which are designed to envelop the prospective buyer into a sensory appreciation of life in one of its many new residential projects. On the day I visited, back in 2010, recorded birdsong was being pumped out of hidden speakers, canvas awnings were dappled with soft spot-lit purples and blues, and potential customers were moving past a series of glass portals, each featuring a different item – a plastic tea set, a pair of football boots, a laptop and a calculator. One window contained nothing but a single coffee-table-sized film book, pinned open on a page about Audrey Hepburn; staring at it I recalled the words of one attendee back at the Next Move conference who explained to me that the satellite city companies were selling not properties, but lifestyles. 'Everything in their show rooms is intended to exude as much contrast as possible with the world "back there" [in Cairo]," he said. "They're saying: "these are the material goods that will feel natural to your family when you join us. They look foreign now, but soon they will feel normal." '

The boxed tea sets and Audrey Hepburn photos didn't only function as marketing magnets for the new developments. They also served to legitimize the entire satellite cities project. In answer to those who accused the gated compound disciples of abandoning their original urban communities in pursuit of self-interest and isolation, Emaar Misr's imagery aimed to reimagine the company's compounds as beacons of civic pride. 'It's where children can play safely, where neighbours foster long-lasting relationships, and where the community really cares,' declared a sign above the maquette of Mivida, a $1 billion Emaar villa complex in New Cairo. Developers defined their projects not as a triumph of individualism, but rather as a progressive national mission to benefit all Egyptians: those who snapped up properties were told they were on the frontline of *nahda 'umraneya*, Cairo's 'urban renaissance'. 'Modern Cairo leaves us isolated now,' Mohamed El Mikawi, the general manager of Al-Futtaim's Festival City – a 3 million-square-metre development in New Cairo modelled on a similar project in Dubai – once told me. 'In the new areas kids will ride their bikes, adults will take walks and meet their neighbours; we're talking about social values being restored.' The villas in

El Mikawi's Festival City were being psychologically stretched to form part of some grand exercise in the common good.

This was the public narrative; its success, though, depended on a darker, private one. The spread of Cairo's *'ashwa'iyat* in the late twentieth century was in many ways a direct consequence of the government's determination to plough state resources into the desert instead of building affordable housing of its own. Now, those very same informal settlements were to be used as justification for the kind of fortified withdrawal that Katameya Heights and Emaar Misr's Uptown were selling to the country's richest. 'Informal housing areas are one of modern Egyptian society's problems,' stated a 1994 article in the state-run *al-Ahram* newspaper. 'They are made up of nests of criminals, beggars, drug dealers and those who flee the law. They are a continual source of disturbance and anxiety for society and represent an axe that will destroy progress. Informal housing areas and their surroundings live with health, societal and cultural backwardness and the spread of social and psychological diseases.'[11] Throughout the 1990s and 2000s, the sense that old Cairo, the 'Paris of the Nile', was irreversibly degenerating echoed throughout the media. Commentators warned that the inhabitants of the *'ashwa'iyat* were not urban and *hadari* ('civilized') but rather rural *fellaheen* – something that didn't belong in the city and was poisoning its lifeblood. 'All the neighbouring villages have become part of the capital, and instead of inculcating them with city ways and civilization, the capital has become sick with all the backwards diseases of the Egyptian villages,' opined one writer in *al-Ahram al-Iqtisadi* in 1990.[12] Almost two decades on, in the aftermath of that deadly Duweiqa landslide in 2008, the same sentiments prevailed. 'The slum-dwellers are not city-dwellers in the proper sense of the word, they are not even citizens,' noted a political sociologist in the English language *al-Ahram Weekly*. 'They tolerate rising heaps of refuse. They live beyond the regulations affecting the residents of the city proper.'[13] Others viewed the residents of informal neighbourhoods as a separate species altogether, part of 'a 'Hobbesian' world of violence and vice'.[14] Reporters who dared to venture into this alien universe spoke of a 'jungle of squatters'[15] dominated by 'raw hot-blooded youth'[16] where young men are 'hunted' by Islamic extremists and locals take the form of 'human herds that were crossing the road dressed in black garb that looked like mourning clothes ... quarrels are common and piles of rubbish are used as playgrounds'.[17] These people, went the narrative, are not our flesh and blood; they are not even of our time. 'In Munira there are no schools, health clinics, social clubs and youth centres, or buses. It is a life belonging to the past ages,' concluded one *al-Ahram* writer.[18] One investigation into the *'ashwa'iyat* uncovered 'carts dating from the time of Methuselah'.[19]

The sentiments were corrosive, but they were nothing new. In the late nineteenth century, the Khedive – Ismail the Magnificent, Egypt's Ottoman viceroy – embarked on the project that would define his reign: the construction from scratch of what we now call downtown, the throbbing polestar of the city. With wide European-inspired boulevards radiating out from squares orramented with fountains, Khedival Cairo offered not only a higher standard of living for the well-to-do merchants, intellectuals and political heavyweights who flocked there, but also a symbolic break with the capital's remshackle old centre – 'Islamic' Cairo's back alleys that seethed with humanity and disorder.* The balconies and balustrades of downtown were presented to Cairo's elites as a way to embrace modernity; they weren't moving into the unknown, they were being thrust into the future.

From the 1990s onwards that process began playing out all over again, except with downtown and other central neighbourhoods now cast in the role of decaying throwback and the gated compounds of the satellite cities taking up downtown's former mantle as a space for psychological liberation from the *fellaheen*. One television advert for Mena Garden City, a 240-acre private compound with round-the-clock security out in 6th October city, featured an Italianate villa from the original Garden City – a neighbourhood in Khedival downtown, just south of Tahrir Square – hoisted up whole by cranes and flown out to its new natural home in the desert. Its occupants had finally been emancipated from the rabble.

Shortly before the revolution began, I was invited to meet Youssef

---

* The term 'Islamic' Cairo, though not particularly helpful (most of the city is 'Islamic') is commonly used in English to describe the older parts of the city around Hussein Square.

Hammad, a sharp, young, Swiss-educated entrepreneur who had worked throughout the Middle East and Europe before winding up as the chief commercial officer for SODIC – one of Egypt's biggest real estate companies and a partner of Lebanese outfit Solidere, the group founded by former premier Rafik Hariri which went on contentiously to rebuild Beirut's shattered downtown in the aftermath of Lebanon's civil war.* Hammad, who hailed from that tiny class of Egyptians for whom the streets of Paris, London or Hamburg are all familiar reference points, was clean-shaven and scented; we sat in a painfully trendy all-glass office out on the Cairo – Alexandria desert road as he fired such platitudes as 'social glue' and 'communities that have a heart, have a soul' at me. SODIC's latest mega-projects were Eastown and Westown – two gargantuan urban hubs based in New Cairo and 6th October respectively, which together were slated eventually to house 100,000 residents, 1.2 million square metres of business space and a staggering array of shops, restaurants and entertainment outlets. The two developments promised to provide everything a full-option city is supposed to provide, and – crucially – they weren't to be gated. 'On our billboards you'll see the words "Time for a different view", but it's not just a slogan – it's something we live and breathe,' Hammad insisted, brimming with corporate enthusiasm. But outside, when I toured the construction site, the realities of social demonization and militarized class division that Westown was built upon were rarely far below the surface. 'It's not just about people who have the money,' explained the SODIC saleswoman, referring to those who might consider buying a property in the new community, 'it's about their social level and way of thinking; their education, their background, their values. Someone, say, who was rich but illiterate and with no social networks – we'd advise him against purchasing property here. Actually we'd tell him we're full. We don't want downtown culture transplanted here, the swearing,

---

* Across its two-decade stewardship of downtown Beirut's redevelopment, Solidere – a corporate hybrid backed by both private companies and public institutions – has been accused by critics of corruption, intimidation of local residents and the pursuit of an urban philosophy which has sucked the life out of one of the Middle East's greatest cities and left parts of it feeling like a ghost town.[20]

the noise . . .' I asked how she could distinguish between the 'right' and 'wrong' kind of person, and she laughed at my naivety. 'It's something you learn. We're trained by SODIC, but it's also natural experience. The point is that we're trying to create the right society.' I pressed her: if the development is not gated, how will SODIC stop the wrong society breaching its borders? 'It's not a gated community, but don't worry,' she smiled reassuringly. 'Security will be at every entrance, ensuring only the right kind of people get in.'

Who were the 'wrong' kind of people for the new, neoliberal Cairo that SODIC and Mubarak were building in the desert? Who were these criminal, beggarly *'ashwa'iyat* residents with their rising heaps of refuse and carts dating back from the time of Methuselah?* The answer was almost everybody. The terrifying 'other' of media imagination and high-end developer sales tours was in reality anything but. By the beginning of the revolution two-thirds of Cairo's population – at least 12 million people – were living in neighbourhoods built since 1950, the overwhelming majority of which were unplanned by the state.† Unlike the satellite cities, they offered a plentiful supply of affordable housing in areas which were socially vibrant and entrepreneurial, and where the shape of neighbourhoods – a dense mix of the residential and commercial, a naturally evolving flow of transport and industry – by and large reflected the collective will of residents rather than the blueprints of a distant city planner. The spread of the *'ashwa'iyat* was a natural consequence of the government's failure to develop any sort of sustainable housing policy beyond a Disneyfication of the desert; informal neighbourhoods have become the very essence of the modern capital, a metropolis which has 'auto-developed' with little heed to top-down masterplans.

Most *ashwa'iyat* neighbourhoods – often incorrectly translated as 'slums' or 'shantytowns' – feature solid buildings that actually tend

---

* Figure in the Hebrew Bible, described as being the world's oldest man, who may have lived for up to a thousand years.
† These proportions are reflected in other Egyptian cities too, though fewer reliable statistics are available outside of Cairo. 'It would be safe to say that informal areas accommodate in excess of 40 per cent of inhabitants in the second city of Alexandria (total population 4.5 million) and probably a higher proportion in the numerous secondary towns in the Delta and Upper Egypt.'[21]

to be more stable than properties in other parts of the city.* Rather than being a homogenous sprawl, informal areas ranged from new to old, urban to peri-urban, middle class to poor, with countless shades and gradations in between; most inward migration into 'ashwa'iyat communities rather than being backwards, rural and anti-modern, comes from other cities, not the countryside, and literacy and poverty rates barely differ from the urban average.[23] Informal neighbourhoods don't threaten the national economy or exist outside of it; they are, without exception, the most economically productive areas in the country, and without them the nation's finances would collapse in an instant.[24] And despite much hyped incidents like the 'Siege of Imbaba' in the early 1990s, when government troops raided an informal Cairo neighbourhood that was said to have declared itself an independent Islamic emirate, sociologists have shown that citizens living in the 'ashwa'iyat are no more 'prone' to extremist radicalization than anyone else.[25] Yet these massive, omnipresent manifestations of staggering ordinariness that define the modern capital for the majority of its residents are, on the whole, officially invisible – in stark contrast with the near-deserted but officially conspicuous satellite cities. On most maps of Cairo, 'ashwa'iyat neighbourhoods are lumped together into an amorphous grey hinterland, or just left blank altogether. 'Such omissions are not mistakes,' says David Sims, the urban geographer. 'The informal city is of little or no interest to modern Cairenes or foreigners who read maps, who banking, travel, or business services, or who need to shop in high-end outlets. In the cognizance of middle-class Egyptians and most government officials, such areas are definitely beyond the pale.'[26]

The exclusion – rhetorical, financial and cartographical – of most of Cairo's population from Egypt's urban future was the natural consequence of an economic programme that pushed tens of millions of

---

* The rare pockets of genuinely slum-like accommodation probably house only 1 or 2 per cent of Greater Cairo's population, yet it is in these neighbourhoods that Egyptian movies purporting to lift the lid on life in the 'ashwa'iyat are always filmed. In other 'ashwa'iyat, construction quality tends to be reasonably high, a reflection of the substantial financial resources usually devoted by owners to their building projects (during the 1992 earthquake, practically all building collapses and fatalities were in formal rather than informal areas).[22]

Egyptians to the periphery. But it also reflected the Egyptian state's symbiotic and often schizophrenic relationship with the *'ashwa'iyat*, communities which the regime was simultaneously dependent upon and terrified of. The existence of informal neighbourhoods insulated the Mubarak regime from grassroots demands for housing; without them, vast numbers would have been homeless, jobless and ready to turn their ire on the ruling class. Moreover, the spread of the *'ashwa'iyat* suited Egypt's existing political model. The state's authoritarianism, based around a clientelist blend of repression and the arbitrary top-down distribution of goods and services in exchange for political support, rested on citizens feeling disconnected from regularized power. Informal communities felt this disconnection more than most, and so when the going got tough residents were more dependent than most on patronage from above. Whether it was an *ad hoc* offer of alternative housing following a natural disaster, or the provision of army water trucks when piped water supplies failed, the reliance of *'ashwa'iyat* residents on occasional acts of elite beneficence served to reinforce the undemocratic nature of the state.[27] The Egyptian state is sometimes described as a 'lame Leviathan'; the maintenance of huge sections of the population in a state of bureaucratic obscurity helped ensure this rickety autocracy just about stayed on its feet.

But for the government, informal neighbourhoods were a double-edged sword. The danger of mostly leaving the *'ashwa'iyat* residents to get on with it was that it gave them the chance to do what the Mubarak regime was constantly telling Egyptian citizens they could never do: build, manage and flourish within environments of their own making. The *'ashwa'iyat* are very far from perfect. Most lack sufficient recreational space and are crowded with narrow, light-deficient streets. The absence of public land has limited the availability of schools, clinics and other social facilities. Environmentally, those built on formerly agricultural and peri-urban land are deeply problematic; thanks in part to Mubarak's rural land reforms, though, many farmers have been left with little choice but to cover their fields in concrete. Yet despite all of this, a culture of *guhood zateya* ('self-help') prevails in most informal neighbourhoods that makes the *faux* communal imagery of the desert's gated compounds – where residents may get to vote on which day of the week their rubbish is picked up and hold neighbourhood parties under the watchful eye of armed security guards – look hollow. Like any community left to work things out for themselves, the inhabitants of the *'ashwa'iyat* tend to prioritize mutual cooperation over transactional competition, with new arrivals selecting plots *'ala'adeena* ('at our measure' – i.e. strictly according to the needs and means of a family, rather than in the pursuit of speculative profit) and residents often voluntarily abandon private ownership of some of their land in order to make space for public roadways.[28] And autonomous social power, directed by people in neither occupational nor material thrall to the state, was inimical to Mubarak Country's political order.[29] 'Together we planned,' explains a resident of Ezbat Khayralla, an informal neighbourhood on the Fustat plateau, to the south of Cairo. 'And this is despite the fact that our *el-nas el-kubar* ['elders' or 'local leaders'] didn't even know how to read and didn't think they knew how to create a vision of the city.'[30] It's this self-confidence that the power-brokers of Mubarak Country found so threatening, which is in part why so much effort was poured into portraying the *'ashwa'iyat* as harbingers of anarchy, and those who dwelt within them as primitive people with little capacity to speak, argue or act as an autonomous collective. Instead they were reconstructed as a menace that could ruin Egypt for all.

Every great metropolis is built on layers of artifice, and Cairo is no exception. Throughout history, the grandiose claims of the city's rulers have rarely matched facts on the ground; residents have always sought to navigate this gap between appearance and reality to their own advantage, relying on their own urban nous to bend an often overbearing and unresponsive bureaucracy to their will. Street-smart ruses have long helped ordinary Cairenes make it through the day, and scrape a living along the way. In ancient Memphis, for example, reigning pharaohs would situate grand palace complexes next to their under-construction pyramids, yet within days of a leader's death these opulent royal courts would be organically transformed into early *'ashwa'iyat* accommodation for the poor. The super-rich have often been brought down to earth on the capital's streets: Mansa Musa, emperor of Mali and the wealthiest person of all time,[31] arrived in Cairo in 1324 with 500 slaves and a hundred pack horses bearing more than 5,000 pounds of gold – and was so throughly fleeced at the Cairene market-stalls that he was obliged to borrow dinars from an Egyptian spice merchant to get home. The providential supply of ancient corpses in Cairo's hinterlands has long provided opportunities for trickery, like the seventh-century practice of taking tourists to see a dance of the dead on Christian holidays when the deceased 'awoke' and arms and legs emerged mysteriously from the ground. When the seemingly insatiable European appetite for mummies sent the price of Pharaonic body parts spiralling during the Ottoman era, enterprising locals simply bought up the remains of criminals, stuffed them with pitch and then left them in the sun to ripen before flogging them for a small fortune.[32] More recently, a law came into force requiring taxi drivers to wear seatbelts; in response, most simply purchased lengths of loose belt fabric that could be draped casually across shoulders and laps. Everybody knows that the way things look and the way things are can be two very different things.

In Arabic, Cairo is *el-Qahira* – 'the Victorious'. To witness a modern victory for breezy improvization over government rigidity, just head to the southern corner of Tahrir Square, where a fourteen storey colossus named the *mugamma'* provides a labyrinthine home to 18,000 civil servants and a Kafkaesque phantasm to everyone else. Nearly all administrative roads, from visa applications to shop permits, fire safety certificates to tax affairs, lead here, and negotiating them can be a soul-destroying experience. Yet amid the countless numbered windows, strictly hierarchical flows of authority and ceaseless demands for carbon-copied paperwork, common sense often prevails; erratic individual working hours frustrate and yet can be bent to personal convenience, essential counter-signatures can be helpfully applied by the pusher of the tea-trolley, a colloquial way through can eventually be charted. In one of Egypt's most famous films, Sherif Arafa's *el-Irhab wel-Kebab* ('Terrorism and the Kebab'), comic legend Adel Imam plays an everyman hero driven to madness in the *mugamma'* when trying to obtain the documents needed to transfer his son between schools. In the midst of protestations he accidentally takes the building's inhabitants hostage, and through his hastily invented demands to negotiators – the first of which is the delivery of some kebab meat – Imam's character exposes the superficiality of government promises and the lengths citizens are often forced to go to make things happen for themselves.

Max Rodenbeck, Cairo's foremost English-language biographer, has described the capital as an 'As If' society, where everyone from top to bottom acts as *if* they were following regulations even as rule after rule is casually broken. I saw the as *if* society in action for myself when the municipal authorities announced plans to beautify Marouf's little downtown streets, part of which involved a repainting job on my brutalist, eleven-storey apartment building. Rather than consult residents on what we might want from such an endeavour, officials acted as *if* this was something that locals had already been clamouring for, and promised to transform the street façade sensitively and competently as *if* they hadn't already resolved to do it on the cheap. And so it was that one morning we woke to the sight through the window of a small army of boys scurrying up and down the exterior of the building on ropes, with large pails of paint strapped to their backs. Paintbrushes and rollers had apparently been deemed surplus to requirements; instead the method of application turned out to consist of a haphazard lunge of the brimming buckets into the sky, accompanied by a vain hope that some or all of the now-airborne paint might find its intended target. The rope-swinging labourers clung steadfastly to that optimism, despite mounting evidence to the contrary. By the end of the process most of the building had been coated in one shade or another of dust-streaked magnolia, as indeed had everything on our balconies and in the street below – including, but not limited to: tables, chairs, doors, hammocks, windows, window shutters, washing lines, clothes on washing lines, the roofs of parked cars, the occasional ill-positioned pigeon and several stray cats. The local authorities declared it a job well done, the painters got (badly) paid, and most of my neighbours bought a load of turpentine and cheerfully got on with their lives. Several weeks after the project was complete, one could still spot emulsion-blotched felines lounging around *tak'ayba* and sleeping on the palace walls.

When it comes to urban illusions, Cairo's grotesque development trajectory under neoliberalism – exemplified at the end of the 26th July corridor by *'ashwa'iyat* towers on the one side and hoardings advertising the desert's gated compounds on the other – has been the grandest con act of them all. The international financial institutions who helped create the economic conditions necessary for such a deception also played a direct role in perpetuating it. In 2008, the Egyptian government collaborated with the World Bank and several other foreign agencies to publish a new urban masterplan entitled 'Cairo 2050', which took the state's existing obsession with desert construction, ramped it up and thrust it several decades into the future.* The 260 PowerPoint slides which set out the Cairo 2050 'vision' imagined a future capital totally unrecognizable from the one that exists today. Residential hubs and government ministries were all transplanted to the sand dunes, and in place of the messy, mixed-up central neighbourhoods of the current old city, computer-generated drawings depicted a holiday and real estate fantasia with capacious boulevards, 2,000-acre business parks designed by celebrity 'starchitects', and a 'tourism oasis' providing more than 5,000 hotel rooms alongside an open-air museum covering virtually all of 'Islamic' Cairo, the capital's historic core. Informal neighbourhoods were nowhere to be seen. In their place stood digitally airbrushed leisure parks and corporate resorts; millions of *'ashwa'iyat* residents were to be shunted out to purpose-built settlement blocs beyond the city's borders, ensuring not only that the gated compounds of New Cairo and 6th October City remained a private playground for domestic elites and foreign visitors, but that the traditional city took on that function as well.

Suffused with the technocratic language of growth – progressive zoning, poverty reduction, Western-style modernity† – the Cairo 2050 plans revealed a bitter distaste for informality among Egyptian politicians and foreign investors, and suggested that, far from merely

---

* Although much emphasis was placed on 'consultation', at the time of Cairo 2050's launch only a tiny fraction of Cairenes had ever heard of the project. Among many moments of absurdity, government officials insisted that 400 local urban planning experts had been consulted on the plans – even though far fewer than 400 urban planning experts exist in the city.
† The aim, according to the official Cairo 2050 presentation slides, was to replace contemporary Cairo with 'a super-modern, high-tech, green, and connected city that can stand shoulder-to-shoulder with the metropolises in the world's most advanced countries'.

talking down the *ashwa'iyat*, the government was now preparing to try to wipe them out altogether. If the regime was privately fearful that such spaces could be incubating outbreaks of political dissent, their fear was well placed. In the run-up to 25 January 2011, protest organizers publicized twenty different places around Cairo at which demonstrators could congregate. All of the location could be found on a map, and when the sun rose that morning, dozens of security trucks lay in wait at each one. But what the organizers hadn't revealed was the whereabouts of a secret twenty-first rallying point, a location that didn't appear on any maps at all. It was the Hayyis sweet shop in Bulaq al-Dukror, a tightly packed *'ashwa'iyat* neighbourhood that lies just west of the Giza railway line. Over 1 million people are believed to live in Bulaq al-Dukror; official documents put the area's population at just under 60,000. Left on the sidelines of a capital being reshaped from above for private profit, many residents of Bulaq al-Dukror read the details of the upcoming demonstration – circulated from hand to hand in printed fliers – with interest. By the early afternoon, at the end of *el-zuhr* prayers, over 300 had gathered at the Hayyis storefront and begun marching towards Tahrir; the crowed swelled as it moved, and by the time police had realized what was happening there were too many protesters to hold off, too much anger to baton-whip back into submission. The start of the revolution was therefore not truly in the city, but in the non-city – those ever-expanding pools of state abandonment which, for so many decades, had been seeping through the metropolis even as those at the top gazed stubbornly out at the sand.

Perhaps some of the Cairo 2050 consultants saw it coming. One of the document's highlights was a vast 600-yard-wide thoroughfare called Khufu Avenue that would run from Sphinx Square to the pyramids and be lined with high-end hotels and office spaces. The proposed road ran straight through the middle of Bulaq al-Dukror, and would have required huge portions of the neighbourhood to be levelled.[33] The opaque nature of Cairo's municipal governance means we were never told the exact route of Khufu Avenue, but it is entirely possible that if the plans had gone ahead the Hayyis sweet shop would have been one of the 220,000 homes and small businesses demolished to make way for it. And although Bulaq al-Dukror has so far been spared the state's bulldozers, many other *'ashwa'iyat* have not been so lucky. Altogether several hundred neighbourhoods have been identified for forced eviction by government officials in recent years, communities that are collectively home to well over 200,000 families. Many have already been cleared, with savage consequences. Residents of informal areas face intense state violence when the day of their eviction arrives: families report watching the walls of their homes being smashed by heavy machinery while relatives cower inside; anyone who resists faces severe consequences from the security services.[34] In 2010 Egypt's government announced it would remove thirty-three 'shack areas' within five years as part of the Cairo 2050 masterplan; in the longer term another 371 districts deemed 'unsafe' by authorities were scheduled to go the same way.

The destruction of the *'ashwa'iyat* neighbourhoods was an attack on the very thing that gives Cairo hope for the future – its dense population and interlinked urban ecology. Perhaps most importantly, the makeover promised by Cairo 2050 sought to create a metropolis in which the anti-Mubarak uprising could never have happened, at least not in the same way. 'It's hard to imagine Egypt's revolution taking place in a gleaming, far-flung city of the future eagerly dreamt of by government bureaucrats and business elites,' observes Cairo-based writer Ursula Lindsey. 'The uprising was shaped and aided by historic Cairo's contours: the densely populated neighbourhoods along which marching protesters yelling "Come on down!" could pick up thousands more; the short distances within the city core; the central, intuitive meeting point of Tahrir Square.'[35] But the battle to resist the splintering of our cities into privatized fragments was not and is not Egypt's alone. From Chonqing to Cape Town to London, market fundamentalism is increasingly fuelling the spread of semi-autonomous urban 'microstates' dominated by walled spaces, the architecture of fear, and deep-seated divisions between economic haves and have-nots. Far from being an outlier, the capital of Mubarak Country was simply in the vanguard of a global trend.

In the thirteenth century, the Syrian governor of Fayoum – an Egyptian oasis lying several hundred miles south-west of Cairo, deep within the Western Desert – made reference to an abandoned village named Zerzura, nestled somewhere, secretly, between the dunes. Two hundred years later, the *kitab al-kanuz* ('Book of Hidden Gems') – a contemporary manual for treasure-seekers which included tips on how to overcome malevolent *jinn* with incantations and fumigations – mentioned Zerzura again, describing it as 'white like a pigeon, and on the door of it is carved a bird'. The book went on: 'Take with your hand the key in the beak of the bird, then open the door of the city. Enter, and there you will find great riches, also the king and the queen sleeping in their castle. Do not approach them, but take the treasure.'[35]

At that point, no one had actually seen Zerzura. But in 1481 a bedraggled camel driver named Hamid Keila stumbled exhaustedly into the Libyan city of Benghazi and told the local emir that he had finally discovered the mysterious desert city. Keila said he had been travelling to the known oases of Kharga and Dakhla from the Nile Valley when a fierce sandstorm unexpectedly lashed his travelling party in the middle of the dunes, killing everyone but Keila himself, who managed to take shelter under his dead camel. Awaking from the destruction to find the desert landscape fatally rearranged out of all recognition by the tempest's winds, Keila – lost, dehydrated and delirious – was met by a group of strange men with fair hair, blue eyes and straight swords (unlike the curved Arab scimitars of the time). Keila explained that the group had carried him back to Zerzura to nurse him, and he reported that the town was full of palms, springs and luxury, and occupied by a people who spoke an odd strain of Arabic and appeared not to be Muslim. He insisted he had been treated with great kindness inside the lost oasis, but had nevertheless decided to escape one night and eventually made it to Libya. The emir was suspicious of Keila, and on discovering a ruby hidden in the camel driver's clothes, he ordered the unfortunate man to be taken out to the desert and have his hands cut off. But from that moment on the legend of Zerzura was sealed. The emir himself became the first of many explorers to try to find it; in common with those who followed, he returned to Benghazi empty-handed.

Over the next 500 years the hope that a hidden valley of life lay hidden in the sand drew fortune-seekers and desert explorers from around the globe, most famously in the 1930s, when a group of cosmopolitan adventurers formed the Zerzura Club in London and swore to track down this long-vanished civilization. Members were drawn from countries that would soon be at war with each other and the story of their forays into the sand reads like a high-octane thriller, each man feigning friendship while double-crossing the others and using the ghost of Zerzura to mask their actual mission: military mapping and espionage.* 'Zerzura is real, not something of the mind,' Abdel Raba Abu Noor, an eighty-year-old inhabitant of Farafra, another Western Desert oasis, once told me. 'But you can only see it when you are lost, you'll never find it if you're looking for it. *Jinns* hide it from sight and make it difficult to enter, but in the right circumstances the oasis will come to your rescue. There's water there, and palm trees and olives, and it can provide you with whatever you need.'

Zerzura may sound implausible, but other 'mythical' oases have been rediscovered in the past, wrenched out of the realm of the fanciful and planted on a real-life map. The sands of the Western Desert are 7 million years old and cover an area the size of the Indian subcontinent; in many places the dunes are virtually impossible for humans to cross. It was once thought that until the Persian conquest, the Ancient Egyptians had no contact with the desert west of Giza; that they believed it was another world, ruled over by Osiris, and that Kharga and Dakhla were inhabited only by the souls of the dead.† For most of human history, those seeking to understand the desert have had to do without Google Maps; little wonder that the notion of a magical city buried deep within that vast dry ocean, one that provided a lost traveller with whatever he or she needed most for survival, took root in so many imaginations down the centuries.

The mystery of Zerzura endures because it is almost impossible to disprove; even under the gaze of modern satellite imagery, the desert

---

* The group included László Almásy, the Hungarian aristocrat and desert explorer who became the basis of Michael Ondaatje's novel *The English Patient* (1992) and a subsequent film of the same title.

† We now know that Egyptians from the Old Kingdom (third millennium BCE) did penetrate deep into the Western Desert; a great deal of evidence has recently emerged indicating links between the Nile Valley and Dakhla oasis, as well as other regions of the desert.[37]

feels enormous and amorphous enough to absorb any fantasies projected on to it. In presenting Egypt's urban future as one that could unfold only in the desert, Mubarak's regime was merely following in the footsteps of many of the country's previous rulers. Most have used the Nile Valley's hinterlands as a canvas on which to draw all manner of unrealistic solutions to national problems, rhetorically following the instructions laid down in the *kitab al-kanuz* all those centuries ago, taking the key from the beak of the bird and making off with the white city's treasure. Looking back over twenty years of structural adjustment under Mubarak – the privatizations, the rural land reforms and dispossession of small farmers, the forced evictions in the cities and the luxury gated compounds in the desert – it becomes clear that several common threads run through all the major reforms enacted in Mubarak Country. One was the reconstitution of the state as a vehicle to promote the interests of domestic and foreign capital. Another was the aggressive attempt to construct new domains in which markets and speculation could flourish, and the relentless – and often violent – attempt to eliminate individuals, communities and social solidarities that might stand in the way of that construction. A third was the way in which these reforms were bundled up in the supposedly neutral language of progress. One modernist mega-project in particular gathered together all of these threads in the biggest, most ostentatious way possible; a project that Mubarak correctly predicted would define his reign. This project took place far, far out in the sand, beyond the fields of Sarandu, beyond the *'ashwa'iyat* of Manshiyet Nasr, beyond the high walls protecting villas in Dreamland, beyond even the old desert oases of Farafra, Kharga and Mut. It was a project as cloaked in illusion as Zerzura. There were various official terms for the scheme, but most Egyptian citizens knew it by one name only. They called it 'Mubarak's pyramid.'

In the late 1990s, just as the most pernicious consequences of the rural land reform legislation and the industrial privatization programme started to take their toll on Egypt's population, Mubarak's government began the development of what was boldly termed a 'new valley' of life in the Sahara. Through a blizzard of press conferences, radio interviews, commemoratively branded cigarettes and even a set of specially commissioned children's story books, the plans were heralded as the saviour of Egypt's economic future: ministers trumpeted the creation of a future home for millions of Egyptians, opening a desperately needed release value for the population pressure bearing down upon an overcrowded Nile. At the heart of the proposal was the construction of a new pumping station in Lake Nasser, the biggest in world history – to be named, naturally, after Mubarak – which would convey water to the spill-off Toshka lakes. From there, a 150-mile canal system would then transport it at ground level to the Western Desert oases, creating 2 million *feddans* of newly arable land (some of which would eventually be assigned to *fellaheen* who had been uprooted in the process). If the plans were ever realized in their totality, they would amount to the most ambitious irrigation project on earth.

Despite intending to devote $87 billion to the New Valley vision, Egypt's government did not deem it necessary to hold any public consultations regarding the project, or produce a single scientific, economic or environmental feasibility report on it for public consumption.[38] Nor were any technical justifications provided for the idea of sending 5 billion cubic metres of scarce Nile water across the surface of one of the hottest deserts in Africa each year, through unlined canals where evaporation loss would be most intense. But Chicago-based Arthur Andersen – an international consultancy firm hired by Saudi prince and prospective mega-investor Al-Walid Bin Talal Bin Abdul-Aziz Al-Saud – was on hand to praise the Mubarak regime for its 'foresight' and talk up the numerous commercial opportunities created by the plans. 'The prince loves the project and is very passionate about it,' gushed Fiona Elgin, an Arthur Andersen spokeswoman.[39] Four years later the firm was convicted of obstructing justice for its role in the Enron cover-up, and had to surrender its professional licence.*

Much like Mubarak's vision of building satellite cities around Cairo, the Toshka scheme was actually nothing new. There had been talk of creating a fertile new valley in the desert ever since the High

---

* The firm was convicted of obstruction of justice in June 2002. The US Supreme Court overturned this conviction in 2005 on the basis that the jury instructions in the original trial did not properly portray the law Arthur Andersen was charged with breaking, but by that point it had already surrendered its professional licence and effectively ceased operations.

Dam at Aswan was constructed under the rule of Gamal Abdel Nasser, though engineers had struggled to work out how to make water from Lake Nasser flow uphill to the higher Western Desert oases. Back then, the option of using massive nuclear explosions to level the desert's gradient was discussed extensively, but the plans never came to fruition and the whole project was ultimately written off as a failure. The Mubarak regime paid little heed. As with the Cairo 2050 plans, any experts who dissented from the government's optimistic narrative were tarred with the brush of being 'anti-modern',* and concerted efforts were made to marry propaganda over this New Valley 'project for the new millennium' to the stigmatization of the old Nile Valley's 'backwards' and 'crumbling' neighbourhoods. Nagwa, a fictional young woman from the near-future who is lucky enough to live in the New Valley, and Salah, her less fortunate cousin who is still stuck by the Nile, are characters created by Abdel Tawab Youssef, a popular children's author much beloved by the Mubarak family.† 'Come and visit us for a few days in a place where you can live in a spacious house with big rooms surrounded by a singing garden,' writes Nagwa in a letter to Salah a story from Youssef's *Wisdom from Toshka* collection.[41] 'No doubt your houses in the Old Valley are small and narrow just like the Old Valley is too small to host its own residents.' When the hapless Salah does eventually leave the Nile behind and arrive in New Valley utopia, he is duly amazed: 'I feel as if I moved to Europe, which my grandfather described to me. Actually, I think that I am in America,' he tells Nagwa. 'Our land is new, but America is no longer new, as it was discovered over five centuries ago,' Nagwa – a nascent artist who adores President Mubarak – replies sagely. 'The New Valley is now counted as "the new continent" that was discovered in 1997.'

In terms of its stated aims, the Toshka vision, inevitably, was a

---

* An example is Dr Mohamed Kassas, considered the 'professor emeritus' of Egypt's environmental movement, who raised doubts about the feasibility of Toshka in 1997 and was promptly removed from the Shura Council. 'The problem with the Egyptian government, and with many governments in general, is that they confuse technical opinion with political stances,' he explained.

† Youssef twice won the Suzanne Mubarak Award, soon after publishing his *Wisdom from Toshka* collection.[40]

dismal failure. Of the 500,000 *feddans* of desert land that were supposed to be greened in phase one of the project, less than 3 per cent were actually irrigated. The ultimate goal – of reclaiming 2 million *feddans* – is now certainly beyond the realm of the fanciful. As predicted by scientists, high saline levels in the sand and the presence of underground aquifers have complicated irrigation efforts, as land reclamation has caused salt to mix with wells and thus reduced access to potable water. On ground that has been reclaimed, the preponderance of clay minerals has caused the big-wheeled structures built to crawl the soil autonomously and provide water to get stuck.[42] The Sheikh Zayed Canal, originally designed to stretch hundreds of miles from Toshka right through the Western Desert and up to Farafra oasis in the north, has failed to make it even a quarter of the way, drying up forty miles short of Baris, the most southerly oasis.[43] And of the little water that is now flowing down the canal, a huge portion is, predictably, being lost to evaporation. *Toshka the Hope*, one of Abdel Tawab Youssef's New Valley children's books, contains one of the few formal acknowledgements of the evaporation issue; in it, classmates of the protagonist, Nagwa, question officials over why canals are being used instead of pipes to transport the water through the desert. 'Will a lot of pure water evaporate, knowing that the region is very hot?' ask the students. 'Don't you believe that we would have taken this point into consideration?' replies the government.

Toshka was never really going to create a new valley of life for Egyptians in the desert, nor provide alternative land for the smallholders and landless *fellaheen* who had been forced off their plots and impoverished by the government's land reform programme. But then the real motivation behind the project was never development; rather Toshka was a political tactic, designed to convince large segments of the population that their government had a plan to tackle long-term social and economic injustice and to deceive them as to what they could expect from their crumbling country in the future.[44] 'It was brilliant in its way, because it was a perpetual long-term solution,' Emma Deputy, a political scientist who has studied the Toshka programme in detail, explained to me. '[It was] something from which no immediate results were expected, but which would provide a massive instant media payoff at a time when, due to the rural land privatizations, Mubarak was facing a wave of serious discontent.' The New Valley enabled officials to present themselves as dealing decisively with growing crisis in living standards, infrastructure and agricultural poverty without genuinely addressing those problems at all. Toshka also intersected neatly with the castigation of the poor and lower classes that accompanied the satellite cities development arc; now not only old neighbourhoods in existing cities could be blamed for the country's ills, but the whole Nile Valley itself.

You don't have to dig far beyond the official publicity to see why neoliberalism's cheerleaders were such enthusiastic adherents of the New Valley scheme. Fayek Abdel-Sayed, general supervisor of the Toshka project at the ministry of public works, confirmed that the government was looking only for large investors capable of building infrastructure by themselves – investors like Prince Al-Walid Bin Talal, the world's second-richest person, who was allocated the first 100,000 *feddans* of future farmland and who in turn contracted a Californian agribusiness named Sun World to develop and manage what would eventually become one of the planet's largest single farms, consuming 1 per cent of the Nile's entire water supply.[45] Arthur Andersen, the prince's American consultancy company, drove home the point about who would be welcome in the New Valley. 'Any small investor getting involved there would probably find it daunting,' explained spokesperson Fiona Elgin. 'Those people will not come for five or ten *feddans*.' So rather than producing their own crops, ordinary farmers arriving from the old valley were expected to work for the multinationals. Egyptian smallholders had been made landless by the hundreds of thousands as a result of the Mubarak regime's fealty to market forces; strangely though, the government's distaste for state support didn't extend to Sun World and other huge corporations like it, all of which were granted twenty-year tax holidays to set up in Toshka and told that up to 20 per cent of its initial capital would be provided by the state. 'The government is doing its best to make investors' lives easier,' reported state newspaper *al-Ahram* with satisfaction.[46]

The role played by Sun World in Toshka's doomed experiment is informative. When Prince Bin Talal announced that the US agricorp would be managing his huge tract of land, the Egyptian government hailed it as vindication of their plans – here, claimed ministers, was an American partner prepared to invest millions in Egyptian agriculture. But as so often in Mubarak Country, the truth was somewhat different. Sun World, which specialized in growing grapes and held the patents on multiple varieties of commercial cultivar, was planning to invest none of its own money in the New Valley project; indeed it wouldn't even pay its own management fees. The reason was that it had recently gone bankrupt and had been taken over by another struggling agribusiness, Cadiz, which in turn was planning to pay off Sun World's debts by selling off its patents and trademarks, including the flagship Superior Seedless™ grape. In other words, rather than producing and selling crops itself, Sun World was now in the business of selling only the names of crops; the business model was simply for the company's product licences to guarantee it a future payment on every piece of fruit that Egyptian farmers employed to labour in the Western Desert might one day grow.[47]

Egypt's farmers once worked on their own plots to provide food for themselves and for fellow Egyptians; now the New Valley was to absorb them as global agribusiness employees instead, living in communities without proper access to water and electricity and toiling in the desert's heat to produce expensive trademarked fruits for export abroad. They were to be managed by a bankrupt company which had invested nothing in the development and would grow nothing itself, but whose costs were being part-met by the government and which would not be required to contribute any taxes to the Egyptian state for two decades. The company's partner was an obscenely rich Gulf monarch who was planning to divert 1 per cent of the Nile's dwindling water supply to his private wealth-generating enterprise, represented by an American consultancy company involved in the largest corporate cover-up in history.

Mubarak once said that the Toshka project marked a shift in Egyptian history,[48] and he was right. From Egypt's fields to its factories, from its towns to its deserts, the transformation of the country under neoliberalism was a pivotal shift in history, one that would ultimately result in revolution. And there was no more perfect embodiment of that shift than this, Mubarak's flimflam pyramid.

3

'I Love to Singa'

During the 1990s, a children's show on Egyptian state television had a regular segment that featured a foreign cartoon. One of these cartoons was a classic Warner Bros short from 1936, 'I Love to Singa'.[1] The animation tells the story of a family of strict classical-music-loving owls, whose peaceful and predictable lives are shaken by the birth of a young owlet who insists on singing jazz numbers whenever the opportunity arises. The family's stern patriarch is appalled at this unsanctioned display of creativity, and eventually ejects his son from the tree in which they've made their home. Alone in the big wide world, the owlet wanders the forest until he comes across an amateur radio singing contest; he enters and performs the cartoon's jazzy title track, wowing his audience. Hearing their off spring's voice on the radio, the owl's parents rush to the tree in which the contest is taking place, and – won over by the young owlet's bravery and imagination – accompany him in a joyous finale rendition of the song. The performance is victorious, and the owlet and his relatives are reunited. 'The message is that by introducing new ideas, defying his elders and essentially being revolutionary, the young owl benefited everyone and saved the family,' Khaled Fahmy, an Egyptian historian who remembers watching the cartoon as a child, told me. As the original film was in English, the show's presenter dubbed it live into Arabic as it was being screened – except strangely, recalls Fahmy, she kept getting the lines wrong. 'In fact, she wasn't just translating incorrectly: she was providing a completely different narrative, one in which the young owl actually betrayed the family and brought trouble and shame on everyone. "See what happens when you defy your parents?" she asked. "See what happens when you don't obey your elders?" It was the complete opposite of the cartoon's real message. At the end of the final scene, the presenter finished up by telling viewers: "Never give in to your dreams. Even dreams have limits." '

Thirty million Egyptians were children in the 1990s; their generation would go on to lead the revolution. One way or another, all were told by the state from their earliest days that dreams have limits: rule was for the patriarch, and politics, change and defiance were not for the likes of them. Bilal Diab, a Cairene activist now in his late twenties, was one of those 30 million, and he heard that message everywhere – in each revelation of torture by the security services, each deadly transport disaster inflicted on Egypt's citizens by an indifferent government, each portrait of Mubarak's face on a wall. 'The mere presence of the president's name was enough to saturate daily life with the ever-present father, regardless of how miserable life was for the ordinary observers of these images,' urbanist Mohamed ElShahed, another child of the 90s, has observed. 'The omnipresence of an ageless Mubarak, often sporting designer sunglasses, created a cohesive reality in an otherwise disjointed urban setting. No matter where you stood, in the street, in the post office, or at work, you were in Mubarak Country, in the reality he created.'² This was the reality of the modern Egyptian state: an impenetrable matrix of political control and financial corruption, off-limits to outsiders. Bilal's young cohort were made to understand that if they ever had grievances, the most they could do was petition the patriarch and his agents, as a subject might humbly petition a kindly monarch. Politics was a scramble for small advantages; it offered no room for those who wanted to reach for anything, least of all the stars.³

By 2008, Bilal was a literature student at Cairo University with little reason to get fired up about the future. He had tried his hand at political activism but found that it was stifled both by the security apparatus – *amn el-dawla* ('state security') agents patrolled the campus and monitored classrooms – and by the narrow horizons of the student body, including himself. "The security services were happy to let protest movements emerge, then they would simply move in and arrest the leaders," he told me. "It was an effective tactic. People were afraid of talking politics; it was a subject to be avoided, and if I ever tried to start a conversation on it people would walk on and avoid eye contact. Our education was all listen and repeat, learning by rote. There was no space for innovation, no space for thinking about how we might build a different kind of country." When news broke that Ahmed Nazif – Mubarak's prime minister and one of the chief archi- tects of the economic reform programme – would be visiting campus to give a lecture celebrating the university's centenary, Bilal and his friends talked about holding some kind of protest. But they had no idea what form it could take. A small demonstration at the university earlier that month, held to coincide with a spate of workers' strikes in the Nile Delta, had simply resulted in multiple incarcerations. 'We thought about trying to hang banners calling for the release of our fellow students, though we knew they'd be taken down straight away,' he smiled. 'Then I thought of submitting a provocative ques- tion on paper, even though I knew it would never be read out. In retrospect, that seems so lame. But we had limited imaginations. That's what Mubarak's Egypt had done to us.'

Working as an Egypt-based journalist in those pre-revolution years, I often found it hard to articulate the size and shape of Muba- rakism, the depth of its toxicity. The regime's commitment to limiting dreams was in some respects its defining feature, but its ubiquity didn't lend itself to daily news stories. One-off tragedies became use- ful ways of telling a more amorphous story. The Duweiqa rockslide, which killed 119 of Egypt's poorest citizens, was a hook on which to hang the social impact of Mubarak's urban development policies. A deadly football riot offered a chance to analyse class divisions and the state's cultivation of a chauvinistic nationalism. When the body of Ahmed Shaaban, a nineteen-year-old who had been on his way to a wedding in Alexandria when he was stopped by police, was found floating among the reeds of the Mahmoudia Canal, I rushed there to write a piece detailing the relationship between systematic state tor- ture and political detachment in the run-up to Egypt's parliamentary elections. But it always felt as if there was something missing from these accounts that was more difficult to put into words and yet more essential than the easy, visceral shock of direct violence. On their own, neither Duweiqa's broken boulders nor Ahmed Shaaban's bat- tered body could transmit the worst aspect of Mubarak's Egypt: the psychological sabotage of its people. Mubarak's ruling class could only survive by painting themselves as guarantors of stability against chaos, and they could only retain and wield that paintbrush success-fully if Egyptians were constantly exhibited – to the world and to each other – as both dangerous and powerless, a sinister pool of iner-tia. 'There is the presentation of Egypt as a country that is intolerant and volatile; that if this regime left it would just become a fanatical, extremist country,' observed Ahdaf Soueif, an Egyptian novelist, soon after Mubarak was toppled. 'We had an enormous sense that we were being deactivated an run down . . . Our heads were being messed with because the message which was coming to us constantly was: "You can't do anything. You have no agency. You are powerless." '[4]

This deactivation took many forms. It was projected through a selective curation of national heritage, through a debasing of Egypt's young people, and through a rigid construction of gender and family. Above all, it was projected through a very specific model of authority that made state power look inevitable and timeless, a natural exten-sion of all the other exclusions that coloured every aspect of daily life for ordinary citizens. Egyptians were effectively told by the Egyptian state that they could never be anything more than the passive victims of history, and it was by overcoming that message that those same Egyptians became history-makers themselves. Everyone involved in the revolution can tell the story of their own personal journey of psy-chological adjustment from Mubarak Country to something new, from one conception of the self and the state to another. The exist-ence of millions of such stories in Egypt is something that the counter-revolution, even at its height, has failed to vanquish.

Bilal's began on the morning of Ahmed Nazif's visit to Cairo Uni-versity. Even years later he grins and shakes his head as he recounts it, as if he can't quite believe what happened next.

On 14 November 1935, nationalist students marched out of Cairo University in protest against British rule. One member of the faculty of agriculture, Mohamed Abdel Magid Mursi, was hoisted aloft by his fellow demonstrators so that he could wave a large Egyptian flag in the air. British troops opened fire. Mursi was killed, and the flag fell to the ground. The moment it landed, another student – Mohamed al-Garahi, from the faculty of humanities – picked it up, and began defiantly to wave it once more. A British officer pointed his gun at al-Garahi, and warned him not to take another step. Al-Garahi, and the flag, marched on regardless. The British officer shot directly into al-Garahi's chest; the young man later died in hospital. According to author Alaa al-Aswany, who wrote about the incident in one of his newspaper columns, 'All Egypt turned out to say farewell to the martyr, who preferred death to seeing the Egyptian flag fall to the ground.'[5]

The mythology surrounding al-Garahi tells us little about the facts behind his death, but a great deal more about the nation which chose to mythologize him. Al-Garahi died as an Egyptian hero in an age when Egypt knew what it was, or at least what it wanted to be: a country steeped in history, master of its own fate and leader of its region. And in the three decades that followed al-Garahi's martyrdom, Egypt rose to fulfil all those expectations and more. Umm Kulthum warbled, Youssef Chahine directed, and Gamal Abdel Nasser was the all-singing, all-dancing leader of the Arab people who faced down Western colonialism and trumpeted Arab nationalism, Egypt-style, across the region. From Algiers to Baghdad, a new political generation inspired by Nasserite pan-Arabism waltzed to Cairo's beat. The Egyptian capital was where wanrabe starlets, intellectual aspirants and national liberation commanders from every corner of the Middle East and beyond aimed to be.* Even those who could never make a pilgrimage to the Nile felt as though they had been there: it was *Egyptian* Arabic that was the lingua franca of the Arab world, *Egyptian* landmarks that formed the visual reference points in every hit film, and *Egyptian* songs that transfixed tens of millions to their radio sets on the first Thursday evening of every month, when *el-sitt* ('the lady': Egypt's popular term for Umm Kulthum) performed her concerts at the Cinema Qasr el-Nil.[6] In 1960, the Hollywood film *Doctor Dolittle* featured a song by Samantha Eggar named 'Fabulous Places', about the desire of a young American woman to break free and visit the greatest, most glamorous cities in the world. Rome,

---

* Egypt was a founding member of the Non-Aligned Movement, made up of countries which positioned themselves outside the Cold War's two major power blocs. The movement's second major summit was held in Cairo in 1964.

London and Paris were name-checked in the chorus. So, too, was Cairo.[7]

If such a song were to be have been written anew in the early twenty-first century, it is doubtful that any Egyptian city would make the cut. In 1967, crushing military defeat at the hands of Israel delivered a body-blow to the country's self-confidence; by the 1970s, rival Gulf states were awash in petrodollars and spending them hand over fist in an effort to become regional superpowers themselves. Egypt, meanwhile, had undergone a geopolitical realignment under Sadat that left it looking more like an American lapdog than a political beast in its own right. And as Sadat's economic reforms and their attendant culture of crude materialism chipped away at loftier intellectual and artistic values, Egypt's reputation as a cultural nerve centre also began to wane. By the latter days of Mubarak's rule, Middle Eastern café TV sets were more likely to be tuned to *Million's Poet*, an insanely popular talent show produced in Abu Dhabi and featuring contestants reciting Bedouin-dialect poetry, than they were to an Egyptian soap opera. Rather than move to the Nile to seek fame and fortune, it was the Nile's residents who were moving in order to escape poverty and stagnation at home. They left to work in the oil-fields or nanny the children of Saudi Arabia, Qatar and the Emirates, or, if endowed with the right education, to staff the clinics, financial centres and engineering firms of Europe and North America. The cultural assets left behind back home were increasingly snapped up by Gulf investors and moulded to the social and religious whims of their new owners: films now had to conform to certain rules of piety, celebrity belly-dancers covered up, and the Saudi proprietor of the Grand Hyatt hotel ordered its entire alcohol supply – reportedly worth $1 million and including several bottles of expensive champagne and vintage cognac – to be poured down the drain.[8] A sluggish and repressive Egypt no longer shaped its own character, never mind that of its neighbours.

Sunk in torpor, Egypt forgot its past, and thus its future. Memory loss wasn't immediate; initially, it appeared as if the new military-bureaucratic caste ushered in by the 1952 coup were determined to reclaim Egypt's heritage in the name of its people. Soon after taking power, Nasser posed for the cameras in front of the colossal Abu Simbel temples, an iconic image designed – like the transfer of an eighty-three-tonne statue of Ramses II to a central Cairene square – to inform the world that Egyptians were now firmly in charge of their own illustrious history. For centuries beforehand Egypt's antiquities had been plundered to tart up the drawing rooms of foreign aristocrats and the squares of Europe's capitals; Nasser's set-pieces signalled that the days when the country's ruins served as private department stores for the rich were over. For the first time a ministry of national culture was established, and a renewed interest in Ancient Egypt captured modern Egypt's streets.

But like the rest of the Nasser-era cultural renaissance, this new-found passion for preserving and disseminating history proved highly selective, geared more towards regime self-preservation than to any real desire to see Egyptians actively engage with their past. Seeking to shore up their political legitimacy, Nasser's Free Officers were determined to insert themselves into a long lineage of nationalist resistance to colonialism. In historiographical terms that entailed promoting and acclaiming anybody associated with anti-British resistance – like the mutinous nineteenth-century general Ahmed 'Urabi, or the early twentieth-century nationalist leader Saad Zaghoul – and condemning or ignoring anything associated with the royal family or its governments. At a stroke Egypt's rich history of nineteenth-century modernism and the cultural renaissance which characterized that formative era – grand leaps in architecture and the arts, the embryonic development of universities, ports, museums and other institutions that would eventually coalesce into the modern Egyptian state – were dismissed and forgotten; the opening of a new chapter, in Nasser's name, rested on a denial of the previous one.[9] Roads were renamed, school curriculums were sanitized, palaces were sequestered by the military elite and venerable repositories of Victorian-era ideals of cultural progress – the Geographical Society, the Institut d'Égypte, the Ethnographic Museum – were left to 'moulder in disuse'.[10] Under Nasser's successors, Sadat and Mubarak, such decay only intensified. Often the deterioration was gradual and muted; sometimes though, it came briskly, and in the form of flames or theft. In 1977 the magnificent Khedival Opera House, set among the gardens of Ezbekiya, burned to the ground. It was replaced with a multi-storey car park. Fire also claimed the Khedive's birthplace, a stunning Ottomanera palace, in 1998. Promised restoration work never materialized. Large parts of the Shura Council building, which housed Egypt's upper chamber of parliament and was the site at which the country's first constitution was signed, were incinerated in 2008. Two years later, in a sign of how undervalued Egypt's non-Pharaonic cultural riches had become under six decades of state stewardship, thieves walked into Cairo's Mahmoud Khalil Museum and carried off a $50 million van Gogh painting. It was the second time the canvas had been stolen. Subsequent enquiries revealed that none of the building's alarms had been working.[11]

This litany of cultural vandalism seemingly mattered little to the state; modern history – the story of the buildings, institutions and struggles which helped establish the contemporary state and slowly transformed Egyptians from subjects to citizens – was generally considered irrelevant or dangerous. The only national heritage deemed worthy of serious attention was the type that arrived mummified, or soared up from the sand. In ever more aggressive attempts to attract tourist dollars, Egypt's unrivalled Pharaonic treasures were gated, plastic-wrapped and commodified to within an inch of their ancient lives, then bundled into a carefully sterilized visitor experience: a four- or five-star hotel on the Nile, organized plexiglass trips to the Egyptian museum and Giza pyramids, a felucca on the river and then on to Luxor, Aswan or Sharm el-Sheikh. The well-connected business magnates who came to monopolize this tightly controlled conveyor belt built up fortunes, while the more immediate historical reference points of 80 million living, breathing Egyptians who occupied the land today were scorned. This regressive notion of Egypt as little more than a kitsch playground of the past became institutionalized and marketed to the world. 'The message is that when it comes to Egypt, there *once was*, and here's *a few highlights of what once was*, and that's about it,' says Cairo urbanist Mohamed ElShahed, who has written extensively about the state-sponsored neglect of the country's *belle époque* history. 'The Sadat and Mubarak regimes have reproduced narratives about Egyptian history that are far more colonial and orientalist than any nineteenth-century colonial orientalist could ever have dreamed of.'[12]

Under Mubarak, Egypt developed a seemingly unbreakable link between tourism and patrimony; the ministry of antiquities was the only government department required by the state to be self-funding, necessitating a relentless search for ticket revenue and removing any incentives to preserve anything beyond blockbuster Pharaonic attractions that were guaranteed to pull in package tours. What's more, the focus on extracting profits from heritage sites meant that Egyptians themselves, most of whom could never afford to pay the tourist-level entrance fees and were less likely to waste money in the adjoining cafés and gift shops, held little attraction to those making decisions about Egypt's past and who should be granted access to it. In 2001 a new entrance and viewpoint for the Giza pyramids was constructed for Egyptian citizens – two and a half miles away from the monuments themselves. The main gate, situated a stone's throw from the pyramids, became the exclusive preserve of foreigners and their tour guides. 'The majority of visits conducted by Egyptians to the site, the plateau, are for fun rather than culture or education,' sniffed antiquities supremo Zahi Hawass at the time. 'People have to understand that it is a sacred, divine place, not a venue for parties, dancing and singing.'[13] Over the following years, under Dr Hawass's supervision, the base of the pyramids was used to stage the World Open Squash Championships, several major international pop concerts (including one by Shakira) and an annual car rally (featuring, according to the ministry of tourism, 400 contestants, 130 cars and trucks, 70 motorcycles, 10 ultralight planes, 3 helicopters and crew from 57 television channels). Meanwhile, ordinary Egyptians were left on the wrong side of a new twelve-mile security fence, topped with infra-red sensors and a network of alarms. A similar sense of exclusion pervaded Egypt's other major historical sites as well. When Mohamed ElShahed tried to visit the gated Egyptian Museum in 2006 with an American friend, he was stopped by security, questioned and made to show ID. His friend was allowed straight in. In the eyes of the state, ElShahed was little more than a trespasser.

This recasting of history as product, visitors as consumers and Egyptians as interlopers impacted anyone living in the vicinity of Pharaonic sites. A long-running plan to transform Luxor – a city of almost half a million people – into the world's 'largest open air museum' and excavate a 1.5 mile-long Avenue of the Sphinxes involved the displacement of thousands, the bulldozing of countless nineteenth century buildings of architectural and historical significance as well as the city's ancient bazaar, and the construction of tourist-friendly plazas and shopping malls throughout the town. New five-star hotels, an IMAX cinema and a golf course are still planned by 2030, despite the forceful resistance of residents living in houses near the Karnak Temple. 'They do what they want, we do what we want,' insisted Zain Sadi, one of the locals affected. 'We will beat and be beaten, we will kill and be killed. After we die, they can take our homes.'[14] President Mubarak and Silvio Berlusconi had been scheduled to open the new boulevard on 20 February 2011; the toppling of Mubarak on 11 February prevented the ribbon-cutting from taking place.

Back in the capital, one of the Mubarak regime's last major development projects was to launch a similar process of tourist-orientated 'regeneration' in the historic neighbourhoods of Fatimid Cairo – home to the bulk of the city's Islamic monuments. In what critics labelled a botched attempt to 'Disney-fy' some of the most important medieval buildings in the Middle East, centuries-old stucco was torn out and replaced with modern plaster, shiny new marble was overlaid on original stonework, and historical monuments deemed insufficiently picturesque were torn down to present favoured sites in artificial isolation.[15] Even more damagingly, the authorities sought to denude the living, breathing core of the city of its people. 'The government is evacuating many of the merchants, artisans, and residents who live in – and give life to – this nucleus of Cairo so that large groups of tourists, directed by signs and guides, will be able to traverse it along designated paths as quickly and summarily as possible,' warned Caroline Williams, an independent scholar specializing in Egypt's Islamic monuments. Nezar AlSayyad, a professor of architecture and urban history and author of several books on Cairo, accused the state of 'museumifying' the city's oldest quarter and transforming it into a theme park rendered in a Western holidaymaker's fantasy of the capital. He highlighted an absurd chain of events involving an eighteenth-century *sebil* – an intricately latticed charitable building designed to provide education and water to the poor – which was stripped of its windows and tile work over a hundred years ago by an American architect who wanted to use them to build an inaccurate replica of the structure in Chicago. Although the replica bore little resemblance to the original, a later restoration of the real *sebil* in Cairo was based on images of the Chicago model. 'Cairo now began to resemble its imagined self,' wrote AlSayyad, 'and had come to derive its new authenticity from its copy.'[16]

The cumulative effect of these policies, according to Mohamed ElShahed, is that most Egyptians in Mubarak Country were 'stuck in the present tense'. That had major political ramifications; with little sense of the agency of previous generations, and the dreams and capacities of those generations to build and shape a state that worked for them, it became much harder for anyone in the present to follow suit. 'The deliberate neglect of 200 years of Egyptian history – the years in which Egyptians began to build a modern state for themselves – isn't coincidental,' ElShahed told me. 'Why did it take thirty years for people to really rise up? Well, partly because we are not aware of our own history. There is enough in Egypt's past not just to generate plenty of money from visitors but also to educate and develop a strong population psychologically. Yet most of it is left to crumble, amid a specific conceptualization of history that is deeply troubling.' Writer Adel Iskandar agrees; only two months before the outbreak of revolution, he warned in his newspaper column of the dangers of a state-curated ahistoricism that ignored the regime's crimes of the past and situated contemporary Egyptians in a seemingly unchanging future. 'While we continue to ignore the symptoms of the gaping wound in our collective consciousness,' he wrote, 'we go on like the living dead, sleepwalking in a seemingly consequence-free environment.'[17] Meanwhile, the man responsible for protecting and nourishing Egypt's connection with its past, Dr Zahi Hawass – self-professed defender of the sanctity of Egyptian antiquities from the ill-educated Egyptian masses, and an intimate friend of the Mubarak family – hawked the treasures of Tutankhamen's tomb around the world on a multimillion dollar tour, armed with his (trademarked) explorer hat, his lucrative contracts with American television networks, and, since 2010, his own clothing line. 'Zahi Hawass is a novel fashion line not just for the traveling man, but the man who values self-discovery, historicism and adventure,' reads the brand's promotional copy. 'Rich khakis, deep blues and soft, weathered leathers give off a look that hearkens back to Egypt's golden age of discovery in the early twentieth century ... Combined with an elegantly themed in-store shop at Harrods, Zahi Hawass clothing will promote a look that is both trendy and casual, conservative and cool.'[18]

The politicized atrophy of Egypt's cultural riches under Mubarak was epitomized on 9 March 2011, when young protesters were dragged from Tahrir Square into the adjacent Egyptian Museum. There, amid the badly kept and dusty remnants of their nation's ancient past, they were brutalized for attempting to rewrite its future. 'The men were being tortured with electric shocks, whips and wires,' remembers Rasha Azab, a political activist who was among the victims. 'The women were tied to fences and trees.'[19] Building work is now underway on a $500 million replacement Grand Egyptian Museum[20] far out in the desert: by extracting the nation's main cultural institution from its capital and population, and leaving the space around Tahrir Square free for the army's electrocutions, Egypt's post-Mubarak rulers are perhaps hoping that in the years to come their battle against history will be victorious, and the state can reaffirm its authority over the past. Despite being sacked from his government duties and handed a prison sentence after Mubarak's fall, Dr Hawass – Mubarak Country's elite gatekeeper nonpareil – certainly believes so.* When I interviewed him in his office soon after the eighteen 'days'† – during which he had spoken out publicly as a staunch defender of Mubarak – he thumped his fist on the desk and showered me in spittle. 'We have always needed a strongman; without one you have chaos,' he boomed. 'Things change, but I am the only one who understands this country's history, who can truly see the past.'[21]

In 2007, Egypt hosted an International Youth Forum at a five-star hotel and conference centre in Sharm el-Sheikh. The forum was

---

* Hawass was sentenced to a year in jail in April 2011, but the conviction was later overturned.
† The 'eighteen days', here and throughout the book, refers to the anti-Mubarak uprising between 25 January and 11 February 2011, with which the revolution began.

organized by the Suzanne Mubarak Women's International Peace Movement, a non-profit organization headed by the First Lady. Several young Egyptians were invited to attend – including Rania a nineteen-year-old freshman at the American University in Cairo, who was asked to facilitate some of the discussions.*

Rania had been looking forward to the event, but once it began her enthusiasm levels dipped sharply. There were hours of predictable speeches and platitudes from officials, but very little actual debate; among the liveried waiters and elegantly carpeted conference rooms, the voice of 'youth' could barely be heard at all. Rania, who describes herself as 'totally non-political' at the time, eventually snapped midway through a session on 'youth and political participation'. 'The whole setup was super extravagant and over the top, with these all-expenses-paid luxuries and ridiculous sermons,' she remembers. 'Suzanne Mubarak spoke and was portraying herself as a great friend of peace and a great friend of youth, and so on and so on. So when I got a chance to ask a question, I simply said, "We're having this big discussion about youth and political participation in this resort in Egypt, and yet outside of here, in the rest of the country, if I actually did any kind of political participation I'd be putting myself and my family in danger." And everything went quiet, and I saw everyone's heads in the audience turn and look at me, and the reaction on their faces was just like "WHAT?!" Then I actually approached Suzanne Mubarak on the stage, and she had all these bodyguards around her, and I just carried on speaking. "You know it's really impressive that this whole conference is happening and the government can manage to pull off something so prestigious, but meanwhile in the rest of Egypt . . ." She cut me off and said, "Why are you saying all that? I'm really surprised that you'd say something like that." And you know what, I think she really was surprised. The attitude of her and her assistant was just like, "Who are you?"'

For most of her adult life, up until she was confronted by Rania, the First Lady had been surrounded by people who bowed and scraped and lauded her every word. On one occasion, at the annual NDP conference, a senior government minister – Aisha Abdel Hady,

* Rania's real name has been changed to protect her identity.

the minister of manpower – stooped down to kiss Suzanne Mubarak's hand as she passed, a tortuously cringing scene that was captured in full by nearby television cameras. Several bloggers at the time observed that the humiliation was not Abdel Hady's, but Egypt's: a throwback to the days of the monarchy in which everyone knew their place and the survival of politicians depended on the whims and graces of their king and queen.[22] In many ways, of course, Mubarak's Egypt was just such a throwback, a nation of bureaucratic viceroys in which position and promotion alike flowed from neither popular legitimacy nor individual competence, but rather loyalty to the emperor supreme – and woe betide those who, like Rania, dared to upset the natural order of things. But Suzanne Mubarak's shock went further than that. Not only had the First Lady been publicly challenged, but she'd been publicly challenged by a young person, one that clearly didn't understand her age group's socially prescribed limits. Mubarak Country's culture of political deference, as evidenced by Aisha Abdel Hady's hand-kissing, was based on the notion of a benevolent father figure shepherding his often wayward flock with firm but fair concern, and that notion shaped social dynamics far beyond the presidential palace or the walls of a Sharm el-Sheikh conference seminar room. After staging her intervention, Rania expected to be accosted by state security; instead, the first threatening phone call she received was from her own father. 'My brother told my dad about what happened, and my dad got really angry,' she recalls. 'He yelled at me over the phone, asking, "Why did you think you could do this? How did you think you could do this?" The way he saw things was that he was struggling to provide the best life possible for his children, and by speaking out I was undermining all of that and putting everything in jeopardy, I was undermining his role as a provider. It made me realize how little there was that I could say that people would actually listen to.' Rania, who now has her own apartment in central Cairo and the independence that goes with it, afforded herself a smile that was part-rueful, part-relief. 'I had a curfew back then, I had to wear the veil. When I was a teenager I told my parents that my dream was to travel the world and live on my own: I was grounded for two months just for saying that out loud. So when the revolution began, I started my own revolution at home as well. Now, when people try and display God-like authority, all I want to do is degrade it.'

Rania's words, and her struggle to project her own thoughts into the world, will be familiar to a vast number of young Egyptians. 'For millennia, Egypt's "fathers" have been omnipresent,' argued Egyptian writer Adel Iskandar in 2011. 'They adorned every public space in the country, from sphinxes in their likeness and obelisks describing their insurmountable achievements, to every government office and street corner decorated with varnished, doctored photos of their younger selves.'[23] The ubiquity of gerontocratic political authority was often mirrored at home. 'I am torn between two fathers,' writes Nada, the fictional nine-year-old narrator of the novel *Farag* by Radwa Ashour, who grows up in the Nasser era. 'Both are from the same generation, both have roots in Upper Egypt, and both are the embodiment of fatherhood. One is a shared public father for everyone, and the other is a personal father. My public father is a leader who is often spoken of in the home, street and school. He is everywhere, like nature. Like the water, air, soil or rays of the sun. My personal, private dad is different. In a moment, I can run into his bedroom.'[24] The institution of the family, both the nuclear family and the broader 'national family', with paternal authority at the helm, is always equated with safety and security; Nada is therefore left disorientated when her 'private' father, a dissident, is imprisoned by her 'public' father, the president.

Paternalism compels infantilism, and the maintenance of both requires an interlocking sense of tradition and crisis – tradition, in order that an imaginary golden age of quiet deference on the part of Egypt's youth can be used as a contemporary reference point to shame dissenters, and crisis so that reckless self-expression by young people can be presented as an existential threat to the social fabric. Mubarak's last decade was characterized by relentless hand-wringing over Egypt's youth 'problem', as the youngest demographic bulged and unemployment spiralled. From the perspective of the state, young people were a danger that needed to be immunized against through government-controlled institutions; a new 'ministry of youth' was established in 1999. But Egypt's young people had little time for the thousands of youth centres, summer camps and sporting contests organized by the ministry, leaving a mosaic of substandard amenities and near-empty halls dotted around the country. The unwillingness of Egyptian teens and twenty-something to channel their energies into spaces monitored and controlled by the state only fuelled further alarm,[25] and in the eyes of many commentators Egypt's youth increasingly began to resemble a shadowy mass that exemplified the national decline in social values – one to which virtually any modern social ill could ultimately be traced. In 2009, a disturbing murder case involving a boy who killed his two young cousins, supposedly to 'burn the heart' of his uncle (who had just fired him from a job), prompted a prolonged bout of soul-searching. The murders, insisted newspaper columnist Tarek Abbas, were part of a new and different Egypt, 'as if I woke up to find myself not by the Nile I know, but instead breathing different air and dealing with different people, becoming scared of things that didn't use to frighten me'.[26]

The truth is that every country has its fair share of random and psychotic crimes; Egypt's annual murder rate was actually the lowest in the world (0.4 per 100,000 in the population – compared to 2.03 in Britain and 5.8 in the US). But that didn't stop fear of a violent crime-wave crashing across the front pages. 'I'm afraid,' explained the popular Egyptian TV presenter Khairy Ramadan in his weekly newspaper column. 'When going to work or when coming back. When I wake up or when I'm sleeping. When my kids are late at school or the club. Throughout the day, I'm really afraid. The danger is everywhere, and killing has been taking place lately for the most trivial reasons. It's not only in the street, but it can reach you at home . . .'[27] When one's environment has become that petrifying, the role of a protective elder – at home or in government – becomes all the more inviolable.

Ramadan's mortal terror crystallized a broader set of social fears, often expressed in the words *fi haga ghalat* ('there's something wrong'), which was bound up inextricably with the issue of 'wayward' youth. It was a lens seized on by neoconservatives in the West; with no agency or identity of their own, the region's young people would surely be easy prey for Islamic militants looking to recruit the next generation of suicide bombers. Samuel Huntington, Donald Rumsfeld and Thomas Friedman all warned of the dangers of youth radicalism in the Middle East; Huntington labelled unemployed young males, who formed large portions of the population in countries such as Egypt, as 'a natural source of instability and violence'.[28] Seen through a prism of fevered suspicion, both at home and abroad, any unfamiliar youth subculture was liable to trigger a bout of periodic hysteria. On a notorious morning in 1997, the doors of seventy middle-class homes in Cairo were kicked in by security forces in full body armour who dragged away the teenagers they found within. All were suspected of practising devil worship (they were just heavy metal fans – a distinction lost on the authorities). Held in jail for between two and six weeks, the suspects were interrogated on an impressively wide range of subjects, including: 'Do you participate in pagan rituals?', 'Do you spit on graves?' and 'Do you skin cats?'[29] A headline in the English-language *Egyptian Gazette* soon afterwards read: 'Mossad Orchestrates Satanic Orgies in Egypt'.[30]

One morning a decade later, about a year after my own arrival in Cairo, I noticed a series of incomprehensible shapes that had been stencilled overnight on to the streets of my neighbourhood; within hours state security agents were questioning passers-by and government street-cleaners were hurriedly removing the paint. The press had a field day: this graffiti was obviously (depending on which newspaper you read) the calling card of deranged anarchists, Shia insurgency cells or jihadist terrorists. The truth, when it came out – that those responsible for the stencils were a group of self-identified Egyptian 'emos' – did little to staunch media consternation.[31] Emos, a musical subculture whose adherents often sport tight T-shirts, skinny jeans and dyed-black fringes, was suddenly the new canvas on to which the rest of society could daub its fears of the youthful unknown. Up to 10,000 Egyptians were members of emo-related Facebook groups, we were informed; all were adherents to a Western, possibly Zionist, cult which glorified homosexuality and threatened to undermine Islam. Discerning readers were offered tips for identifying emos: they were 'driven by punk and emotion', wore 'guyliner' and 'manscarer' and were to be found 'loitering in streets . . . often dismal and in tears'.[32] The backlash against a group of youths whose worst crime was probably an over-abundance of My Chemical Romance songs in their record collections actually began before the street-art controversy, when the host of *el-Haqeeqa* ('The Truth'), a top-rated talk-show on Dream TV, devoted an entire episode to the phenomenon. In it he grilled a number of self-identified emos, including one gutsy student named only as Sherif, who persistently interrupted the presenter and callers to insist that the emos were not an organized movement and were not all gay. 'The idea is that there is nothing wrong with admitting that you are emotional,' Sherif said defensively. The host, Wael el-Ibrashi, was sceptical. 'Look, no one can tell you how to wear your hair,' he conceded. 'But when that becomes a group philosophy, it's worrying.'[33]

Egyptian emos were few in number, but el-Ibrashi's anxieties were part of a much larger social pathology: in the twilight years of the Mubarak regime, any form of group identity or playful ritual unsanctioned by the state was a source of consternation for patriarchs big and small. The act of seeking and creating one's own forms of fun and individuality presupposed a set of assumptions about self, society and life that were at odds with the paternal state, and therefore hazardous. 'What possible injury is done to the ideological state by the innocent act of flying kites, by the joyous movement of the body in a private wedding festivity, or by the exchange of harmless smiles between timid teenagers in the tense moments of backstreet love?' asked sociologist Asef Byat in his study of Egyptian youth, which saluted the 'creative inbetweenness' of young people who found ways to both fit in with and subvert entrenched social conventions. Anti-fun ethics, Byat went on to argue, amounted to a particular technique of power, 'a discursive shield that both legitimizes and insulates moral or political authority by binding it to "what is not to be questioned", to the sacrosanct, the untouchables'.[34] The state feared anything that might bring a culture of 'daddy deference' to an end.

And the fear was well founded. Of the scores of young people I have interviewed since 2011 about their experiences of the revolution, the vast majority began their tales of the eighteen days with an account of how they confronted, persuaded or outfoxed their parents in an effort to escape the house and join the demonstrations: my notes are littered with blazing rows, defiant messages pinned to bedroom doors, inelegant clambers out of first-floor windows. For many, just like for Rania, the revolution blew through the home as much as

Tahrir Square. Of course, respect for elders and the family hasn't disappeared. But in many classrooms, kitchens and conference centres, infantilism is no longer the default mode. In the moment after Mubarak's departure was announced, the father of revolutionary activist Gigi Ibrahim called her to ask about the future. 'He's asking me what happens next,' grinned Gigi in response. 'My dad, asking me! That never happens!'[35] Increasingly, Egypt's young people feel that such an altered generational dynamic should be the norm, not the exception. And this rejection of paternalism has structured and sharpened every key episode of political turmoil since the revolution began, including Sisi's vigorous efforts to re-establish himself as the national patriarch. I've witnessed many street battles between protesters and security forces in Egypt over the past few years; they are often chaotic and fragmentary, and – if one is embedded on the demonstrators' side of the barricade – characterized as much by rapid-fire acts of human kindness as by unadulterated rage. But the occasion on which I saw and felt Tahrir to be at its most awesomely furious was not during a street battle at all, but rather in the immediate aftermath of those few minutes on the night of Thursday, 10 February 2011, when the packed square fell silent to listen to what most people fervently believed was going to be Hosni Mubarak's resignation speech – only to hear the dictator announce that he would be staying in power. There were not enough radios to go round; an acquaintance, Fakhr el-Sanoury, was able to listen through earphones plugged into his phone, and had the unenviable task of becoming a temporary mouthpiece for the president, repeating Mubarak's words to a large crowd that gathered expectantly around us. 'I am addressing the youth of Egypt today in Tahrir Square and across the country,' muttered Fakhr nervously, pointing repeatedly at the earphones to underline the distinction between himself and the most hated man in Egypt. 'I am addressing you all from the heart, a father's dialogue with his sons and daughters. I am proud of you.'[36] It was not just Mubarak's refusal to step down that sent a livid, guttural roar thundering into the night sky at that moment. It was the words he used, the language of paternalism being deployed to pacify a people for whom such paternalism was the very source of their discontent. It demonstrated in an instant that no matter what concessions were offered, no matter what pseudo-reformist rhetoric was spouted, this was a man and a regime that could never understand the sort of Egypt Fakhr and his friends were fighting to create.

Two scenes:

One. It is 2008, a year after Rania confronted Suzanne Mubarak in Sharm el-Sheikh, and, 200 miles away in Cairo, eighteen-year-old Mariam Kirollos is crossing the street. It is 11 a.m. A man drives up beside her and, without warning, attempts to pull her forcefully into his vehicle. She manages to wriggle free and runs off down the street, but the driver gives chase. Eventually Mariam bursts through the doors of a pharmacy and begs for help. The pharmacy owner tells her there is nothing he can do. 'At that moment my first thought was, everyone is going to rape me in this pharmacy,' remembers Mariam. 'It was only when I pleaded with him and said things like "What if I were your daughter, wouldn't you protect me?" that he finally locked the door and stopped the driver from reaching me. Then he took a long look at me, shook his head and said, "Why aren't you well-dressed?" I looked down at my clothes. I was wearing sweat-pants, my brother's T-shirt, glasses and had my hair pinned up. I looked back up at him and said, "I don't know what else I can do." '

Two. It is 18 January 2011, and a short video is uploaded to the internet.[37] It is plain and grainy, depicting a young Egyptian woman sitting in a room with white walls and a grey door. Her name is Asmaa Mahfouz, and she is twenty-five years old. She speaks directly to the camera, and begins by observing that in recent days four Egyptians have set themselves on fire in an attempt to replicate the self-immolation of Mohamed Bouazizi in Tunisia and spark a copy-cat revolution. One of the four has just died of his burns. She tells the camera that she has one simple message: she will go down to Tahrir Square on 25 January to protest for honour, dignity and human rights, and others who hate this government's corruption and violence should do the same. Her call appears to be universal, but she then switches to masculine pronouns and begins specifically addressing Egypt's men. 'Anyone who sees himself as a man, should go out to protest,' Mahfouz insists. 'Whoever says that women should not go down [to Tahrir] because they could be maltreated or because it is improper . . . should show some honour and manhood and go out to protest . . . If you are a man, you should go out to protect me and protect any girl who is out to protest.'[38] Seven days later, tens of thousands of men and women take to the streets.

In Mubarak Country, power wasn't just old – it was male. The state's self-construction along familial lines begat an authoritarian leader to whom anyone could appeal for clemency, but only from a position of juvenile dependency and gratitude – never from the standpoint of being an equal political participant. And just like the generational divide, the gendered aspects of this relationship were reflected in many other spaces as well, including the Cairene pharmacy where Kirollos had desperately sought help and the YouTube video in which Mahfouz called for the protests that would culminate in revolution.

In the two scenes above, Kirollos and Mahfouz were both – in very different contexts – making appeals to men. In each case, the young women found themselves having to confront and in some ways bolster the rigidity of established gender roles, roles which controlled and delimited men's lives as well as women's. Within Mubarak Country's model of the loving, stable family, men had to be honourable protectors and providers; women were always a wife, a mother, or a wife and mother-to-be. Those operating outside this familial context, and who refused to couch their demands in the manner of a child beseeching a parent, were often presented as an eccentric menace; in this arena, women are fallen and little more than prostitutes, and men are *baltageya* ('thugs') or *baltageya*-to-be.[39] It was a dynamic that coloured relationships in the home and on the street, and shaped not only the daily reality of political authoritarianism but even forms of dissent to it as well. Kirollos was forced to make herself into a daughter in order to get the pharmacist to fend off her attacker; self-determination over her body came at the price of dependency. Mahfouz wanted to subvert the patriarchal state, but felt compelled to appeal to conventional notions of masculinity and femininity in order to do so. When it came to gender, resistance and reinforcement were often bound up together.

The struggle by Egyptians to fight gendered exclusion has a long and nuanced history. As the revolution grew, many of its street symbols became female: the pharaoh queen Nefertiti still stares down from countless Cairene walls in a gas-mask given to her by contemporary graffiti artist el-Zeft, and more modern icons of women's liberation such as Huda Shaarawi and Doria Shafik have also been held aloft at demonstrations. But the stories of these two legendary feminists are a reminder of the scale of the challenge faced by those fighting regressive gender binaries. Shaarawi, most famous for the moment in May 1923 when she arrived in Cairo's central station and dramatically removed her veil,* grew up in the segregated universe of the *harem* and was married off to her cousin at the age of thirteen. She spent her life breaking taboos: doing her own shopping at local department stores, chairing political meetings in the absence of her husband, who was a prominent activist, and founding her own organization, the Egyptian Feminist Union, which made major strides in the battle for women's suffrage and other political and social rights. Her campaign for the establishment of women-led social services in Egypt dealt a powerful blow to popular assumptions about female visibility in public space and the need for women to be 'protected' through incarceration at home or the presence of male chaperones outside of it. But as an upper-class woman, much of her activism was shaped by her economic privilege. Some scholars have accused her of having a romanticized and passive perspective of poor women, one in which their route to salvation appeared to lie chiefly through the philanthropic activities of the rich.[40]

Doria Shafik, by contrast, came from a more ordinary background.[41] She reached adulthood in the 1920s, just as Shaarawi's activism was at its peak, and spent the rest of her life elbowing her way into domains that had previously been the sole preserve of men; by the early 1950s, the country's religious establishment, its colonial rulers and its liberal elites had all become targets of her inexhaustible militancy. In 1951, the 42-year-old Shafik formed the first all-female paramilitary units to join the anti-British resistance movement; that

* Ironically, given the subsequent importance attached to this moment, the veil at the time was worn only by relatively prosperous urban women and as such wasn't a major issue for the majority of Egyptian females; Shaarawi herself dedicated little of her campaigning energies in this direction.

same year she led a crowd of 1,500 demonstrators and stormed a session of the Egyptian parliament in an effort to win women the vote (the franchise was eventually extended in 1956).* Shafik appeared to be the perfect poster-girl for Nasser's Egypt, and yet her political agitation – she transformed her feminist magazine, *Binat el-Nil* ('Daughters of the Nile'), into a political party soon after independence, and became an outspoken critic of the president's policies and governance style – was considered a step too far by the new ruling class. In 1957, after launching the second of two hunger strikes and promising to maintain it until death unless Nasser's dictatorial rule came to an end, she was captured by security forces and placed under indefinite house arrest. There she remained in seclusion for almost two decades, the woman who did so much to break open space for women outside the home condemned to a permanent existence within it. Shafik finally ended her own life, by jumping off her balcony.

Battles over gender intersect with all manner of other social dynamics; attempts to isolate them rarely pay dividends. Sha'arawi was active in a period in which much of the public discourse around feminism had been framed not by a woman, but a man: Qasim Amin, a late nineteenth-century reforming judge who is often referred to as the Arab World's 'first feminist'. Amin spoke passionately on the issue of female emancipation and published an influential pair of books on the subject. Yet, as historians have subsequently pointed out, Amin's 'feminist project' was not the work of Egyptian women seeking equal citizenry, but rather of Egyptian men seeking inclusion in a very Western conception of modernity.[42] Amin's main interaction with women was likely to have come only within his own aristocratic family circle, and possibly with prostitutes,[43] though that did not prevent him from representing all of them in considerable and often contemptuous detail in his works. To Amin, an avowed Darwinist and fervent supporter of British occupation, the social position of women was a key metric by which the compatibility of Egypt – and

---

* Although Egypt's 1956 constitution introduced the idea of universal suffrage, voting by women was not made obligatory – unlike for men – and female voters were forced to demonstrate their literacy before being able to cast a ballot. Shafik criticized the reforms as discriminatory.

thus Egyptian men, and thus himself – with 'civilized' Europe could be measured; 'if Egyptians did not modernize along European lines and if they were unable to compete successfully in the struggle for survival they would be eliminated', he warned.[44] Amin's problematic attempts to use women's bodies to project his own distinctions between social progress and backwardness, with little thought to the autonomous choices of women themselves, was a pattern repeated across women's rights campaigning throughout the twentieth century, and it looms larger than ever today.

In the decades since Shafik was imprisoned in her own home, 'colonial feminism' has been joined by another regressive appropriation of feminist struggle: 'state feminism'. The advent of post-colonial military regimes across the Middle East has often been accompanied by government efforts – piecemeal, but real and significant nonetheless – to incorporate women as formally equal political subjects with the same juridical status as men. But at the same time the state's patriarchal architecture has been annealed, ensuring that no one, male or female, is ever afforded the status of political *citizen*, someone with the power to make democratic choices of their own.[45] Under modern Egypt's power configuration, certain females – like Suzanne Mubarak – have attained individual empowerment within the bureaucratic and political apparatus, but these supposed flag-bearers for female advancement have in reality often been staunch defenders of the status quo, under which political paternalism remains uncontested and hopes for more egalitarian social relations are left forever unfulfilled. State feminism ensures that policies aimed at legally extending women's rights come with a trade-off in the form of state control over the content and scope of women's political agendas; women's rights becomes a separate, sanitized set of issues from everything else, and more radical challenges to the state are contained.[46] Shafik refused to be controlled in such a manner, and was placed behind walls for it, walls she escaped only through death. Her story underlines the paucity of state feminism on its own as a tool for real change.

As part of the state's attempts to consolidate, control and delimit feminist movements, President Mubarak founded a National Council for Women by presidential decree in 2000, an organization that was headquartered in the NDP building in downtown Cairo and run by his wife.* By that point, however, Egypt's gender norms were increasingly coming under pressure from multiple sources. As in many other areas of public and private life, the expansion of media outlets – from new private newspapers to online forums – was prising open fresh areas of discussion and making old certainties look mutable; marriage and family came under the public spotlight like never before. In 2006, a young woman launched an anonymous blog about her attempts to find a husband, and her posts – sharp, satirical and scathing in their excoriation of traditional gender roles surrounding matrimony – became so popular that they were turned into a bestselling book and a major television sitcom. The woman, who later revealed herself to be Ghada Abdel Aal, a 27-year-old pharmacist from Mahalla, poked fun at the ritualized charade of parental matchmaking, but she also made more profound jibes about the manner in which the social pressure to marry was gendered, raising questions about the whole model of familial identity. 'Society needs to stop confining women solely to the role of bride,' she wrote, in easily accessible colloquial Arabic which helped fuel her massive readership. 'Because when things fall apart ... they feel like worthless good-for-nothings, and they sit and complain, like I'm doing to you right now ... If I don't get married and if I don't have children and if I can't follow society's grand plan, I will always have my independent nature and I will always have my own life and I will never be ... a good-for-nothing.'[47] Such sentiments provoked disquiet among some commentators; as Abdel Aal acknowledged herself, marriage is a 'really sensitive subject' and she was approaching it in unconventional ways. 'The depiction of a single woman's quest for a partner makes many uneasy because Abdel Aal effectively reverses the active-passive binary that has historically dictated the rules of marriage in Egypt: men choose while women comply,' wrote Hanan

---

* The NCW pursued some progressive reforms, including much needed changes to the personal status code which granted women the right to a *khul* ('no fault') divorce and more custodial and decision-making powers over their children. But – more importantly from the state's perspective – it also provided Egypt with a regime-friendly representative in the international galaxy of women's rights campaigning, and successfully sucked international donor money away from less compliant NGOs.

Kholoussy, a professor at the American University of Cairo, who pointed out that the bifurcation of gender roles around marriage is even reflected in the Egyptian Arabic verbs used to describe the act: a man marries (*yigawwiz* – an active verb), while a woman is married off (*titgawwiz* – a passive verb).[48]

Abdel Aal wasn't the only Egyptian woman making trouble, and headlines. Shortly before Abdel Aal began her blog, a celebrity paternity scandal involving one of the country's most famous young actors gripped the media. After falling pregnant, Hind el-Hinnawi, a costume designer on a television comedy (titled, ironically, 'When Daddy Returned'), filed a lawsuit against Ahmed el-Fishawy, a star of the show, claiming he was the father of her child. Outrageously, the pair were not married, at least not in the normal, official sense. Hinnawi alleged they had secured an *urfi* marriage, a contentious form of Islamic matrimony allowing couples to become betrothed in private according to the terms of a contract drafted by the pair of them, and often used to 'legitimize' premarital sex theologically. For his part, el-Fishawy initially insisted they had never even slept together (he later admitted to the affair). Hinnawi's high-profile legal attempts to force her one-time lover to undergo a DNA test to establish paternity broke multiple taboos surrounding sex, relationships and most importantly the agency of women – who in such situations were usually expected quietly to terminate the pregnancy, thus maintaining the myth of the virginal bride for her future husband and protecting time-honoured notions of the family. 'Society is ready for a million Hinds to have abortions and deceive their future partners rather than stick with the truth,' declared Hinnawi's attorney after winning the case.[49] Attiyat el-Abnoudi, a renowned Egyptian filmmaker who supported Hinnawi through the case, agreed. 'The whole society says: "No! No! No! Don't say this. It's shameful. It's a scandal. Go have an abortion. This girl was not well raised. She's loose,"' observed el-Abnoudi, who went on to become the child's godmother. 'The importance of this case is that it is out in the open. The whole society has to question whether it is only her, or whether the society is changing. Young people want to make love without getting married.'[50] To the surprise of many, Hinnawi's immediate family took her side as well, making supportive public statements that shocked conservatives. 'I don't make the link between honour and sex,' said Hamid Abdo el-Hinnawi, Hind's father. 'Honour is one thing and sex another. Any guy or girl can have sex without sacrificing their honour.'[51]

The Hinnawi case and Abdel Aal's blog were among many public frenzies over perceived deviance from social and sexual norms. There was also the arrest of a middle-class civil servant and his school-teacher wife for hosting 'swinger sex parties',[52] revelations of unmarried sex in monasteries, football hotel rooms and the cockpits of EgyptAir planes, and the publication of *Noon*, a novel by feminist author Sarah el-Mougy about a divorced woman who prefers extra-marital sex to the traditional confines of spinsterhood.[53] Professions of establishment outrage over all these incidents were really part of a reaction to Egypt's 'marriage crisis', a malaise that dominated both domestic and international coverage of Egypt. An extension of *fi haga ghalat* ('there's something wrong') and Egypt's 'youth problem', this marriage crisis presupposed the existence of a fast-growing army of disaffected, sexually frustrated young men who could not afford to marry and were thus detached from the infrastructure that guaran-teed everyone's security. The country's structural adjustment reforms and associated poverty were making the expensive institution of mar-riage, an important social marker of adulthood, harder than ever for many young people to attain. But the media brouhaha revealed more about the centrality of family and authority to almost every area of public life than it did about marriage itself. 'Marriage, it seems, is regarded as a barometer of the nation's social progress, political well-being and economic health,' argued Kholoussy. 'The 'marriage crisis' is about much more than matrimony. It serves as a platform for debates about materialism, privatization, social customs, unemploy-ment, gender roles, Islamism and the performance of the government.'[54] The 'crisis' was really that in the late 2000s notions of marriage, and thus traditional family and gender roles, were in flux.

All of this raised the possibility of change, and in Mubarak Coun-try change was something to be halted. It was maybe unsurprising, then, that such a moment of sexual fluidity would be underpinned by the spectre of sexual violence in public spaces, as the state sought to re-discipline women straying beyond the boundaries of the author-itarian family. Nowhere was this more visible than at opposition protests. Since the early 2000s gangs of *baltageya* had been sent in by the security services to either attack demonstrators or mingle with them whenever political rallies took place, with a brief to wreak havoc – damaging property, attacking civilians, shouting extremist slogans – in order to help the state frame these peaceful movements as something criminal and terrifying.[55] The aim was to render opposition events both hyper-visible to the wider public and utterly alien, and to activate latent phobias based around gender and class (the uncontrollable frenzy of the poor, male mob) in an effort to delegitimize them. The state wanted to depict political protesters according to the old orientalist conventions of the 'Arab Street' – something brutal and irrational.[56] By the middle of the decade, protest organizers had found ways to hit back: 'respectable', upper-middle-class women moved to the foreground of marches to contradict this narrative of terroristic masculinity. It was a canny move, precisely because the state had worked so hard to frame women as pious and moral, a symbol of gendered security.[57] Now that those same women were confronting state brutality in a public setting, the regime's demonization of opposition activity began to ring hollow. Mubarak's counter-attack was to target female protesters directly. At a protest outside Cairo's Journalists' Syndicate in 2005, which came to be known by activists as 'Black Wednesday', security forces surrounded the rally then opened a path for *baltageya* to swarm over and assault women ('You want to demonstrate against Mubarak,' said one such attacker as he penetrated a woman with his fingers. 'This is what Mubarak's doing to you. He's screwing you').[58] State-imposed sexual aggression was designed to undermine the respectability that protesters were using as a shield against the regime's violence, and turn the figure of the pious woman pursuing legitimate anti-government protest into a physical impossibility. 'Women who protested were sexualized and had their respectability wiped out,' writes Paul Amar, an academic specializing in gender and security governance in the Middle East. '[This was done] not just by innuendo and accusation, but literally, by sexually assaulting them in public and by arresting them as prostitutes, registering them in court records and press accounts as sex criminals and then raping and sexually torturing them in jail.'[59]

Alongside episodes of visibly political sexual violence came another phenomenon: seemingly indiscriminate sexual attacks on Egyptian women by large crowds of young men during public holidays, a time at which many Egyptians traditionally take to the streets to stroll and shop, especially in downtown Cairo. The experience of being caught up in such an attack must have been horrific, not least because of the lack of assistance forthcoming from the police. Eyewitness accounts agree that security agents stood by and allowed the violence to proceed unhindered, while those who made it to a police station and tried to file a crime report were told, 'What do you want us to do? It's *eid*. Happy *eid* to you too!'[60] Interpretations of these assaults differed sharply among different activist groups and NGOs working in the field of women's rights, as did the assignment of responsibility for the attacks. For some civil society organizations, the problem lay in a culture of 'libidinal perversion' among working-class boys. Their solution was to shame men and demand a ramping up of the authoritarian security apparatus needed to enforce discipline: more police, more CCTV, a safer and more sanitized urban space.[61] Such calls were articulated through awareness efforts that were heavily supported by the international constellation of donor-sponsored women's rights initiatives. The Egyptian Centre for Women's Rights began a 'Safe Streets for Everyone' campaign and took out radio spots featuring celebrities exhorting men to 'respect themselves';[62] the youth group Kelemetna took a similar tack, using the slogan 'Egypt still has real men' and bemoaning the fact that in the past 'men were more gallant and protective'.[63]

This insistence on 'respectability' may have been well intentioned – who can disagree with the suggestion that men should be held accountable for sexual harassment and violence? – but it let the police state off the hook (indeed it posited security forces as the solution rather than the problem) and reinforced the elitist idea that public space was the natural domain of the decorous upper classes, now being 'overrun' by undisciplined youth from the edge. Not everyone linked the rights of women in public spaces to class-based appeals for a more 'honourable' manifestation of Egyptian masculinity. Some initiatives were more subtle in their approach, such as 'HarassMap', an effort to combine SMS reporting with mapping technologies to create a real-time picture of harassment hotspots,[64] or the legal battle undertaken by Noha Roushdy, a 27-year-old filmmaker who broke new ground in 2008 by overpowering a man who had groped her on Cairo's streets, forcing him into a police station and pursuing a court case which resulted in him being imprisoned for three years.[65]

A more radical approach was also adopted by the el-Nadim Centre, an organization which campaigned throughout the Mubarak era against police torture. El-Nadim had tracked and exposed different forms of sexual violence by the state for years, and sought to find ways to challenge it without reinforcing gender norms: assaulted protesters were not fallen women whose respectability needed rehabilitating, but rather agents of political change; harassment was not a timeless problem of masculinity, but a specific perversion practised by a repressive security state; shame and immorality were to be located inside the web of the security services, not only among working-class boys; prostitutes were workers whose public rights were being violated by state violence, not trafficking victims to be 'rescued' and protected; sexual violence could not be seen as a problem experienced only by heterosexual women under attack by heterosexual men, but rather was a pathology that reached across gender and class divides to reveal the brutality of the state – including, for instance, the government's assaults on young male prostitutes.[66] Beyond these example, however, much of Egyptian civil society's reaction to the sexual assaults consisted primarily of 'depoliticized' lobbying – not to undermine gender norms, but in favour of better protection from the state.

The state's own response, meanwhile, was to vacillate between ignorance and exploitation. Initially, harassment remained invisible to the gatekeepers of top-down, state feminism: Habib el-Adly, then minister of the interior, stated simply that 'sexual harassment does not exist'.[67] 'Egyptian men always respect Egyptian women,' Suzanne Mubarak declared breezily in 2008, a few weeks after hundreds of women were attacked during *eid*. 'Maybe one, two or even ten incidents occurred. Egypt is home to 80 million people. We can't talk of a phenomenon. Maybe a few scatter-brained youths are behind this crime.'[68] But when it became apparent that the women's rights NGO sector was for the most part ignoring the role of the police state in generating sexual violence and blaming social groups that were also targets of the regime's apocalyptic crisis discourse, the security establishment swung enthusiastically behind the anti-harassment campaigns – 'protectively' detaining women in public spaces and rounding up working-class boys en masse in the name of virtue.[69] In late 2008, in the space of just one week, Cairo police arrested more than 400 males aged between fifteen and seventeen years old on the charge of 'flirting with girls'. A controversy that at times threatened to expose a system of repressive policing and state torture instead became appropriated by the NGO establishment and the security apparatus as justification for acts of social cleansing and the maintenance of emergency law. Presenting sexual harassment as something distinct from politics enabled both government voices and critics to reproduce narratives that blamed women for the violence they experienced. A mass assault against women in 2006 was blamed by police on 'provocation' by the belly-dancer Dina.[70] In 2008, posters were circulated depicting two lollipops, one wrapped in its plastic cover and pristine, the other 'unveiled' and covered in flies, with the tagline 'You can't stop them, but you can protect yourself'.[71]

Even many of those who at the time stood in public opposition to both the regime and the Islamists and were keen to condemn these attacks, like author Alaa al-Aswany, casually rescored traditional gender roles in their efforts to convince others that such violence was unacceptable: 'The girls who were assaulted were not prostitutes or delinquents, just ordinary Egyptians like my wife or your wife, my daughter or your daughter,' al-Aswany wrote in his newspaper column.[72] The possibility of any woman existing outside those static categories, or indeed of 'prostitutes' or 'delinquents' also having the right to walk through the streets unmolested, seemingly remained beyond imagination.

Neoliberal. Ahistorical. Static. Old. Male. This was the Egyptian state that Bilal Diab confronted on the day of Prime Minister Ahmed Nazif's visit to Cairo University in 2008, the state that told him and his contemporaries that even dreams had limits. That morning, the campus looked more like the interior ministry than a seat of learning: shops were shuttered up, outside materials were banned from the grounds, and security forces were everywhere. Nazif was supposed to be addressing 'the student body', but guards on the doors had been instructed to keep out any young troublemakers, and they knew Bilal's face. He was turned away from the grand hall where the speech would take place, and only managed to slip through by crouching down and smuggling himself inside a group of supportive students, before secretly finding a seat up in the balcony. The stage was hung with thick red curtains and crowned with a large portrait of Mubarak. At a trestle table sat Hany Helal, minister of higher education, and Ali Abdel Rahman, president of the university, and at the podium stood Nazif. The prime minister was bespectacled, a short white moustache complementing his trim white hair, and he gripped the wooden lectern with both hands, reading from a sheaf of notes. He spoke sternly and sonorously to his mute audience, handing them down a checklist of mantras: Egypt's future was bright, he explained, and the growth of the internet was making it easier than ever for the country's youth to express their opinion. At that moment Bilal rose to his feet. '*Ya ra'ees, ya ra'ees,*' he yelled with all his might into the silent auditorium, addressing the prime minister. 'Egypt's youth are behind bars!'

To the assembled dignitaries on the stage, it probably wasn't Bilal's words that were so shocking; it was the fact that he was using his voice at all. In Mubarak Country, Bilal was supposed to be inert; his voice was not meant to exist. By speaking out without permission, he briefly upended the state's entire supervision of age, gender and history, just as hundreds of thousands of his fellow citizens were doing in their own way throughout the final years of the regime. 'Education is *zay el-ful* ['like a flower' – i.e. perfect, beautiful], the university is *zay el-ful*, there is bread and freedom!' roared Bilal sarcastically, as Nazif's student audience broke into thunderous applause and security agents rushed towards the balcony. 'Release Egypt *ya ra'ees*! Release Egypt!'

PART II

Resistance Country

PART THREE

Resisting Chopin

4

The Colonel's Revenge

Darkness had fallen on the night of 5 August 1882, when Lieutenant Howard Vyse, of the King's Royal Rifle Corps, set out from Alexandria on the eastern bank of the Mahmoudia Canal and began moving south. His men were silent, and nervous. Three weeks earlier the Royal Navy had taken the city following a two-day bombardment from the ocean. The attacks had killed hundreds on shore and sent fores searing through one of the world's greatest ancient ports; according to one naval officer, the artillery blasts were so intense that at their height, 'the roar of the guns and the shrieks of passing shot and shell were alone audible'.[1] When the British finally landed they found a town in chaos, with infrastructure in disarray and Bedouin looters ghosting through bombed-out ruins. The soldiers were here to protect Egypt's beleaguered monarch, Khedive Tawfiq, who had abandoned the capital to escape a tidal wave of anti-colonial sentiment. Propped up by British guns and banknotes, the Khedive was unable to command meaningful support from the majority of the country's population. The British had advised him to flee the country secretly on one of their frigates or a passing mail-ship but he refused, preferring instead to take refuge in Alexandria's magnificent waterfront palace at Ras el-Tin. There, surrounded by acres of fig trees and a ring of British military steel, he paced the hallways and watched his shrinking empire descend into war.

Ten miles inland from the coast, at Kafr el-Dawwar – a small settlement nestled among the Ptolemaic rocks and old cemeteries of the northern Delta – an Egyptian revolutionary army under the leadership of Colonel Ahmed 'Urabi lay in wait. 'Urabi hailed from relatively humble origins. The son of a village leader, he was among the first generation of Egyptian *fellaheen* to break into the higher ranks of the military, rising to become one of the Khedive's most trusted advisers. Beyond his army service, 'Urabi garnered a reputation as a fine orator and determined advocate for the rights of native Egyptian in a society still dominated by foreign aristocratic castes; contemporary sources talk about long lines of supplicants queuing outside 'Urabi's house to beg for his assistance. Wilfrid Scawen Blunt, the dissident British poet and activist who became one of the colonel's most ardent supporters, described him as 'tall, heavy-limbed, and somewhat slow in his movements'. 'Urabi, continued Blunt, 'seemed to symbolize that massive bodily strength which is so characteristic of the laborious peasant of the Lower Nile . . . He was one of themselves, they perceived, but with their special qualities intensified and made glorious by the power they credited him with.'[2]

Dissatisfied with the pace of reform under the Khedive, 'Urabi gradually emerged as a powerful nationalist rival to the royal family, and in the late 1870s he came out in open mutiny. Despite 'Urabi being formally declared a rebel and traitor, his appeal to the Egyptian people to liberate themselves from European control resonated widely; since then, the colonel's revolt had spread to every corner of the country. By the spring of 1882 he had effectively taken charge of Cairo, forcing the Khedive to flee to Alexandria. Now, on the edge of the Mediterranean, 'Urabi was closing in on Tawfiq once again. Pro-royal spies and scouts were dispatched from the port city out into the countryside under the cover of nightfall; they reported that 'Urabi had asked for one-sixth of the male population from every province in the land to lay down their tools, leave their families and come and join him in the trenches so that the British advance could be halted and the stranglehold of Egypt's imperial-backed monarchy broken once and for all. A pasha loyal to the Khedive who managed to pass through rebel territory and get to Alexandria revealed that "large numbers of soldiers were flocking to 'Urabi from the villages, [and] arms were being distributed to all comers'.[3] Egyptians called 'Urabi *el-Waheed* ('The One'), and they were answering his call.

For the British, who held hefty financial interests in Egyptian bonds and the Suez Canal, 'Urabi's nationalism was a cancer that could not be allowed to spread. From his base on the banks of the

Mahmoudia Canal at Kafr el-Dawwar, the renegade colonel had the only water supply into Alexandria at his mercy. By late July, the canal level had started dropping, and the only water trickling into Alexandria was salty: just as the British feared, 'Urabi had dammed and leeched the waterway. Time was running out. In desperation, the Khedive himself implored his British patrons to launch an assault on rebel lines. 'He pointed out that it was most necessary, as "Urabi's power had become so great as to spread terror and consternation in the minds of all the natives,' recorded Charles Royle, a British naval officer who took part in the invasion and later wrote up a diary of his experiences. 'His possession of the country, and especially of Cairo, His Highness added, left at his mercy the families and property of all who remained loyal to the Khedive.'[4] With revolutionary forces expanding by the day and alarms in the city sounding every night, the British decided they could wait no longer. And so an expedition down along the canal to Kafr el-Dawwar was dispatched, and with no little trepidation. 'Urabi's chief strength, warned the acting British consul-general, lay 'in his unscrupulous and barbarous mode of warfare'.[5]

That night, Lieutenant Vyse had 800 men, eighty mounted infantry and a naval nine-pounder gun behind him on the eastern bank. Across the canal a further 500 men and another nine-pounder proceeded in tandem. Less than half a mile further to the west, 1,000 British marines and an armoured train – sporting a forty-pounder gun, a Nordenfelt, two Gatlings and two more nine-pounders – crept along the railway track which followed the path of the canal towards the capital. The plan was for the three streams to meet at the point where the canal snaked closest to the railway line, which was marked by a white house on the waterside, and then advance together. But the British were strangers to this terrain; the fields of the Nile Delta were best navigated by Egypt's farmers, and most of them had thrown their support behind 'Urabi. So Vyse's soldiers had no way of knowing that there was more than one white house on the bank of the canal; the three armed columns ended up halting at different places, leaving themselves exposed along a diagonal line on the very cusp of 'Urabi's trenches. The mistake was a fatal one. Confused by the disparate British lines, Vyse rode ahead into the blackness to investigate, and through the gloom a single Egyptian bullet whistled through his femoral artery. Ten minutes later, he was dead and the British army was in retreat. 'Urabi sent news to Cairo that the colonialists had been triumphantly repulsed; at Kafr el-Dawwar, a line of independence had for ever been drawn.*

'This is the stopping point,' says Magdi Sharabaya, sweeping his arm across the bank. It's an autumn evening in 2012 and the light is fading fast; over the canal in front of us, a blue footbridge skims low above the water. At a faded-pink bus stop, a gaggle of *tuk-tuks* waits to meet the next arrival; bored drivers are swapping cigarettes and fiddling with mobile phones. In the thirteen decades since Lieutenant Vyse's fatal last mission, Kafr el-Dawwar has been transformed from farmland into a major industrial city, but until recently the spot where 'Urabi dug his trenches was still just about in the countryside, a quiet hinterland that lay out beyond the town's borders. Today though, as in most of the Nile Delta, urban growth is carpeting the nearby fields with bricks and mortar. On the far side of the canal a whole new neighbourhood has arisen in the space of only a few years, and a row of furniture-making workshops now faces out on to the water. 'Before "Urabi's stand, the invaders thought they could march and blast their way through Egypt's soil,' continues Magdi, a local labour activist with a grizzled chin and a wide smile. 'They thought the Egyptians were weak. But at Kafr el-Dawwar they learned otherwise. We were the role models for resistance then, and we're the role models for resistance now.'

Mubarak Country was a place of economic injustice, political exclusion and psychological deactivation; it was also a rich and nuanced collage of resistance. Three major strands of unrest shaped Mubarak's reign, each developing independently but also gradually

---

* Some British military historians have since cast the initial Kafr el-Dawwar skirmish as nothing more than a reconnaissance mission that went wrong and handed an unfortunate propaganda gift to the enemy. Egyptians have always interpreted the event as an assault which was successfully repelled; either way, what is undoubtedly true is that 'Urabi's defences at Kafr el-Dawwar held British forces at bay for five full weeks, forcing Britain's Lieutenant General Garnet Wolseley to redeploy down the Suez Canal instead.

supplying collective confidence to the others – especially in the dictator's final decade – and eventually coalescing in revolution. One of those strands concerned the struggles of local communities over economic privations and the increasing absence of government services to which they believed they had a right. Another was the explicitly pro-democracy movement that mounted small but game-changing street protests in Egypt's largest cities. But the first strand, and arguably the most critical, was the fight-back by workers against the structural violence and redistribution from poor to rich that accompanied neoliberalism. This chapter traces that fight-back, and it starts in Kafr el-Dawwar because the city and its mythology symbolize a distinct period of labour activism in Egypt, which began under Nasser and ended with Mubarak's presidency – one in which both the state and workers were framed as being on the same side of a broader battle against colonial opposition. By the twenty first century, economic liberalization under the tutelage of the international financial institutions had eroded that alliance, and workers increasingly saw the state itself as the facilitator of colonialism of a different order. In the final years of Mubarak's reign, workers embroiled virtually every category of workplace you can think of in confrontation. By 2011, they would play a critical role in toppling the president altogether.

Despite his dramatic stand at Kafr el-Dawwar, 'Urabi's revolt was ultimately unsuccessful. After failing to penetrate his defences in the Delta, the British switched directions and instead swarmed down the Suez Canal – which 'Urabi had left undefended after receiving a bogus promise from the canal's French developer, Ferdinand de Lesseps, that the area would not be allowed to become a war zone. From Suez the occupiers pushed on to the capital, encountering the remainder of 'Urabi's forces at Tel el-Kebir and killing more than 2,000 of them along the way. Twelve days later Khedive Tawfiq was formally reinstated as Egypt's leader and 'Urabi was sentenced to death, although his punishment was later commuted to banishment for life in Ceylon (modern-day Sri Lanka). The British went on to rule Egypt both directly and at arm's length until 1952. But although the colonel died in obscurity, the historical memory of his cause and the victory he scored over the colonialists at Kafr el-Dawwar, however fleeting it proved to be, lived on. Today you can find streets and neighbourhoods named after 'Urabi in places as diverse as Gaza and New Orleans. 'God created us free, and didn't create us heritage or real estate,' 'Urabi is said to have told Tawfiq after being admonished by the Khedive for daring to defy the power of royalty. 'I swear by god, that there is no god but he; no bequeathing, no enslaved any more.'

Historians now suspect that 'Urabi never spoke those words; indeed there is doubt that the colonel's final verbal showdown with Tawfiq, long ingrained in the minds of Egyptian schoolchildren and the inspiration for several films, painting and songs, ever took place at all.[6] But that made little difference to the legend.

Once Gamal Abdel Nasser came to power in 1952 and began his historiographical revolution, the story of 'Urabi and the ordinary Egyptians who left their workplaces to come and fight for liberation alongside the best of Egypt's officer class became increasingly prominent. Nasser's industrial policy was based around the reorganization of Egypt's labour force into a series of deeply hierarchical and compulsory monopolies – placing most workers inside huge, vertically integrated production chains that ran from raw materials to finished product, pumping out vast quantities of cement, for example, or textiles, or steel, often in towns almost entirely devoted to a single sector. Part of the social contract that Nasser was offering to the Egyptian people was a shared notion that the exclusionary state – while remaining closed to any democratic influence from outside Egypt's military elite – stood shoulder to shoulder with ordinary workers in the country's quest for independence and dignity; together, as they had done under 'Urabi, high-ranking generals and the population they protected would face down foreigners and feudalism. The tale of Kafr el-Dawwar helped bolster this narrative, as did more recent episodes of anti-imperialist activism like the organization of Egyptian workers at the Suez Canal in 1947 to block the passage of a Dutch ship, the *Volendam*, which was en route to suppress the independence movement in Indonesia. Of course, when paternal rulers and the grateful ruled are bound together in common purpose, there is little scope for division. Nasser saw his ideology as synonymous with working-class interests, which meant it was never in working-class interests to challenge his ideology. Agitation by workers acting autonomously from the state was not to be tolerated.

But there is also another history of labour activism in Egypt: one of workers using mass strikes on their own initiative to force concessions from employers and governments and to reshape their world for the better. The world's first recorded labour stoppage was in Egypt, more than 3,000 years ago; hereditary craftsmen downed tools under Ramses II while building the tombs of the pharaohs that would later come to be known as the Valley of the Kings, and secured themselves extra food rations as a result.[7] More modern examples abound as well. In 1882, the year of 'Urabi's battle at Kafr el-Dawwar, the coal-heavers of Port Said downed tools and brought the city's docks to a standstill.[8] They were followed in 1899 by the Greek cigarette-rollers of Cairo, and later by the tramway operators in Alexandria, the Italian labourers building the original Aswan dam, and most notably the cabbies of the capital, who brought bedlam to the city in April 1907 with a mass strike that provoked waves of unrest throughout the working population.[9] The *'arabagi* ('taxi drivers') were angry at the activism of the British-run Society for the Prevention of Cruelty to Animals in Egypt, which disapproved of the treatment meted out by cabbies to their horses and had succeeded in obtaining thousands of convictions for animals cruelty. When up to 5,000 taxi drivers coordinated a mass stoppage one day, they ended up surrounding police stations and blocking tramways in a display of collective power that swiftly inspired other workers to follow suit. 'The recent strike of cab-drivers, which occasioned so much inconvenience in Cairo, is, it seems, indirectly responsible for unending disturbances,' wrote one disgruntled European at the time in a letter to the English-language *Egyptian Gazette*.

Daily one hears of some fresh disturbance among employés, who up to the present time have been perfectly contented with their conditions. One day we wake up to find the streets crowded with bands of ruffianly silk-weavers, who parade the town and molest innocent pedestrians, or damage valuable property; then again, it is printers, who forcibly demonstrate their grievances to uninterested passers-by. So the idea has spread, affecting every kind of trade. To-day we are threatened by a strike of bakers.[10]

A growing labour movement, strengthened by the emergence of embryonic trade unions, continued to undertake major actions and extract significant victories right up into the early 1950s; huge strikes by Egyptian workers at British army camps in Suez helped hasten the end of occupation.

The ascension of Nasser's Free Officers, however, heralded a new corporatist mould of worker–employer relations that would not be fully broken for half a century. In the first few years following independence, the state went to extraordinary lengths to ensure that the word 'strike' disappeared from the political lexicon.[11] Perhaps appropriately, the army's violence against workers began at Kafr el-Dawwar, which by the 1950s had become an important centre for spinning and weaving. Barely two months after the coup, soldiers moved to brutally crush a series of labour riots in the town. In a stark message to the rest of Egypt's workers, two local union leaders, Mustafa Khamis and Mohamed el-Baqri, were condemned to hang on Nasser's orders. By 1957 worker movements had been entirely subsumed into a state-controlled labour federation and purged of militants; trade unions were now an arm of the state, designed not to transmit the will of members upwards to those in power but instead to serve the regime as a static resource, something which could be mobilized to produce displays of political support in the streets or at the ballot box whenever such support was deemed useful.[12] Any dissenters from among the ranks of labour activists were imprisoned.

In spite of such oppression, Nasserism's particular set of relations between labour and the state was never solely imposed on Egyptian workers from above. Nasser's policies promised – and delivered – concrete material gains for most Egyptian citizens: free education and healthcare, guaranteed employment for university graduates, a higher standard of living. The social contract was a way of co-opting working Egyptians, and selective historical memory – like the veneration of events at Kafr el-Dawwar during the late nineteenth century – helped build ideological consent for the whole enterprise. But this did not mean that workers remained passive. On the contrary, as Nasserism gave way to Sadat's *infitah* and labour conditions deteriorated, the Egyptian working class continued to organize, and often to fight. Throughout the 1970s and 80s, confrontations in big industrial centres like Helwan were commonplace, and certain factories – such as the ESCO mill in Qalyub, just north of Cairo – became known for their volatile workforces.[13] By and large though, these struggles tended to be framed by a 'moral economy' consciousness – a sense that the social pact was being violated, and an attempt to persuade the state's custodians to fulfil their pre-existing obligations.[14] In response the state would usually call on the security forces to quell any sit-ins and contain the unrest, before quietly giving in to most of the workers' demands.* In Kafr el-Dawwar, for example, workers' strikes in 1984 against the government's raising of food prices grew into a three-day, city-wide insurrection; factory employees and urban crowds 'cut telephone lines, started fires, blocked transportation and destroyed train carriages'[15] and, despite the imposition of a curfew, clusters of young men crept out on to the streets each night to hurl rocks and firebombs at police positions on the far side of the Mahmoudia Canal. The protests succeeded: once demonstrations began, the government rolled back the new price rises almost instantly and increased the size of subsidized bread loaves.[16] So this was an era in which the Egyptian working class played a key role in shaping the pact governing state–society relations, as well as being shaped by those relations itself.[17] Compliance with the social contract did not equate to quietude among Egyptian workers, especially not in proudly unified communities like Kafr el-Dawwar where the passing of the years can be parsed and referenced with each surge of factory militancy; on the contrary, it was an active choice and one that could and would be reversed if the state ever failed to keep up its end of the bargain. 'When you try and handcuff people here, they respond in anger,' Magdi Sharabaya, the local labour activist who had shown me the location of 'Urabi's trenches, told me as we made our way from the canal bank back up to the car;

* In 1986 security force conscripts rioted themselves. The unrest began on 25 February after *amn el-markazi* recruits heard rumours that their three-year compulsory service was going to be prolonged by an additional year; 17,000 conscripts mutinied in the capital and destroyed two hotels. Mubarak ordered in the army to crush the mutiny, which ended after three days with 107 people killed.

he was among the many arrested during the uprising of 1984. 'In Kafr el-Dawwar, handcuffs never survive for long.'

The arrival of structural adjustment in the early 1990s and the intensification of neoliberal reforms a decade later altered this state–labour dynamic irrevocably. The globalized production and supply circuits of the twenty first century require a different kind of work-force, one that is organized not into giant single-sector factory towns but rather small and specialist private-sector hubs scattered across many national borders; today, raw platinum extracted from a mine in South Africa may be sent to Ulsan in South Korea to be fashioned into engine components, then on to a satellite city near Cairo to be assembled into cars, and on to a boat at Suez, to be sold in a show-room in Berlin. In Egyptian towns such as 10th Ramadan or 6th October, employees in industries like engineering, pharmacology or electronics were brought together in small numbers and kept rela-tively isolated from one another; the immediate worker-to-worker connections and institutional memories of labour struggle that had once dominated big, all-encompassing industrial centres such as Kafr el-Dawwar largely became a relic of the past.[18]

Meanwhile, Kafr el-Dawwar itself entered a tailspin of decline. After we left the canal, Magdi and his colleague, fellow labour activ-ist Rashad Bassyuni, took me on a tour of the old factory quarter – a walled city within a city, now many years past its prime. There used to be a cinema in this labyrinthine compound, as well as a tennis club, workers' houses and a patchwork quilt of streets that linked up each element of the massive spinning and weaving complex to the next, totally dominating one whole bank of the canal. Moving around, it was clear how conducive such a space must have been to organized resistance; one way or another, workers spent most of their time inside this tightly integrated world – sharing stories, aspirations and a collective identity closely bound up with the history and phys-ical fabric of the factory neighbourhood. As a social unit, they never felt secluded. Now, most of the quarter was a ghost town. Rusting electrical wires drooped balefully out of crooked lamp-posts; piles of rubbish, often still smoking from the afternoon heat, oozed out from behind buildings boarded up with corrugated iron sheets, and spilled across the roadways outside. At one point Rashad asked me to stop the car and got out to examine a dilapidated building more closely. After a few minutes, he climbed back in with a wistful smile. 'That was the school run by the factory managers, which the children of workers would be sent to if they misbehaved,' he explained. 'The headmaster was "Eissa Shahin, and everyone was scared of him. I went to school there.' Rashad had turned sixty a few days earlier; for a few moments he just stared through the car window at the old school and the empty street around it, lost in memory, until a group of goats searching out food amid the rubbish piles wandered across the path and shook him from his reverie. 'The whole of Kafr el-Dawwar society was once here,' Rashad sighed as we drove back out through the gates.

The mothballing of much of Kafr el-Dawwar's old factory quarter was part of a global trend towards economic activity becoming more dispersed, and workforces more physically atomized. But although neoliberal reforms disrupted older patterns of worker mobilization in Egypt, they did not destroy the ability of workers to mount resistance against employers and governments. In fact, neoliberalism opened up new pressure points that could be used to strike directly at the state – fuelling creative forms of struggle that would scarcely have been imaginable under Nasser or Sadat. One of those pressure points was the neoliberal economy's heavy reliance on transport and communications. Between 1990 and 2010, Egypt's imports and exports rose four-fold and six-fold respectively; by the last decade of Mubarak's rule, Egyptian workers – dockers, port workers, airport staff and Suez Canal employees, as well as local transport operators, communications workers and logistics specialists – concentrated in areas where domestic production intersected with international connections had never been a more important cog in the economic system, and hence never more capable of striking the regime where it might hurt the most.[19] The new façade of competition and pluralism which accompanied free market reforms masked the fact that whole chunks of not only the national economy but also the regional and global economies had all become highly dependent on a powerful core of workers who, if they wished, could bring billions of dollars' worth of financial activity to a standstill in an instant. By the dawn of the revolution, for example, Egypt's telephone sector had been liberalized and boasted at least three major multinational mobile companies. And yet all of these companies still depended wholly on infrastructure maintained by the formerly state-run Telecom Egypt, which also managed all internet connectivity between Asia and Europe, and on whose fibre-optic cables the Gulf kingdoms relied to access global financial markets.[20] Telecom Egypt employed nearly 50,000 people; the leverage those workers could wield by acting collectively was virtually unparalleled.[21]

A second pressure point was the imposition of new constraints on the state's ability to repress worker militancy. In the past, mass strikes and sit-ins were viewed by ministers almost wholly through a political and security prism: with a compliant state media on side, the level of violence meted out against workers by police or soldiers was of little concern, as long as the militancy could be contained and compromises struck in order to get production back on track. But structural adjustment prioritized the economic dimension of production over any political or social concerns; the aim was profit at any cost. That meant that in Mubarak Country, where growth was dependent on continually attracting overseas investors, who had to be convinced that Egypt was a stable place for them to sink their fortunes, any levelling of live ammunition at a workplace became somewhat problematic – particularly given the growth of a noisy independent media scene in the mid-2000s that quickly dispatched dedicated labour correspondents to every flashpoint. Now, as one labour activist put it, 'They did not want to scare away the investors by invading plants with armoured cars and armed soldiers like they used to do . . . who would want to invest in such an atmosphere?'[22]

Most importantly though, the state's embrace of neoliberalism destroyed the old corporatist pact that supposedly bound rulers and ruled together. The social contract never allowed for workers' lives becoming harder and their jobs less secure, nor the diminishing of free access to healthcare and education due to the imposition of 'cost-recovery mechanisms' and privatization by stealth in schools and hospitals, nor the flagrant devotion of public resources to a tiny band of the country's elite. Nasserite rhetoric about a regime and labour force united against the domestic bourgeoisie and Western imperialism could hardly withstand the corrupt selling-off of so many national assets to foreign investors at below-market prices – investors who often went on to fire huge numbers of staff, chip away at workers' rights and drive down salaries. The anti-imperialist hero-ics of Colonel 'Urabi had once helped legitimize Nasser; in Mubarak Country, where the regime acted as courtier to Washington and Tel Aviv, they served only to illuminate the gulf separating the president from Egypt's nationalist icons of old. Mubarak supported the US and Israel in their invasions of Iraq and Lebanon respectively, worked closely with the Israeli security establishment on upholding the siege on Gaza, and signed large trade agreements with the Israeli security establishment on upholding the siege on Gaza, and signed large trade agreements with the Israeli state providing for the export of subsi-dized natural gas from Egypt to Israel and the creation of special 'QIZs' ('Qualifying Industrial Zones') in which economic partner-ships between the two nations could flourish. As Egyptian labour expert Anne Alexander observes, the regime breached its own anti-imperialist rhetoric; under those conditions, class tensions which arose under neoliberalism could no longer be glossed over by a top-down appeal to nationalist sentiment.[23] 'It's crucial to see that the working class withdrew from the social contract from below,' she told me. 'Ironically, neoliberalism liberated workers from Nasserism to the extent that they had nothing to lose but their chains.'

In 1994, 7,000 evening-shift workers in the textile factories of Kafr el-Dawwar launched a spontaneous sit-in to protest against recent staff layoffs; riot troops were swiftly dispatched to contain the strike and four civilians, including a ten-year-old boy, were killed as a result.[24] A week later, the government reinstated all the previously sacked workers. It proved to be the last major industrial showdown of the old era that conformed to the traditional template of worker–state relations. With the structural adjustment programme now underway, both Egypt's economy and the mode of its economic con-flicts were about to change for ever. About seventy miles south-east of Kafr el-Dawwar, in another of Egypt's great textile cities, a new template for labour militancy was about to be established. The name of that city would eventually become synonymous with Mubarak-era revolt.

*

When employees of the Misr Spinning and Weaving Company in Mahalla talk about their place of work, they tend not to bother with the statistical superlatives: Egypt's biggest factory, 1,000 acres of machinery, 300,000 spinning machines gobbling up 1 million quintiles of cotton a year, the largest textile plant in the entire Middle East. Instead, they often refer to the way in which Mahalla's existence seems to transcend physical space and dominate the entirety of one's mental landscape. 'When I was a child I used to think the factory was the whole of Egypt,' says one worker. Another claims, 'The factory lives inside of us, just as we live within its walls.'[25]

Since its inception in 1927, Mahalla has been a cauldron of rebellion. Workers staged their first strike there in 1938; nine years later tanks entered the plant for the first time to suppress protests over the sacking of labour activists. By the mid-1970s, when company employees were returning home from war in the Sinai to find that Sadat's much-trumpeted 'peace dividend' had provided them with barely enough to feed their families, workers began breaking into the comparatively luxurious apartments of high-ranking engineers, taking the food they found there, and dangling it down on ropes to the restless crowds below. 'They eat chickens and pigeons, we're tired of eating beans,' chanted the strikers. 'And the beans are tired of us!'[26] In 1988 strikes started spilling beyond the factory walls for the first time and into the city centre; workers made a coffin and put Mubarak's picture on it, prompting a full-scale deployment of security forces. 'The workers believe they own this factory,' says one labour activist from the plant. 'They are willing to give their life for it.'[27]

In December 2006, the factory's 27,000 staff made an unpleasant discovery then they collected their pay cheques: a two-month bonus, recently promised by the government to employees of all state-run enterprises that managed to reduce their losses, like Mahalla, was missing. Managers and government officials claimed that Mahalla was exempt from the bonus on a technicality, and dismissed workers' grievances. In response, employees refused to cash their cheques. They gave bosses three days to rectify the situation. Their bosses would have been wise to do so.

The Mahalla bonus spat came at a volatile moment for state–labour relations. The preceding decade of neoliberal reform had witnessed a steady growth in collective labour actions, as workers began to transition from the old social contract to a new and more antagonistic paradigm. By 2004, when Ahmed Nazif – the prime minister who would drive through the most far-reaching of Mubarak's neoliberal reforms – was appointed, the number of strikes and work-place protests was already tripling year on year; by the end of 2006, when Mahalla's staff realized their pay packets were incomplete, labour activists were documenting an average of five incidents every week.[28] Some of these mobilizations caught the public eye, not least because they brought the contrasting outcomes of neoliberalism for Egypt's population into such sharp relief. The staff of Ora Misr, for example, a Spanish-Egyptian building materials company, staged a remarkable nine-month sit-in after bosses chose to fire the entire workforce rather than pay out compensation for the firm's illegal use of asbestos; forty-six Ora Misr workers contracted lung cancer in the factory, and eighteen employees died. But the extent to which these actions were geared explicitly towards attacking the Mubarak regime remained patchy. Some of the Ora Misr workers went on hunger strike: 'I don't care if this hunger strike kills me,' declared one labour leader, 'either we die from starvation because we now have no money to survive, or we die from cancer and asbestosis. They are killing us whatever way you choose to look at it.'[29] Yet despite the emotive language, the workers' demands were still couched in the form of an appeal to the existing official apparatus governing labour relations. Strike leaders called on the state-controlled official trade union federation (ETUF) to negotiate on their behalf alongside several government ministers; their goal was to secure concessions from within the state, rather than challenge it more fundamentally. Of course with the state so brazenly reconstituting itself in the interests of big capital, any push-back by workers against the effects of neoliberalism had significnt political implications. But the fact remained that, up until 2006, few of the labour mobilizations threatened to rewrite economic reality in a way that might begin to break the exclusionary state wide open. In Mahalla, that changed.

After three days of waiting for management to rectify the bonus omission, female employees in Mahalla's garment factory downed tools and began occupying the plant's main courtyard. 'Here are the

women! Where are the men?' they chanted, shaming their male colleagues into following suit. Before long up to 10,000 workers had
gathered in protest, and central security forces swiftly deployed
around the edge of the factory site and throughout the city. Many
inside the factory gates were expecting a repeat of what had happened in Kafr el-Dawwar in 1994, but this time the troops stood
back, watching nervously, and made no move to break up the crowds.
'They were shocked by our numbers,' remembered Mohamed
al-'Attar, one of the leaders of the strike. "They were hoping we'd fiz-
zle out by the night or following day."[30] By nightfall, however, there
was no sign of anyone wanting to stand down. Some men entreated
female workers not to sleep in the factory but rather go home to their
families; they were given short shrift. "The women almost tore apart
every representative from the management who came to negotiate,"
explained el-'Attar. "The women were more militant than the men.
They were subject to security intimidation and threats, but they held
out." Three days and nights later, a panicked government announced
that the workers' demands would be met after all, and the strike days
would be considered a paid holiday. Emboldened by their success,
workers went on strike two more times over the coming months
after yet more broken promises from management, and once again
their demands were met. More important than the paper settlements though was the manner in which they were reached. On the
sixth day of the second labour stoppage, a meeting took place that
undermined the entire infrastructure of the post-1952 state–labour
dynamic, and helped revolutionize workers' perceptions of what
could be achieved through self-organized collective action. The meeting, which lasted five hours, consisted of the president of Egypt's
official trade union federation, along with the head of the company
and local ruling party leaders on one side of the table, and twenty-five
workers' leaders on the other – all of whom had been elected democratically by the striking workers themselves.[31]

The set-up of that meeting was transformative, for two reasons.
Firstly, by placing ETUF alongside the state and bosses, it made visible the fact that, despite its rhetoric, ETUF was little more than
an extension of regime power, working in the interests of capital. As
the state's only official trade union federation, ETUF had complete

formal control over Egypt's trade unions and no worker collectives were allowed to exist outside it. Far from standing up for workers, ETUF's senior officials had long replicated the patriarchal-infantile relationship of the state and society at large – stifling most autonomous labour actions and serving as an enthusiastic promoter of structural adjustment. It was a key thread in the web of state authority that bound Mubarak Country together; now, it had been disentangled from the workers' movement and thrust firmly on the other side of the battlelines. The second reason was that in place of a formal, ETUF-affiliated factory committee to 'negotiate' with, an alliance of neoliberal interests was being forced to deal directly with democratic workers' committees. Not only had ETUF been expelled from the workers' struggle; it had been replaced. Now, through their own stubbornness, organization and strength, the Mahalla workers had broken the state's monopoly over 'legitimate' worker militancy and paved the way for the entire economic apparatus to be shaken from below. It was a significant development, one which quickly produced political ramifications. For the first time, some of the strike leaders began to frame their actions explicitly as an anti-regime movement with national implications; in 2007, a new strike call emerged from Mahalla, making demands not just on behalf of Mahalla employees but in the name of all Egyptian workers, in the form of a greater national minimum wage. 'We will not be ruled by the World Bank! We will not be ruled by colonialism!' chanted factory staff, in video clips that were uploaded to blogs and swiftly spread online.[32] Sayyid Habib, a prominent strike organizer, announced simply: 'We are challenging the regime.'[33]

Events in Mahalla sent shockwaves through Egypt's textile industry. Most of the sector's 100,000-strong public-sector workforce swiftly took advantage of the situation to issue their own demands, demands that struck right at the heart of the country's growing inequality under neoliberalism. Thanks in large part to Egypt's accession to the World Trade Organization in 1995, which opened up the domestic market to foreign competition, sales by local textile manufacturers halved in the early 2000s while clothing imports jumped 500 per cent.[34] To compound the drop in local demand, Egypt's government – under direct pressure from the World Bank – was busy dismantling the economic security of textile workers in an effort to make the Egyptian industry a more 'competitive' component of the global textile market and boost the profit-streams of foreign investor partners such as Marks and Spencer, Calvin Klein, Walmart, Gap and Lev's.[35] The result was that in the early 2000s a third of Egypt's 100,000 garment workers lost their jobs, and those left behind experienced a 4 per cent fall in real-term wages.[36] In that context, the concessions sought by restless employees in Mahalla and other textile centres were not unreasonable: workers called for an average raise of less than 100 EGP (approx. £10) per person in the form of an annual profit-sharing dividend, representing a total cost to the state of 13 million EGP. That same year, the government spent 500 million EGP alone on refurbishing ministerial offices.[37] But the speed at which they succeeded revealed the regime's panic, and encouraged more radical labour activists to push further. In the remaining textile plants at Kafr el-Dawwar, a statement signed by the 'Workers for Change in Kafr el-Dawwar' began circulating across the factory floor barely a month after the conclusion of a successful strike. The leaflet called not for more pay rises, but for what the authorities feared most – better coordination between employees in different companies and cities that were undertaking labour action, and the development of solidarity links between them.[38]

In the final years of Mubarak's rule, Egypt shuddered with a strike wave so vast that academics labelled it the largest social movement seen in the Middle East for half a century.[39] In 2007, not a single day went by without a labour protest occurring somewhere; by the end of the year, teachers, doctors, train drivers, government data collectors, educational administrators, Suez Canal navigators, regional revenue collectors, nurses, university professors, metro employees, paramedics, health insurance workers, civil servants at Cairo's al-Azhar, Sunni Islam's highest seat of learning, civil servants in the ministry of manpower, prosecutor's office employees and staff at the forensic medicine department had all joined the unrest, professing not just localized grievances but a common, collective suffering fuelled by the widening cleft between prices and wages that structural adjustment had delivered.[40] These mobilizations took many different forms but nearly all of them followed Mahalla's lead in several key respects. In the past, most labour actions had taken the form of the *i'tisam* ('sit-in'), whereby employees would occupy the workplace and *keep working* in an effort to remind bosses and ministers of their role in upholding the social contract; the goal was to shame the authorities into respecting worker demands, and as a result production often rose rather than fell during these periods. After Mahalla though, workers began using the *idrab* ('strike') as their primary tactic instead – a sign not only that Egypt's working class were increasingly rejecting the Nasserite notion of employees and the state being partners in production, but also of a growing consciousness on the part of workers regarding their collective economic weight under neoliberalism, and how they could apply it most usefully.

Workers no longer cared about rebuilding their partnership with managers; now the goal was to hurt Mubarak Country's alliance between capital and state as sharply as possible. Oil workers in Suez began timing strike actions to coincide with the arrival of large oil shipments; cement plant employees in Torah arranged their strikes in such a way as to prevent their product being shipped out at all, maximizing financial losses for the company.[41] And whereas labour actions used to be brief – most lasted less than twenty-four hours, with long-running disputes like Ora Misr a rare exception – now, as in Mahalla, strikes which lasted several days or more became the norm. This shift was not just quantitative. Longer strikes, which by their very nature usually involve overnight occupation of the workplace, require grassroots organization: rotas for sit-in duty, committees to ensure worker security and to protect machinery in case bosses accused strikers of sabotage, mechanisms to obtain and distribute food, water and sleeping materials.* All of this forced workers to begin creating new methods of resistance themselves, and allowed time for word of strike action to spread to other workplaces and other communities, expanding the potential for solidarity actions.[43] After 2006, Mahalla's next strikes lasted six days, and Kafr el-Dawwar's protest went on for nine. In the Abu Makaram textile

---

* At the Kafr el-Dawwar sit-in in 1994, workers claimed that state security agents infiltrated the factory and set fire to a portion of it in order to provide justification for troops to launch their deadly storming of the site.[42]

company in Sadat City, workers struck for almost three weeks.[44] In 2009, a strike at the Tanta Flax and Oil Company lasted for more than six months.[45]

In April that year, just as the Tanta strike was getting underway, I spent a morning standing in the street in front of Egypt's State Circus interviewing the resident clown, Refat el-Grasy, who had joined his colleagues in a walk-out. Instead of unpacking his spinning plates and oiling his unicycle in preparation for the stage, the 52-year-old was holding a placard and shouting slogans at passing cars. 'We can't live on our current wages and we don't want to see this place privatized,' he told me. 'We'll keep on walking out here for as long as it takes for our voices to be heard.'[46] El-Grasy, who had been employed by the circus his entire working life, was probably Egypt's most colourful striker that April morning, but in other respects there was nothing unique about him. By that point, analysts estimated that almost 1.5 million Egyptians had participated in labour protests of one sort or another in recent years.[47] And yet there was something particularly emblematic about the decision of circus staff to join the strike wave and gather in their tattered performance garb outside the faded technicolour big-top on Cairo's Agouza corniche. When the veteran Helw family circus – which had been performing in Egypt for generations – was given a permanent home on the Nile and relaunched as a national circus by Gamal Abdel Nasser in 1966, it was part of a wider attempt at a government-sponsored cultural renaissance including ballet, folk art and Arab musical institutes: a statement of what post-colonial Egypt could be. But Egypt's subsequent decline sucked the lifeblood from the circus; standards slipped, audiences fell, and on the night of 12 October 1972, the circus's star lion, Sultan, mauled his trainer Mohamed Helw to death in the ring, in front of the audience. The Egyptian author Yusuf Idris was a spectator in the big-top that night and wrote a famous essay about the incident, 'I am Sultan, the Law of the Jungle', which was published in *al-Ahram* a few days later. 'In the tremendous shock of the event, Idris saw something fearsome in the human side of the tragedy, symbolising not only the state of the circus at the time, but also the political and social life of Egypt,' wrote the economist and essayist Gamal Amin. 'He concluded that the lion's attack on the trainer was an allegory for the state of Egyptians of that time – fearful, defeated, their high ideals lost, and their dreams of heroism and glory destroyed.'[48]

Three decades later, under Mubarak's neoliberalism, the state circus seemed to once again be holding up a mirror to the nation. Given the unprecedented chasm between a tiny group of the rich and the growing poor, Refat el-Grasy's clowning felt hollow: starved of public funding, like most Egyptian institutions, the tattered circus tent was letting in the cold night air, the bleachers were dilapidated, and the artists and crew behind the production were each taking home less than 250 EGP (£25) a month.[49] Some staff were even harder off. Suleiman 'Ashur Suleiman, a 53-year-old workman who had served the circus loyally since he was twenty years old, had a monthly salary of 100 EGP (£10). His poverty meant he could never marry, and to save money he slept on the floor of the circus between the animal cages. One night in January 2002, after the evening's performance had come to an end and Suleiman was picking his way across the cages, he slipped and fell partially into the tiger enclosure; the tiger, Muhsin, jumped up and tore at his leg. From his hospital bed, surrounded by TV cameras, Suleiman told reporters that he thanked God for having survived the accident but was fearful that he might now lose his job – so fearful, in fact, that he expressed his anxiety on this front to every visitor he received. Millions of Egyptians watching at home looked upon Suleiman – a humble older man who had spent his entire life working hard in an incredibly dangerous job for the state, yet was pitifully paid, had no pension, retirement benefits or health insurance, knew that there was no other job out there for him, and had been stripped of his dignity to such an extent that he was left to sleep each night among the animal cages – and they saw themselves.* At that time, the circus seemed to symbolize a sense of hopelessness under the economic devastation of neoliberalism. By

---

* Media coverage of the incident speculated that to cut costs, the circus management had replaced some of its animal feed – usually buffalo or beef – with donkey meat, which is considerably cheaper. Donkey meat, however, has a higher proportion of sugar and is close in taste to human flesh, hence why it is never supposed to be used as feed for lions and tigers. Gamal Amin wrote at the time that the entire accident seemed to revolve around hunger: '[Suleiman] was hungry and the tiger was hungry, and so, it seems, is a good proportion of the Egyptian population.'[50]

2009, though, when Refat el-Grasy and the clown's colleagues had walked out to join the strike wave, the circus symbolized resistance.

One of the most crucial elements of this resistance – and one of the reasons why it posed such a threat to the state – was the increasing readiness of Egyptian workers to operate outside official state-sanctioned trade union structures. The self-organization of workers in Mahalla and their refusal to negotiate with ETUF had demonstrated that collective, autonomous activity was possible during moments of heightened industrial conflict; the question now was whether anybody could make the next critical leap forward and establish a permanent, independent trade union – something that would defy the law as it then stood, and break six decades of state control. The answer came from an unlikely source. In September 2007, 50,000 local property tax collectors began organizing protests outside the Property Tax Authority (PTA) headquarters in Giza, just as Mahalla's victories were sending the textile industry into convulsions. PTA staff, unlike other types of tax collectors, were employed locally through provincial councils rather than directly through the ministry of finance, and had seen their already meagre wages – between 200 and 400 EGP a month – dissipate over many years.[51] What began as a relatively small and politically isolated episode of labour unrest – just one among so many rebellions in the broader strike wave – grew over the next three months into a national sensation, as striking PTA staff from all over the country gathered outside government buildings in Cairo and outsmarted the panicked regime into total capitulation.[52] In the course of their occupation, workers turned nearby roads into a carnival of protest that befuddled the security forces and won the hearts of local residents, who helped supply the campers with food and water. One of the strike leaders, Mahmoud 'Uwayda, described the scene when his twenty-two bus convoy of PTA employees from one part of the Nile Delta arrived at Hegazy at the same time as another delegation from the region. 'We were greeted with open arms and cheers, by smiling, laughing, cheerful faces as if we had known them for years ... The drums, tambourines and megaphones, the joy and the shouting, some people cannot believe that the numbers on that day were more than ten thousand. And everywhere you heard the beautiful chant "a decision, a decision . . . we're not going home without a decision.'[53] When strike delegates first attempted to speak with Minister of Finance Youssef Boutros-Ghali, the minister's head of security told them he was busy meeting IMF officials. A month later, Boutros-Ghali was sitting down with strike leaders directly, and agreeing to their demands.[54]

Up to this point, the end of a successful strike usually meant the end of any independent strike committee; this time though, workers felt differently. 'If we lose our committee, we will lose a weapon which we sweated and struggled to create, and it will give the state and management a chance to attack us again,' warned Kamal Abu Eita, one of the primary strike organizers.[55] Abu Eita believed the best chance of maintaining the committee and transforming it into something more durable was to ensure its governance wasn't constituted from above by a small number of prominent faces; an entity in that form would be too easy for the state to swat away. Instead, he argued, a permanent committee should consist of delegates from every office and governorate, democratically elected and accountable to workers – in other words 'the property of tens of thousands of property tax collectors; they would build it themselves so that they would defend it, and be ready to protect it'.[56] By the end of the following year, Egypt's first independent union in more than half a century – the Real Estate Tax Authority Union (RETAU) – was born. In the final years of the Mubarak regime, postal workers, teachers and others would follow suit with their own independent unions, standing firm against both security intimidation and legal challenges. ETUF, once the commanding pillar of the Nasserite corporatist pact, was rapidly becoming irrelevant.

On 6 April 2008, Mahalla workers walked out from their factory yet again, this time in protest at the failure of Mubarak's government to raise the national minimum wage – which, at 35 EGP (approx. £3.50) per month, had been unchanged since 1984. Opposition activist networks in Cairo and elsewhere called for a general strike to support them. Since the start of the strike wave in the mid-2000s, a pendulum had been swinging between workers' mobilizations and pro-change political protests in Cairo and Alexandria, two currents that the regime were hell bent on keeping apart. 'For the first time in decades,

the demands raised by workers over their local or sectional grievances provided the starting point for a chain reaction which detonated
a national political mobilisation against the regime,' observed Anne
Alexander and Mostafa Bassiouny.[57] The government were well
aware of the significance of this moment. In a show of dictatorial
strength, riot troops deployed to every major city in the country. In
an eerily quiet Cairo that morning, I remember walking through the
haze of the April *khamseen* – the annual hot, dry wind that whips in
from the desert and curdles the air with dust – past truck after truck
of security forces parked in the road leading from my apartment to
Tahrir Square. It was the first large-scale open deployment of authoritarian violence I had seen with my own eyes since arriving in the
country, and it was chilling. In the square itself, platoons of plain-
clothes thugs stood in formation on each corner, watched over by
sunglass-sporting state security generals who chewed gum and occasionally adjusted their earpieces. The display of force worked, at least
in the capital. The streets stayed largely silent, and the entwining of
labour and opposition protest that the state so feared did not materialize. In Mahalla, as ever, things were different.

In the neighbourhoods surrounding Mahalla's massive Misr Spinning and Weaving complex, police had swooped pre-emptively in the
night to arrest the strike's main leaders. Dawn rose on a factory that
had already been occupied by riot troops. Prevented from accessing
their workplace, employees gathered instead outside the factory gates
and were soon joined by tens of thousands of local residents. No one
knows who threw the first rock, or tore down the first Mubarak pos-
ter. But by the afternoon, an urban insurrection greater than anything
seen in Egypt since the anti-Sadat bread riots in 1977 was decisively
underway. Central security forces fought cat and mouse battles with
youths in the backstreets, the city's railway lines were cut, and astonishing images – of Mubarak's photo lying on the asphalt as hundreds
and hundreds of Egyptians surged towards it with their feet held
aloft, ready to stamp – began leaking out on to social media. 'People
burned the picture of Mubarak because they wanted him to feel the
suffering of the street,' said Amal al-Said, a factory worker who had
been working there since 1984.[58] Troops arrested hundreds and fired
tear gas, rubber bullets and live ammunition into the crowds, killing

166

three people, including a fifteen-year-old boy. After several days of fighting, security forces reasserted control of the town and set about rounding up perpetrators. The uprising generated almost no coverage in the international media, and no major Western political leader spoke out on the matter. A few months later, the IMF elected Youssef Boutros-Ghali, Egypt's finance minister and a major player in the structural adjustment programme, as its new chair of the International Monetary and Financial Committee, the principal policy-setting organ of the organization.[59] In the aftermath of such concentrated unrest on the streets of Egypt, stemming from the policies that Boutros-Ghali and the IMF had been forcing through, it was an audacious appointment. The echo chamber of international finance was seemingly determined to ensure that no amount of grassroots protest would be allowed to disrupt the equilibrium of neoliberal reform and the self-authored, self-congratulatory reports that saluted it. They failed; in less than three years Egypt's revolution would begin – and Youssef Boutros-Ghali would be a wanted criminal on the run.

'God created us free, and didn't create us heritage or real estate,' Colonel Ahmed 'Urabi supposedly told Khedive Tawfik more than 120 years ago. 'Urabi's appeal to the Egyptian people was based partially on nationalism, but his revolt was animated too by a desire for individual dignity and collective autonomy; the idea that Egyptian citizens were more than passive pawns to be moved around on someone else's chequerboard. Back in 1882, that chequerboard was European imperialism and the players were foreign colonizers working in partnership with local elites. In Mubarak Country, the chequerboard was the empire of neoliberal capital, and once again external forces formed an alliance with the domestic ruling class to carve Egyptians and their nation into real estate so that it could be gambled, sold and speculated on to make money from money for those with power. The last stand at Kafr el-Dawwar by 'Urabi and the many ordinary Egyptians who joined his revolution became part of the foundational mythology-that Nasser later used to justify the rise to governance of Egypt's top military generals and the exclusionary state they constructed – the same state that Mubarak and his supporters at home and abroad depended upon to ram through structural adjustment while preserving their own regime. Mubarak saw himself as hailing from the same lineage of patriot officers as 'Urabi, Nasser and Sadat but in truth he was as detached from his people as Tawfik. In Mubarak Country, 'Urabi's real legacy could be seen in the sit-ins, strikes and protests that roiled through the state in the final years before the revolution – and began to prise it open for ever.

5

'Who told you we were weak?'

On a bright Friday before dawn in November 2007, Maher Youssef Ibrahim – known to everyone as Hagg Maher – was shaken awake by his cousin. 'It's the general – he's in the garden and he wants to talk,' came the whisper. Maher, a large man in his forties, rubbed his eyes and pulled on some clothes before stepping outside on to his lawn which stretched all the way down to the Nile, bordered by Victorian-style lamp posts along the sides and a row of small trees on the riverbank. Two wicker chairs stood in the middle of the grass; waiting behind them, in full uniform, was General Arabi el-Maseri, an Egyptian naval commander. Through the mist, the general spoke. 'If you have anything of value here like a fridge or a television,' he said, nodding towards the house, 'then take it now. This is our land, and today we are reclaiming it.'

Maher nodded slowly, and took a step towards him. 'General, you are our guest on this island, and I must offer you something to drink,' he replied. 'The sun is about to come up – let us take some tea in the field.' They walked together through an adjacent stretch of farmland, down paths that Maher knew were being watched by friendly eyes – eyes belonging to people who would know what to do. Finally they came to rest in Maher's field, and the farmer issued a warning. 'You are a guest on Qursaya Island, and no harm will come to you,' he repeated. 'But if one combat soldier as much as sets their foot down on Qursaya's shore, we are ready with sticks and stones to repel them. You will lose.' General el-Maseri told him it was too late. With the sun breaking over the water, he lifted his walkie-talkie and pressed a button. The invasion of Qursaya was about to begin.

*

Qursaya began life as a small glob of earth in the middle of the Nile, situated across from the giant Ma'adi apartment blocks that dominate the skyline towards Cairo's southern quarters. Until the 1970s, the island existed only for half the year, when the river level fell low enough to expose it. During those months it was used as a waystation for boat people from Upper Egyptian towns such as Qena, Sohag and Minya, who came down the Nile each year on feluccas with the seasonal flood and exchanged their lentils, beans and pottery for oil and aluminium in the capital. From above, the shape of this ephemeral mud bank resembled *qursa* – a small, round loaf of flat bread, often baked with dates, records of which stretch back to the thirteenth century[1] – and in honour of this, locals named it 'Qursaya'. Once the newly built Aswan High Dam began regulating Egypt's annual floods and granted Qursaya a degree of permanence, enterprising Cairenes started to extend it. 'It was just two or three families at first, who came from [the nearby and larger] al-Dahab island or from the Giza mainland,' said Mohamed Abla, an artist who has made his home on Qursaya. 'In the winter they would dig up mud and pack it with wire and bamboo before drying it and adding to the island.' Land reclamation was followed by the cultivation of crops by farmers, and soon fishermen took up residence as well. By the end of the decade there were at least a hundred people living there; by the turn of the millennium, Qursaya's population stood at more than 2,000. No bridges connect it to the mainland; access is via a steel-cable ferry, hand-operated by the ferryman. Mohamed Abla, whose art ranges from abstract depictions of the river to collages of satirical anti-government newspaper headlines, believes the geography of the island makes it unique. 'It's a village in the very heart of busy Cairo,' he said. 'There is a special psychology here. It's a community of farmers, but at the heart of the metropolis; here we travel between two cultures every day, rural and urban, and we rely totally on the ferry boat to take us back and forth. It's our only connection between the two worlds, which feels fragile. But at the same time, empowering.'

In 2001, a cabinet decree was issued ordering that all land on the Nile's two main agricultural islands in the capital – al-Dahab and al-Warraq, both of which lie close to Qursaya in the shadow of el-Munib Bridge, which carries the ring road across the river – was to be expropriated for unspecified 'public use', and all residents evicted. Like most informal settlements, the communities on these islands had up until that point been 'off-map', and largely ignored by the government. Al-Dahab and al-Warraq, despite being home to more than 100,000 Egyptians between them, had no secondary schools and very few city services; the isolation of Qursaya, relatively tiny in comparison to its neighbours, was even more complete.[2] But the extension of the el-Munib bridge at the turn of the millennium raised the possibility of ramps being constructed to carry traffic to and from the islands, and that in turn exposed the land on them to potential speculative development. The prime minister defended the state's seizure of al-Dahab and al-Warraq by claiming that it would help protect the environment; the minister of housing insisted the decree was aimed at 'sprucing up unplanned areas' and argued that the existing residents were few in number and lived in 'run-down' houses. Egyptians who lived in those run-down houses occupied al-Munib bridge in their thousands on the day the decree was announced, waving signs that read 'No to investors' and bringing traffic to a halt. Over the following days an unlikely alliance of informal community groups and well-connected environmental activists, hailing from very different social backgrounds, mounted an effective campaign against the government plans. Without even a façade of 'public interest' to expropriation, the decree had laid bare the extent to which regime policy was being geared towards the interests of private financiers rather than local Egyptians. Prominent cultural figures joined the chorus of protest, and one NGO began a legal challenge against the ruling. Once the issue had become a *cause célèbre*, some local politicians – including influential members of the NDP hierarchy – also took up the residents' campaign.[3]

Taken aback by the scale of opposition, ministers rescinded their decree the following month. But the state hadn't given up on the idea of clearing the Nile islands for private development; it withdrew only to plot an alternative way forward. In 2004, the appointment of Ahmed Nazif's liberalizing government ratcheted the economic reform programme up a level and generated fresh hunger among regime-allied businessmen for new investment hotspots and opportunities to enclose and commodify the commons. To Egypt's financial elite, Qursaya, one of the last green and non-urbanized spaces in the capital – where slender egrets stood hunched over fields of silt and prowling cats laced low between the reeds – flickered enticingly.

In 2005 Mohamed Aboul Enein – an NDP lawmaker, tourism and ceramics tycoon, and senior Mubarak-era official – purchased a villa on Qursaya, and began making bids to nearby farmers for their fields. Most refused, even when they were offered double the market price; their land wasn't a financial asset to be traded, it was a home, a community and a way of life. According to Mohamed Abla, that's when Aboul Enein innocuously raised the possibility that the government might seize the territory by force. Sure enough, one morning in September 2007, letters arrived through the door of several residents on the island, each signed at the bottom by Egypt's prime minister, the defence and agriculture ministers, and the governor of Giza. They were mandatory eviction orders.[4] At a hastily convened public meeting on his private boat, Aboul Enein – playing the disingenuous role of concerned village elder – told residents that if the army ever arrived on Qursaya to enforce the eviction orders, 'we will respect them and invite them for tea, and never try and do anything against them'. Abla, who has a crop of black curly hair and a bushy moustache, was sitting in the audience; he asked why Aboul Enein thought that men with guns should be allowed to occupy their homes and take away farmers' livelihoods without any resistance from the community. Aboul Enein replied that the residents had no choice because they were weak. The mood on the boat darkened. 'Who told you we were weak?' Abla shot back. 'We are strong, we are going to win and you are going to lose. These people are a lot stronger than you, and you should take heed.' Residents remember Aboul Enein laughing, and asking what weapons these people had to fight with. 'We have art,' shouted Abla, prompting more guffaws. The meeting broke up in disarray.

After its previous attempt to seize al-Dahab and al-Warraq, Egypt's government had elected to pursue different tactics on Qursaya – hoping to avoid the public backlash which sunk their project last time round. Rather than make a prominent announcement regarding state expropriation, this time the state targeted families individually and offered no explanation for its actions. The regime was gambling on the fact that compared to those of the larger islands, Qursaya's community was much smaller, and stood less chance of building alliances with celebrities and getting its message out to the independent media. 'We were singled out by the regime because they had tried and failed with al-Dahab and they thought this island is small and the people are very simple,' explained Abla. 'They thought they could do it very quickly and nobody would notice.' More importantly, the government brought in a new player that they hoped would silence any criticism in the press and terrify residents into submission: the Egyptian army. The notion of a country's armed forces being involved in a domestic dispute over residential and commercial land may sound curious, but in Mubarak Country the connection was logical. Since the beginning of structural adjustment, the military had been foremost among the speculators driving Egypt's vast property bubble, and with good reason: in 1997 all 'undeveloped' land in the country was formally placed under army control, while the top brass had the power to designate any other patch of ground as a military asset for security purposes. The armed forces enjoyed other privileges too which afforded them a leading and lucrative role in Egypt's real estate boom: huge production facilities for brick and cement, access to an unpaid labour force through military conscription, and the ability to crack down on workers and protesters with legalized violence. The country's generals put these advantages to profitable use. As the desert compound frenzy reached its zenith in the mid-2000s, senior military officials – who already controlled a huge economic portfolio covering everything from washing machines to pasta – became ever more important landowners and investment partners to the private sector.* When new recruits or conscripts first take their military oath, they 'swear to God to be a loyal soldier to the Republic of Egypt, protecting its security and peace'. There is currently no mention of any duty to attack fellow-countrymen in order to forcibly open up new financial markets for the rich to speculate on. But now, in the aftermath of the meeting on Aboul Enein's boat, soldiers began circling Qursaya in naval skiffs, disrupting the cable ferry and firing water cannons to intimidate those on shore.

---

* Like every aspect of the military's economic empire, details of the exact extent of land ownership by the generals are shrouded in secrecy and there are no figures publicly available.

Hagg Maher was one of the residents served with an eviction notice. His father and grandfather had been among the original farmers on the island, and the family's rhythms – cultivating crops, feeding live-stock, selling milk and fish on the mainland and meat during the *eid* festival – have been the template of rural existence on Qursaya for decades. 'We're all linked here, and the way of life makes it a peaceful place by nature, with peaceful people in it,' he told me. So when the army landed on the island one day and told twelve locals, Maher among them, that they should bring their ownership papers to a bur-eaucratic office in order to receive government certificates confirming their rights to their land, he believed them. 'But it was a trick,' he smiled ruefully. 'The next thing we know we're on military police buses to C28 [Cairo's notorious military court].' Maher was brought up on thirteen charges, including conspiring against the regime, use of force against the military, ownership of illegal weapons and illicitly obtaining foreign funds. 'When they read them out to me I laughed and said: "Why don't you add number fourteen as well – my assassi-nation of Sadat? You guys should be charged with being idiots."'

To secure their release, Maher and the others were forced to sign papers formally relinquishing any claims to their land, as well as promising they would never step foot on Qursaya again or fight against the Egyptian armed forces. Any breaches of these conditions, they were told, would result in military prosecution. When the farm-ers eventually made their way back to the island, they found that their fields had been strewn with bamboo and set alight by soldiers. The community huddled together to debate what to do next. Back in 2001, the residents of al-Dahab and al-Warraq had successfully appealed to select members of the NDP elite to intercede on their behalf with the national government; in Qursaya, however, the NDP parliamentary representative for the island was Mohamed Aboul Enein, the very man driving their eviction. If the regime's aggression was going to be resisted, the Qursayans realized, they would have to resist it themselves. 'After that we got organized,' explained Mohamed Abla. 'We held events – music, pottery-making, readings and exhibitions – to try and get journalists interested in our story, to raise the profile of Qursaya. We collected blankets and set up shifts; we had people guarding the island every fifty metres around the shore, twenty-four hours a day. They slept there with a stick or a bag of stones or empty coke bottles, ready to attack anyone who tried to invade. No guns though. We protected ourselves with the things we found on the island. By day we were making noise, and by night we simply waited.'

The wait didn't last long. And on the morning Maher was woken up by his cousin with the news that General el-Maseri was in the garden, Qursaya was prepared. At the first sight of the military man in Maher's fields, his neighbours had begun quietly going door to door, stirring the islanders. Now, as the motorboats whirred into action and bore down upon the shoreline, a pair of youths ran to the island's two places of worship – Ramadan to the north mosque and Abdel Mowaty to the south – and used the *muezzin*'s microphones to rouse residents to their defences. Yells of 'The army is coming!' boomed out from every loudspeaker, and within moments Qursaya's riverbank was alive with people taking up positions overlooking the water's edge.

Dr Mohamed Mustafa was already awake, rushing out of his house in his winter pyjamas and *shib shib* ('flip-flops'). As one of the island's few professionals – most of the residents were *fellaheen* – he, along with Mohamed Abla, had been among the first people Hagg Maher had called when it became clear the army assault was underway. Mustafa rushed towards Maher's fields to remonstrate with the general, only to spin back around when he heard the troopships had chosen his own garden as their landing point. 'It was a military manoeuvre – they had selected the strategic beaches and jetties they would need to get a foothold on the island then overwhelm us,' the doctor told me. 'When I entered the garden I found the troops had already made it on to the lawn, and were surrounding my daughter and her young children. I walked right up to them and pushed the nearest officer, who swung his gun and bayonet towards me in surprise. "This is live ammunition," he yelled at me and cocked the trigger. I just put my hands up and said, "Shoot me then."' By this time word had spread through the loudspeakers that the doctor's house was the frontline, and young people were arriving in their dozens armed with sticks and stones. The soldiers kept their guns raised and stood uncertainly as more and more Qursayans piled into the garden. For a few moments, the two sides faced each other in absolute silence. 'Get off our land and back on to your ships now, otherwise there will be a catastrophe,' shouted one of the young people. The officer shook his head, and a rain of rocks began pouring down on the troops.

For the rest of the morning and afternoon, war was waged in the middle of the Nile. On Dr Mohamed's lawn, soldiers slipped and stumbled as they backed off from the onslaught of stones and bottles, unsure as to whether or not they should fire back into the crowd. 'At the end of the day, these young conscripts are farmers too,' reflected the doctor later. 'They're scared as well, and don't want to have to kill fellow Egyptians. Their orders were coming from above.' One soldier dropped his gun, which was quickly picked up by the crowd and brandished back at him; another officer, attempting vainly to stand his ground, had his arm broken by a local with a stick. Among the fiercest combatants were the women of Qursaya, several of whom dragged an army tent – which soldiers had been trying to pitch in the garden as a temporary base – down towards the water. 'Some of the rocks were flying past the soldiers and hitting the troopship on the river,' remembers Dr Mustafa. 'The glass windshield of the boat started to smash and the captain – who could only see now by craning his head over the windshield and into the path of the missiles – began to panic and reverse the boat away from the shore. That terrified the rest of the soldiers on the land, and they began dropping their guns and running back to the boat.' It was only a temporary retreat, but over the next few hours, as another army ship was brought in to bolster the invading forces and more landings were attempted at different locations around the island, residents held their ground every time, often linking hands to create a human barrier to the shore. Each time troops were forced to back off, some islanders dug shallow graves on the water's edge and wrapped themselves in white shrouds before lying down within them – a message that they would rather die here than let the army seize this land. 'Everyone came down from their homes: men, women, children, everybody,' recalled Abla. He and Maher had stayed with the general, arguing and imploring him to call off his troops, and they could hear the panicked reports coming through the walkie-talkie from officers all over the island being beaten back by the resistance of the Qursayan people. 'One after the other they came through crackling and shouting "It's very difficult sir, we're coming under attack from rocks and we can't do it." By late afternoon, they had given up trying to land. No ammunition was fired, and no one from the island was hurt. We had beaten the Egyptian army, and we knew that after that nothing would be the same again.'

In the final decade of Mubarak's reign, acts of communal resistance of the sort carried out by the people of Qursaya became a second major current of unrest which, alongside labour protests, began to shake the foundations of his rule. As with the strike wave that was inflaming Egypt's workplaces, communal protests – mobilizations which brought together residents of a specific neighbourhood, village or town – usually began over localized grievances, but they soon assumed a more political character and undermined the authority of the regime in ways that transcended the parochial.

Firstly, discontent was usually sparked by issues that flowed directly from the neoliberal, patriarchal nature of the state in Mubarak Country. Shortages of basic resources – such as drinking water, subsidized bread or the fish that once swum freely in rivers, lakes and oceans – were often a direct consequence of the dictatorship attempting, as part of the structural adjustment reforms, to convert something which most Egyptians understood as a shared right into a saleable asset instead. Furthermore, the decisions which led to social goods being privatized or public access to them being restricted were invariably taken in a high-handed manner at the top of the bureaucratic apparatus with no meaningful consultation. Ordinary citizens were rarely offered any formal outlet through which they could push their case, leaving them with a double sense of exclusion. The story of Qursaya is a typical example of this: a commonly held good on which many people's welfare and security depended (the island's land) was summarily appropriated by the state so that it could be transformed into a private possession (real estate), and the first residents knew about it was when eviction letters dropped through their door. 'The authorities don't speak to us at all. It's as if we don't exist. Nobody pays us the slightest attention,' Dr Mohamed explained at the time. 'We just want them to reveal what they are doing and make us feel that we are not just numbers.'⁵ The issue was a local one, but it was derived from a set of economic relations and a system of governance that stretched far beyond the doctor's garden or Hagg Maher's fields. The more often communities were exposed to local injustices, the more apparent that fundamental reality became.

Another recurring feature of communal protests was that over the course of popular mobilizations, assumed distinctions between different levels and agents of the state often began to dissolve. In the past, Mubarak's regime had been served by a mythology of separation between the office of the president, the cabinet and the many lower organs of authority that transmitted the violence and forced dispossession of the state down to its citizens on the ground. This 'separation' encouraged disgruntled Egyptians to channel their anger towards one element of official power while appealing to another for intercession on their behalf. Such appeals, whatever form they took, always helped to insulate the state as a whole from dissent. If a local corruption scandal led to outraged residents calling on the prime minister or the president to step in and defend their rights, Mubarak's dictatorship could breathe a sigh of relief; it was the sort of sentiment that afforded Mubarak a high degree of protection, as junior officials, governors and even cabinet ministers could easily be sacrificed to placate popular fury. Such a mindset reinforced the fiction of Mubarak Country being a nation of benign paternalism, one in which nothing more than an occasional rotten apple could be found hanging on an otherwise benevolent bureaucratic tree. Sometimes communal petitions were presented the other way around, with Egyptians depending upon select local members of the ruling elite to advance their cause within the national corridors of power – as happened during the government's failed assault on al-Dahab and al-Warraq, when residents won the support of key NDP bigwigs for their campaign. This too strengthened the state's clientelism: for citizens, access to the state and influence within it could only be obtained via the supply of political support to the state's representatives. Concessions, if they ever materialized, arrived in the form of largesse from above, not via the active involvement of citizens entitled to participate in decisions that shaped their land, lives and livelihoods.

But in the run-up to revolution, that separation mythology began unravelling – with immense political significance. Many of the communal protests in the mid and late 2000s were so fierce that the regime had to marshal a huge range of resources to try to contain them – the deployment of the army on Qursaya, for example – and in the process fabled divisions between different arms of the state started, slowly, to collapse. Before the attempted invasion of Qursaya, many residents had long maintained great respect for the armed forces. By the time I visited, they were queuing up to share stories they had unearthed of military corruption; Mohamed Abla described the island's resistance to me as 'a real revolution against Mubarak, against the government and against the army – because all of those things became the same'. A similar mental shift took place among the workers in Mahalla when they forced representatives of ETUF, the state's official trade union federation, to sit down on the same side of the table as bosses and government ministers during strike negotiations. ETUF was ostensibly an institution that represented workers' interests, yet through collective struggle the Mahalla employees proved the fallacy of that claim. Exposing ETUF as a pillar of the existing political order helped illuminate the entire web of state power that Egyptians would eventually rise up against in 2011. In the same fashion, communal protests like Qursays's moved many Egyptians away from viewing one particular area of state bureaucracy as greedy, corrupt or oppressive; now, those adjectives were increasingly applied to the state as a whole.

Lastly, community-level mobilizations often brought impoverished Egyptians, for the first time, into direct confrontation with security forces. The manner in which the state chose to react to protests provided communities with unvarnished field experience of the brutality of police rule, not only radicalizing those involved but also offering practical lessons on how to fight back. In the final years of Mubarak Country, those practical lessons spread. Varied efforts to disrupt the state were undertaken by countless groups of Egyptians – cutting roads, occupying bridges, fighting soldiers – and collectively they imparted a sense of what autonomous organization could achieve, even if victories were short-lived. Come 2011, the implications of that street-level education became clear, as tens of thousands of citizens used a brilliant array of tactics to fight running battles with the state's gendarmerie, and won.

A hundred and twenty miles north of Qursaya, on the shores of the Mediterranean, lies Borg el-Burullus. Known simply as el-Borg to its inhabitants, the town is situated on the north-eastern edge of Burullus, one of four immense lakes that crest the furthest reaches of the Nile Delta. Sandwiched between the lake and the sea, the centre of el-Borg is dominated by a warren of narrow, brightly painted alleyways marking out the old fishermen's quarters; almost everyone in the vicinity makes their living from one body of water or the other, and the rise and fall of open fish stocks directly correlates with the comfort or poverty of over 100,000 people in the region. In recent decades, though, Burullus has witnessed no rises in fish stocks, only falls. The fish and the lake they live in have perished in tandem, along with much of the wetlands and arable land nearby. In the past fifty years, Burullus has shrunk by more than 35,000 *feddans*, losing almost a third of its original surface area. Of the fifty-two separate fish species that were recorded in the lake at the turn of the twentieth century, only thirty-three now remain.[6]

The problem in Burullus is part of a bigger problem in the northern Nile Delta and Egypt as a whole: the country most closely associated with the world's longest river is suffering from an acute shortage of water, and its deficit is only likely to get worse.[7] In Mubarak Country, when this issue was discussed at all among those in power, two main explanations were usually proffered: population growth and global climate change. Both are relevant. The Delta was once nourished by the water and silt that washed in with Egypt's seasonal floods; since the construction of the High Dam at Aswan in the 1960s those floods have ceased, and in their place a network of irrigation canals has ferried gallons of freshwater from the Nile's two tributary branches across to where it's needed. But increased water use upstream, in part due to the sheer volume of people living in the Nile Valley, has taken a toll. Egypt currently has only 700 cubic metres of freshwater per person (m^3/pp), well short of the 1,000 m^3/pp the UN believes is the minimum needed for water security. Demographic pressures over the coming decades will cut that down further, possibly as low as 450 m^3/

pp, and climate change will only compound the situation.[8] Any temperature rises which accompany global warming will result in more of the Nile evaporating before it ever gets to the Delta; the amount of river water reaching lakes like Burullus is set to drop by 70 per cent over the next half-century.[9] To make matters even worse, Egypt's northern region – already among the top three areas on the planet most vulnerable to any rise in global sea levels – is being hit by coastal erosion, enabling the spread of salinity through the fields and damaging soil fertility. Experts at the country's Soils, Water and Environment Research Institute predict that wheat and maize yields could drop by 40 and 50 per cent respectively across the next thirty years, and if even the most optimistic climate change predictions materialize, flooding from the sea could displace millions of Egyptians from one of the most densely populated regions on earth.[10] 'The Delta is a kind of Bangladesh story,' Dr Rick Tutwiler, director of the American University in Cairo's Desert Development Center, told me. 'You've got a massive population, overcrowding, a threat to all natural resources from the pressure of all the people, production, pollution, cars and agricultural chemicals. And on top of all that, there's the rising sea. It's the perfect storm.'

Under Mubarak, these facts became weapons. Egypt's ecological challenges were harnessed to the government's exclusionary development agenda, and blame was pinned on those most affected by them: the poor. Ministers developed a neo-Malthusian narrative of environmental doom which closely echoed the 'anti-modernity' discourse applied to inhabitants of the informal *'ashwa'iyat* settlements; the prevailing notion in official circles was that Egypt's impoverished masses were anti-green – through their breeding, their littering, their lack of education and their feckless waste of resources – and that millions of ordinary citizens were therefore incompatible with the country's future. As with the exaggerated horrors of 'slum' neighbourhoods, most of which weren't slums at all, this formal concern for the environment ran skin-deep. Its real purpose was to legitimize state assaults against marginalized communities and give government schemes orientated towards the growth of private wealth a *faux* patina of social responsibility. It also helped curry favour with IFIs and foreign investors who had their own corporate social responsibility checkboxes to adhere to. Hence why the attempted forced evictions on al-Dahab and al-Warraq islands were initially justified by the prime minister as being necessary on environmental grounds, despite the fact that the islands were already far more ecologically vibrant than they would be under any of the commercial development plans envisaged by officials.

Similar arguments were deployed by the state when it tried to clear parts of the informal Ard el-Lewa neighbourhood in Giza for a new road designed to speed relatively rich commuters to and from the 6th October satellite city, and again in an attempt to clear out the capital's pottery community in Mar Girgis, who stood in the way of a series of lucrative new tourism developments planned for the Coptic Cairo area in the run-up to the millennium.[11] In each instance, the appropriation of land by the state was justified in part by claims that the regime was liberating the area from environmental vandals. Of course the residents of Ard el-Lewa, accused by the state of being environmentally unfriendly, drew far less on the country's scarce water supplies than did the permanently green golf courses in Mubarak's upmarket desert compounds, a new motorway to which apparently necessitated the bulldozing of their community. The pollution emitted by the potters of Mar Girgis pales into insignificance when set alongside the ecological harm associated with the Sun World Superior Seedless™ Grape folly in the New Valley, or the rest of Mubarak's Toshka pyramid. But the government's green sympathies were selective. Little was said, for example, about the fact that large corporations had helped turn lakes in the Delta like Burullus into little more than drainage pools for the country's pollutants; 65 per cent of urban industries in Alexandria disposed of their waste fluids in nearby Lake Mayrut.[12]

Behind the veil of government rhetoric, it was often ordinary Egyptians – especially the *fellaheen* who worked the land – who were most aware of Egypt's environmental predicament and conscious of the need to manage resources sustainably; naturally green agricultural techniques were passed down from parents to children. Pressure from IFIs to liberalize the country's agricultural market and maximize revenue-generating export crops, however, threatened to undermine this knowledge. 'Local and historical awareness of the land and its nuances is being lost with each generation, not least because the supply of agricultural information is being more and more centralized in university faculties which teach only chemically intensive farming,' Ahmed el-Droubi, formerly of Greenpeace Egypt, explained to me. 'These experts go and tell the farmers "This is what you have to go and do," and consequently the farmers cover their crops in pesticides. Meanwhile, they often have a small little patch next to their own house where they grow food for their own family in the traditional way, and that patch is always fine!' By way of contrast, many of the government's supposed ecological experts doubted whether climate change was real or were convinced that the problem was so great as to render any human intervention useless. 'It's down to God,' one environmental officer for a major Delta town once said to me with a shrug. 'If the Delta goes, we'll find new places to live. If Egypt was big enough for Mary and Joseph, then it will be big enough for all of us.'[13]

When it came to their disappearing fish stocks, though, the fishermen of Lake Burullus were less concerned with God and more interested in USAID (United States Agency for International Development). They knew about the water shortages that stemmed from over-demand upstream, and about the threat posed by climate change to the coastal region, but they also knew that something else was disrupting the lake's environment – something the regime was not so keen to talk about. As far back as 1982, reports by the American government agency were flagging up the 'highly profitable' potential for intensive commercial fish farms to be established in the lakes of the northern Delta;[14] by 1999, when structural adjustment was in full swing, US experts were recommending that such private farms be given 'initial use' of the dwindling supplies of freshwater, and providing guidance on how to ensure exclusive leases on the farms were constructed and managed.[15] Fish farming is the commercial raising of fish inside enclosed tanks or cages; in Egypt, this translated into the transformation of the shorelines of the Delta lakes from public domain to corporate fortress, complete with armed guards and prowling dogs.[16] Businesses with the right connections, often NDP politicians and local bureaucrats, were in the best position to grab and defend the leases; in many cases they have since expanded their

farms well beyond their original sizes. Ordinary Egyptians, especially small-scale subsistence fishermen, have seen their access to the
lake restricted as a result and the delicate ecological balance of the
water has been shattered. Land reclamation on the lake's margins, in
part to provide the infrastructure for the fish farms, has destroyed
85 per cent of the lake's marshes and, as well as damaging the marine
environment, this has eroded the breeding and staging grounds for
several under-threat bird species, such as the ferruginous duck and
the little tern. 'The NDP government dried out the land for investment purposes,' says Rabaa Shahawy, a local activist. 'With official
help, tycoons were given hundreds of *feddans* on the edge of the lake
to turn into fish farms, and that destroys the lake's ecology which we
all rely on.'

I met Rabaa in the Mahsen Eissa coffee shop in el-Borg, back in
2012. The *ahwa* had a battered 25th January revolution sign tacked
to its steps and an Egyptian flag fluttering above the doorway; inside
posters of local celebrity Hamdeen Sabahi, a Mubarak-era opposition leader and post-Mubarak presidential candidate, were plastered
over every available piece of wall. Hamdeen (as he is universally
known) gazed out with a comforting smile from beneath a shelf housing the shisha pipes; he looked down authoritatively from a special
Hamdeen calendar pinned above the coal repository; his dreamy eyes
commanded adoration through a stack of coffee pots on the counter.
As I entered, a somewhat cumbersome sheikh winched himself up
and waddled past me towards the mosque across the road, yelling
praise for Hamdeen to no one in particular. Rabaa, middle-aged,
bearded and clad in a white pinstripe shirt overlaid with a black pinstripe jacket, nodded gravely as he stood up to receive me. 'Here,' he
declared, with appropriate bombast, 'Hamdeen is a red line.'

Rabaa's first task was to introduce me to the 'respectful revolutionaries of the Burullus rebel army', about twenty of whom were packed
into the *ahwa* and sitting all around us. Rabaa, who explained with
no little degree of pride that he was the commander of this unofficial
platoon, was a ball of grandiloquent energy; rarely, though, has a
general looked more at odds with his footsoldiers. The group around
us seemed almost exclusively comprised of sixty-something *m'assal*
('unflavoured tobacco') smokers who slumped semi-comatose on

benches in their *gallabeyas*, puffing silently on their shisha and responding with a glacial dip of the head whenever their exploits were fervidly recounted by their chieftain. 'In Burullus,' thundered Rabaa with a dramatic sweep of his arm, 'our entire existence has been a life of resistance, because our entire existence has been a life of repression.' The rebel army nodded imperceptibly, and took another drag on their pipes. That's when the stories began.

The location of Burullus, on the most central and northerly point of Egypt's landmass, has led to it being the gateway into the country for many an armed column over the centuries. Locals are rightly proud of their history of putting up anti-imperialist defences: in 1956, at the height of the Suez War, fishermen here played a key role in resisting British forces, and Burullus was the location for the legendary kamikaze lunge of Jules Yussuf Jamal, a Syrian – believed by some historians to be fictitious – who is said to have rammed his speedboat into an approaching French warship, sinking both and killing himself in the process. Those who go out on boats here are famed for their skill and courage, a reputation burnished in 2009 when two of them – Adl Mohammed Abaidi and Shahat Ragab Morzi, the latter only seventeen years old – helped outsmart a gang of Somali pirates who had taken them hostage in the Gulf of Aden. The story of their audacious escape features a satellite phone hidden in a wash bucket, bandanas that served as a secret signalling system, and a swashbuckling final showdown on deck.[17] 'Somali pirates have terrorized the whole world, including the Americans, yet Burullus fishermen brought them back in handcuffs,' declared Rabaa, prompting a quiet rumble of approval from his soldiers.

But it was something closer to home that put Burullus on the map in the twilight years of Mubarak Country. In the summer of 2007, around the same time that Qursaya's islanders were first beginning their fight against forced eviction, el-Borg's entire supply of piped drinking water was suddenly cut off for fifteen days. Three years earlier, under pressure from the World Bank, the government had consolidated water utilities into a single commercial holding company and moved it beyond parliamentary oversight. Now a separate board of directors was required to seek joint ventures with private companies and distribute water at a profit. The sector's workforce was reduced, domestic water prices rose, and the growing scarcity of freshwater from the Nile encouraged the new operators to funnel as much of it as possible towards high-value customers in the gated desert communities around Cairo and upmarket resort towns on the north coast, with concomitant cut-offs in poorer, rural settlements such as Burullus.[18] As rumours spread that those with high-level security contacts – or who could afford to bribe the right people – were enjoying access to a second, working water line, Rabaa and others met in the Mahsen Eissa coffee shop one morning at seven and decided to make a stand on the international coastal road, a major highway running east to west through the Delta which cut through the south of al-Borg town. 'We had reached the tipping point of our patience,' recalled Rabaa. 'The people of Burullus have been facing oppression for so long that our minds are wired to take the initiative and launch resistance when needed.'

The motley crew made its way through the populous Shouri neighbourhood, rounding up disciples to their cause. The first to join was the local bread shop owner, and more soon followed, including hundreds from surrounding villages who drove up in trucks. Many had already seen their incomes depleted by the government's effective privatization of their fishing lake, from which they had subsequently been excluded; the privatization of their drinking water, and now their exclusion from it in the middle of a baking summer, was the final straw. By the time it reached the coastal road the crowd was more than 3,000 strong. Residents swiftly rolled huge logs on to the tarmac, severing the motorway completely apart from a small gap through which demonstrators planned to let ambulances pass if needed. The ensuing traffic jam stretched for fifty miles and took fourteen hours to clear. With the presidential convoy due to drive along the highway later that day, security forces immediately deployed to the area and ordered everybody to disperse. The protesters refused. That same afternoon, miraculously, water returned to the pipes. 'We insisted on waiting a few hours to make sure it wasn't a trick, and then, at 8 p.m., we packed up our protest and reopened the road,' grinned Rabaa. Something small but substantial had just occurred; ordinary citizens, out of the gaze of the national media and with no NDP big-shots to protect them, had taken the law into their own hands, confronted the state and rectified a grievance. 'It raised our awareness regarding what we could achieve and gave us confidence to go out and do it,' confirmed Rabaa.

It gave others confidence as well. In an attempt to contain any unrest and cast events in Burullus as a purely local problem with a local solution – a classic exercise in separation mythology – Mubarak dismissed the governor of Kafr el-Sheikh, the governorate to which Burullus belonged. General Salah Salama, the former head of Egypt's State Security Investigations, was personally detested by many of the Burullus protesters; I was told he had rudely insulted many of them, and his departure was a cause for popular celebration. But if Mubarak thought that such a move would insulate the broader state from dissent, as it had done so many times before, he was mistaken. By the end of the summer, drinking water shortage and associated communal protests had spread to settlements in Cairo, Dakahlia, Gharbia, Minya, Qalyubia, Fayoum and Munifiya.[19] In the Giza neighbourhoods of Faisal and Haram, protesting locals mirrored the tactics in Burullus exactly, threatening to block the capital's ring road if supplies weren't restored immediately. In el-Marg, on the other side of the city, citizens eschewed security warnings and simply cut off the local highway – stranding an entire cavalcade of government ministers in the process. 'These events are a rebellion against the ruler, a disorganized revolution,' Dr Abd el-Wahab al-Masri, an, Egyptian intellectual, wrote in the independent newspaper *al-Masry al-Youm*.[20] 'Egypt is now witnessing a state of general desperation among the Egyptian people because of a government that has pursued a free-market policy and left people to the vagaries of supply and demand,' 'Asim al-Dassuqi, a contemporary history professor, warned in the same publication. '[The regime] is leaving the people to businessmen and investors, with no intervention to protect their rights.'[21]

The 'revolution of the thirsty', as the water protests were soon dubbed, took many observers by surprise, not least because it emerged amid an explosion of labour unrest that had already stunned Egypt and brought many workplaces to a standstill. Strikes and sit-ins had never been so prevalent, but still, they were hardly a new concept; these determined and confrontational communal protests, on the other hand, appeared to be of a different ilk – pitting regular Egyptians from all over the country against the state with alarming regularity. And the summer of 2007 proved to be only a dress rehearsal. The following year Kafr el-Sheikh's new governor took a unilateral decision to reform the local system of bread subsidies. The new rules prevented people buying discounted wheat themselves, forcing them to purchase subsidized pre-baked loaves from official bakeries instead. Under a different model of political governance, one in which the needs and perspectives of citizens were transmitted upwards to those taking executive decisions within the state, the governor would have quickly learned that although this rule change might have been logical in urban areas, in Burullus it could never work. The majority of men in the region are fishermen and spend days at a stretch isolated out on the water; their habit was to take wheat with them and bake their own bread on the boats, but now that option was being snatched away without any consultation. In properly functioning state, this misunderstanding could have been quickly rectified and exceptions to the new system established. But this was Mubarak Country, and so things played out in a very different way. 'We had been negotiating with the governor for a month, but nothing changed because the mentality of the regime was so rigid, so ignorant of ordinary people like us,' said Rabaa. 'It was the women who felt the impact of the bread crisis first, and they led the sit-in; spontaneously we all began to move towards the coastal road, as if that was now the natural thing to do when we were angry. No one had planned it, but you could feel the anger all around you. That's where the violence began.'

This time, the regime was ready. Riot squads were dispatched to the motorway and fired volleys of tear gas in an attempt to stop the community from blocking it; more than eighty people were injured in the ensuring clashes. 'They had their weapons, but we had the local intelligence,' Rabaa explained with a knowing smile. 'The fishermen of Burullus are very adept at understanding weather patterns, and through cat and mouse confrontations we managed to position ourselves so that we were upwind from the troops, and all the tear gas they fired blew back in their faces. They have their bombs and arsenals, we have our brains.' It took a hundred arrests and a region-wide curfew to break up the demonstration, but as with the 'revolution of the thirsty', Burullus's new 'revolution of the hungry' quickly spread.

In Fayoum, just south of Cairo, hundreds of rural women surrounded the governor's office over the failure to distribute subsidized flour effectively; across the rest of the country, eleven people died as a result of bread-related unrest.[22]

In Egypt's calamitous seven-year drought of 1065–72, bread prices soared to an unimaginable 12 dinars a loaf (the equivalent to about £130 today) and rumours abounded that some Cairenes were so desperate for food that they fitted meat hooks to ropes outside their windows and fished unlucky pedestrians off the street for dinner. At the height of the famine, one wealthy widow pawned a necklace worth 1,000 dinars; the payment she received was just enough to purchase one sack of flour, most of which was stolen by a hungry mob outside the city gates. With the small fistful she had left, the widow baked a biscuit which she then carried to the door of the Caliph's palace. 'People of Cairo!' she shouted to a gathering crowd. 'Blessings on our master al-Mustansir! Providence has proved the goodness of his rule, since I have bought this biscuit for 1,000 dinars!'[23]

Egyptians have never been afraid to expose the arrogance and failings of their rulers. The bread riots of 1977, after Sadat terminated subsidies under the orders of the IMF and World Bank, were a warning shot: citizens were capable of fighting back against the spread of any free market doctrine that denied them social and economic rights. 'Those of my age, we have this memory and we have kept it with us,' says Mohamed Abla, the Qursayan artist, who joined the protests in Alexandria back then and set about occupying tram stations, stopping traffic and destroying pictures of the president. 'It was something very strong. This is the generation that went on to lead the struggles of the 2000s, and 1977 was that germ of influence. We lodged it in our minds, we knew it was possible. We knew we could do it.' The governing class was adept at surviving such crises through a canny blend of co-optation and repression. But each cycle of contestation between citizens and the state emboldened Egyptians, and fleshed out the size, shape and vulnerabilities of their opponent. And by the 2000s, amid the neoliberal makeover of Mubarak Country, it wasn't just one large issue like bread prices that was galvanizing protest and educating communities in the practise of revolt, but countless smaller issues, all stemming from the chasm that stood between the nature of the state as it was and the nature of the state as Egyptian citizens needed it to be. Just as his participation in the unrest of 1977 gave Mohamed Abla the confidence to fight the army in 2007, so the battles of that later period laid down a path to the subsequent revolution.

Qursaya and Burullus are two examples of communal protests, but there were untold others: riots over butane prices in Sharqiya, clashes with police over unsafe housing in Alexandria, showdowns with security forces in the aftermath of fires in Sayida Zainab, demonstrations against poor sewage facilities in Giza, over rockslides in Duweiqa, against forced evictions and land speculation in Fakhariya, and many, many more. In 2009, a rumour spread through the informal settlement of Ezbet el-Haggana in Cairo that the entire district was about to be razed by the government. Thousands of residents took to the streets, and when Mubarak's anti-riot troops were deployed to contain them, Haggana locals responded with such fury that most security forces fled the neighbourhood in terror; some ended up under siege in a nearby police station, watching helplessly through the windows as their vehicles were burned to the ground outside. Add that to the resistance mounted by hundreds of rural villages like Sarandu against Mubarak's IFI-sponsored land reform, not to mention the workers' strikes, and the impression – sometimes given in the media – that Egypt was inert and its citizens docile until the day revolution exploded in January 2011 is rapidly exposed as baseless. Mubarak Country created so many marginalized spaces in which citizens had no choice but to fight in order to put themselves back on the map and survive that it became, simultaneously, Resistance Country, one in which every town, village, neighbourhood, office and factory in the land was a potential site of struggle. But for all this blossoming of localized unrest that forced the regime to play whack-a-mole on a near-daily basis, by the end of the decade protests in Egypt were still yet to coalesce into a unified assault on the state. For that to happen, something universal, an injustice that could be felt by every Egyptian citizen, no matter where they lived or worked, was needed. That injustice took place on 6 June 2010, when a young man named Khaled Said stepped out of his apartment near the Mediterranean seafront at Alexandria, and walked over to his local internet café.

6

Enough

Khaled Said was a quite young man and often preferred to spend time on his own than in the company of others. The 28-year-old had friends, and saw them regularly, but he was also devoted to his twelve pet cats (when times were hard, he sometimes skipped meals so that he could afford to buy them food) and enjoyed flying kites alone down on the Alexandrian beaches by his home. The air is lovely out here, despite the roar of traffic on the el-Geish road; if there's not too much haze, you can see all the way down the seafront to Ras el-Tin, the palace where Khedive Tawfiq took refuge during Colonel 'Urabi's rebellion all those lifetimes ago. The waves aren't big, but the rocks on the shore are uneven and so foam spills upwards where the water tumbles off sharp angles and into crevices. If you stand parallel to the coastline, and get it just right, you can barely hear anything but city noise on one side and almost nothing but an enormous, infinite silence on the other. Both feel equally loud as they press down upon your ears.

Khaled's family have kept his bedroom as it always was. It's small; his sister, Zahraa, had to stand back in the doorway to give me space to look around. Aside from the bed most of it is taken up by an intricate sound system, hand-spun out of car batteries and fragments of old radios. Khaled would practise rapping in here until the early hours, but he was usually too shy to perform in front of others. It was only later, after they retrieved his bashed and purpled body from the morgue, that family members searched Khaled's computer and found video recordings of him singing self-penned anti-government songs to the camera. They discovered something else too: footage of local police officers apparently dividing up the spoils of a drug haul between themselves – just before he was murdered, so the story goes,

Khaled had somehow obtained the footage and posted it online. 'It wasn't just a beating gone wrong, it was a public execution,' his mother, dressed all in black, told me in the front room. 'The officer was heard by witnesses phoning his superior and saying, 'It's done, the issue is over.'

'They killed him in broad daylight, and now they are going after young people everywhere,' she added, after a long pause. 'The youth have declared "We are all Khaled Said," that's their slogan, and the police are responding by saying, "yes you are – we will deal with you like we dealt with him." '

Sidi Gabr police station is a squat, two-storey building in the eastern part of the city. Locally, people call it the 'butchery'. One evening in June 2010, two officers set out from the station in search of Khaled. They found him sitting in an internet café, just down the road from his apartment. As they hauled him out and pummelled him to death in front of witnesses – his head was smashed repeatedly against a marble staircase in the lobby of the building next door – the officers had no reason to think that this particular act of state violence, in a country so abounding in acts of state violence, would attract undue attention. In the end though, it attracted a vast amount of attention – so much so that you can now find images of Khaled's face pasted into blog posts and daubed on to walls all over the world. Part of the reason for this was that Khaled came from a respectable middle-class background. The relatives of poorer victims of police brutality are usually easier for state security agents to intimidate into silence and their stories gain little traction in the media, but Khaled's family, while by no means well-off, felt economically secure enough to put themselves on the line and speak out. Another reason was that Khaled had no known affiliation to any particular religious or political movement; as he was unattached, everyone could claim him as their own. More importantly, Khaled's death attracted attention because it took place at a particular moment in Egypt, a moment in which, after all those labour strikes, all those communal protests, all that relentless inequality and economic hardship, the old rules just didn't seem to fit any more. In different ways, many people could feel that moment. It was taut and muffled rather than loud and all-looming, a vague staining of the atmosphere just waiting for a spark. The fate of Khaled

Said was one such spark. Slowly, but unstoppably, it helped set Egypt ablaze.

If you were a young person in Egypt in the late 1990s and wanted to demonstrate against the government, the choices available to you were pretty limited. The Muslim Brotherhood were large and well organized – but many of its cadres were in jail, and the movement's leadership ordered those still at liberty to shy away from direct criticism of the regime or its security forces. Sometimes, during protests, Brotherhood members tried to hush anyone who spoke out against state violence, or to drown them out with more supportive, pro-police chants.[1] Moreover, the Brotherhood were Islamist, which meant that unless you shared the movement's belief that the Quran should guide all areas of social and political life, signing up was hardly a viable option. Then there was the old left, comprising organization like el-Tagammu' and the Nasserite parties who occasionally staged tightly sealed spectacles of dissent on their office balconies in downtown Cairo. But many of their members looked as ossified as Mubarak, and their rhetoric was stale and often Stalinist – bound up in the ideological battles and personal gripes of a previous generation, not the struggles of today. Some of their leaders seemed more like pawns of the regime than adversaries of it: props in an elaborate piece of 'democratic' stagecraft designed to provide Mubarak with a fig-leaf of political plurality while closing down the space for genuine debate. The surge of labour actions and communal rebellions that shook Egypt in the late 2000s were still many years away, and difficult to engage with directly if you didn't work in a factory or office that was walking out on strike, or live in a village or neighbourhood that was facing down government forces. Protest, of the pro-change, pro-democracy sort that directly targeted the regime and its institutions, wasn't entirely unknown. But it was minimal, and constrained. When Hossam el-Hamalawy first began life as a student in 1995, he felt suffocated; it was hard to imagine how disconnected pockets of dissent might one day prise open their doors and start breathing in the streets. By the time Hossam graduated, all that had changed.

Hossam was the son of a university professor, and his family ranked among the educated middle classes that had seen their real-term incomes fall away under Mubarak's economic reforms – leaving them endowed with a social prestige that far outstripped their financial resources. 'My father had to enslave his arse at work to earn enough money to pay for my schooling,' remembers Hossam, who studied economics at the American University in Cairo (AUC), one of Egypt's top-ranking educational institutions. 'You had this two-tier student body at AUC: the children of the elite who had their Jaguars and Porsches in the car park, and then the kids of the civil servants and so on whose parents were spending two months ahead of every semester scraping, and saving, and doing endless calculations about how they were going to afford the fees.' Hossam was intellectually curious but found lectures a frustration: most of his professors stuck faithfully to the country's structural adjustment script, which meant that the public sector was almost always denigrated, privatization lauded, and discussion of economic alternatives virtually non-existent. Hossam wanted to know more about Egypt's big loan deals from the IMF and World Bank, but his probing questions – about conditionality and accountability, about whether or not these tranches of international financing were helping to pay for the government's highly aggressive 'dirty war' against Islamist insurgents in the country's south during the same period – were generally left unanswered. And outside the classroom, things weren't much better. University campuses were one of the few spaces in which the regime granted some limited leeway for political activism; by and large, students were able to hold meetings and even conduct small (and heavily policed) demonstrations, but only as long as they remained safely inside college walls, concentrated on foreign issues, and avoided drifting anywhere near sensitive red lines like the presidency. 'You knew exactly what the limits were: nothing domestic, nothing that involved stepping outside, nothing that had anything to do with police brutality or Mubarak – I mean, you could never even mention Mubarak's name,' says Hossam. 'If you strayed beyond that then you risked getting kidnapped, you risked getting shot.'

But forcing political subjects into neat little boxes and keeping them there is tricky: debates over flashpoints abroad quickly exposed contradictions and malpractices with roots much closer to home. Over time, students like Hossam who were interested in international affairs found themselves wandering on to dangerous terrain almost by accident, and it was a radicalizing experience. A student walkout in solidarity with Lebanon in 1999, when the country was under Israeli bombardment, led inevitably to discussions about Palestine and its geopolitical situation, which in turn shone a spotlight on Mubarak's government – a close ally of the Israelis. 'We found ourselves asking why our country was opening an embassy for Israel at a time when the Palestinians were still denied their own state,' recalls Hossam. 'Why is our government able to send troops to control our demonstrations on campus, but not send a single soldier to help the Palestinian cause? Why does Mubarak export cement to Israel, who will then use it to build settlements on Palestinian land? I think for lots of us on campus who were politically active at that time, this notion – that the road to Jerusalem lies through Cairo, that to liberate Palestine you have to liberate Egypt first – really began linking things up for us and training our attention on the regime here. You would be having a conversation about Gaza, and a few minutes later you were suddenly talking about bilharzia [a parasitic disease that has killed many Egyptian farmers] and the government's counter-insurgency tactics in Upper Egypt.'

Enthralled, Hossam became more active. He sought out like-minded members of the student body who were also eager to prod at the limits of 'acceptable' political activity. He joined the Revolutionary Socialists, an opposition movement that had a tiny yet committed presence at the university. And he almost cried when he was surreptitiously handed a copy of the organization's underground monthly magazine – *al-Ishtiraki al-Thawri* ('Revolutionary Socialism') – and came across the phrase 'Mubarak the dictator' for the first time in his life. 'Back then I never thought that I would ever see those words written down in Arabic on a page,' he says.

In September 2000, Israeli Prime Minister Ariel Sharon made a highly provocative visit to Jerusalem's Temple Mount, Palestinian demonstrators faced off with Israeli Defence Force soldiers, and the Second Palestinian Uprising began. Hossam was about to be exposed to many more unexpected things. Ripples from the intifada were felt across the Arab World; in Egypt those ripples sent protests tumbling out beyond the campus walls, and Hossam still recalls the chill that went down his spine when he first marched through the streets of downtown Cairo and heard chants comparing Mubarak to Sharon. 'It was something from another planet,' he grins. 'I was used to seeing twenty people marching – now it was thousands, and Mubarak was the target. I remember thinking, this is it. It felt like revolution was going to start the very next day.' In reality, it would take another decade for Mubarak to be toppled. But by escaping their regime-sanctioned protest ghettos, Hossam and others like him who mobilized over Palestine helped kick-start a wave of political activity in Egypt that over the coming years would sweep across a landscape littered with red lines – carving out a path to revolution in the process.

What emerged from the early Palestinian solidarity demonstrations was a long series of political tremors that openly pitted protesters against security forces in Egypt's streets, shattering illusions of grassroots apathy and helping to render the violence of the state frighteningly visible to many Egyptians who, up until that point, had rarely witnessed it with their own eyes. Only a fraction of the population were ever directly involved in these rallies and marches, but those involved punched above their weight. Initially confrontations were relatively brief and fuelled by events beyond Egypt's borders; with each fresh trigger point though, new protest norms were noisily established and the cross-hairs of resistance moved closer to the core of the Mubarakist state. The security services learned a lot during this period; manoeuvres carried out by Egyptian troops to break up protests a decade later during the revolution were honed throughout the early and mid-2000s: police vehicles driving in zig-zags through crowds of demonstrators to try to mow them down, armed police aiming their guns at civilians' eyes.[2] But activists learned a great deal too, not least how to tease out the state's weaknesses and test its resilience, as well as how to go about constructing a new political platform – something that was far removed from the moribund world of the official 'opposition' parties, something around which ideologically diverse and tactically disjointed individuals and movements could come together and collaborate. By the end of 2000, twenty NGOs and countless independent campaigners had pooled their resources to form the Popular Committee to Support the Intifada, an umbrella front which attracted leftists, Brotherhood members and Arab Nationalists alike and sent trucks seeking Palestinian solidarity donations out into some of the poorest neighbourhoods in the capital.[3]

After Palestine, the next convulsion arrived on 19 March 2003, when George W. Bush made a televised address to the American nation. 'My fellow citizens, at this hour American and coalition forces are in the early stages of military operations to disarm Iraq, to free its people and to defend the world from grave danger,' he announced from the Oval Office. 'These are opening stages of what will be a broad and concerted campaign.' In Egypt, activists called for a rally in Tahrir Square the following night to protest against the war and their own government's close ties with Washington. They expected a few hundred to attend; instead 40,000 showed up, occupying the square for more than twenty-four hours and chanting *el-shari' lina* ('the street is ours'). On the fringes of Tahrir, lines of riot troops amassed and waited for orders from a government that suddenly appeared uncertain; inside, posters of Mubarak were set on fire and further taboos went up in smoke. Eventually the square was cleared with brutal force, and a renewed backlash against all forms of street mobilization followed. But those twenty-four hours of occupation left an indelible impression on those that took part. 'After that, we felt like no matter how dark things were, we could always find room for manoeuvre,' said el-Hamalawy. One activist at the time declared gleefully: 'This is the first time we've made it out of the cage.'[4]

Although anger over international issues often mutated into domestic criticism of Mubarak's regime, it wasn't until 2004 that the president became an explicit target of a demonstration from the outset. On 26 June of that year UN's International Day in Support of Victims of Torture – 500 protesters broke new ground by gathering outside the general prosecutor's office in Cairo to denounce police abuse and regime violence within Egypt itself. They were quickly surrounded and penned in by a thick ring of security forces, but by taking the barbarism of Egypt's dictatorship as the starting point for a mobilization on the streets the event drove a huge leap forward in activist confidence. 'It was one of the first protests aimed – from the very beginning – at a domestic issue and the crimes of this regime, and it worked,' says Hossam. 'We were realizing that all regimes were susceptible to pressure. Even this one.' Less than three months later, seven veteran activists from different political backgrounds – among them Islamist, Coptic and Nasserite – had dinner together and floated the idea of building an organized front against Mubarak, one that would echo the Popular Committee to Support the Intifada, but this time with renewed focus on oppression here at home. By the end of 2004, Egypt's Movement for Change – which became better known by its main slogan, kifaya! ('Enough!') – had staged its first rally and issued a founding statement that drew a clear line from geopolitical unrest to the main institutions of Mubarak Country. 'We believe there are two grave dangers which beset our nation today,' read the statement, which attracted hundreds of signatories. The dangers, it went on to explain, were 'the odious assault on Arab native soil' and a 'repressive despotism' in Egypt which could only be addressed by removing the presidency's monopoly on power. 'They are two sides of the same coin, each nourishing the other and neither curable alone,' the statement concluded.[5]

Over the next two years, Kifaya reordered the topography of political dissent in Egypt. Its relatively non-hierarchical structure and cross-ideological support base reflected global protest trends in the 1990s and 2000s; activists on the left were increasingly moving away from rigid political party models aimed at seizing conventional power, and towards looser social movements within which autonomous elements could flourish.[6] In Egypt leftists and Islamists, long suspicious of each other's political activities, were now building coalitions. Under the umbrella of Kifaya, associational groups – 'Doctors for Change', 'Teachers for Change', 'Journalists for Change' – formed and brought professionals on to the streets. Tareq el-Bishry, a widely respected judge, called on Egyptian citizens to 'withdraw their long-abused consent to be governed'; a wave of sustained judicial activism quickly followed. Perhaps most significantly, Kifaya supporters mobilized in places previously thought of as off-limits to protesters: they arranged flash mobs in popular neighbourhoods, engaged in 'guerrilla' activism – where small groups of activists would flood public parks and plazas with flyers and attempt to engage passers-by in political discussion – and expertly exploited new media spaces which had been thrown open by the internet.

Kifaya's heyday coincided not just with the rise of blogs and social media (Hossam's website '3arabawy', which hosted photos and chronicles of opposition protests, became a key resource for campaigners), but with a small, limited flowering of privately owned mass-market media; new newspapers like *al-Masry al-Youm* used coverage of Kifaya to distinguish themselves from the state press, and some local satellite channels – not to mention foreign imports such as al-Jazeera – followed suit. Bodies on the ground were still few in number, but those involved now had a chance to reach millions more on their sofas at home. 'As someone who came from a slightly older generation where Mubarak had for so long been a red line,' says Hossam, 'I was shocked that all these kids were getting involved in Kifaya who weren't familiar with those taboos and had no fear when coming up with anti-regime initiatives.' Demonstrators marched through crowded Cairene neighbourhoods like Shubra chanting 'Down with Mubarak', and taunted the plain-clothes thugs who were paid by the state to confront them with songs alluding to their pay cheques: *'ya 'ishreen gineih, bit ooloo eih?'* ('Hey twenty pounds, what are you saying?') After initially ignoring the movement, Mubarak was eventually rattled enough to denounce it publicly; he accused Kifaya members of being the paid agents of foreign forces. 'I could have organized paid demonstrations to shout "not enough",' the president insisted defensively.[7]

Despite its prominence, Kifaya as an organized force was not long-lasting. Critics – from sections of the radical left as well as communities beyond Kifaya's heartlands of Cairo and Alexandria – accused it of being too middle class, too well educated and urbane, too disconnected from the daily lives of ordinary Egyptians. In truth, as neoliberal reforms intensified the economic privations suffered by most of the population, the tactical usefulness of an explicitly pro-democracy front simply began to fade, and other forms of protest – such as the mobilization of factory workers in Mahalla or the cutting of roads by villagers in Burullus – began to dominate the landscape of resistance instead. But the movement had served a crucial purpose, not least by normalizing the sight of opposition protest on Egypt's streets and visibly challenging the regime's grip over public spaces. The ugly frontline of Mubarak Country's political defences was no longer buried away in police station basements or behind the walls of state security headquarters out on the desert road; instead, ordinary

Egyptians saw uniformed agents of their government shoot and beat their fellow citizens in broad daylight – citizens who looked nothing like the terrorists the regime always claimed to be hunting down beyond the capital. 'By 5 p.m. on Saturday, Tahrir Square resembled a military zone,' began one domestic newspaper report on a Kifaya rally in 2005. 'Thousands of anti-riot police, special forces, hundreds of plain-clothes policemen, high-ranking police and State Security Investigations (SSI) officers were deployed in Tahrir and the surrounding streets. Khaki police trucks and armoured vehicles completed the picture.'[8]

The state was strong enough to see off Kifaya's troublemakers on a day-to-day basis, but each time it was forced to drag all this war furniture into the capital's commercial districts just to shut down a single demonstration, the existence of an alternative narrative – one that revolved around a fundamental reimagining of how power in Egypt was distributed – was simultaneously telecast to a considerable portion of the population, just at a time when Egyptians were beginning to search out non-state news sources for themselves. The equation of Mubarak with stability and Egyptians with political inertia – a familiar tune hummed by both regime supporters at home and Egypt's allies in the West, and sometimes repeated uncritically by the international media – was becoming harder to sustain, though that didn't stop the dictatorship's backers from trying. 'I'm pleased to welcome my friend, Hosni Mubarak, to my home,' beamed George W. Bush from his Crawford ranch in 2004, before going on to praise Mubarak's 'years of effort on behalf of the peace and stability of the Middle East'.[9] In 2006, the BBC marked twenty-five years of Mubarak's rule with a profile declaring that the president 'probably does enjoy huge support in the Egyptian street', adding, for good measure, that he had 'presided over a period of domestic stability and economic development that means most of his fellow countrymen have accepted his monopolization of power in Egypt'.[10]

That piece was published in the aftermath of the unprecedented labour strikes in Mahalla, the continuation of violent struggles between *fellaheen* and landlords in the countryside, and an anti-government demonstration outside the Judges' Club in Cairo that brought thousands of riot troops on to the streets and saw uniformed police clubbing protesters and journalists in broad daylight. As unrest spread, it seemed, in some quarters at least, only to grow more invisible. 'Why does the myth of passive, politically apathetic Egyptians refuse to die?' asked Egyptian blogger Baheyya at the time. 'Stupid and false mantras, parroted often enough and by ostensibly learned people, will stick and spread like thick algae over a deep pond. Fortunately, however, algae have no roots, leaves, or stems. So even if they spread and multiply, they can always be easily brushed aside to reveal the crystal-clear water underneath. As Egypt's streets are once again enlivened and energized by collective action and protest, and a thousand reform manifestos bloom, and people demand unconditional democracy, the algae-peddlers and hawkers will work overtime to spread their concealing, falsifying fare. Brush them aside.'[11]

Although he didn't realize it at the time, when Hossam first began his tentative conversations about Palestine and bilharzia with fellow students back in those early university days, he was contributing to the start of a political protest movement that would, along with the other strands of anti-regime resistance, ultimately churn the cornerstones of the Egyptian state. From the Nile-side clubs where Egypt's elites rubbed elbows and relaxed, the water looked calm and the sweet tea was served as efficiently as ever. But in places like Sarandu, Qursaya and the Cairo University hall where Bilal Diab roared out his challenge to Prime Minister Ahmed Nazif, streets and minds were being contested and the tumult was growing stronger. It's not that Egypt's political power-brokers couldn't feel it – only that they couldn't silence it. The ruling class, emboldened by steadfast international support, was not about to abandon an exclusionary, patriarchal state that had worked so relentlessly, for so long, in its favour. A diet of limited concessions, co-optation and violent repression had succeeded in warding off trouble in the past; surely it would work again. The club members thought this old-school armoury would be enough to shield their world from change, that the fear barrier would stand firm. They hoped there would be no tipping point to prove them wrong. They hoped in vain.

'We thought they would just interrogate him,' said Hassan Mosbah, the owner of the internet café from which Khaled Said was dragged by policemen on 6 June 2010. 'But they took him as he struggled with his hands behind his back and banged his head against the marble table inside here.'[12] Mosbah went on to explain how Khaled was pulled into the lobby of the building next door, from which he never came out alive. An investigation into Said's death by the Egyptian Organization for Human Rights revealed that two passers-by, who happened to be doctors, attempted to revive the unconscious young man when they saw him on the floor. Even as they did so, the two officers carried on battering his corpse. Other locals who saw what was happening were too scared to intervene.

It didn't take long for photos of Said in the morgue – his skull and jaw fractured, his face shredded and mangled almost beyond recognition – to start circulating on social media. When the ministry of interior put out a statement claiming that Said was a deserter from the army and a drug user, activists dismissed it as a lie and held a demonstration outside the ministry headquarters calling for the minister – the notorious Habib el-Adly – to resign. In the scuffles that followed, many, including Hossam el-Hamalawy, were attacked by security forces in the streets. Within weeks the *Kullna Khaled Said* – 'We are all Khaled Said' – Facebook page, secretly administered by a young Egyptian journalist named Abdelrahman Mansour and the Egypt-born, Dubai-based Google executive Wael Ghonim, had attracted hundreds of thousands of supporters. Members of the group began to come together in creative ways that would maximize public sympathy and draw the starkest line possible between the behaviour of protesters and the police: filling a public square to sing the national anthem, for example, or stretching out across the seafront in silence, each person wrapped in the Egyptian flag. Whatever they did, wherever they did it, Mubarak's security forces would, without fail, find them, stop them and beat them.

Kullena Khaled Said resonated with many Egyptians because it didn't rest on specificities; if you didn't have experience of working in a textile mill or resisting eviction from an *'ashwa'iyat* neighbourhood, then conflict there was easier to explain away – but encounters with the police were universal. The regime spent twice as much money subjugating its citizens as it did on providing them with healthcare, and under permanent Emergency Law the shadow of an arbitrary and unaccountable security apparatus touched most corners of the country.[13] At one time or another almost everybody had been stopped and humiliated at a police checkpoint, held their tongue when being forced to pay a bribe to a traffic marshal, moved quickly away from a commotion in the street for fear of being scapegoated when the security forces arrived. Everyone knew too that people sometimes disappeared into police stations or state security buildings and never came out.* Between April 1993 and April 2004 there were 532 recorded cases of police torture, 120 of which resulted in death (the actual numbers are likely to have been much higher); during one fifty-day period alone, coinciding with the NDP's annual conference in 2005, ninety citizens were tortured by the security services, seven of whom died.[14] Videos – of a child arrested for stealing a teabag who later died from electrocution burns, of a microbus driver who tried to intervene in a dispute between his relative and a police officer and ended up being sodomized with a stick – circulated freely on a growing number of internet sites dedicated to their exposure. People knew it happened, they just never thought it would happen to them. But Khaled Said – the an impeachable, well-mannered youth from a respectable family – really could have been them, or their son, or brother, or cousin. 'We are all Khaled Said' wasn't just a slogan, it was a devastating statement of fact.

After the diffuse convulsions of the past decade, one could argue that Egyptians needed Khaled Said to tie it all together; that if he hadn't been murdered, legend would have had to conjure his story into existence regardless. In some ways, that is exactly what happened. Said was undoubtedly killed at the hands of a rotten police state, and his death was unquestionably a gross injustice. In the aftermath of that atrocity, though, a portrait of Said emerged that in its saint-like purity and straightforwardness could never do justice to a real, complex human life. The actual Khaled Said, rather than the beatified version of him that was adopted by many who were desperate to see change in Egypt, had gone AWOL during his mandatory

---

* Of course, it was the regime's adroit maintenance of a large and thinly veiled state torture apparatus that made it such an attractive partner to the Americans during the CIA's extraordinary rendition programme.

military service and did take drugs; his family apartment in Alexandria, which Said often had sole use of while his relatives stayed in Cairo, became a regular hangout for a motley assortment of shady friends.[15] Acquaintances who have looked carefully into the circumstances surrounding his killing are sceptical of the idea that it resulted from the posting of a video depicting police corruption, as textbook as that explanation sounded. Some think Said really was in possession of *bango* (low-grade cannabis) when the officers caught up with him, and that he had been set up deliberately by a contact who was working as a police informant; the cops were always on the lookout for drug arrests to fill quotas, or to earn bribes, or sometimes to establish a hold over certain individuals which could then be exploited in the future, and this arrest may have simply, and horrifically, gone too far when Said, quite rightly, resisted. None of these facts remotely justifies his fate, but they were all airbrushed out of the picture in the summer of 2010 as a complicated, troubled young man in life became a parable of virtue in death.

The transformation was, perhaps, an inevitable one given the role Said unknowingly played in unravelling Mubarak's dictatorship in that final, heady year. Once protests over the murder began to spread and exposed a chink in the regime's armour, few people outside government circles had any interest in correcting the myth of the perfect martyr, and so understandably it intensified and proliferated. 'The stage was set, the script was written, and it now awaited the "appropriate" actors to show up and play out their assigned roles,' observes Amro Ali, an Egyptian political analyst who was a neighbour and contemporary of Said's, and who has written extensively on the construction of his legend. The 28-year-old 'became the answer to redress all the lives taken away and injustices suffered in the past . . . Khaled became the human face of Egypt's tragedy, [and] also its digital youth.'[16] As Ali has observed, other victims of police killings in Egypt – many of them less 'fashionable' owing to their poverty, geography, religion or gender – have never been afforded the attention and veneration bestowed upon this single case. Said's story speaks volumes about the social filters all of us, including progressive anti-government activists, deploy when highlighting state abuses which – through the tragedy of their regularity – have somehow to be ranked and sifted.

Perhaps the saddest aspect of the mythology surrounding Khaled Said is that the real man who died had far more in common with most young Egyptians than the flawless cipher which replaced him, and symbolized the perversity of Mubarak's Egypt in a much sharper way. Educated, frustrated and thirsting for a getaway, Said, like millions of his peers, saw no future for himself in the country of his birth; he lived in Alexandria, once one of the world's greatest metropolises, yet according to his Facebook page yearned to emigrate to its namesake, Alexandria Bay in New York. He fled army conscription because most conscript duties are hard, futile and punitive; drugs, and the internet, were a source of escapism, and marriage seemed like a distant dream. Like everyone in Mubarak Country, Said deserved so much more.

As 2010 rolled on and the air grew tighter, Egypt's absurdities seemed to vibrate at an even higher pitch than usual, and citizens were fighting back. Fury over the government's corrupt and inequitable urban development projects, including the cut-price land sales through which mammoth satellite cities such as New Cairo and 6th October had been created, escalated. A campaigning lawyer named Hamdy el-Fakharany launched a series of lawsuits over the sales; as a result, the flagship Madinaty complex was ruled by a judge to be illegal.* Having launched the New Valley Toshka Lakes project several years earlier in a blaze of publicity, the regime was by now desperate for everybody to forget about it: state media reports on the topic had dwindled to near-zero. But Egyptians refused to forget. In those final months, before everything changed, online searches for Toshka and the New Valley were ninety times higher than the average in previous years; at his regime's moment of crisis, Mubarak's pyramid was coming back to haunt him.† Meanwhile, amid all the fallout from Khaled Said's murder, the officers of Sidi Gabr police

---

* Hisham Talaat Moustafa, director of Madinaty's parent company TMG, had by this stage already been found guilty of arranging the murder of his Lebanese pop star girlfriend. TMG's lawyer argued that Fakharany's legal challenges would frighten off foreign investors and 'open the gates of hell'; Prime Minister Ahmed Nazif concurred, warning that Egypt would be committing 'economic suicide' if any land sales were annulled.

† During the eighteen-day anti-Mubarak uprising itself, Egyptian online interest in Toshka was 20,000 per cent higher than usual.[17]

station proved that their methods were unchanged and their spirit unbowed. In early November, the body of nineteen-year-old Ahmed Shaaban was found floating among the reeds of the Mahmoudia Canal, the channel into Alexandria along which Colonel Vyse had met his end 138 years previously. Shaaban had been picked up by police as he made his way to a wedding; officers claimed he had deliberately drowned himself – in water so shallow that it could barely have reached his knees. A few days later, Shaaban's uncle stood in front of a local journalist's video camera and addressed Mubarak directly. 'You are at war with your own people,' he said softly. 'Your gang is running loose killing citizens, and all you care about is the presidential chair.'

I sought out those who had seen the inside of Sidi Gabr's cells and found Mohamed Ibrahim, an electrician, who had been talking on his mobile in the street one day when a group of officers suddenly bundled him into a Toyota van. On the butchery's upper floor they had strapped him down, stretched his leg out and stamped down on it, snapping the bone in two places. 'I immediately felt numb and let out a scream, but it was like shouting into the desert,' Ibrahim told me from his bed, in a tiny apartment he shared with his elderly mother. His face was cut and bruised, and his leg in a cast and bandaged. 'Nothing I could say had any impact: they just kept yelling the most terrible insults, kept on proving their power over me.'[18]

At the end of the month, with speculation mounting that Hosni Mubarak was preparing to bequeathe the presidency to his son Gamal, the NDP engineered itself 97 per cent of the vote in the first round of parliamentary elections. As Egypt teetered, the message from the patriarch was clear: I may be old, but I will set the terms of my own departure and there will be no vacuum for you to fill. The fences we have built around this state will remain intact, he seemed to say: no compromise, no opposition, no surrender. I thought about the words of Zahraa, Khaled Said's sister. 'Change will not come from this government's version of democracy, it will come in the shape of a tidal wave from below,' she had suggested, as she stood on the apartment balcony looking down towards the sea. 'Maybe the torture and murders carried out by our policemen will set that tidal wave in motion.'

That winter was the chilliest I'd experienced in my time in Egypt. Street vendors hawked richly patterned blankets folded into cellophane suitcases; in the markets, boxes containing Chinese-made electric heaters were stacked atop one another in precarious jumbles. Up high, above the city's heaving tower blocks that stood sentinel against the worst of the cold, the wind often lashed with a ferocious bite. In January I visited my friend Waleed Shamad, who lived with his parents on a downtown rooftop, and we sat with scarves around our faces looking out over an apricot dusk, talking about weddings and revolution. Almost 1,500 miles away, Mohamed Bouazizi had finally died of the burns sustained from his self-immolation outside the governor's office in Sidi Bouzid, Tunisia; following weeks of street protests, the country's president, Zine El Abidine Ben Ali, had fled the country by plane. From our vantage point that evening, looking west towards the Nile, the Sahara and – far beyond – a liberated Tunisia, the Egyptian capital below felt tranquil. But there were fires burning around us too, and they were engulfing our conversations: over shisha, during football matches, and up here on the parapet as we sipped cans of pineapple fizz and watched the sun disappear behind a smoggy horizon.

According to a television newsreader, the latest Egyptian to set himself ablaze was a 35-year-old who had moved to the capital some time earlier in the hope of finding work and saving enough money to buy a home and get married. The lack of job opportunities had driven him to despair; he had doused himself in petrol and lit a flame – the twelfth such incident that week. Al-Azhar released a statement reiterating Islam's opposition to suicide, the Egyptian government issued new restrictions on the purchase of bottled gasoline, and Finance Minister Youssef Boutros-Ghali – the man who once blithely insisted that Mubarak's regime had 'taught the Egyptians to accept anything' – dismissed any suggestion of the immolations leading to revolt. 'It's an attempt to imitate things that won't happen in Egypt,' he said. 'Egyptians are different from Tunisians.'[19] Yet still, the fires kept coming. 'That could have been any of us,' said Waleed, when we talked about the conditions, the frustration and the feeling of hopelessness – or was it hope? – that could drive somebody to such an act. The son of Sudanese migrants, Waleed had lived all twenty-seven years of his life under the presidency of Hosni Mubarak; like so many of his contemporaries, he was university-educated, still living in the family home – in his case a set of thin-walled rooms constructed unofficially on the rooftop – still unmarried, still relying on scraps of informal work here and there to get by. Waleed didn't like the idea of anyone taking their own life, but he shared the pain of those who had tried to do so. 'Not having a regular job affects every aspect of your life practically and psychologically; almost everybody I know of my age is still unmarried and dependent on their families – it makes you feel hopeless,' he explained. Tunisia, he told me, was a counterweight to that desperation, an antidote to torpor. 'I'm so proud of the Tunisian people. When you see a friend or brother succeeding in some great struggle, it gives you hope, hope for yourself and hope for your country.'

I asked Waleed if he was going to attend the anti-Mubarak protest that had been planned for Egypt's Police Day – a national holiday aimed at celebrating the country's noble and patriotic security forces. On the *Kullena Khaled Said* Facebook page, where the demonstrations had been publicized, people were calling it 'Revolution Day' and posting bullish comments: 'If Tunisia can do it, why can't we?' read one. 'We will either start living or start dying on January 25th.' Waleed shrugged. His group of friends made no attempt to disguise their latent hostility to the regime – indeed, they revelled in it. But the risks of active opposition appeared too high, the personal costs too great, the prospect of success too slender. Could 25 January tip the scales? 'It's not as if we want to sit here passively and accept the situation,' Waleed insisted, defensively. 'The problems come from the government, but the instinct of our generation is to avoid the state, not confront it. I know that there are big demonstrations planned for next Tuesday, but we're taught from birth to be fearful of the police. They know how to hurt you, and hurt the ones you love.' Besides, 25 January was the day of our friend Gomla's wedding, he reminded me. And no one misses a wedding.

A few days before 25 January, I drove to Mahalla to watch a group of activists affiliated with the April 6th movement try to drum up support for Revolution Day. 'April 6th' was a youth organization that took its name from the date of the proposed general strike in April

2008, the day in which Mahalla began its own short-lived intifada; its members understood the importance of links between the restless labour movement and pro-democracy, pro-change political activists who tended to move and campaign in different circles. But those links were still tenuous, and no one could say how many workers would mobilize on the 25th. I watched the young people meet up with a group of local political elders in the city from the established – and discredited – formal opposition parties. The veterans advised them against holding up banners and chanting in the streets that day; the youth activists broke away to hold their own discussion, and then politely announced their intention to ignore the elders' advice. They stood around Mahalla's main square, flagging down motorists and handing out leaflets urging people to protest on Police Day. Some passers-by were curious, others hostile. Many expressed sympathy, but warned of chaos. 'I've never been on anything like this before, although my brother's friend was attacked by police back in April 2008,' said one 26-year-old motorbike rider after he stopped to see what all the commotion was about. I asked him if he'd go along, and he looked unsure. 'Circumstances have got pretty bad now, and I think changing the big sharks at the top is probably the only way we can make things better. I'll try and make it.'

The demonstration in Mahalla that day was never more than fifty-strong, but after leaving the streets the activists whooped, hollered and high-fived each other, their faces flushed with excitement. They finished up by singing the Tunisian national anthem, which ends with the words: 'When the people will to live / Destiny must surely respond / Oppression shall then vanish / Fetters are certain to break.'* Driving back to Cairo that evening, I allowed a little bit of myself, for the first time, to believe. Maybe, I thought. Just maybe.

The morning of the 25th felt bright, and expectant. I woke up to a text from Waleed, telling me not to forget about Gomla's wedding. I promised I'd try to make it. In the end though, I never did.

---

* Several different translations of the poem by Abu al-Qasim al-Shabbi on which the Tunisian national anthem is based are in circulation, and the differences between them are significant.[20]

7

'The streets are ours'

My notebooks are as raw as my memories. Two of the spiral-bound ones are twisted, their spines dislocated from the pages; when you pick them up, they spill sheets carelessly upon the table. The handwriting is hurried, messy – words have been snatched hastily to the paper amid drumbeats and shouts and gas and flight, and they've brought bits of that universe with them: grubby stains, smears of rock dust, strange ink. Pens were dropped all the time in the struggle and new ones borrowed, so sentences appear in different colours and some of them are splotched by teardrops. Many pages are torn, and a few are missing. It's as if the notebooks refused to stand separate, refused to seal themselves off into tidy organs of record while revolution raged around them. During those eighteen days in Tahrir, I filled five journals with thoughts, quotes, yelled names and scribbled phone numbers. With most shops closed, stationery supplies were hard to come by so I had to make do with whatever was available. The last notebook is actually an address book grabbed from an empty hotel gift shop, a preposterous-looking substitute with tan stitching across the cover and gold leaf daubed around the edges. Because it was designed for Arabic script and I write my notes in English, I flipped the address book over before using it – inadvertently upending a map of the globe printed on the first page. I don't remember when, but at some point during the uprising – maybe in a quiet corner of a field hospital as I waited to speak to a harried, blood-spattered volunteer doctor, or maybe crouched and panting behind a makeshift barricade, gulping down water offered by a stranger – I wrote in big letters across that map: 'The World Turned Upside-Down'. The words are underlined with such intensity that the pen's nib has punctured the paper.

Or maybe it was when I found myself sitting alone on the floor of an upstairs room, inside the house on the corner. The house is old, at least a century old and maybe much older, but I don't know anything about its history, nor do the neighbours I've asked. It sits, abandoned, at the end of the alley which leads off from my street, and commands a fine view: the criss-cross flyovers of Abdel Munim Riyad, the terracotta walls of the Egyptian Museum, and the wide, multi-laned approach road to Tahrir. It must have once been a grand residence, for there is a marble staircase – each slab now mottled and cracked, or occasionally absent altogether – and huge tiled windows, the glass in them long broken. On the outside of the building, there are gargoyles peering out of the stucco. For years, before the revolution started, I walked past those gargoyles each morning and wove them unconsciously into my sense of time and place in Egypt: they were the watchmen of my walk home, the reference point of a departing lover's final text message, the silent audience to a dozen moments of private joy, or loss, or validation, or depression, or everyday unkempt ordinariness. They belonged to me in a doggedly personal way, the same way that the cigarette kiosk on the opposite pavement and its surly teenage vendor and his ringtone collection and the argument we once had about Marlboro *abyad* belonged to me, the same way the clothes shop a bit further down Mahmoud Bassiuny Street and its ragged mannequins and hand-painted discount signs belonged to me, the same way that all those things belonged uniquely to anybody who ever moved through that little patch of the city. The same way the stuff of the streets, any streets – their objects, their furniture, their roughage, and all the silly and epic thoughts we individually infuse them with – belong, in distinct and identical ways, to everyone.

And now those same building-blocks that we all use to envision and understand our immediate environment, to root ourselves within it, had been transformed into something else. The clothes-shop shutters had been wrenched off their hinges to serve as a rampart against crude missiles. The cigarette kiosk was a gunman's shield. And the house on the corner was a guerrilla base, the farthest outpost of a dishevelled, heroic network of defences for the square. Young people smashed rocks against the ground and formed lines to carry heavy bags of stones up to the rooftop, where make-do military commanders – an agronomist, a university lecturer, a mechanic – tried to strategize and marshal our revolutionary energy. Everything was make-do, because make-do is all you have when you try to make and do something entirely new against the forces of old. I joined the rock-carrying line and pitched in right at the doorway to the house, just below the gargoyles, because like my notebooks I couldn't seal myself off into something separate, something objective, from the beautiful thing that was happening around me. And then I went inside, and found an empty room, and sat on the floor, and wrote. I wrote while the chaos of battle, of revolution echoed around me.

Those days turned the wide world upside down, and they turned our own, intimate worlds upside down, and sometimes – amid the adrenaline, and the pain, and the hope, and the fear – it was hard to know the difference.

The marches broke through police lines on 25 January, again and again, in Shubra, and Sayeda Zainab, and Giza, and Ramses; so many marches and so many broken police lines that everyone's geography – the security state's geography, the protesters' geography – got smudged. Those were the first hours, and for some they were perfect. 'My dream is to live like this, breaking through police lines,' a young man called Ahmed Ashraf told me, grinning. He worked in a bank, and I met him for about twenty seconds on the corner of Qasr el-Alyni, as we surged back and forth through the tear gas, backing away when the police lines charged, then reforming and charging ourselves to repel them from the square. I never saw him since. He was one of hundreds of Egyptians I would meet in the following days, weeks and years in the din of street-fighting, where there is no time for a proper chat, no time for in-depth interviews, no time for sober analysis. Just two strangers, a pair of lives intersecting at a revolution and finding a way to help one another with no questions asked or explanations provided; just a few words exchanged, and – if I was lucky – the barest of biographical details. The revolution has provided Egypt with millions of these moments, tiny irrepressible political grenades that detonate inside the imagination and make you look at the people around you, and the systems you live under, and your power to change them, with wiser, brighter eyes. Youssef Hisham, a 25-year-old filmmaker, provided another of those moments soon afterwards, when the security forces retreated from Tahrir and – for a few hours – *el-shari' lina*, the streets were ours, and I went wandering around the square, drinking it all in. 'I don't belong to anything, just Egypt,' Youssef told me, unprompted, as we passed each other on the grass. 'Here, we are in the centre of everything.'

The Egyptian state could not leave its people at the centre of everything for long. Communications were patchy, so in the early evening of that first day I left Tahrir to find a working computer and file my newspaper story. When I came back out into the streets at Abdel Munim Riyad, a vehicle nearby was engulfed in flames and something had shifted; a human wave was rolling out from the square and crashing towards me, and before I could move it had swallowed me up and there were shouts and bodies everywhere, and then the briefest, eeriest emptiness as it thundered past and left me standing alone on the tarmac. Then, suddenly, two men – burly, leather jackets – were on me, a blizzard of punches and kicks. They hauled me from the ground and frogmarched me behind police lines, slapping the back of my neck with metronomic regularity. As we walked, other security agents milling about – strutting, sweating, puffed up with their reclamation of this space from the interlopers – took turns to run up and aim flying kicks at my stomach. They took me to their makeshift holding pen, one of dozens that must have sprung up across the country that night. This one was the ground-floor lobby of an apartment building on the edge of Abdel Munim Riyad, right next to the cigarette kiosk, opposite the house on the corner. Other captured protesters were also being shuttled towards the doorway, where two lines of central security forces waited with sticks. One by one we were made to run, stumble and crawl through a gauntlet of beatings to reach the lobby inside. The furniture of the familiar yanked into something new. As I ran, stumbled and crawled, those gargoyles looked on.

We were made to stand silently in a line facing the wall; any who tried to turn around, or sobbed too loud, or recited Quranic verses, or ventured a shout of defiance would have their heads smashed from behind against the brickwork, or were simply dragged away. The rest of us just stood, and waited. Eventually we were told to sit. Then they hauled us outside again, one by one, back through the gauntlet, and into a dark green police truck, banging our heads on the metal frame as we were forced in. It was dark inside, and stacked with a heap of humanity, bleeding and bruised. Someone heard an officer count us: we were forty-four in all, herded into a space that could comfortably fit no more than ten. The heavy metal door swung shut and was locked behind us, and then, after a pause, the truck began to move. There were no windows, just a handful of thick metal grates through which orange streetlight would occasionally stream and dance across our faces. They had taken the wallets and phones of most of us back in the lobby, including mine, but a few had somehow kept their mobiles hidden and my dictaphone was still in my pocket; I took it out, and began recording.[1]

Despite the violence, people were excited, giddy even. Those who collapsed from the suffocating heat were helped to their feet; messages of support were whispered, then spoken, then yelled from one side of our mobile jail to the other. 'The police attacked us to get us out of the square; they didn't care who you were, they just attacked everybody,' a lawyer standing next to me, Ahmed Mamdouh, said breathlessly when I asked him to speak into the recording device and explain what was happening. 'They . . . hit our heads and hurt some people. There are some people bleeding, we don't know where they're taking us. I want to send a message to my wife; I'm not afraid but she will be so scared, this is my first protest and she told me not to come here today.' Later he told me: 'As I was being dragged in, a police general said to me: "Do you think you can change the world? You can't! Do you think you are a hero? You are not!" ' We swayed silently for a bit, letting the throb of the truck's engine and the moans of the injured wash over us. 'I think he's wrong,' said Ahmed, finally. 'I think we're changing the world right now.'

We wended our way at high speed through the city, each sharp turn and bump in the road flinging us wildly into the floor, ceiling, walls and each other. With no windows, navigation was hard but others were able to spot an occasional identifying landmark through the metal grilles and realized we were heading out of town, into the desert. On more than one occasion, the truck stopped, the single door was opened, and armed police appeared at the entranceway, shouting into our throng for 'Noor'. Noor was the son of Ayman Nour, a prominent political figure who had challenged Mubarak for the presidency in 2005 and been thrown into jail for his troubles, becoming something of a *cause célèbre* at the time. His prominence in influential diplomatic circles meant that the arrest of his son was likely to provoke more trouble for the Mubarak regime than it was worth; orders had seemingly come down from on high for Noor – and Noor alone – to be released. But Noor, with a dignity and calm that moved me deeply, refused to leave unless all of us were freed alongside him. Frustrated, the officers swore and slammed the metal door shut again, and we continued our journey into the unknown. Before that evening I had never met Noor, though I have since come to know him as a committed and courageous revolutionary. I'll never be able to tell if his insistence on remaining with us that night saved our lives, but two and a half years later – after thirty-seven prisoners locked in a police truck suffocated to death when an officer threw a tear gas canister inside[2] – I began to think it might have.

By the time we reached our destination – state security headquarters in Obour, a satellite conurbation deep in the desert fringes – the heat was unbearable and many of my fellow prisoners were in a bad way. Some had lost large amounts of blood, and others had fainted. One was struggling desperately to breathe; those with medical experience shouted at everyone to give him space and some air, and warned that he was slipping into what looked like a diabetic coma. For an hour we hammered on the insides of the now-stationary truck and screamed out, 'Help, a man is dying in here'; for an hour we were met with nothing but silence, interrupted only by short bursts of rhythmic banging on the truck's outside walls – the security forces trying to disorientate and intimidate us. Then commotion, and the truck began to tip violently from side to side. In the frenzy, a resolution was made to charge at the door if it opened at any stage, no matter who or what was on the other side. We heard the lock turning, and those at the front steeled themselves for a leap into a different kind of darkness. A police officer appeared and for a moment we all locked eyes with him; then he made a grab for the nearest inmate and began to haul him out for another round of beatings. With a cry, we surged forwards and knocked him flat, before spilling out past the watching troops and into the desert night. The diabetic was carried from the truck. With their quarry fanning out across the sand and cars rapidly approaching – Noor's family had got wind of his location and sent out a rescue party – the police reluctantly withdrew back into their security building. It had been only a momentary insight into the underbelly of Mubarak Country, the briefest of windows on to a violence that was commonplace for thousands of Egyptians stuck on the wrong side of the police state. But it brought home to me what was happening that day, what was being fought against and how fiercely that enemy would defend itself.

That night, the state newspaper *al-Ahram* ran a front-page story describing the many visits made by ordinary members of the public to police stations throughout the day in order to hand bouquets of flowers to officers and thank them for all their work. Such is the absurdity of power on the brink of collapse: its most violent impulses are exposed as the froth drains away, and so are its most comical unrealities. On the outskirts of el-Obour, we found ourselves many miles from home, shorn of money and mobiles, with no idea of what was happening back in Tahrir. But we knew we were free. And we knew that something ferocious, colossal and indescribable had started.

The building that stands at number 26 Ramses Street is twelve storeys high. We're not sure exactly what floor houses the central internet exchange – the place which fibre-optic cables carrying virtually all of the web traffic between Egypt and the rest of the world run into – and we don't know exactly how those cables were shut down. Engineers could have tampered with the software mechanisms that manage the network, or they may have simply turned off the power to the massive router banks which the system relies upon to stay functional.[3] Either way though, shortly after midnight on Friday 28 January 2011, someone at 26 Ramses Street found a way to hit the off switch. We like to think of the internet as something almost intangible, and thus inexplicably robust – no single person, or government, could ever reach all those infinite nodes and lines, those humming servers and vast grids of data; no single entity could ever turn out all those lights. But in Egypt, someone did. Within minutes, citizens of one of the most densely wired, technologically advanced countries on the planet were digitally severed from the rest of the world, and from each other. It didn't matter. They came out and made a revolution anyway.

Twelve hours later, I was sitting with an eye surgeon outside el-Istiqama mosque in Giza, waiting for the end of *el-zuhr*, the midday prayers. His name was Dr Gihad el-Nahary, and he told me he was here to liberate his country. 'I missed my chance to revolt before,' he said with a playful smile. 'I'm not going to make the same mistake now.' The streets around us were hushed and stiff, lined with police truck after police truck, so many they looked like toys. Inside the mosque, and on the grassy hillock outside it, the faithful worshipped. From atop the motorway flyover that ran level with our position and among the huge stone pillars below the security forces watched, and waited. Soon the sky would be fat with smoke and tear gas, shouts and explosions, sirens and whistles. But that moment, just before the prayers ended, was still, completely still. 'People don't just live on bread, they live on liberty,' said Gihad. He was fifty-two years old and he seemed unnervingly peaceful and content, his eyes half-closed and face thrust up to the sunlight, as though he'd been waiting for this his entire life. Later I heard many Egyptians use those exact words to describe their feelings that day, but Gihad was the person who seemed physically to embody the sentiment most completely. 'We don't need leaders, we are the leaders,' he added, eyelids still shuttered, head angled to the sky. They were the last words he spoke to me. Immediately afterwards we were shaken by an almighty bang, and a roar went up from the crowd: *el-sha'ab, yureed, isqat el-nizam.* 'The people, want, the downfall of the regime. The people, want, the downfall of the regime.' It has an irrepressible sonic energy of its own, that chant, and it sent us hurtling down the hill and into the streets.

When I remember 28 January, it is as a triptych. The first panel is Haram Street, the long avenue that connects Cairo to the pyramids, and on this day it is a war zone. Scattered by security forces who are spraying death from the main road, protesters are regrouping in the backstreets behind Haram and chanting *wahid, itnayn, el-sha'ab el-masri feyn?* – 'One, two, where are the Egyptians?' They are calling to those watching from their balconies to come down and join them, and many do; some of those that can't, throw down bottles of water instead and yell support. A group of kids rushes past carrying a bucket of black paint to throw at the windscreens of armoured police vehicles on the main road; they want to blind the security forces, just like they keep blinding us with gas. People are wheezing, staggering and trying to acclimatize to unfamiliar surroundings – after the surges forward and the brutal firing back, groups have been dispersed and no one can find their friends or family any more. And yet no one is isolated because everyone is shouting encouragement at each other, sharing water and tactics and rumours. Mobiles aren't working, so there's nothing to tweet, nothing to post, only a street to win. We edge forward, on to an overpass; some young kids are breaking rocks off the kerb and running across a rubble-strewn no-man's land right up to the police, who rise out of hatches at the top of their vehicles with guns in their hands and take aim at those approaching. It's surreal, this tableau with its almost farcical imbalance. The protesters are ragged, and bare; the security forces, on the other hand, are all straight lines, swaddled in thick plastic, glass and metal. When the shooters emerge from the hatches they look like part of the machine, inanimate cogs being snapped up into place and back down again with a push of a button or a pull of a lever. It's hard to believe they are humans, like us, and that despite all the weaponry and body armour their hearts must be pounding and their heads swimming in disbelief, as ours are. These policemen can pick out one, two, three protesters at a time from their hatches, but more and more keep pouring out of the backstreets and suddenly there's too many to aim at and a driver panics, slamming the vehicle into reverse and skidding wildly around, sending the hatch crashing back on to the shooter's head.

No one has taught these kids how to do this, how to use nothing but speed and rocks to outmuscle an armoured platoon bristling with rifles and helmets and shields and trucks and canister after canister of tear gas – so much tear gas, forever mushrooming inside our lungs and choking us from within – but they are making do, and winning, and gradually the crowd is learning and copying and advancing, and the police are in retreat. From up here, crouched behind some twisted railings for cover, I can see the whole Cairo skyline, and in every direction there are streamers of gas and columns of smoke twisting high into the air. 'Wake up Egypt, raise your voice – your silence is what kills us!' the people around me are chanting. 'We are change!' I crouch and I wonder. No internet, no mobile, no way of knowing – except by that skyline, and the story it tells. Across the capital, and across the country, I realize, the things I'm seeing here are being repeated, again and again.

The second panel of the day's triptych is at the Nile, when we tried to cross towards Tahrir. Closer to the square, I find out later, a monumental battle is raging on Qasr el-Nil bridge; demonstrators sat and prayed as they were pummelled by water cannon, then rose up and fought as they were riddled with bullets. But where I am, on Galaa bridge – Qasr el-Nil's twin sister, which connects the other side of Gezira Island to the western shore – the ground has already been liberated and the security forces pushed back. Only two police trucks remain, along with a handful of abandoned and hugely outnumbered conscripts. As the protest crowds converge on them, there is terror in their eyes; they retreat inside their vehicles and barricade the door. Earlier I had seen a fleeing *amn el-markazi* ('central security forces') soldier drop his helmet and shield as he backpedalled away from protesters, only for those advancing to pick the items up, surround the young man, and hand them back. 'We are not your enemy,' they told him. 'We are like you. Join us.' But here the mood is different; protesters have died to win this little patch of street and force open a path for marchers in the west of the capital to converge upon Tahrir – just as many have died all over Egypt to win their own little patches of street and prise the regime's fingers from the country's asphalt.

Many of those still standing are wounded and angry, and some want revenge. The crowd is pressing closer to the trucks and arguing about what to do; some are urging restraint, others are baying for payback. The doors may be locked but eventually they will be forced open, and clearly no one from the state is coming to the conscripts' rescue. The conscripts yell through the windows that they will come out and the crowd quietens and tenses; I look around at hundreds of faces – sweaty, dust-smeared, blood-streaked – all trained intensely on the door. The lock turns and the door swings open, and there at the doorway is a man – a young man, as young and scared and hopeful and defiant as the rest of us – who has stripped off all his armour, all his weapons, even all his clothes but for his trousers and a plain white vest. We can see that behind him, his colleagues have all done the same: an act of submission, a plea for clemency. A couple of hotheads in the crowd lurch forward, but others hold them back, and we all wait for the man in the doorway to speak, a tiny bubble of silence holding firm for a fleeting moment in a city echoing like never before with noise. What must be going through his head at that moment, as he looks out on the crowd, and the river, and the country burning beyond, on his world turned upside down? 'I am not afraid of you,' he begins boldly and I can feel the crowd stiffen, but then his voice drops and he looks around and picks out someone to talk to, an individual to lock eyes with. 'I am afraid . . . of losing my job and ruining my family,' he continues. And there are murmurs, and nods, because people understand this. They don't forgive the things the young man has probably done that day, and certainly not the regime that told him to do them, but they can feel his pain. 'Mubarak is in his castle and has abandoned you to your death,' a woman near me in the crowd shouts back. 'Give him up and join us!' There are more nods and shouts of approval, and the man in the doorway is nodding too. But he must get his men to safety, and after much discussion a ragtag but effective double-line of protesters forms to give them secure passage to a nearby police station.

The final panel of my triptych is underground, at least partially. A colleague, Dalia Awad, and I have been desperately trying to get back across to the east bank of the city to find out what is happening in Tahrir, but on the other side of Gezira every bridge is blocked by clashes. Swimming hardly seems an option – our notes and recording equipment would be drenched, the currents are unpredictable and there is live gunfire ricocheting around the river – but what about the metro? Of course the trains won't be running, but could we walk through the tunnels? We flag down a car and beg the driver to take us to a station, any station on the west bank; he lets us in and skitters off at high speed through Giza, passing pockets of utter devastation – debris, twisted metal, burning vehicles – amid long stretches of total calm. Everyone in the city is either hiding or fighting, and barely any other motors are on the road. We reach a station and descend into the city's bowels. An empty ticket-hall, a deserted pair of platforms, frozen lifts and a few relics of normality – a no-smoking sign, an advert for a mobile phone company – strangely scary because isolated normality only accentuates the apocalyptic. Dalia and I slump back on a platform bench, and for a moment we are both awash with exhaustion. And then, incredibly, a tingle moves through the air, the one you can just about feel somewhere in your torso before you actually hear it with your ears, the tingle that rises from a metal rail that is starting, very gently, to sing. The tingle that can only mean a train is coming. We stare at each other and then collapse in laughter, because the whole thing is so absurd.

The eastbound train is almost empty as it pulls into the platform, and we don't catch sight of the driver. Some of the carriage lights are out, others are flickering. Who is running this train, and why, and what dangers could there be further down the tunnel in a city pockmarked with fires and warfare? There's no time to think it through, so we jump on. The first couple of stations we reach on the Giza side are like the one we boarded at: empty but open, and the train stops at each with a forlorn sense of duty. Then we are under the Nile and approaching Sadat, the metro station directly beneath Tahrir. Dalia and I stand and brace ourselves, but the train isn't slowing; we hurtle through a darkened platform and from the light of the train we catch a brief glimpse of shadowy figures moving around beyond, across the big expanse of polished granite that connects the different lines, and we can hear bangs. Were they police, or protesters, or looters? In whose hands was the square, and why didn't the train stop? And then, before we can work out the answers, swoosh – the tunnel shutters our view through the windows once more, and reluctantly we sit back down. We don't stop at Naguib either, or Ataba. And then abruptly the train pulls into the vast station complex below the Ramses rail terminus and grinds to a halt, the doors sliding open and the carriage's electrical hum shutting down: a grating sound, then a whimper, then nothing. Only one or two fluorescent strip lamps in the station are working, and the platform is almost completely dark; from the light of the train we can see there are pieces of rubble strewn across the ground, and broken glass. No one else is getting on or off; in fact there is no other human in sight. Echoing through the air is the sound of distant explosions, but the tunnels are a warren and we have no idea where they are coming from; occasionally a human cry bounces off the walls and it sounds as though it belongs to someone in our immediate vicinity, but it's just a trick of the ears, and our hearts are thudding. The driver must still be in his cab, but he hasn't moved or made a sound and we have no idea if he is friend or foe, whether it is safer to seek him out or to venture alone into this gloom that speaks of something happening, something violent. We decide to step off the train, and take another leap. On the walls above us, the name of this stop can just be made out in large-font English and Arabic letters, illuminated by the flickering bulbs inside the carriage and clouded with swirling dust. This is Mubarak station, and it is devastated.

We cling to each other and crunch across the station concourse, using the light of our otherwise useless mobile phones to plot a path. Our eyes are pricking, then stinging and then scorching as we make for an exit staircase, and we realize that tear gas has been pumped into this subterranean labyrinth. Maybe it is still being pumped in right now, and maybe we are heading directly towards those who are doing the pumping. They might shoot us on sight when we emerge at street-level. But we cannot stay down here, we will choke and eventually collapse, and there will be no one around to help us. As we near the surface the gas is thickening and neither of us can see; we're blinded by tears and convulsing with coughs, and as we get closer and closer to the street I know we have no choice but to run into the fresh air no matter what is waiting up there, because otherwise we will be incapacitated. We're huddled together and stumbling, somehow into the open, and we can hear the sound-junk of battle all around us, and through blurred and streaming eyes I can see the sky has darkened and night is falling. And now we run together, and we have no idea where we are or what is happening, and we can hear shots but our vision is scrambled from the gas and we don't know where they're coming from, and it feels as if the gas is following us everywhere; we run and run and trip and rise and run some more and then, all the energy gone, we crumple against a wall, and cough, and blink, and slowly, slowly, the pain begins to lift. And we look around at our surroundings and realize we are in the Turgoman neighbourhood, near the central bus station, and that mercifully there is no gas here – just spores still clinging to our clothes – and there is no one shooting at us, and, for now at least, we are safe.

The streets are empty, but a local – he must have seen us from his apartment – has come down to bring us water, and we kiss him on both cheeks again and again and laugh once more, because we are stupidly grateful to be alive. He tells us that a battle has been raging all afternoon for control of the Ramses plaza and the access it provides to Tahrir from the east, and that we must have surfaced from the station just as the police were retreating. And we grab him, suddenly, and ask him about the square – what has happened in the square? Has the square been taken? Who has won the streets? And he nods and points towards Tahrir which is a mile or so away, and that's when we first see the huge plumes of smoke rising from the NDP headquarters, which lies just past the square's north-west corner. 'The protesters have it, and the security forces are fleeing,' he tells us. And then he blesses us, and turns to leave. And Dalia and I glance at each other once more and smile, and look back at the twisty columns of smog the NDP building is belching into the twilight. The sun has set on Egypt's day of rage. *El-shari' lina*. The streets are ours.

During the mid-twentieth century reign of King Farouk, the playboy monarch commissioned a statue of his grandfather Khedive Ismail to be made abroad, and – as he waited for its delivery – had a pedestal built for it in Cairo's central square. It was Ismail who had ordered the transformation of that square from a patchwork quilt of green fields and royal gardens into a symbol of his country's urban modernization, and it was he who named it Midan Ismailia, after himself. Farouk wanted to honour his predecessor's legacy by installing a bronzed reminder of what top-down power and munificence can achieve. But the Egyptian people had other ideas. They used the square as a place to congregate and protest – first against British occupation in 1946, then again in 1952, sparking the Great Fire of Cairo and eventually Gamal Abdel Nasser's coup, which brought Farouk's reign to an end. A few weeks after Farouk was forced to abdicate the throne by Egypt's new military masters, the statue he had ordered belatedly arrived in the country. It never was placed on its pedestal.[4] In 1960 Midan Ismailia was officially renamed Tahrir – the Arabic word for 'liberation' – and for many years the pedestal stood there empty; a symbol in its own right, perhaps, of a very different kind of power than Farouk had in mind. In the 1970s, building work began on the metro station below the square, and the pedestal was removed. Tahrir Square has often been the place Egypt's rulers have come to spell out a vision. And it has often been the place where Egypt's people fought back with visions of their own.

There is a danger in projecting too much of the revolution on to this single square, and thus confining the revolution in space and time. Egypt's generals have tried to physically do this by building walls and metal fences on the square's main corners, and foreign leaders have spoken approvingly of the Tahrir spirit – because from afar, packaged up in that iconic stretch of concrete and grass and lauded with bromides, it seemed that the revolution could be strapped tight to a particular corner of the world and made safe. Focusing too closely on Tahrir ignores a panoply of revolutionary struggles, and it leaves the factories and farms and schools and alleyways and minds in which revolution is raging dangling far off the edge of the page, alongside the dozens of other city squares across Egypt where battles were won and occupations mounted. But still, Tahrir was special. Not because it was all the revolution consisted of (it wasn't), not because it was the revolution's mouthpiece (it wasn't), and not because it was the most media-friendly window on to Egypt's turmoil during those heady days (it was, and that was part of the problem). It was special because it embodied something more fundamental about the revolution – an act of creation, one that has coloured Egypt's politics irrevocably ever since. In Tahrir, Egyptians built something different from Mubarak Country: a different set of borders, a different set of social relations, a different narrative about who they were and what they could do. Everyone, including me, wrote about the inventive food supplies and toilet systems, the hijacked power cables and tented schools, the in-house hairdresser and exuberant street weddings. But these weren't just elements of a temporary mini-state, scores in the sand by which distance from the regime could be measured. They were the physical embodiment of a genesis that stretched far, far beyond Tahrir's limits, a sense of activation that wrenched the centre of the state down to the streets, down to the people, and recreated Mubarak Country from within. Now, when I look back at Youssef Hisham's words on 25 January about Tahrir being at the centre of everything, I finally understand them. It was the existence of Tahrir – this Tahrir, the one where people chanted collectively but also often wandered about singing softly and delightedly to no one but themselves, the one where corporate advertising was torn down and replaced by people's billboards – that held the promise of no one having to shout into the desert any more, like the Alexandrian electrician Mohamed Ibrahim had to in the Sidi Gabr butchery. It held the promise of those on the margins populating the state, because they were populating the streets. Despite everything, I believe it still holds that promise.

Shahenda Maklad, the Kamshish teenager who took on the feudalists and had now reached her early seventies, was to be found in Tahrir during those days. So too was Mohamed Abla, the artist from Qursaya Island who had helped to fight off the army's invasion. He ran workshops in the square for children who wanted to express what they were seeing all around them through pieces of art; 'Everything is changing, and everywhere I look, the world is painting new pictures for us,' he beamed.[5] Mohamed Radi, the young man who was among those arrested and charged in the hamlet of Sarandu for resisting Mubarak's land reforms, and who had subsequently fled police custody and escaped to Alexandria, would have passed by Abla's workshop. Before the revolution started Radi had tried and failed to flee Egypt on a smuggler's boat to start a new life in Europe; now, after watching six days of anti-government protests by the Mediterranean in open-mouthed wonder, he had decided to travel down to Tahrir instead and join the occupation, despite officially being a wanted man. 'I felt a full wave of freedom wash over me . . . my fears of prison disappeared,' he grinned. Bilal Diab, the Cairo University heckler, set up camp in the *midan* and shouted 'a million Bravehearts!' as he gestured all around him; Hossam el-Hamalawy was pacing around nearby, snapping photo after photo of the crowds and using the electrical points and wi-fi routers rigged up by activist geeks on the grass to upload his snaps to the '3arabawy' website and the world. Rashad Bassyuni, the retired labour activist in Kafr el-Dawwar, spent the whole eighteen days in the square, and there met dozens of property tax collectors in REATU, Egypt's first independent trade union, members of which established a permanent presence in Tahrir.

ETUF – the state's official trade union federation – attempted, unsuccessfully, to mobilize workers against the revolution and bring them on to the streets to defend Mubarak; some believe that in desperation, ETUF head Hussein Megawer teamed up with oligarchs like NDP stalwart and Qursaya land baron Mohamed Aboul Enein to hire thugs and lauoch the 'Battle of the Camel', an infamous attack on the square which was successfully repelled. Workers were at the forefront of the days of fighting that had enabled the revolution to reach this point: those killed by Mubarak's troops on the days of rage included a welder, a plumber, a cement factory mechanic, a stonemason, a shoemaker and a microbus driver.[6] The Egyptians most directly afflicted by structural adjustment had brought protest from the margins into the core of the capital. Now, as the eighteen days rumbled on, they swept revolution back out again from Tahrir to workplaces up and down the country; on the final days before Mubarak crumbled, workers in the transport, petroleum, steel, fertilizer, cement, textile, printing, military production and many, many other industries came out on strike to apply a final dose of pressure on a broken dictatorship, pressure which sealed Mubarak's fate.

The martyrs were there in Tahrir too: in the chants of the occupiers, in the posters erected by their families, in the private stories those posters sparked off whenever you encountered one. And their presence gave everyone strength, because it was not just about grief, but about finding strength in that grief that could be shared around and allow everyone to continue. Lotfi Abdel Latif had been caught up in street-fighting in Imbaba when he found a small child torn by shrapnel wounds – security forces had been shooting at protesting crowds to disperse them. 'He grabbed the boy and went up to remonstrate with a riot policeman, asking why they were firing live bullets into the air at the Egyptian people,' said Azzam Abdel Latif, Lotfi's father. 'The policeman fired two bullets into my son's chest, and he died instantly.'[7] Lotfi was twenty-eight years old when he was murdered. Azzam and his wife, who described themselves as totally non-political before the revolution, buried their child, then came straight down to Tahrir. They carried a picture of Lotfi's face and a copy of the autopsy report, which they mounted alongside it – whether as proof, or an assertion of grief, or an attempt to contrast their son's vitality with the state's cold bureaucracy, I couldn't really tell. 'I only had one son and I lost him to these protests; if I did have another, I would tell him to come down and join this,' Azzam told me. 'We must bring down Mubarak. If I see the president, I'll get him myself.'

Day and night, and especially at night, Tahrir felt like Tahrir. Not like a travelling circus, or a Hyde Park festival, or the world's biggest street party, or any of the phrases everyone fell back on to try to convey the atmosphere and dynamism of this space, even though none of them was equal to the task. In Tahrir, you could walk for hours across a giant carpet of human activity and constantly find unexpected little circuits of energy – a poetry reading, a political debate, a bawdy peal of laughter – that drew strangers together and made you feel that you were plugged into something gargantuan. 'I've never had any love for Mubarak or his system before, but my mind – like everyone else's – has always been sealed from the possibility of change,' an engineer in his forties named Atef Seif el-Din told me, after I found him picking litter in the square. 'And honestly, when I began chanting for my, rights and the government security forces fired tear gas at me, that seal was broken for ever.' He said that picking litter was his duty, and in terms of upending Mubarak's psychological sabotage of the Egyptian people, I guess it was. 'We've taken control of our streets from the police and whereas they threw bombs around, the people want to prove they can look after it better. This is our country; we're not thieves, not looters, we're just taking back what is ours from the forces of corruption. Trying to keep the square clean is a symbol of that.' Tahrir drew its pulse from its constituent elements, but it also conferred vitality on those within it, and made them agents of their own destiny. Shady Alaa el-Din, a young hotel worker who I befriended during the eighteen days, was one of many who said as much to me, as we sipped tea in the *midan*. 'What we've done in Tahrir, what you can see there – it's perfect,' he said. 'Before, I wanted to leave Egypt, and I asked myself, "Where can I go? Where can I live like a human?" Now I realize this place is Egypt, this place is in Tahrir Square. I think that feeling is spreading to the rest of the country, and I want to be a part of it.'

Of course Tahrir wasn't really perfect: not as an occupied space, not as a revolutionary strategy, not as an alternative political community. The dynamics of the square were volatile, and assaults on its sovereignty – both rhetorical and physical – bred paranoia and defensiveness at times, sentiments that could sometimes manifest themselves in the *midan* as internal censorship and even violence. But how could it be perfect, when it was a living, breathing, perpetual feat of learning and invention? If perfection is the litmus test for legitimate expressions of change, challenges to the status quo can only ever arrive from on high, and thus offer no real challenge to the status quo at all. Tahrir could only ever have been messy, only ever have been imperfect, and in that way it attained a scrubby sort of perfection unique to itself. As Egyptian newspaper editor and thoughtful revolutionary Hani Shukrallah once reflected, 'no popular revolution is ever fully prepared for the tasks, vision and aspirations that set it into motion. For a people to garner the courage and will to rise up against oppression, rather than to submit, subvert and make do, they need to reach for the stars, yet the stars are invariably beyond reach.'[8]

Subsequent chapters of Egypt's revolution and counter-revolution have also tarred the 'Tahrir-as-utopia' chronicle, especially in the eyes of foreign observers; on many occasions I've read a sarky comment below an Egypt-related news article, mocking – with a peculiar and savage glee – those who dared live a dream like Tahrir, dared to partake in this act of inception. The crux of the argument is always that these people were naïve fools, who have rightly been brought back down to earth with a bump. The commenters almost seem affronted that anyone could have grasped for the sky like that, that someone ever had the audacity to think and act and forge Tahrir. They sound defensive over never having taken that leap themselves, and delighted when those who did met walls on the way, because they think that those walls retrospectively justify their own timidity. It's always comforting to play the role of the rational, time-worn realist, because it's always more comforting to accept the world as it is rather than brave failure in pursuit of change. If believing in a different world and beginning to build it is the hallmark of a naïve fool, then let the fools spread far and wide. Those who experienced Tahrir first-hand and the millions more worldwide who were inspired by its energy know that the solution to hitting walls isn't to stop leaping, but to leap higher, and get others leaping with you.

When Tahrir was threatened, it was more alive than ever – a moving grid of cross-cutting grooves along which currents of defence, defiance, treatment, rescue and remembrance all flowed at once. Lookouts scamper up walls and lamp-posts to report on the impending danger. Those on the ground find a rock and bang metal railings, alerting the square and intimidating those advancing towards it. Revolving lines of revolutionaries approach the front line, using anything they can for cover and falling back when they are tear-gassed; as they retreat, others are waiting with soothing liquid to squirt into stinging eyes, and others pour forward to take their places. Motorbikes shoot across the debris of the front line to pick up the injured and carry them to a field hospital, sometimes in the face of sniper fire; the long lines of blood-drips left by the wounded are later framed with rocks as a mark of memory, of presence. Usually Mostafa Bahgat would be there, the revolutionary cameraman *extraordinaire*, standing tall with his fiery red hair and looking almost serene amid the chaos – no flak jacket, no helmet, just open to the elements and seemingly immune to the dangers fizzing through the air around him. 'Much of the time I'm not even looking at the viewfinder; instead I'm glancing all around me, calculating what's going to happen next and whether or not I need to move,' he tells me.[9] Safety equipment would stop him being hyper-attuned to the elements and the street-fighting on all sides of him: the shifting position of the combatants, the direction of the wind, and the precise location of every lamp-post, phone box and scattered piece of metal that could be pressed into use as an emergency barricade. Despite his reputation, he is not invincible; there are eight pieces of ammunition lodged deep within his leg, and his own incredible footage shows security forces aiming their weapons straight at him, time and again. But he keeps coming back, keeps recording history. 'My strongest tactic is to think back to when I was younger. As a child we jump, roll, hide and play all the time; it feels instinctive to move around in a creative way. Those instincts don't leave us, and now I know what I can use them for.'

The field hospitals are the best and worst of the square; chaos and fear, but also desperate hope. One of them is the mosque at the back of Hardees, right off Mohamed Mahmoud Street – just a narrow passage really, sandwiched between two tall buildings and partially roofed. The prayer mats are soaked through and the volunteer doctors are running around trying to prioritize their patients, save lives, reassure friends, preserve evidence – a box of .22 calibre shell casings, proof the regime is using live ammunition – and clear room for the next delivery of lifeless souls from the frontline, all simultaneously. 'We're advising people to halt the assault on the interior ministry because the police there have snipers and the youths have nothing but stones,' says Dr Ahmed Ali, an oncologist who is now doing emergency surgery. 'They don't stand a chance – but they keep going on anyway. And as long as they keep going, we will too.' When someone dies – and on the worst days someone was always dying – their bloodied clothing might be hoisted on a stick and marched out of the field hospital, into Tahrir, where chants for the martyr would then rock the square. And yet no one is dissuaded. 'Those [pro-Mubarak forces] throwing missiles from the outside are using sharp rocks which split the face into two pieces,' explains another doctor, Samar Sewilam. 'Ninety-nine per cent of the patients I've treated go back to the front-line to continue the fight. They ask me to stitch them up and then they instantly return. "Just stitch me up and let me go back," they always say.'

What does it do to you, to throw yourself into this sort of medical work, in squalid conditions, in a place you might be bombed or shot or tear-gassed at any minute, with the barest of resources, and deal with the fragility of human flesh and the ferocity of human emotions, day after day, night after night? On the other side of the *midan*, on the approach road from Abdel Munim Riyad just opposite the Egyptian Museum – where revolutionaries linked arms to protect the building and reclaim their heritage from a government who had reduced it to a commodity – I asked Dina Omar, a cardiologist. The night before was the battle of the camel, when pro-regime thugs on horses and camels were paid to lay siege to the square with clubs, machetes and shards of glass; at one point a bus of *baltigayya* breached Tahrir's defences and drove right into the field hospital there, forcing doctors to pick up their patients and run for their lives. Revolutionaries protected themselves from the rocks raining down on them with whatever they could lay their hands on: there were helmets made out of water bottles, helmets made out of colanders, helmets made out of cardboard, helmets made out of bread, but it was never enough to stop the injuries mounting. Dina was living and working in Beirut when the revolution started; she flew back to contribute. The thirty-year-old had to endure her mother begging her not to go, and overcome the fury of her brother who tried to block her from moving her car, all so she could reach Tahrir and do this draining work hour after hour in the impromptu roadside clinic. 'From a medical point of view we did amazingly; even in the middle of a war zone we managed to keep most of the needles sterile, and when we couldn't sterilize them we didn't use them – it is better to bathe and clean a wound and leave it unstitched than it is for them to contract HIV or hepatitis,' she says. 'I treated over 200 patients that night, two of whom died in my lap. One 23-year-old was brought to me seemingly unconscious, with his head wrapped in bandages; we tried CPR for several minutes but it was clear we were too late. It was only when someone else ran up to us with a towel wrapped around a complete human brain that I realized what had happened – we turned the patient over and saw that the whole back of his head was missing. And of course there was no time to shed a tear. "*Yalla*" ("let's go"), I said, "next patient."'

Many stayed all night in the square; those who didn't went home, where the work continued. The police had been beaten out of Tahrir but the regime withdrew them everywhere and opened the jails; not to emancipate political prisoners, but to send criminals into the streets, a final act of psychological sabotage designed to sow destruction inside newly expanded imaginations. But people were getting used to doing things for themselves now, and so they started forming local militias to guard their neighbourhoods. They were rough-hewn at first, and then they developed identification and communication systems, shift rotas, ways to better command the streets.

In Heliopolis, residents repelled thieves by pouring scalding water from their balconies; in other corners of the city, I found out to my amazement that some friends had got hold of guns. 'It's a strange feeling defending your own community, fear mixed with intense pride,' one told me. 'People are coming together in a way they never have previously. It's really liberating – before we lived in fear of the police and never had the chance to take responsibility for our own communities, but now we are in control. It's a continuation of the revolution, bringing it out of the main squares and into our homes.'

In my own neighbourhood, Marouf, residents brought down metal rods and kitchen knives to be shared among the volunteers, who set out on patrol past the mechanics workshops, around Abu Tarek's *kushari* emporium, on laps of the old palace. As a weapon, Mahmoud Omar, the dreadlocked father who lived opposite and whose apartment was once a mini-hub for celebrities of the downtown arts and music scene, carried his camera tripod. 'We are looking to see whether we recognize the person, and if not we ask them questions to test their knowledge of the area,' he explained. 'Everybody is very tense, because it's dark, it's cold, and it's very disorientating out here – we are very wary of any approaching cars or motorbikes. Earlier some thugs on a motorbike attacked a lone soldier and stole his weapon; luckily we apprehended them and tied them to a lamp-post, and then helped the soldier back to his tank. Tonight we are disorganized because we are not experts in urban security, we're learning as we go. Tomorrow will be different.'

Those in power have for many decades attempted to reshape our understanding of politics and the language we use to describe it. Under neoliberalism, the economic realm has supposedly become inoculated from politics; they have tried to shrink what we think of as 'legitimate' dissent into a space small enough that it can play out within the system – a matter for rational discussion, for NGOs and civil society, for gradualism and reform. If you have a political problem, then shake the tree: sign a petition, donate to charity, form a pressure group. When society is nothing more than an agglomeration of individuals motivated by personal self-interest, what else is there to do? But Egypt's revolution, at its most dynamic, has not sought merely to shake the tree. It has sought to uproot it, and grow something else in its place.

As Mubarak wobbled, politics at the top was still the same old game of exclusion. Foreign Minister Ahmed Aboul Gheit warned against revolutionary 'adventurers' being allowed to take power. Omar Suleiman, Mubarak's spymaster and newly appointed vice-president, decried this 'creative chaos' that threatened to upend politics as he knew it, and warned once again that Egyptians were not ready for democracy. King Abdullah of Saudi Arabia dismissed revolutionaries as 'infiltrators'; he called Washington to insist that regime change must be avoided at all costs, and promised to bankroll Mubarak through any economic difficulties.[10] Tony Blair hit the airwaves to describe Mubarak as 'immensely courageous' and 'a force for good' – 'I don't think the West should be the slightest bit embarrassed about the fact that it's been working with Mubarak,' he insisted.[11]

Some months later, I met a man named Aladin Tawfiq Harkan, who had worked for Tony Blair when the former British prime minister visited Egypt on holiday. Mubarak and Blair were so close that the latter enjoyed complimentary flights, private tours of the pyramids by antiquities supremo Zahi Hawass, and the free use of two government villas in Sharm el-Sheikh – a generous gift that was paid for, of course, by the Egyptian people.[12] Harkan was Blair's driver during the trip; as a highly ranked army sniper, he was carefully vetted and well-trusted by senior members of the security establishment, living a life of relative comfort and enjoying regular postings abroad to European cities such as Vienna and Budapest. 'Back then I lived far from politics,' he told me. 'We had everything in Sharm, even though everything was about money and bribes and my friends and family couldn't afford a smile. I didn't use to care about what was beyond my eyes.' On 20 January 2011, he had taken a break and returned to his home village, near Tanta in the Nile Delta. On the 25th he heard rumours of protests in Suez and Cairo, but paid them no heed and cursed the troublemakers. By the 28th whispers of unrest were getting louder, though his village was quiet and he still saw nothing of import on the state television channels. Intrigued, he told his wife and children he was going to head into Tanta to see if anything was happening. 'I left my house that day as a passive man, and returned as a revolutionary.'

What he found on the streets of Tanta was a massacre; communications had been cut and the security forces were shooting openly at the protest crowds. Aladin is a huge man, and was once very strong; he told me he suddenly felt a fire inside, and waded into the mêleé to retrieve those who had been injured, carrying them to safety on his shoulders. In the streets he came across his friend Gaber, doing exactly the same thing, and the pair exchanged astonished smiles. A few minutes later Gaber himself was shot in the stomach; Aladin needed every last ounce of strength to lift him and stop his innards from spilling out into the dust. The fighting raged for forty-eight hours, and towards the end of it Aladin was hit with birdshot – first in the legs, then in the eye. The latter blinded him; that night in hospital, his head swathed in bandages and his eyes seeing nothing but darkness, fellow patients screamed at him to run because the security forces were charging through the wards and gunning down anyone who looked like a protester. That's what Mubarak's stability and courage looked like; that was the experience of an Egyptian who ferried the Blair family from villa to beach to gourmet restaurant and back again, and then had to listen to his former passenger describe the dictator who had brutalized him as 'an immense force for good'. Long after Mubarak had fallen, on one of the many occasions in the ensuing years when Tahrir once again flared into life as a weapon of resistance, Aladin was still there, urging people to stay, urging them to make this their new reality. 'This square is Egypt, the Egypt I want to live in,' he repeated, again and again. 'This is our future, now.'

Tahrir attempted a different type of politics, one based not on hierarchy but on mutual trust, not on concessions and crumbs falling from above but on roots and vines growing from below. Towards the end of the eighteen days, a self-appointed 'Council of Wise Men' – a band of elders who presumed, unilaterally, that they could command the support of Tahrir and the trust of the regime – decided they were going to meet Suleiman and negotiate, reach a compromise within the system. 'The opposition leadership is so divided that no clear option is available outside the ruling establishment,' explained political analyst

Diaa Rashwan at the time.[13] The thought that revolutionaries might have loftier objectives than just swapping one dictator for another had apparently not occurred to him. In Tahrir, where a haphazard but constantly refined system of debate, delegation and agreement was cautiously emerging (outside the ruling establishment), more radical demands were being articulated and the tree-shaking Council of Wise Men was irrelevant. 'These so-called prominent opposition figures can do what they want with regards to speaking with the government, but they have nothing to do with those on the ground here,' Amr Gharbia, a revolutionary activist, shrugged. 'When the government shut down the web, politics moved on to the street, and that's where it has stayed,' said one youth. The novelist Ahdaf Soueif watched the proceedings with amazement; this was Mubarak's psychological sabotage being actively undone. 'Genuine opposition politics in this country has always relied on people taking the initiative, and that's what we're seeing here – on a truly astounding level,' she told me. 'There is more transparency and equality here in Tahrir than anything we've ever seen under the Mubarak regime; anyone and everyone can have their say, and that makes the demands that come out of the process even more powerful.' If you sat anywhere in Tahrir in those days, you sat in the middle of a spontaneous political discussion, and you were compelled to join in. It was the opposite of elite politics, the opposite of exclusion. Foreign Minister Ahmed Aboul Gheit had warned of revolutionary 'adventurers'; the square, effortlessly, made adventurers of everyone within it.

As the clock ticked over to 11 February, someone in London sent me a text. 'With you tonight in disgust, with you tomorrow – again – in hope,' it read. The world was watching, and the Egyptians did not let them down.

Later, my friends Karim and Simon claimed the tipping point had been their casual stroll to Amo Hosni, a fast-food chain with a branch in Heliopolis, by the presidential palace. We had gathered outside the palace, along with what felt like most of Egypt, and they had ducked out of the massive rally to grab a burger. As they walked back along Ahram Street, an army officer apparently looked out of the window and saw them biting into their food. 'Picture the scene,' Karim insisted, to whoever would listen. 'The president is prevaricating. The crowds are building. The military high command are torn – can they protect Mubarak, or will the size and fury of the streets be too much for them? An officer peers out of the window and sees two young protesters sauntering along the pavement with such confidence, chomping on their burgers with such casual insouciance, that he realizes they have no choice. "Sir," he reports back, "it's no good. Hosni has to go." '

Hosni went, and the world blurred with colour.

In the midst of the epic, always, the absurd. Nothing this vast and all-encompassing could play out without trailing clouds of wit and whimsy in its wake. 'In the name of God the merciful, the compassionate,' announced Vice President Omar Suleiman to the nation, looking like the second-or third-tier villain in a low-budget zombie flick. 'Citizens, during these very difficult circumstances Egypt is going through, President Hosni Mubarak has decided to step down from the office of president of the republic and has charged the high council of the armed forces to administer the affairs of the country. May God help everybody.' The statement was recorded in such a rush that Suleiman's assistant, Major Hussein el-Sherif, was accidentally standing in shot behind him. El-Sherif unwittingly took a starring role in the most famous thirty-seven seconds of television in Egypt's history; this being Egypt, #MBOS – 'The Man Behind Omar Suleiman' – was quickly photoshopped into every iconic photograph imaginable. Today, if you trawl the web, you can find el-Sherif peering out curiously behind Hitler as the Führer addresses the Reichstag, sharing a platform with Martin Luther King during the 'I have a dream' speech, and watching on as the Lion King's 'Mustafa' surveys his kingdom.

As the now ex-president's family piled into an army helicopter to escape the capital and begin internal exile in Sharm el-Sheikh – gaudy holiday home for the Blairs, that most ostentatious of monuments to Mubarak Country – his wife Suzanne apparently climbed out of the chopper at the last moment and rushed back inside the presidential residence. Impatient guards assumed that she had forgotten something and gone to fetch it, but after she remained absent for a few minutes they broke protocol by bursting in uninvited – only to find

the now-former first lady prostrate on the floor, sobbing uncontrol-
lably. 'Do you think they can get in here?' she howled to the officers.
'Please, don't let them come here!' We have this account from Abdel
Latif el-Menawy – the head of Egypt's state news output and thus a
serial regime apologist who, like so many who grew plump in the
service of Mubarak, has since carved out a career by unconvincingly
marketing himself as a dyed-in-the-wool revolutionary – and so it
must be taken with a hefty pinch of salt. But it was a popular version
of events, because it confirmed everything that many Egyptians
thought about the Mubaraks: the vanity, the arrogance, the determination that their world was theirs alone and, even in this final hour
as the planet's oldest country climaxed in revolution, it could somehow be sealed off and sterilized from outsiders.

Afterwards there would be parties: on the tops of burnt-out police
trucks, where Egyptians turned death-traps into dance-floors; in
the cramped confines of Stella Bar, where Simon led a round of 'the
people *have* brought down the regime' and, one by one, the entire
drinking den joined in and grew louder and louder until the walls
were shaking and we all collapsed back in our seats in a drunken,
dizzy rapture; at the house of our friend Sarah Carr, where people
brought along specially baked Mubarak cakes and sung and jumped
and jived, before scattering joyously into the night whispering giggly
fuck-yous to the army's curfew. But the moments that struck me in
the immediate aftermath were the quieter ones. A phone call from
Ahmed Mamdouh, my lawyer companion from the police truck, getting through to me just as we were marching back towards Tahrir
and chanting for the martyrs – his voice barely audible through his
tears. The television interview with Khaled Said's mother, in which
she announced that the following day, for the first time since her son's
death, she would wear white instead of black. And the sight of a
very old man in the square whose name I never discovered. He was
hunched and frail, standing peacefully on his own in the middle
of the pandemonium around us with his walking stick, and simply
beaming – at the fireworks, at the dancers, at everything. No one else
seemed to notice him standing there alone so silently, proudly and
happily, dressed in what looked like his best clothes – a slightly frayed
three-piece suit, dark green and weathered by the years, but clearly

cared for with great personal attention. I sat on a low wall and watched him, and thought about all the things this man must have seen through his life: the wars and births and deaths, loves which rose and died. And I thought about how – purely because he didn't look at all wealthy – this man had been done down by the Mubarak regime and its international advocates for so many decades, and how now, towards the end of his existence, he got to soak *this* in and stand so tall. It was all projection; I didn't know the man, I didn't get to speak to him, and his circumstances could have been completely different from those I imagined. But I thought nonetheless about how quietly contented he appeared, how adrift from the boisterous energy of the youth around him he was but how utterly delighted he seemed to be with it all regardless. And for the first time since the revolution began, I cried without a tear gas canister in sight.

PART III

Revolution Country

8

The Old Ways and the New

Nobody loves the Cairo ring road; they only endure it. They sit behind the wheels of private cars and fiddle impatiently with the radio dial, or they perch up in the cabins of lumbering, overweight trucks and bellow their horns, or they slump into the passenger seats of half-broken taxis and feel great lakes of sweat expanding slowly, and unstoppably, across their backs. More than sixty miles of dusty asphalt loops endlessly, high above the city, shouldering motorbikes and microbuses* and wooden carts sagging low with the wares of street vendors. Everyone moves at breakneck speed, or they don't move at all. It takes only a few moments for the entire highway to congeal and switch from race-track to traffic clot. This happens every morning and every afternoon, and when it does there is nothing to do but wait.

Apart from the long tailbacks, there are two things these days which are notable about the ring road. One is the prevalence of checkpoints along it. Some are permanent and others are makeshift: you turn a corner and suddenly there they are, a line of metal barriers jutting across the highway, patrolled by overheated men clutching weapons and clad in tan or black. Often there are a couple of tanks, or armoured personnel carriers, or dark green police vans parked behind the stopping-point and coils of razor wire thrown haphazardly across the lanes. Security personnel force all vehicles to slow

---

* Microbuses – small privately owned passenger vans that provide a more informal alternative to government-run buses and metro trains – are a central feature of Cairo's transport network. Drivers charge cheap fares and zoom all over the city with both aggression and panache.

down and crawl through a small gap. Faces are scanned; some are beckoned over to the side of the road, where ID cards are demanded and questions asked. The air around these checkpoints is stale; it smells of state control, of authority and obedience. If you look the wrong way, or say the wrong thing, or wear the wrong clothes when you pass through one of these checkpoints, your journey on the ring road will come to an end. Mahmoud Hussein, an eighteen-year-old student, was stopped by officers at a checkpoint up here on 25th January 2014 – three years exactly since the beginning of the revolution – because he was sporting a celebratory 25th January scarf and had the words 'Nation Without Torture' scrawled across his T-shirt.[1] He was taken to a nearby police station, beaten and electrocuted, and thrown into jail. At the time of writing, he had been held in detention for more than 500 days without charge.

The other notable feature of the ring road over the past few years is the gaps that have appeared in the low walls which line the overpass. They are rough and jagged, peering out over huge mounds of sand and dirt that have been banked up underneath the highway to form illicit ramps between the ring road and the communities living in the shadows below. For many decades the inhabitants of these communities – many of which are informal 'ashwa'iyat – had been forced to share their environment with the underbelly of the highway, without ever having access to its tarmac. Their homes, cafés and shops commingled with giant concrete pillars holding up the road, stanchions of separation that threw daily life into darkness and lent each neighbourhood a ceaseless backdrop of rumbles and roars. Now, without asking anyone for permission, residents have decided to end this isolation and build their own unofficial access points to the ring road; today their *tuk-tuks* and pick-ups and family wagons are wobbling their way up on to the fast lane at pace, with a cheerful indifference to formal rules.

The security checkpoints and the informal access ramps represent two very different understandings of power and space in revolutionary Egypt, a country which is also – simultaneously and inextricably – counter-revolutionary Egypt: home to both a whirlwind of change and its symbiotic opposite, the struggle to prevent change from materializing at all. One vision is of public space being back in the hands of its self-appointed custodians, those who know best how to rule it. The other is of people physically remaking their city, and their country, for themselves.

In June 2011, about five months on from the moment Mubarak was forced out of the presidential palace, I found myself sitting in the living room of a tiny apartment on the edge of eastern Cairo, not far from the ring road, listening to a young woman explain what had happened a few nights previously, when men with guns had burst in through the front door. 'The first thing they did was grab my new-born from my arms and slap me in the face,' she told me, cradling a baby and wiping away some tears. The apartment was sparsely furnished, but the woman and her husband had managed to add a few touches of individuality in the time they'd been there: there was a pair of frilly pink cushions angled carefully up against each other on the sofa, and behind them a display case crammed with inexpensive but diligently polished glass crockery and ceramic trinkets. It reminded me of childhood, and long, lazy afternoons spent at my grandparents' flat in Hastings. 'Then they threw the baby back to me,' the woman continued. 'My husband tried to rush forward to defend us but they forced him to the floor and beat him, all the while shouting, "This will teach you not to protest against us." '

As we talked, more women – hearing there was a journalist in the building – entered the apartment and jostled to tell their own stories of the raid. The space was so small, and the noise so loud, that it was difficult to separate out all the details. The women spoke of police and military troops forcing their way in to homes and blindfolding those they found inside; almost everyone had a husband or a brother who had been taken away into detention. The housing project that we sat in was named after Suzanne Mubarak and had been built several years earlier to accommodate Egyptians displaced from informal settlements nearby in the Manshiyet Nasser district. Some had lost their homes in the 2008 rockslide at Duweiqa; others had been evicted by the state. According to housing activists, the evictions were part of a government plan to clear and beautify the neighbourhoods around Uptown, the luxury residential compound being constructed on the Mokattam clifftop by Dubai-based property developer Emaar.[2] Ten thousand basic but functional units had been completed, arranged into a series of identical six-storey blocks, yet despite an urgent demand for affordable accommodation in the area the women said that up until the revolution started, many of the units had been left empty. 'It's corruption,' claimed one of them. 'The security people here paid bribes and got the apartments for themselves, even though they were meant for us. They've kept them empty so they can sell them on in the future and make a big profit.' During the eighteen-day uprising, as the president was being toppled, these women and their families had taken advantage of the chaos and broken in, depositing their meagre possessions and setting up home. Now, the state wanted these squatters out again; the army had been dispatched in an effort to intimidate them.

A couple of weeks after I visited the Suzanne Mubarak housing project, security forces attacked again in the early hours of the morning; videos show troops firing weapons all over the place as a large crowd of people, including children, run screaming in search of safety. This time, the apartments were successfully cleared. With nowhere else to go, the families that had been living within them built makeshift shelters outside in the street: 'walls' were formed out of bed-slats and mattress springs, and blankets served as roofs. Yassin Salah Eddin, head of the local district council, justified the violence on the grounds that, up to that point, 'the state [had] lost its authority' and 'a show of strength' was needed. 'All I want from the state is four walls, nothing else,' said Amal, a domestic cleaner and grandmother who was among those evicted. 'I had that, and they took it away.'[3]

Does the story of the Suzanne Mubarak housing project belong in an account of the Egyptian revolution? The Supreme Council of the Armed Forces (SCAF), which is comprised of the Mubarakist state's most senior military generals and assumed formal power after Mubarak fled, would argue not. That summer, in 2011, SCAF issued a statement praising Egypt's 'glorious' revolution but warning that in the months following the president's successful ousting some elements of society had been trying to 'disrupt public order' and 'obstruct the functioning of the state'.[4] It insisted that 'all options were open' when it came to dealing with such elements. At the time of the statement, popular protests had shut down the country's administrative nerve centre, the *mugamma* building in Tahrir Square, and thousands of demonstrators calling for housing rights – including some from the Suzanne Mubarak project in eastern Cairo – had occupied the road outside the state television building at Maspero. Camped out alongside them were the relatives of Egyptians killed by police during the anti-Mubarak uprising, who were appealing for justice and accountability, Coptic youth activists demanding an end to sectarian discrimination, and poultry vendors protesting about ongoing corruption within their industry. SCAF was drawing a clear line between demonstrators who had mobilized to bring down Mubarak on the one hand, and groups like these on the other, including Amal and her fellow evictees – Egyptians who seemed intent on harnessing revolutionary energy towards something that went beyond Mubarak and demanded a different sort of state. The generals saw these people as dangerous. 'The Supreme Council of the Armed Forces is aware of plans to harm the country,' asserted their statement, adding that these included 'protests and strikes . . . that negatively affect citizens and stop the wheels of production from turnings'.[5]

According to SCAF, along with many other elite forces both inside Egypt and abroad, the revolution was a popular movement against Hosni Mubarak and came to an end, victoriously, at the moment he was flown off to Sharm el-Sheikh. This narrative of the revolution depends upon a certain conception of the modern Egyptian state, one that sees it as a neutral, autonomous machine designed to protect its citizens, advance overall prosperity, and mediate conflicts between different segments of society. On this reading, Mubarak and his cronies had made their way to the top of the state and exploited its powers to enrich themselves through corruption and prolong their rule with violence; now that he was gone, other, more enlightened people – eventually, people who were elected by Egyptians themselves – could take control of that state apparatus and put it to good use. This is a deceptive analysis. In reality, the state is not something detached from the political oppression and economic exclusion that characterized Mubarak Country, it was the very instrument of that oppression and exclusion.

Long before Mubarak ascended to the presidency, the Egyptian state was made up of vast, overlapping networks of authority and patronage: each dominated by different elites, each generally balancing the others out to ensure the whole system was maintained in a durable equilibrium. It retains that structure today, many years after Mubarak departed. Some of these networks take the form of government institutions, like the interior ministry and information ministry, while others operate on a more local level through Egypt's regional governorates. Certain networks tend to lurk below the radar, like the General Intelligence Services or the Military Intelligence Services, and some, like the web of high-level business connections at the top of the old National Democratic Party, don't have proper names at all. The most powerful individuals within the Egyptian state operate across several of these networks at the same time; they know how to manipulate their deep elements – hidden levers of power buried carefully below layers of public administration – as well a their broader, shallow components, such as the presence of retired army generals in almost every governor's office, almost every privatized company board, and almost every state contractor in the land. The survival of the state in its present form depends on multiple mechanisms of popular exclusion – political, economic, cultural and psychological – that lock most citizens out of these networks, mechanisms which have developed out of the country's colonial history and its long tradition of military dominance, as well as more recently its economic restructuring according to neoliberal principles. Collectively, these mechanisms ensure that state institutions and the domains of governance they preside over remain enclosed within private fiefdoms, to which ordinary Egyptians enjoy no admittance.

The creation of an Egyptian state in which the families evicted from the Suzanne Mubarak housing project could secure decent homes instead of living in makeshift shelters on the street would necessitate much more than the downfall of a single president, even if his replacement were chosen by a popular vote. At a bare minimum, it would require a different kind of economic model, where residents weren't evicted to make way for speculative high-end property development, and a different kind of security apparatus, one that didn't receive several times more state funding than the housing budget, and the prevalence of a different set of social norms, in which violence by the state against unarmed civilians is considered repugnant rather than routine. It would require many of the state's domains to be democratized, and the various elites who control each of them, and in whose interests the state currently operates, to be weakened. Such elites are not identical: at the broadest level there are the higher echelons of the military, a bureaucratic order that manages the state's activities, and a capitalist class that derives rents from the state's control and commodification of Egypt's assets, plus many subdivisions below them. The make-up of these elites isn't static and their relationships with one another aren't immutable; sometimes internecine conflicts break out between them and at times of crisis, as in recent years, rival elites have sought to harness unrest to gain an advantage. But all share a common interest in protecting the inviolability of the system as a whole. Mubarak Country is the landscape controlled by this undemocratic power grid, and the revolution is fighting to liberate it.

When the revolution broke out, on 25 January 2011, it threatened to do much more than force out Mubarak and propel a new set of faces into the higher reaches of this state. It plunged the state itself into the most devastating crisis it has ever faced and whipped up a storm that, initially at least, rearranged the terrain of Mubarak Country almost beyond recognition. With the existing power structure and all its mechanisms of exclusion now peppered with breaches, Egyptian citizens were able to scurry over many of the state's defences and looked poised to infiltrate some of its innermost sanctums. Ordinary people seized back resources, like the Suzanne Mubarak housing project units, that they believed had been unjustly appropriated from them, and they underwent a psychological shift: elite appeals for state authority to be respected now fell on deaf ears, and the threat of state violence no longer commanded fear. The state as it is currently constituted could not, in the long term, withstand such a metamorphosis, and over the past half-decade those that profit from it have done everything in their power to restore the old patterns of politics and beat the intruders back. Starting with the ousting of Mubarak, they have sacrificed successive prime ministers and presidents, invited rival counter-elites to enter the establishment system and help re-seal its walls, disingenuously adopted the language of revolution in an effort to sap the strength of protesters, and unleashed waves of terror to subdue Egypt's population back into quietude. In this endeavour they have often been assisted by international allies, in the Gulf and in the global north. There are many foreign governments which gain a great deal from the existing set-up of the Egyptian state and also worry that the revolution against it, unless checked, could inspire similar movements in their own countries against their own mechanisms of political and economic exclusion, many of which are interconnected with those operating in Egypt. Domestic elites have been aided too by the rivalries of some Egyptian opposition forces, both liberal and Islamist. Some of these movements have labelled themselves as revolutionaries but are actually reformists: keener on penetrating the existing state structure and holding it for themselves than they are on demolishing it altogether.

Many of these measures have been successful; for now, the state in its traditional form lives on. But Mubarak Country has been fragmented by the ongoing revolution and counter-revolution. Within it, new spaces have emerged – radical, imaginative pockets of Egypt in which life and politics play out in a completely different way from anything that has been done before: factories effectively run by their own workers, villages that have declared their independence, alternative security collectives dedicated to resisting sexual violence, major energy projects that have been seized and transformed by locals, sending state officials and their gendarmes running to the hills. These alternative spaces are often isolated from each other; many get swiftly closed down by the authorities. But extinguishing them altogether has proved impossible. They form a splintered Revolution Country, and many of the Egyptians who helped to force these spaces open, or who have had some experience, however fleeting, of moving within their borders, now walk around with an altered sense of what is normal, and what is possible, and think in a way that is incompatible with the conventional system of authority. From inside these spaces, the old state can look like an anachronism.

And so, although the political gains that accompanied the first wave of revolution have largely been reversed, Egypt exists today in a prolonged moment of flux, in which the long-running custodians of the state are continually trying to stitch their stronghold back together and rule as if nothing has changed – as if all Egypt was still Mubarak

Country – while significant portions of the citizenry exist within an entirely new political culture that no longer accepts the structure of the old state at all. The country's great divide is not between secular Egyptians and Islamists, or between those cleaved to some traditional notion of Arab or Muslim identity and those embracing liberal Western modernity. It is between those who see themselves as part of the new landscape, made up of all these tenuous little zones in which the old ways have no legitimacy, and those who still support the old ways and wish to draw the revolutionary storm to a close. You will find Muslims of every political persuasion on both sides of this divide, just as you will Christians. There are young people on both sides of this divide, and older people. There are poor people to be found on both sides, and rich people, and those who use social media and those who don't; there are artists on both sides of the divide, and newspaper columnists, and trade union leaders, and soldiers, and intellectuals, and people from the north, and people from the south, and people from everywhere in between. Of course there are other, very real divides as well – along sectarian, geographical and class lines, to name but a few – and these faultlines are important too; sometimes they cut across the clash between two irreconcilable political cultures, and sometimes they become conflated with it. But while the influence of these other faultlines rises or falls with the daily twists and turns of post-Mubarak Egypt, they are not the underlying fissure which is animating this era. It is in the context of a struggle between the old ways and the new that everything else is taking place, and it is that struggle that will continue to bring turbulence to Egypt in the years ahead. Since Mubarak fell we have been told time and again that the storm is now over, that people like the women of the Suzanne Mubarak housing project are irrelevant, and that Egypt has returned to the days when the state's foundations were solid and the authority of those inside it uncontested. These claims are wrong. The truth is that we stand at the beginning of a long and deep-seated revolutionary moment, looking out over a hurricane that will cause Egypt to shudder for a very long time to come.

The eighteen-day anti-Mubarak uprising was the first flashpoint in a cycle of confrontations provoked by the fundamental clash between

Mubarak Country and Revolution Country, between the old ways and the new. These confrontations have often pitched revolutionaries against counter-revolutionary forces, but they have also involved fighting among rival elites as they seek to take advantage of the tumult and expand their areas of influence, and among reformist forces as they attempt to keep each other at bay and grab institutional power for themselves. Each cycle usually involves the steady accretion of political tension, the initial indifference of the state's proprietors, an unexpected trigger point that brings protesters to the streets, then a series of responses by the state in an effort to halt popular mobilization: attempts to delegitimize demonstrators as unpatriotic or non-revolutionary, repressive violence, limited concessions, then finally a shuffling of the establishment deck – prominent individuals are jettisoned, new ones brought into the fold – in an effort to split the protest movement and reconsolidate the security of the state as a whole. The tranquillity that follows is never more than surface-deep, because the core gulf between state and citizenry remains unresolved.

When the uprising against him began, Mubarak told Egypt's citizens that they had to make a choice between chaos and stability. In the end, it was the broader elites surrounding him that made that decision. With each passing day he remained in office, the struggle against the president attained greater radicalism; the state's incumbents dumped him in order to preserve their idea of stability. But Mubarak's departure failed to silence the streets. 'I used to hunt for where protests are, now everywhere I go there is one,' tweeted activist Gigi Ibrahim under the hashtag #PostMubarakConvenience. SCAF's attempted distinction between 'authentic' anti-Mubarak protesters and the 'troublemakers' and 'thugs' continuing to agitate for change now that he had gone was policed with staggering brutality: thousands of Egyptians who mobilized in public over the coming months were captured and beaten, and many were subjected to military trial. Mubarak was packed off to prison, but so too were hundreds of revolutionaries. In Tora, Egypt's most notorious political jail, Mubarak-era icons who had fallen out with SCAF generals found themselves caged next to the same youths who had fought to bring them down. And yet revolutionary momentum persisted: security headquarters were ransacked, regime-friendly bosses were hounded out of workplaces, dreams remained alive. One group of incarcerated activists wrote to human rights campaigner Heba Morayef: 'As long as there is hope, nothing is impossible.'[6] They were right. On the ring road, photos appeared of soldiers kissing babies, but the next cycle of confrontation was already on the horizon. Initially a small minority, those speaking out directly against military rule were growing in number. By the summer of 2011, opponents of SCAF had mustered enough support to reoccupy Tahrin. The state responded with new civilian front-men, new cabinets and new consignments of tear gas – even, in October, a massacre of Egyptians taking part in a Coptic Christian demonstration, broadcast around the world – but to no avail. By the end of autumn, there were hundreds of thousands back in the streets once again.

These confrontational loops weren't merely a consequence of the state's determination to resist all but the most cosmetic of changes. They were a product, too, of the nature of the revolutionaries themselves and the sort of revolution that many of them were fighting for. Those actively battling the state since the revolution began – by which I mean those trying to dismantle the state as a whole, breaking down those core networks of elite authority and the neo-colonial exclusions they are built upon rather than protesting on behalf of one factional rival or another which aimed to seize the state for itself – have sought to create new forms of sovereignty that don't mirror the power structures of Mubarak Country. These revolutionaries have adopted, often at great personal cost, consistent positions against authoritarianism, and those positions have pitted them against Mubarak, against the army generals that succeeded him, against Mohamed Morsi and the leadership of the Muslim Brotherhood, and against the military regime and their self-professed 'liberal' allies who subsequently forced Morsi out and regained power for themselves. One way of attempting to form a different kind of state, without the authoritarianism, violence and patriarchy of the current one, would be to take temporary control of the state's existing formal institutions and then exploit their clout to begin transforming the country.

This has been the initial model of many of the world's most famous revolutions: French radicals agitated through the *ancien régime*'s

Estates-General before storming the Bastille; Russia's revolutionary upheaval began via the provisional rule of the Tsar's Duma. By and large, though, Egyptian revolutionaries have never pursued this strategy. They haven't viewed power as something just 'out there', to be captured; they've understood it as something diffuse, scattered across complex domestic, regional and global nodes.[7] Through this lens, resisting power means much more than replacing those that wield it. It means a reimagination of how power functions, and the opening up of a space in which that reimagination can take place. It means a rejection of rigid hierarchies and ideological blueprints, of charismatic leaders and the obedience they crave. 'During the eighteen days you wouldn't find demands [for a specific political platform],' said one of those living within Egypt's new political universe, when asked to explain what they were striving for. 'Our demand was, "I don't want this kind of power to be practised on me. I want my body and soul to be respected. I want to be who I am. I want my dignity." That's why I tend to disagree with people who say this revolution doesn't have a direction or a compass. It has one, but it's a new one; it's a revolution on the form of the revolution itself.'[8]

The organizational aspects of the revolution have therefore developed beyond the state rather than in parallel to it, not so much 'leaderless' as 'leaderful': comprised of many groups and individuals that make contingent alliances with one another but retain their political autonomy as well. Some of these alliances have had official names, like the Revolution Youth Coalition, the Revolution Continues Coalition and the Road to Revolution Front, but many others have remained informal and nameless, ravelling together when needed and then disbanding into the wind. What brings them together is a rejection of elite binaries – 'us or chaos' – and the conviction that politics and life can and must find better forms than the status quo. They believe that the discovery and implementation of those forms are not preordained but will develop out of the very struggles being waged against those who seek to deny their existence. Inspired by the *horizontalidad* social movements of Latin America over the past two decades, this sort of rhizomatic organization – similar to the structure of roots underground, which spread far and wide and have many diverse buds of activity rather than a single centrepoint – was the natural outcome of the oppositional activity that had taken place during the Mubarak era. Under Mubarak, the regime prevented any large organized and radical alternative to the dictatorship from emerging on an institutional level, which meant that for their own survival activists had to remain loose, dispersed and flexible. In Egypt's revolutionary era, the continuation and deepening of that form of political struggle has proved sensationally effective at delivering wave after wave of crisis to elites inside the state. Without an obvious trunk to chop down and eliminate, or a visible ideology or individual to discredit, the state has often floundered in its attempts to draw mass revolutionary protests to a close.

As a result, state authority has waned sharply at times, while the individual and communal agency of Egyptian citizens has expanded. And it is this sapping of stature on the one hand and the invigoration of it on the other that has enabled the various stretches of Revolution Country – uneven, fragile but vital – to materialize. The forces supporting the state and those they pay to defend them cannot police every corner of Mubarak Country at every hour of the day; to a great extent, their power rests on norms that are threaded through the nation's social fabric: respect for one's elders, popular deference to the patriarchs, belief in *haybat el-dawla* – the prestige and inviolability of the state. But from the draughty halls where popular neighbourhood committees have met in order to organize their own gas cylinder distribution and circumvent local politically connected business magnates, to the university lecture halls where students no longer tolerate being educated by rote, to the empty affordable housing units being broken into and occupied without permission by impoverished young women and their families, the revolution has generated spaces in which those norms no longer apply. Such spaces don't exist in isolation from the rest of Mubarak Country. Like the informal ramps up to the ring road, they are dotted alongside and within a landscape still largely under authoritarian control, and most Egyptians traverse both sorts of terrain every single day. But their persistence is what keeps the long revolution alive. Hence why the head of the municipal district council blamed squatting at the Suzanne Mubarak apartment blocks on the state's loss of authority, and why he argued that a 'show of strength' was necessary in an effort to restore it. Hence why the experiences of those women absolutely belong in an account of the Egyptian revolution: because they tell the story of a democratic citizenry emerging, albeit one still ruled by a despotic state that rejects the possibility of any such democracy existing.

The closest historical parallel to this is not Gamal Abdel Nasser's coup in 1952, which left most Egyptians still estranged from the Egyptian state, but rather the stream of revolutions that swept across Europe in the late 1840s, in which certain segments of society attempted for the first time to enter politics – hitherto the sole preserve of armies, monarchies, noblemen and the Church – rupturing the existing model of state power but, at least initially, without sustainably replacing it with something new. Those European uprisings appeared at first to have failed, as the old order clung on to formal rule. But the maelstrom they engendered continued for many decades and ultimately transformed the nature of the modern state as we know it. The Egyptian revolution has likewise thrust long-excluded segments of the population – not just the bourgeois, as in 1848, but a far broader group of citizens, including many of those most marginalized by market fundamentalism and military autocracy – headlong into the political arena, exploding the old ways though struggling, so far, to articulate the new.

At times, leaders embodying the old ways have and will continue to command support from sections of the population enthused by the new who believe that this particular figurehead or that one can help effect the transformation in these moments, far from remaking the state, many Egyptians have become ardent supporters of traditional state authority. But their backing of each reconstituted eliteregime is conditional, and easily withdrawn when they are let down once again. 'This is not something that ends tomorrow, or in a year, or three years, or even with Sisi or whoever follows him,' argues Khaled Fahmy, the historian. 'We are in the beginning of a long, long phase, and speaking as a historian I recognize that this moment is one that Egypt has never witnessed before, ever. That's not to say political mobilization and change is somehow contrary to the Egyptian "nature"; we know that it is not. This is not something that contradicts the overall trajectory of Egyptian history. But the scale of it is something we've never previously seen. We have never witnessed something so big, so deep, and so profound.'[9] Mona el-Ghobashy, an Egyptian political scientist, has argued that thanks to the revolution, only one thing is certain: 'The Egyptian state is no longer off limits to the Egyptian people.'[10] She is right, and yet the state itself acts as if those limits remain.

But by not attempting to seize state power directly for themselves, revolutionaries have also afforded elites time and space to regroup after each cycle of confrontation, to plot new strategies for survival, and rebuild the repressive institutions necessary to fight back. In the weeks and months following the anti-Mubarak uprising, as it became obvious that felling the president would not on its own be enough to quell protest and protect the ruling class, SCAF scrambled to find a new formula for power – one that could somehow dampen the revolution's energy, draw people off the streets, and yet leave the broad outlines of state authority intact. The military needed a political settlement that combined procedural democracy – the Egyptian people would clearly not be sated by anything less – with practical autocracy, and to that end they needed a new partner in the ruling enterprise. That partner was the Muslim Brotherhood.

The Brotherhood, whose leaders had been negotiating with the regime since 1 February 2011, well before Mubarak departed the presidential palace, were in many ways the state's ideal collaborator for 'project stability'.[11] The organization's leadership was innately conservative, believers in strict hierarchies of power who frowned on attempts to upend the status quo. They were also staunchly committed to neoliberalism. Many of those who mobilized in the streets during the anti-Mubarak uprising were Muslim Brotherhood members or sympathizers who shared the revolution's aim of building a different kind of state – even if the sort of state they sought to build was different from that pursued by the democratic left – and whose political and economic priorities were far more radical than the organization's senior officials. But after so many years in the cold, those officials were determined to use the opportunities thrown up by the revolution to move into the closed centre of state power, even as the revolution sought to smash it open, and hence they signed up to a 'transition' plan that would revolve around a series of elections – elections which only the well-organized Brotherhood were ever likely to win. Unlike the Brotherhood, revolutionaries had no experience running for office. They had never created institutions for that purpose, partly because of the historical restrictions placed upon them and partly because of their particular interpretation of state power and the way in which they wanted to defeat it. The political structure of the Brotherhood, on the other hand, was an almost exact mirror of the political structure of the state: a clear pyramid of authority, a plexus of shared business interests, family ties and regional loyalties, a long tradition of formal organization and obedience.[12] Brotherhood activists drew on religion to justify their support of SCAF; campaigners insisted that opposition to the constitutional amendments proposed by the generals in order to facilitate their transition plan was an affront to God and Islam.[13] Revolutionaries, meanwhile, resisted the rush to the ballot box because they could see that post-Mubarak Egypt was shaping up to be much like Mubarak's Egypt, only with some new faces at the summit, and that elections on their own, designed to formalize the revolution and sanitize it before it penetrated the heart of the state, would not be enough to achieve change. They sought a democracy with depth and meaning – not a democratic façade that legitimized the old ways and shut down the new. They have often been criticized for this approach, and some criticism may be warranted. But it is worth bearing in mind that we have a concrete example of a political force that did take the route of more conventional political organization and electoral participation, and we know what that achieved: once inside the state the Brotherhood did nothing to unpick it, and were eventually swept away by the very forces they worked so hard to accommodate and compromise with.

In mid-November, before voting could begin, a massive uprising erupted against military rule; in the clashes that followed, more than a hundred lost their lives. The November uprising adhered to the now familiar cycle: ministers resigned, successive speeches were made from on high, unrest only mounted. It was eventually overcome by two things: the ferocious violence of the Egyptian army and the support given to that army by the Brotherhood. At the height of the clashes, members of the Brotherhood came down to Mohamed

Mahmoud, one of the main streets that leads out from Tahrir Square, and linked arms to try to prevent revolutionaries from reaching the security forces – to prevent them from winning a battle that could have sounded the death knell for the police state. Few who were there will ever forget that the Brotherhood's highest echelons were keener on protecting the state and its practitioners of death from revolutionary pressure than they were on supporting the revolution. Few will forget that as Egyptians like Ahmed Harara – who lost one eye at the hands of a police gunman on 28 January and then the other in the same fashion during the street battles of Mohamed Mahmoud – sought to push a tottering military government over the edge, the Brotherhood went out to campaign in the parliamentary elections and hold SCAF's tattered 'transition' plan together. Nawal al-Saadawi, an Egyptian feminist and novelist, declared that Mohamed Mahmoud was the 'unmasking' of the Brotherhood, who had 'tried to co-opt the January revolution and make deals with the people in power while the blood of young people flows in the streets'.[14] In later years, when revolutionaries commemorated those clashes, they hung a banner across that iconic road which read 'Revolutionaries only: entry prohibited for Muslim Brotherhood, Army and *felool* ['remnants of the old regime']'.

Mohamed Mahmoud has been likened to that original day of rage back on 28 January, but in truth it felt different: partly because the direct involvement of the armed forces was teaching revolutionaries so much more about the shape of the state they were up against, and partly because the bloodshed at times felt even fiercer. We saw protesters scrawl their parents' contact details on their arms before entering the fray so they could be identified more easily if they died; we saw American-imported teargas so strong that there were jokey chants about the people wanting the regime to bring back the old stuff; we saw morgues run out of coffins. I remember the jolt that ran through me one evening after dark when I passed a middle-aged couple walking through a scene of devastation in Talaat Harb Street towards the fighting, each silent, each looking straight ahead, each clasping the other with one hand and carrying a rock in the other. I remember too the nausea that washed over me when I first saw the footage of Egyptian soldiers dragging dead bodies along the street and piling them in the corner like trash.[15] Hossam el-Hamalawy, the revolutionary socialist behind the 3arabawy website, was asked by a television journalist if this was Egypt's second revolution; exasperated, he replied: 'No, we're just finishing off the first one.' Khalid Abdallah, revolutionary and actor, surveyed the carnage and pointed out that every Western leader who had tramped ostentatiously through Tahrir for a photo-op after Mubarak fell and then offered unconditional support for the SCAF 'transition' was complicit in this orgy of death, complicit in counter-revolution.

Rumours proliferated that senior generals, including the head of SCAF, Mohamed Tantawi, came close to fleeing the country as the uprising reached its peak. We may never know how true they were, but if the Brotherhood had stood with the revolution at that moment, a very different Egypt might have emerged from the wreckage. Instead they turned their backs on the martyred and their attention to the polling booth. Revolutionaries are sometimes asked, especially by Western commentators, why they didn't campaign more effectively for support in that first post-Mubarak parliamentary election, which began in the middle of the Mohamed Mahmoud bloodshed; why they weren't on their soapboxes giving speeches and scanning the skyline for voters. The answer is that it's hard to do so when your mouth is full of gas and your eyes have been blinded by birdshot.

And so elections proceeded. The Brotherhood went on to become the largest party in parliament and win the presidency. On the ground, everything felt different, but in the formal realm the revolution had so far succeeded only in ushering a new counter-elite into the corridors of power. The arrival of the Brotherhood in the state's private enclaves caused much resentment among the existing military-bureaucratic caste, who had always viewed senior Brotherhood leaders as mortal enemies. But, for the time being, the survival of the existing state apparatus was more important than personal rivalries. The Brotherhood's attempt to safeguard elite power was the first betrayal of the revolution by Egyptian reformists – but not the last – and it provided the exclusionary state with a critical lease of life.

In June 2012, Mohamed Morsi was elected president. Some revolutionaries boycotted the poll altogether, but after a fatal vote split in the first round – candidates broadly aligned with the revolution polled more than either Morsi or Mubarak's last prime minister, Ahmed Shafik, but the division between them enabled the latter two to proceed to a run-off election – the Brotherhood's representative appeared to others to be the lesser of two evils, particularly when he adopted an explicitly revolutionary platform during his campaign against Shafik and promised to deliver on the demands of Tahrir Square. As a reformist, committed ultimately to building from the state as it was, rather than from a venture on the ground to reimagine what the state could be, Morsi was never going to be the vehicle through which the revolution ultimately triumphed. But there was hope, among the optimists at least, that – despite the Brotherhood's defence of SCAF in 2011 – once in office he would follow through on his rhetoric and assemble a coalition of political forces that could fight to expand elected areas of the state against the unelected, and begin to disassemble some of those military, bureaucratic and financial networks that Revolution Country was up against.

The optimists were to be bitterly disappointed. Once he had the tools of the authoritarian state at his disposal, Morsi turned upon the revolution – breaking strikes, beating protesters, censoring creatives, defending the security apparatus against popular demands for reform and resisting any moves towards transitional justice. Far from taking on the old regime, Morsi was intent on cohabitation. Mohamed Ibrahim, an old hand from the Mubarakist security apparatus, was appointed minister of the interior and charged with clamping down on demonstrations. To codify the ruling settlement that had secured his power, Morsi retired some of the military's old guard and promoted a new generation of army leaders, including a new defence minister: Abdel Fattah el-Sisi.* Fresh protections for the military's

---

* Some analysts at the time interpreted the retirement of Tantawi and the army's chief of staff, Sami Anan, as a revolutionary attack by Morsi's government against the military's power base. In reality, it was an institutionalized entrenchment of the status quo. Tantawi and Anan were intimately associated with Mubarak and (as noted by a 2008 cable from the US embassy in Cairo, released by Wikileaks) strongly resented by the majority of army officers – in the longterm their positions were clearly untenable. But before removing them, Morsi took care to consult other senior military generals about the changeover and secured their full approval for the move.

reserved bastions of influence – including an institutionalized right for generals to force civilians through military tribunals – were woven, against popular opposition, into Egypt's constitution. It quickly became clear that Morsi's ascendancy was part of an authoritarian solution to the challenge of incorporating some popular recruitment into high office without allowing Egyptian citizens to overrun the state: the aim was to subdue unrest in order that Egypt's traditional power configuration, now mildly rejigged to incorporate the Brotherhood, could re-solidify. In Morsi's first one hundred days as president alone, there were 200 reported cases of police brutality. 'Torture is more violent and the sexual abuse involved is increasing,' said rights activist Aida Seif el-Dawla at the time, 'and a torture chamber now exists wherever there are security forces.'[17]

It wasn't just the violence that marked out Morsi's presidency as a bone-tired by-product of Mubarak Country; it was also his infantilizing tone, the staid way in which he presumed that the old mental infrastructure of ruling class power could continue without interruption. One of Morsi's first acts in office was the holding of an 'open house' where aggrieved citizens could come and present their petitions for change at his feet. But 1,000 Egyptians hadn't laid down their lives so that those who lived on could wait for social justice to be dispensed from above on a whim. Morsi patronized and hectored opponents, shunned attempts at compromise, and appealed time and again, just as his military partners always did, to the supremacy and inviolability of the state. At one point, he even began emulating his predecessors' physical tics. During the protests that erupted under military rule in 2011, SCAF General Mohsen el-Fangari had addressed the nation. Abrasive and accusatory, el-Fangari insisted that the armed forces would not tolerate protests that 'harmed the nation's interests', and – unforgettably – wagged his finger at the camera as he spoke, in the manner of a schoolmaster ticking off a naughty child. The next day that same finger was lampooned in spray-paint on a hundred walls in Cairo, a Facebook group named

---

Rather than face trial for their crimes against Egyptian citizens, as revolutionaries had called for, Tantawi and Anan were awarded several distinctions of state by Morsi, as well as *de facto* immunity.[16]

'Fangari: You cannot threaten us' was attracting thousands of new members by the hour, and a fresh set of rallies and sit-ins were scheduled for the coming weeks.

Yet when Mohamed Morsi took to the airwaves a year and a half later, in response to another tsunami of popular discontent against a controversial presidential decree he adopted exactly the same tactic, dispensing a musty blend of threats and bribes from on high and repeatedly jabbing at viewers with his finger. 'Your Excellency the President, Egyptians will not stand for being shouted at or pointed at with your finger,' wrote activist Nawara Negm in *al-Tahrir* soon after. 'Especially when your suit is too big and the sleeves are too long and reach halfway down to your fingers, and your finger sticks out of the sleeves and we can't see the rest of your palm.'[18] As the blogger Baheyya argued, Brotherhood rule was simply

> the old politics of elite machinations, excluding the little people from 'high politics' by throwing them some economic crumbs, or trying to shush them with talk of threats and conspiracies. That notion of limited democracy, of kissing up to the people until you have their vote and then ignoring them completely for four years, is expired for Egypt. Already under Mubarak's vicious autocracy, Egyptians were crafting the most ingenious means of having their say on public matters, even when their say 'didn't change anything'. Now that everything's changed, they're punishing every official who dares overreach. No Egyptian president now can afford to act like a boss who knows best. Consent must be secured not just at the ballot box, but at every critical juncture.[19]

But SCAF and the Brotherhood had been locked together in a shared undertaking to defend the state, and rather than genuinely engage with a restless populace their attention shifted to the division of the spoils within. Organs of institutional power – now occupied both by the old guard and the reformist newcomers – became contested battlegrounds, with both Brotherhood figures and *felool* members jockeying for position. Egypt's constitutional assembly was on the front line, as were administrative positions in the governorates and the whole of the judiciary. Of course these contests remained off-limits to regular citizens. For those outside, striving for their rights – to their cities, to their farmland, to a life free of poverty and an economy that worked for the many not the few – the state remained as aloof as ever.

Yet the game Morsi was playing was a dangerous one. It involved both empowering old elites on the one hand, allowing oppressive organs of the state to build up their strength once again, in an effort to repress revolutionary tremors from below, and also simultaneously sparring with those same elites on the other, whenever he felt the newfound privileges enjoyed by the Brotherhood at the top of the pyramid were being encroached upon too extensively. As mutual animosity grew, long-term occupants of the state's main institutions began effectively to boycott Morsi's presidency, refusing to follow his orders and throwing up judicial and bureaucratic obstacles in his way. In response, Morsi sought to insulate his office further and further from the rest of the state's infrastructure. Later, the Brotherhood would correctly claim that the deep state had been scheming against them, but their mistake was to assume they could sideline revolutionaries and outfox it on their own. Morsi made no efforts to build a durable coalition with his revolutionary opponents because he saw them as more of a threat than the old guard; instead it was to fellow Islamists that he turned for support, handing a propaganda gift to the deep state.

In late November 2012, Morsi issued a constitutional declaration which effectively placed him above the law and granted the president's decisions immunity from all legal oversight, a move which – though rescinded, for the most part, some days later – sparked a whole new wave of revolutionary confrontation at the *itthadeya* presidential palace in December 2012. Internationally, some on the left looked at these protests and saw a democratically elected and representative government being challenged by upper-class liberal snobs, but their reading was skewed.[20] True, among the activist tents and bright green lasers you could find demonstrators wearing Prada trainers who were more concerned about the advent of Islamists at the top of the state than they were about the revolution, but in the main the anti-Morsi marches and rallies were driven by an acute anger and mass repudiation of the way in which Egypt's elites – including both the Brotherhood and the police state they had initially allied with – were selling out the

Egyptians' struggle for change. Regional headquarters of the Brotherhood's Freedom and Justice Party were set ablaze; at *itthadeya*, protesters broke through barricades and reached the palace walls.

Morsi was a leader tasked with keeping a lid on the revolution, and the old custodians of the state would tolerate him only for as long as he carried out his prophylactic role effectively. The events of late 2012 revealed that this 'masterful authoritarian solution' to the quandary of marrying exclusionary politics with mass demands for change had not succeeded. Protests against Morsi's rule grew larger and larger with each passing month he was in office, culminating in a series of mass demonstrations that brought millions back on to the streets in the summer of 2013. Both the Brotherhood and the military had underestimated how fundamentally Egypt had changed on the ground; amid the blossoming of Revolution Country, the Brotherhood-bolstered forces of order could not bring the Egyptians to heel.

When the anti-Mubarak uprising began in 2011, Egyptian revolutionaries were the darlings of the global press. Now that they had refused to be sated by pseudo-democracy and had insisted that elections would not dictate the limits of their struggle, they lost their media shine. It was popular in some quarters throughout this period to claim that Egyptians didn't know how to 'do' procedural democracy; *Time* magazine even labelled them the 'World's Worst Democrats'. I didn't meet any *Time* reporters on parliamentary election day in late 2011, but I did watch thousands of people queuing patiently for hours in the mud outside polling stations in Manshiyet Nasr, just as they were in Shubra el-Kheyma, in Imbaba and in countless other communities across the country. In those queues I saw Egyptians who believed this ballot was their opportunity to finally muscle on to the formal political map, Egyptians who were seizing that opportunity with unbridled enthusiasm and both hands. At the Ahmed Orabi secondary school in Duweiqa, where ballots were being cast, I sat with the headteacher, Mahmoud Hassan Mohamed, as the polling station's various cast of characters – soldiers, judges, electoral administrators and the odd lost voter – drifted in and out of his ground-floor office; no matter who came through the door, Mohamed greeted them with a smile that stretched from ear to ear. 'We have created Tahrir here in our little school,' he beamed.

Later that day I met Magdy Mustafa in Sayeda Zainab, a beautiful neighbourhood just south of Cairo city centre; he was the father of a martyr, 24-year-old Tarek Mustafa, who had been shot dead by a policeman in Sayeda Zainab Square during the eighteen days. 'Ask anyone, and they'll tell you Tarek was loved beyond belief by all who knew him,' Magdy told me. 'He was a graduate from the faculty of commerce, yet in Mubarak's Egypt that meant he could only get a job quarrying rocks for the metro system. In late 2010 he was laid off and left with nothing. He lived in a country where another young man of the same age might live in a villa and have a car worth 2 million gineih, the kind of man who will happily throw 5,000 gineih at the feet of a belly-dancer. Meanwhile, my son couldn't afford a one-gineih cup of tea. So he joined the uprising and said he would document this struggle against injustice with his camera. I was supportive of him and the revolution from day one. I never expected I would be making such a sacrifice.'[21] I asked Magdy why he was voting, and he replied that it was because the revolution – a revolution against the inequality and gunfire borne by his son, against the way the old state had shunted people like him to the periphery – had not yet been completed. 'This vote today is a way of keeping it alive,' he explained. 'Because what's changed is that there is no longer any fear in the hearts of the Egyptian people; when a police officer walks alongside you he now has to do so as an equal, not a master. Those in power know that they must show humility to two things: God and the Egyptians. Today, we're reminding them: if you disrespect the Egyptian people, we will make mincemeat out of you.'

Like millions of their compatriots, Mahmoud and Magdy believed in the revolution's promise of a truly democratic Egypt, and they believed – initially at least – in the assurances of Egypt's elites when they were told that elections would deliver that democratic Egypt to its citizens. In the past half-decade there have been nearly a dozen national elections; Egyptians have 'done' procedural democracy more than virtually any other people on earth, so much so that they have invented a new term to describe the system of government inflicted upon them since Mubarak fell. *Dimooqrateya* is the Arabic word for democracy; many now talk instead of living under the rule of *sundooqrateya*, a (ballot) 'boxocracy'. They have tested that system, and they have found it wanting. The Egyptian people have discovered that ballots alone are not enough to remake the state; they have discovered that *sundooqrateya* has nothing to say about accountability for state crimes, that it is silent on social justice, and uninterested in ending the economic violence still being wreaked on the Egyptian people in the name of progressive reform. They have watched *sundooqrateya* remain mute on the institutional support for police abuses, and on the building of a different kind of Egypt: an Egypt where citizens aren't evicted on the whims of tycoon developers, where land and water are collective resources held by citizens rather than becoming the private playthings of millionaires, local people have a say in what their villages, towns and cities look like, and the political system works in the interests of citizens. They have concluded that genuine change will not flow from a solitary appearance at a ballot box twice a decade in order to select between various members of a political class who share to many of each other's values, a political class which uniformly demands that voters return home and stay quiet on all the days in between.

Throughout Morsi's tenure, the Brotherhood equated the entire revolution with *sundooqrateya* and insisted that the 51.73 percent share of the vote he had received in the presidential run-off election placed his actions beyond reproach and made protests against him illegitimate. But this minimalist interpretation of democracy wasn't peculiar to Egypt's Brotherhood: it was borne along by the ideological currents of our age. In procedural democracies all over the world, citizens have been told that popular sovereignty extends to an occasional pick-and-mix between politicians whose ideological differences are microscopic and whose ability to reshape the dynamics of power on our planet stands at virtually nil. We've been told that protest – legitimate protest, rather than irresponsible troublemaking or extremism – consists of utilizing our 'vote' as free market consumers, of donating to an NGO, of marching down public streets every now and then in an orderly fashion under the approving gaze of the authorities. Neoliberalism's separation of the political and economic realms, its faith in markets and its struggle to void domains over which citizens might collectively practise authority, has conspired to enforce a gradualist notion of political change: one in which expressions of dissent are to be sounded wholly within the prevailing system, a 'consumerist' and 'stakeholder' parody of transformation in miniature. Under the assumption that liberal capitalism has emerged victorious and now stands uncontested as the prevailing orthodoxy of our time, truly transformative projects to remake societies and states are consigned to the murky fringes of political behaviour, or merely dismissed as relics.

It was into this pasteurized world that Western elites sought to shepherd Egypt's revolution: the anti-Mubarak uprising was framed as the country's entry ticket to liberal modernity instead of any kind of offensive against the power configurations that affect us all. When international leaders toasted Tahrir, far from encouraging the revolution it was a way of delimiting it inside the procedurally democratic, capitalist-friendly, gradualist model of change. It was that delimited revolution which brought David Cameron and his arms dealers to Cairo weeks after Mubarak fell, which led Hillary Clinton to wax lyrical about the 'peacefulness' of Egypt's struggle – because resistance must never be violent, no matter how much violence the system throws at you – and which then US Defense Secretary Robert Gates sounded so thrilled about when he congratulated the Egyptian army on 'empowering' change. It was that delimited revolution that has since been marketized by corporations and advertisers; by late 2011, the London Chamber of Commerce was holding conferences for weapons manufacturers in which the 'opportunities' thrown up by Arab revolutions were picked over,[22] and an international PR and communications agency, JWT, of which Vodafone – which had switched off its services at the height of the anti-Mubarak uprising at the regime's request – was a client, was busy producing an advent in which the mobile phone company took credit for the dictator's downfall.[23] When large numbers of Egyptian citizens rejected those sorts of limits being placed upon their revolution and poured back out on to the streets, knowing that collective mobilization was not antithetical to democracy or elections, but was rather participatory politics by other means, Western observers changed their tune.[24] Prime-time American news host Fareed Zakaria wondered whether the Arab Spring had 'lost its appeal' and posited that Egyptians had a civilizational opposition to democracy.[25] CNN and

Foreign Policy magazine both asked whether the revolution had been 'worth it'.[26]

Mohamed Morsi might have been asking himself the same question. In an effort to mount the summit of Mubarak Country, the man popularly derided as the 'spare tyre' – a reference to the fact that he was only the Brotherhood's second choice for presidential candidate, after their preferred representative was disqualified – had offered himself up as a buffer between Revolution Country and the state, granting the occupants of the latter as much leeway as possible to end the revolution's storms as long as the Brotherhood could join the party. He showed no interest in confronting or resolving the central contradictions of revolutionary Egypt, and as a result he engendered a groundswell of popular opposition that threatened to overwhelm the state's defences once more. Amid the spiralling unrest, the state incumbents that Morsi had done so much to defend spied their chance: to quell the opposition by piggy-backing on anti-Morsi sentiment and ejecting the Brotherhood back out into the cold. Now it was time for the old guard to take back power for themselves.

In those final, fateful few months of Morsi's rule, the interlacing of Mubarak Country and Revolution Country grew more extensive, the shifting of authority between state and citizens occurring so fast it could make you dizzy. 'In Cairo these days the pavements disappear under your feet as the stones are pulled out for use as ammunition,' wrote Ursula Lindsey in early 2013. 'Barriers spring up overnight, turning familiar neighbourhoods into strange mazes. Ancient buildings go up in flames. And every day there are new warnings, slogans and portraits sprayed on the walls.'[27] She went on to point out that the turmoil was directed beyond the Brotherhood: it was a rejection of the old ways that Morsi's reign had placed in sharper relief than ever, and it was scaring defenders of the state right across the supposed Islamist/secular divide. 'Only 6 per cent of Egyptian men are over sixty. They lean back in their office chairs, in their seats on TV platforms, trying to look relaxed but clinging to their armrests. The Islamists, the generals, their secular opponents – they all seem to think they can cleave some advantage from the chaos, that they can use the young men in the street against each other. In any case, they don't know how to stop it. The young men are angry and unafraid.'

In his bid to survive, Morsi pulled out all the stops: anti-Brotherhood activists disappeared from rallies and were discovered brain-dead in hospitals; the old rhetoric of pernicious foreign hands and Zionist agents returned to the foreground of government speeches. People like Mohamed el-Guindy and Gaber Salah, known as 'Jika' to his friends, became immortalized in a thousand protest chants. The former died after four days of torture at the hands of police; the latter, a sixteen-year-old, was murdered at a protest against one of Morsi's decrees. Just before leaving his house on the final day of his life, Jika wrote on his Facebook page, 'If I fail to come back, I ask the people to continue with the revolution and claim our rights.' Anger on the streets soared. If the unrest continued, it seemed inevitable that Morsi would either be overthrown directly or forced to call early elections. No one knew what permanent damage might be inflicted upon the state by such an outcome, what radical currents might be unleashed. The generals had no desire to find out.

Within their predicament, the army's top brass spotted a golden opportunity to strike back at the very counter-elite they had grudgingly admitted into the state's fold in the first place. A military manoeuvre against Morsi had two advantages. Firstly, it would eliminate a political rival from all those networks of privilege and patronage they had been forced to share with the Brotherhood. Secondly, by capitalizing on the very real popular anger against Morsi for his betrayal of the revolution, the military could once again – as it had attempted to do with Mubarak – try to build a firewall between the most visible personification of state authority and the deeper architecture that lay beneath it. By eliminating Morsi before the people did, and by reframing his misdeeds as crimes against the state, rather than crimes against the revolution, the generals hoped to present themselves as the nation's saviour and twist popular anger 180 degrees. Mubarak Country wasn't the problem: just Mubarak, and then Morsi. And because, unlike Mubarak – an air force general who emerged from within the military's own ranks – the Brotherhood were something 'other', something that looked different from the state's traditional public face, the solution to Morsi's perfidy could be recast as a return to some more familiar faces; not a different kind of state, after all, but a return of the old one that in reality had never gone away. The revolution's sole aim, according to the generals, was now the removal of the Brotherhood and a reclamation of the prestige the organization had leeched from the old ways. Revolutionary struggle now lay in strengthening – not emasculating – the state in order to make that happen. Egyptians, they gambled, would embrace a military strongman who could shore up the old ways and dismiss Islamist trespassers from their fortress.

And so from early 2013, the armed forces and various *felool* elements began actively to support and co-opt the anti-Morsi protest movement, steering its oppositional momentum away from the state and towards the increasingly beleaguered Brotherhood. Debate has since raged over whether mass mobilization or elite conspiracy was the driver of Morsi's downfall, but the two are not mutually exclusive. Street protests against the Brotherhood were real and they were revolutionary, but there was a failure on the part of many involved to discern the ways in which the deep state was able to channel developments to its advantage. The security apparatus that Morsi had fought so hard to protect threw its weight behind a huge national anti-Morsi petition drive named *tamarod* ('rebel'), which claimed to secure 23 million signatures. The businessmen that the Brotherhood had defended used their media outlets to demonize the Islamists. And it was here that the revolution suffered its second betrayal by reformists – this time of the liberal and secular variety. Despite having little influence on the streets, the National Salvation Front (NSF), an alliance of establishment opposition politicians, had taken a formal organizational lead in battles against the Brotherhood, and often claimed, wrongly, to speak for the revolution's cause. But as the state's involvement in proceedings became clearer, the NSF – rather than pursuing an independent agenda against both Morsi and the military generals – opted to form opportunistic alliances with the 'steel heart' of Mubarak Country. In doing so, they became a counter-revolutionary mirror of the very people they swore to destroy.[28] Egyptians were once again being told that a slightly reconfigured ruling class would solve all Egypt's problems, that a shake-up of the state's custodians was all that was needed for the revolution to succeed. Weary and desperate, and repulsed by the Brotherhood's vision of political change, many believed it. It would be a fatal mistake to underestimate the extent to which the hijacking of revolutionary tactics and language by the counter-revolution succeeded in winning popular support.[29] Revolutionaries who raised slogans against the army or interior ministry as well as the Brotherhood began to find themselves hushed at demonstrations; a movement that once fought police officers off the streets started carrying them on its shoulders. By the end of June 2013, millions were calling on the president to fall and the army issued a final ultimatum to Morsi. Before protesters could oust the 'spare tyre' themselves, Sisi moved to do it for them – and lap up the public's adulation.

For many revolutionaries, those early summer nights were exhilarating, and terrifying, and traumatic, all at the same time. Again, grassroots unrest had electrified Egypt's elites into crisis mode; for the third time in as many years, they had been forced to reshuffle the top deck in an attempt to stop the revolution from bringing the whole house of cards down. The reactionary settlement reached by the generals and the Brotherhood had decisively been broken: in some ways it was a dramatic affirmation of the revolution's potency. And yet the outcome was also emblematic of the revolution's weaknesses. The old state remained standing, its traditional occupants were out of the wings and back on centre-stage, and the army's canny manoeuvring and skilful manipulation of revolutionary rhetoric had won it abundant backing from a public exhausted by economic hardship and three years of turmoil. Most corrosively, the regime's attempt to reorientate the revolution's faultlines – from horizontal to vertical, people versus state to people and state versus Islamists – took on a chilling new dimension. The old political culture was suffused with violence; it drew on a communal memory of coercion as the only effective instrument through which to achieve public order.[30] Now, as the state was hauled back up off its knees, that celebration of duress was married to a vicious dehumanization; under a 'War on Terror' strapline that was slapped across television broadcasts and newspaper front pages alike, Sisi sought to rob Brotherhood supporters not only of their nationality, but of their lives. Thousands of Morsi sympathizers and other opponents of the military had gathered in Rabaa

and Nahda, two large squares in Cairo, to protest against his ousting. In the name of 'stability', Egypt's government launched an attack
that resulted in the bloodiest massacre in the country's history.

And so Egyptian names were again scrawled on arms as protester's
battled against being reduced to a number in a morgue, or merely
consigned to the ranks of the uncounted. Among footage of besieged
mosques, robocop machine-gun fire and the dreadful sight of people
throwing themselves off bridges to escape through a maze of police
bullets, it's that little detail – the writing on the arms – that disturbed
me the most.[31] As the efforts by volunteers to collect and catalogue
the belongings of the dead, some of whom risked their lives to retrieve
plastic bags stuffed with scraps of non-life as army bulldozers closed
in,[32] writing your own name on your arm feels like the most basic
affirmation of presence in the face of a state committed to inflicting
absence: absence of a heartbeat, absence of humanity, absence of
anything but a narrative in which everything is black and white and
people are units to be slotted into pre-drawn political templates.
Writing a name on an arm says, devastatingly, 'No – I was here too.'
The authorities counted 638 corpses, the Brotherhood more than
2,500. "It was raining bullets," recalled one survivor at Rabaa. "We
didn't hear any warnings, nothing. It was like hell."[33] A protester and
medic at one of Rabaa's field hospitals recounted how each floor of
the building, from the basement upwards, gradually filled up with
bodies, as snipers' bullets pounded the hospital door.[34] Later, he said,
security forces burned down the hospital with the dead still stacked
up inside. By and large those bodies belonged not to the Brotherhood's leaders who had done so much to protect the police state
from revolutionary efforts to undermine it, not to the Brotherhood's
leaders who appointed Sisi and the interior minister, Mohamed
Ibrahim – chief architects of the crackdown – against the protests of
revolutionaries. By and large they belonged to ordinary Egyptians,
many of them Brotherhood rank-and-file, who believed in the revolution's aspirations and paid for that belief with their lives.

The Rabaa and Nahda massacres were a tragedy for Egypt's
revolution because they involved such an overwhelming loss of
life, and because in their totality they tried – and in the short term
succeeded – to drown out the voices of those seeking to remake the

state. The relentless imposition of state violence creates binaries as well as bodies: you are either with us or against us, pro-military or pro-Brotherhood, an Egyptian or a terrorist. When everything is an either/or, and the contours of struggle are set from on high, it becomes that much harder to believe in the sort of alternatives thrown up by Revolution Country, because every line of independent thought is subjugated by a more fundamental dichotomy: on whose side do you stand? Judith Butler, the feminist philosopher who has faced opprobrium for her condemnation of the Israeli occupation of palestine, has spoken of how her critics seek to destroy the conditions of audibility and force a reality in which one cannot speak out against injustice, a reality in which words of dissent cannot even be heard. How Egypt's defenders of the status quo, forced on to the back foot by the revolution, had similarly longed to destroy the conditions of audibility. In their 'War on Terror', they finally found the enemy, the fight and the stage on which to do so. In this arena of guns and certainties, it felt as if the revolution's real struggles were fading to black.[35]

Revolutions always involve counter-revolutions and are a series of skirmishes won and lost – but this loss was of a different order. It was not just deaths that had to be mourned, but the glee with which those deaths were met by so many of the living. Outside active revolutionary circles, justified hatred of the Brotherhood's leadership and its counter-revolution was so intense that it blinded millions of Egyptians to the role played by the military in that same counter-revolution. A renewed assault on the state looked more daunting than ever; hope, felt many, had been snatched away. 'My cynicism was deep and heavy to budge, but it evaporated over the course of those weeks,' wrote Yasmin el-Rifae of the eighteen days, 'and I've kept it sternly in check ever since; choosing, every time things got violent or dispirited or stagnant, to see the possibilities people were working for all around me.'[36] After Rabaa, she continued, it felt as if that ability to keep cynicism at bay had been stolen from her. Omar Robert Hamilton concurred. 'We thought we could change the world,' he stated. 'We know now that that feeling was not unique to us, that every revolutionary moment courses with the pulse of a manifest destiny. How different things feel today.'[37] Emboldened by their successes, the generals and their security apparatus moved quickly to unleash the rest of the classic authoritarian armoury: a protest law which forbade unsanctioned marches and rallies, a terrorism law that allowed authorities to denote anyone the state disliked as a militant, a military decree that placed all public property under army control.

Sisi sought an Egypt in which those that looked different were distrusted, where revolutionary activists would be swept from the streets or taken at night from their beds, where citizens' agency was destroyed. 'When I put all my clothes on together and laid my blankets on top of each other I thought that there are people who live in shacks or on the streets and that they have less clothes and less blankets than I do,' wrote revolutionary activist Alaa Abd El Fattah, back in prison once again under Sisi – as he had been under Mubarak, as he had been under SCAF – along with almost 20,000 others. 'But after the coldest night, when I decided that I had to block the windows in my cell, I realized that even the homeless can get up at any time they choose and try to deal with the cold. They may find a solution or they may not, but the feeling that an authority decides with bureaucratic randomness when to open my door or when I might find a bit of cardboard to block the window or when the guard on duty will get permission to bring a ladder so he can climb it and block the window is so oppressing that it hurts.'[38] Journalist Laura Dean described the kitchen table of her friend Hossam Meneai, an artist and filmmaker, and the cold tea and lemon slices left behind after he was arrested and removed by security forces. 'Activists of all political persuasions are in jail, along with others who have no idea why they are being held,' she wrote. 'The message: the cold tea and rotting lemons could be on anyone's table.'[39]

On 25 January 2014, the third anniversary of the revolution's first moments, pro-Morsi protesters were greeted with bullets, and so too were revolutionaries who tried to mobilize against the regime's false dichotomies – those who stood against both Sisi and Morsi, against the Brotherhood's vision of exclusion and the army's. More than 1,000 were arrested that day; some talked later of police cells with walls that were smeared with blood.[40] From journalists, especially foreign ones, the state – and, devastatingly, many civilians – demanded either fear or fawning; those displaying insufficient quantities of either found themselves imprisoned, deported, attacked in the streets. The question of how far Egypt's struggle could ever be shared by outsiders on the ground had always been a fascinating and fluid one: what were those of us without Egyptian heritage doing when we chanted *tahya masr* – 'Long live Egypt!' – at revolutionary rallies, what collective were we trying to make ourselves a part of? Personally, I saw those chants as support for a struggle for justice in my adopted homeland and as part of something broader, global, and Egypt's revolutionaries, by and large, seemed to welcome that support. But following Sisi's rise, the question stopped being academic. Reporter colleagues were assaulted and taken to court; many people, journalists and others, Egyptians and foreigners, headed for the airport. The metric of revolutionary progress was now framed by the government and most media outlets along chauvinistically nationalist lines, as unity between the army, police and people against intruders, rather than as a struggle for bread, freedom and social justice – and many of us, because of the colour of our skin or the notebooks we held in our hands, looked dangerously like intruders. Revolutionary rhetoric had been twisted by the generals to mask a return to total political control of society by the state, and of the state by a revitalized ruling caste. True to form, Tony Blair was quick to offer his support. 'Right here in Egypt I think it is fundamental that the new government succeeds, that we give it support in bringing in this new era for the people of Egypt,' he declared. 'And, you know, we can debate the past and it's probably not very fruitful to do so, but right now I think it's important the whole of the international community gets behind the leadership here and helps.'[41]

In March 2014, when Sisi announced that he would run for president, he revealed how painful the revolution had been for those charged with sealing the state from the masses. 'What Egypt witnessed in the last years in politics or media, internally or externally, is this country being occasionally trespassed,' Sisi declared. 'It is time for this disrespect and this intrusion to stop. This is an esteemed country, and everyone must know that this is a decisive moment – that disrespecting Egypt is an adventure with consequences.'[42] Like his forerunners in the post-Mubarak era, he couched his warning in the language of ultra-jingoism and hinted that this 'threat' consisted of shadowy foreign infiltrators. But the real infiltrators he was cautioning against were the Egyptian people themselves. His message to them was that after years of disruption, it was time to bring the revolution to an end.

In the early nineteenth century, two pivotal events contributed to the founding of the modern Egyptian state. The first was a massacre of the Mamluks, the caste that had ruled Egypt for hundreds of years, and the consequent rise of Ottoman commander Mohamed Ali as leader.[43] The second was the attempt by Ali to found a modern army, based on conscription. When the draft orders went out, in 1822, Egypt's population rose in fury. Over the next two years, revolts erupted in every region of the country; in the south, a revolution of 30,000 peasants spread from Esna to Aswan, bringing Ali's nascent state to the brink of implosion. Staring at defeat, the pasha took a momentous decision and ordered his military's First Brigade to launch an assault directly against the revolutionary communities, killing 3,000 men, women and children. The modern Egyptian state was founded on that act of violence; the first-ever combat operation conducted by its army was directed against its own citizens. As the historian Khaled Fahmy has pointed out, the price of immediate political victory was a social and moral defeat. Ali's promises of a 'national revival' ultimately met with failure, because they rested on the promise of a state intent on subduing and humiliating its citizens. Sheikh Mohamed Abdo, Egypt's late nineteenth century Islamic scholar and liberal reformer, concluded in 1902 that 'Mohamed Ali was a fine merchant, farmer and soldier, and a skilful tyrant – yet he was an oppressor of Egypt and a killer of her real life and spirit.'[44]

The post-Morsi era likewise began with a political victory for those at the top of the state. But what price the foundation of Sisi's Egypt, and the acts of murder and division it has been predicated on? In an effort to shut down Revolution Country, the state pressed Egyptians to turn in on themselves. A microbus passenger turned provocateur spoke of rebellion on a journey; when a fellow traveller agreed with her criticisms of Sisi, she hauled him off the bus and denounced him as a terrorist to the security forces.[45] Schoolchildren were detained for sporting potentially seditious stickers on their pencil cases. A man who named his donkey 'Sisi' was thrown into prison. Three *al-Jazeera* English journalists were raided in their hotel room and later found guilty in court of aiding terrorism; footage of their arrest was leaked to Egyptian television and set to the soundtrack of Hollywood sci-fi thriller *Thor*.[46] A fictional puppet, Abla Fahita, was accused of being an Islamist sympathizer; the authorities agreed to investigate.[47] Egyptians who had been arrested by police for attacking Brotherhood headquarters during Morsi's rule were now placed in handcuffs on account of their supposed membership of the Muslim Brotherhood.

The security establishment basked in rediscovered glory; now that they were no longer being directed by the Brotherhood, its members could do no wrong. When two low-ranking police officers abducted and raped a young woman, popular television host Amany al-Khayat dismissed the incident as a ploy aimed at discrediting the interior ministry.[48] Meanwhile, Egypt's armed forces amazed everyone by coming up with a device which they claimed both detected and cured HIV, AIDS and Hepatitis C. 'I take AIDS from the patient, and feed the patient on AIDS, I give it to him as a kofta skewer to feed on,' explained General Ibrahim Abdel-Atti. 'I conquered AIDS with the blessings of my Lord, glory to him, with a rate of 100 per cent.'[49] Wael Eskander, journalist and revolutionary, declared that Sisi's Egypt was where logic came to die. 'The emperor organizes the circus,' he said, 'but this time you don't even need to get off your couch to go and cheer.'[50]

Under Egypt's latest strongman, in large part due to Morsi's disastrous year in power, the networks of exclusion that shield the state from opposition are now far stronger than they were in the first eighteen months of the revolution, a period which ran from the toppling of Mubarak to the first set of presidential elections. Much of the old left, including figures such as Shahenda Maklad, the Kamshish firebrand, and Kamal Abu Eita, leader of the country's first independent trade union, identified in the Brotherhood a greater danger to the revolutionary project than that posed by the military, and have thrown their support behind Sisi. Younger revolutionaries have split on the issue of whether or not to build an alliance with Islamist protesters – who continue to bear the brunt of the regime's repression – while at the same time struggling themselves to avoid being targeted by the security forces. The divisions among those who reject Sisi's rebooted authoritarianism are deep, and they are bitter; meanwhile, a culture in which criticism of the state is taboo and self-muzzling is pervasive has gained ground once more.

And yet, behind Sisi's headline triumphs, the state continues to suffer from many of the same fragilities that were exposed when the revolution erupted half a decade earlier. The military proprietors of the state have flourished most when they have been partnered with civilian front-men, but no such front-men are left; Sisi's direct assumption of the presidency leaves his junta more exposed than ever when the winds next shift, when the next wave of confrontation roils Egypt once more. In terms of public support, the regime is able to generate plenty of buzz, but little by way of depth. Sisi styles himself as a contemporary Nasser, an authoritarian nationalist who brooks no dissent but delivers social goods to his people in return for their political passivity. But what social goods can he deliver? As long as the 'War on Terror' continues to play out successfully, the generals can probably count on some people wearing Sisi masks and buying Sisi chocolates. But if that 'war' begins to lose its way, there will be nothing for them to hide behind when citizens turn their attention once again to economic injustice, to the violence of the security apparatus, to their political marginalization, to all of the state's ongoing mechanisms of exclusion; nothing for the generals to sacrifice for survival when the inadequacies of the old political model are wrenched back up through the topsoil.

The Muslim Brotherhood conceptualized Egyptians in such a way as to appeal to Western governments and the financial institutions they dominate: a people who abrogate their voice to a stagecraft of procedural democracy and limit their political participation to election days before returning home and quietly embracing neoliberal austerity. The army, aided by its 'liberal' allies, views the Egyptian people as steadfastly loyal to the military, ready to march in defence of the national and secular state against a fifth column of Islamists and foreign spies; these Egyptians abrogate their voice to the state in return for protection from trespassers, and likewise remove themselves from politics so that capital accumulation by the state and its partners can continue unchecked, so that the 'wheel of production' can keep on turning. But there is also Revolution Country's vision of the Egyptians, the people – as Anne Alexander and Mostafa Bassiouny put it – who comprise 'the vast majority of Egyptians: the urban and rural poor; the small traders and artisans; industrial, transport and office workers; teachers and health workers . . . They are the heart and soul of the January Revolution'.[51] They are the squatters of the Suzanne Mubarak housing project, like the grandmother Amal, whose simple demand – for a state that can provide her with four walls – remains a revolutionary threat that the old order simply cannot eradicate. The state wishes to remake these people in its image, but the people have it in them to remake the state as well. On the informal ramps up to the Ring Road and in the other ever-widening crevices of Sisi's Egypt, these people are speaking out – and abrogating their voice no more.

On the fourth anniversary of the start of the revolution, Mosireen, the revolutionary media collective, launched a new video, entitled *We Emptied Our Pockets of Joy*. Against a backdrop of revolutionaries once again confronting police violence on contested stretches of asphalt, the narrator declares: 'We'll go back to not letting the state into our streets. What drove our folks to fight will drive us to fight too. We used to face Morsi down with rocks for hours. The gas would kill us but we weren't afraid. Mohammad al-Guindy died for that. So did Jika. You kill millions and want us to be silent? We won't.' The video concludes with the lines, 'The youth keep having kids, the kids have kids and they all keep getting burned. I won't keep silent. You're oppressors . . . We'll clean the country up and we'll wage a war for it, against you, just like we did against Morsi. We used to fight with stones and we weren't afraid. The best of our youth fall and die. And we keep going.'[52]

9

Sheep Manure and Caramel

There is an awkward silence in the room as Madame Daniela looks us slowly up and down. Dissatisfied with the results of her initial scan, she tilts forward her thick black sunglasses and repeats the action, this time with her heavily made-up face scrunched into an asymmetrical canvas of contempt. She shakes her head, parts her lips as if to form some words, and then abruptly thinks better of it. After a long pause, she turns incredulously to Seif, her security director, who is standing nervously to attention at the end of her desk. 'You say these are journalists?'

Seif, a large moon-faced man who is spilling slightly out of his tightly buckled braces and sweating profusely, gulps twice and shifts his weight from one foot to the other, considering his options. He eventually decides that the situation demands a bout of firm, authoritative hedging. 'Journalists,' he replies gravely, 'is indeed what they claim to be. But of course, people are not always who they claim to be.' Another silence ensues, and a clearly discomforted Seif, feeling perhaps that his acumen in this regard is not being sufficiently appreciated by the assembled party, attempts to drive the point home. 'In fact, I have found in life that people are often not who they claim to be. Anyway, whoever they are, they were discovered in one of the chemical mixers.' Madame Daniela's eyes widen. 'They were *inside* one of my chemical mixers?' she says disbelievingly, pivoting her withering gaze back around towards me and my colleague Effat. 'What on earth were you doing inside one of my chemical mixers?'

It's a sweltering afternoon in October 2012, and the four of us are standing in a palatial office suite some thirty miles south-west of Suez. Around us lies the main factory compound of Cleopatra

Ceramics, one of the largest ceramics plants in the Middle East and home to thousands of workers. From this sprawling desert complex, everything from tiles to toilet basins is made and exported to more than a hundred countries around the globe. Its owner, Mohamed Aboul Enein – the former NDP stalwart and owner of vast tracts of land on Cairo's Qursaya Island, where locals accuse him of conspiring with the army to terrorize the local population into giving up their homes – has recently declared himself, with a characteristically modest flourish, 'one of the noblest businessmen in the world'.[1] His wife, the immaculately coiffed Italian-born Madame Daniela, is Cleopatra's vice-president, and the disparity between our respective appearances is contributing to her obvious distaste at our presence in her office. She is clad in a black-print dress with a string of pearls around her neck, a jewel-studded bracelet on each wrist, and a cloud of expensive perfume that glides with her back and forth whenever she paces the room. Effat and I are both wearing jeans and T-shirts smeared with dust and dirt, and our odour speaks more of the realm of a localized toxic spillage than of the cosmetics floor of a chic department store. She motions us to sit, and I thank her for inviting us in. 'I didn't invite you and your friend to my factory, Mr Shenker, and yet here you are, crawling around in my chemical mixers,' she shoots back, with – it must be said – admirable precision. 'That, young man, is the problem.'

Madame Daniela is right. For the post-Mubarak industrial tycoon, the discovery of uninvited journalists crawling around one's chemical mixers certainly is a problem; not so much in itself, but because it hints at a broader reality of Egypt's revolutionary era. The problem is that the lines of authority which once structured production here at Cleopatra Ceramics are now smudging. Before 2011, it would have been virtually impossible for an outsider to walk in through the gates without prior permission from management and probably some vetting by state security as well; today, though, Madame Daniela's sphere of absolute power extends no further than the walls of her office suite, and control of the factory floor has been diffused in many directions. That's why Effat and I were able to tour Cleopatra at our leisure in the company of independent labour activists, and why we were able to breeze past security guards who once obeyed management orders without question but now operate in multiple jurisdictions – part Mubarak Country, part Revolution Country. It's why we were able to climb inside a chemical mixer to see Cleopatra's working conditions with our own eyes, and interview employees who are tired of the old ways and are imagining a future in which they might seize control of this factory and run it for themselves. The problem is that between revolution and counter-revolution, the outlines of workplace dominion – like most areas of the Egyptian economy – are up for grabs, and there is precious little that Madame Daniela can do about it.

On 24 February 2013, a man entered Egypt's High Court, walked past security guards, climbed several stairwells until he reached the roof, and tried to throw himself off. He later told passers-by who prevented him from jumping that he had launched a lawsuit against members of the Mubarak family for their sequestering of illicit gains before the revolution, along with the NDP businessman Ahmed Ezz and a national bank; on discovering that the public prosecutor had opted not to pursue his case, the man decided to end it all. Media coverage of the incident was limited, but ten days later another man climbed to the rooftop and followed suit – this time with a young child in his arms. Once again, quick reactions from onlookers managed to prevent the jump and save both lives. According to those on the scene, the latter man was an employee at a paper company who had recently lost his job after the firm's owner fled the country. 'He said that he is doing this because he can't afford to raise his son,' claimed Mahmoud, an eyewitness.[2]

It was Egypt's political economy – the specific type of capitalism which dominated the country prior to the revolution, and the way it was entwined with the structure of the Egyptian state – that gave rise to the social explosion of 25 January 2011.[3] And it is the unfulfilled, popular demand for social and economic justice that has remained the perpetual engine of the revolution ever since, even as the political winds around it have twisted and turned. 'I saw freedom, a freedom no one's ever seen before,' said Ahmed Hassan, a young Egyptian from Shubra (where unemployment was running at 30 per cent before the revolution), on how those days in Tahrir transformed his expectations for the future.[4] 'God willing, I will find work. Now, after an employer finds out I was part of the revolution, he will never treat me badly like before. *Mustaheel!* "Impossible!"' Like millions of others who participated in the past half-decade's uprisings, Hassan wanted the revolution to deliver more than the odd election; he dreamed of a post-Mubarak future in which poverty, inequality and precariousness were no longer the norm, a future which requires a different sort of economic model from the neoliberal status quo. Despite the fight-back of the state, in hospitals, airports, sculleries and steel plants, not to mention the Cleopatra Ceramics shopfloor, attempts to actualize those dreams continue.

Barely a week after Mubarak's fall, a new word entered Egypt's political discourse: *fi'awi*, which means something of or related to *fi'a* ('a group'), but was used to describe anyone still agitating for change in their workplace or the streets, particularly in relation to economic concerns. Almost immediately after taking power, the military generals issued a communiqué which outlined the negative impact of continued protests and strikes on the country's fragile economy and urged labour and professional syndicates to help bring about a swift return to 'normality'; soon afterwards, another army statement adopted a more menacing tone, warning that *fi'awi* demands were illegitimate and pledging to pursue agitators through legal means in the name of 'protecting the security of the nation and its citizens'.[5] The accusation was that instead of acting in the broader national interest, participant in *fi'awi* protests were taking advantage of the political turmoil during this exceptional moment of state weakness to hold those in power to ransom and extract unreasonable concessions. The Muslim Brotherhood's spokesman, Essam el-Erian, quickly echoed the military's sentiments, accusing *fi'awi* protests of 'undermining national consensus'. So too did Usama Haykal, editor-in-chief of the liberal Wafd Party's daily newspaper, who cautioned that *fi'awi* mobilizations could destroy the gains of the revolution. Over the next few months Finance Minister Samir Radwan claimed that *fi'awi* actions were costing Egypt over 20 billion EGP, prominent TV personalities and newspaper columnists condemned *fi'awi* rallies as 'continuous, hysterical and vengeful', and the country's grand mufti, Ali Gomaa, declared that 'instigators of *fi'awi* demonstrations violate the teachings of God'.[6] On 23 March, the government – in virtually its first ever piece of post-Mubarak legislation – approved a law banning any assemblies, strikes or work stoppages that might 'impede private and public businesses', and ordered transgressors to be punished with huge fines and a prison sentence. The message was clear: *fi'awi* was antithetical to the revolution.

The rhetoric surrounding *fi'awi* – a word previously devoid of any normative connotations, but which was now intimately associated with selfishness and private, sectoral interests – was the first weapon fired by Egyptian elites in an attempt to counteract revolutionary demands for an economic upheaval. The stakes were enormous. In calling for bread, freedom and social justice, revolutionaries were directly undermining a central premise of neoliberal ideology: that the state's political realm should be divorced from its economic model, and that governments must divest themselves of any influence over the latter, allowing the marketplace to dictate affairs instead. By targeting the Egyptian state with their social justice demands, and by identifying its current formulation as a barrier to collective economic security, revolutionaries shattered this artificial distinction between the political and economic spheres; *fi'awi* was a way for elites to try to place the latter beyond the reach of demonstrators. The term was so loosely defined that it could be applied to any rally, march, strike or sit-in aimed at confronting the current distribution of wealth, and the sentiments behind it quickly assumed an institutional form as well. In March, Egypt's newly revised post-Mubarak constitution, drawn up by a committee appointed by the generals and supported enthusiastically by the Muslim Brotherhood, was unveiled; despite 85 per cent of Egyptians telling pollsters that socio-economic issues were their primary concern, the final document contained barely any references to socio-economic rights at all.

SCAF's generals had good reason to fear any democratization of Egypt's economy. As we've seen, the Egyptian military-industrial complex – far from opposing Sadat's *infitah*, or the Mubarakera turn to neoliberalism – had by the start of the millennium fully embraced the reforms that accompanied the IMF's structural adjustment programme, particularly once it became clear that army-run enterprises were to remain immune from privatization and that army top brass would be among the first to benefit from profit-making opportunities in the new era. What's more, Military Inc. – as Egypt's huge network of army-controlled companies and conglomerates is sometimes known – had been able to carve out lucrative new revenue streams under Mubarak by expanding its production of war matériel into commercial areas. By the outbreak of revolution in 2011, the army's economic scope had grown so wide that it was directly involved in sectors as diverse as maritime transport, oil, renewable energy, real estate, ports and dockyards, private shipping maintenance, fertilizer production, railway wagons, computer hardware, pipelines and smart cards.[7] In 2012 a revolutionary activist created a video and PDF package showcasing all the logos, websites and products associated with military-controlled companies that he could find (no mean feat, given that much of this information is classified as a state secret and dissemination of it can lead to jail); scroll through it, and images of everything from bottles of drinking water to women's lingerie fill the screen.[8]

This economic empire was increasingly predicated on lucrative partnerships with international corporations – from Italian petro-chemical outfits to vast Gulf-based conglomerates like Kuwait's Kharafi Group, which through its Americana food subsidiary operates KFC, Pizza Hut and Krispy Kreme outlets across the Middle East. Close financial integration with multinational capital was nothing new to an institution that had long enjoyed transatlantic financial ties worth hundreds of millions of dollars to outfits like arms manufacturers Lockheed Martin and the consultancy firm Deloitte;[9] now though, civilian partners such as Tesco, Macy's and Costa Coffee were also being swept up into Military Inc.'s economic domain.[10] For SCAF, the revolution's noisy denunciations of economic injustice therefore represented more than just a challenge to the military's vehicle of political control, the state; inextricably, they also threatened to torpedo the army's private financial fortunes.

During the eighteen days, when Mubarak carried out his final cabinet shake-up in a doomed attempt to cling on to office, NDP stalwart Samir Radwan had replaced the notorious Youssef Boutros-Ghali as finance minister. In the months following Mubarak's fall, Radwan began working on a budget that he thought would please his new military masters, one that eschewed radical reform but was expansionary enough to deliver modest increases in social services and public sector wages, and thus garner enough popular support to quieten the streets. The generals were having none of it. Radwan was quickly given his marching orders and succeeded by Hizam al-Beblawi, a former adviser to the Arab Monetary Fund known for his ardent support for free markets.[11] Talk of a new minimum and maximum wage was replaced by a focus on subsidy cuts, some of which struck directly at Egypt's poorest citizens, and a slew of IMF and World Bank prescriptions designed to reassure foreign investors, including the issuing of dollar-denominated treasury bills to guard against inflation and a refusal to lift the country's debt ceilings, were adopted in their entirety.

The military's aim was not only to gear macroeconomic policy-making towards defending the neoliberal state during this crucial period of 'transition', but simultaneously to position itself as the sole gatekeeper of investment opportunities in post-Mubarak Egypt; it was the generals that would determine who got access to private wealth-creation, and who would be locked out. Under SCAF, a highly selective 'anti-corruption' campaign by the government saw domestic tycoons most tainted by their association with Mubarak, along with some of the army's economic rivals, thrown unceremoniously to the wolves; civilian businessmen with strong links to military companies went largely unmolested. Meanwhile, foreign firms weighing up Egyptian investments were offered the kind of insurance no money could buy if they partnered with the military: the use of Egyptian soldiers to secure corporate assets, at a time when political instability made such guarantees a key requisite for entry into the Egyptian market. The Kharafi Group, for example, was given an armoured guard (complete with tanks) to ensure safe delivery of equipment to one of its power plants.[12] The generals succeeded in awarding themselves the power to determine both winners and losers at the commanding heights of Egyptian capitalism; with that level of military muscle, civilian elites both local and international became bound to the army's ongoing control of the state.[13]

But the military's most important function in this period was to discipline any Egyptian citizens who refused to fall into line. Under

SCAF rule, numerous labour mobilizations erupted that went far beyond a desire for pay rises or better working conditions and hammered directly at the command exercised by the armed forces over the economy: there were protests at companies run by the army, protests at companies run by retired generals, protests against the militarization of key industrial sectors. In many cases, corporate management was able to call on military police to come and disperse these demonstrations, forcing strikers back to work. When employees of state-owned Petrotrade, a part of Military Inc., began an open-ended strike the day after Mubarak's resignation, they were joined over the following weeks by thousands of others across the industry; the army's response was to infiltrate the strikes,* abduct the strike leaders, send them for military trial and lock them up in prison.[15] Similar aggression was deployed against Suez Canal employees who blocked train lines in protest at their unjust treatment at the hands of military bosses, and against workers at the military-owned Arab Organization for Industrialization (a collection of twelve army production plants) who had created Facebook pages criticizing their military administrators. SCAF members understood that such activities represented more than self-serving 'opportunism' on the part of workers: they were gross acts of defiance against the core infrastructure of Mubarak Country, and if violence was necessary to bring them to a halt then so be it.

But to beat back Revolution Country and maintain the fiction that Egypt's existing economic arrangements could be spun out and insulated from a merely 'political' uprising, the military did not act alone.

The Muslim Brotherhood were first out of the blocks when it came to supporting the army's *fi'awi* narrative, a position which was entirely consistent with the party leadership's economic values by the time the

---

* 'Petrojet employees were approached by an individual claiming to be a co-worker, suggesting that they attack the army soldiers stationed around Parliament. When asked for his company number, the man replied that it was 500, and when he was told there was no such number, he attempted to flee. He was caught, beaten and handed over to army soldiers. [Newspaper] *Al-Wafd*'s report includes a photo of the ID card allegedly taken from the man, identifying him as National Security Agency officer Ahmed Salah Eddin.'[14]

anti-Mubarak uprising began in January 2011. It hadn't always been this way: historically, the movement's economic policies have been riddled with contradictions, blowing to the left or to the right depending on contemporary political contexts and the shifting social base of the organization's membership. In the pre-Nasser years, for example, the Brotherhood combined a virulent brand of anti-communism and alliances with both the monarchy and conservative nationalists on the one hand with a fairly ambitious manifesto of progressive land reform, nationalization and state-led economic development on the other.[16] Yet by the Sadat era, the group's grassroots following had waned and links between the leadership and their supporter base all but vanished. From a mass movement of nearly 500,000 Egyptians in the 1940s, the Brotherhood had shrunk by the late 1970s into a society of only a few hundred. Most of them were businessmen with close ties to Saudi Arabia who had made their fortune out of the president's *infitah* programme – and were keen to help him resist perceived threats from the left to the new socio-economic hegemony.[17] The rise of these Brotherhood business moguls was dramatic; come the 1980s and the dawn of Mubarak's rule, some 40 per cent of all private economic ventures in Egypt were believed to be connected to Brotherhood interests.*[18] As a result, when structural adjustment arrived in the 1990s and began to wreak its social misery, the Brotherhood's top lieutenants – vastly rich men like Khairat el-Shater, the organization's first pick for the presidency before Mohamed Morsi – were never going to offer by way of criticism anything more than one-off denunciations of corruption from a strictly moralistic standpoint. Some leftist elements within the organization, such as former deputy supreme-guide (leader) Mohamed Habib, did take a different tack – they were keen to oppose privatizations and support the growing workers' struggle, a sentiment shared by many of the Brotherhood's cadres on the ground. Internal battles were fought by the rebels,

---

* The joint business empire between Khairat el-Shater and Hassan Malek alone is believed to comprise seventy large companies in sectors as diverse as land reclamation to construction and clothing, with subsidiaries operating across Turkey, Algeria and sub-Saharan Africa. Many are registered in the name of the children and other relatives of senior Brotherhood operatives, but their corporate boards are almost entirely made up of high-ranking Brotherhood members.[19]

and lost. By the 2000s, the organization had settled on a strongly pro-market discourse – albeit one that incorporated some populist critiques of neoliberalism – and argued that private charity could be an effective substitute for far-reaching economic change aimed at delivering social justice.[20]

What was surprising about the Brotherhood in the revolutionary era wasn't, therefore, the fact that its leaders were willing to take to the army's barricades to defend neoliberalism; it was that their desire to appease existing economic elites ran so deep that the Brotherhood actively went out of their way to rehabilitate even Mubarak's most blatant fraudsters. In October 2011, one of the movement's leading lights, Hassan Malek – a rich businessman who inherited his father's textile empire, was imprisoned twice under Mubarak, and went on to build profitable IT, furniture and export companies – gave a high-profile interview to Reuters in which he declared that Mubarak's economic policies had been 'on the right track'. "We can benefit from previous economic decisions," Malek explained. "There have been correct ones in the past. Rachid Mohamed Rachid [Mubarak's former minister for trade and industries] understood very well how to attract foreign investment and his decisions in that area were correct."[21] Rachid had been the man behind some of the most unpopular neoliberal lurches under Mubarak, responsible for privatizing large swathes of the industrial sector and stripping away workers' rights in an effort to attract ever-greater levels of foreign investment. By the time Malek started publicly venerating him, Rachid had already fled the country, been found guilty *in absentia* of embezzling public funds, sentenced to five years in jail, fined 15 million EGP, and been declared a fugitive by Interpol.[22]

But the Brotherhood's new-found esteem for Rachid was no isolated blip; with the party assuming the presidency, more of Mubarak Country's neoliberal titans saw their reputations publicly laundered. Soon after Morsi took office, Malek boasted that 'mechanisms are currently in place to effect reconciliation with former regime businessmen who have currently absconded abroad', and cited both Yassin Mansour (the billionaire chairman of Palm Hills, one of the companies embroiled in the notorious scandal surrounding the state's sale of public desert land to private developers) and tourism tycoon

Hamed el-Chiaty (whose assets had been frozen by several countries under the international sanctions regime) as examples of those who, 'God willing', would soon return to Egyptian shores.[23] In early 2013 Malek hosted an exclusive gathering of wealthy exiles and potential investors in London's five-star May Fair Hotel. 'Most of these investors, they own large projects in Egypt,' he explained at the event. 'Their coming back mostly would be a sign of reassurance to others who might want to invest their money.'[24] It would be a sign of reassurance too that, under the Brotherhood, post-Mubarak Egypt would guarantee business-as-usual for those seeking to make rampant private gains. Malek's message was that capital had nothing to fear from revolution, and that those who flouted the law in pursuit of personal profit could count on protection from the country's latest political masters.

Under Mubarak, the highest echelons of the NDP provided an institutional nexus between business and state; now, in the Brotherhood era, a new organization named the Egyptian Business Development Association (EBDA – the word *ibda* means 'start' in Arabic) was formed to play a similar role. It was led, naturally enough, by Malek; Bloomberg described its members as 'Brothers of the 1 per cent'. The board of EBDA claimed they wanted to bring about an 'economic revolution' in Egypt;[25] what they actually sought was economic stasis, the only difference from the past being better access for themselves to the bounty. Tycoons such as Malek and fellow EBDA members Safwan Thabet (chairman of beverage giants Juhayna) and Mohamed Moamen (owner of the restaurant chain Mo'men) had grown rich under Mubarak, but their Islamist leanings classified them as a political threat to the regime and as such their accumulation of wealth had been somewhat held in check by periodic security crackdowns. 'They allowed me to reach a certain level, but there was a ceiling,' complained Malek, when asked about his economic activities in the old days.[25] In the new Egypt, things would be different – and for that to happen, things would have to stay the same. Instead of critiquing the high-level cronyism and nepotism that had manacled Egypt's economic development under Mubarak, EBDA turned its rhetorical fire on the public sector: more privatization was needed to stamp out graft, insisted the Brotherhood, more foreign investors must be wooed.[27]

'Today, there are 6 million government employees and a culture of corruption has long been embedded in the system,' warned Malek darkly. 'The issue needs to be tackled and should be considered a major priority by the next president.'[28] At a revolutionary moment in which that neoliberal mantra, 'There is no alternative', was finally being eroded, the Brotherhood fought with all their might to shut down any discussion of what alternatives might look like, both within their organization and outside it. 'The core of the economic vision of Brotherhood, if we are going to classify it in a classical way, is extreme capitalist,' explained one former member who eventually quit in exasperation.[29] 'They [the Brotherhood leadership] tightened the screws on anyone who had different ideas about economics,' said Mohamed Habib, who had once been the organization's deputy guide.[30]

Upon assuming the presidency, Morsi did all he could to continue tightening the screws, starting with the maintenance of a decree – originally issued by SCAF and ratified by the Brotherhood-dominated parliament – exonerating from prosecution any entrepreneurs previously found guilty of corruption.[31] He then moved to roll back one of the biggest socio-economic gains delivered by the revolution so far: a legal challenge against the fraudulent privatization programme carried out under Mubarak. In September 2011 an administrative court had declared three of Mubarak's most high-profile privatizations to be unlawful and ordered the companies in question to be returned to the state. Among them was the iconic Omar Effendi department store chain and the huge Tanta Flax and Oil Company which in 2005 had been sold off to Saudi investors for EGP 84 million (barely a third of its estimated value a decade earlier), and whose workers went on to play a key role in the labour struggles of the late 2000s.[32] The court rulings sparked copycat legal actions by workers across Egypt's privatized industries, and sent a fresh wave of energy surging through the labour movement. The fight-back against market fundamentalism provoked critical questions about what it meant to be a citizen, and what kind of state citizens wanted to be a part of. 'Before I felt that the company was mine, now I feel like a slave,' said one employee of textile firm Polvaraat, when asked why public ownership was so important to him.[33] Public ownership was important for the

Brotherhood too – it had to be resisted. With a new president and elected civilian government finally in place by the summer of 2012, Morsi's prime minister, Hesham Qandil, was legally obliged to implement the court orders and begin a process of renationalization. Qandil refused. In April 2013 another court handed down a suspended sentence of one year in jail to the prime minister for flouting his legal duties. Morsi's regime simply ignored that ruling as well.

Morsi's privatization scandal was only the start. When revolutionaries demanded transitional justice – not just for the violence committed by the state against protesters, but also for Mubarak Country's economic crimes, such as the creation of corrupt monopolies which had deprived the Egyptian people of fair prices for years – Morsi responded by appointing the holder of a vast Mubarak-era dairy monopoly as his new minister for trade and manufacturing. When questions arose over the future of QIZs – special free trade areas set up in partnership with Israel under Mubarak and heavily criticized by the Brotherhood in opposition[34] – Morsi dispatched a delegation to Washington to explore the idea not of closing the controversial zones, but of expanding them. 'A lot of people are making good business out of that [the QIZ agreement],' explained Prime Minister Qandil. 'We want to make sure we do the right thing for them to flourish.'[35] Only a day after awarding himself vast new constitutional powers in December 2012, Morsi quietly issued a presidential decree making it easier for the government to impose its own supporters on trade union boards, reversing much of the momentum behind the independent trade union movement that had been building since before the revolution.[36] Those beyond Egypt's borders who insisted upon viewing Morsi as a progressive and a democrat found it increasingly hard to maintain their position, as the Brotherhood battled tooth and nail for Egypt's *ancien régime* reactionaries and fought back brazenly against any attempts to democratize control of the country's wealth.

And like SCAF before it, the Brotherhood regime understood that one of its primary tasks in defence of the state was to punish those violating the economic consensus. The highest ranks of the Brotherhood and Egypt's armed forces may have disagreed on some things, but they were always clear about their common enemy: those left marginalized by neoliberalism who felt empowered enough by the revolution to disrupt the status quo. In April 2013, on the back of a new wave of workers' struggles that echoed the huge mobilizations witnessed before the revolution between 2006 and 2010, Egypt's train drivers launched their largest nationwide strike in three decades in an attempt to win better pay and conditions. Morsi's minister for transport responded by forcefully conscripting the striking drivers into the army, transforming their work stoppage from a civilian matter into an act of martial sedition and exposing them to military trial. Responding to the conscription, a coalition of independent trade unions and revolutionary groups said in a point statement:

> The Egyptian government – rather than thinking about how to implement workers' demands, which are the genuine expression of social justice and one of the fundamental slogans of the revolution – has spent two years experimenting with new ways to try and break the movement. Sometimes it smears the workers, claiming that they are exploiting the revolution for their own sectional demands, and at other times it uses all forms of victimization including dismissals and imprisonment on charges of striking ... What is happening here is an attempt to terrorize the drivers from exercising their constitutionally enshrined right to strike by prosecuting them under military law.[37]

The army quickly moved to enforce the order, founding up almost a hundred workers and detaining them inside military barracks in Sharabiya. 'The Morsi administration's targeting of strikers has proven to be much worse and more oppressive than the actions of the Mubarak regime,' explained train driver Ashraf Momtaz.* 'The army held us as if we were war criminals.'[39] This was the real 'economic revolution' that Hassan Malek's EBDA fought to bring about: one that would turn the clock back to the days of unfettered Egyptian

---

* As further evidence of Momtaz's point, a few months earlier five union leaders at the Alexandria Port containers Company were sentenced to three years in jail for leading a strike back in 2011. These were the harshest prison terms handed down to any striking worker since the death of President Sadat.[38]

neoliberalism when the pursuit of private riches remained unencumbered by workers' resistance, to the benefit of both elite Brotherhood and army brass.

In April 2011, World Bank president Robert Zoellick addressed an audience in Washington and offered his take on how the West should respond to the Arab uprisings, sparked by the self-immolation of street vendor Mohamed Bouazizi in Tunisia. 'The key point I have also been emphasizing and I emphasized in this speech is that it is not just a question of money. It is a question of policy,' Zoellick argued. 'Keep in mind, the late Mr Bouazizi was basically driven to burn himself alive because he was harassed with red tape.'[40]

When the Egyptian revolution began, it imperilled global neoliberal forces in two ways: firstly by threatening the profitability of existing and future foreign investments in Egypt, and secondly by undermining the ideological strictures of market fundamentalism – the supposed disjunction between politics and economics, the illegitimacy of protests outside the realm of procedural and consumerist democracy, the notion that big questions about state and society were all but settled. Zoellick's audacious reframing of unrest in the Middle East as a popular cry for more economic liberalization was part of a retaliation by a chequerboard of cross-border entities representing elite financial interests, from Western politicians to international financial institutions (IFIs), multilateral development banks (MDBs), transnational corporations and conservative think-tanks, intent on shifting the revolutionary narrative away from social justice. The following month, most of these institutions came together in Deauville, France, to form the Deauville Partnership with Arab Countries in Transition, dedicated to ensuring the continuation of economic 'stabilization' and 'reform' programmes in countries rocked by revolution.[41]

The aim of the Deauville partners was to keep multinational capital fused with whatever political models emerged from the region's massive anti-government uprisings. It was the start of a multi-pronged campaign to outflank revolutionaries by taking command of transitional economic knowledge production for themselves.[42] Without the assistance of this international ruling class, it is safe to say that neither the Egyptian military nor the Muslim Brotherhood could ever have succeeded in keeping Revolution Country at bay.

From the earliest days of structural adjustment, Egypt's transformation had profited IFIs and MDBs directly; international institutions were closely enmeshed with the Egyptian corporations and political figures which both army generals and Muslim Brotherhood leaders fought so hard to protect once the revolution was underway. In 2005, for example, the World Bank put $50 million of its own money into the privatization of the Omar Effendi department store chain through its private sector lending vehicle, the International Finance Corporation (IFC) – one of several Egyptian government sell-offs which would later be deemed illegal in the court ruling that President Morsi chose (illegally) to ignore.[43] A whistleblower eventually revealed that NDP bigwigs, presided over by Mubarak's minister of investment, Mahmoud Mohieldin, had pressured the valuation committee to under-price Omar Effendi and thus defraud the Egyptian taxpayer; as a result the state treasury lost nearly $100 million, 2,000 workers lost their jobs, and investors – including the IFC, which directly owned 5 per cent of Omar Effendi's new shares – cashed in.* In Egypt Mohieldin was deemed a criminal by activists and had lawsuits filed against him; Robert Zoellick, by way of contrast, called him an 'outstanding young leader' and appointed him as a managing director of the World Bank.[45] The IFC's embroilment with Mubarak Country went further: in 2010 it partnered with the European Investment Bank (EIB), the commercial lending outfit of the European Union, to pour tens of millions of dollars into a new investment fund named InfraMed – chaired by Rachid Mohammed Rachid (the Mubarak-era trade and industry minister and subsequent Interpol fugitive that the Brotherhood were so keen to acclaim). InfraMed's co-investors included the Egyptian investment bank EFG Hermes, whose private equity arm was part-owned by Gamal Mubarak.[46] That meant that, by investing in InfraMed, EU taxpayers were going into business with not just the Egyptian government, but the Mubarak family

---

* Omar Effendi was one of the three privatizations annulled by the courts after Mubarak fell; Mohieldin was named in that court ruling as a 'responsible party' to the scandal.[44]

itself, the very dictators that EU leaders would later queue up piously to condemn.[47] And the InfraMed deal was no one-off; in the decade leading up to the revolution, the EIB and IFC plunged €370 million into EFG Hermes between them.[48] 'What is apparent,' noted a report by Counter Balance, a coalition of NGOs who work to hold the EIB to account, 'is that "development" banks played important roles not only in financing but in legitimizing Middle Eastern despots. They provided what EFG Hermes, in reference to itself, calls "a vote of confidence ... from a reputable institution like the EIB". From the perspective of developing country elites, that "vote of confidence" and the political and financial protection that comes with it, is what the EIB and its ilk are for.'[49]

Engagement with the daily nuts and bolts of regime profiteering went beyond specific corporate investments; without the support of global institutions, Egypt's neoliberal makeover under Mubarak would never have been possible. Every phase of economic reform since the country's original IMF loan in 1991 secured not only verbal support from global technocrats and unwavering tick-box approval from the IMF, but also something more tangible – critical funding sourced from IFIs and MDBs, money which itself came from foreign governments and foreign taxpayers, and ultimately enriched Egypt's autocrats. USAID and the World Bank directly contributed more than $2 billion to the country's highly controversial financial sector reform programme alone;[50] across the 2000s, the EIB provided almost €4 billion of financing to projects in Egypt.[51] Zoellick's 'revolution against red tape' shtick was a way of trying to get everyone to look the other way, and from the moment Mubarak was ejected, other representatives of multinational capital scrambled to reinforce it.

David Cameron was the first world leader to beat a path to Tahrir Square; in an indication of where the UK stood with regard to the Arab uprisings, his trip was part of a regional tour to promote the British arms trade.[52] 'This is a moment of great opportunity for Egypt,' the British prime minister declared, before going on to speak of the importance of economic reform. 'It is a great opportunity for us to go and talk to those currently running Egypt ... and to see what countries like Britain and others in Europe can do to help.'[53] Barack Obama announced that the US was seeking to support 'positive change in the region . . . through our efforts to advance economic development for nations that are transitioning to democracy', and promised that IFIs would help 'stabilize and modernize' Egypt. 'The goal must be a model in which protectionism gives way to openness,' he continued. 'America's support for democracy will therefore be based on ensuring financial stability, promoting reform, and integrating competitive markets with each other and the global economy.'[54] The Institute of International Finance, a lobby group for the world's biggest financial institutions, also chipped in. 'As momentous as the current security and political restructuring challenges may be, it is absolutely critical that the transition authorities also place a high priority on deepening and accelerating structural economic reforms,' the Washington-based organization claimed in a report. 'Transition and subsequent governments must articulate a credible medium-term reform and stabilization framework that addresses the need for higher growth and job creation.'[55] Even as Egyptians were celebrating their success at bringing down Mubarak and mourning their dead, a revolution driven in large part by the iniquities of capitalism was being reclassified as a mobilization of aspirant capitalists. 'The forces of the market have come to the Arab world – even if governments didn't invite them in,' wrote prominent neoliberal economist Hernando de Soto in the *Financial Times*. 'Political leaders must realize that, since Bouazizi went up in flames and his peers rose in protest, poor Arabs are no longer outside but inside, in the market, right next to them.'[56] Egypt's problem, according to the global economic soothsayers, had not been too much neoliberalism, but too little.[57]

Duly endorsed, capital got to work. In a made-for-TV moment, US senators (and former presidential candidates) John McCain and John Kerry rang the opening bell of the Cairo Stock Exchange in June 2011, declaring Egypt under SCAF open for multinational business. 'We are both extraordinary committed to what is happening here in Egypt,' gushed Kerry.[58] America's own military-industrial complex swiftly stepped up its sales to the Egyptian army. The revolution had never given arms companies much pause for thought; on 10 February 2011, for example – the eve of Mubarak's resignation, when millions around the world were glued to the drama in Tahrir Square unfolding on their TV screens – executives at American military shipbuilders

Swiftships signed off a $20 million contract with the Egyptian navy. Over the next two years, contracts for fighter jets, tank materiel and combat training worth a cumulative $203 million were struck between American weapons manufacturers and the military government of Egypt.[59] Meanwhile, as the SCAF–Brotherhood political settlement began to take shape, delegations from Morgan Stanley, General Electric, Apache Corporation, Morgan Chase and General Motors touched down in Cairo airport to break bread with the Islamists.[60] Lindsey Graham, a Republican senator in South Carolina, took a group of colleagues to meet Khairat el-Shater, the organization's leading 'Brother of the 1 per cent'. 'He is the behind the scenes guy,' concluded Graham. 'Very impressive.'[61]

But all this was small fry when set alongside the real transmission line of neoliberal expansion in post-Mubarak Egypt: public-private partnerships (PPPs). PPPs are a tricksy piece of financial alchemy first developed by the British government in the early 1990s; they proliferated under Tony Blair's New Labour government before being exported all over the world. PPPs enable a government to shift the costs of certain services and infrastructure projects off its balance-sheets by contracting them out to the private sector instead; in most cases, an agreement is signed between a public authority, a private consortium and a bank specifying that the consortium will build, maintain or run a certain public asset (such as a hospital, school or railway line), receiving in return both a proportion of income from that asset and some of the investment risk associated with it. The theory is that the private sector will bring a higher degree of efficiency to major projects and relieve governments of having to find investment money upfront. From Canada to Croatia, the reality has proved very different. Because it is invariably more expensive for the private sector to borrow money than it is for a government, PPPs nearly always end up costing more than an equivalent public project. As PPP operations are motivated by profit rather than the universal provision of a social good, the services they deliver often tend to be decrepit or patchy. And despite all the rhetoric on 'risk-sharing', the fact that PPP contracts cover essential public infrastructure means that ultimately all the risk is retained by taxpayers – if a PPP proves to be unprofitable the private firm can always pull out, safe in the knowledge that the state simply cannot allow such projects to crash. In Britain, home to a series of PPP scandals including the botched semi-privatization of the London Tube system, a *Financial Times* report in 2011 concluded that the state had been saddled with over £20 billion worth of 'extra' borrowing costs – the price of forty major new hospitals – as a consequence of the 700 PPP agreements signed by successive governments (another £4 billion has been pocketed by consultants and lawyers).[62]

As formerly collectively owned assets in the West have been swept en masse into the marketplace, investors have had to work harder at finding new social goods to commodify – and it's to the global south that many of them have turned. As a corollary of structural adjustment programmes, PPPs have been promoted by the 'international community' as a quick-fire way to ramp up infrastructure development at little cost to poorer states, and aid donors – such as the World Bank – have used their financial clout to force through many such privatizations against heavy public opposition. Often, it's been moments of political turmoil that have thrown up the most fertile territory for appropriation, such as Eastern Europe in the 1990s following the collapse of the Soviet Union. As formerly communist nations emerged 'blinking into the light' of Western capitalism, the international community – led by neoliberal economists like Harvard professor Jeffrey Sachs – quickly began administering a rapid privatization programme that would transfer previously public assets into speculators' hands. 'Despite economists' reputation for never being able to agree on anything, there is a striking degree of unanimity in the advice that has been provided to the nations of Eastern Europe and the former Soviet Union,' noted Lawrence Summers, the World Bank's chief economist, in 1994. 'Privatization, stabilization, and liberalization ... must all be completed as soon as possible.'[63] The outcome of these policies for most of Eastern Europe was economic failure and a scarcely believable level of corruption; in fact, the economic data shows that the more closely countries followed neoliberal strictures, the more relentlessly its people suffered.* The suffering, of

---

* Harvard and Cambridge economists have collated relevant statistics on twenty-five post-communist nations between 1990 and 2000, and demonstrated an empirical link between neoliberalism and poor economic performance.[64]

course, was not universal. Local kleptocrats with the right connections secured financial windfalls of epic proportions, as did foreign investors who were quick to jump on the commercial bandwagon.[65]

At the heart of the economic remodelling of Eastern Europe was the European Bank for Reconstruction and Development (EBRD), a development bank under the joint ownership of several countries (including the United States and members of the European Union) that was created in 1991 as a vehicle for free market reform in the former Soviet bloc. From the outset the EBRD had a particular passion for PPPs, and their implementation, from Sofia to Zagreb, has proved to be a catastrophe for ordinary citizens: drinking water that became undrinkable, wastewater systems that cost double their estimates and left taxpayers footing the bill, huge motorway projects that served only to line the pockets of politically connected crony capitalists.[66] Despite all the mounting evidence discrediting the public value of PPPs and other market-orientated reforms, the EBRD has continued to plough the same ideological furrow; in November 2013, the bank acknowledged that after twenty years of neoliberalism, Eastern European nations were falling behind in the wealth stakes – and then explained that the solution was for structural reforms to be relaunched and intensified.[67] The EBRD's problem is that successive waves of privatization in the former Soviet bloc have left behind relatively few assets that are still open to commodification. The Arab revolutions, however, brought a new economic playground on to the horizon.

In February 2012, a year after Mubarak's fall and just as some of Egypt's workers' movements were attempting to organize a general strike, the EBRD published a technical assessment of Egypt's economy. Cairo was a long way from the bank's Eastern European roots, but the similarities – and the appeal for the EBRD – were obvious: a country in political crisis undergoing a fundamental transformation, and, despite Mubarak's 'privatization a week', somewhere that still boasted a large number of public assets that had not yet been carved up for the market. In its review of previous liberalization efforts, the EBRD report noted primly that structural adjustment in Egypt had so far met with public opposition, fuelling 'acute social stress' and a 'perceived lack of fairness'.[68] 'Privatization,' the authors explained, 'was seen to benefit well-connected elites, and job creation suffered as large segments of the economy, especially smaller businesses, did not benefit from the opportunities opened by reforms.' Of course the EBRD's answer to such neoliberal flaws was, just as Zoellick, de Soto and others like them had been arguing, yet more neoliberalism. 'These were, however, pathologies linked to the implementation and focus of reforms, and in fact their incompleteness, rather than [issues] inherent in market-oriented economic systems,' the EBRD report continued. 'Market economies can be fair and inclusive.' Under the heading 'Transition Gaps', the report went on to identify Egypt's agricultural, manufacturing, services, energy, financial and transport sectors as ripe for further privatization via both PPPs and other commercialization mechanisms; urban water supplies, sewage systems, Cairo and Alexandria's mass transit networks and the national railway and road systems were all specifically flagged up as potential state assets that could be handed off to public-private partnerships. Little wonder that at a follow-up meeting in October 2012, the EBRD's directors concluded: 'Egypt is a country where the Bank can carry out its purpose and functions . . . namely "to foster transition towards open market-oriented economies and to promote private and entrepreneurial initiative".'[69]

The EBRD's privatization blueprints are only the beginning. The EIB has also been pushing aggressively for more public-private partnerships – issuing a press release on 8 February 2011, before Mubarak had even been forced from office, in which it demanded that southern and eastern Mediterranean countries, including Egypt, 'make themselves more attractive for foreign direct investment', and announcing the launch of 'an ambitious programme of technical assistance to encourage the use of public-private partnership contracts' in an effort to capture as much as possible of the estimated €300 billion that will be invested in public utilities in the region over the next twenty years.[70] The US too has pledged $1 billion worth of investments in Egypt through OPIC, the Overseas Private Investment Corporation, that has a government mandate to support American investment in emerging economies and 'foster the growth of free markets'. Agencies like OPIC intend the main driver of such growth to be PPPs: an OPIC statement in 2011 promised to use

Obama's Egypt money to 'identify Egyptian government-owned enterprises investing in public-private partnerships in order to promote growth in mutually agreed upon sectors of the Egyptian economy'. Without a hint of irony, the press release concluded:

> Today, the people of the Middle East are providing the world with an example as inspiring as that offered by the people of Central and Eastern Europe twenty years ago after the fall of the Berlin Wall. Then, OPIC backed the new democracies with over $3.8 billion in investments, spanning nearly 150 projects ... OPIC is now striving for similar success in the MENA region, in the months and years ahead.[71]

And a myriad of other, smaller multilateral agencies are following the lead of institutions like OPIC, the EIB and the EBRD. ACDI/VOCA, for example, a private Washington-based international development organization that often administers USAID programmes, had already been pushing public-private partnerships in Egypt's agricultural sector for years before the revolution, including a major programme with Heinz encouraging smallholder farmers in Upper Egypt to switch to export-based tomato crops (even as domestic food prices spiralled to crisis levels).[72] Now it has spied an opportunity for further PPP expansion; in 2013 it held a major conference at a five-star Cairo hotel that brought together investors, banks, consultants and others to celebrate Egypt's 'significant untapped potential to develop agribusiness'.[73]

Egyptian PPPs dredge Mubarak Country's interdependence between state and global capital to the surface, but the relationship between these two forces has never been an even one: it is mediated, in reality, by a mountain of external debt. This provides international financial institutions with an immense amount of leverage over the state, regardless of which type of leader is fronting it. The signing of Egypt's original IMF loan deal in 1991 ushered in two decades of structural adjustment in which fresh loans were repeatedly taken on in a quick-fix effort to gloss over the country's economic woes; by the start of the revolution, Egypt's total foreign debt had reached $35 billion. But the net transfer of money over this period did not flow from the international community to Cairo – quite the opposite. Between 2000 and 2009 Egypt paid out almost $25 billion worth of interest payments to lenders, yet in the same period, its debt obligations *rose* by 15 per cent. Over those years, the amount paid out by Egypt to its debtors exceeded its income from external loans by more than $3 billion;[74] in other words, the more Egypt paid, the more its obligations grew, and the more external debt the regime decided to take on yet again to meet the next round of payments. None of this debt was acquired by or voted for by ordinary Egyptian citizens; indeed a significant proportion of it was spent on weaponry and security personnel so that the state could crush any attempts by citizens to reform it.[75] But it is Egyptian citizens who are now, in the post-Mubarak era, responsible for the debt's voracious interest payments, both directly – through the burden placed on their tax contributions – and indirectly, through the absence of public services such as new schools and hospitals and trains, things for which there is no money in the treasury because such a large proportion of national wealth must be set aside to service Mubarak's loans.

Even apart from the calamitous impact that structural adjustment policies – whose implementation the original IMF loan was predicated on – have had on Egypt's poor and middle classes, it is clear that this external debt trap has been a terrible deal for Egyptians. Given the nature of Mubarak's authoritarianism a very strong case could be made that loan obligations should be audited and the majority of them classified as odious and illegitimate – a move previously pursued by other countries emerging from dictatorship, like Ecuador and Argentina.* But post-Mubarak, the state's custodians – both military and Islamist – have never entertained the possibility of such an audit. Instead they have called for something else: the acquisition of billions of dollars' worth of fresh external debt, in the form of both heavy borrowing from the Gulf region and new IMF loans. Like the South African state, which opted after apartheid to continue repaying apartheid-era government debt – constricting the incoming administration's economic resources and policy options – Egypt's rulers have used international loans to ensure that procedural

---

* Odious debt is a legal theory which holds that loans acquired by governing regimes for purposes that do not serve the interests of the country, such as oppressing citizens and denying them their rights, should not be enforceable.

democracy at home remains, ultimately, a choiceless democracy for its people. 'Foreign debt is not a neutral form of "aid" but an exploitative social relation established between financial institutions in the North and countries in the South,' points out Adam Hanieh, an economist. 'Trapped in this relationship, countries become dependent upon a continuous stream of new loans in order to service previously accumulated long-term debt. It is a means to deepen the extraction of wealth from Egypt and – precisely because of the continued dependency on financial inflows – serves to chain Egypt to further structural adjustment measures.'[76] *El-gilla asbah karamilla?* ('Does sheep manure turn into caramel?') is an Egyptian proverb reminding us that things we know to be unpleasant aren't likely to suddenly become wonderful. Perhaps a more appropriate proverb for both domestic and foreign elites with regard to Egypt's external debt would be *timoot el-raqqasa we wustaha biyil 'ab.* It means 'The belly-dancer dies and her waist is still moving' – in other words, old habits die hard.

Each element of Egypt's socio-economic counter-revolution – the military, the Brotherhood and the captains of international capital – has followed a near-identical script. Egypt must get back to economic growth: to do so the country needs more debt, its assets need more privatization, its citizens need more austerity, its dissenters need more muffling in the name of security and stability.[77] Ironically, since the revolution began, it is ordinary Egyptians rather than foreign investors who have been propping up the economy: remittances from Egyptian workers rose 40 per cent in 2012 to top $19 billion, staving off the worst of the country's balance of payments and currency crises, while domestically the bank deposits of Egyptian citizens have been converted, through the use of treasury bills, into a key source of finance for the government in its battle to plug the budget shortfall.[78] The bulk of funding for a new extension to the Suez Canal, one of the Sisi regime's first major infrastructure projects, was 'crowd-sourced' from private citizens via the sale of investment certificates.[79] These are the same citizens that the state continues to lock out of economic decision-making, the same citizens that it refuses to meaningfully redistribute wealth to. But they are also citizens who are no longer willing to surrender questions of social justice to the 'experts'. Over the past half-decade, a plethora of alternative economic ideas – from the modest to the visionary – have emerged from worker collectives, economic rights campaigners and revolutionaries: a new system of budget transparency, an alternative tax structure that shifts the burden from poor to rich and imposes windfall levies on foreign corporations who profited excessively from their alliance with Mubarak's dictatorship, renewed resistance to more tranches of international debt. Every new round of IMF negotiations since the revolution began has been met by protests in the streets; a satirical ode to the IMF, performed by Egyptian musician Yasser el-Manawahly and uploaded to YouTube, has gone viral. 'Oh monetary fund, poison in honey,' el-Manawahly croons in Arabic over images of cooking gas running out and electric fans coming to a standstill during power cuts. 'You help me build my home, you help me seed my land, without you life sucks . . . You plan our future, and control my decisions . . . Live with dignity, with my head held high, who'd hold it for me except monetary fund.'[80] IFI orthodoxy may be axiomatic to Egypt's elites, but in Revolution Country rival economic possibilities are still singing out.

When Ibrahim laughs, everyone follows suit. His chortles are deafening enough in open space, but right now Ibrahim is confined inside a twenty-foot long metal drum, the ceiling of which is too low for him to stand, and Effat and I are confined in there with him. 'Don't wipe your sweat!' he booms joyously, as the pair of us make futile attempts to mop our brows and shield our eardrums. 'We're all sweaty! Join the party!'

Ibrahim and his colleagues on the maintenance team are tacking up rubber insulation inside one of Madame Daniela's chemical mixers, and beckon us to join them through a tiny crawl-hole in the drum's base. There's a small lantern inside for light, and no ventilation; the drum feels like an oven. Apparently, this is nothing. When the mixer is on, it draws together several muddy chemical rivulets that run through the factory floor, belching heat and fumes up through the grilles, before churning them all into a smooth liquid base that will eventually be baked into tiles. The tank heats up to 180 degrees centigrade and adjustments to the bolts are often needed while it's running – each maintenance worker can manage only about twenty seconds next to the burning walls before jumping back and letting someone else take a turn. Sometimes there are malfunctions inside the mixer during operations, and rather than shut down the production line for repairs the workers are forced to make adjustments from a porthole in the roof, hovering above the boiling slurry and reaching in with a spanner. A single slip could mean serious injury, or worse; a welder was killed in a nearby section of the factory back in 2010. Ibrahim grows serious for a fleeting moment, setting down the lantern. 'I'd just like the managers to experience this for a few seconds,' he says through the darkness. 'That's why we're fighting, pure and simple.' Then it's back to a steady stream of bawdy jokes, to which Ibrahim's two assistants offer a rolling, appreciative soundtrack of chuckles. But nothing is funnier than my next question: why isn't anyone wearing safety equipment or goggles? 'Safety equipment! Goggles!' erupts Ibrahim with a cackle. 'I remember those. We last saw them four years ago, on a morning when Mubarak had a tour of the factory. The next day, they disappeared.'

Safety goggles are almost impossible to find in the Cleopatra Ceramics factory, or at least they were along the vast bathroom fittings and tile production lines on the day I visited. Nor could I see any protective gloves, or overalls, or footwear, or face-masks. Most employees work in T-shirts and flip-flops, tending to the chemical streams, operating the tile kilns, casting the moulds, polishing the ceramics and moving, wrapping and loading the finished product or to huge pallets with export destinations scrawled haphazardly on the side: Uganda, Italy, England. Many parts of the factory are clouded with a choking acrid dust that worms its way up your nostrils and down your throat and leaves your face caked in an off-white silt. Apart from those in the chemical mixer, the worst conditions are probably in the mould-room, where workers like Hisham each cast twenty toilet bowls a day. Above them hangs a sign depicting a pair of gloves, with the instruction 'Wear protection!' printed in English and Arabic. As a gloveless Hisham bends over each mould, he uses the hem of his grit-streaked fake Arsenal shirt to wipe his eyes. 'They want us to produce and produce and produce. Like animals, or machines. Sometimes I go a bit mad in here and start thinking that

I've become an animal or machine.' Brightening, he points at my notebook. 'Write that down! These [toilet bowls] might be for Britain. Maybe someone will read my words in your book while sitting on one of my toilets.'

Back in 2006, just as the main period of Mubarak-era labour unrest was taking off, the staff at Cleopatra Ceramics went on strike for better wages and conditions. Workers managed to obtain a modest salary increase, but the dispute threw their lack of power inside the factory into focus. The sit-in crawled with state security operatives who threatened strikers openly, underlining just how closely aligned Mubarak's state was with Cleopatra's owner (and leading NDP parliamentarian) Mohamed Aboul Enein. The morning after an agreement to end the stoppage was finally signed, security forces kicked down the doors of the strike leaders and dragged them from their homes; each was held in detention for ten days, then either transferred or fired. 'I remember standing there as Mr Mohamed [Aboul Enein] screamed through a megaphone at us, saying that there was no authority in the country that can make him pay a penny more to his workers than he wanted to, and that any dog who walked out of the company would never walk back,' remembers Mohamed el-Khawaja, a Cleopatra employee. Back then, he was also a member of the NDP. 'I wasn't particularly political and I never really thought about it – an NDP membership card gave you access to things, and so it seemed sensible to join.' The 2006 unrest forced Mohamed to interact with more politicized colleagues for the first time and even play a part in collective decision-making. 'There was a lot of fear back then. Anyone who spoke out, you wouldn't know what happened to them. At election time we would all be bussed out to the appropriate place to vote for Aboul Enein; there was no accommodation so we slept outside in the cold where there was no shelter, and dogs roaming.' After the strike, Mohamed's enthusiasm for the NDP began to wane; for his own protection he initially remained a member of the party and in 2009 even helped organize a local NDP youth conference, but by the following year he'd had enough. Less than twelve months later, he became a militant strike leader.

I'd first met Mohamed the night before my visit to Cleopatra, in the company of a veteran Suez labour activist named Sa'oud Amr. Sa'oud knew the history of the Suez region inside out: he spoke of the 1.5 million Egyptians who had built the Suez Canal in the nineteenth century for French developer Ferdinand de Lesseps, of how de Lesseps's name was used by Nasser as a code word in a 1956 public radio speech, signalling the Egyptian army to launch a surprise assault on the British and seize the Canal for themselves. He talked of the nationalist mythology that has permeated Suez for decades. 'It was in Suez that Egyptians were first successful in their agitation for equal rights at British companies; many of those who led the anti-British strikes in the dying days of colonialism hailed from Suez; it was at Suez that Egyptian workers first withdrew from British army camps,' Sa'oud explained. He was dressed gloriously in a neatly tucked red and blue pinstripe shirt and blazer, and as he reminisced he smoothed down his moustache impulsively and adjusted his glasses, as if his words were not enough to mop up the excitement of his tale. 'It's always been an industrial city, a city where workers come together and find ways to form movements and fight. Labour struggle is embedded in Suez; governments and investors come and go, but they can't uproot it.'

For our meeting, Sa'oud had brought me to a café overlooking a stretch of wasteland separating Port Tawfiq, the spot where the Suez Canal meets the Red Sea, from the rest of Suez itself. From our vantage point, 100,000-tonne container ships appeared to float ethereally through the sand dunes on the other side of the canal; we sat on plastic chairs under a fraying sun shade and darkening sky while stray dogs scampered across the open scrub and came to investigate our shisha pipes. As well as Cleopatra's Mohamed el-Khawaja, there were several employees of the huge Sokhna dockyard sitting around our table. All were currently engaged in their own labour mobilization against multinational port owners DP World, who also run docks in London, Vancouver, Rotterdam and Dubai. Over the course of the evening, news was shared from the Suez Company for Fertilizer Production where workers had downed tools in protest at the hazardous air they were forced to breathe under the factory's public-private partnership management, and from the Suez Steel Company in nearby Ataka, where police trucks and armoured personnel carriers had surrounded the factory gates in an attempt to snatch strike leaders as they entered or left the premises. 'We're sensing our possibilities, but at the same time realizing how hard the regime and the rich will fight to stop things changing,' said Mohamed, sweeping his arm across the city.

During several hours of conversation, everyone told similar stories of working life since January 2011: the initial panic by bosses when the revolution began, the swiftly proffered concessions to workers in an attempt to ward off unrest, the slow realization that management and owners were just playing for time and trying to pull the wool over workers' eyes. 'Mohamed Aboul Enein came to us [after Mubarak's resignation] and said, "I'll give you all your rights,"' recalled Mohamed. 'Madame Daniela, his wife, did the same. The very fact they were talking to us seemed like a huge victory; before they would just come, put their feet up and fire a worker, and anyone who talked would be sent to the police station. So this conversation felt like a big step forward. But it turned out to be just words, all lies. They never did anything for us. All those years of no healthcare, no services, all the medical problems that come with the nature of our work, no compensation for the risk we take in that factory. We realized the problem wasn't to do with these individual demands. The problem was the political and financial power of the bosses we were dealing with. The problem was who controlled the factory.' Mohamed said that since the start of the revolution, from the perspective of Cleopatra's workforce, Aboul Enein's ownership role at the ceramics plant had become inseparable from the role he and other magnates played at the national apex of business and politics: they hated him for oppressing workers in the factory, and they hated him for the part he played in oppressing Egyptians more generally, especially revolutionaries. During the eighteen days, the occupation at Tahrir was attacked, notoriously, by thugs on camel-and horse-back; the figures behind that assault were allegedly a clutch of Mubarak-era oligarchs, Aboul Enein among them. Aboul Enein and several others were later arrested and charged with inciting the killing of protesters; the evening I met the Suez labour activists, all defendants had just been acquitted in court. Mohamed could barely disguise his fury at the verdict, lighting cigarette after cigarette and regularly breaking off our discussion to pace around the table in consternation. 'In the factory, in the court, Aboul Enein *is* the counter-revolution,' observed Sa'oud with a sigh. I asked if I could visit Cleopatra the next day. 'Yes,' replied Mohamed. 'Give me a lift to work tomorrow morning and I'll take you inside.'

At Cleopatra, workers have occupied the factory on multiple occasions since the start of the revolution. But unlike in 2006, they are no longer prepared simply to stand around while Aboul Enein yells insults at them through a megaphone. Each mobilization has been massive, with four or five thousand employees walking out a time, and the goal of each protest has been about far more than improvements in pay and conditions: with each iteration of unrest, workers have presented yet another unequivocal, non-negotiable rejection of Aboul Enein himself, and the Mubarak-era investor class that he represents. Mohamed showed us a video of an occupation shot by the revolutionary media collective Mosireen. 'The government cannot be a government for businessmen,' insists one worker, to the camera. 'When we made the revolution, we did this in order to eliminate the government of businessmen. We demand a government that represents the people.'[81] In early 2012, both Aboul Enein and the national minister of labour were captured and held overnight in detention by hundreds of Cleopatra workers in Cairo, who released their quarry only when the army intervened to broker a deal. On other occasions, Cleopatra workers have blocked streets in the capital[82] and stormed government offices in Suez.[83]

The struggle to 'cleanse' Cleopatra and other workplaces of mini-Mubaraks like Aboul Enein is known in Arabic as *tatheer*, literally 'purification'. It has sent the fight for collective democracy waged by many of Cleopatra's employees in recent years – in Tahrir, in Suez's el-'Arbaeen Square and within countless other public spaces – out beyond the streets, and back into the workplace. In the course of all these protests, some Cleopatra employees have stopped seeing themselves as employees at all, but rather as custodians of a shared, productive resource that should be pressed into service for the good of all Egyptians; in other words, they have started thinking like a state – a process that has potentially serious implications for the existing one. 'We are forming a committee, composed of all the political forces in the governorate and some of the departments here [in the factory], like storage monitors, sales, and security,' explained one worker during a stoppage in early 2012. 'We are planning to proceed on schedule and sell our product, and pay out wages . . . Workers can take the factory and own it. This factory belongs to the workers, it was founded and built by the workers. These workers are the most rightful people to take over this factory and run it.'[84] Recently, staff had also started taking solidarity actions with strikes at other industrial plants in the Suez region, and building wider alliances; Mohamed told me that during their latest stoppage, when workers were running out of food and reduced to climbing palm trees on the factory lawns to retrieve dates, local Bedouins began organizing to bring them milk and bread. 'People inside and outside these walls want change,' he said as we drove up to the factory compound. 'We are pulling together to survive, and to win.'

Cleopatra's story – one of successive attempts to force out regime remnants who continue to live and rule by the old ways – is a story shared by thousands of workplaces across post-Mubarak Egypt. The workers involved are not a homogenous bloc; some are more militant than others, and the degree to which the participants of each struggle see themselves as linked to other workforces in other industries varies across time and place. But the sheer volume of mobilizations is astonishing. In 2011, the first year of the revolution, there were nearly 1,400 work stoppages and other labour protests across the country.[85] In 2012, there were over 3,800 mobilizations over economic rights and social justice, the majority of which were labour actions – more than in any single year under Mubarak, even at the height of the pre-revolution strike wave. By the start of 2013, episodes of labour unrest had reached 800 a month: a work-related protest or strike somewhere in the country for every hour of every day, and more than 5,000 throughout the whole year.[86] In 2014, long after Sisi had seized power and clamped down on all forms of protest, more than 2,200 labour protests were still recorded.[87] The biggest single cause of labour unrest – right up to and including strikes during the Sisi era – has been some form of *tatheer*; these struggles have helped keep Revolution Country alive. Cairo's metro workers have struck in protest at what they say is the denigration of a vital public service by managers still allied to Mubarak. When the metro company's chairman was sacked by authorities in an effort to bring the walkout to an end, employees elected to carry on striking until he faced prosecution on corruption charges.[88] At the Torah Starch and Glucose Manufacturing Company in Helwan, where management planned to dismantle machinery and destroy production lines in order to turn the site into a shopping mall, employees went on strike to thwart them: 'Today I am no longer imprisoned, physically or otherwise – and I have the freedom to speak,' explained Abdullah, one of the many Torah employees who decided that the factory floor no longer belonged to his bosses.[89]

By raising demands that go beyond what elites dismiss as 'sectional' interests, such as pay and working conditions, Egypt's labour force has used *tatheer* to expose and confront the inner workings of the neoliberal state: its rules and linkages, its leading characters and the channels through which their power is conveyed. Illuminating this ecosystem shatters the myth of its inevitability; it forces the possibility of alternatives. 'This is not investment, it's colonialism,' chanted striking employees outside the gates of Telemisr, a massive electronics manufacturing company that was gutted to provide speculative property gains for investors following privatization.[90] Workers at SUMED, a petroleum pipeline company, and Bitcino/Legrand, manufacturers of door entry systems, have downed tools in opposition to outsourcing and the use of temporary contracts; civil aviation workers at Cairo airport have mobilized in opposition to the power exercised by Military Inc. over their workplace, and denounced the involvement of Mubarak-era aviation ministers in the post-Mubarak political scene. Actions like these have exposed as fallacy the notion that regime change can mean anything without radical economic rebuilding. Critiques of the workplace have become critiques of the state, and vice versa: the very feedback loop that elites have battled so hard to prevent. 'The company is itself, in origin, a source of tyranny, and is built on illegitimacy, and has leeched my blood, and the blood of the people,' argued a striking worker at Petrojet – one of Egypt's biggest oil conglomerates. 'Our problem is not what they call *fi'awi* ("sectoral") sit-ins. What is that term?! What are *fi'awi* sit-ins? I'm saying, save me – hunger has consumed my guts.'[91]

That is not to say that workers have succeeded in achieving all their wider demands. Examples of employees actually seizing control of production have been episodic and uneven: before the revolution, two factories in 10th Ramadan City, an industrial satellite town north-east of Cairo, experienced periods of self-management,[92] and since Mubarak fell another firm in the same city – Kouta Steel – has also been taken over by staff, after the owner failed to pay them for several months.[93] Far more common is the situation found at Cleopatra, where transitory stretches of worker occupation have been sandwiched between management initiatives – often temporarily successful – to draw strikes to a close. This back-and-forth has placed Cleopatra and many other factories in a grey zone, within which workers feel semi-liberated, old bosses remain in place, and paths of authority become muddied.

But although few borders have been permanently redrawn, there have been plenty of provisional glimpses of Revolution Country in the workplace. Many of those glimpses have been fuelled by the continued expansion of Egypt's independent trade union movement, which did so much to undermine Mubarak's rule. Cairo's Manshiyet el-Bakri Hospital, for example, has undergone sustained periods of collective management by staff following the establishment of an independent trade union in 2011. One of its doctors, Mohamed Shafiq, had volunteered at Tahrir field clinics during the anti-Mubarak uprising; on returning to work, he found the hospital in a state of radical foment. '[I] found a revolutionary mood,' he explained. 'Even people who supported Mubarak were saying the situation in hospitals couldn't continue. So I did a leaflet with doctors' demands. Unlike previous experiences of petitioning, nearly every doctor signed. It was amazing. A number of nurses asked to sign [too]. At first I said no. There has always been an invisible barrier between doctors and nurses. But so many asked that I thought, why not?'[94] In the end, not only were nurses allowed to join, but also ancillary and maintenance staff like porters and cleaners. Within a fortnight members of the new union held elections to choose representatives; they built their own glass-fronted ballot box, and drafted in members of the independent bus workers' union to supervise the vote. Then, armed with a self-practised democratic legitimacy, the process of *tatheer* began. 'We rearranged the hospital and the budget,' said

Shafiq. 'Our manager refused to implement these changes. Hospital managers are small dictators – Mubaraks. So we told him to go and not come back.' For the first time ever, a vote was held by workers to decide who should run the hospital administration; when union representatives contacted the ministry of health to inform them of developments, they were met with spluttering disbelief. 'You can't elect your director!' replied a shocked official. 'You can't elect your father!'

Ezbet el-Haggana lies south-west of the Cairo airport fence, across the busy Suez road. As a densely populated *ashwa'iyat* settlement, it is invisible on most official maps. To its east is Nasr City, a middle-class suburb boasting wide avenues, franchised coffee shops and regularized rhythms. In every other direction lies sandy edgeland: epic skies, trunks of asphalt road, high walls lined with incongruously perfect shrubs – the hallmark of private military enclaves.

In the not too distant past Haggana was a desert hamlet populated by families of Egyptian coastguard soldiers who were based nearby; the area was under army control, and the conurbation was so socially and geographically marginal that it was known officially only as 'Kilometre 4.5' – a reference to the distance along the highway between the settlement and Heliopolis, its nearest recognized town. Most of the inhabitants were of Nubian and Sudanese origin, and they built their houses in the traditional single-storey Upper Egyptian style, with red bricks and mud ceilings. Back then the whole community comprised less than a square mile, bordered by the motorway to the north and a line of high-voltage electricity cables to the south. Today, 1 million people live here. The buildings are so tall and the alleyways so thin that daylight is often hard to come by, even on the hottest summer's day. During the final months of the year, when policemen are seeking to complete their annual arrest quotas, young men from Haggana avoid leaving the settlement and walking around the rest of Cairo alone; they claim that if any officer stops them and checks their IDs (which always includes details of the bearer's home settlement), an incriminating 'Kilometre 4.5' is enough to land you in a cell for the night, regardless of whether or not you've done anything wrong. 'The first battle for much of the population here is just to officially exist,' says Abdel Abou Ela of el-Shehab, an NGO that organizes social work in the neighbourhood. 'So often they just get lost in the bureaucracy, and fall between the cracks.'[95]

Nahmido Saeed Salah knows what it's like to fall between the cracks. As a domestic worker for an upper-middle-class family in Nasr City, she spent fifteen years making the daily journey there from Haggana, picking up food and other groceries for her employers along the way. Over the next twelve hours or so she would collect dirty laundry, wash clothes and bedding, sweep up dust, polish wood, clean ceramics and generally beautify each room, scrub the toilet and shower, deal with tradesmen, make tea, cook dinner and beat out the carpets. For all these chores, her basic salary was around 600 EGP a month – or 20 EGP (£2) a day. One afternoon the 42-year-old was accused by her employer of stealing some silver cups. Nahmido insists she did no such thing, and suspects that her husband – who she says was having an affair at the time and trying to break up the marriage in a way that would be materially advantageous to him – set her up. Whatever the truth of the matter, she was dismissed immediately without debate, compensation or notice. 'There was nobody to defend me,' she told me when we met in a dusty office at the heart of Haggana. 'I began to think of all the other stories I'd heard about domestic workers being abused, beaten and exploited, and I realized that if we had something like a syndicate to represent us then life would be much better.'

As the size and scope of the independent trade union movement has grown within the revolution, workers on the furthest margins of Egypt's economy – from Nile felucca-boat captains to downtown street vendors – have decided they too can and should start organizing collectively. The embryonic Ezbet el-Haggana Domestic Workers' Union, of which Nahmido is a co-founder, is just one example of a growing trend; independent unions are starting to upset conventional power structures outside the formal workplace as well. Domestic servants in Haggana who were already members of a local *gam 'eya* – a grassroots savings cooperative – began discussing the potential for an independent syndicate as far back as 2010, but it took the uprising against Mubarak to convince them that such a thing might ever be possible. As word spread organically through Haggana's back-streets, women began coming forward with their stories – of being sexually assaulted by male members of employer families, of being forced to clean kitchens while recovering from a broken leg, of suffering injuries at work and then immediately being dismissed so that employers could avoid taking any responsibility for their maidservant's welfare. Samah Hagazu, a 35-year-old domestic worker from the neighbourhood who had recently joined the union, said that she had once been hit by a car on her way to an employer's house. Despite the fact that she had worked full-time for the family for seven years, 'they pretended they didn't know me because they didn't want to be responsible for my medical bills. They acted like they'd never seen me before. I got nothing, and had to pay for all the medical costs myself.' Now the new union wants to use its collective bargaining power to make employers sign contracts with domestic workers – something virtually unheard of before the revolution – and educate members on ways to protect themselves from harassment, maltreatment and forced prostitution. Ultimately, there is hope that the union could become a central employment office, guaranteeing the sort of things workers elsewhere often take for granted – fixed salaries, health insurance and retirement benefits – as well as finding work for all who need it. 'We want to feel that we haven't just been used and used and for years with every drop of usefulness squeezed out of us, and then abandoned at the end with no compensation,' said Nahmido.

With the new union's ambition has come pride. 'Our role in the economy is absolutely central; if my job isn't carried out correctly, others can't do their jobs either,' explained Mona Saad, a young domestic worker who was busy researching similar initiatives in Thailand and the Philippines. 'If I don't clean the house of a doctor properly, and I cause him or her stress or trouble, that doctor can't go out and do their job properly. So I deserve my rights and respect within my workplace.' Nahmido, who believes that confronting popular misconceptions about 'menial' workers must be the first step of the struggle, agreed. 'Before I was ashamed to say I was a domestic servant because the idea and the image that society had of us is so wrong,' she added. 'We're seen as low-class, or even as thieves. But through this union route, I've discarded my shame – I can go into the street and say out loud that I'm an employee of a household, a house manager, someone who helps other women to do their job better and enables other women to play a better role in society by taking care of their house for them. I am proud of my job; I work hard and I sweat and I clean and I wipe so that I can make money to raise my children. You know, we ourselves didn't realize how important we were before we started organizing like this. Doing this has made us feel that we are something, that we can make our voice heard.' I asked the women whether they had faced resistance to their union activities from other members of the Haggana community, and Mona smiled. 'We've had our fair share of laughter and mockery, with people making fun of the idea that women could organize in this way, but we've proved them wrong with our actions.' What about her husband? 'He's seen the work we've put into this,' replied Mona. 'Joke about it? He wouldn't dare.'

Despite its extremely limited resources, the Ezbet el-Haggana Domestic Workers Union has already produced a draft model contract and is beginning to attract new members from other informal settlements as well. But the road to legal recognition and formal affiliation with an independent union federation is a long one. The women involved lack the finances needed for consultations with lawyers and administrative assistance; many of those they are keenest to represent, such as live-in child servants, who count among the most vulnerable category of domestic workers in Egypt, are also the hardest to identify and reach. As they grow larger, they will also have to confront stereotypes that remain prevalent among certain sections of the independent union bureaucracy, especially the old Nasserite left: that proper labour activists are male and work in a factory, that women engaged in 'menial work' have no business organizing on the ground for themselves. But the independent union movement generally is no revolutionary panacea: half a decade into its existence it remains dangerously fragmented and politically isolated, leaving its leadership prey to co-optation by non-revolutionary forces.

That is exactly what happened when Kamal Abu Eita – leader of the property tax collectors who formed Egypt's first independent union, and subsequently head of EFITU, a federation of independent syndicates – accepted a job as minister of manpower in Sisi's first cabinet following the overthrow of Mohamed Morsi. To the dismay of many activists in the labour movement, for whom Abu Eita had long been a hero, he quickly began using language that was eerily familiar to anyone who witnessed SCAF's brutal crackdown on labour struggles during its initial period of post-Mubarak rule. 'Workers who were champions of the strike under the previous regime should now become champions of production,' declared Abu Eita, before urging employees to take to the streets to support the government's 'War on Terror'.[96] Abu Eita's story is a salutary reminder of why revolutionaries wanted to avoid 'seizing' state institutions in the first place; without creating a different kind of power and alternative forms of sovereignty, individuals that move inside the system, however seemingly radical at the outset, tend to mould themselves to the state's values rather than the other way round. Within weeks of the coup, strikers at Suez Steel and the Scimitar Petroleum Company were both forcefully put down by soldiers. At the Abboud Spinning Company in Alexandria, security forces opened fire on striking workers with live ammunition. Multiple union leaders have subsequently faced arrest and state torture.[97]

The appointment of Abu Eita to government is part of Sisi's efforts at bringing a decade of virtually non-stop labour struggles in Egypt to an end. By incorporating a Nasser-type social contract between workers and regime into their relentless invocation of *haybat el-dawla,* or 'state prestige' – the notion that the state as a whole is inviolable, a red line which protesters must not cross – the generals are hoping to persuade workers that rather than setting themselves up as adversaries of the military junta, they will begin to see their role in capitalist production as one of partnership with Egypt's benign political elites; that chauvinistic nationalism can be successfully wedded to neoliberal appropriation in the service of foreign and domestic capital. Popular hatred of the Brotherhood has been harnessed by the state to fight back against *tatheer*; regime-allied media outlets have painted attempts by workers to remove 'mini-Mubaraks' from their workplace as a dastardly fifth column spreading 'Brotherhoodization' from deep within the factory floor.

But unlike Nasser, Sisi has provided Egyptian workers with no material gains or grand ideological vision in return for their quietude and the violence needed to enforce it. Instead, he has promised to deliver an even deeper dose of austerity. 'If I make you walk on foot, can you stand it?' Sisi asks rhetorically, in a secret tape outlining what economic hardships Egyptians can expect to endure under his rule – one of several recordings of his private conversations with advisers that have leaked out into the public domain. 'If I make you wake at five o'clock in the morning every day, can you stand it? If we become short of food, can you stand it? If we lack air conditioning, can you stand it? Can you stand it if I take away subsidies in one go? Can you stand that from me?'[98] Subsidy reforms enacted in the Sisi era have targeted the poor over the rich and resulted in staggering price hikes. The cost of low-grade fuel, for example – the type used in general transportation and cheaper vehicles – has risen by 78 per cent; by contrast, the price of Octane 95, per cent more commonly used by luxury cars, has risen by only 7.[99] Industrial tycoons with close links to the state continue to see many of their basic supplies heavily subsidized, driving up corporate profits; since the revolution began, Egypt's billionaires have seen their wealth grow by 80.[100] Meanwhile, per cent household electricity bills have soared by 30 per cent, and 5 million more Egyptians have slipped below the national poverty line.[101] 'I would like to tell you that Germany reduced 50 per cent of the salaries for its austerity plan, and people accepted that,' Sisi is heard saying to a colleague in another leaked tape. 'When South Sudan seceded from the north in order to become independent, it cut salaries by 50 per cent. People said nothing . . .'[102]

For multinational financiers, the story of Sisi's presidency so far has been a happy one. A new investment law immunizing contracts between the government and corporations from any third-party legal action – effectively placing business interests above democratic sovereignty – was drafted within weeks of Sisi taking power. Several global corporations holding investments in Egypt have already launched legal actions against the state in an attempt to quash the small number of post-Mubarak economic reforms that have arguably been geared towards social justice rather than against it. Mexican cement giant CEMEX has sued over the threat of renationalization; Veolia, the French waste and energy outfit, began a lawsuit following the introduction of a new minimum wage.[103] In the future, this new investment law will make it even easier for international companies to shield private profit-making from any collective oversight by the Egyptian people. As one newspaper put it, 'This isn't Egypt after the revolution, so the new narrative goes; it's Egypt before the gold rush ... The [investment] law leaves the door wide open for corruption.'[104] In March 2015, an international Egyptian investment conference – sponsored by Saudi Arabia and held in Sharm el-Sheikh – saw more than $30 billion of government deals signed with the private sector.[105] Investment itself is not necessarily a bad thing; what is disturbing is the belief, seemingly held by both the Sisi regime and its international allies, that these sort of deals alone can rescue Egypt's economy, without any consideration of the social and political context they are being struck in. 'Egypt's current investment framework continues to favor the interests of multinational corporations over the interests of the public,' concluded a report by the Egyptian Center for Economic and Social Rights in 2015.[106]

Sisi's retooled state has to offer investors new opportunities for capital accumulation; just like in the Mubarak era, many grand and ultimately unfeasible mega-projects are being rapidly sketched out in ministry offices to help answer that very need. Sisi has enthusiastically embraced the Mubarakist urban development plan, Cairo 2050, and announced plans to extend it by constructing an entirely new capital city – New New Cairo – in the desert, at an estimated cost of £44 billion.[107] A huge scheme to widen the Suez Canal has already led to the forced eviction, without consultation or compensation, of residents from up to 5,000 homes; engineers and economists have described the regime's financial rationale for the project as wildly unrealistic.[108] Meanwhile, Mubarak's pyramid – the failed Toshka project in the New Valley – continues to bleed the Egyptian treasury dry, while rural smallholders and Egypt's landless, the supposed beneficiaries of Toshka, carry on sliding into poverty as land privatization distils agricultural wealth into fewer and fewer hands.

The biggest winners from all this have been the Gulf governments – long the principal funders of counter-revolution in the Arab World – and the private capital they are enmeshed with. Riyadh and Abu Dhabi have backed Sisi's regime to the tune of billions of dollars in an effort to guarantee his survival, and it is Gulf companies that are reaping the benefits; in the agribusiness sector alone, for example, firms from Saudi Arabia, Kuwait and the United Arab Emirates now control more than half of the Egyptian milk market, half of the domestic poultry market, 45 per cent of the sugar market and 42 per cent of the edible oils market.[109] Under Sisi, Emirates property developer Emaar, owners of Uptown Cairo, have been given permission to build another new high-end gated compound on the fringes of the capital; the development includes a new private road, the construction of which will require the demolition of a local residential neighbourhood named Jabal el-Ahmar. The generals are, of course, doing very well themselves: of the fourteen companies listed by the government as eligible to bid on contracts relating to Sisi's Suez Canal widening scheme, almost all were joint ventures between the Egyptian military and private Gulf conglomerates; since Morsi's removal, major infrastructure contracts totalling billions of dollars have been handed directly to the army by the state.[110] Not that the Egyptian armed forces aren't grateful for the largesse. In June 2014 the military grandly announced it was 'donating' £90 million to the Egyptian treasury in a gesture of goodwill. The money was drawn from the budget of the National Service Projects Authority, the only institution tasked with maintaining any regulation over the economic empire of Military Inc.[111] A new military production company has since been created, specializing in the development of – among other things – sports facilities, tourist resorts, hospitals, public relations and advertising. [112]

The consensus among Western economists on Sisi has, according to the *Financial Times,* been 'so far, so good'.[113] In early 2015, the IMF – conducting its first major survey of the country since 2010 – praised Sisi's 'turnaround' of the economy. 'Following four years of political uncertainty and economic slowdown,' declared IMF Mission Chief for Egypt, Christopher Jarvis, 'Egypt has chosen a path of adjustment and reform which, if followed resolutely, will lead to economic stability and growth.'[114] In neoliberal, autocratic Egypt, the more the state changes, the more it stays the same.

And yet, for all this fresh wealth appropriation and the violent implementation of Mubarakera economic norms, pockets of Revolution Country continue, obdurately, to blossom. In February 2014, ahead of Sisi's much anticipated announcement that he would run for the presidency, over 250,000 workers joined a national strike and brought down the military junta's interim cabinet – led by neoliberal 'technocrat' Hazem el-Beblawi – in the process. 'For the past six months [since Sisi's rise to power], the people waited for the government to be the government of the revolution – as they had promised,' said Hoda Kamel of EFITU, the independent trade union federation. 'But when January came, people realized it was a trick.'[115] For every Kamal Abu Eita who has been co-opted by the regime, there are others – like Fatma Ramadan, a long-time labour activist and fellow EFITU board member – who have publicly denounced the jingoistic 'wheel of production' narrative so beloved by the old state, and who are urging the labour movement on to another round of revolutionary resistance. In an open letter to workers in July 2013, at the height of the state's crackdown on political opponents, she wrote:

> Egypt's workers dream of freedom and social justice, they dream of work at a time when thieves who are called businessmen close down factories to pocket billions. Since before the 25th of January you have been demanding your rights, and your strikes and demonstrations for the same unanswered demands continued after Mubarak's overthrow. Both the Muslim Brotherhood and the military have negotiated left, right and centre, not once having in mind your demands and rights. All they have in mind is how to put out the sparks you have lit with your struggle in times of darkness . . . Do not be fooled into replacing a religious dictatorship with a military one.[116]

It is the persistence of people like Ramadan that demonstrate the basic contradictions of Egypt's neoliberal state remain acutely unresolved.

As we climb down from the chemical mixer, Seif, the Cleopatra security director, is waiting 'You better come with me,' he barks, and leads us over to Madame Daniela's offices. There, after admonishing us, she begins to speak.

Madame Daniela talks of the injustices visited upon Aboul Enein, her husband, since the revolution began, and of the ingratitude of her workers, 'who have no ability to compromise'. Having initially been infuriated at our infiltration, she now seems relieved to have an opportunity to chat, to expound, and to connect, however briefly, with the outside world. To Madame Daniela, these offices have become an island of traditional certainty, surrounded by a sea of anarchy that has flooded across the rest of the factory, the rest of Suez, and the rest of Egypt at large. Some days the waves seem to recede; on others, they lap ever closer to her feet. 'This country is in major trouble,' she proclaims, in Italian-accented English. 'The economy has gone down, material prices are up, the banks have no liquidity.' She takes a piece of paper from her desk and draws a line on it with a biro, indicating an unbreachable divide. 'The culture of this country is never compromise. Egyptians seem to want to fight, everybody wants all of what they want.' She waves a hand back towards the factory floor and then trails off into silence. 'But I don't think there will be revolution again,' she says, finally. It's almost as if she's speaking to herself, an exercise in private reassurance. 'I don't believe there is one Egyptian willing to make revolution now.' She stares questioningly at Effat, but continues before he can comment. 'No more revolution. Everyone is too afraid of the future.'

It is interesting that Madame Daniela believes that fear of the future will check revolution, rather than fuel it. What the status quo looks like, of course, depends very much on whether you sit in the Cleopatra office suite or inside one of the chemical drums – or outside the factory fence altogether, searching desperately for work. I ask her about the terrible labour conditions at the company, and she defends them by positively comparing the ceramics plant to the squalor of her employees' homes. 'Did you see, in their homes, what is the condition of these people? Most of these people in their home, they live together in the same room . . . They are poor. If we gave them the safety equipment, they would sell it.' We point out that this might be a sign she is not paying her workers enough, and she looks defensive. 'I protect my workers very well,' she replies. 'Every time someone dies, I visit their home.' I ask whether she visited the home of the welder who died on the production line in 2010 when a dropped cable electrified the puddle of water at his feet. His colleagues told me that if he had been wearing safety shoes, he would not have been killed. 'If" is a word you can say here a lot of times,' she retorts. 'I want to tell you that sometimes accidents happen because of the non-efficiency of the workers. For every Italian worker, you need twenty Egyptians to get the job done. And even then, they are not equivalent to one Italian.'

Seif, the management security director, has been glancing nervously at his mobile phone throughout this interview; now, unable to contain himself any longer, he leans over and whispers something urgently into Madame Daniela's ear. She purses her lips, and then stands. 'Well, it's been a pleasure to meet you,' she says abruptly. 'It's time for you to go. For your own safety, leave the complex right now.' Before we have time to ask anything more, we are ushered out of the office and through the doors of the building, narrowly missing a forklift truck that is whizzing past towards the main factory entrance gate as we go. In every direction, workers are streaming off their production lines and out towards the entrance gate; some are armed with sticks and clubs. There is an excitable hum of chatter, blended with the roar of lorry engines as they too motor towards the throng around the entrance. Curious, we push through the crowds – to find Aboul Enein's chauffeured black saloon, halted and surrounded by Cleopatra staff. Employees are circling the vehicle and chanting furiously: for Aboul Enein's imprisonment, for their rights, for a takeover of the factory. 'You don't have any camels or thugs to protect you now, you son of a bitch,' yells one man in overalls. Another approaches the car with a knife, though he is restrained by colleagues. From the back of a flat-bed truck, Mohamed el-Khawaja addresses the crowd and appeals for calm.

Aboul Enein, freshly returned to his ceramics empire after being acquitted in court of leading the counter-revolutionary 'Battle of the Camel' charge against Tahrir during the eighteen days, was besieged that day by workers who have decided that they no longer belong to him, or to his company, or to the economic system he represents. It was a scary, exhilarating sight, and a perfect microcosm of the economic turmoil in post-Mubarak Egypt. Aboul Enein was still in charge, still ensconced in a chauffeured car, and still had the neoliberal state and its allies firmly at his back. Yet the man who once so unassailable that he could berate his own striking staff through a megaphone and – clasped securely in the folds of a political system configured precisely to protect his interests – insist nobody could make him do a thing he didn't want to, was now being frog-marched to his own office against his will for negotiations with Mohamed, an independent labour activist who was once a member of the NDP. As he was shepherded past me and Effat, surrounded by chanting workers, he stared straight ahead with what looked like a mixture of defiance and fear.

That night, when Effat and I returned to downtown Suez, we met up with Mostafa Deraa, a 31 year-old Suez native who is following in the footsteps of local labour stalwarts like Sa'oud Amr and throwing himself into a new era of worker activism. Growing up in this heavily mythologized region had given Mostafa a taste for rebellion; while schoolchildren in other places took class trips to the zoo or a museum, Mostafa's teachers took him to the sites of famous military battles, many of which lie right on the city's doorsteps. In late 2011, as Suez revolutionaries clashed with army forces and both sides took hostages from the other in an attempt to strengthen their position, Mostafa was one of those called in to meet a senior general and begin negotiations. 'The general stared at me and shook his head, then asked me: 'Why are you doing this? Aren't you afraid?' I smiled and explained that we had been playing in the ruins of our wars with Israel, France and Britain since we were kids. We watched tanks roll by – it's what we grew up with, it's in our blood. 'Army strength doesn't frighten us,' I told him. 'We know we can beat anyone if the cause is right.' The sort of nationalism that Sisi depends upon for survival cuts both ways.

Excitedly, we told Mostafa what we had witnessed that afternoon: the showdown with Madame Daniela, the wildcat strike, the seizure by workers of Aboul Enein. The young man simply shrugged. 'This sort of thing is happening every day in Suez, and in Egypt more generally,' he explained. 'The worker is always fighting against all forms of exploitation, whether it comes with a cigar or a beard. Our struggle has always been for an economy run by the workers, not by the "investors" – the revolution has just made that struggle even more real than it was before.' He started telling us a story he'd heard regarding a German woman who claimed she'd survived cancer after following the Egyptian revolution on television from her hospital bed: 'If they're brave enough to overthrow Mubarak, I'm brave enough to beat this disease,' Mostafa quoted, or claimed to quote, with a rapturous smile. 'You have no idea what this revolution means to us, how deep it runs and how impossible it will be to defeat.'

His phone buzzed; it was Sa'oud with some news. Mostafa creased his brow as he listened, and then swore. He ended the call and informed us that some of the union leaders from Sokhna port that we'd met the previous evening had just been fired by bosses at DP World – part of a new management crackdown on labour activists. Protests would now be held across town. 'There could be 20,000 on the streets tomorrow, and the security forces will be scared shitless,' Mostafa said. He called for the bill and sprung up to leave – there were organizers to phone up, rallies to schedule, arrangements to be made. 'You see,' he grinned, turning one last time before reaching the door. 'It's like I said: we make gains here and losses there, everything is up and down all the time. But nothing's still. It's a battle that's underway. Mubarak's economy, the investors' economy, your [the West's] economy: it's never ever had a fight on its hands like this one. Trust me. I know who's going to win.'

IO

'Now we make our dreams
real in the daytime'

When I asked Mastour what it was like to meet the president, he shrugged and wrinkled his nose. The reaction took me by surprise. The previous day, Mastour and some fellow Bedouins had made a 400-mile round-trip to Cairo in order to attend a public reception at the presidential palace; I'd been expecting photo slideshows, gossip about the furnishings, eye-rolling at the airport-style security. Instead, Mastour had the air of a man who was struggling to understand why anyone would consider a meeting with the president to be noteworthy. In fact, he was slightly affronted; if anyone should feel honoured by the encounter, he implied, it was the president – not him. 'Before the revolution, sure, it might have been something special,' Mastour eventually conceded. 'But now . . .' He trailed off and stared at me, as if the matter was so obvious that it was almost demeaning to put it into words. 'Now there's no value whatsoever in the government. It's nothing. Look at the coastguard out there – they don't dare come near us. In Dabaa, authority lies with the people.'

It was late 2012 and the two of us were standing on a small hilltop in Dabaa, a two-hour drive west from Alexandria, looking out over the Mediterranean. The ground around us was reddish and fleshy, scarred with little ravines through which water once ran. In the distance there were a few tyre tracks and a smattering of goat droppings; beyond that, only the low waves of the sea. Mastour Abdel Wanis Salah – known universally in Dabaa as Sheikh Abu-Shakara – went on to explain that these days it tended to be communities like his that issued invitations to meetings and politicians who were forced to answer them, not the other way around. A few weeks earlier, then-president Mohamed Morsi had accepted an opportunity to come and address community delegates in the nearby town of Marsa Matrouh, Egypt's last major conurbation before the Libyan border; he was greeted by 4,000 angry protesters demanding that the presidentially appointed regional governor be sacked. The governor was duly removed, though that did little to mollify the Bedouins of Dabaa. They had a deeper struggle to contend with, and at this particular moment Mastour – tall, broad and crowned in a red tarbouche – was perched on top of it: a small, empty depression, about sixty feet in diameter, chiselled into the earth at our feet.

Mastour walked slowly around the depression's circumference and traced its edges with a piece of driftwood. Within this crater, Egypt's government plans to lay the foundations of a 5,000 mega-watt nuclear reactor. In most countries, citizens like Mastour do not get to trample at will over the place in which a series of sensitive nuclear and security installations are being constructed. Post-Mubarak Egypt, however, is nothing like most countries.

Daba' is the Arabic word for a female hyena. Popular legend has it that one of them once lived in the nearby mountains and could be heard cackling into the night for miles around, which is how the Bedouin settlement originally gained its name. Mastour grew up on this land, like generations of his family before him. When he was a child, these beaches and soft hills were his playground. He capered around among farmers and fishermen, watching them hunt quail and catch migratory birds in big nets strung up along the seashore, and he tended to the family's fruit and olive groves which sprang out of the sand thanks to a freshwater well sunk by his grandfather in 1962, a well that still irrigates Mastour's cantaloupes, tomato vines and corn plants half a century later. At the end of each working day, the community traditionally came together to socialize on a limestone plateau that abuts the water and sets brilliant white rock alongside the azure of the ocean. Mastour has happier memories of this little spot than of anywhere else in the world. 'We've been here as nomads for thousands of years,' he told me, pointing out the hilltop cemeteries above the water in which Dabaa's Bedouins have long buried their dead. 'Our ancestors are in this place.'

In 1981, Egypt's rulers decided they wanted something else in this place as well: a $5 billion internationally financed nuclear power plant. Dabaa was chosen because of its coastal location (nuclear plants require vast quantities of water for cooling, and so are nearly always built close to the sea) and low risk of seismic activity, and because the topography of the region was considered suitable for construction. The government's site selection study also noted the area's 'low population density'.[1] In one of his final acts before he was assassinated, President Sadat signed a decree authorizing the appropriation of Bedouin land at Dabaa for the project. Mastour and his fellow residents were neither consulted nor adequately compensated over the decision, but initially that didn't seem to matter as the decree was never properly implemented – Chernobyl's horrors a few years later knocked global confidence in nuclear power and plans for a reactor at Dabaa, like so many other Egyptian mega-project blueprints, were left to gather dust on ministry shelves. But in 2003, Mubarak's government switched tack and decided it wanted the land after all. At a stroke the area was engulfed by army, police and bulldozers; to force the community into compliance, soldiers first demolished the Bedouin's water towers before driving across the land bellowing threats into megaphones. No one resisted, although according to Mastour many of the older sheikhs rushed to the cemeteries and fell to their knees, weeping, as the security forces moved in. The eviction occurred right before the harvest, and Mastour only just had time to throw the lid over his grandfather's well and cast one last look back at his blossoming olive groves before being hauled away. It would be nearly a decade before he saw them again.

In the years that followed, the displaced Bedouins launched various lawsuits and pressed for a proper compensation package as well as an official inquiry into whether locating a nuclear reactor in Dabaa was appropriate. But the idea of reclaiming their land never crossed their minds; for one thing the authorities had quickly constructed a well-guarded wall and metal fence around the nuclear site and topped it with barbed wire, and for another the notion of openly defying the state just seemed fanciful. The limestone plateau where Bedouins had gathered socially was now enclosed behind the state's fortifications; when the community tried to muster a bit further down the coast instead, outside the nuclear area, police chased them away. 'They told us our tiny stores of cooking gas, which we used to cook meals by the sea, were a safety hazard to the nuclear plant,' recalled Mastour. Meanwhile, no one knew what was going on behind the perimeter walls; any rare attempts to infiltrate the site or protest nearby were met with brutal security crackdowns. Scraps of news would leak out only when the press published occasional reports of elite-level infighting over Dabaa's fate: Ibrahim Kamel, an NDP tycoon, owned a tourism complex further along the coast and allegedly wanted the reactor site moved so as not to depress the value of his hotel, whereas Gamal Mubarak was convinced that the Dabaa project must go ahead, and in 2010 made a forceful speech committing Egypt to a nuclear future. Nobody ever asked the Bedouins what they thought. 'Since 1981, up until today, not a single official lecture, workshop, conference or consultation has been held to inform local people of what nuclear power involved,' said Mastour. 'All we knew of it was arrests and beatings.'

In early 2011, two things happened in quick succession that transformed Dabaa's local struggle into something much bigger. The first was the outbreak of revolution, which infused with a sense of possibility communities all over Egypt that had grievances against the government. The second was something entirely unexpected, which took place 6,000 miles away in the tiny Japanese town of Okuma, in the prefecture of Fukushima. It was early afternoon there on 11 March when an earthquake began forty-five miles out at sea; within an hour, a tsunami up to twenty-three feet high was washing across long stretches of the Japanese coastline, killing thousands and breaching the seawall of Fukushima's nuclear power plant. By the next day a nuclear meltdown had occurred, radioactive materials were escaping into the atmosphere, and the world was contemplating the worst nuclear disaster since Chernobyl. In Dabaa, Mastour and his friends watched the news unfold with a mixture of disbelief and horror. The fight against – Dabaa's nuclear reactor was no longer only about stolen land; it had become a battle to save Egypt from the risk of nuclear annihilation.

For the local community, the next few months were a whirlwind. Hunched over laptops in the reception room of Bedouin elders, Mastour and others began reading up on nuclear reactors and the dangers associated with them. As the weeks went by they reached out to

scientists and environmental movements, not just in Egypt but further afield in America, Europe and Asia as well, and invited technical
experts to come and give them educational talks on the issue. They
learned that a huge tsunami had struck the Mediterranean and devastated Egypt's coastline back in the fourth century AD, and that
geologists believed the same thing could happen again.[2] They saw the
government's safety assurances being exposed as fallacious, after it
was alleged that Mubarak and his former prime ministers had been
illegally dumping nuclear waste in the Western Desert for years.[3]
They tracked the outbreak of mass protests against nuclear power in
India, and cheered when huge street mobilizations forced the governments of Germany and Switzerland to tear up nuclear construction
projects and begin phasing out old nuclear power stations. 'All this
awareness was new,' explained Mastour. 'It emboldened us.' The
Bedouins wrote a fresh round of letters to every relevant government department they could think of, outlining their firm opposition
to the Dabaa reactor and demanding that their land be returned.
They did not receive a single reply. It was at this stage, said Mastour,
that the community decided that it would no longer wait for collective rights to be granted from above. In mid-November, they began a
sit-in.

Initially, officials continued to ignore the protesters, but when
Mastour and his colleagues blocked the gates to the nuclear site and
prevented workers from entering it, the authorities were riled. A military detachment was sent to the occupation and a brigadier general
stiffly informed those gathered there that unless they dismantled their
tents and cleared the area immediately, 'there would be consequences'.
Mastour recounted what happened next with an enormous grin.
'Sheikh Abdel Aziz, one of our elders, rose slowly from the ground
and stared the general in the face. 'If you kill one of my men, I will
kill ten of yours,' he told the general calmly. 'I have weaponry that is
far superior to your own.' Flustered, the officer withdrew; from that
day forth the sit-in grew and grew, and by early January 2012 there
were as many as 5,000 protesters every Friday massed outside the site
entrance, watched over by approximately 1,200 armed soldiers on
the other side of the wall.

It's impossible to predict the final spark that will set a clash alight

in Revolution Country; it can be as dramatic as a murdered demon-
strator, or as seemingly inconsequential as a door accidentally closed
in someone's face. All that can be said with any certainty is that
whenever stand-offs between citizens and the security forces endure
and harden, whenever the tenacity of the former spirals and the
morale of the latter begins to sap, something always, inevitably,
breaks. So it was in – Dabaa on Friday 13 January 2012, after *el-zuhr*
prayers, when a quarrel broke out between a soldier and a local
youth. No one can remember exactly what it was about. All that matters is that at one stage in the altercation a rock was thrown from one
side of the wall to the other; in an effort to calm the situation a few
soldiers fired into the air, only for Bedouins with guns to respond in
kind. Some even exploded dynamite that is usually used for deep-sea
fishing; panicked by the noise, the security forces sounded the alarm
and began closing all gates to the site. Energized by the chaos, the
Bedouins surged forward. In a matter of hours, one of the most
closely guarded security installations in North Africa fell into the
hands of local people.

On the internet, you can watch videos of that January battle – the
rock-throwing, the confusion and then, most thrillingly, the moment
the wall was breached. Bedouins swathed in headscarves tear at the
bricks with their bare hands, take long run-ups to the wall before
aiming flying kicks at it, and even begin reversing into it with pickup
trucks. On top of the wall, in a nod to Berlin in 1989, young boys
direct proceedings and yell their acclaim for the efforts of comrades
below. In the background, through the gates and through punctured
holes in the brickwork, official trucks and military vehicles can be
seen reversing wildly and speeding off in fright. But what the videos
don't show is the reaction of the Bedouins once the security forces
surrendered and they were able to cross the divide and walk back
across their territory for the first time in years. 'There were tears and
blood everywhere,' remembered Mastour. Ambulances were allowed
through to treat the injured, who numbered forty-two soldiers and
ten Bedouins; as night fell, a camp was constructed just inside the
newly reclaimed stretch of sand. As Mastour talked, he welled up
and choked with emotion. 'We camped through the night and at first
light we all rose together and went to see the eemeteries where our

ancestors are buried. To the government's credit, they had respected the sanctity of the cemeteries and left the dead undisturbed. But after that each person went to check on their old homes and farmland. It was happiness and sorrow all at once: joy because we were back but terrible horror, shock and sadness, at the condition of the land.' Mastour discovered his olive grove overrun by goats; neglected for so long, the cantaloupes and tomatoes were dead, though he has since managed to coax the latter back to life.

The Dabaa coast is bewitching. After two successive cycles of human destruction – once in 2003 when soldiers evicted the Bedouins and tore down everything they'd constructed, and then again in 2012, when the Bedouins reclaimed their land and destroyed everything the state had installed – the landscape now is a strange commingling of the natural and the half-built. We drove down roads bordered with fiery red heather, the clouds above throwing huge shadows over neat rows of olive and fig trees, most of which were dead and desiccated, thrusting spiky wooden claws out of the sand towards the sky. 'We knew they must have damaged the land and destroyed our buildings, but it was different to actually having to confront that fact with our own eyes when we finally made it back here,' said Mastour. 'To see the place where a tree once stood, a tree where you would sit each day under the shade and eat a fig, and now to see a stump there instead, that's very hard. All those memories were erased, and not a single person in this community ever benefited from that erasure.'

After winning back their territory, the Bedouins were initially cautious; who knew when the army might return and start opening fire on those inside the nuclear compound? But as the weeks went by, confidence grew, and by springtime people were planting new crops and gathering recreationally on the limestone plateau once again. Mastour's three daughters were all born after the original eviction and had never seen their family land; that year though, they spent the entire summer camped out on the coast and splashing about in the sea. The authorities, stunned by events at Dabaa, initially engaged in a war of words between different security agencies over what had happened; when MPs demanded answers from the defence ministry, a military representative told them the only way to have stopped the infiltration would have been to open fire on Egyptian citizens. 'We cannot shoot our own people,' he added plaintively. 'It is a sensitive issue.'[4] A few weeks later officials promised to form a new committee examining the future of Dabaa – this time taking into account the views of Bedouin landholders – but no further steps were taken in that direction and the community heard nothing more until after Morsi's election in July, when the national Nuclear Power Plants Authority issued a statement informing them that they were encroaching on public property. 'No person or entity may use or build on the land without the authority's consent,' it affirmed.[5] The Bedouins' response was equally terse. 'The state insists on pushing ahead with its nuclear project on our lands,' announced Mehanna Abdel Hamid, Dabaa's *umda* (the local mayor), at a hastily convened press conference, 'but the only way they will be able to continue with this project is over our dead bodies.'[6] In post-Mubarak Egypt, old ways were floundering in the face of the new. 'The problem,' acknowledged an astute official in the ministry of electricity, 'lies in the lack of the people's confidence in the government in general.'[7]

In common with countless small communities across Egypt, the Bedouins of Dabaa had wandered on to the threshold of some of Revolution Country's haziest and most important frontiers. Like the staff at Cleopatra Ceramics, and other workplaces where pockets of alternative, unstable authority have materialized within existing power structures without overwhelming them completely, Egyptians like Mastour embody the country's ongoing moment of mutability. Some of the revolution's core dynamics are at play inside communal revolts such as Dabaa – new forms of organization outside the traditional political arena, direct confrontation with state violence and, crucially, the chalking up of victories over Mubarak Country that would never have felt possible before the revolution. These struggles have not emerged from nowhere; in most cases they are fuelled by grievances which stretch back years or even decades, built on that culture of resistance which flowered in neighbourhoods, towns and villages right across the country towards the end of Mubarak's reign – from uprisings against rural land reform to the battles waged over military appropriation in Qursaya, or water provision in Burullus. And yet the revolution marks a rupture with that earlier period, as well as a line of continuity. Demands are now couched in a manner that undermines the very 'inviolability' of the state that its elites rely upon for survival, because they come at a moment in which the myth of state omnipotence has been shattered. Through mobilizations like that at Dabaa, many Egyptians have moved beyond seeking better care or compensation from the government; instead through the nature of their demands, they have challenged its authority to maintain any hold over them at all. When the state is ejected from its own nuclear site, it serves to blunt the regime's defensive armoury; it's not just land that has been snatched away, but an entire system for maintaining its rule.

When the Bedouins first reclaimed their land at Dabaa, the state media quickly fell back on an age-old 'anti-modern' caricature, long applied to any Egyptian daring to stand in the way of a top-down government mega-project. Just like those who resisted the New Valley Toshka plans, or the forced evictions that accompanied Cairo 2050, Mastour's community were depicted by the press as unsophisticated shepherds, trampling blithely over the very essence of Egypt's scientific future. In the newspaper *al-Ahram*, early reports from Dabaa asserted that the Bedouins had broken into locked safes and stolen radioactive material; that they had blown up a nuclear reactor; that they had caused $80 million worth of damage. Government minister Faiza Aboul-Naga, one of the most toxic old-regime hangovers that have continued to pollute the post-Mubarak era, told journalists that the storming of the Dabaa site was an act of pure looting, and that 'rioters stole computers, earthquake monitoring systems, transformers and cables'.[8] None of that was true: there was never any reactor on the site, because construction work on a reactor had never commenced. Nor, obviously, was there any radioactive material left knocking about in safes that could be jemmied open with a crowbar. Photos published in the state press purporting to show goats swarming over hi-tech nuclear equipment were actually taken during the era of army control; soldiers had made money on the side by allowing a few herds of livestock in to graze, but according to locals the images were released later to reinforce the notion that Egypt's progress was being undermined by foolish nomads. As one human rights advocate pointed out later that summer, in reality the 'reactor site' consisted of nothing more than the empty depression which Mastour had sketched out for me with a piece of driftwood. 'As you can see here, this is what our nuclear power plant in Dabaa looks like after thirty-one years of work,' Ahmed Mansour laughed. 'This is not a nuclear reactor, as the media portrays it to be. Yet the newspapers call local residents thugs, traitors and terrorists for allegedly infringing upon this site.'[9]

But post-Mubarak, the state is finding it a great deal harder to make such tired charges stick. Mastour and his fellow community members have proved deft at sidestepping the marginalization intended for them by the state's modernity discourse; after seizing back their land they worked tirelessly at forming new links with environmentalists and scientists to demonstrate to the Egyptian public that the fight-back against a nuclear reactor should be a mass struggle, not just a local-ized land rights dispute. As a consequence, international solidarity with their cause quickly mounted. On 11 March 2012, the first anni-versary of the Fukushima disaster, Bedouins held a colourful protest march through Dabaa; among the journalists to attend were a news crew who flew all the way from Japan. At the same time, they suc-ceeded in reframing public debate about where Egyptian national interests really lie when it comes to long-term development, and about what a democratized energy system – stripped of corruption and secrecy – might look like. 'We remain completely opposed to any nuclear reactor being built here, but that doesn't mean we take no interest in the question of how to solve Egypt's energy problems or want to avoid debate about the best way to develop this land,' Mas-tour told me. The Bedouins were full of ideas about expanding communal farmland, starting a programme of tourist development in the region under local grassroots control, and exploiting the area's potential abundance of renewable energy riches to help supply the national grid. '[Nuclear power] is a technology that will make us even more dependent on private companies,' says Ahmed el-Droubi, a Cairo-based environmental campaigner who argues that the reac-tor's need for foreign experts and materials is a clear threat to the country's long-term security, and who was among many in the capi-tal to join the Bedouins' cause. 'We'll be importing a minimum of 80 per cent of materials and knowledge, and relying on the countries we import from to deal with the uranium after.'[10]

The existence of communities like Dabaa poses substantial questions for anyone who believes that, when it comes to state authority, Egypt's clock can simply be rolled back to the Mubarak era. What happens to the old ways when aggrieved Egyptians refuse to be bought off or coerced individually, but insist instead upon being viewed as a collective – with rights and responsibilities that trump the state's? What happens when local squabbles enable citizens to start thinking like a state themselves, framing the terms of national debate and formulating national policy from below? Like most self-contained slithers of Revolution Country, Dabaa's formal 'liberation' has proved ephemeral. In 2013, the intelligence services negotiated a deal with Bedouin leaders that temporarily dampened down hostilities and allowed state officials to reenter some sections of the planned nuclear site; the community have been promised a meaningful compensation package and local jobs, as well as closer consultation on any future development. The government may keep its promises, or it may not. Either way though, the Bedouins are watching, and waiting, and ready to rise again. 'This is the new Dabaa, where people have no fear of the police and refuse to be labelled as simpletons who should keep quiet and know their place,' smiled Mastour.

The problem for the state is that even as it attempts to reconstitute the old circuitry of elite power and crush dissent on the streets of Egypt's major cities, as if nothing has changed it is being forced to confront hundreds of far-flung Dabaas and potentially millions of Mastours within them, for whom nothing is the same as before.

The coastal road east form Dabaa to Damietta is over 200 miles long, and clouds began to black-blot the sky as I drove. By the time I arrived on the far side of the Nile Delta, fat raindrops were thumping the asphalt. Today, Damietta's gates were open, but not so long ago they had been padlocked shut, with tanks stationed on one side and a population in revolt on the other. Scrawled graffiti was visible on street corners: 'No to the factory of death' and 'No surrender before they leave'. This was a town that spoke not just of battle, but of occupation and siege.

The story of Damietta's 'factory of death' began in 2006, when Agrium, a Canadian fertilizer giant, struck a deal with an Egyptian state-owned chemicals company to build a $1.2 billion plant in the area that would convert natural gas into ammonia and urea. What began as a convoluted local dispute would eventually progress into a full-scale urban insurrection, revealing much about ongoing sources of instability in the post-Mubarak era. Agrium's plant was to be located on the island of Ras el-Bar, just north of Damietta, at the point where the Nile's eastern branch empties out into the sea. The island had been designated a special industrial zone by the Egyptian government, guaranteeing factory owners a profitable combination: plentiful supplies of natural gas and easy access to the port for distribution. But locally there were fears about the ramifications of constructing such a large chemical complex in a densely inhabited location, and by 2008 demonstrations had broken out against the project. Agrium, which insisted that its pollution outputs were half the level permissible under Egyptian law, argued that similar factories in built-up areas of Canada and France had provoked no opposition, and claimed that the campaign against them was being whipped up by provincial elites who cared little about the environment but were intent on defending their own special interests.[11] To an extent, that was true. The governor of Damietta, who had his own plans to transform Ras el-Bar into a lucrative tourist concession, had formed an alliance with a series of local tycoons in an effort to protect their property investments on the island; in Mubarak's Egypt, this was the one kind of lobby group capable of getting its way. After a parliamentary inquiry and much negotiation, a settlement was reached which saw the majority of the venture shift into the hands of MOPCO, a state-owned industrial giant, with Agrium retaining a minority stake. More importantly, the authorities announced that the factory would be moved. Locals were told the new site would probably be in the industrial desert area of Sokhna, near Cleopatra Ceramics, some 150 miles to the south. In the end, the factory was rebuilt 200 feet away on the mainland, across the water from Ras el-Bar and directly opposite its old location. What's more, MOPCO announced it would be adding two extra urea lines at the new site, tripling the factory's production capacity. The original anti-factory business group, now that they had secured their goal of saving Ras el-Bar island for high-end tourism, declared themselves satisfied and wound down their campaign. Poorer groups who had been part of the protest movement, including the inhabitants of Sinnaniyah – a small village bordering the new factory site – were left to continue their efforts alone. 'The case of Agrium is like the revolution in general; made by the people and hijacked by others,' explained Hassan Sharaawy, a resident of Sinnaniyah and one of the Damietta protest leaders. We were sitting in a first-floor office in the centre of town; rain lashed against the shutters and trickled down the wall. 'Our case was hijacked by the businessmen, but we won't allow them to succeed.'

In the aftermath of the relocation, corporate politicking gave way to ground-level campaigning, and the struggle against the chemical plant entered a new phase. Since its original construction, multiple reports, commissioned by different actors, have reached differing conclusions on the impact of the factory. Some supported the protesters' claims, others dismissed them In July 2011, a team of researchers comprising both local representatives and national academic experts reported back to the cabinet with thirteen specific criticisms of the plant's ecological footprint, including allegations that it drew freshwater from the Nile and discarded industrial waste into the river.[12] The team recommended a series of measures that would rectify the situation, and local residents offered to end their opposition if the factory acted upon them.[13] They were rebuffed. 'The committee put down on to paper the things that we knew with our own eyes,' said Hassan. 'We lived their conclusions for ourselves, finding fish half-dead and being told by the labs that they are suffering from cancer. We couldn't give up, it's too important – this is an issue which ties together the Nile, tourism, wildlife, people's livelihoods.'

A twin-pronged strategy of legal manoeuvres against MOPCO on the one hand and regular displays of collective strength in the streets on the other – including the draping of black banners from balconies throughout Damietta – began to gain momentum. Whether or not the factory is giving fish cancer remains a disputed question. But the whole project was textbook Mubarak Country: no consultation, no compensation, no suggestion that anyone but an aloof state had the right to take decisions which convulsed ordinary people's worlds. In the absence of any official presentations to or discussions with the local community, rumour – accurate or otherwise – filled the void.

And as the factory expansion plans gathered steam, so too did public scepticism. 'MOPCO 1+2 [the plant's planned extensions] will be built over our dead bodies,' Sharaawy told me. 'I come from Sinnani-yah; my family have farmed there for generations, although I now work in the furniture business. For us, the problems with the factory aren't academic. I see fish dying, I see strange things in the water, I see summer holiday places becoming unusable. There are plants growing with thick layers of strange waste on them, and the migrating birds don't come through here any more. We have temperate weather here and you always used to see them, but not any more. That water channel was where fish specifically came to lay their eggs, but now they don't. The environment here is changing, and no official will convince me otherwise.'

Post-Mubarak, rallies and restlessness intensified. By September 2011, a picket of the factory had succeeded in shutting operations; even after the machinery was wound down, protesters agreed to disperse only when smoke – the company insists it is just water vapour – stopped pouring out of the plant's giant chimney. Less than a month later, the chimney spewed into action again. Hassan was among the first group of locals who headed straight back towards the factory to resume the picket, but this time they found an army guard waiting at the gates. 'I spoke to the commanders and told them not to use force on us; I said that this was a problem that required a political solution, not a security one,' recalled the 47-year-old. 'At 3 a.m. on the fourth day of *eid*, the officers assured me that peaceful demonstrators would not be attacked. It was a promise that lasted less than a day.' That evening, according to residents, twenty *amn el-markazi* ('central security forces') trucks and three army vehicles surrounded protesters – who at this stage numbered about 150 – and began launching tear gas at them. 'Our only defence was rocks. There were hundreds of gas canisters being fired, an endless barrage – people were fainting and collapsing all around me. I had the feeling of a human who is dying, and I could have been killed twenty different times.' Those on the scene say they were saved only by the bravery of local families who rushed to bring them onions, which help ameliorate the effects of the gas. News of the violence filtered back to the city, and within hours Damietta's protest camp was growing exponentially as thousands streamed in to join the clashes. Faced with relentless, hostile rock-throwing by a growing crowd, security forces were made to retreat and Damietta's residents launched a full-time sit-in. In the negotiations that followed, officers assured residents that a political solution to the stand-off was being worked on, and promised that there would be no repeat of the previous night's violence.

That evening, spirits at the sit-in were high. One protester in particular – a nineteen-year-old upholsterer named Islam Abdullah – seemed invigorated by the communal solidarity; he bustled up and down the lines of protesters, smiling at everyone and making tea for all. He was so enthusiastic that he rose at dawn the following morning to help prepare breakfast for the camp. That was the moment that soldiers flooded the sit-in, firing live ammunition. At 5 a.m. Islam was killed by a single bullet.

The Egyptian state has murdered many of its citizens; before the revolution, security forces had no reason to think they were risking a city-wide insurgency every time they did so. In Damietta, Egyptians showed them that Revolution Country was different. As Islam's life slipped away, in nearby villages and throughout the main city people scrambled through the streets with megaphones, screaming 'The army is killing the people, come down and defend Damietta.' Hundreds of thousands answered the call. Within hours Damietta's railway line, most of its industrial sites and all of its busy trade port were cut off and placed under the control of demonstrators. The army, which had swiftly fanned troops out throughout the city as unrest spread, was overwhelmed by the strength and scope of the rebellion. Assaulting an isolated protest camp was one thing, but this was a full-on uprising; using weapons to restore order would mean shooting virtually everyone in sight. Soldiers, nervous and uncertain, eventually lowered their guns and backed away. Jubilantly, ordinary citizens seized the streets and formed *ligan sha'abeya* ('popular committees') to run the city. The main entranceway to Damietta was blocked off. Seven months on and more than a hundred miles away from the anti-Mubarak occupation in Tahrir Square, far from the international news cameras, Damietta had liberated itself spectacularly from within.

The square where Damietta's residents held their original anti-factory sit-in lies a few hundred yards south of the MOPCO gates. It was here that most of the initial clashes with the military unfolded, but little evidence of the bloodshed is left now. Timber companies sit on two corners of the junction, and a railway track bisects it in the middle. Fruit and vegetable vendors and rug merchants are dotted on the roundabout, above which a huge billboard advertises air-conditioning units and Nesquik chocolate. With the city at one side of the square and the port at the other, the whole place has a no-man's land atmosphere to it, and feels slightly forlorn. For those who lived through the battle though, it is a site infused with revolutionary significance. Hassan and one of his colleagues, a large, rambunctious man named Amr with a fulsome grey beard and a heavy laugh, had brought me here to talk through the beginnings of the uprising, and for a while they simply stood without words, solemnly surveying the scene. It was Amr who broke the silence first, regaling us with tales of both farce and unlikely heroism which played out during the struggle. The details were impossible to verify, and some of the stories sounded completely outlandish – such as the supposed kidnap by protesters of twelve soldiers in their APCs, who were then held as 'prisoners of war' ('We released them because we didn't want to insult the army,' chortled Amr), or Amr's infamous one-man conquest of a tank roof (the soldiers inside apparently drove around desperately twisting the gun turret left and right in an effort to shake him off) – but they were also irresistible Damietta's occupation lasted for eleven full days, and in this city the period has been granted the honour of the definitive article, spoken of as reverentially – if not more so – than the eighteen days of the anti-Mubarak uprising that launched the revolution. 'During the eleven days we were in such control of the city that the head of security was calling and pleading with us to let food in for the central security troops,' said Amr as we drove north of the square and up towards the factory. 'The guys who were beating us needed our help to get the fuel to carry on!'

As in all occupations, systems quickly sprang up to adjust to and augment the new reality. Those guarding the city entrances were given papers detailing essential supplies that should be allowed

through to the civilian population, including food, petrol and medicine; citizen patrols were set up to keep the peace. 'Not a single
lightbulb was damaged, nothing was destroyed,' said Hassan proudly.
'That stands in our favour. I can't say we were happy with the situation but we had no choice; we'd reached the end of the road and
every other method of opposition had been exhausted. It was their
use of force which took us to this situation, and we made the best of
it.' Out in the Mediterranean, dozens of ships had to anchor in open
waters, unable to approach the darkened port and its turbulent city.
But the situation could not last. Despite popular attempts to keep
supplies flowing, the unrest had choked off the passage of basic
goods, and it was the poor who were hit hardest. 'The price of a gas
cylinder increased five-fold, and although support for the occupation
remained solid we knew that we couldn't allow ordinary people to
suffer,' said Hassan. A decision was taken to end the city-wide uprising but continue a sit-in at the gates of the MOPCO factory,
preventing it from operating. That sit-in would eventually last ten
months, with the factory lying dormant for four of them.

Amr and Hassan took me along the industrial zone's perimeter, at
the end of which stood the high walls of MOPCO. The road was
almost completely deserted and the few people we passed – including
one farmer leading a solitary cow along the base of the grey ram-
parts, enabling it to graze on scattered clumps of weed – were dwarfed
by the skeletal machinery which soared up into the sky on the other
side of the wall. The land looked barren, but to Amr it was an open
history book and he read each mound and ditch out loud with care.
'Here is where we cut an inflow pipe to the factory,' he said, pointing
at a dirt trench in the road, 'and here is where we built our sandbag
barricade, which was six feet high.' The weather was worsening
again as we closed in on the factory itself; we switched to Hassan's
car and I ducked low to avoid the suspicions of a soldier guarding the
entranceway to the industrial zone with an APC. The ruse worked,
and we were able to get right up to the MOPCO fence, behind which
lay a sleek dreadlock of green and silver pipes. A huge advertising
hoarding which once proclaimed the name of the factory had been
pulled down by revolutionary youths during the sit-in, leaving behind
an empty shell of metal panels peeling off into the wind. Beyond,

huge water drums were visible and the air was thick with ammonia, pricking our eyes. We climbed a large quartz pile – silica is extracted locally from the rock – and were able to look out right across the factory site, as well as over the water channel to the vast empty space on Ras el-Bar Island where the plant used to stand. The site was shorn of all its palm trees, and the air was cold and weird. 'When I look at this, I wish I had a bomb and could just blow it all up,' said Amr softly, gesturing at the chemical plant. Hassan beckoned us down. 'Only the wind is making the ammonia bearable,' he said. 'On a windless day your eyes and lungs wouldn't cope with standing this close.'

MOPCO is now up and running once again, the outcome of a fresh set of negotiations with residents which finally brought the sit-in to an end. The company's managers promised to comply with the thirteen recommendations made in the contested environmental report, abandon the factory's controversial expansion plans, and build a new desalination plant in Damietta to compensate for the factory's consumption of freshwater. They also dropped all legal actions against anti-factory activists. In an effort to calm Damietta's population, the authorities have vowed that if those promises aren't kept, the factory will be closed. As in Dabaa, outright revolt has been downgraded to uneasy compromise, with a cowed state forced to bow, partially at least, to the will of local people. But in the process, an entire community has been radicalized by their fight with Egypt's security forces and by a collective experience of self-rule. 'We had a revolution here in 2008 over the factory, and another in 2011. If they break their assurances again, there will be a third,' said Hassan. 'We're simple people, but never think that we're not aware of our environment and those seeking to destroy it. There's no man who can fail as long as his cause is just and righteous.'

We drove about half a mile east, to the underbelly of a bridge linking Ras el-Bar to the mainland; this was the site of the ten-month sit-in. Locals are now building a mosque here which they plan to name *masgid el-ribat*, a clever piece of Arabic wordplay which derives from the idea of people who persevere and sacrifice, people who never leave. 'We're building it because we're staying,' said Amr as he used a nearby agricultural tap to wash for prayers. 'What happened here was amazing, so amazing. Almost a year here, throughout the winter. At times it was so cold at night that we all had to huddle together for warmth, twenty to thirty of us squashed together like children.' Both Hassan and Amr, in common with other protest leaders, had been invited on expensive international junkets by Agrium, the Canadian chemical company, in an effort to win them over. Both have refused. A shady-looking man on a motorbike appeared and watched us intently before moving away and speaking hurriedly into a mobile phone. It was a police informant, and time for me to go. As I said my goodbyes, I told Amr that I wished I could have stayed longer. He smiled. 'Don't worry, you'll have plenty of time to come back. We'll be here for ever.'

Ask any Egyptian for an example of the Mubarak regime's corruption, and there's a good chance they will cite the export of natural gas to Israel at heavily discounted prices. Analysts estimate that the lucrative deals struck by politically connected operators involved in the project cost Egypt $11 billion in lost revenue, and the scandal continues to reverberate: Egypt is facing up to $20 billion worth of international lawsuits after cancelling some of the commercial contracts involved, and the Sinai pipeline used to transport the gas to Israel has been the target of repeated bombings.[14] Since Mubarak was overthrown, struggles over energy and the environment have been a perpetual feature of Revolution Country. Be it against nuclear reactors, chemical plants, power stations or pipelines, popular campaigns have thrown some of Egypt's deepest faultlines into focus: the infringement of community rights, the lack of state transparency, the need to shift sovereignty out of the realm of foreign corporations and markets and bring resources under democratic control. Dabaa and Damietta are only the beginning: over the past half-decade, protests have erupted against a World Bank and EIB-funded power plant in Abu Ghaleb in northern Giza;[15] at a public-private partnership oil refinery in Qalyubiya, north of Cairo;[16] at the site of a proposed BP gas-processing plant in the small Delta town of Idku, east of Alexandria;[17] at a fracking operation run by Dana Gas, an Emirati energy outfit, at Kom Ombo in the governorate of Aswan.[18] A nationwide campaign against coal, imports of which have risen following pressure from the politically connected cement industry, has brought together local groups from all over the country and forced the government on to the defensive.[19] Over the coming years, these struggles can only intensify: huge new offshore drilling concessions and fracking contracts have been awarded by Sisi's regime to some of the world's biggest oil and gas corporations, and new extraction projects are in line for billions of dollars in funding by international financial institutions like the European Bank for Reconstruction and Development, the institution that has long been lobbying for the privatization of Egypt's major infrastructure classes. Under Sisi, Egypt – once among the world's biggest gas exporters – has begun the process of privatizing both its electricity and gas sectors; the government is now renting huge floating import terminals to plug frequent power shortages.[20] Opposition protests are focused on far more than the issue of the country's energy mix, or its pollutant levels, crucial though those concerns may be. At stake is the fundamental process of decision-making in post-Mubarak Egypt, and thus the nature of the state itself: in an age of revolution, are Egyptian citizens willing to have choices about their environment made for them? The answer, so far, has been no.

The reality is that communities across Egypt have been refusing to allow the state to make decisions for them on virtually every issue of importance since the day the revolution began. Egyptians with homes have been fighting off forced evictions; Egyptians without homes – like the families of the Suzanne Mubarak housing project – have been breaking into the empty properties of financial speculators and squatting, seizing from the state both land and housing for themselves. In 6th October City, entire neighbourhoods have been informally occupied by citizens who have gone on to build their own unofficial shopping centres and transport terminals; in Cairo's Bassatin district, 900 families have taken up residence on abandoned land, renaming their new neighbourhood after the 25th January revolution. On Qursaya Island, where residents fought off the army back in 2007, naval skiffs have attacked once again: soldiers stormed the island at 4 a.m. one Sunday shooting live ammunition, spraying birdshot and shouting *allahu akbar* ('God is great') as they chased and gunned down residents fleeing for their lives. Many threw themselves into the river to escape the bullets, only for the soldiers on land to continue firing at their bodies in the water. Three members of the community died, but when those who survived travelled across the mainland and began blocking roads in furious protest at the violence, hundreds of citizens who lived nearby chose to join them. 'This country is an erupted volcano,' declared Sayyid Mohamed, a local salesman.[21] Their pressure has paid off: Qursayans are now back in control of their island once again.

On the way back from Egypt's north coast, I stopped at a place named Tahsin which lies in the governorate of Dakahlia, at the heart of the Nile Delta. The village was founded by Nasser in the 1960s but initially there was no arable land here; it took years of work by the sixty families who were settled in the area to cultivate the fields and conjure fruit, cotton and corn out of the soil. By the 1990s, their hard work was under threat: Mubarak's Law 96 forced farmers who had lived in Tahsin for thirty-plus years to 'bid' for their long-held plots at market rates, forcing many into penury. Failure to meet payment deadlines led to several *feddans* being seized by the government, and hundreds ended up in debtors' prisons. Meanwhile, the community was almost completely cut off from government services; locals called it 'a village without a village', and compared it to a cemetery. 'For years we've called out, but to no avail,' said one resident. 'You'll only have heard about us in the obituaries,' observed another.[22] Following the outbreak of revolution, Tahsin's citizens decided that their isolation – and immiseration – was coming to an end. At the top of their list of demands was a new tarmac road to replace the two-and-a-half-mile dirt track which ran to the nearest town, Beni Ebeid; in the absence of proper healthcare or educational facilities, the track was a lifeline to residents and yet the state of it made travelling incredibly arduous, even by car. Every villager is able to recount stories of women in labour dying on the roadside while trying to reach the hospital in town, or of children left paralysed because of the delays in reaching medical care. After Dakahlia's governor promised to pave the track by June 2012, residents were optimistic. But the deadline came and went, and no asphalt road appeared. So villagers gathered together in a popular assembly – 'We have no single leader, but rather horizontal decision-making,' a revolutionary youth,

Mostafa Salah, told me – and voted to declare their independence, as well as to begin a campaign of mass civil disobedience.

Tahsin isn't the first Egyptian community to detach itself from the rest of the country. During the 1919 revolution against British colonialism, the town of Zifta – a mere fifty miles away in Gharbia, across the eastern branch of the Nile – also declared its independence from the empire, in solidarity with the nationwide uprising against imperialist forces. According to contemporary reports, townsfolk seized the train station and telegraph office and formed a revolutionary council; the London *Times* reported breathlessly that an autonomous flag had been raised by the newly independent republic. Such historical parallels were not lost on Tahsin's contemporary revolutionaries. 'We are a village living under an unjust regime, like the British occupation was unjust and the [subsequent] regime that calls itself Egyptian is unjust,' one resident told Mosireen, the revolutionary media collective. 'They declared independence, and so do we.'[23] A letter was dispatched to the president informing him of developments. 'From the residents of Tahsin village to the president of the republic,' it read.

> We announce that as of today we have seceded administratively from Dakahlia Governorate and its oppressive rulers. We emphasize that we abide by the laws of the Egyptian state and fall under the authority of its police, army and presidency . . . We are 3,000 citizens, and just a quick glance at our conditions would make you feel that we are altogether left out. You will see the oppression, corruption, poverty, persecution, illiteracy, disease and misery that we suffer. Mr President, we are strangers in our own country.[24]

Over the coming weeks the entire village went on strike, and anything to do with the government – from rubbish trucks to a parliamentary delegation – was barred from entering. 'People felt as they did during the anti-Mubarak uprising, but even stronger because this was something we were making ourselves,' grinned Mostafa, 'a mini-revolution of Tahsin with all the things that involves: cameras, protests, banners and everything. The more government ignored us and the more stubborn they proved, the more energized we became.' By the end of the year, two more Dakahlia villages had followed suit, making independence declarations of their own.

Tahsin's story is remarkable, but it also demands caution. Even after 'independence' villagers went out of their way to pledge the loyalty of their new dominion to the wider Egyptian state; ultimately the independence declaration was a creative stunt to secure attention and win concessions from a government that has always played off village against village, town against town, community against community as a means of keeping its citizens dependent on a system in which material resources are distributed by elites. Revolutionaries generally seek to break and remake the state, not secede from Egypt altogether. But Tahsin matters because of the process that led the village to this stage. Across decades of government neglect, the community became used to taking matters into their own hands; residents told me they had researched and funded the installation of the water, drainage and electricity systems themselves, and built the local mosque. At each popular assembly, contributions for these services are worked out on the basis of family circumstances; those that can't afford to pay anything are able to offer crops instead of cash. The triple experience of state abandonment, self-determination and revolutionary upheaval gave citizens of this tiny community the confidence to pit themselves against a vast system of political authority. Although 'independence' won't last, that confidence will. Since 2011, many Egyptian citizens have also experienced some form of state abandonment, self-determination and revolutionary upheaval. The question for the state is where their confidence will lead next.

Damietta, Dabaa, Tahsin and all those other sites of communal resistance are gashes – small and fragile, but real – on the map of Mubarak Country, each with its own collective memories that contradict Sisi's attempted appropriation of the revolutionary narrative. Those fighting to defend the old ways have worked hard to remodel popular struggle from a movement against the state into a movement in favour of state supremacy against a terrorist spectre. Even on Egypt's margins, their efforts have had an impact. In Dabaa, Bedouins say that one of the reasons they reached a compromise deal over the nuclear site with the intelligence services in 2013 was that they feared being labelled as Islamist insurgents by the government and ultimately suffering the same fate as Muslim Brotherhood protesters in Rabaa Square.[25] In Burullus, the lakeside fishing community whose residents repeatedly cut off the main coastal highway in the late 2000s in protest at bread and water shortages, an ongoing campaign against rich and powerful fishery operators – who are accused by locals of shooting at small-scale fishermen and cutting their nets to keep them off the lake – has been coloured by accusations of Muslim Brotherhood affiliation, a quick and easy way to drain legitimacy from opponents and promote fear.[26] But although the state has managed, in some quarters, to temporarily refashion the story of the eighteen days to its own benefit, it has not yet succeeded in doing the same with the eleven day occupation of Damietta, or Tahsin's independence declaration, or any of the countless other mini revolutionary uprisings that have come to pass a long way from Tahrir. Those gashes on the map endure.

Mostafa, Tahsin's revolutionary youth activist, and I stepped out into the last of the winter sun and strolled around Tahsin's quiet backstreets, alleyway browns and rural greens leeching slowly out of focus as the sun set over to the west. At the house of the village's aged sheikh, I was introduced to other villagers, as the sheikh himself smoked his *m'assal* pipe and nodded along to their stories with a gurgle of throaty grunts and wheezes. 'When I grew up here there were twelve of us who went to school, and we had to walk several kilometres to the schoolhouse, barefoot even in winter,' remembered Samir Abdel-Hady, a Tahsin resident. 'Sometimes when we arrived the teacher would well up with tears at the sight of us. It's this experience which persuaded me to ensure my children never go through the same thing. Now my daughter is already prepared to fight for the future. We're demanding the very minimum of humanitarian life for the children of tomorrow.' The sheikh, who had been fighting back a coughing fit, spluttered his agreement. 'I want to live with a clear conscience with regards to what I leave behind for the children,' he said. 'And that includes how much they believe in themselves. State security used to chase us in our homes, now they don't dare come to the village because they know that the people here are no longer scared. After one of our general meetings, one resident told me: "I will not live as a third-rate citizen any more. I have withdrawn my acceptance of the status quo." This is the fruit of the 25th January revolution, and there's no turning back.'

Darkness was coming, and it was a long drive home. Samir and Moustafa led me back to my car. As we walked, I shared some of my fears about the counter-revolution, but the pair insisted that their confidence was unshakeable 'We're no longer hoping that things will get better while we sleep,' said Samir, as he clasped my hands. 'Now we make our dreams real in the daytime.'

11

Writing Walls

When I grew up I found I had a hundred dreams
Not one of them seems to come true
Please tell me wise one, what is this story . . .
I can't breathe, I feel tied up, there's no more truth
This is my time, this is my place
This is my life, one day we'll look back
No one feels for me, the world is closing in
I found everything all twisted and turned . . .
But in the end, the end of the story
The train passed. The train passed.

Okka and Ortega[1]

24 January 2014. Revolution birthday eve, and in central Cairo the roads are quiet. On every approach to Tahrir, armoured military vehicles squat below the mid-afternoon sun. Helmeted soldiers stare out from behind metal barriers on to long tracts of tarmac, occasionally brushing away a fly. In the centre of the square stands a small brick plinth – the remains of a grand circular folly, built by the authorities to honour the 'martyrs of the revolution' two months earlier and largely destroyed by protesters the following day. Around it lies nothing but empty grass, and around that nothing but empty streetscape.

Listen to my story of a revolution
It turned their worlds around . . .
Those who started it were boys and girls
All they saw was pain and torture . . .
They tricked us and changed the regime

351

They told us life would be good
It all turned out to be an illusion
He who screams and asks for his rights
They shoot him like a slave . . .
What have we done with the blood of victims
You stole the revolution in the end
You who are silent, why are you silent?
Did your brother not die?

DJ Figo[2]

Out on the edge of the capital, north of the airport road and far from Tahrir Square, a grid of interlocking concrete avenues and muddy cut-throughs called Madinat el-Salam is very much alive. Laundry flaps from the balconies of brutalist apartment blocks, and sheets occasionally blow down into the middle of giant football games that are playing out in the shadows below. On street corners chickens peck around the bases of tobacco kiosks, whose flimsy walls vibrate to the sound of music piped from speakers nestled into beds of chocolate bars and cigarette packets. At the far end of the main thoroughfare, a mound of car tyres is burning; around it children are letting off fireworks and banging drums. There is a fairground in the central square, where three rides on the carousel can be bought for a *guineih*. An open-backed truck rumbles past, laden with sound equipment and hollering youths. They are getting ready for a wedding. It will take place that very night, in one of the many side-alleys that lead off from the square.

Where is the Egyptian of before?
There's no money, not even a penny
That's it
I'm broke . . .
There's no more flirts, no more shirts . . .
I went home drunk
I screamed at my father while I was wasted
I'm good like this
I'm fine like this . . .
We are masters
In this world we are known

Okka, Ortega and Weza[3]

After dark, hundreds will cram into the side-alley and dance. They will twist and contort themselves, wrap limbs around each other and then snap away with a crack or unravel effortlessly like parting water. They will mosh and sway, their beads of sweat illuminated by green laser pens and smoking flares. They will turn each other into musical instruments, and writhe in time to the beats on stage. Up on a platform, a crew of young men will hold a microphone in one hand and a bottle of Stella beer in the other, immersing the crowd in a sonic landscape of energetic synths and profane, auto-tuned vocals. Crunk-like calls and responses will bind performers and audience together in a waterfall of noise. The sound is restless, raw and irresistible, and in these parts it can be heard not only at late-night wedding parties but also from *tuk-tuks* pumping it out of Chinese-manufactured MP3 players; from rooftop coops where pigeon-keepers lay out their mobiles and broadcast it to their flock; from wastelands on the edge of town where kids park their motorbikes, rig up speakers, and pass away the hours by shimmering through scrub to the rhythm. It comes from a world of dusty teenage bedrooms, illicitly downloaded mixing software and mistranslated YouTube tutorials. Polite society hates it, radio stations won't play it, the old established players in the record industry ignore it. But millions love it. It is music from the margins, for the margins, in an Egypt where the margins will not fade away.

> *I'm going to talk about each street*
> *Break down any barriers*
> *This is the way of our streets*
> *Lions standing everywhere, all the cowards run*
> *This is our address*
> *Welcome to el-Salam*
>
> DJ Figo and Alaa Fifty[4]

To put the cultural moment from which this music has emerged into context, it is worth going back several years: to about 7 p.m., on Wednesday, 22 October 2003, to be precise, when the expectant hush which had fallen upon the Small Hall of the national Opera House, on the southern end of Cairo's Zamalek Island, finally gave way to thunderous applause. Up on stage, Sudanese author Tayeb Salih had just concluded the International Conference on the Arab Novel by announcing the winner of that year's most prestigious writing prize: Sonallah Ibrahim, prolific novelist and grandee of the Egyptian literary scene. Smiling and shaking hands, Ibrahim slowly made his way up to the podium, where the rest of the judging panel – distinguished writers from across the region – awaited. Alongside them stood Farouk Hosni, President Mubarak's minister of culture, and Gaber Asfour, general secretary of the government's Supreme Council of Culture, as well as other regime functionaries and assorted journalists. Egypt's literati had packed out the auditorium; they were eager to see what Ibrahim, former political prisoner under Gamal Abdel Nasser, would have to say now that he had been embraced by the state and brought in from the cold. The clapping eventually died down, and Ibrahim, leaning into the microphone, began to speak. 'Initially, his tone is contained, his voice sad,' reported Arabic literature professor Samia Mehrez, who was in the audience that evening. 'Gradually it rises: loud, powerful, angry and passionate.'[5] The minister and his colleagues exchanged nervous glances as Ibrahim, his trademark round eyeglasses balancing precariously on the bridge of his nose, hit his stride and the television cameras kept rolling. 'I have no doubt that every Egyptian here is aware of the extent of the catastrophe facing our country,' Ibrahim declared, prompting vigorous nods and murmurs of agreement from the back of the hall where the younger generation was seated, and stony silence from the establishment figures positioned around him on the stage. 'It's all aspects of life. We no longer have theatre, cinema or scientific research; we just have festivals, conferences and false funds. We don't have industry, agriculture, health or justice. Corruption and pillage spread. And anyone who objects faces getting beaten up or tortured. The exploitative few have wrested our spirit from us.' Ibrahim looked up from his notes, and completed his speech with a flourish: 'All that's left for me is to thank those who chose me for this prize, but to say that I won't be accepting it because it is from a government that, in my opinion, does not possess the credibility to bestow it.' With that, Ibrahim walked off the stage and was enveloped in a crush of kisses and wild cheers as he made his way towards the exit. 'You have given us hope!' shouted many from the audience. Hosni and Asfour, awkward and exposed, could do nothing but scratch at their suits, gaze out from the platform, and wait in vain for the tumult to die down.

Ever since Mohamed Ali began laying the foundations of the contemporary Egyptian state in the early nineteenth century, the government has attempted to produce and administer an orthodox literary establishment – a domestic intelligentsia that the country could call its own. A thriving arts scene was seen by many liberal Egyptians as part of the nation's passport to European modernity, and the construction of the Arab World's first indigenous printing house – Bulaq Press, whose first publication was an 1822 Arabic–Italian dictionary – served as a source of national pride.[6] Since then, books have, by and large, been published by state-run publishers and printed by state-run printing houses; literary prizes – and the funding that goes with them (the award spurned by Ibrahim was worth 100,000 EGP, approximately £10,000) – have been the preserve of state-run cultural bodies. For its part, the literary establishment has generally returned the government's favour, not only by respecting certain red lines but also through its depiction of the state as secular, avant-garde and a patriotic partner for progress – something distinctly removed from the forces of Islamism that would surely seek to turn back the clock and impose theocratic limits on creative expression. Literary imagery has often been deployed to reinforce the state's paternal vision of itself; the metaphor of family as nation, and nation as family, is a trope that can be found across a wide swathe of twentieth-century Egyptian novels – from Naguib Mahfouz's famous *Cairo Trilogy* to Latifa al-Zayyat's *The Open Door*.[7]

But the relationship has never been entirely harmonious. Egypt's authorities have been quick to take action against authors and publications deemed dangerous or offensive, often in an attempt to placate Islamist critics and achieve some short-term political gain. Censorship is omnipresent; in 1966 the entire initial print run of Ibrahim's first novel, *That Smell*, which recounted his time in jail as a result of Nasser's anti-communist crackdown and had been self-published on what Ibrahim called a 'shabby little printer', was confiscated by government censors, and all existing copies were ordered to be pulped. As a result, for many writers the state has long occupied an ambiguous position as both patron and persecutor; despite some misgivings, alliances with the military-bureaucratic complex have been essential for survival. 'These alliances have impacted the prospects of the autonomy of the cultural field at large and have allowed the state to manipulate the cultural producers in its own game of power,' Mehrez, who is one of Egypt's foremost cultural critics, has warned.[8] When Ibrahim arose to address the Opera House so dramatically that late October evening, he wasn't merely taking a public swipe at the Mubarak regime. He was prodding, deftly, at the complex and often compromised bonds between Egypt's cultural producers and their political leaders; his nonacceptance of the award excoriated not only the state, but also the unofficial accords that so many of his colleagues had reached with it.

But these alliances have never been static. Ibrahim's intervention arrived at a moment in which the connection between Egypt's cultural intelligentsia and the state was undergoing a series of quiet ruptures – just as Mubarak Country more generally, in the decade leading up to revolution, was undergoing multiple quiet ruptures of its own. In 2001, a ruckus over the banning of three allegedly pornographic novels provoked a rare confrontation between the government and leading writers. And censorship wasn't the only bone of contention. In 2005, less than two years after the Opera House drama, a fire broke out during a theatrical performance at the Beni Suef Cultural Palace, just south of the capital; the venue was overcrowded, fire exits were closed, safety equipment was locked away in an inaccessible location and emergency crews arrived late and unprepared. Forty-six people lost their lives in the blaze – an appalling act of state neglect and cultural vandalism, even by the Mubarak regime's standards, and one that thrust a further wedge between the state and discontented artists. By that time several writers, including Ibrahim, had already joined a group named Writers and Artists for Change which aligned itself with the opposition Kefaya movement and declared that it wanted to 'liberate imaginations from self-censorship' and help carve out a 'different space for dissidence'.[9]

Writers and Artists for Change, much like the rest of the Kefaya movement, faded from prominence fairly quickly. But although few writers continued to mount explicitly political campaigns against the government, other more subtle changes were afoot. Foremost among them was the emergence of a new and younger wave of novelists who rose slowly to prominence throughout the 1990s and 2000s, and who seemed intent on breaking with their literary forebears and tearing up all the old rules. Distant from and uninterested in the cultural orthodoxy, voices from the periphery of Egyptian society, such as former manual labourer Hamdi Abu Golayyel or Bedouin Miral al-Tahawy, began shunning the state-run publishing houses and turning to places like Dar Merit – an independent publisher whose office block in downtown Cairo was shared with the Egyptian Angling Association and an orthopaedic surgeon – to bring out their work instead. I visited Dar Merit in early 2010 and found chain-smoking writers bunched up on threadbare sofas; precarious towers of books took up every available inch of carpet space, each stacked floor to ceiling. 'We can't compete with the big firms in terms of profits, but the new wave of authors will always be sitting here,' Mohamed Hashem, Merit's 52-year-old founder, told me with a grin. 'Yes, we have poverty and limited resources. But we also have the future.' His writers' novels abandoned the traditional iconography of family and nation; instead of monumental epics that spanned the generations, this 'heretical' literature was slim and sharp and nihilistic, recounting madcap journeys into a neoliberal world of personal isolation and social atomization. These writers mocked and twisted traditional allegories: Adil Ismat's *Fear of Death* opens with the expiration of a family patriarch and his "constant order like that of the days . . . the resounding voice of the father with the grammatical rules of classical Arabic in different corners of the house," while Ahmed al-Aidy's psychotic joyride *Being Abbas al-Abd* urged its protagonist to "burn your history books and forget your precious dead civilization . . . you're on your own now'.* The cultural establishment hated these works; newspapers ran campaigns against the authors, and literary journals refused to publish them.[10] The authors didn't seem to care.

---

* Critiques of the family/nation metaphor are not exclusive to literature. Mohamed Abla, the artist who lives on Qursaya Island and joined the resistance there against invasion and occupation by the army, has also subverted this trope in his work; one of his first solo exhibitions following the fall of Mubarak was entitled 'My Family, My People'.

Al-Aidy, in his novel, placed himself in the 'I've-got-nothing-to-lose-generation': a generation in crisis that arranged hookups by scrawling mobile numbers on the toilet walls of upmarket shopping malls, a generation of the microbus and of arranged dates in coffee shops, a generation for whom hope in the 'Generation of the Defeat' that preceded it had been extinguished.

When the revolution began, then, it did so against the backdrop of a literary landscape that was already restless. The breach represented by the anti-Mubarak uprising though, and particularly by its attendant experiences of collective occupation, resistance and victory, was of a completely different magnitude from anything before it. Many writers did more than observe these events; they lived them, and then found that existing literary vocabulary was unequal to the task of conveying the intensity of that lived experience on the page. 'It is not only a question of taking the necessary distance, but how can you expect me to write while I'm being overwhelmed by the events and far too directly related to them?' asked novelist Khaled al-Khamissi.[11] He wasn't the only one to be afflicted with revolutionary writer's block. 'In Egypt, in the decade of slow, simmering discontent before the revolution, novelists produced texts of critique, of dystopia, of nightmare,' observed author Ahdaf Soueif. 'Now, we all seem to have given up – for the moment – on fiction.'[12] The tension between engaging with fast-moving political developments and detaching oneself sufficiently to observe, process and transmit them, the difficulty of chronicling a 'rupture in reality', left many writers in a state of creative paralysis, even as they spent their days immersed in the dynamic bustle of rallies, protests and squares. 'Attempts at fiction right now would be too simple,' explained Soueif. 'The immediate truth is too glaring to allow a more subtle truth to take form. For reality has to take time to be processed, to transform into fiction.'

Those who did attempt to articulate the revolutionary moment in book form were forced to contend with a series of knotty questions. What did it mean to try to chart a rebellion from within it, especially when – at a time when elites and revolutionaries were wrestling over the right to speak in the revolution's name – the narration of revolt was in many ways inseparable from the act itself? With so much change on the streets, and so little change inside the systems of the state itself, how best to interpret and convey the concept of revolution when both its classical definition – as a cycle, in which history always, inevitably, recurs – and in its newer sense – as a complete transformation – appeared simultaneously to be true? Could revolutionary conviction make room for personal doubt on the page, or would that represent some sort of betrayal? 'Heretical' writers had, before the revolution, been narrating tales of individualism as a way of undermining the old iconography of family and nation, using characters who appeared powerless and disenchanted to subvert the state's discourse of a collective acquiescence to authoritarian rule. But the revolution was an act of intense collectivity, the opposite of atomization or disenchantment. And in post-Mubarak Egypt, nobody needed novelists to subvert the government's rhetoric when half the population was revelling in open disrespect for the state and every teenager had a parody of a SCAF communiqué sitting on their Facebook wall.

So where did that leave literature? Writers on revolution found, as writers on revolution have always found, that existing literary forms were incapable of providing answers, and so they were forced to find new ones. Mona Prince, for example, in *Revolution Is My Name,* her 2012 memoir of eighteen days in Tahrir, begins with a collage of media fragments – news clippings, social media posts, cartoons, jokes and warnings – to explore the ambivalence and fragmentation of that time in the square, as well as its certainty and coherence; as the book progresses, Prince, when describing the demonstrating crowds, switches constantly and seemingly unconsciously between the pronouns 'I', 'they' and 'we'. *Blacklist,* a novel by acclaimed lawyer-turned-author Ahmed Sabry Abul-Futuh, is told through the eyes of that omnipresent and ambiguous Egyptian character type of the past few years: the *baltagi* ('thug'). By using the lens of crime and revenge to spin a revolutionary yarn, Abul-Futuh was trying to find a way of putting the counter-revolution at the heart of the uprising; the implication is that the two are not discrete historical phases, but have always been entwined.[13] Like all novelists confronted by Revolution Country, both he and Prince have been grappling in real time with the fact that 'revolutions are not stories. They are not poems. Revolutions are not texts nor are they primarily textual in nature.

Revolutions are events. They are projects and processes, made and sustained by people insisting on living lives of dignity.'[14] At the same time, as Arabic professor Elliot Colla argues, 'Stories make revolutions, insofar as they are part of what mobilizes people to go to the street. Horrifying tales of torture, abuse and corruption. Inspiring fables of resilience, imagination and effort . . . Reading, writing and revolution, then doing it again. Not so much separate activities, but stages in a single process of action and reflection.'[15]

Literature finds it hardest to respond at speed to fast-changing events; songs, poems and street art tend to have shorter gestation periods than novels, and are better placed to reflect political turmoil as it unfolds. And yet literature's pre-revolution trajectory – close entanglement with the state at some levels, opposition to it and the emergence of generational tension at others – mirrors, to some degree, that of almost every creative form in modern Egypt. And just as the revolution challenged writers to unpack their craft and even redefine it in order to acknowledge changing times – inventing new formats and techniques to capture and transmit a changed reality, and bringing previously marginalized voices to the fore – so too were practitioners of other arts pushed into similar challenges. Common to them all has been the struggle to tell revolutionary stories, at a moment in which the revolution itself remains an open-ended story. From painting to dance, music to media, this process has repeatedly broken open new spaces for cultural production, performance and distribution.

Nowhere is this truer than in the realm of graffiti. A negligible, minority pursuit before the revolution started, it has become so pervasive since then that empty walls in Egypt's major cityscapes have at times felt less like the norm and more like a delayed inevitability – a blank concrete canvas, merely waiting its turn to be filled in. 'There's a rush to it, an adrenaline shot,' Amr Nazeer, a graffiti artist who became famous for spreading a clenched fist symbol – the logo of revolutionary youth group 'April 6th' – through the streets of Cairo, told me. 'The first time I ever did graffiti, before the revolution, I'd never felt so scared in my life. We stencilled and sprayed, and then we hid and watched. It took the police about fifteen minutes to find it and start radioing their bosses, calling for reinforcements. My legs

and knees were literally jerking. But I realized that tension, that fear –
that's what I love about it. You should have fear, because the point is
you are going to where they don't want you to be.'

Under authoritarianism, public art – official murals, nationalistic
imagery, portraits of the president – seeks to render the abnormal as
ordinary; public space is saturated so extensively with the presence of
the state that the possibility of alternative forces emerging appears
non-existent.[16] That totality of control is a powerful weapon in the
hands of repressive regimes, but it is also a vulnerability; if your legitimacy is based, in part, on the absence of visual dissent then it doesn't
take much for a critical artist to produce something that – however
outwardly innocuous – could be interpreted by viewers as defiance,
and thus for your legitimacy to waver. In 2010, for example, a young
artist and musician named Ahmed Basiouny produced a performance
piece in the grounds of Cairo's Opera House entitled *30 Days Running in the Place*, in which he simply jogged on a treadmill inside a
transparent rectangular box for a few hours every day, while colourful television monitors displayed how much energy he had used up
and the sweat from his body was collected in a bottle. At the end of
thirty days, he tossed the contents of the bottle into the dust and
walked away. No one could accuse Basiouny of political agitation.
Yet after thirty years of Mubarak's rule, anyone passing by may well
have drawn the inference that Egypt's citizens were running in perpetual stasis, and that three decades worth of collective sweat had
been of little consequence.[17] What gave the piece its power was not so
much its content, though, but Basiouny's presence: the insertion of a
nonconformist flicker on to that landscape of state authority, a way
of saying to the state 'your power is not so total after all'. On 28 January 2011, three days into the anti-Mubarak uprising, Basiouny was
shot dead by police as he protested in Tahrir Square. By that stage,
the capital and many other towns and cities across Egypt were already
awash with graffiti. The spray-painted slogans, subversive cartoons
and portraits of revolutionary martyrs constituted another form of
radical visual presence that told the state, and Egypt's citizens, that
power in the streets was no longer under lockdown; that spaces once
artificially bleached by autocracy had now been polluted by dissent,
and ennobled.

Since the revolution began, successive regimes have attempted to corral it physically by building giant walls out of granite blocks on the edges of Tahrir Square and other rallying points throughout the country. Wherever these walls have appeared, graffiti artists like Amr Nazeer have flocked and reimagined them with spray-cans. In 2012, one such wall, built to separate Tahrir from Sheikh Rihan, one of the streets leading to the interior ministry, was painted, block by pains-taking block, with an exact replica of the road behind it – complete with buildings, trees and pavement. By turning Mubarak Country's defences transparent, revolutionaries refused to accept their existence at all. 'Those walls were beautiful, because they were meant to divide but they actually did the opposite and brought us together,' Nazeer told me. 'We worked together in a team to change the meaning of those walls, rather than on our own in the shadows, and the people around us in the streets were involved from the beginning. And since then, that sort of teamwork has become normal.' Graffiti hasn't just expanded in the age of revolution from a tiny subculture to a major form of cultural communication; as a medium, it has undergone a qualitative change, bringing into groups artists who had previously guarded their independence with fierce pride, and turning their work from something relatively passive – made silently under the cover of night, and 'received' by passers-by the following day – into something active, produced in daylight under the watchful eyes of citizens who are free to criticize, applaud or join in with the graffiti as it comes into being.

'The revolution completely changed the dynamic between graffiti artists and the people,' Soraya Morayef, one of the most respected chroniclers of the post-Mubarak graffiti scene, explained to me. 'Beforehand, there was a line between them. The artists were afraid of conversations; there was never direct access between artist and audience, never really a space in which passers-by could engage with the artist and ask, "What are you doing? And why?"' In Revolution Country, by contrast, graffiti artists have often found themselves live-painting, in real time; drawing scenes of battle from inside the battle itself, watching protesters respond to the art as it unfolds and responding to those responses as the work continues. Morayef describes the scene in Cairo's Mohamed Mahmoud Street, a focal point for political graffiti, on the nights of February 2012 following the deaths of dozens of football fans in the city of Port Said – violence that many suspected had been orchestrated by the military regime. Most of the victims were supporters of the Cairo club al-Ahly, and as survivors arrived back in the capital and held funerals for those killed, bloody fighting with security forces broke out on the streets. 'All the [graffiti] guys were down there, painting, and as they created these portraits of the Port Said martyrs there were literally mourners passing by them,' Morayef remembers. 'One group saw the walls and started crying; when I asked them what was wrong, they said, "That's our best friend, we just buried him."' Once the clashes started there was a field hospital set up right by the walls; the guys would paint, then stop and throw rocks, run back, talk with the ultras who were protesting, argue with religious guys who were criticizing them because graffiti is *haram* ['forbidden'], do some more painting, throw some more rocks, and so on. It was graffiti as three-dimensional performance. The story of that wall, at the end of it, was about much more than thirty metres of painting: it was the story of the painting being created and the context it was created in, as well as the story of the boys who had died.' Like the generation of writers who previously turned inwards in an attempt to unpick state power, only to find that sort of narration disrupted irrevocably by revolution, graffiti artists were unable to seal themselves off from Egypt's turmoil and pronounce on it from afar. They too have been 'bombarded with collectivity'.[18]

The incursion of graffiti artists into public spaces has been repeated by those working in other mediums. Organized arts events like '*el-Fan Midan*' ('Art is a Square') and 'D-CAF' ('Downtown Contemporary Arts Festival'), have brought participatory theatrical and musical performance to the streets; impromptu flash-mobs, meanwhile have become a colourful form of protest (during Morsi's tenure as president, the Muslim Brotherhood were treated to mass displays of everything from classical ballet to the Harlem Shake by opposition demonstrators). The revolution has unsealed the physical edges of multiple cultural forms, even if other lines of division between artists and audience, such as class and gender, remain persistent and problematic. 'There were lots of things we didn't do before the revolution, not necessarily because they were impossible to do – although that's what we told ourselves – but because *we* couldn't do it,' says Sondos Shabayek, an actor and director. 'There was a lot of self-censorship.' Shabayek is one of the founders of the *Bussy* project, which before the revolution collected women's stories of daily life in Egypt, from the comical to the disturbing, and turned them into performance pieces. Back then, the process of trying to stage the pieces was as important as the pieces themselves; it probed the boundaries of regime authority (their first outdoor performance was in a car parking space), of social tolerance (some of the stories were considered so inflammatory they had to be mimed rather than spoken out loud) and of their own fear. But after living through the start of the revolution and experiencing the occupation of Tahrir Square as a 'festival of shared, casual story-telling', Shabayek felt her internal self-censor fade away. Since Mubarak fell, *Bussy* has been performed in the women's carriages of Cairo metro trains, and a new project, *Tahrir Monologues* – developed out of protester accounts of the eighteen days – has been staged everywhere from the underside of Cairo's Mokattam clifftop to the gaps between tables and chairs in roadside cafés. 'When we performed in the metro carriage, we'd just start without any introductions,' Shabayek told me. 'On one occasion a woman screamed that we were terrorists and tried to get others to call the police. On another occasion one older woman asked us to stop because it was making her feel sick, but then some young girls at the other end of the carriage got into an argument with her because they wanted to carry on listening. I don't think any of those people would have been there, or had those debates, if we had performed that night on a stage, in a theatre, instead.'

In her previous life, Shabayek was a journalist. When the revolution began, she was juggling theatrical work with various reporting and editing duties at independent outlets like the newspaper *al-Masry al-Youm* – but the experience of protesting in the afternoon, and then reading on the pages of the evening newspapers, politicized distortions of the very events she had been a part of persuaded her to abandon a career in the media altogether. The enmity she felt towards the mainstream press was shared by many citizens, stoked by years of misinformation and craven coverage of the regime. But the fictions propagated by the major newspapers and television channels in the early days of the anti-Mubarak uprising – that revolutionaries were spies and foreign agents, for example, that they were paid to protest and were receiving free food from KFC – were of a different order. Although some protesters later took to satirically waving Colonel Sanders placards, at the time these falsities were terrifying. 'I remember in the square how these headlines, which were so often lies, could influence our lives as protesters,' Shabayek says. 'Not just our day-to-day lives in Tahrir, but literally whether or not we would be seen by the rest of the country as good people or bad people, whether or not we would live or die. That felt filthy, and it was all in the hands of those making the news.'

While Shabayek's experience of revolution persuaded her to abandon the media industry, others have attempted to reinvent it. And like Shabayek's theatrical forays into the women's metro carriage, that process of reinvention has meant the establishment of new platforms – physical and virtual – in which journalism can flourish. Momen el-Mohammady is a bespectacled forty-something from Asyut whose name used to appear on bylines in *al-Ahram*, the government's biggest daily newspaper. Now it appears on Facebook posts instead; el-Mohammady's critiques of Islamic theology and religious discourse are read by thousands; his pieces have been turned into a bestselling book, and he speaks at packed-out public events throughout the country. 'My first ever Facebook post was in the summer of 2011,' he explained, when we met in a Cairene coffee shop. 'It was about different ways to understand *sharia* [religious law]. I didn't have any followers back then, it was just a piece to share with my friends. But the more I wrote, the more I saw my follower count creep up, sometimes by a hundred or 200 every day. There was a hunger for real debate that readers weren't getting elsewhere; people started arguing with each other in the comments section, suggesting certain topics for me to write about. During the day I was stuck behind a desk at *Ahram* being told by my editor, "Please don't write this or that, don't criticize the military, remember that you are one of our writers and you have a responsibility . . ." And then by night I was writing my own posts, whatever I wanted, from cafés and from my bedroom, posts which were real and generating curiosity and discussion, and which were really popular. So one day, I just walked out of *Ahram* and left.'

In the post-Mubarak era, El-Mohammady is one of many who have carved out mass audiences for themselves through the means of social media. Self-published online journalism is a way of bypassing the state's propaganda grid, whose lines of transmission run not only from government media outlets but also from supportive private newspapers and television channels with corporate owners that share the state's agenda. But it also comes with its own set of limits. Audiences tend to be self-selected, leaving writers preaching to the converted. Readership is restricted to those with internet access. And although comments on el-Mohammady's articles are a vibrant forum for discussion, the articles are still very much his and his alone; others can consume them privately, but the relationship is pedagogical – a one-way virtual performance. That lack of meaningful engagement with readers is a problem el-Mohammady himself is keenly aware of. In an effort to address it, he often uses social media channels to announce forthcoming trips to different governorates; within hours of each message he is invariably flooded with offers of accommodation and a venue at which to give a talk – sometimes a grand public hall, other times a cramped family sitting room. 'This was the most important aspect of it all for me,' said el-Mohammady. 'Going beyond the screen, into real places – it's very powerful.'

Other citizens of Revolution Country agree, and they've gone much further. In December 2011, Egyptian soldiers launched a violent attack on a revolutionary protest camp outside the government's cabinet offices, just south of Tahrir Square. In statements that were broadcast repeatedly that evening on dozens of television channels and transcribed in every major newspaper the following day, a military spokesman told reporters that army personnel had acted with restraint. Independent newspaper *Tahrir* responded with the front-page headline *kazeboon* ('Liars') above a now iconic photograph of the army dragging a woman along the street during the clashes, exposing her electric-blue bra, as a soldier stamped down viciously on her chest. The juxtaposition of formal narratives and images which lay bare their mendacity was jarring and effective, and activists began extending the idea by creating video mash-ups online which placed footage of the military's brutality alongside official denials. Some began projecting these videos into any corner of the city capable of absorbing them – the painted sides of a building, a fold-out projector backdrop in a back-alley, a white bedsheet strung up between a lamp-post and a tree. '*Askar kazeboon* ('The Military Are Liars') was born.

The Kazeboon movement is leaderless and non-hierarchical; anyone can download short films from its website or Facebook page and organize their own local screening. It builds on a broader model of public media that has gained momentum since the outbreak of revolution, one that deliberately enmeshes journalists and audiences rather than severing them from each other, and which takes as its starting point media as a revolutionary strategy rather than as an object of private consumption. It is the model adopted by radical media collective Mosireen, which has built up an unparalleled archive of revolutionary footage. Mosireen's short films explore everything from episodes of police violence to workers' occupations; many of the videos depicting demonstrations, street battles and community struggles have been shot not by the professional media corps but by participants themselves. The formula has proved popular: over the past half-decade, Mosireen's YouTube channel has ranked among the most watched non-profit YouTube channels not just in Egypt but across the world. At their downtown Cairo offices, Mosireen members offer training in filming and editing to anyone who's interested; like Kazeboon, the collective often attempts to screen its footage in public spaces - including Tahrir Square itself. A spin-off project, *Tahrir Cinema*, seeks, like Kazeboon to pose transformative questions about what the media is, and who it is for. The aim is not just to replicate the existing mass media battleground and hustle for audience share with commercial and political rivals, but rather to create something that can take media into new places altogether – not least the physical battlegrounds of the revolution itself. 'The liberation and transformation of quotidian, everyday spaces has been one of the paramount features of the Egyptian revolution; any media that would claim to be revolutionary must engage with and take place within these spaces,' explains Sherief Gaber, a member of Mosireen.

'The goals of Kazeboon and *Tahrir Cinema* were not only reaching the most people, reaching people who had not seen these images before or producing a counter-narrative. The goals of these initiatives also became changing relationships between media and publics. In other words, activists sought to make media public and work differently than as a tool for the transmission of information.'[19]

Like post-Mubarak graffiti artists, Egyptians who produce public media are forced to cope with a panoply of live responses to their work; the very point of a Kazeboon or *Tahrir Cinema* screening is to create a sense of communal possession over the images being projected, and that shared ownership can have unpredictable consequences. Film showings are often attacked by the security forces, hired thugs or just hostile passers-by, and there is always a plan made in advance detailing who will grab the equipment and run, and what escape routes they will use. Even when screenings aren't broken up prematurely, they always divide opinion among those watching: some cry, some shout, some cheer, and some shake their heads and dismiss the activists as troublemakers. These reactions, and the kerbside discussions they engender, are not side effects – they lie at the core of public media's purpose. Just as power for the video projector is usually hijacked from the electricity cables running up nearby streetlights, so the impact of the footage is derived from staging it in the same spaces in which the struggle between Mubarak and Revolution Country is being waged day in, day out, both on the streets and within citizens' interactions with each other. And there is no pretence at objectivity here. 'Documenting, distributing, and archiving the present is not an academic exercise,' says Gaber. 'Our desire is for these images to incite, provoke, and spur to action.'

Out in Madinat el-Salam, down a residential alley and through the doors of a nondescript storage unit, Ahmed Farid Sayed has been subverting conventional media images as well. Sayed is a third-year student in tourism and hospitality who wears a black leather jacket and paint-spattered jeans, and has a permanently bashful look on his face – half humble-shy, half boyband-smirk. There are two rooms here. The front one is plain and empty. The back one contains two plastic chairs, a computer, a tower of speakers and a mixing deck propped up on a trestle table. The walls are painted black and there are no windows; the only light comes from a UV lamp hanging from a tangled wire in the ceiling. Sayed double-clicks on a couple of desktop icons linking to pirated versions of Fruity Loops and Acid Pro, both pieces of music-mixing software, and opens a file named 'Figoooooooooooo'. He smiles as the lyrics – drawn from a long tradition of Egyptian popular folk, but set to a rugged drum track heavy with sub-bass and hip-hop beats – fill the room: 'Like trees / I go and come with the wind / [But] however far I go / I'm still in my place / my place is here.' The 22-year-old nods along and mouths the words, pausing only to adjust some synth parameters and fiddle with his hat before looping the track round once again. 'My new song,' he beams, once it's over. 'What do you reckon?' Sayed is DJ Figo, juvenile godfather of the *mahraganat* music scene, and this is his lair.

As with most young Egyptians, Figo's youth played out to a bifurcated soundtrack. The songs he grew up with were either heart-wrenching warbles from mid-twentieth century musical royalty like Umm Kulthum and Abdel Halim Hafez, or modern, clean-cut bubble-pop from Arab superstars such as Amr Diab and Tamer Hosny, whose airbrushed faces adorned advertising hoardings along the desert highway linking el-Salam to the capital. By his mid-teens Figo was getting into DJ-ing and being asked to play at local parties, but the music available to him felt stale. In search of something different, he looked up remixes of popular Egyptian tunes online, but the tracks he discovered still lacked originality and oomph. That's when he first consulted an Arabic–English dictionary and tentatively typed in the words 'how to make beats' on YouTube. 'I couldn't understand the voiceover on the videos, so I just tried to work out what was happening by pausing and looking at the screenshots,' he explains. Figo spent six months scrutinizing the tutorials, learning how to add in layers of sound element by element – cymbals, bass, drums – and control the speed. His computer was gradually swamped by viruses and malware as a result of all the illegal software downloads, but in among them on the hard drive lay scraps of sound that Figo had created; the start, maybe, of something new.

A group of friends began congregating in Figo's bedroom. One was called Alaa Fifty, a local boy who had been flogging scratchy recordings of his own rap songs to passers-by in el-Salam's streets. Sessions would stretch long into the night, headphones and microphones passed back and forth as Alaa and others dropped lyrics and Figo blended them in with basslines produced on the mixing software and samples he found on the internet. One day an acquaintance of the group announced that he would soon be getting married in Matariya, another low-income neighbourhood to the north-east of Cairo, and asked if they would create a song for the wedding. 'I spent longer on it than anything I'd worked on before,' Figo tells me. 'The groom kept asking, "When will it be ready?" and I kept replying, 'It will be ready when it is perfect.' With an almost spiritual reverence, Figo hums the tune and taps out the song's beat on a plastic chair, using his laptop keyboard as a stage-prop piano. At the wedding, '*Mahragan el-Salam*' ('Salam Festival') sent the crowds into rapture – it was grimy, infectious and real, like nothing they had heard before. There was nowhere you could buy this song, and no home for it on the internet, but Figo's friends had it recorded on their phones; they began sending it to their friends, who sent it on to their own friends in turn. From Matariya and el-Salam, mobile to mobile, the track spread to Ain Shams, Ezbet el-Haggana, el-Marg, and dozens of '*ashwa'iyat* on the fringes of the city. Figo even heard reports of it being played in the Delta, as far north as the eastern governorate of Sharqiya. The phenomenon of *mahraganat* music was underway.

Mahraganat is the Arabic plural for 'festival'. As Egyptian cartoonist and culture critic Andeel points out, it is also used as colourful slang to identify something as 'extravagant, loud, full of happiness, and sometimes extremely messy'.[20] That's an apt description of the sound that Figo and his crew have cultivated; it's a chaotic roar of pure energy, unbound by convention. This is a genre in which it's OK to make loads of noise, to throw in yet another layer of hypnotic sampling, to swear and strut and shout. 'We don't deal in organized verses, we take words from the left, from the right, from wherever there is something that can make people dance,' says Figo. Critics accuse *mahraganat* practitioners of sounding ugly and robotized, but that's the point: its appeal lies in the fact that pretty much anyone with a laptop can produce their own tracks, evening out sonic imbalances with AutoTune and chucking anything they want on the pile, from snatches of classical Egyptian ballads to jingles from breakfast cereal commercials and gripes about the cigarette vendor on the corner. *Mahraganat* is the sound of Egypt's underdogs jostling for attention, and although it first emerged before 2011, it is in Revolution Country that the genre has mushroomed far and wide. During the anti-Mubarak uprising I remember trying to escape tear gas along the corniche and hearing this strange music as I ran, pulsing up through acrid fog from the low-rent pleasure boats along the Nile. Mona Prince, author of *Revolution Is My Name*, recalls dancing in Talaat Harb Street on the 28th January 'day of rage', alongside *tuk-tuk* drivers who had driven defiantly across the river from the informal settlement of Bulaq al-Dukror and were using their vehicles' speakers to fill the air with *mahraganat*. *Tuk-tuks* are supposed to be banned from downtown Cairo's Europeanized boulevards and restricted to the back-alleys of peripheral neighbourhoods, but here they were anyway, a convoy of the edgelands at the centre of a city that no longer knew who was on the edge and who was at the centre. 'What is this music?' asked Prince as she swirled, laughing until her eyes watered. 'Where did you guys get this?'[21]

Today *mahraganat* has matured beyond its humble beginnings, but not outgrown them altogether; even as Figo and the new generation of singers and producers that have followed in his wake achieve local stardom, they have remained living and working in the same neighbourhoods they grew up in – the same neighbourhoods whose sense of social exclusion helped power both *mahraganat* and the revolution in the first place. The notion that this music is intimately connected with Egypt's margins is something its practitioners are explicit about. Weza is a *mahraganat* artist from Matariya. 'For them,' he says, in reference to the rest of society, 'we don't exist.' Sadat, part of Figo's crew in el-Salam, agrees. 'If you haven't been to Salam,' he insists, 'you can't understand what I say.'[22]

Mahraganat music embodies something critical to the revolution, not because of any political prescriptions or dutiful moralizing – little of that can be found in the songs – but via a gleeful reclamation of sonic space by citizen outsiders. These beats betray a mischievous cynicism that is wired with possibility, an expression of post-Mubarak Egypt's shakily democratic subconscious' where life is often crap, hope is omnipresent, the old rules are broken and revolutionary protest chants are a reference point understood by anyone who cares to listen.[23] One of the most popular tracks, developed by former ringtone-salesman and PC repairman Amr Mohamed (street name 'Amr 7a7a' – the '7' represents the aspirated Arabic letter 'H', so the name is pronounced 'Amr Haha'), takes the revolution's most famous slogan, 'The people want the downfall of the regime' and irreverently twists it: the song starts with a rendition of the national anthem, played on a rubbish keyboard, followed by the sound of a smashing window and the lyrics: 'The people want five *gineih* phone credit / The people want to bring down the regime / But the people are so damn tired . . .' As Sadat argues, this sort of content, in this sort of register, isn't detached from revolutionary turmoil – it is the turmoil. 'If I talk about something that happens, that's politics,' he says. 'If I talk about the situation of a country through a story of youth, that's also politics. Politics doesn't have to involve the government, or the regime. What we talk about exists in the streets. That's why people listen.'[24]

One of Sadat's songs includes the line: 'What's the story? / We're in the story, from the beginning.' Part of *mahraganat*'s appeal is who it pisses off as much as who it attracts; the self-insertion of the marginalized into the story of post-Mubarak Egypt – and the backlash from those who are used to ignoring such characters altogether – is the essence of revolutionary struggle, and *mahraganat* reproduces that faultline on a digital mixing deck. 'You'd only like it if you like the taste of liver sandwiches from the dirtiest of Cairo's carts,' observes Andeel. 'It's going to be difficult for you to like it if you're the kind of person who asks the waiter in the shisha place for the plastic thingy that they put on the tip of the pipe to make it less contagious.' The music's power, Andeel argues, is to remind those in Egypt who pay a great deal of money to get away from Figo and the type of people who dance to his creations that such people still exist and aren't going away. Every time elites try to dial down the volume, kids in places like el-Salam respond by turning it up. 'These kids know what it feels to burn a police vehicle and how to transport a wounded protester on a stolen bike,' Andeel writes.[25] 'These kids know there are people in the country who are much richer than them, who don't like them and think they are disgusting. They respond with insanely annoying music. It's a generation of confrontation. It knows that something is not fair. For now the response is as sweet as music. Later it's going to be more than that.' As Figo told me in his studio, his face glowing in the purple UV light, 'I didn't think I was interested in politics before the revolution. I was interested in finding a way to make myself heard when it felt like the whole world wanted to forget me. Now I know that's what politics is.'

Like any alternative art form with a claim on 'authentic' roots, mahraganat has now found an appreciative middle-class audience; Amr 7a7a and Sadat play a weekly night at the After Eight nightclub, where bouncers enforce a dress code and the cover charge can be up to a quarter of the monthly minimum wage. Some mahraganat devotees have bemoaned the 'takeover' of the genre by the privileged, but cultural mediums always mutate and find fresh audiences. Watching Figo perform on a downtown Cairo stage is very different from watching him perform as he hangs off a speaker stack at a street party in el-Salam, but both performances are magnetic. And like the public media initiatives pioneered by Mosireer, *Tahrir Cinema* and Kazeboon, both performances represent the encroachment of something unnatural on to the old landscape of the state. These faces and images are refusing to ask permission for their presence any more. It's all part of the same dynamic that has seen informal street vendors flood Egypt's public squares since the revolution began, the same dynamic that has inspired residents of poorer neighbourhoods to start painting their water and electricity pipelines with brightly coloured paint – to highlight the government's neglect of public services, to seize ownership of the environment, to say, as graffiti artist Amr Nazeer puts it, "I'm here too."[26] On his laptop, Figo has caught the sound of Egyptians who believe, one way or another, they can remake their world. "It's a fundamental shift," says Elliott Colla, Arabic professor. 'Before, the initial assumption regarding anyone doing anything on the street was always "Who let you do that?" Now the initial assumption is "I can do that." '[27]

Egypt's 'revolutionary art' has given rise to a thousand colourful magazine features and video news packages in the international media in recent years. But although cultural expressions in Egypt have assumed new and different meanings in the context of revolution and counter-revolution, the term itself is problematic. It suggests that a certain subset of painting, sculpture, poetry, literature or performance can be hived off and endorsed with a revolutionary ID badge, and it ignores the existence of most of these art forms before the revolution began, depicting the country pre-2011 as some sort of acultural wasteland. It also raises awkward questions: who gets to define what revolutionary art consists of, and does the definition (or definer) change along with the evolution of events on the ground? In a scathing critique of 'revolutionary art', Andeel has demanded to know whether or not the four-fingered 'Rabaa' symbol – an expression of support for former president Mohamed Morsi, or the Muslim Brotherhood, or general opposition to Sisi, depending on who you ask – would be placed in the category of 'revolutionary art' if it had been 'designed by an artist connected with international art institutions and speaking good English'.[28] Andeel might have gone further: would an adoring mural of President Sisi vanquishing Morsi, spray-painted at night on to a side street off Tahrir Square, make it into the revolutionary cultural canon? What makes art revolutionary – the characteristics of the artist, the content or location of the artwork, or the political perspective of the viewer? The few artists brazen enough to label their own work explicitly as 'revolutionary' have tended to produce things which are trite and kitschy – weary protest clichés hauled uncritically from street to canvas, page or screen. Reviewing a 2011 collection of film shorts by young Egyptian directors entitled *Tamantashar Yom* ('18 Days'), cultural critic Ursula Lindsey observed that almost all of them 'make use of political symbolism so pointed it amounts to assault by metaphor. Even the better ones cannot seem to resist final shots that thuddingly overplay their hand: an embrace in front of a tank; a blood-soaked banknote; a confession by a murdered political prisoner that simply reads: "Freedom . . . freedom . . . freedom".'[29]

Andeel's question raises a related issue when it comes to thinking about the cultural impact of Egypt's current fragmentation between Mubarak and Revolution Country, which is that many people to whom the term 'revolutionary's is often applied by outsiders actively shun the label themselves. Take football, for example – Egypt's most vibrant form of popular culture, and the realm in which one particular group of individuals, the 'ultras', have made a name for themselves as cadres fighting on the frontline of the revolutionary struggle. The existence of Egyptian ultras – a hardcore set of supporters identified with a particular football club – dates back to the late 2000s; well before the anti-Mubarak uprising began, rival ultras groups were traversing many of the rifts and fractures that would later become central to Egypt's present revolutionary moment. By forming collectives that were independent of the state and parallel hierarchies at the local club level, and by seeking to reclaim autonomy over secured spaces – in this case, the *curva* stands at football stadiums where the most ardent fans congregate – the ultras set themselves on a collision course with club elites and the regime's security forces, and became adept at fighting both.

'We weren't just some fans union or pressure group,' Mohamed Beshir, a founding father of the UWK ('Ultras White Knights', an ultras movement linked to Zamalek Sporting Club, a Cairo football team) told me. Beshir is better known by his moniker GemyHood; once one of the country's most notorious ultras, he has since been spurned by his former comrades after writing a book about his experiences. "The police and the government feared us because we found an area we could control, and they want control of everything. We had our own rights and our own ideas which had nothing to do with them, we believed in football owned by the supporters. And so of course, it was a battle." The ultras were known for violence – against players, police and rival ultras groups – but they also embodied something else: an alternative politics of fun that paid no heed to the state's core paradigm of patriarchy and stability. Beshir showed me videos of his crew's antics: an avalanche of shoes thrown at the underperforming Zamalek squad during a friendly match in 2008, riots on an army base in Gharbia in 2009 when Zamalek travelled there to play the military football team, a tussle between a police officer and an ultra in front of 10,000 fans in the stand that led to half the stadium singing songs about the security forces being pimps. In the context of Mubarak Country, the ultras' contempt for social norms and their almost nihilistic embrace of chaos represented something meaningful.[30]

When the revolution began and propelled all sorts of Egyptians into the streets, it was the ultras who had the greatest experience of guerrilla fighting; stories abounded of ultras groups which had been historic foes now standing side by side to hurl rocks at the central security forces and defend Tahrir from the regime. And just as the ultras were at the forefront of resisting state violence, they were also among its most prominent victims; the Port Said massacre in 2012, which was memorialized in real time by Cairo's graffiti artists, claimed more than seventy lives – most of them from UA07 or 'Ultras Ahlawy', a group linked to Zamalek's rivals al-Ahly SC. As a result, the fact that the ultras constituted an institutionalized, albeit anarchic, wing of the revolution appeared self-evident; activists embraced them, and academics wrote long think-pieces about their interventions into the political sphere. Yet the ultras themselves, at least as a community, rejected that notion altogether. 'The people who talked like this about the ultras have nothing to do with football,' insisted Beshir. 'They don't understand what we're about. I'm fighting the police for my own reasons; if my friend is in jail, and I have a history of war against the jailers, then I attack the authorities according to my own rules, not the rules of the activists. There are the people who call themselves revolutionaries and they have their own language and their own internet forums and they write their own things and that is all fine, but it's not our language.' Beshir told me that ultras got so tired of the 'revolutionary' label that at some protests they began chanting *aha el-sawra* (roughly, 'fuck the revolution'). 'Why not?' replied Beshir, when I raised my eyebrows. 'Lots of ultras support the revolution, yes. But stop calling the ultras revolutionaries. We play by our own rules – people can't put me in a box, I destroy boxes!'

Regardless of Beshir's boxes, Egypt's ultras do play a revolutionary role; they represent certain notions about society and the state that counter-revolutionaries are highly fearful of, ideas that the counter-revolution has been forced into existence to resist and remove. But the ultras' irritation at being lumped together by outsiders into some all-encompassing revolutionary bloc is a reminder of how much nuance is needed to navigate the post-Mubarak cultural terrain. From performance art to popular sport, Egypt's cultural realm has been electrified by revolution and counter-revolution alike, but not everything new, or different, or spray-painted on a wall is 'revolutionary' by definition, just as not everyone calling themselves an 'ultra' is necessarily seeking to undermine the state. Radical cultural expressions have been quickly appropriated – by political opponents, by counter-revolutionaries, by profit-seeking corporations. Coca Cola has sponsored major graffiti 'events' in poorer Cairo neighbourhoods as part of its corporate social responsibility programme; foreign NGOs have tried to seize ownership of the street art scene;[31] regime supporters have used graffiti to 'reclaim' the el-Shuhadaa ('Martyrs') metro station, once named after Mubarak, in the former dictator's name. A group calling itself the 'Badr Battallion', named after the Egyptian military's crossing of the Suez Canal in the 1973 war, has set itself up to fight back against more subversive forms of street art practised by the likes of Amr Nazeer; under Mohamed Morsi's rule, some Muslim Brotherhood supporters formed an organization called 'Ultras Nahdawi' and used the tactics and trappings of the football ultras movement to try to defend their beleaguered president from revolutionary pressure in the streets. For every Mosireen and Kazeboon video uploaded to the internet and shared through social media, there is another featuring a montage of Egyptian army triumphs, overlaid with a soundtrack of nationalist anthems.

In a dispiriting turn, some of those cultural figureheads most closely associated with the revolution when it first began have now joined the chorus of pro-state cheerleading. Certain sections of Egypt's orthodox literary field have reprised their old role as 'ally' to the state against the forces of Islamism and imperialism; as the Sisi regime readied its massacre of Muslim Brotherhood supporters at Rabaa, Alaa al-Aswany, Mohamed Hashem of the Dar Merit publishing house and many other literary figures who originally supported the revolution – even Sonallah Ibrahim – were among those to speak out in defence of military rule. For some, the government – as both patron and persecutor – has been embraced with affection once again. Gamal al-Ghitani, an author whose 1963 novel *Zayni Barakat* – an allegory of Nasserism set in sixteenth-century Egypt – is widely considered one of the defining post-colonial critiques of charismatic, authoritarian leadership, labelled Sisi's ascent 'a miracle of history' and celebrated the deaths of Muslim Brotherhood supporters at Rabaa as 'excellent' and something that should be extended.

Al-Ghitani has actually been close to state power for many years, so perhaps his admiration for military violence under Sisi should come as no surprise. But the echoing of his views by other, tradition-ally more insurgent literary icons suggests something more than just an instinctive opposition to Mohamed Morsi and the rule of the Brotherhood, understandable as that opposition may be. In a period of immense political complexity, al-Ghitani and his generation of Egyptian intellectuals seem, as critic Ahmed el-Shamsy puts it, 'to yearn in their old age for a repetition of what they were part of as young men: the elating days of Nasserite optimism and common pur-pose, which somewhere, inexplicably, took a wrong turn and ended in the dark dungeons of the security police ... Their advocacy appears rooted in the conviction that given a second chance, the promises of that era will at last be fulfilled.'[32] But the great rallying cries of Nasserism – anti-colonialism and social justice – have with-ered on the vine of Sisi's Egypt, leaving nothing but the worst of Nasser's project remaining: the hysteria, the dehumanization, the worship of a strongman for whom dissent is intolerable. Under those circumstances, renewed faith by the intelligentsia in a state hitched to the old ways, even as a temporary strategic move, is hard to fathom. In August 2013, 150 leading writers and publishers signed a state-ment condemning Muslim Brotherhood 'terrorism'. Discussing the shift undertaken by most of the literary class towards cheering on the state, Elliot Colla observed: 'If there is lasting impact it will not be in the political arena, but in the field of literature itself. What is at stake is nothing less than the ability of writers and critics to create their own spheres of autonomous thought and action.'[33]

To complicate matters further, the unstable borders between Mubarak and Revolution Country have, under Sisi, closed in on Egypt's cultural rebels – just as they have on those fighting for an eco-nomic alternative to neoliberalism, and on local communities seeking to recalibrate their relationships with the state. Under both Morsi and Sisi, acts of government censorship have escalated once again, particularly in the media where satirical voices – from newspaper cartoonists to topical comedians, such as internationally renowned talk show host Bassem Youssef – have found themselves on the wrong side of not just the law but also the reactionary sympathies of the moguls who employ them. Journalists, when it comes to thinking about the state, have been presented with a choice between either flattery or banishment; those who pick incorrectly, or hadn't realized they were being made to pick at all, have generally ended up behind bars, or dead. Reporters who believe in holding power to account are incompatible with Sisi's Egypt, to the extent that their very identity and humanity are called into question.

Mohamed Fahmy, an Egyptian-Canadian correspondent with Al-Jazeera English who was jailed along with two colleagues, ostensibly for 'spreading false news' and 'harming national unity' but in reality for the crime of journalism, has been forced to renounce his Egyptian citizenship in an effort to be released and deported; in Mubarak Country, one cannot be a citizen and question the state. 'The media's priority,' announced Sisi in an August 2014 meeting with major media figures, according to an account published by *al-Masry al-Youm*, 'should be to highlight the dangers to Egypt's national security.'[34] Sisi went on to criticize press coverage of a recently leaked video showing an orphanage supervisor brutally beating a child in care, insisting that it wasn't 'the right time' to be focusing on such issues. 'Sisi responded to a suggestion to empower youth,' continued the report, 'by saying that he doesn't have a problem with the youth but he doesn't have the luxury to experiment at this phase.' Mainstream newspaper editors agree; deviations from the official narrative are now to be avoided. 'We reiterate our rejection of attempts to doubt state institutions or insult the army or police or judiciary in a way that would reflect negatively on these institutions' performance,' claimed seventeen of them in a joint statement in late 2014, before going on to assert 'total confidence' in all government bodies and promise unwavering support for any measures undertaken by the state 'to confront terrorism'.[35] Many prominent media personalities have been quick to toe the line: 'I would say anything the military tells me to say out of the duty and respect for the institution,' claimed Ahmed Moussa, a popular TV host.[36] The regime's hostility to non-conformist journalism reflects how uncertain it is about its long-term grip on post-Mubarak Egypt. It's not the right time to empower youth, or to talk about child abuse in orphanages, because it's not the right time for anything but the buttressing of the state: its strength, its unity, its prestige. It's not the right time for experimentation, because in the course of the revolution that strength, unity and prestige have looked more vulnerable than ever before.

Courageous Egyptians continue to find cracks in the façade of consensus; the brilliant, pioneering and self-critical journalism produced in English and Arabic by *Mada Masr*, the online news outlet, remains a go-to resource for anyone seeking an alternative lens on events, and journalists working within compromised media outlets have themselves been brave enough to speak out against repression – after the statement by newspaper editors pledging fealty to the state, hundreds of their staff signed a petition condemning their bosses' crackdown on freedom of opinion as itself a from of terrorism. But the halcyon days following Mubarak's fall, when videos circulated of Abdel Latif el-Menawy, head of Egypt's state news, being chased out of his office building by his own staff, feel very far away. Egypt today remains one of the most dangerous places on earth to be a journalist, and as the counter-revolution has gathered pace other cultural producers have also found themselves fighting for survival.[37] In July 2014, a week after he went missing, the body of nineteen-year-old Hisham Rizk – graffiti artist, cartoonist and 6 April revolutionary – washed up in Zeinhom morgue, supposedly after being found floating in the Nile. Informal street vendors have now been chased back out of Tahrir Square by the state; the march of the margins, in all its forms, is being faced down by Sisi at every turn. Yet despite its horrors, this backlash is a sign of a brittle regime. A state secure in its hold over the citizenry has little need to live in terror of notebooks, nut-sellers and paint tins. Each muscular enforcement of cultural unanimity can also be read as an admission of weakness. 'The best you can do is fight walls,' concludes a poem once scrawled next to a piece of anti-Mubarak graffiti in Cairo's Mohamed Mahmoud Street, 'and claim victory over colours and lines.'[38]

One of the reasons this fight over walls is so acute is because Egypt's revolution, at its most basic level, has become a battle over memory: the memory of what the state is and what the state does, the memory of what Egyptians themselves have achieved, of who they are and what they struggled for. Egyptian elites have never trusted the citizenry with knowledge; hence an education system based on learning by rote, and a national archive staffed by people whose job it is to keep researchers out, not encourage them in. 'Reading is potentially a suspicious activity,' says historian Khaled Fahmy, who spends much of his professional life locking horns with librarians, 'and those responsible for these cultural institutions therefore view themselves as custodians of knowledge, and consider their prime task to be to strive hard to protect and safeguard knowledge, but never to disseminate or produce it. Knowledge for them is thus akin to raw data, data that has to be protected, hoarded and preserved.'[39] For the post-Mubarak political classes, amendments made to the official historical record in light of revolution have remained an elite affair: a rewriting of the history of the 1973 Arab – Israeli war, for example, to play down Mubarak's status as an air force hero and talk up the role played by rival generals.[40] The Brotherhood's leaders, for their part, used their time in power to try to etch out the rest of Egyptian history altogether. 'There's a concerted effort by the Brotherhood to erase and keep everyone in the present,' says urbanist Mohamed ElShahed. 'For them, January 25th was day zero.'[41] Against all of this, the revolution has sought to break open and democratize memory. One of the first things revolutionaries did after Mubarak had been toppled was storm state security headquarters and post online the documents they found there. The sort of cultural production pursued by Amr Nazeer in his graffiti, or by Sondos Shabayek in her *Tahrir Monologues* performances, amounts to an entirely new and unsanctioned layer of historical memory being applied to Egypt, one that the counter-revolution cannot allow to take hold.

It is telling that whenever the state has built its own official 'memorials' to those killed in the course of revolution, revolutionaries have almost immediately destroyed them – including the grand circular folly that this chapter opened with, reduced to a small brick plinth and a pile of rubble by Egyptians who rejected the state's right to assume control of revolutionary memory. It is just as meaningful that some of the state's most famous revolutionary victims have been killed while trying to carve out a revolutionary memory of their own – including Shaimaa el-Sabagh, a young poet and mother in her thirties, who was gunned down by police in January 2015 on her way to Tahrir Square to lay flowers in honour of the martyrs.[42] Videos circulated online showed the moment the security forces fired their weapons; the interior ministry offered no justification for the shooting, but initially suggested it could be the work of 'Islamist infiltrators'.[43] History is battered via bricks and bullets, again and again, in a battle to inscribe the future. The government's forensics authority later pinned the blame for what happened on el-Sabagh herself. 'According to science, [she] should not have died,' a spokesman said. 'Her body was like skin over bone, as they say. She was very thin. She did not have any percentage of fat. So the small pellets penetrated very easily, and four or five out of all the pellets that penetrated her body – these four or five pellets were able to penetrate her heart and lungs, and these are the ones that caused her death.'[44]

Amid the state's unreality, is it any wonder that *mahraganat* music, the sound of something real, has commanded such an audience? When it was time for me to leave Figo's studio in el-Salam, he jumped in a *tuk-tuk* with me and we drove out to the edge of town where my car was parked. The *tuk-tuk* driver had Figo's entire back catalogue on an mp3 stick; festival music, played at its eardrum-wrecking loudest, accompanied us all the way. As we neared the end of the drive, we came across a group of teenagers on a side road, spraying walls to advertise the upcoming wedding of one of their friends. '*Amm Figo!*' ('Uncle Figo!') they yelped in excitement, when they saw who was riding in the *tuk-tuk*. The groom – a taciturn eighteen-year-old with the wispy beginnings of a moustache and gelled-back hair – was bundled to the front of the crowd to shake Figo's hand. After hugs and blessings, Figo agreed to do a set at the wedding. He said his good-byes and headed off to the studio, but before getting in the car I ran back to the groom and asked him what having Figo perform at his wedding would mean to him. A smile crept across his face. 'It means the man who makes our music will be there,' he replied. 'Now everyone will dance.'

12

Body Paint

In 2003, students taking exams at a high school in Sohag, a city in Upper Egypt, were asked to write an essay on one of two topics: the environment, or the role played by Arab armies in standing up to Israel. One of the students, a teenager named Samira Ibrahim, chose the second. In her essay, Ibrahim argued that historically Arab armies had failed to stand up to Israel, and that the Palestinian people had been betrayed as a result. The following day, state security agents entered the classroom during lessons and pulled Ibrahim out for questioning. The school's headmistress attempted to stop Ibrahim being taken; in response, the agents hit and kicked her.

Ibrahim, the daughter of a known Islamist sympathizer, was investigated for forty-five days. Eventually, the authorities decided that, as a minor, she could not be imprisoned. Instead, they took her father. He had emerged from his latest jail stint only five days previously; now he was thrown back behind bars, this time for five years. When I met Ibrahim, on the top floor of an upscale Cairo café in early 2014, I asked if her father had been angry at her about what happened. She laughed softly, and shook her head. 'My father is sixty-five years old, and he has spent thirty-five of those years in prison,' she replied. 'Perhaps one day I'll be able to match his record.' She told me that the incident had radicalized her. Before it happened, her father's diatribes against the regime were an abstraction. Afterwards, they took on greater meaning. 'The regime and state security are responsible for who I am today,' she said. 'They awoke this political personality inside me.'

Sohag is a small and congenial provincial capital, situated about halfway down the Nile between the tip of the Delta in the north and the Sudanese border in the south; the river runs wide here, and the bridges low. After school and university, Ibrahim got a job as a marketing manager at a local private firm. Life was comfortable enough, if predictable. Then came the fall of Tunisia's President Ben Ali in January 2011, and the call for demonstrations in Tahrir Square. On the morning of 25 January, Ibrahim's colleagues were surprised to find her desk empty; she had spent the whole of the previous night on a microbus en route to Cairo, arriving at 8 a.m. to find a strange and silent city with its shops shuttered up and its highways lined with security forces. 'I roamed around looking for something, any kind of protest spark, but I couldn't find it,' she remembered. 'I kept seeing other young people walking on their own or in little groups, walking around like me and making eye contact with each other. And then suddenly a lady wrapped in an Egyptian flag just screamed "*yasqut yasqut Hosni Mubarak*" ("Down, down with Hosni Mubarak") and it was like a weight had been lifted off everyone's shoulders – we all began running and converging and chanting. It was the most exciting moment of my life.' From that moment onwards, Ibrahim stayed in the square – through the eighteen days, through those early moments of SCAF rule, through the rapid disillusionment with military government and the beginning of a new stage of revolutionary struggle against the generals. Soldiers dispersed Ibrahim and her fellow demonstrators once, but the revolutionaries returned: they pitched tents, drew placards and sung songs about Tahrir belonging to the people. Then, on 9 March they heard the rumble of tanks approaching.

Ibrahim was standing outside the 'Kentucky' as it is known, (KFC) outlet holding a protest banner when security forces approached. They told her to leave, and she refused. 'I have my ID, and it's my right to be here,' she replied. So they grabbed her, pulling her hair and dragging her by her clothes to the grounds of the nearby Egyptian Museum. She was met by an officer she didn't know. 'Hi Samira!' he said. 'I've been expecting you! Come and say hello!' She walked towards him, and he electrocuted her in the stomach.

A few weeks after I met Ibrahim, President Sisi gave a speech in which he asserted that the moral reform of the Egyptian people was a leader's responsibility. 'The law alone isn't enough, we need to utilize other tools, such as the media, education, places of worship and the family,' he insisted. 'Do you want to know what I will do as president? I'm saying it loud and clear: state institutions, namely those with educational, religious and media roles, have to help us regulate morals that we all think are problematic.'[1] Later that year, following Sisi's coronation, Egypt's education ministry added a new subject to the school curriculum: 'Intellectual and Moral Security'. The purpose of the new subject, according to a ministry-affiliated think-tank, was 'to reform errant behaviour that threatens security, to cultivate students' love of their country and their sense of belonging, and to include subjects that are concerned with intellectual security'.[2] The think-tank advised school officials to open up a database of any students who appeared resistant to such reform.

As the revolution has led Egyptian people to try to remake the state, the counter-revolution has led the Egyptian state to try to remake the people. Like all other areas of society, the identities we use to define who we are as individuals and communities – gender, sexuality, nationhood and religious belief (or lack of it) – have been muddled and shaken by the past half-decade's turmoil, and within the commotion Egypt's old guard has identified something powerful, and dangerous. Ibrahim's tale, and that of other Egyptians in the chapter, is a story of the state battling to protect itself through the imposition of a very specific type of identity on its citizens, with rigid parameters. Simultaneously, it is a story too, of certain citizens refusing to adhere to that identity, of those parameters being ruptured. Egypt's rulers want to inscribe their power on Egyptian bodies, weaponizing whatever deviation they can find from state-sanctioned norms as a means to isolate and humiliate the wayward, forcing them back to the fold. They believe that the salvation of Mubarak Country will come from a reimposition of the familial model, around a patriarch – male, heterosexual, devout and patriotic – who embodies the ideal Egyptian; in Sisi, they have the apotheosis of what every citizen should aspire to be. Some who don't or can't meet the criteria, such as women and Coptic Christians, are to be tolerated as long as they accept their subordinate role within the national family. Other subversions – homosexuals, atheists, foreign refugees – are beyond paternal redemption; they threaten everyone, and can be afforded no place in Sisi's Egypt at all. 'Egypt believes that the traditional family is the natural and fundamental core unit of society,' the country's ambassador to the United Nations, Amr Abul Ata, declared in late 2014. 'This healthy family environment cannot be achieved without [the] state's and society's total engagement in the protection of the family.'[3]

Under the latest iteration of military rule, those who betoken difference of any sort have been targeted relentlessly: men hauled by police from bathhouses in front of prime-time television cameras, women sexually assaulted at political protests, Syrian migrants tortured and deported. But the official baiting of social minorities is about much more than majoritarian bullying. It is about underscoring a distinction between 'us' – those loyal to the patriarch and embraced by the state – and 'them', and ensuring that all Egyptians, regardless of their social identities, fear placement on the wrong side of the line. Those posing the fiercest menace to Abul Ata's 'healthy family environment' are actually any Egyptians, be they male, female, Muslim, Christian, straight or gay, who have come to view themselves as autonomous citizens, rather than as dependants. The revolution has created very many of these people, just as very many of these people have created the revolution. Those with one foot in Revolution Country are wary of paternal authority in all its forms. They won't allow their access to public space to be mediated by their gender, they no longer follow orders from the clerics at their place of worship, they do not envision Egypt as a family unit in which they are consigned socially or politically to the status of children. Mohamed Tolba, a big-bearded Salafist in his mid-thirties, and Tony Sabri, a 21-year-old Copt, are two such Egyptians. Their tales are very different, and their religious backgrounds cast them, conventionally, as enemies. They have never met. But both are a source of existential angst to the state, and both, by structuring their lives around the new ways rather than the old, are fighting on the same side of Egypt's most important post-Mubarak divide.

Tolba's beard – which tumbles all the way to his upper chest, black on the sides and grey in the middle – is the only aspect of his appearance that fits the media caricature of Salafists. The day in January 2014 when I visited him in his Cairo office, a cramped corner of a Zamalek Island residential block, he was dressed in a grey hoodie and an outsized red bomber jacket; an iPad was tucked under his arm. He greeted me with a wide-beam smile and looked pointedly at the iPad before rolling his eyes. 'I know, right – Salafists don't have iPads, they've never heard of Dell . . .' He showed me to a seat. 'People think all that stuff because Salafism is popular among the poor. The poor don't have laptops, but it's not because they're Salafists or anti-modern. It's because they're poor.'

Tolba was born to a liberal family and led a rebellious youth, up until the age of twenty-one, when a close friend of his died in a car accident on a mountain road in the Eastern Desert. 'It was a turning point, the sort of thing that either drives you away from or brings you closer to God.' He pushed back his glasses and ran a hand through tufts of short, curly hair. 'I decided to get closer.' When he eventually became a Salafist, Tolba's parents were appalled. 'They thought I would be dragged away by state security, or blow myself up as a terrorist. But I was happy – I'd found something in my life, and I felt satisfied with it.' His parents' apprehensions, though, were understandable. Salafism has many strains, but as a broad generalization its adherents take guidance from the original text of the Quran and Hadith; more recent theological scholarship is rejected. Although Tolba's religious identity had little in common with those responsible for Islamist terror attacks in Egypt during the 1990s, the regime's anti-insurgency crackdown fuelled official suspicion of any Muslim who placed himself outside the religious mainstream; the 9/11 attacks in 2001, and Egypt's subsequent participation in America's 'War on Terror', isolated Salafists even further and rendered them a direct target of the security forces. 'The lectures I went to were in secret locations – people's apartments, mainly, because Salafi preachers were kept out of mosques,' Tolba told me. 'We couldn't walk around in groups, or gather at a friend's home for dinner. If we did ever get together we'd have to leave and disperse before 10 p.m., because after that there were checkpoints on the road.' On one occasion, said Tolba, he and a group of friends had been playing PlayStation at a fellow Salafist's apartment and lost track of the time; suddenly, they realized it was 1 a.m., and the guests quickly left and went their separate ways. 'We had forgotten to check our watches because we were having such fun and were so relaxed. Four hours later, the security forces raided the apartment we'd been in. It was a fifth-floor apartment – they sent armed soldiers to guard every floor, from the first up to the eighth, then they hauled our friend out and into the road, blindfolded him and drove him away. Of course the first thing you have to do when you hear about something like that is delete the friend's number from your mobile. Because you know he is being questioned in a 'tough' way, and that he will be made to give names, and that you are probably next.' Tolba himself was detained twenty-two times before the revolution; he has never been charged with or convicted of any crime.

If there's one single incident that epitomizes Tolba's dislocation from the state in those difficult years, it was the time he attempted to drive to Hurghada, the beach resort on Egypt's mainland Red Sea coast. It was 2003, just after the start of the Iraq War and around the same time that Samira Ibrahim, almost 300 miles away, was sitting down to write the essay composition that would eventually land her father in jail and set her on a path to Tahrir Square. Tolba had only been a fully fledged Salafi for a year; just married, he decided to take his new wife for a holiday weekend. 'I was so excited that I had my swimming trunks on while driving so I could jump in the ocean as soon as we arrived.' After almost five hours in the car, the young couple drew up to a police checkpoint. 'The guy was surprised to see me,' recalled Tolba. 'He said, "Where are you going?" I told him I was going to Hurghada. The officer laughed, and said, "You're going to Hurghada? Why?" I told him I was going to swim. He shook his head and handed me back my licence "I'm sorry," he said, "but you can't use this road. You have to turn back." ' Tolba wanted to argue his case there and then, but there were soldiers with guns surrounding the vehicle and his wife was distressed. 'I took the U-turn, and we drove in silence. Eventually she fell asleep. I felt so down. You want to treat your wife, be a source of support and love for her, and instead she sees you being humiliated like this. I'm not a criminal, why should I be banned from a public road in my own country? As I drove back, I got angrier and angrier; it was late now, and getting dark. Then I suddenly thought, I don't have to put up with this.'

The only other highway into Hurghada was the mountain road through the Eastern Desert where his old friend had been killed, but despite his reservations Tolba decided to take it and swung around once again. 'I drove very fast because I wanted to get to Hurghada before my wife finished her sleep, and surprise her.' Tolba was tired, frustrated, and wracked by memories of his late friend, and the drive was gloomy and hazardous – but he almost pulled it off. About twelve miles outside the resort, though, he encountered another checkpoint; instead of waking up to sand and waves, Tolba's wife awoke to the sight of security forces brandishing automatic weapons at her. Tolba, still in his swimming trunks, got into a fight with officials and had his identity card seized at gunpoint; the couple were eventually let into Hurghada but he was ordered to report to the local state security headquarters the following day. 'It was my first time being interrogated in a state security office, though rooms like that would become a home from home over the following years. They do all the tricks: leave you waiting for hours, put you under a single light just like in the movies. They questioned me all day, and eventually told me I could go. As I got up I said, "I have a question." The security agent looked shocked. "You don't ask questions, I'm the only one with the right to ask questions," he replied. "Well, I will borrow your right for a minute and ask this," I said. "If I was a terrorist planning to bomb the city, do you think I would arrive with a full beard?"'

By the time Tolba was released, the weekend was over; he never did get to swim in the Red Sea. 'Want to know the first thing I did after Mubarak fell?' he asked me, grinning. 'I took my wife to Hurghada and went swimming.'

Tolba went on to do something else as well. In April 2011, he was invited to meet representatives from Mobinil, one of Egypt's biggest mobile phone networks, in his capacity as sales manager for a major international IT company. Tolba needed to brief his colleagues beforehand but many were out of the office, so he called one of the company's secretaries and asked her to schedule a meeting for everybody in a nearby branch of Costa Coffee. To his surprise, the secretary refused. 'She said, "No, I'm not falling for that one,"' Tolba recalled. 'I asked her what she meant. "You're making fun of me!" she replied. "What, a Salafist is going to have a meeting in Costa? And drink cappuccino?" Then she hung up on me. I was genuinely shocked.' When Tolba complained about the incident to other, non-Salafist colleagues, he discovered that they shared the secretary's incredulity that a man like him could or would ever enter a Western coffee franchise. In response, when Tolba returned home that night, he created a Facebook group named 'Salafyo Costa' (Costa Salafists) and invited all his colleagues to join. It was intended as an inside joke. Today, the group has more than 200,000 followers and has become a vibrant, online forum for multi-faith political discussion and cross-community engagement. There are Christians on the leadership board as well as Muslims, both Salafists and Muslim Brotherhood sympathizers. Under a circular maroon logo, which unapologetically rips off Costa's own, the group has produced awareness videos tacking everything from sectarian tensions to mental illness stigma, organized medical caravans to conflict flashpoints around the country, and joined demonstrations against anti-Christian violence and military rule. Most famously, they have put on inter-religious football matches – not with mixed teams, as Tolba is delighted to point out, but with Salafists lined up directly against Copts. 'Let's have a real experience!' he cried with enthusiasm. 'The government arranges all these official interfaith dialogues where old men that no one trusts any more kiss each other and pose for the cameras. There's nothing real about it. In a football match you have everything: the happy moments, the bad moments, the solidarity and fighting, the kicking and the swearing. Everyone sees the real side of each other, and they become closer because of it. It's not plastic, or artificial.'

Salafyo Costa and its larger-than-life founder offer an insight into the plurality and fragmentation of the Islamic landscape in Egypt, something conspicuously absent from the monolithic blocs of 'religious fundamentalists', 'religious minorities' and 'secular Egyptians' often depicted in the mainstream media. In the past, Salafists have tended towards isolation – in part due to the state repression exerted against them, but also because of a doctrinal inclination in favour of communal purity. 'It's partly down to choice,' said Tolba. 'We build our own islands, our own ghettos, and the discrimination just reinforces it.' Salafyo Costa is a bridge out of that isolationism, pursued enthusiastically by some, and it has angered senior members of the Salafi establishment: Sheikh Mohamed Abdel-Maqsoud, a leading Salafist authority, has condemned Tolba as 'compromised' and 'ignorant'. But Abdel-Maqsoud's irritation stems from more than a handful of multi-faith football matches. Part of what Salafyo Costa represents is a growing disengagement by ordinary Salafists from traditional leaders, a pattern repeated across the Islamic spectrum in Egypt – from Sufi orders to Sunni scholars at al-Azhar. When anti-Mubarak protests were first planned for 25 January 2011, those in positions of theological authority across nearly every strand of Islam in Egypt either ignored the event or directly prohibited their followers from participating; despite that, many deeply religious Egyptians opted to join the frontlines at Tahrir Square anyway. The subsequent toppling of Mubarak and the national flowering of a revolutionary discourse legitimized those independent thinkers. It also weakened the many sub-state religious autocrats who duplicated the state's paternalism, and could once depend upon the obedience of those below them.

This has been a source of major disruption within Islamist movements. The Salafists, for example, traditionally avoided political engagement but there are now several Salafi political parties. Tolba is one of many who have joined post-Mubarak revolutionary rallies against the instructions of senior sheikhs; he was injured in the Mohamed Mahmoud clashes of November 2011, when Egyptians rose up against military rule. The past half-decade, according to Islamist intellectual Ibrahim el-Houdaiby, has 'challenged the governing perceptions of leadership and led to a redistribution of power within Islamist groups ... The power of initiative-taking has been inspired and magnified by the revolution, and poses a clear challenge to the leadership of Islamist factions.'[4]

El-Houdaiby is well acquainted with this sort of tectonic movement. He was once a member of the Muslim Brotherhood, an organization modelled on strict notions of hierarchy and deference to one's elders. In the late 2000s though, throughout the years running up to revolution, he was among a group of young Brotherhood bloggers who exploited new forms of communication on the web to give the movement's youth cadres an unprecedented independent voice – one that was often explicitly critical of the Brotherhood's conservative leadership.* Most of these bloggers were eventually forced out of the

---

* There were of course incidences of Muslim Brotherhood speaking out against the movement's elders before the late 2000s. In a 2002 letter to *al-Hayat* newspaper for

organization and many went on to play prominent roles in the revolution: Abdelrahman Mansour became the Arabic administrator of the *Kullena Khaled Said* ('We are all Khaled Said') Facebook page which helped build the 25th January protest, for example, and Mostafa al-Naggar assumed a key position in Mohamed ElBaradei's National Movement for Change. But in the post-Mubarak era, the repudiation of paternal authority within groups like the Brotherhood has continued, and expanded. When the organization's guidance council expelled Abdel Munim Aboul Fotouh, a leading reformist within the movement, for going against the leadership's wishes and running for president, hundreds of young Brotherhood members followed him out of the door and formed their own breakaway party, *al-Tayyar al-Masry* ('The Egyptian Current').

Mohamed Tolba, who almost joined the Brotherhood himself before eventually opting for Salafism, believes that open opposition to gerontocracies – not just in the shape of the state itself, but within other institutions that dominate citizens' lives and help structure and delimit individual identities – is near-universal, and it has the old guard, be they Salafist, Brotherhood, Sufi or secular, intensely worried. 'Back in the early 2000s, when I was still being courted by the Brotherhood, I asked them what would happen if I disagreed with a decision taken by a Brotherhood leader,' Tolba told me. 'They said there was no space for disagreement, only obedience – we may give you the reasons for a decision or we may not, but either way you have to follow. I said not to all that and became a Salafist instead, now the revolution has spread this feeling everywhere.' Since Mubarak fell, the Salafist political party *al-Nour* ('The Light') has had to contend with its own internal youth rebellions, as has Mohamed ElBaradei's secular *el-Dostour* ('The Constitution') party; members of the latter held protest sit-ins at their own party's offices in both Cairo and Alexandria.[5] 'In Tahrir, I watched Marxists pitching tents next to

---

example, young members questioned the leadership's compliance with Egyptian state security forces and called for a greater embrace of street protests. But the frequency and reach of the dissent articulated by the 'Brotherhood bloggers' was a new phenomenon.

*al-Gama'a al-Islamiyya,** recalled Tolba. 'There's a big split in our country, but deep down I don't think it's a religious one.'

A moment earlier, Tony Sabri had grabbed my fingers from across the table and thrust them into his mouth. Now carefully, and slowly, he was sliding them one by one across his gums. A waiter drifted over to offer us some more coffee; after a single glance at the scene in front of him, he assumed a look of mortal terror and then turned on his heels and fled. I murmured something awkward and apologetic, but Sabri merely shrugged and made a grunting sound. It may have been a word, but with his mouth otherwise occupied it was somewhat hard to tell. Hedging my bets, I nodded vigorously in reply, wondering silently what exactly I was supposed to be feeling for. Sabri, who had matched a black T-shirt with thick-rimmed hipster eyeglasses, appeared entirely unperturbed. 'Ddjjjyyyuu sshhhhee?' he exclaimed finally, as I came across a small round bump, hard and protruding, above a broken tooth. He extricated my hand, and offered me a tissue. 'Birdshot, from police guns. I got it at *itthadeya*.† Apparently it's safer in than out.'

Sabri sports his battle scars with pride, and with good reason too. He is one of many Christian youths who have spent the past few years undermining father figures both national and closer to home; no mean feat for members of a community whose leader holds the title 'Patriarch of All Africa', among many others. The Coptic Church, believed to have been founded by Saint Mark the Evangelist on a visit to Egypt in the year AD 48, is one of the oldest Christian institutions in the world. Today, the Coptic pope presides over a flock that is at least 8 million strong, approximately 10 percent of Egypt's total population, and bolstered by a Coptic diaspora that stretches across Europe, North America and Australasia.[6] Copts have played a critical role in most of Egypt's great social and political transformations, including the 1919 revolutionary uprising and the opposition movement in the mid-2000s (one of Kefaya's most prominent founders, George Ishaq,

---

* 'The Islamic Group' – a formerly armed Islamist movement labelled as a terrorist organization by the US and the European Union.
† A reference to the clashes outside the presidential palace in December 2012, under Morsi's presidency.

is Christian), and they have not been afraid to hold power accountable within their own ranks either. The 115th Coptic Pope, Yousab II, was kidnapped by his own laity in 1954, after presiding over a period of mounting corruption and nepotism; he was eventually rescued by police, but forced to abdicate anyway a year later. Since then, though, the papal authorities have by and large kept a firm grip over internal dissent – aided in part by a close alliance with successive Egyptian governments, in which the pope lends political support to the ruling dictator and is, in return, recognized by the state as the sole political representative of the Coptic people.* Despite official rhetoric about national unity, the deal has allowed the Church to dominate every aspect of Coptic social life – walling the community in.[7] 'The Church from the beginning has been a regime of its own, a state within a state,' says Sabri. 'Shenouda [the pope in office for the entirety of Mubarak's reign] followed Mubarak everywhere.'

In the late 2000s though, much as younger followers of the Muslim Brotherhood were starting to challenge the concentrations of power within their own institution, the Coptic Church's absolutist clasp over its membership began to face some serious subversion of its own.[8] New lay groups formed to demand internal reform of Church institutions; at the same time, pressure was mounting over the Church's restrictive 'personal status' laws which prevented most Copts from being able to divorce and remarry, while tension over the Church's official response to sectarian assaults against Christians threatened to boil over. In many parts of Mubarak's Egypt, the decline of open civic space in which citizens could come together and develop a shared communal identity helped fuel a retreat into religious polarization, as did the growth of economic insecurity as a consequence of market reforms; with the state no longer providing many key services, citizens were forced to turn to rival religious establishments to fill the gap. When local disputes over dwindling public resources occurred, they often ended up assuming a sectarian

---

* A rare exception to this was when Pope Shenouda fell out with President Sadat in 1981 and was sent to internal exile at an ancient desert monastery. Soon afterwards, Sadat was assassinated; the Pope's exile came to an end under his successor, Hosni Mubarak.

hue, with Christians – nearly always the more marginalized of the communities – suffering the worst of any subsequent unrest.

On the night of 7 January 2010, Christian worshippers leaving a Coptic Christmas Eve church service in the Upper Egyptian town of Naga'a Hammadi were sprayed with bullets from a passing car; nine people died, including a Muslim passer-by. By the end of the year, a row over the construction of a new church in the Omraneya neighbourhood of Giza, in western Cairo, had led to open street battles between Copts and the security forces in which two Christians were killed. When I visited the area, soon after the clashes had taken place, I found the road towards the church littered with chunks of asphalt torn from the flyover above; around a set of children's funfair rides, a plastic splash of painted-neon off the pavement, lay spent tear gas canisters and the debris of broken Molotov cocktail bottles. I didn't realize it then, but this scenery was to become a familiar urban backdrop over the months and years to come. 'I fought for Egypt in the 1967 and 1973 wars, and was a PoW in Israel; you could say that I've spent the whole of my life on the frontline for my country,' Peter Gobrayel, a local Copt in Omraneya, told me. 'Now, speaking honestly, when I see the nation burning I just want to add petrol. I am an Egyptian first and foremost, and yet my country seems to want to eradicate me.'[9]

A few weeks later, on New Year's Day, a bomb exploded in Alexandria outside the Two Saints Church, as the congregation streamed out from a service; twenty-three people lost their lives. 'That's when I started joining the demonstrations,' Sabri explained. 'The official line from the priests and the pope was always "we don't retaliate". Two days after the bombing, one of the bishops publicly thanked Mubarak and [then interior minister] Habib al-Adly for all their "reconciliation efforts". But we'd had enough of the official line.' That night, and on subsequent ones, Coptic protests erupted on Cairo's streets; rocks were thrown by both demonstrators and riot troops, and police cars were set on fire.[10] 'We know who is organizing these demonstrations and who is taking part in them, and we do not agree with them,' Pope Shenouda said in a television interview, as the violence raged. He went on to reaffirm his support for Mubarak. 'It is in our nature to desire a quiet life,' he added. 'We don't like to take part in demonstrations or things like that.'[11] When I reminded Sabri of the pope's words, he snorted. 'I remember us facing down lines of security forces, and singing at them that a revolution was coming, that we wouldn't be slaves any more. That was just over a fortnight before January 25th. I guess we understood more about what was going on than the pope did.'

When the national revolution began, the highest echelons of the Church – like their senior counterparts in Islamic communities – ordered its members not to participate. In common with many of their fellow Muslim citizens, large numbers of Christians chose to ignore that order. At Tahrir, in Alexandria, throughout the Delta and in Suez, Copts and Muslims fought side by side to reclaim the streets from Mubarak's security forces; when the dust cleared, the Church's political legitimacy was in tatters. Radicalized Coptic youth, meanwhile, felt the wind at their backs. 'We were swapping phone numbers, making arrangements, forming new institutions of our own,' said Sabri. 'For as long as I could remember, old men in the Church spoke for us. Now we talked with our own voices.' Christians began a long-term sit-in on the road outside the Maspero state television headquarters, just north of Tahrir Square, and before long the Maspero Youth Union – the first of many revolutionary Coptic alliances which came together in open defiance of the Church leadership – was formed.* Sabri was a member, and the young man's activism landed him in military detention for three days. But his newfound friendships, including a close relationship with a fellow Coptic revolutionary named Mina Daniel, kept him bright-eyed and buoyant; despite the hardships, everyone was fired up by the future. Then came 9 October.

Sabri unspooled his memories from that day in between a series of long and intensely focused silences; each was filled by the sounds of tinny pop music emanating from the café's speakers and other mundane noises from the land of the living, and by the tears which slowly

---

* Maspero was chosen by Christians as a site of protest to distinguish their activities from the occupation of nearby Tahrir Square; there were fears Coptic protests in Tahrir would be subsumed into the broader revolutionary movement, and possibly provoke sectarian hostility. Maspero was also closely associated with the state media apparatus, which many Christians believed was responsible for stoking anti-Coptic bias, and had been a rallying point for the community before the revolution as well.

clouded Sabri's eyes. The protest march that afternoon, from the northern Cairene neighbourhood of Shubra to Maspero, had been called in response to a dispute over the destruction of a church in Aswan; in reality, though, it was also an affirmation by Copts of their right to rally, in the face of a Church leadership which still believed it could arrogate its members' political voices for itself. Demonstrators came under attack long before they reached Maspero – stones were thrown at them from a bridge above Shubra Street, and more violence broke out near the *al-Ahram* newspaper buildings soon afterwards – but it was only when they made it to the Nile, around the corner of the Ramses Hilton hotel tower, that the army's massacre truly began. 'Some people had already been shot dead by the time the APCs arrived,' said Sabri. 'They drove through the crowd and crushed us, again, and again and again. It was like using the other end of a pencil, when you keep going back to rub something out.' On video recordings of the atrocity, filmed from above, you can see the squat armoured personnel carriers twist and turn and zig-zag into densely packed swarms of protesters on the road, who scatter away in all directions before regrouping in the space left behind, like a school of fish trying to escape a snapping shark. After each pass, in the APCs' wake, a few more still bodies remain lying on the tarmac. Eventually, one of the military vehicles takes a run-up and slams on to the raised pavement at the bottom of the 6th October bridge, where dozens had thronged in the hope that it might prove a refuge from the slaughter. First you see the carrier's giant front wheels rise high in the air and fall, as they encounter and then flatten some formerly living resistance. The rear wheels follow suit, before the APC clanks back down on to the road and drives on. Before 9 October I had never imagined what it might look like to ram a box of hard, reinforced metal at high speed into a soft mound of human flesh. At Maspero, Egypt's military generals showed us all.

Mina Daniel, Sabri's friend, was walking at the front of the march that day. Born in an Upper Egyptian village near Assyut, Daniel was raised by his older sister Mary and brought to Cairo as a young child. 'We couldn't stay there,' Mary told me when I visited her home – a small apartment in a crowded Ezbet el-Nakhl block up towards the ring road, north-west of the airport. The scratched green walls were hung with pictures of saints and photos of Daniel; below a flickering light in the hallway was a revolutionary sticker declaring 'Strikes Are Legal Against Poverty and Starvation' in Arabic, and a small framed tapestry that spelled out 'Love Never Fails' in English. 'It was all the time. My uncle was listening to a verse from the Holy Book once, and was beaten on the back of the head for it. When members of our family complained to the police, we were arrested. Cairo felt like it would be an escape, a new start. The cycle of life is different, there's less time for sectarianism.'

In el-Nakhl the family's existence was tough and precarious, but living in a huge metropolis exposed young Daniel to sights he'd never seen before – fabulous wealth, grinding poverty, the novelty of an air-conditioned bus. 'He was always so interested in the world around him, so keen to grow his awareness,' said Mary, who is in her early forties. She was wearing a red-checked gown and as we talked she turned her face up towards the light, her eyes squeezed tight. Through the open window, which overlooked a dark and narrow alleyway, flies buzzed around each other and the high-pitched babble of a children's cartoon show floated up from another flat below. 'He looked like a Pharaonic man. Even as a child he had the mentality of a wise, old person: he intervened in arguments to bring them to an end, he was never materialistic, never interested in money or clothes or shoes.' After school, Daniel wanted to study archaeology but never got the grades; he turned to street politics instead. In those early days of Coptic youth activism, Daniel was at the forefront – not in drawing sectarian battlelines against Muslim neighbours, but in persuading everyone to frame their struggle around social justice instead. People said he resembled Che Guevera, and Daniel cultivated the image: he kept his hair long and shaggy, and often quoted the Argentine revolutionary in his political conversations. He was vehemently opposed to Christian-only demonstrations. On one occasion before the revolution, when sectarian tensions flared in the working-class Cairene neighbourhood of Bulaq following a Coptic protest against discrimination, Daniel spoke with both sides. 'He told them, why are you fighting each other? Both Muslims and Christians are poor, both can't find proper housing, both are suffering,' recalls a friend. 'In the end, the Muslims joined the Christians in the protest. Mina had that kind of charisma . . . When he talked, people listened.' [12] Mary told me that her younger brother, despite being frustrated in his chosen career, remained fascinated by history and certain that better education and an appreciation for the past could help bring Egypt's problems to an end. 'The Pharaohs are my grandfathers, he always said.'

At Maspero, Daniel was shot dead by an army soldier with a single bullet to the shoulder. He was twenty years old. Mary, who had been further back than Mina when the violence started, was fighting to escape the gas blooms and confusion when she found out that Mina had been hit. On state television, news anchors had been showing edited footage of the bloodshed and telling those watching at home that soldiers were under attack by Christians; a call was issued for citizens to 'come and protect your armed forces'. In central Cairo, groups of Muslims took to the streets with knives; others came down from their homes to protect Coptic protesters. 'I could hear anti-Christian chants through the smoke,' said Mary. 'Everything was in chaos, one moment you would come across pools of blood, the next minute a thug armed with a sword.' Mary and some other demonstrators found a taxi willing to let them in, and they drove fast towards the Coptic Hospital where Daniel had been taken; she thought he had only been wounded. 'On the way I got a phone call from people there. I asked how Mina's injuries were, and they said, "Mina is not injured. He is a martyr now."'

Out of all the 'snapshots of horror', as he describes them, that Tony Sabri witnessed that day – a soldier aiming a gun at his head before turning at the last moment to fire at someone else instead, corpses tumbling into the Nile, an older priest stumbling through the carnage in order to reach bodies lying in the road so that he could gently close their eyes – the one he remembers most vividly is the sight of Daniel, face creased into a grin, waving back at him in Shubra Street as the march got under way. A few hours later, Sabri caught a brief glimpse of his friend through the tear gas smog, throwing stones at the APCs that were mowing demonstrators down, trying to stop them in their tracks. He never saw Daniel alive again. "He was the best man that I ever loved, and I lost him," said Sabri. 'I think we went from whispering "down with military rule" that day, to screaming it at the top of our lungs.'

Twenty-eight people lost their lives at Maspero; several years later, the only people to have faced justice are three soldiers, each handed down a jail sentence of between two and three years for negligent driving.* Two Christian survivors have also been jailed, for allegedly handling army weaponry. At the time, before the uprising the following month which almost brought Egypt's military government to its knees, no one knew quite what to make of the massacre politically; it was only after the Mohamed Mahmoud clashes, where the battlelines between revolutionaries and the army became so visibly entrenched, that the events of 9 October were retrospectively incorporated into the revolutionary canon. Victims faced a double erasure: death at the wheels of military vehicles and death again through being refused any acknowledgement or presence in the public realm, where government officials and army spokesmen issued brazen denials that any massacre had taken place. But political deaths are living things, contingent on the politics around them. Less than one year later, both regime stalwart Ahmed Shafik and the Brotherhood's Mohamed Morsi used images of Mina Daniel in their election campaign for president, appropriating his memory to boost their own revolutionary credentials in the hopes of furthering what would turn out, in both cases, to be their own counter-revolutionary bids for power.

Another year on, the memory of Maspero became contested once again, as the army carried out another massacre of demonstrators in Cairo – this time of Muslim Brotherhood supporters at Rabaa and Nahda squares – and debates raged among revolutionaries about what lines of connection could be drawn between the two events. Ultimately, although the killings occurred in very different contexts and cannot be equated with each other, I believe they do share a common thread. Both were enacted by a military determined to publicly accentuate the state's prohibition against popular protest. And on both occasions they did so by targeting a community whose identity

---

* The full verdict, reached by a military court in September 2012, was on the charge of 'involuntary manslaughter'. It found the soldiers in question guilty of 'negligence and absence of caution, while driving armoured personnel carriers in an arbitrary fashion . . . leading to them hit the victims'.

had been shifted by the state outside the borders of the national family, a community that the generals knew few would dare to rally behind. For that reason, Maspero – not just for its brutality, but for the insight it provided into the struggles yet to come – was terrible, and emblematic. As Mosireen activist Sherief Gaber has written, 'Maspero was not the last massacre we would see, but it remains singular as a pivot on which so much other political memory swings.'[13]

Since Maspero, the Christian community, much like the Brotherhood and the Salafists, has been further fractured by dissent from within. Pope Shenouda passed away in March 2012; his successor, Pope Tawadros – whose name was drawn from a chalice by a blindfolded altar boy, out of the three that made it to the final shortlist – has continued to align himself to the old state, and appeared alongside Sisi on live television when the latter announced his popular coup. Tawadros's public support for the constitutional referendum that paved the legal path to Sisi's presidency provoked a massive backlash among the younger laity, as did his comments about the Arab revolutions being an 'Arab Winter' engineered by people with 'malicious motives'. In 2014, when asked questions about the Sisi regime's human rights record, the pope replied, 'You want to talk about human rights while there is terror and crime?'[14] A senior bishop, admitting that the organized Church had attempted to mobilize votes for Sisi, insisted that this was about 'patriotism, not politics'.[15] In a display of defiance, worshippers at the main Coptic cathedral in Cairo have, since the ascension of Tawadros, sometimes used coordinated silences to signal their disapproval of the government whenever the names of political leaders are mentioned from the pulpit.[16]

In the aftermath of Morsi's downfall and the Rabaa massacre, the Maspero Youth Union has had to contend with splits and internal turmoil, as has Mohamed Tolba's Salafyo Costa movement. The military generals have sought survival through social polarization and the erosion of sub-state solidarities, and no group of Egyptians, however radical, has entirely managed to escape the lines of division they have sown. But increasingly, the revolution's own battlelines are clear. Alongside Islamists and 'secular' activists, Coptic youths defying the government's anti-protest law have been among those swept up in Sisi's 'War on Terror'. Many have been charged with 'membership of

a banned terrorist organization' (the Muslim Brotherhood). On protesting that they are Christian, not Muslim, some have had their legal
accusation rewritten to accuse them of membership of the April 6th
group, the anti-regime revolutionary movement that has no religious
affiliation; others have simply been ignored. In the end, the juridical
details don't matter. For the state, the task is simply to shift any rebels
outside the familial fold, using whatever indictments are at hand. The
goal is to place dissent beyond the realm of the possible, however
absurd the formalities.

Some Egyptians have fought back in imaginative and admirably
absurd ways of their own. In 2013, a campaign to cover up the 'religion' field on national ID cards – the carrying of which is mandatory
by all citizens – gained momentum: many stuck paper over the text
which identified them as either Muslim, Christian or Jewish (the only
three options) and scrawled 'none of your business' over the top of it
instead. One enterprising citizen replaced their religion simply with
the word 'Sponge', from 'Spongebob Squarepants'. 'Critics have misunderstood the campaign's point. It is not a campaign against religion
or religious identity,' explained British-Egyptian journalist Sarah
Carr, who started the trend.[17] 'It is about preventing the state from
poking its nose in matters that do not concern it . . . and from having
any role in defining, controlling or exploiting religious identity.' But as
long as the counter-revolution prevails, behind pious official homilies
about Christians and Muslims being as one, the generals must and
will ensure that the religious identity of every citizen remains uncovered
and firmly on display. To prevent the virus of new politics from spreading, Egypt's old guard must transform the people into carriers for
despotism – and to that end, the sharp demarcation of religious identities is a weapon that Mubarak Country desperately needs.

For seven long hours after Samira Ibrahim was first attacked in the
gardens of the Egyptian Museum, she remained trapped in what she
calls 'a party of torture', alongside dozens of other protesters snatched
by soldiers from Tahrir. 'They were throwing water over our bodies,
then applying electric shocks. It was like a television being turned on
and off, on and off. We would faint for moments at a time, and then
wake up. And I was thinking all the while, I was thinking a thousand

times in my head: are you the people we carried on our shoulders? We celebrated you!' At one point a civilian who had somehow got into the grounds pleaded with officers to let the women go. 'We know these girls,' he told the general in charge, 'Let us take them home and we won't let them come again – if they do, then take them!' The general refused, telling the man that Samira and the others had been found in a whorehouse. After darkness fell, the protesters were loaded on to buses and taken to the C28 military prison on the Cairo – Ismailia desert road. There they were made to pose for photographs with bottles that looked like Molotov cocktails, screamed at by officers who told them they had ruined the country, and beaten in shifts throughout the night. Officers told them that anyone who spoke would be buried.

In the morning, Ibrahim was taken into a room with a large window and an open door where a female medic was waiting. Ibrahim presumed she was going to be patted down and searched, but the woman told her to take off all her clothes. Around the door and on the other side of the window, male soldiers and officers were watching and laughing. Samira asked the medic to close the door and window; in response a male officer entered the room, hit her and electrocuted her. She was returned to her cell. Later soldiers separated the female prisoners into 'girls' (unmarried) and 'women' (married); Samira was in the first group. An officer announced he was going to check whether or not they were prostitutes. Samira recounts what happened next:

> They took the girls one by one. I didn't object, didn't talk. Then the woman said, 'Lie down, for "Sir" to examine you.' 'Sir' was dressed in army colours. I took off my pants, they told me to raise my legs. And I . . . A man? Was going to examine me? I was naked, it was like a show with people watching, all those officers and soldiers. I asked her to please reduce their numbers. The man electrocuted me in the stomach and I was getting very badly insulted. I surrendered. If this is a doctor – what is he checking for five whole minutes? You answer that question for me! It's just humiliation, they're breaking you. They are breaking you so you don't even think of asking for Egypt's rights, so that you don't even consider demonstrating against oppression.

He's an officer, dressed in army clothes. She was standing near my head. I even asked her to cover me, and move to the side. No. One of them was playing with his mobile. Look at the degree of humiliation, look how much they humiliate you. How much they break ... How much they break you. After he 'examined' me, he told me I have to sign a statement that I'm a 'girl' – meaning a virgin [...]

They put us back in the cells after the examination, they took each group back to its cell. I was in shock. I had never imagined that they would do something like this. Not in my wildest thoughts would I have expected this from them. The surprise was that they had special forces – practising on us. The people who went quiet after going home, it's because of what they've seen. Now I expect anything from them, they're capable of anything. After what I saw the army do, nothing can surprise me [...]

On that day, I truly wished for death. I kept telling myself people get heart attacks, why don't I just have one and die? Whatever I tell you about that day, if only that was enough for them [...] They humiliated us. They humiliated, do you understand? We wished we were dead. I felt envy. Others had died, why couldn't I have died too? Why wasn't I dead?[18]

Some months later, an up-and-coming SCAF general defended the army's forced invasion of Ibrahim's genitals along with those of six other female protesters, by claiming it was necessary to carry out so-called 'virginity tests' (an examination to check whether the hymen is intact, even though the result provides no conclusive indicators of virginity).[19] 'The procedure was done to protect the girls from rape, as well as to protect the soldiers and officers from rape accusations,' said the general.[20] Ibrahim was raped to stop her claiming she was raped, ran the general's argument; only a rapist state could defend its women's honour. That general's name was Abdel Fattah el-Sisi.

There is nothing new about the use of military doctors to impose control over Egyptian women's bodies. The country's first school for girls, which opened in 1832 in the Ezbekiya Gardens district of Cairo, specialized in midwifery. Subsequent historians have hailed it as a key pillar of the nineteenth-century Egyptian *nahda* ('renaissance') under Mohamed Ali – but after a close study of the archives, contemporary historian Khaled Fahmy reached a different conclusion. 'The school was not established with the purpose of disseminating knowledge, let alone "empowering women," he has written, 'rather, its main purpose was to serve the new army founded by Ali a few years earlier.'[21] The chief task of newly trained midwives was to check prostitutes for sexually transmitted diseases that could disable soldiers who visited them; just as important, though, was their role as forensic doctors in police stations, where they performed virginity tests on women whose male relatives suspected them of having extra-marital sex. Documentation arising from these examinations could be used by men to claim compensation from the offending party. "Police records are replete with cases in which the female medical practitioner used degrading phrases, such as "She was found to have been previously used," and "The hymen was torn a long time ago," observes Fahmy. The impulse to categorize female citizens through a strict duality – obedient mother or daughter on the one hand, fallen whore on the other – is hardwired into the DNA of the modern Egyptian state; almost two centuries later, the language of institutional patriarchy has barely changed. 'The girls who were detained were not like your daughter or mine,' claimed Major General Ismail Etman, one of Sisi's SCAF colleagues, in relation to the virginity tests.[22]

For many protesters, one of the most electrifying elements of the Tahrir occupation was simply how different it looked. The visible, public presence of Egyptians who paid no heed to Etman's binaries – that felt like a revolution in itself. Kholoud Bidak, a radical feminist in her thirties who has become one of Egypt's leading campaigners for marginalized social groups, told me that on her first glance at the square, she became '100 per cent sure' that more than anywhere else in the world at that moment, *this* was the place she most wanted to be. 'I could see women, I could see groups of LGBT Egyptians, and I'm not only referring to people whose sexual identities I already knew. I'm talking about people I'd never seen before, and their appearance. I mean, you could just tell. I'm talking about dykes, I'm talking about gay men with make-up, I'm even talking about transgender Egyptians. They were there, and they were standing proud.

Because this thing that we had started, this thing that Tahrir had become, it was so much bigger than someone criticizing how you look. We had taken the square and the feeling was simply "What can we do now?" It was such a spontaneous feeling that we didn't even need to discuss it: of course we will spend the night in here, of course this is the street, and of course it's ours.

'Well, you can make fun of me for saying this, but . . . I would say I'm quite a realistic person. The definition of utopia is something I'd read about a lot of times, and whenever I'd discuss the word with friends or lovers or whoever, we'd agree that you might find a moment of utopia but it could never actually manifest itself as a place, because you can't really live such a thing. It needs to be outside this galaxy, somewhere else. But I really found utopia during those eighteen days. Really. There are no words to describe it. You can take as many sentences as you want, and you can arrange them in a paragraph however you want, and still: the people who were there will understand what I mean, and the people who weren't will not.'

Reclaimed places like Tahrir were communal sites, but they also enabled the creation of intensely individual realms in which personal identities could be interrogated, sifted and owned. As conventional social precepts were being challenged on the streets, though, not least the exclusion of women from public space, institutional politics strove to reinstate them.

When Mubarak fell, the body that replaced him the Supreme Council of the Armed Forces – (SCAF) – was comprised entirely of men. One of SCAF's first acts was to appoint a committee overseeing amendments to the constitution: a committee comprised entirely of men. In the meantime, day-to-day running of the country was delegated to an interim government comprised entirely of men, with the single exception of Fayza Aboul al-Naga – an unreconstructed Mubarakist who was to remain Egypt's only female minister for the rest of its revolutionary 'transition'. SCAF's championing of gender inequality was abetted by a popular association of formal women's rights, particularly in the area of political representation, with the Mubarak regime – just at a time when the Mubarak regime was political poison. Mubarak-era legislation that had established quotas for female MPs in parliamentary elections was now dismissed by opponents as one of 'Suzanne's Laws' (named after Suzanne Mubarak, the president's wife and chair of the state-run National Council for Women), and successfully abolished. The result was that in the 2011–12 parliamentary elections, the first of their kind in post-Mubarak Egypt, only seven women won seats – 2 per cent of the total.* The commencement of Morsi's presidency six months later did nothing to redress the institutionalized exclusion of women at the top of the Egyptian state. Morsi had promised if elected to appoint a woman to the vice-presidency and publicly decried the absence of women in senior leadership positions, insisting his government would 'put an end to any attempts to marginalize women, diminish their rights, or suppress their freedom and dignity'.[23] Like most of his guarantees regarding democratic pluralism, Morsi's rhetoric turned out to be worthless: no female was ever made vice-president, and only two women were granted places in his thirty-strong cabinet. Of the hundred Egyptians tasked by Morsi with drafting the constitution that would supposedly protect and empower every citizen and define Egypt for a generation, ninety-four were male.

Morsi's leeriness at the idea of women occupying political roles was grounded in his organization's regressive gender politics. The Brotherhood's ideological lens on the subject can be seen in an article on their Arabic-language website back in 2007, entitled 'Your daughter is a wife of the future – how should you prepare her?!' The piece explains that children are a gift from God and given to guardians for safekeeping and protection. As such, it is a mother's duty to prepare the daughter for her inevitable future role as an adult: namely as a keeper of cleanliness and order in the home. 'A girl in a house is like basil and so she must leave a good impression,' the article says. 'The most laudable characteristic that we want to inculcate in girls from an early age is cleanliness. It is not a trifling matter but rather must be inculcated in girls from when they are small.'[24] As Osama Salama, a 'family expert' for the Brotherhood, puts it: 'A woman needs to be confined within a framework that is controlled by the man of the house.'[25] The corollary of women belonging in the home is that they

---

* Two more women were included among the bloc of ten MPs unilaterally appointed by SCAF.

are trespassers elsewhere; this perpetual undercurrent of expulsion rests on the notion of female bodies as 'precious stones' or 'fragile candies' (both examples of imagery used in Brotherhood literature)[26] – always inanimate objects, always unwelcome on the public stage, and always at fault if they place themselves outside the secure, protective glow of the family.

This undercurrent bubbled below the 'jurisprudential' decision made by the organization in 2007 to forbid women from the Egyptian presidency.[27] It's the undercurrent that led Morsi's government to reject a global UN declaration calling for an end to violence against women and a recognition of their autonomous social, cultural and sexual rights. 'This declaration, if ratified, would lead to complete disintegration of society, and would certainly be the final step in the intellectual and cultural invasion of Muslim countries, eliminating the moral specificity that helps preserve cohesion of Islamic societies,' decried the Brotherhood in a press release. Warning that the declaration would 'destroy the family, the basic building block of society', the Brotherhood went on to outline 'what decadence awaits our world, if we sign this document': contraception, the criminalization of marital rape, the replacement of 'guardianship with partnership' and the cancellation of the need for a husband's consent if women want to travel or work were all among the consequences cited. 'These are destructive tools meant to undermine the family as an important institution; they would subvert the entire society, and drag it to pre-Islamic ignorance,' concluded the statement.[28] And it's the undercurrent that fuelled the Brotherhood's continued defence of female genital mutilation under the Morsi administration, despite the practice being unlawful in Egypt.[29] Egyptian academic Mariz Tadros has said that mutilating bodies is the Muslim Brotherhood's gift to Egyptian women.[30]

The Brotherhood's misogyny warrants the fiercest resistance – and yet much of the backlash against it, both within Egypt and abroad, has done little more than reproduce the patriarchal assumptions that critics claim to oppose. In fact, almost every discussion of gender in post-Mubarak Egypt, even by those who view themselves as on the progressive side of the argument, has tended to involve the reduction of women to passive ciphers. Whether it is the Brotherhood treating females as objects that must remain pure and untouched so as to better represent nation and faith and to defend a particular set of values against Western imperialism, or whether it is the Brotherhood's enemies touting the exposure of female hair and flesh as a yardstick for cultural liberation and modernity, women's bodies are invariably cast as social signifiers in a way that men's bodies never are. At the time of Morsi's inauguration, for example, sections of the Egyptian media went into hysterics over the appearance of his wife, who wore a headscarf and preferred the traditional name Umm Ahmed ('Mother of Ahmed') to her legal name, Naglaa Ali Mahmoud. 'She can't be an image for the "ladies" of Egypt,' argued one Zamalek banker. 'If you travel to New York or wherever, people would make fun of you and say: "Your first lady wears the *abaya*, hahaha,"' observed an engineering student, adding, 'Previous first ladies used to be elegant.'[31] What was at stake here was not the agency of Umm Ahmed, but the exploitation of her as an inert symbol of *difference*, one that the Zamalek banker and the engineering student were using in an attempt to confer superiority on themselves. 'We Egyptians love representations,' wrote the academic Zainab Magdy in an article on the furore. 'We don't want to be told how to dress; but we want to tell Umm Ahmed that she should dress in certain way because she represents Egyptian women ... The obvious question is, was Ms Suzanne Mubarak a representative of those who reject Ms Ali? The more I read about Ms Ali, the more it hits me how deep the conviction [is] that women are objects to be told how to dress because they represent something: a country, other women, a religion, their family, their upbringing and so on and so on. And the saddest thing is the women are propagating this thought without realizing its danger.'[32]

Umm Ahmed's headwear was a pretext for Egypt's rich to demonize the poor, but this sort of objectification can be found well beyond the Egyptian upper classes. On her blog, feminist writer Sara Salem has collected a number of European campaign or advocacy posters over the years that use Muslim and Arab female bodies to demonize Muslims and Arabs: a mocked-up photo by the International Society of Human Rights, a German NGO, which equates the status of a woman in a *burqa* to that of rubbish bags (tagline: 'Oppressed women are easily overlooked'); two pictures set alongside each other by a right-wing political party in Sweden, one depicting four young, naked female models standing in pristine water, the other showing older women with headscarves bathing in a muddy pool. The notion that women's 'status' can be evaluated primarily through their hair, skin and shrouding, and that the visibility of female bodies must be *the* metric of gender progress, is one that has characterized external coverage of the revolution from the beginning, fuelling a journalistic obsession with 'finding' Egyptian women on the streets and detailing their clothes and headwear (or lack of) whenever quoting them. What is ultimately being signposted in this sort of coverage is the supposed gulf between oppressed women *there* and liberated women back home in the West. By concentrating on objects like the headscarf that are visibly foreign and different, this sort of 'gender sensitive' reporting often masks bigger questions which aren't so easily 'detached' from the West: the exploitation of women in Egypt's export-orientated textile factories, for example, or the violence inflicted upon women by a state which enjoys the West's political and financial support.

Of course this sort of gender discourse is also shorn of historical context. Eight hundred years ago many women were treated like slaves in Europe, while females in some parts of the Islamic empire enjoyed significant rights and power; the reality is that neither Islamic nor European culture is homogenous, and neither is historically immutable. It relies, too, upon extrapolations that are never applied to the West: Morsi's misogyny, for example, is taken to represent a general Muslim and Arab 'problem' with women, whereas sexist remarks made by the British prime minister, David Cameron, in parliament, or the fact that his government's austerity policies have been shown to disproportionately impoverish women,[33] or indeed the misogynistic antics of the political Christian right in the US, carry no such equivalent meaning for Christianity or the West. When it comes to Egypt, however, everything is framed through the plight of oppressed women. Within this clichéd mould – repressive Muslim men, passive Muslim women – even the outliers gain currency. When an entirely fake story surfaced about Egypt's new Islamist parliament preparing to introduce a law legalizing necrophilia (the 'farewell intercourse' legislation would apparently 'allow husbands to have sex with their deceased wives up to six hours after death' – women don't get more passive than that), global media outlets such as the feminist blog *Jezebel*, the *Daily Mail*, the *Huffington Post* and Swedish newspaper giant *Dagens Nyheter* all regurgitated it, even though the briefest minute of web searching or phone-calling would immediately have revealed it to be a hoax.[34] Such idious doesn't arise from nowhere: it's the product of a false dichotomy that presents all Arab women as static emblems for one cultural ecosystem or another, a champion for either the bikini or the *burqa*.[35] 'In both cases, it is not women's best interests that are at heart,' argues Sara Salem. 'Women who cover their hair in the Netherlands are seen as oppressed by their own culture/religion/men; and women who wear miniskirts in Cairo are seen as oppressed by consumerism and a culture obsessed with women's bodies and sex. And within these binary discourses, how free are we, as women, to choose what we want to wear, be, think, feel, or do?'*

One evening in late 2012, Mariam Kirollos was walking through a large protest rally in Tahrir when she heard screaming. Kirollos, the young woman who was attacked by a car driver back in 2008 and forced to take refuge in a pharmacy, had become intimately acquainted with the square and its rhythms ever since the first day of the revolution, when she defied her parents by pinning a note reading 'Down with Mubarak' on her bedroom door and escaping out to join the demonstrations. Like Kholoud Bidak, Kirollos used the word 'utopia' when talking to me about the eighteen-day anti-Mubarak uprising, and the visibility of women in this public, political arena. 'You had the *niqabi* women, the women with the veil, the women with the *hijab*, the women with the hair, the woman with the short dress, the

---

* Public debate over women's agency amid the revolution spiked in October 2011, when a twenty-year-old Egyptian woman, Aliaa al-Mahdy, posted a nude picture of herself online, above a statement reading: 'Put on trial the artists' models who posed nude for art schools until the early 70s, hide the art books and destroy the nude statues of antiquity, then undress and stand before a mirror and burn your bodies that you despise to forever rid yourselves of your sexual hangups before you direct your humiliation and chauvinism and dare to try to deny me my freedom of expression.' The post was viewed nearly 10 million times. Al-Mahdy later left Egypt and allied herself with 'Femen', the Paris-based self-described 'sextremist' feminist group who have faced accusations of Islamophobia.

woman who is painting, the woman who is taking pictures, and it just felt great,' she said. 'It felt amazing.' After Mubarak fell, Kirollos became a prominent figure at revolutionary gatherings, leading protest chants and – to the amazement of bystanders – carrying a large drum. ('If women in Egypt are expected to play instruments at all,' Kirollos explained, 'it's the piano or violin. Never the drum!') The sonic might of street marches was intoxicating; sometimes she drummed so intensely, for so long, that her fingers started bleeding. On this particular evening though, the 22-year-old had left her drum at home.

Stories of mass sexual assaults at protests, of the type carried out by the Mubarak regime at the opposition rally outside the Journalists' Syndicate in 2005, had been circulating for months, and multiplying. Kirollos and a few friends had decided to wear pink ribbons and move around Tahrir together, scouring it for any signs of attack. She was just on her way to pick up her ribbon when she heard the cries, and instinctively ran towards them. 'It was a woman, and she was in a fucked-up state,' Kirollos told me. 'She was saying "it's my fault", over and over again, "it's my fault, it's my fault . . ." At that stage I didn't know how to deal with survivors of sexual assault, so I just hugged her and just said, "My name is Mariam Kirollos, here is my phone number," and I repeated this maybe about a dozen times. And she hugged me. I took her away. I was really stupid, and did everything you shouldn't do – starting with asking her what happened. She explained that she had been surrounded, that three of her friends were still trapped inside the attackers' circle and she couldn't reach them, and she just kept saying "I can't, I can't . . .". I made sure she got out safely, and then found all these men surrounding me and shouting, "Why is she crying, stop her crying, she shouldn't be crying." All I could feel was that at this point I didn't want to see a single man in front of me. Suddenly I looked up at them and said, "If it wasn't for you and your dicks, and how you act and . . . She should cry! She should scream! She should punch you in the face!" I was going crazy, because I was not only witnessing sexual violence, but I was also witnessing how this sexual violence is socially represented and diminished. I was furious.'

From Mubarak through to military rule, Mohamed Morsi, and

then back to the generals once again, successive leaders of the Egyptian state have presided over an institutionalized epidemic of violence directed against the bodies of Egyptian citizens who dare to enact political presence by joining protests in the street. Security forces have exploited tropes of passive femininity to target both men and women, attempting to 'emasculate' the former through sexual assaults and re-impose state-centric masculinities in the process. But it is women who have borne the brunt of sexual violence at demonstrations. Most attacks follow the same grim pattern. The first common feature is isolation; in the crowds, friends are separated from each other, and the targets find themselves surrounded by at least one ring of men. As Egyptian newspaper *Ahram Online* summarized in February 2013, 'a group of men usually form two lines and begin snaking through the square, while chanting and singing. Once they find a victim – usually one or two women standing alone – the group forms a U-shape and then a complete circle around them, trapping them inside.'[36] Sometimes the attackers form several concentric circles to help them fend off any attempts from outside to stop the assault. According to Hatem Tallima, of the Revolutionary Socialists, 'The men in the circle immediately surrounding the woman begin to strip the girl. The second circle includes men who claim that they are helping the girl. The third circle try to distract the people in the square from what is happening.'

The next common feature is disorientation; in a flurry of hands, fists and shouts, the protester's sense of space and time is blurred and they find it impossible to distinguish potential allies from attackers. 'Some looked like thugs, some looked like normal people,' remembers Yasmine el-Baramawy, who was pinned by a mob to a car bonnet in Tahrir at a November 2012 protest against Morsi's constitutional declaration; her attackers whispered, 'We are going to fuck you' in her ear and left her covered in blood and excrement.[37] 'It was as if I was in a washing machine, being pushed and pulled and grabbed,' she says. 'I didn't know what was happening to me or when it would end. I thought that I would faint or die. But I didn't.'

The third common feature is extreme violence; far more than delivering sexual gratification for the individual attackers, the assault is clearly aimed at terrorizing the protester and anyone else who might consider demonstrating on the streets. Weapons are often used, not only to remove layers of clothing quickly – a process which can leave gaping wounds on the protester's body – but also to penetrate the genitals; on several occasions blades, sometimes blunted, sometimes sharp, have been used to rape women. Even when no weapons appear, the intensity of the attacks has been exceptional. 'The way they were throwing me around was as if I was a not a human, but a piece of garbage,' recounts a journalist who was attacked in June 2012 while covering protests, and taken to a nearby apartment building. 'Again I was surrounded, this time from all sides in the middle of the floor. There was even a man lying on the floor being stepped on by the others, forcing his fingers between my legs. That happened from all sides and more fingers at the same time. I was sure that they wouldn't stop before I was lying dead in that hallway. I really tried to fight and protect my body but it was impossible. Every time I tried to kick out more hands were between my legs and every time I tried to hit someone or remove hands, my shirt was even more ripped and my breasts pulled. For one second, I had the chance to hurt one of the men back. I pressed my finger, with all the power I had left, in one of his eyes but he just continued hurting me with his fingers.'[38]

The fourth common feature is an explicit link between the violence of the state and the violence being meted out against the protester. Sally Zohney, an anti-harassment activist, recalls being shoved inside a clothing store during the June 2012 rallies – in a desperate attempt to fend off the attackers, the women working in the store were pushing on the glass door to keep it closed, while the attackers attempted to force it open from the outside. 'I heard the attackers screaming, "Get out! We'll have a party on you, just like the police!" ' The Arabic phrase *ihtafal 'ala* ('to have a party' on someone) is used colloquially to mean hurting or humiliating someone and taking pleasure in their pain;[39] the echoes in language used by government security forces and supposedly 'civilian' mobs is no coincidence. In a similar vein, when Ola Shahba, an activist with the Socialist Popular Alliance, was assaulted outside the presidential palace during the November 2012 protests, she found it wasn't only Salafists and Muslim Brotherhood supporters who were seeking to violate her bodily integrity (some yelled, 'You hate God this much?' as they beat her). After her attackers eventually took her to a police officer, he told the men, 'Whatever you want, I will do it to her.'[40]

Where have these horrors come from? There have been hundreds of documented sexual assaults at protests since the start of 2011; in just one week of demonstrations surrounding Mohamed Morsi's removal as president in late June and early July 2013, 186 separate attacks were recorded by activist groups.[41] They have taken place under military rule and under Islamist rule, and almost nobody has been brought to justice for these crimes. The attacks are not random, not spontaneous, not merely a product of crazed young men's 'libidinal perversion'; they nearly all bear the hallmarks of high-level organization and deploy tactics that are near-identical to those used during sexual assaults against protesters during the Mubarak era that we know were arranged and perpetrated by agencies of the Egyptian state. In the post-Mubarak era, definitive proof as to who is behind the violence has been difficult to secure. What we do know is that more than one attacker has admitted to being paid for his work; in late 2012 a man told reporters that he had been given money to 'go out and sexually harass girls, go out and hassle them, and try to touch them, to the point that they'd leave the demonstration'.[42]

We know that these assaults clearly serve two related goals of the Egyptian state – to reinforce an 'authentic' division between male and female gender roles, and to expel anyone articulating an autonomous political voice from Egypt's public spaces. We know that most campaigners on the issue, and survivors of the attacks, are sure that to some extent such violence has been curated by those political powers, acting through segments of the security establishment that have a vested interest in thwarting efforts to remake the state from below. Azza Suleiman, director of the Center for Egyptian Women's Legal Assistance, is confident that the 'first actor' in these assaults is the interior ministry. 'The message to women is, "You should stay at home, you should stop protesting, you should feel stigmatized," ' says Hania Moheeb, who was attacked in January 2013 and believes what happened to her is inseparable from the revolutionary struggle. 'The justice I need is the justice [for] the Egyptian people. The success of the revolution will be success for them.'[43]

Some senior figures within the Islamist establishment have sought to shift the blame for these incidents on to women themselves. 'Egypt's girls are not a red line,' Sheikh Abou Islam, a prominent Islamist, told the al-Hafez television network. 'These women who are naked, indecent and prostitutes are not a red line, they are going there to be raped: nine-tenths of them are women crusaders and the other tenth are women who have no men to control them, they are widows who have no one to revere or to put them right – shame on you, where is your femininity? Where is the femininity that is due by religious law? These women are like ogres with their unruly hair . . . she-devils called women.'[44] And we know that those running the state, both Islamist and military, also embrace the notion that women should 'take responsibility' for entering protest spaces, and hold those that choose to do so in contempt. In 2013, Rida al-Hifnawi, Shura Council member for the Brotherhood's Freedom and Justice Party, made the following declaration following attacks on women during a revolutionary rally: 'Women should not mingle with men during protests . . . How can the interior ministry be tasked with protecting a lady who stands among a group of men?'[45]

After demonstrations erupted against Egypt's military in late 2011 following the circulation of the 'blue bra' photograph, showing a soldier stomping down on the exposed chest of a female protester as she is dragged along the street, retired major-general and SCAF adviser Abdel Moneim Kato said that those marching should be 'sent to Hitler's ovens'.* We also know, from the testimony of Samira Ibrahim and many others, that the state itself uses sexual violence as a means of disciplining its citizens as a matter of course, and that its agents act with impunity. Aida Seif el-Dawla, psychiatry professor and founder of the el-Nadim Center which helps rehabilitate victims of state violence, says that attacks by the security forces against detained females are 'massive' and 'systematic'. 'The grabbing of breasts and sexual verbal abuse is routine for women,' she adds.[46] The el-Nazra Institute for Feminist Studies has decried the 'militarization' of the state's abuse of female human rights defenders, labelling it as 'targeted' and 'institutional'.[47]

---

* Other members of SCAF later attempted to distance themselves from Kato's comments.

The state implicitly condones violence against women in the private sphere as well as the public by its ambiguous legislation on rape and sexual abuse, by failing to prosecute perpetrators under existing laws, by marginalizing the vulnerable through sexist and restrictive personal status regulations, and by providing zero support for those affected.[48] The upshot is that 99.3 per cent of Egyptian women report being sexually harassed in public, and nearly half say they have experienced some form of domestic violence in the home; it is not just in city squares that Egyptian women have to fight for the right to their own bodies, but on the microbus, in the metro carriage, at the office and behind the closed doors of family apartments as well. In the past half-decade, two young Egyptian women have lost their lives as a result of fighting back: Shorouq el-Tarbi from Gharbia, in the Nile Delta, whose harasser ran her over as he attempted to flee the scene, and Eman Moustafa, from rural Assyut, who was on the way to buy cement from the village market in the autumn of 2012 when a man named Ramadan Salem drove up alongside her on his motorbike and groped her breast. She spat in his face, at which point he drew a gun and shot her dead. She was sixteen years old. Outside dedicated activist circles, the murder generated little interest. Dalia Abd el-Hameed of EIPR, the human rights group that took up the case on behalf of Moustafa's family, proffered a simple explanation for the lack of national attention: 'She was poor, she was young, she was a girl, and he's from Upper Egypt.' In other words, Moustafa had every attribute of the socially invisible. 'He killed her,' continued el-Hameed. 'He killed her just because she defended herself. The mere fact was that she just didn't accept what's very accepted in society. When you don't accept the norm, society punishes you. And he punished her.'[49]

The state didn't shoot Moustafa, but it did help provide the context in which such a shooting could take place. Its message, consistently, is that men are responsible for protecting 'their' women from other men, and that women are responsible for what happens if they choose to stray beyond the limits of male protection; unyielding gender identities delimit men as well as women. And as the revolution has disrupted those identities, so the state has responded by attempting to marginalize women further. Azza Suleiman points out that the security apparatus often explicitly connects the gender issues with the revolution, even when confronted by 'non-political' cases of sexual violence. 'I have women that come to us [to open a police file] after an argument with their husbands,' explains Suleiman. 'The police say, *khalli el-sawra tinfa'ik* ["Let the revolution help you"].'[50] From Eman Moustafa in Assyut, to the sexual assault survivor that Mariam Kirollos encountered in Tahrir Square, the enforcement of stringent, conventional ideas about masculinity and femininity is a key pillar of the state's survival strategy in the face of revolution, and it is from here that the horrors of mob sexual violence at protests have emerged. Assaults on women in Tahrir and at other protest locations are meant to shame not just the individuals concerned, but the wider citizenry of Revolution Country as well.

The screams Mariam Kirollos picked up in the square that night were heard by other revolutionaries too. Soon, many of them came together to form OpAntiSH (Operation Anti Sexual Harassment, pronounced phonetically: op-an-tish), less a single-minded rescue group and more a protean revolutionary movement dedicated to fighting sexual violence at protests, supporting those who are attacked and struggling against the patriarchal foundations that enable such assaults in the first place. At a typical protest rally in Tahrir, OpAntiSH will place three large groups in the square – each comprising between twenty and thirty volunteers, both male and female, wearing distinctive white T-shirts. The *midan* team distributes flyers with information about how to respond to sexual violence and hotline numbers on which assaults can be reported. When cases are logged, the intervention team attempts to reach the site of the attack and extract the protester from the scene – often fighting off attackers themselves in the process. The safety team then gives whatever support they can to the survivor, be it taking them to a safe house, accompanying them to hospital or merely sitting down and talking the whole episode through. The operation is coordinated by a control centre near the square. The work is exhausting, dangerous and deeply traumatizing; volunteers risk their life on every occasion they attempt to end or prevent an attack. Their priority during a mob assault is keenly focused: never on capturing perpetrators – unless that option presents itself and the survivor is keen for it to happen; never on recording documentary evidence of the attack; always on getting the protester out of the circle, and to safety.

The scenes of violence witnessed by volunteers aren't easily forgotten. 'It's religious people who define hell and heaven, but if you ask me I'd say this is hell on earth,' says Kholoud Bidak, who works with OpAntiSH. 'I'd rather have a bullet between my eyes and die peacefully than be in some of those situations.' But the work has also exposed volunteers to some of revolution's brightest fires. 'In response to a horrifying social phenomenon . . . they had decided to counter its madness with their own brand of madness,' wrote Wiam el-Tamami, who signed up with OpAntiSH in July 2013, at the time of some of the worst episodes of mob sexual violence Egypt has witnessed since the revolution began. 'I marvelled at this group, how they joked about the food, how they mentioned nightmares in passing; I had not seen what they had and could not fathom the burden they were bearing. I could not possibly understand what it feels like to be there, though the idea haunts me: to hold your hammering heart in your hand and willingly enter these circles of hell . . . What does brushing up against that darkness do to you for the rest of your life? And then to still be able to laugh, to get up every day, to believe . . .'[51]

Nobody at OpAntiSH believes that it is the duty of 'honourable men' to defend 'passive women', nor do they appeal to the safeguards of an authoritarian state in order to cleanse Egypt's streets from the threat of gender violence. Some other initiatives against assaults at protests and against sexual harassment in public spaces more generally – like male-only rescue teams, the formation of protective male cordons around females who want to attend political marches, or the *ifdah mutaharish* ('Expose the Harasser') Facebook group which calls for the reinforcement of security forces in crowded places and new surveillance systems to put in place by the government – risk reproducing the marginalization of women that the sexual assaults are aimed at in the first place. Refusing to see an increasingly armoured state as the 'solution' to sexual violence – and an appreciation of the state's role in fomenting such violence – remains crucial to OpAntiSH's philosophy, one that situates gender violence firmly within a revolutionary attempt to remake the state rather than as a separate issue which can be spun off and tackled in isolation under the rubric of 'women's issues'. The movement's founding statement explicitly declares that the regime is involved in perpetrating harassment, and questions the wisdom of handing individual practitioners of sexual violence over to an unreconstructed police force and legal system.*

The debate over how best to frame gender struggles in Egypt, at a time when the country is caught so intensely between the old ways and the new, is a vital one. Already, during the sexual harassment episodes of the mid-to-late 2000s, a split had developed between self-described women's rights organizations working within the formal NGO structure on one side and more radical movements on the other. In the post-Mubarak era, that split and the questions it poses have assumed fresh relevance. To what extent should grassroots activists enter and cooperate with the state-sponsored 'women's rights' arena, at a time in which the very nature of the state is being challenged?† Is calling for 'protection' from the state more progressive in the context of a revolution than it is under a relatively stable autocratic regime, or less so? How potent can new initiatives to unify gender struggles be, if the same old faces and classes dominate all decision-making?‡ What productive steps, if any, can be taken by organizations that claim to resist patriarchy in the home and yet actively support the patriarchal character of military rule – so much so that they end up condoning military attacks on women?§ Is a

---

* At the time of writing, OpAntiSH had suspended its ground operations because of the danger posed to volunteers. For now, it continues as an online community, with members determined to reactivate the movement fully as soon as circumstances allow. For more on OpAntiSH, see the group's Facebook page (https://www.facebook.com/opantish/info).

† The National Council of Women was refounded in early 2012, with all members appointed by SCAF. It was immediately criticized from all sides of the political spectrum for being little more than a reconstitution of the old regime-friendly organization it had been under the leadership of Suzanne Mubarak.

‡ The Egyptian Feminist Union – the entity originally founded by Hoda Shaarawi – was refounded in late 2011 and claimed more than 1,000 affiliations by smaller groups.

§ The new Egyptian Feminist Union and the Egyptian Center for Women's Rights both adopted positions of support for the military during the summer of 2013; the latter issued a press release following the Rabaa and Nahda protest camp dispersals congratulating the interior ministry on its operation.

focus on 'rights' for women merely a way of individuating the gender struggle and detaching it from larger communal and social movements? All these questions are pieces of a much bigger one, a question which has hovered over most 'civil society' initiatives over the past half-decade: is this revolution ultimately about improving regulatory frameworks – in other words, forcing the existing state to guarantee better personal rights from above – or is it about the spread of emancipatory imagination that could lead the Egyptians to reconstruct the state themselves from below? And are these two models of change inherently contradictory, or can they exist side by side?

As well as OpAntiSH, there are powerful examples of individuals and bodies active in Egypt who insist upon viewing feminism as an inherently political issue, bound up with the distribution of power in any given society and all the class, ethnic and other faultlines that involves – the previously mentioned el-Nazra Institute for Feminist Studies is one, the el-Nadim Center another. But they remain in the minority. During the *eid* holiday in July 2015, the ministry of the interior deployed a special unit of female police officers to combat sexual harassment in Cairo; when videos circulated of one such officer dragging an alleged offender into a movie theatre before repeatedly administering electric shocks to his body, some campaigners hailed it as a watershed moment while others refused to celebrate such a display of state violence.[52] 'You have to be conscious of class politics in Egypt,' Martina Rieker, director of the Institute for Gender and Women's Studies at the American University in Cairo, told me. 'When you look at what the women's movement actually is, it's not even a middle-class but very much an upper-class phenomenon. I'm not saying upper-middle-class people can't have radical politics, but there is clearly a lack of a mass base and we have to at least acknowledge that fact when we are talking about the women's movement. Where are the troves of working women who have to navigate Egyptian cities each day? Why are they not part of this movement, part of these formations?' Rabab al-Mahdi, a political science professor, agrees. 'Most women's rights NGOs have defined a limited agenda of their own that prioritizes a certain identity for women,' she argues, 'one based solely on their gender as opposed to their class or location or even their most pressing concerns.'[53]

*

When Egypt's old military-bureaucratic complex wrested full control of the state back from the Brotherhood, much was made by the generals and their supporters about the difference between this new, secular regime and the social conservatism of the Islamists that had gone before them: unlike under Morsi, Sisi's Egypt would be one where the liberty of personal faith, expression and identity could flourish. 'The real Islamic religion grants absolute freedom for the whole people to believe or not believe,' claimed President Sisi in early 2015. 'We are not gods on earth, and we do not have this right to act in the name of Allah.'[54] Within four weeks of those remarks, the following things happened in Egypt. A government education office carried out a ceremonial burning of eighty-two religious books deemed to conflict with national values; patriotic music was played over loudspeakers as the fire raged.[55] An administrative court declared that it was lawful for the state to expel or bar entry to gay foreigners in order to 'protect public interest and religious and social values', and upheld the deportation of a Libyan man on the grounds of homosexuality.[56] The chairman of the Journalists' Syndicate, Diaa Rashwan, called on members to report any colleagues 'proven to have incited against the army and police'.[57] And Sisi's religious endowments minister announced the formation of special community groups with the purpose, among others, of 'spreading awareness on the threats of atheism, Shi'a, [and] Baha'ism'.[58] All this occurred against the backdrop of a new presidential decree prohibiting insults to the national anthem or flag (a crime now punishable with imprisonment), the establishment of a committee tasked with exploring the widespread installation of surveillance cameras across public spaces in Egypt, and the formation of a new community police force which will grant patriotic citizens power of arrest, so as to aid the regular security forces 'in facing crime, enhancing a sense of security among citizens and . . . creating a culture of security'.[59]

Sisi, like Morsi, is determined to exclude Egyptian citizens from politics. To administer this exclusion the Egyptian state seeks daily to expose, manipulate and punish social differences; when people are divided and scared of being cast out of society, those inside Mubarak Country's citadel can sleep safer in their beds at night. It has always been thus, but the revolution has posed a greater threat to the existing state than anything it has had to contend with previously. Consequently, in Sisi's Egypt, the repression of social minorities via the enforcement of a chauvinistic nationalism – dependent on hyper-masculine imagery, the muscularity of the authorities, perpetual moral panic, the dutiful subordination of those below the patriarch and the scapegoating of the marginal – is harder, faster and more ostentatious than almost anything that has passed before.

In October 2013, a small gym in el-Marg – north-eastern Cairo's most far-flung neighbourhood, a straggly collection of streets and buildings that bleed into the desert and suck in its dust – was raided by police, who arrested at least fourteen of the men inside. Local newspapers reported that the users of the gym were *shawazz* ('perverts') who went there to practise *fahesha* ('immorality'). Less than a month later, a private party in a villa out in 6th October City was interrupted by security forces bearing handguns who announced they were looking for 'effeminate' men, 'ladyboys' and *khawalat* (a derogatory term for homosexuals); ten guests were detained on suspicion of *fujur* (which translates as 'debauchery' but is used in Egyptian legal parlance to refer to consensual sexual relations between men). In 2014, a raid on a Turkish bathhouse in downtown Cairo was filmed for prime-time television; presenter Mona Iraqi confronted the men with their role in 'spreading AIDS' as they were bundled into the back of a police truck, wrapped only in spa towels. Nearly all Egyptian men arrested for their sexuality are later subjected to anal examinations by police doctors. 'First we make them take the prostrate position – the position that Muslims take when they pray,' explained Dr Maged Louis, deputy director of the Forensic Medical Authority, and chief of forensic medicine for the Cairo police district. 'Chronic homosexuals' are identified by the shape of their anus, which according to Louis, 'won't be normal any more and will look like the female vagina'.[60] Human rights organizations have condemned such examinations as illegal under international law and morally abhorrent; international medical experts have confirmed that the test has no basis in medical science, and that Louis's assertions are 'categorically not true'.[61]

Throughout history, Egypt's queer community – whether they be men and women who identify as part of a consciously gay 'scene' (entry to which is often structured around class and wealth) or simply individuals who engage in homosexual relations – have been scapegoated by the state whenever the governing regime is keen to trumpet its social values, most notably in 2001 when a high-profile police crackdown on the Queen Boat, a known gay hangout on the Nile, ended in fifty-two men being placed on trial; LGBT rights activist Scott Long called the incident 'just an experimentation with a different sort of demons'.[62] Under Sisi, those trumpets are sounding once again. In the immediate aftermath of Mubarak's removal, a nascent gay rights movement had seemed to be coalescing in Egypt. Like Kholoud Bidak, the activist who recounted her experience of the eighteen days earlier in the chapter, many queer Egyptians found camping out in the square to be a transformative experience. 'For the first time, we weren't aliens,' explained one gay man. 'The main challenge was to prove that, 'Yes, I sleep with men, I may be effeminate – but you have to respect me because I'm standing next you in this fight.'[63]

Locations where gays and lesbians could come together – everywhere from beauty parlours to underground nightclubs – proliferated, and the growth of smartphones and technology enabled more Egyptians to pursue homosexual encounters than ever before. A revolutionary graffiti mural depicting two policemen kissing alongside the slogan 'Cops are gay' was amended to read 'Homophobia is not revolutionary' and images of the updated stencil circulated widely. In May 2012 a 21-year-old man from the Nile Delta named Ramy Yousef posted on Twitter: 'I'd like to say that I am gay, and I'm proud of who I am. Here I come out.' His family responded by forcing Yousef from their home, but activists saw glimmers of hope; government attitudes towards homosexuality under Morsi's reign remained resolutely hostile ('Gays are not real people,' an Egyptian diplomat declared at a conference in Geneva) but neither were there any prominent crackdowns on homosexual activity. Then came the resumption of military government. ' "We're all Sisi," ' warned Long, correctly, 'and anybody who doesn't look safely, nondescriptly, heterosexually Sisi-esque enough will be in trouble.'[64]

In the first two years of Sisi's rule, over 150 Egyptians have been arrested because of their sexuality by the morality police, and more than a hundred have been jailed for debauchery. Many have fallen victim to honey-traps set by security agents posing as gay men looking to arrange sexual encounters on the internet. The makers of the international mobile app 'grindr', which connects men looking for casual same-sex encounters, have started posting messages to Egyptian users warning them that profiles on the site could be police officers in disguise; media outlets have reported the existence of gay men who try to 'attract sympathizers to the terrorist [Muslim] Brotherhood' by having sex with them.[65] Transgender Egyptians have faced worse cruelty than most; dozens have been arrested and tortured, while newspapers and television shows engage in ritual mockery and humiliation of their families.[66] 'Look what recklessness can result in – you could end up with a man,' chat show host Basma Wahba warned the male partners of transgender women, before professing herself to be 'shocked and disgusted' by this 'unnatural reality'. 'It's all because we stopped listening to our parents.'[67]

Who is entitled to their own identities or bodily integrity in Mubarak Country, at a time when the revolution fights to unpick it? The regime would have the world believe that it wants Egypt to be open, inclusive and forward-looking, especially in the domain of women's rights. Following sexual assaults against women who took to the streets in the aftermath of Sisi's presidential inauguration in the summer of 2014, the new leader paid a visit to the hospital bed of one of the survivors and promised her a state-funded spiritual pilgrimage to Mecca to assist with her convalescence. Nine men were subsequently convicted of involvement in attacks, and the majority were handed down life sentences. A presidential decree has now, for the first time, made sexual harassment explicitly unlawful. The former secretary-general of the government-affiliated National Council for Women (NCW), Mona Omar, insists that 'Women's rights under the rule of President Sisi [have] improved.'[68] But what sort of rights is she talking about? The legal reforms put in place are badly needed, but they have been accompanied by a far bigger raft of laws, prosecuted with far greater ferocity, that prevent any citizen, including any woman, from having a political voice of her own. The anti-protest law forbids demonstrations, new civil society legislation prevents feminist activists from operating independently, the terrorism law casts dissenters – including, seemingly, those dissenting from the sexual 'norm' – as enemies within.

One of the revolution's biggest accomplishments was to shift the battle against patriarchy out of the draughty halls of state councils and on to the streets; now Sisi is presenting Egypt's women with a new patriarchal bargain in order to turn back the clock – give up independent organizing and relinquish your political agency to us, then you will be protected. The limits of that protection, and the fate of those who refuse the bargain, have been demonstrated by the current doyenne of Egyptian state feminism: Mervat al-Tallawi, Suzanne Mubarak's replacement at the National Council for Women. In her former position as minister for social solidarity, al-Tallawi played a key role in the drafting of new restrictions against NGOs; at events part-organized by the NCW, people holding up placards condemning sexual violence have been arrested.[69] Ahead of the army's attack on protesters at Rabaa, al-Tallawi – who has been a steadfast supporter of military violence, even when directed at women – insisted that females were present at the rally only because protest organizers had kidnapped them and forced them to service male demonstrators sexually in an act of 'jihad intercourse'.[70] Since then, she has observed that "it is impossible that a paramilitary organization like the police would commit crimes of sexual violence in Egyptian prisons'.[71]

In a television interview in early 2014, Sisi expressed his 'astonishment' at the 'awareness' of Egyptian women, and said they could contribute to the country by going around the house and saving electricity, turning off the lights. He claimed he could count on female support because women were the 'calm' and 'soft' voices of the household. 'I am talking about the Egyptian woman who maintains her household, turns off the heater and the stove,' Sisi continued. 'I'm asking you now to preserve our bigger house – Egypt.' He went on to say that it pained him when Egyptian women were hurt, as such actions contradicted the principles of chivalry. 'On a personal level – and I hope no one misunderstands me – I love Egyptian women,' he concluded. 'All Egyptian girls will be my daughters.'[72] At a presidential campaign event with female supporters, Sisi was interrupted by cheers from the crowd, at which point an organizer intervened. 'When the leader speaks, everyone should be quiet,' the organizer explained.

But to Sisi's frustration, Egypt today is full of people who refuse to be quiet – including Mohamed Tolba, Tony Sabri, Mariam Kirollos and the OpAntiSH team, and of course Samira Ibrahim, the woman whose sexual assault by the state he publicly defended. After her virginity test, Ibrahim was taken to a military court and charged with attempting to assault army officers, carrying Molotov cocktails and knives, breaking curfew, obstructing traffic, vandalizing cars and the destruction of pavements. No matter that she was carrying no weapons when arrested, had committed no violence against any military personnel, and was taken from Tahrir at half-past three in the afternoon (curfew began at 2 a.m.); she was not allowed to speak in front of the judge, got beaten and dragged away before his eyes, and was handed down a one-year suspended prison sentence. That should have been the end of the matter; Ibrahim was expected to return home and internalize her shame, quietly restoring her stolen honour. Instead, she publicly revealed what had happened to her at the hands of the Egyptian army. 'No one stained my honour,' Ibrahim wrote on her Twitter account, after coming forward with her story. 'The one that had her honour stained is Egypt. I will carry on until I restore Egypt's rights.'

She has since dragged the Egyptian armed forces through the courts, both in Egypt and abroad, at the African Commission on Human and Peoples' Rights; although the doctor who raped her has avoided justice, the military has been sufficiently embarrassed by the furore to announce it has ended the practice of virginity testing altogether. The historian Khaled Fahmy labelled Ibrahim's actions the single most important revolutionary act of its time.[73] Like Shahenda Maklad, the rebel teen from Kamshish who is more than five decades her senior and who led a march through the streets of Cairo to protest against virginity testing, and like many others is still fighting for the revolution today, Ibrahim shook the state simply by insisting that her voice and her body were her own.

Epilogue: Journeys

In mid-March 2015, I flew into Sharm el-Sheikh airport. The runway sits on a flat strip of sand between the Red Sea and the city's 'Ring of Steel' security wall, beyond which the Sinai mountain range, dotted with sunken canyons and high gardens filled with pomegranates, almonds and mulberries, stretches for more than a hundred miles to the north. There were helicopter gunships circling low around the airport perimeter as I landed, and the highways from the airport were lined with Egyptian Special Forces units – balaclavas over their heads, black goggles over their eyes – baking silently in the desert heat. Large billboards were dotted around the town, featuring the word 'Welcome' in English, alongside the logos of major Egyptian and multinational companies. At the International Congress Center, behind a series of military checkpoints, signs proclaimed 'Egypt The Future' and flags fluttered in the wind.

Inside the centre, corporate executives and Western politicians were slapping backs and breaking bread, leaving a trail of Danish pastry crumbs in their wake. Christine Lagarde, managing director of the IMF, was there, and so was Sri Mulyani Indrawati, managing director of the World Bank. John Kerry, the US secretary of state, gave a speech in the plenary hall, as did Tony Blair, Britain's former prime minister, and Philip Hammond, the country's foreign secretary; eighteen current kings, presidents and heads of state were seated among the audience. High-level delegations from China, Russia, France, Germany and Spain were in attendance, along with representatives from the European Investment Bank, the European Bank for Reconstruction and Development and the African Development Bank. Senior bosses from Coca Cola, Unilever, Siemens, Allianz and oil giants BP, BG and Total all took the stage at keynote sessions.[1] Lunch was sponsored by CI Capital, the after-dinner 'cocktail fun party' by telecoms billionaire Naguib Sawiris. 'The images that have been coming out of this part of the world have been, by the nature of media, unrepresentative of what's happening on the ground,' Ahmed Heikal, founder and CEO of Qalaa Holdings, one of the largest private investment companies in the Middle East, told me. 'We want to convey the normal, more representative part of the story, which is that Egypt is open for business.'[2]

Four years, one month and seventeen days since Egypt's anti-Mubarak uprising erupted the corridors of counter-revolution were busier and more convivial than ever. 'Conferences likes this change the image,' Sir Martin Sorrell, chief executive of WPP, the world's largest advertising agency, explained to me in a side room off the main lobby. He had just got off a plane and was wolfing down some breakfast on the go; the conference schedule was frantic, and Sorrell – one of the main organizers of the event – was struggling to make all of his meetings. 'It changes the atmosphere, it changes the perception, and given what's happened to Egypt in the past four years, obviously the brand has changed and there's a necessity to reposition it.' He ran through his company's various attempts to woo Sisi at the last World Economic Forum in Davos, and the network of public relations consultants and brand advisers that since then had been working around the clock to remarket both the Egyptian president and his country to the world. I asked whether Egypt's current turmoil – the political violence, the terrorist bombings; the insurgency raging not far away from us in northern Sinai – made stability and investment a difficult message to sell on the international stage. He gestured at the hubbub around us, and smiled. 'In a world where CEOs are trying to get top-line growth ... well, to put it very crudely, a 90 million population country doesn't fall down from the sky very often,' he replied.

Over three days, 'Egypt The Future' – or the Egypt Economic Development Conference, to give the event its full name – attracted 3,500 delegates and tens of billions of dollars' worth of foreign investment deals. New investment and bankruptcy laws, timed to coincide with the conference, offered investors new incentives and protections including special dispute-resolution mechanisms to shield their operations from the Egyptian courts, and permission to abandon privatized projects without penalty. As part of the legislation, state officials were granted the right to sell, rent and dispose of public property for investment purposes by direct order, without having to carry out a public tender, and to do so for free; both state officials and investors were given blanket immunity in relation to the handling of public funds.[3] New tax cuts and fiscal exemptions for corporations were announced as well. Diplomatic approval was universal. 'They seem to be taking the right steps in a lot of different directions,' declared a representative of the US State Department.[4] 'Egypt has been able to demonstrate its sheer commitment to transforming its own economy through the right policies, through the right regulatory reforms, as well as presenting the right set of investment opportunities,' beamed Sultan Ahmed Al Jaber, minister of state in the United Arab Emirates.[5]

This was a national coming-out party for the planet's most ancient country, as it outgrew its moody adolescent years of revolutionary upheaval and finally embraced the modern world. Special pull-out supplements and customized content packages associated with the conference ran in all the major Egyptian newspapers, as well as the *Wall Street Journal*. When attendees weren't applauding the various Gulf monarchs who had funded 'Egypt The Future', or ransacking the lavish refreshment tables, they were firing up the specially commissioned 'Marketplace' smartphone app, a sort of neoliberal Tinder where 'leaders and game-changers' could arrange to come together for 'brain dates'. Around the coffee dispensers and bilateral breakout spaces, there was an all-pervading buzz of positivity and freshness, as if an economic strategy centred on foreign direct investment, GDP growth and autocratic military rule had never been pursued before. If the weekend had come with a soundtrack, the *Lego Movie*'s 'Everything is Awesome' would have been an appropriate choice. Sisi said Egypt was on 'a path to the future' and received a standing ovation; to enthusiastic cheers, Christine Lagarde declared that 'The journey to higher growth has already begun.' From exile, the surviving leadership of the Muslim Brotherhood issued press releases insisting that Egypt 'is not for sale', seemingly forgetting that exactly the same business elites had been flogged to and fawned over by Mohamed

Morsi as well. 'The government of current President Abdel Fattah al-Sisi has embarked on an ambitious economic reform agenda,' concluded *Foreign Policy* magazine, citing constructive meetings between the Egyptian investment ministry and American multinationals such as Exxon, IBM and Kellogg. 'These, then, are the fruits of a return to the strongman era of Egyptian politics.'[6]

At the conference, no one talked much about the other fruits of that era: the virginity tests and the protest law, the thousands of political prisoners behind bars, the ninety detainees who were killed in state custody in Cairo alone the previous year and the police stations now so infamous that locals had dubbed them 'graves of the living'.[7] It would have felt impolite, even unseemly, and anyway some of the websites detailing the violence – including that of Human Rights Watch, which has labelled Sisi's assault on the Rabaa protest camp one of the largest state massacres of demonstrators in modern history – were blocked on the conference WiFi.[8] 'I think those are political, not business questions . . .' said Jeff Immelt, the CEO of General Electric, when he was asked whether there was a trade-off between democracy and economic 'stability'. 'Frankly speaking, I'm not at all competent on that,' said Richard Attias, the conference producer, when I raised the issue of Shaimaa el-Sabagh – the young mother and poet shot dead by security forces a few weeks earlier as she attempted to lay a wreath of flowers in Tahrir Square. 'I think you should ask the local authorities . . . It is not by excluding a country from the global community that you will help them solve their internal deep issues.' Tony Blair insisted that Egypt needed 'efficacy' and 'leadership', and praised Sisi for understanding the modern world. 'Look, I'm absolutely in favour of democracy and I think that, in the end, all countries as they develop will go to a situation in which the citizens elect the government,' he said from the stage. 'But I also think you've got to be realistic sometimes about the path of development, and that sometimes you will have a country [with] not what we would call 100 per cent Western-style democracy, but on the other hand is going in a direction of development that's really important.'[9] A few days before Blair's speech, the Egyptian government hanged the first of more than 700 Islamists sentenced to death since Sisi assumed the presidency.[10]

Blair, Attias and Sorrell are part of an interconnected grid of high-level country branding specialists tasked with helping Sisi's regime reshape Egypt's image in the international arena. The event was put together by Richard Attias & Associates, a strategic consulting firm owned by Sorrell's WPP that shares its London headquarters with Global Counsel, the lobbying outfit run by former Labour minister Peter Mandelson, who publicly campaigned on behalf of Gamal Mubarak when the revolution first began.[11] Mandelson is also a chairman and international representative of the financial consultancy company Lazard, who have been hired as economic advisers by Sisi's government; his close ally Blair has advised Sisi too, as part of an Emirates-funded consultancy programme.[12] Among Global Counsel's clients is British energy giant BP, whose chief executive Bob Dudley was, alongside Blair and Sorrell, another star turn at the conference.[13] 'You can almost feel the economic engine of Egypt starting to rev up,' claimed Dudley in a keynote speech, after announcing a new $12 billion BP investment package. 'We are very pleased to be part of that.'[14]

Country branding is a fast-growing industry. States have always attempted to market themselves as tourism and business destinations; now though, governments – especially ones tainted with a reputation for human rights abuses – can call upon a vast array of dedicated, global consultancy experts, fluent in what Bell Pottinger, one of the largest players in the business, calls 'the dark arts' of identity management, in order to refashion themselves.[15] A great deal of effort is made to keep these practices secret; the details or even mere existence of contracts between national governments and public relations firms are often not publicly disclosed, and journalists attempting to report on them have found themselves the target of legal action.[16] Undercover investigations and leaked documents have revealed that Bell Pottinger, which counts the Mubarak regime among its former clients,*[17] seeks to exploit privileged access to Western political

---

* In 2010, I was telephoned by a representative from Bell Pottinger, who explained that the firm was undertaking consultancy work with the Egyptian government to assess how it could improve its communications with international journalists and ensure the country was portrayed more positively in the foreign press. He asked me

leaders for lobbying purposes, massages Google search result rankings and the content of Wikipedia pages, and places favourable opinion pieces and country supplements in prominent news outlets in order to serve their clients' agendas.[18] Media manipulation is a key tool in the armoury; an internal report on the company's services for Belarus – the country known as 'Europe's last dictatorship' – following a parliamentary election in 2009 in which every single seat was 'won' by the president's supporters, includes recommendations from Lord Bell on how to 'seize the strategic initiative and turn the international news coverage away from the fact that no opposition candidates were elected, and that the OSCE [Organization for Security and Co-operation in Europe] reported the count as "seriously flawed" '.[19] The rebranding of nations is now such a major business sector that it even has its own league table, providing rankings of which countries are on the rise or fall.[20]

The job of country branders is to select certain national values and narratives – commercialized heritage, low-wage and placid workforces, strong governments with a friendly attitude to neoliberal reform – that are intelligible and attractive to global capital, and to steer them to the foreground; collective expressions of national identity that conflict with the PR 'hymn sheet' are sidelined or suppressed.[21] Through this prism, every aspect of a nation's common memory and culture is assessed according to its usefulness in generating revenue and political legitimacy for the ruling forces, rather than any role it might play in fostering a sense of community within the country concerned. In Egypt's case, the marketing message at the Economic Development Conference was clear: with ISIS on the march and the region destabilized by extremism, Sisi was the only man who could simultaneously protect Egypt from imminent collapse and open the

---

for any thoughts on the latter, and – as this was soon after the murder of Khaled Said by policemen in Alexandria – I suggested that one way to ensure Egypt was portrayed more positively in the foreign press would be for the state to stop beating citizens to death in the street. "Yes, of course," the representative stammered, "but, er . . . well, to be honest that's not really the sort of thing we had in mind." I asked him what sort of thing Bell Pottinger and the Egyptian government did have in mind. "Well," he replied, "do you, for example, have any ideas about how to make the emailing out of press releases more efficient?"

country's resources up to ever greater levels of financial speculation and appropriation; under his supervision, the thorny issue of mass revolutionary uprisings could be safely left to moulder in the history books.

Meanwhile, there was more palatable historical imagery for delegates to enjoy. In the congress centre's main lobby area, between stands for investment banks and property developers, a large multimedia display from the Bibliotheca Alexandrina – a modern iteration of the Library of Alexandria, supposedly the ancient world's greatest ever depository of knowledge – projected stirring images of Egyptian pyramids, temples and tombs to complement the corporate ambience. A nearby timeline of modern Egypt's 'milestones' included references to economic liberalization reforms in the 1990s and 2000s, but no mention of the massive protest movements that swept Mubarak, the architect of those reforms, from power. In Sharm el-Sheikh, marketing professionals were offering the world commodified Egypt: an old Egypt, where things used to happen under the stewardship of the pharaohs, and a new Egypt, where things were going to happen under the stewardship of global business titans and domestic elites. Egyptians themselves, then and now, remained inert, or invisible.

It is instructive to discover what this fantasia Egypt, so beloved by the international community, looks like; to see which kind of people are brought into focus and given a voice, and who is pushed to the edge. In the run-up to the conference, as part of the national rebranding programme, an expensively produced music video was commissioned by the Egyptian government to draw investors and tourists from the Gulf region. Entitled 'Egypt is Close', the video depicts a visitor from the Gulf wandering around an immaculate Cairo, where prominent Egyptian celebrities – dressed in the traditional garb of the humble Egyptian – glow with delight at successive opportunities to serve the visitor some coffee, take him on a felucca ride or drive him around in a taxi.[22] Actual Cairenes, who would have been cleared from the streets and kept behind well-guarded barriers to enable filming to take place, are nowhere to be seen; there are no informal 'ashwa'iyat residents, inhabitants of the non-city, in the video, nor any of those who have spent the past few years tearing up downtown Cairo's paving stones – all replaced and polished for filming, of course – to hurl at the security forces. Such Egyptians occupy the places where the camera lens grows fuzzy, where no one would notice if you slipped out of shot altogether. The message for any potential foreign visitor, as the cartoonist and critic Andeel has observed, is that Egypt is close and cheap, that everybody there is poor, and if you come and visit you'll feel like a king by comparison. 'The video is humiliating and embarrassing, and it's an extension of a low vision for what making a living and sorting things out means in the minds of those who decide how Egyptians will live,' Andeel writes. 'If this country's foreign policy is going to totally rely on begging and aid, and if the people living in it are not going to have a say in who's going to rule them or plan for their lives, it's even more miserable that those who decide everything will also decide the image and reputation of their subjects, as well as the channels through which their relationships with the surrounding world will happen.'[23]

Mubarak Country, Egypt as imagined by those who believe the old ways must hold firm, now lives on through the leadership of President Sisi; its vision of 'Egypt The Future', on sale at the Sharm el-Sheikh conference, is one in which Revolution Country – those spaces and minds where new ways of thinking predominate – is beaten back into smaller and smaller pens, with any ineradicable remnants carefully screened off from public view. But although the state's practices today involve much that is familiar from Mubarak's days, they are not identical – for the simple reason that the Egyptian people themselves have changed so profoundly. The exclusionary model has never been entirely static; it has always had to shift and adapt to maintain supremacy, at no point more so than with the start of the revolution. Since January 2011, Egypt's citizens have propelled themselves unstoppably on to the political stage: time and again, and against the odds, they have made their presence and autonomy felt by brazenly contesting different variants of regime power, in the streets and in their communities, from Mubarak to SCAF to Mohamed Morsi. At every turn, voices have suggested that this time, with this leader, the revolution must really be over; at every turn, those voices have eventually been proved wrong. It is because Egyptians have been so stubbornly resistant that Egypt now, caught in its moment of flux between the old and the new, is being ruled by a system that is more subtle than textbook authoritarianism: it is tyranny blended with a façade of proto-democratic features, a language of authority that echoes authoritarian Nasserism but at the same time sits comfortably with Western notions of liberal modernity.[24] Sisi's state constantly invokes 'the people'; it has to, because the people will not go away. But to reconstruct those people in order to ensure they pose little danger to the neo-colonial model, the regime has been forced to find new ways to try to deactivate them and deprive them of meaningful democracy. Here, the window-dressing of Western procedural democracies – as well as the many dysfunctional elements of such systems, which collectively ensure that sovereignty is never truly displaced from the top – has proved exceedingly useful.[25]

Regular elections, strict consensus around an ever tighter embrace of markets, the careful curation of what sort of collective activity is seen as reasonable and what sort of protest is illegitimate, the balancing out of 'individual rights' with a broader context of national stability and security: all these are now entrenched features of post-Mubarak Egypt. They enable Egypt's rulers to adopt some of the terminology of revolution – sanitized revolution, that is, where resistance is subordinated under the logic of capital and unsanctioned forms of mobilization are rejected – and thus to differentiate themselves from the hated figures of the past, while at the same time framing Egypt's development arc as something recognizable and benign to the international community. And yet these features are married to a discourse of chauvinistic hyper-nationalism and rigid social conservatism designed to turn individuals against one another and encourage citizens themselves to denounce any solidarities that might undermine the state. 'Take care when you are demanding your rights, take care, don't lead us astray with you,' Sisi warned in a speech in early 2015. 'I'm not saying protesting is rejected, no. I'm just saying we have given protests a certain standing that is, appreciated, but those 90 million want to eat, drink, live and feel secure about their future.' He went on to admit to some 'violations' of human rights by security forces. 'We do not approve of them,' he said, 'but this is an exceptional stage in Egypt's history.'[26] It was a nuanced performance, combining a veneer of legal equality and freedom with an old-school articulation of division and threat. Protest is not rejected, it even has a certain standing – but then again, potential terrorists are everywhere; phone numbers and photos of dissenters will be posted on government-run Facebook pages to encourage public shaming and vigilante discipline; journalists will be imprisoned; in the interests of national security, all parties participating in the parliamentary elections will be encouraged to band together and form a unified list.[27] Voluntary servitude to despotism will be harnessed from below, as well as imposed from above. And capitalism, through it all, will be presented as the pathway to agency, prosperity and liberty; not a theory to be questioned, but a reality to be accepted and lived within. At the Sharm el-Sheikh conference, Sisi's real message to the world was that even when a revolution was thrown at it, the state was able, ultimately, to survive and thrive. His promise was that after half a decade of turmoil and missteps, the custodians of the old ways had figured out the answers – and foreign partners could rest easy once again.

So it was that delegates at 'Egypt The Future' were treated to projections of the country's Pharaonic ruins at the Biblotheca Alexandrina stand, instead of being shown pictures of the obelisk inscribed with the names of more than 1,000 martyrs killed by the state, which revolutionaries once built and erected in Tahrir Square.[28] Hence why they were able to enjoy 'authentic' Bedouin dance performances in the foyers of their five-star hotel resorts, while real Bedouins, whose tribal land was appropriated by the state in partnership with multinational companies many years ago to facilitate the Sinai tourism boom, were stuck on the wrong side of a twelve-mile security fence;[29] why the Bedouins of Dabaa, who demonstrated a more radical concept of sovereignty and a more potent understanding of resistance than the one on offer here when they stormed the government's nuclear reactor site, were nowhere to be seen on the conference shuttle bus. Delegates could watch Bob Dudley, chief executive of BP, give a major speech at the conference, yet they heard nothing from the people of Idku, a small community just east of Alexandria, who have spent years fighting off an attempt by BP to build a gas processing plant there on a beach used by local fishermen. 'This is our land, where our parents and grandparents are from,' one Idku resident told a campaign video by media collective Mosireen, which went on to highlight BP's commercial dealings with dictatorial regimes in

Azerbaijan, Algeria and Angola and its alleged complicity in the actions of Colombian paramilitary death-squads.* 'As long as we're here no one can come and take it over.'[30] After cutting roads, occupying construction sites and holding massive rallies, the people of Idku succeeded in driving BP out in 2013; they won national support from Egyptians for whom memories of the Mubarak regime's flagrant gas export corruption scandals – when Egypt's natural gas reserves were sold abroad at below-market prices while Egyptians themselves were burdened with rising energy bills and frequent power cuts – remain painfully fresh.[31] 'British Petroleum is an agent of, and I know this sounds harsh, of looting . . . of looting this natural gas for the benefit of European nations,' says Saad al-Shalaby, a citizen of Idku involved in the campaign against BP. 'How should I allow you to come divorce me from my land? . . . What sort of tyranny is this? What sort of imperialism is this?'[32] 'Egypt The Future' is a professionally marketed brand for a country in which inconveniences like the people of Idku are not supposed to to trouble Bob Dudley, or any other delegate, ever again.†[33]

Mido was working as a boat mechanic in Port Said, on the northern tip of the Suez Canal where the waterway meets the Mediterranean, when one of his neighbours – a high-ranking member of the local security apparatus – asked him to take a look at a vessel with some engine problems.‡ 'All my life I've loved the sea,' he told me. 'I love everything to do with it.' It was early 2015, soon after the Egyptian Economic Development Conference in Sharm el-Sheikh, and Mido and I were seated in the cramped smoking yard of a west London coffee shop, sipping hot drinks and stamping our feet to chase off a family of rats that had set up camp in some nearby bins. Over the

---

* An allegation which BP vigorously denies.

† BP's close links with the British government and the 'revolving door' between the two institutions are well documented. Former BP chief Lord Browne was appointed to the UK Cabinet Office in 2010; at the time of writing former BP executive John Manzoni is the chief executive of the civil service, and the recently retired head of the British intelligence services has a seat on the BP board.

‡ Mido's real name (along with some biographical details of his story) have been changed to protect his identity.

coming months we met many more times, in cafés and bookshops and parks around the city, but no matter where we were Mido's eyes would dart around apprehensively as we spoke, scanning the surroundings for danger. He is a large man in his early forties, powerfully built, yet his facial features betray a child-like vulnerability: his skin is tense, his mouth pulled inwards. 'Every hour of every day I'm carrying all this weight and stress inside of me,' he once said to me. 'My chest is tight, I feel so much pain. Sometimes if I talk to myself then I can calm myself down, but I'm scared people on the street will think I'm crazy.' He explained that he'd taken to wearing a broken Bluetooth earpiece out and about, so that if passers-by saw his lips moving they would think he was having a conversation on the phone. Mido is one of the most softly spoken and empathetic human beings I have ever encountered; my impression is that he wears the earpiece not to avoid the social stigma of being thought of as crazy, but because he doesn't want to alarm anyone, and that the thought of upsetting a stranger, even accidentally, is abhorrent to him. 'I see people in the streets and on the bus and in the cafés and they are laughing and happy, and I struggle so hard to imagine what they're feeling and feel it myself,' he confided. 'But I never can. I never can reach the place they're in.'

When Mido went to take a look at the boat belonging to the Port Said police colonel, he saw something he shouldn't have seen: tucked away in the hull was evidence of an illicit smuggling operation. Terrified, he finished fixing the engine and went to settle up with the colonel, pretending nothing had happened. But the colonel stared at him intensely throughout their conversation, and it was clear that he knew Mido had discovered his secret. Some days later, Mido was walking his dog along the beach when the colonel appeared and asked him directly about what he had witnessed inside the boat. Mido feigned innocence, but the colonel could tell he was lying. Calmly and nonchalantly, he explained some of the details of the smuggling network, and said that now Mido was aware of the situation he could come on board as a mechanic and help service the boats. Mido politely declined, and the colonel's face darkened. 'It wasn't a request,' he told Mido, 'it was an order.'

The moment at which Mido knew he was really in trouble was when people with *wasta* – friends of friends with 'connections' or 'influence' – stopped returning his calls. He had tried to laugh off the anonymous phone threats that preceded that moment, though they upset him more than he cared to admit, and he'd even plucked up the courage to face down the colonel directly at another one of their 'accidental' meetings on the beach. 'If anything happens to me, I'll expose you,' Mido warned him. The colonel stared straight back at him. 'I'm going to finish you,' he replied, before walking away. Mido thought it might be bluster, but he didn't sleep well that night, or the next. It was only when he mentioned the colonel's name to local contacts, people Mido thought might be able to help protect him against the colonel, that he began to get an inkling of what he was up against. 'They told me, "You have to do what he says,"' recalls Mido. 'Or they just hung up. They were scared as well. I realized I had to run.'

Mido had never been political. It was the late 2000s, and the revolution was still a long way off. 'My friends used to laugh because someone would mention a famous politician's name over shisha and I wouldn't even know who it was,' he remembers. 'I was always reading magazines about boats, I didn't follow the news. I mean, I saw the bribes and corruption everywhere, and I hated the power police officers had over you at a checkpoint, the way they would force a bribe out of you or call you a motherfucker, the way they had no respect for people. But I never thought about how it all linked together. I was wearing blinkers, and the colonel tore them off.' Mido left Port Said, hoping to escape the smugglers' attention, but he soon discovered the colonel had invented a legal case against him concerning financial irregularities, in the hope of forcing him home. A judge issued a summons relating to the case; if Mido didn't return to the city to answer it, he would be formally declared a fugitive and eventually flushed out. Reluctantly, he came back. Determined to show he could not be intimidated, Mido went straight to the public prosecutor's office to insist that the case was a fabrication; the 'incriminating' documents were blatant forgeries, not even in his handwriting. Outside the building, a group of men were waiting for him in the street. They were dressed in plain clothes, but carrying police radios and guns. In among the flurry of sticks and rods and punches and kicks, one of them shouted in Mido's ear that they were going to do things which would make him wish he were dead, make him beg to be allowed to lick the colonel's feet. Mido stayed at a friend's house that night on the edge of the city, bloodied and bruised and shivering in terror. When he risked going back to his old apartment to retrieve some stuff, the same men were there, waiting for him, as they were when he visited the offices of a local handwriting expert in an effort to prove his innocence. 'My mother and father are dead,' Mido told me. 'I don't have connections, I don't have power. I used to be able to lift a 900cc motorbike up six flights of stairs. But here, I had no strength at all. I didn't know what to do. I went swimming each day to try and clear my head and soothe the wounds, and I realized there was no way to beat these people. I realized I was alone, that I couldn't win.' Under the cover of night, Mido fled Port Said once more; in his absence, a judge found him guilty of the trumped-up charges, and sentenced him to prison.

By the time Mido reached Cairo, it was January 2011. He made it to the British embassy and obtained a short-term student visa to the UK; until he could find a way to get out of Egypt he kept moving, from town to town, city to city, in an attempt to avoid being arrested and forcibly returned to the colonel. One day he was travelling by rail through the Nile Delta when the train suddenly came to a stop; the line had been cut by protesters. Mido climbed out of the carriage to see what was happening, and learned that a huge anti-Mubarak uprising had broken out across the country, and that the police were on the run. 'My emotions were so conflicted,' he said. 'I wanted to grab a megaphone and cheer with the crowds, I wanted to shout the name of [the police colonel] in Tahrir Square and say, "Everyone, let's get this guy too! He is corrupt and violent and he is part of Mubarak's system, part of everything that is wrong with this regime!" But I also felt fear. Because the country was in chaos and there were thugs everywhere, and I realized it would be easier than ever for the colonel to pay someone to shoot me. I had to get out.' Amid the confusion of revolution, he did.

Like many of the Egyptians I met in places such as Tahsin, Qursaya, Damietta and Sarandu, Mido owns a black folder that is stuffed to the brim with foolscaps of bureaucracy. He holds on to it stiffly; the contents make his heart pound and his head ache, but they are all he has to remind him of an officially verified existence, a place, however tenuous, on someone else's map. In Egypt, the documents tend to consist of historical land deeds, letters from municipal authorities, contested judgments from lower courts. Mido's papers, on the other hand, are nearly all stamped with a crowned shield of the British monarchy's coat of arms – the crest of the UK Home Office. When he first arrived in Britain with his student visa, Mido didn't tell the border staff he wanted to apply for asylum because he didn't know what asylum was. He was just glad to be thousands of miles from Egypt, thousands of miles from anyone who wanted to hurt him or make his life miserable. After the student visa expired, he stayed on in the UK, trying to find work and build a life. One day he had a brief run-in with the police. It didn't result in any charges, but as a consequence of the encounter his immigration details were checked. Because he had overstayed his visa, he was detained at the Harmondsworth Immigration Removal Centre near Heathrow airport, and placed on the Detained Fast Track system – which provides for the accelerated deportation of illegal migrants from Britain. Mido didn't understand what was happening. 'I could hear planes all the time, just beyond the walls, and I spent every minute wondering when I would be put on one of those planes,' he told me. 'It was torture. A different kind of torture from Egypt, but still torture.'

Harmondsworth, which holds more than 600 detainees, is the biggest immigration removal centre in Europe. In 1970 it became the first such centre in the UK to be outsourced by the government to a private company; since then, huge swathes of the British custodial system, as well as other core public services, have been privatized or placed under the supervision of public-private partnerships.[35] The initial contract was handed to Securicor, now part of G4S, which runs outsourced government operations around the world. Among other things, their Egyptian office is responsible for security on the Cairo metro network; G4S revenue from Egypt has doubled in recent years, and its former director has boasted of how the company has benefited from revolutionary unrest.*[36] In 2010, Jimmy Mubenga, an Angolan migrant, died at the hands of three G4S guards who were in the pro-

---

* G4S Egypt was given the opportunity to provide a comment on the company's operations for this book, but declined to do so.

cess of deporting him from the UK; an inquest heard that the guards ignored Mubenga's desperate cries for air as they pinned him down, handcuffed, to an aeroplane seat.[37] All three were eventually found not guilty of manslaughter.[38] It was later revealed that two of the guards had racist text messages on their phone. One of them read:

> Fuck off and go home you free-loading, benefit grabbing, kid producing, violent, non-English speaking cock suckers and take those hairy faced, sandal wearing, bomb making, goat fucking, smelly rag head bastards with you.[39]

By the time Mido was locked up in Harmondsworth, management of the centre had passed to an American company called the Geo Group. Under Geo control, six detainees died in custody, including an 84-year-old man with dementia who was left in handcuffs for several hours, even after his heart had stopped.[40] The UK Home Office said it was a 'sad case', but that it could not comment further.[41] Harmondsworth is now run by the Mitie Group PLC, which also holds British outsourcing contracts for the maintenance of public schools built under the private finance initiative, for the provision of care workers in the community, and for the cleaning of privatized railway services. At Campsfield, another immigration removal centre run by Mitie, detainees have held two hunger strikes to protest against their treatment by staff, and one migrant has committed suicide.[42] A major fire at the centre in 2013 was blamed partly on the fact that the company had neglected to install any sprinklers.[43] Mitie, which took in revenue of £2.3 billion in the financial year ending in April 2015, are being paid £180 million by the British state to manage Harmondsworth and an adjacent immigration removal centre; key details of the contract are shielded by law from public oversight.*[44] When news of the deal came through, Alex Sweeney, the company's business

* The Home Office was given an opportunity to provide a comment on Mitie Group's operations at Harmondsworth for this book, but declined to do so. A Freedom of Information request by the author for the redacted parts of the Home Office's contract with Mitie PLC was rejected under the exemption provided for in section 43(2) of the Freedom of Information Act, 'where disclosure would prejudice commercial interests'.

development director, wrote on Twitter that it was 'a great day in the office'.[45]

Inside Harmondsworth, Mido's life was contorted into something he doesn't have any words for; he tried to find the right way of describing it, in English and Arabic, but the scale of the task was beyond him. Journalists are barred from immigration removal centres, as are cameras and camera phones, but undercover video footage that emerged in 2015 showed rooms in Harmondsworth overrun by pests, piles of food rotting in the kitchens, drainpipes overflowing and cells infested with bed bugs.[46] A Home Office representative at the centre told a covert reporter that the ban on photos and filming was to prevent detainees sending out images of fighting, acts of self-harm and 'these bad conditions like the rats and whatever other shit that's in here', because the government 'don't want the bad publicity that would entail'.[47] Mido told me he saw inmates cutting themselves on the face with razor blades and swallowing them whole in an effort to get hospitalized and halt their deportations. He grew sick himself, and developed serious mental health problems. At one point, while waiting outside the doctor's office for a medicine prescription, Mido got into an argument with the centre's head of security, who then summoned other staff to forcibly hold him down and 'restrain' him. 'I saw the beatings in Egypt all over again, it was like a videotape running through my head,' he said. 'At night when they locked me in the cell I felt like I couldn't breathe. I'm used to the sea, to swimming and being underwater, yet being in that cell was the only time I felt like I was choking.'

Mido submitted an official claim for asylum in the UK and was sent by the Home Office for a medical assessment. The doctor rushed Mido through his story and took a cursory glance at his injuries; in the doctor's report, which amounts to a few handwritten scribbles on a pre-printed template, he said that there was no indication of Mido having been tortured. A subsequent medical assessment from inside Harmondsworth reached the opposite conclusion and a third, independently commissioned assessment, by an organization named Medical Justice, found fifteen major scars on Mido's body as well as numerous other wounds and abrasions; the doctors declared that these were 'highly consistent' with Mido's account of abuse and torture in Egypt, and that after extensive interviews with him they could detect 'no evidence of any deception' in his story.* But the original, mistaken medical report had been enough to place Mido on the government's Detained Fast Track to deportation, and 99 per cent of migrants in that system have their asylum claims rejected, regardless of their circumstances.†[48]

Like the management of the centres themselves, medical care in most British immigration removal centres has been privatized. Mido's initial assessment was carried out by a company called Primecare, which is owned, via a series of parent companies – Nestor, Allied Healthcare and Acromas – by three major private equity outfits controlling cumulative funds of more than $130 billion. Among the firms' other business interests is a tourism company that offers luxury holidays in Egypt; one of the three has been in negotiations with Kharafi, the Kuwaiti conglomerate partnered with the Egyptian army on power plant operations in the Nile Delta.[49] Mido was eventually granted an interview with a Home Office official to determine the validity of his asylum claim. His assigned solicitor met Mido for the first time five minutes before the interview began, and the Home Office provided Mido with an Algerian interpreter who did not speak Egyptian dialect. Mido was interrogated for four hours and asked 170 questions during the interview; the official transcript contains dozens of mistakes. The following morning, he received a letter refusing his asylum claim and ordering his deportation back to Egypt. He was given forty-eight hours to appeal. 'They kill you by paper, they kill you by bureaucracy, they kill you by a "thousand paper cuts",' said Mido. 'They kill you by a mistake on a document, by a misspelled name, by going round and round. They get in your brain, they break you, and they kill you.'

Like his original claim, Mido's appeal was rejected. Since then the UK government has twice attempted to put him on a plane back to

---

* I have seen all of the medical reports mentioned, as well as Home Office letters and many other documents related to Mido's case in both Egypt and the UK, all of which appear to support his account of events in Egypt and the UK.

† In June 2015, the British High Court declared key parts of the Detained Fast Track system to be unlawful, a decision which was subsequently upheld by the Court of Appeal.

Cairo. Pilots are responsible for the safety of all passengers on their aircraft and can refuse to fly an individual if they believe he or she may pose a risk to themselves or others; on both occasions, Mido was inspected prior to take-off and declared unfit to travel. Due to his medical condition, he was eventually released from Harmondsworth but placed under strict supervision requirements that would enable the Home Office to monitor his movements and enforce the deportation order at a later date. In desperation, Mido absconded; he is now, once again, on the run. 'I can't go back to Egypt, because I will die there,' he said, as we sat on a park bench in central London and watched squirrels chase each other across the branches of a nearby tree. 'And I can't go back to a prison cell here. Both are death sentences for me. I'll end my own life before either of them happens.' These days he moves from place to place, sofa to sofa; he calls it 'a life on rails' because all he can think about each moment is how to eat, where to sleep, whether or not he will be captured, and what will happen to him if he is. 'I don't know why they do this, why they try and make people hate each other so much,' he told me. 'It feels like the wrong people get the rights, and the right people don't get anything. In Egypt, and here.'

Capita, the UK's largest private outsourcing company, is contracted by the Home Office to track down people like Mido who have been ordered to leave Britain but are now missing. Capita are given a bonus for each migrant they find and deliver, under a payment system worth up to £40 million.[50] If Mido is eventually found, it will likely not be a British police officer that arrests him but a corporate bounty-hunter – contracted by one neoliberal state to help facilitate the removal and transfer of undesirable individuals to another. The degree of wilful harm and bureaucratic absurdity varies between these states, as does the absence of democracy. But like all neoliberal states, both are well-versed in the art of barbarization, and in both the line between corporate power and political authority is becoming so blurred that at times it can be hard to pin it down at all. Under Mubarak, Egypt's business magnates were also its ministers and political power-brokers, and vice versa. Since the revolution began, elections have come and gone but each regime they have anointed – from Morsi's Brotherhood to Sisi and the razzmatazz of his Sharm el-Sheikh economic conference – has continued to privatize, to maintain austerity, to warn citizens that there is no alternative but to stay the course.

In Britain, where prospective migrants can avoid Mido's fate provided they have at least £2 million in available bank funds and are willing to spend £8,900 on a fast-tracked Tier 1 visa for high net worth individuals,[51] voters are free to choose between the Conservative and Labour parties, but not to elect a government that might roll back private outsourcing and afford Mido and others like him the humanity to which they are entitled. Capita's former chairman loaned Labour £1 million; two shareholders in Capita's rivals, Serco, which also runs immigration removal centres in the UK, are Conservative members of the House of Lords.[52] G4S has a former government minister, Whitehall advisers and civil servants on its board; in the US, Geo Group has provided almost $5 million in campaign finance contributions over the past two decades, with money disbursed to both Republicans and Democrats.[53] Mido has crossed many borders in search of bodily integrity, autonomy and democratic citizenship, but they remain elusive. Violence has shadowed his journey, and so too has a system in which formal politics serves not the many but the few.

The revolution that Egypt's citizens have mounted against the neoliberal state is the property of all who believe in an alternative future, wherever they may be. And to the frustration of those who seek to neutralize it, that struggle – precisely because the forces ranged against it are so globalized – cannot be contained. Rachid Mohamed Rachid, Mubarak's former minister of trade and industry who has since been convicted of embezzling public money, stashed $30 million in a Swiss tax haven run by HSBC, one of the biggest banking groups in the world.[54] The twelve F-16 fighter aircraft, twenty Harpoon missiles and 125 M1A1 tank kits that President Obama authorized delivery of to the Egyptian government soon after the Sharm el-Sheikh economic conference, will be built, in part, by American workers; American taxpayers are funding the $1.3 billion of annual military aid supplied by the US to President Sisi.[55] Campaigners attempting to fight back against the growing ascendancy of corporate power over democracy, particularly in the realm of multilateral trade deals that allow companies to sue governments which compromise their financial interests, are able to cite Egypt as an example of why vigilance is so necessary; the country is facing legal action by French outsourcing giant Veolia – formerly contracted to run waste management services in Alexandria – after revolutionaries forced ministers to implement a meaningful minimum wage.*[56] Veolia's compensation claim will be heard at the International Centre for Settlement of Investment Disputes, an entity run by the World Bank that is shielded from any democratic oversight by national citizens. 'It is good to see that Egypt is open for business,' declared the World Bank's managing director at Sharm el-Sheikh's 'Egypt The Future' conference. 'We should now work hard to push the door as wide open as possible.'[57]

But it is revolutionary Egyptians who have pushed doors open: not for the World Bank's model of business and development and the expired notion that political progress inevitably accompanies free market reforms, but for the possibility of something different. And they are by no means on their own. In recent years, a spirit of protest and resistance has swept many corners of the planet; the debates lived out by Egyptian revolutionaries – over what sort of governance structures their lives, whether or not they should aim to seize state power, how best human beings can find the space in which to imagine and implement alternate forms of sovereignty and the courage to stand up to the brutality that will confront them along the way – are debates which are playing out everywhere. On 25 January 2014, *the anniversary of the start* of Egypt's revolution, the anti-austerity party Syriza won power in Greece. Syriza's struggles in government have brought the limits of democrotic sovereignty under neoliberalism into sharp relief, and similar radical movements are gathering momentum in Spain, Portugal and Italy. From Southern Europe to India and Palestine, the inevitability of neoliberalism and the dangers of sectarianism and extremism have been entwined by elites in an effort to stymie the emergence of what those in power fear most: transformative ideas – of the sort that Egypt has produced, and which Sisi is struggling to

---

* King & Spalding, the international law firm representing Veolia in the company's case against Egypt, was given the opportunity to provide a comment regarding the legal action for this book, but declined to do so.

expunge – ideas that lead to practices that might just change the world. 'Your war is our war, and your stability is our stability,' Italy's prime minister, Matteo Renzi, told Sisi at the Sharm-el-Sheikh conference. 'The issue is not about Egypt or the region only, but also about Italy and the rest of the world.'[58]

All narratives of revolution are outstripped by events; this one has been completed at a time when the counter-revolution is in full flow and the revolution's days seem at their darkest. But it has been written in the conviction that Egypt's moment of flux between old and new, itself part of a global moment of flux between old and new, is not yet over, and that even fiercer battles are still to come. 'Many are tired,' Noor Noor, the young revolutionary with whom I found myself locked up in the back of a police truck on the night of 25 January 2011, admitted to me recently. 'This is a group of people that has spent the past few years consistently running for their lives. There is an adrenaline rush that will keep you going to a certain extent and stop you feeling the scars, but eventually it runs out and then the scars and the post-traumatic stress and the exhaustion make themselves known. There has to be rest, and recuperation, but that's not the same thing as hopelessness. Because a significant proportion of the Egyptian population no longer think about themselves and about politics in the same way, and are no longer prepared to put up with the old crap in the long term. We may not be in power, but we are not alone.' How many others outside Egypt are no longer prepared to put up with the old crap? 'The Arab uprisings point to the hope, necessity and potential that rebellion holds,' argues Adam Hanieh, a Middle Eastern scholar. 'This promise of revolt remains ever-present in the political moment – it extends beyond the Middle East and belongs to all who seek a different world.'[59]

Sisi's rebooted patriarchy necessitates a constant stream of promises from his regime: of economic progress and security to his domestic audience, of fertile new grounds for speculation and accumulation to his international one. Mubarak had the Toshka lakes; at the Sharm el-Sheikh economic conference, Sisi unveiled his own flimflam pyramid – an entirely new city, New New Cairo, slated to one day occupy an area in Egypt's eastern desert as large as Singapore and form the biggest purpose-built capital in human history.[60]

Alongside a downtown green space twice the size of New York's Central Park and a theme park four times bigger than Disneyland, the focal point of New New Cairo will, according to a promotional video aired at the conference, be a civic square that is 'open to all'. At the presentation in which the new capital was announced, no one mentioned that old Cairo once had a civic square open to all, and that it was opened up not by the state, but by its citizens.

Of course New New Cairo, like Toshka and the New Valley project before it, will never resemble the computer-generated slides that were used to promote this sterilized city of the future; likely as not, it will never materialize at all. But Sisi is hoping that mirages like New New Cairo or his regime's much hyped extension of the Suez Canal,* will buy that much more time for the old ways, and it is time that he and the Egyptian state desperately need. In order for Sisi to survive, Egypt's 'War on Terror' can never be wound up, but its relentless quest for new targets has begun to implicate Egyptians – like football legend Mohamed Abu Treika and comedian Bassem Youssef – whose popularity outmatches even the president's.[63] Promising eternal protection against enemies within and abroad – 'I am willing to stand against the whole world, but you have to be with me,' Sisi has told the Egyptian people, 'otherwise I can't' – carries risks as well as rewards; hyper-nationalism is a dangerous fire to play with when so little of substance lies behind it. The backlash has been unpredictable. By 2015, another prominent footballer, Ahmed Marghany, had publicly labelled Sisi a 'failure' (he was subsequently fired by his club);[64] even some of the public intellectuals who loudly supported Sisi's ejection of the Brotherhood were beginning to express reservations about his rule. 'Slipping into the past – which means opening war on the future – is more dangerous for the country than terrorism's bullets

---

* The opening ceremony for the New Suez Canal project, which took place in August 2015, was sponsored by a roll-call of Mubarak-era industrial tycoons including Mohamed Aboul Enein (of Cleopatra Ceramics), Ahmed Ezz (of Ezz Steel), and the Talaat Moustafa family (owner of the Talaat Moustafa Group conglomerate, whose real estate arm was at the centre of several land sale controversies).[61] During the inauguration, Sisi paid tribute to police officers and civilians who had been the victim of terror attacks, but made no mention of the ten Egyptians who died while working on the new project.[62]

and explosive devices,' warned Abdullah al-Sinnawi, an old leftist newspaper editor who has generally been a staunch ally of the president, in an opinion piece that directly contradicted Sisi's justification for his rule. Al-Sinnawi went on to accuse Sisi's regime of 'normalization' with the past and claimed there was a threat of the revolution being hijacked once again. 'If society's discontent starts to reach the boiling point then political equations are likely to be completely over-turned,' he wrote. 'No one has the right to gamble with the country's future.'[65] Lawyers, many of whom had initially expressed backing for Sisi owing to the Muslim Brotherhood's attempted manipulation of the judicial system, have engaged in mass strikes during his presidency to protest against attacks against their profession and the use of state violence in police stations;[66] in the government's inevitable chasm between revolutionary rhetoric and reality, between how power is conceived by citizenry and state, there is a sense that the vast apparatus upon which Sisi relies to coordinate his rule is beginning to fragment and slip out of his control.

Meanwhile, as adverts for New New Cairo are plastered up on the ring road, the economic policies that Sisi's Egypt remains bound to continue to reproduce forgotten and marginalized spaces in the old cities – the real cities – where real Egyptians already live. Beyond the pro-state bombast, there is an eerie familiarity to Egyptian news-paper headlines these days. As in the late 2000s, the stories speak of official neglect: an escalation of water shortages within poorer communities; ferry disasters, industrial fires and hospital failures claiming multiple lives; sit-ins held by public sector workers outside the cabinet office to protest against low wages. These are the conditions under which shoots of resistance grew once before – coalescing into a challenge that took the repressive and seemingly impregnable state by surprise, and plunged it into chaos. At Matariya, a low-income neighbourhood in the north-east of Cairo, police battle protesters every Friday, chasing scarf-swaddled teenagers down alleyways so narrow that locals are able to thwart the movements of the security forces merely by placing a rubbish bin outside their front door.[67] Many of those demonstrating are Islamist, but not all; a cycle of state violence and resistance – the neighbourhood's police station has twice been set ablaze since the revolution began – has helped to radicalize a generation of local youth from across the political spectrum. Among the many Matariya residents shot dead by the state in 2015 is a local mahraganat DJ, inspired by el-Salam's DJ Figo; dozens more have been killed by police who patrol the area in roving armoured personnel carriers, and drag prisoners back to their headquarters to torture. And still, the demonstrations continue.[68]

Despite all this, Egypt's revolutionaries have to contend with several weaknesses of their own. Beyond the wave of state repression that has depleted their ranks and disrupted any attempts at organization, as well as the devotion – however shortlived it may prove – that Sisi has secured from large sections of the population, there are also deep disagreements within the democratic left over where to turn next and how best to prepare for the next round of mass confrontation with the state when it arrives. Yet Matariya's body count, like the body count that has accompanied every 25th January anniversary since Sisi took power, is indicative of the president's vulnerability too, and that of the wider system of violence and corruption he depends upon. Ultimately, Mubarak Country is built on an assumption of fear and dependency; pre-revolution and now, it relies not on a stable system of governance, but on the perpetuation of mental shackles, on a belief that nothing more is possible. The problem with mental shackles is that poverty and exclusion tend to rust them, and they are hard to maintain when new generations, new minds, keep bursting on to the scene. Perhaps that is why Sisi, who claims that all of Egypt's youth are his children, has been particularly determined to oppress the very youngest. In October 2013, several school students aged between twelve and fourteen were arrested for protesting in eastern Cairo; a few weeks later, fifteen-year-old Khaled Mohamed Bakara was thrown in a military prison after his pencil case was discovered to contain anti-Sisi imagery.[69] The following month seven girls under the age of eighteen received sentences of up to eleven years in jail for allegedly taking part in a demonstration in Alexandria.*[70] These are not the actions of a state that is confident in its own survival; they are the actions of a state which knows its authority has been irreparably damaged, and that Revolution Country clings on amid the fissures.

---

* The sentences were later overturned.

At the end of one our meetings, I showed Mido the video on my phone of the schoolchildren in Zawyet el-Dahshour playing at revolution: marching towards an imaginary police line, falling back under a barrage of imaginary tear gas, gathering themselves together again and chanting for the downfall of their headmaster. Mido would have provided me with a neat ending if he had punched the air and declared himself awash in newfound optimism; if he had proclaimed his renewed faith in an Egypt he could one day return to without fear of arrest or torture. But he was too weary, too scared, too busy struggling in a daily scrabble for survival on the underbelly of modern Britain, to get swept up by a grainy minute of footage shot 5,000 miles away. Before we parted, though, he asked to take a look at the video one more time. 'You know there are two versions of me inside, fighting each other always,' he said, as we walked towards the door. 'There's the one where all this pain feels for ever and I can't see a way out, and there's the one that knows it will get better. The one that believes eventually I'll be able to make my own decisions, and live my own life the way I want to live it.'

Notes

PROLOGUE: 'THE PEOPLE WANT . . .'

1. 'Company Profile', ASEC Engineering and Management: http://www.
   asec-engineering.com/Site/CompanyProfile/History-Milestones.aspx /
   'Our Heritage', Qalaa Holdings: http://www.qalaaholdings.com/
   our-heritage / 'Ciments Français in Egypt', Ciments Français: http://
   www.cimfra.fr/ENG/Ciments+Fran%C3%A7ais/Ciments+Fran%C3%
   A7ais+worldwide/Egypt/ / Italcementi Group: http://www.italcemen
   tigroup.com/ENG
2. '50 Helwan Cement workers sacked', Ikhwanweb (2 July 2007)
3. Ibid.
4. '2007 Annual Report', Italcementi Group: http://www.italcementi
   group.com/NR/rdonlyres/FD20FC80-8CEF-444E-9AE2-03194F423
   F4F/o/ANNUALREPORT 2007.pdf
5. John Lanchester, *How to Speak Money* (Faber and Faber, 2014)
6. Maha Abdelrahman, *Egypt's Long Revolution: Protest Movements
   and Uprisings* (Routledge, 2014), p. 17
7. Testimony provided by Aida Seif el-Dawla and the el-Nadim Center,
   2006. Words starred out in original testimony as published by el-Nadim.
8. 'Egypt: Reforms trigger economic growth', IMF Middle East and
   Central Asia Department (13 February 2008)
9. Alaa Al-Aswany, *On the State of Egypt: What Caused the Revolution*
   (Canongate, 2011), p. 21
10. '"Work on him until he confesses:" Impunity for Torture in Egypt',
    Human Rights Watch (2011)
11. Author interview with Kamal Abbas
12. 'Why the Middle East matters – a keynote speech by Tony Blair', The
    Office of Tony Blair (23 April 2014)
13. Jared Malsin, 'Egypt's revolution comes full circle: Court orders
    Mubarak's release', *Time* (21 August 2013)

14. Ian Lee, 'Mubarak cleared: Drama not over yet, but Egypt's revolution is dead', CNN (29 November 2014)

15. Simon Mabon, 'Egypt's full circle as failed revolution lets the military's grip strengthen', SBS (29 January 2014)

16. Rebecca Banatlava, 'Now Hosni Mubarak has been acquitted, it's safe to say that the Egyptian Revolution is officially over', *Independent* (4 December 2014)

17. Matthew Taylor, 'Anti-cuts campaigners plan to turn Trafalgar Square into Tahrir Square', *Guardian* (22 March 2011); Andy Kroll, 'The spirit of Egypt in Madison', TomDispatch (27 February 2011)

18. Nir Rosen writes elegantly on this subject in Adel Iskandar and Bassam Haddad (eds.), *Mediating the Arab Uprisings* (Tadween Publishing, 2013), pp. 11–20

19. Paul Sedra makes this point well in 'Roundtable on the language of revolution in Egypt', *Jadaliyya* (12 August 2012)

20. George Orwell, *Homage to Catalonia* (Penguin, 2000), p. 195

21. With thanks to Adam Hanieh, who uses a similar formulation in his excellent *Lineages of Revolt: Issues of Contemporary Capitalism in the Middle East* (Haymarket Books, 2013), p. 15

22. David Sims, *Understanding Cairo: The Logic of a City of Control* (AUC Press, 2010), p. 3

23. Video at YouTube: http://www.youtube.com/watch?v=7xdXMyd6SGA

1. 'THIS IS OUR EGYPT'

1. M. R. El-Ghonemy, *The Political Economy of Rural Poverty: The Case for Land Reform* (Routledge, 1990), cited by Ray Bush in Rabab El-Mahdi and Philip Marfleet (eds.), *Egypt: Moment of Change* (AUC Press, 2009), p. 52

2. Farouk inherited 20,000 *feddans* from his father Fuad, and added another 80,000 to the royal pile under his own reign, plus a further 150,000 in the name of limited companies which remained under the control of the monarch – Henry Habib Ayrout, *The Egyptian Peasant* (AUC Press, 2005), p. 17

3. Ibid., p. 16 and Bush in *Egypt: Moment of Change*, pp. 52–3

4. Beshir Sakr and Phanjof Tarcir, 'Rural Egypt returns to the ancien regime', *Le Monde diplomatique* (October 2007), and Hamied Ansari, *Egypt: The Stalled Society* (SUNY Press, 1986), p. 27

5. Ansari, *Egypt: The Stalled Society*, p. 31

6. Ayrout, *The Egyptian Peasant*, p. 33

7. Ibid., p. 111

8. Patrick Richard Carstens, *The Encyclopaedia of Egypt during the Reign of the Mehemet Ali Dynasty 1798–1952* (FriesenPress, 2014), p. 203

9. Yasmin M. Ahmed and Reem Saad, 'Interview with Shahenda Maklad', *Review of African Political Economy*, Vol. 38, Issue 127 (2011), pp. 159–67

10. Tarek Osman, *Egypt on the Brink* (Yale University Press, 2011), pp. 219–20

11. Officially, 'punishments' meted out by the HCLF ranged from the sequestration of land – and deportation of landowners and their immediate families from the area – down to the stripping of formal titles from alleged feudalists. Claims of coercion and violence by HCLF members arose later during the trial of those responsible for investigating Salah's murder, where witnesses claimed murder suspects were beaten with clubs in public and subjected to sexual abuse. Although the claims are certainly feasible, the entire court case was highly politicized which casts some doubt on the reliability of such testimony – Ansari, *Egypt: The Stalled Society*, pp. 45–6, 103–4.

12. Ibid., p. 39

13. Gamal Abdel Nasser, speech on 26 October 1964 in Alexandria, as he survived an assassination attempt by a member of the Muslim Brotherhood.

14. David Harvey, *A Brief History of Neoliberalism* (OUP, 2007), p. 20

15. Ibid., p. 37

16. D. Hirst and I. Beeson, *Sadat* (Faber and Faber, 1981), cited in El-Mahdi and Marfleet (eds.), *Egypt: Moment of Change*, p. 3

17. Ansari, *Egypt: The Stalled Society*, pp. 19–20

18. Ibid., pp. 46–7

19. Ibid., p. 48

20. Bush in *Egypt: Moment of Change*, p. 56

21. Marfleet in ibid., p. 21

22. Ansari, *Egypt: The Stalled Society*, p. 21

23. Y. Sadowski, *Political Vegetables? Businessman and Bureaucrat in the Development of Egyptian Agriculture* (Brookings, 1991), cited by Ahmed El-Sayed El-Naggar in *Egypt: Moment of Change*, p. 35

24. Osman, *Egypt on the Brink*, pp. 135–6

25. Ibid., p. 130

26. Mark Blyth, *Austerity: The History of a Dangerous Idea* (OUP USA, 2013), p. 162

27. Timothy Mitchell, *Rule of Experts: Egypt, Techno-Politics, Modernity* (University of California Press, 2002), p. 277

28. Ibid., pp. 277–8

29. Anne Alexander and Mostafa Bassiouny, *Bread, Freedom, Social Justice* (Zed Books, 2014), p. 48

30. Ibid., pp. 49–50

31. Marfleet in *Egypt: Moment of Change*, p. 4

32. Monthly report of Egypt's ministry of finance, July 2011

33. Mitchell, *Rule of Experts*, p. 272

34. El-Naggar in *Egypt: Moment of Change*, p. 35

35. Egypt's GDP growth ranged between 4 and 6 per cent from 1994 until 2000, then dipped slightly in 2001 and 2002 before climbing again through the rest of the decade, up to a high of 7.2 per cent in 2008 – World Bank data

36. El-Naggar in *Egypt: Moment of Change*, p. 47

37. 'Egypt Country Assistance Evaluation' World Bank (June 2000), cited in Alexander and Bassiouny, *Bread, Freedom, Social Justice*, p. 97

38. Adam Hanieh, *Lineages of Revolt: Issues of Contemporary Capitalism in the Middle East* (Haymarket Books, 2013), p. 78

39. Ibid., p. 82

40. Bush in *Egypt: Moment of Change*, p. 61

41. Dan Murphy, 'Discontent flaring in rural Egypt', *Christian Science Monitor* (6 May 2005)

42. 'Egypt: Attacks by security forces in Sarando', Human Rights Watch (17 March 2005)

43. Fawaz A. Gerges, 'The end of the Islamist insurgency in Egypt?: Costs and prospects', *Middle East Journal*, Vol. 54, Issue 4 (Autumn 2000), p. 592

44. All examples from Bush in *Egypt: Moment of Change*, pp. 61–2

45. Karim El-Gawhary, 'Nothing more to lose', *Middle East Report*, Issue 204 (Autumn 1997)

46. Cited in Bush, *Egypt: Moment of Change*, p. 62

47. Hanieh, *Lineages of Revolt*, pp. 88, 94, 96–7

48. Reem Saad, 'Social and political costs of coping with poverty in rural Egypt' – Paper presented at the Fifth Mediterranean Social and Political Research Meeting, Florence & Montecatini Terme, organized by the Mediterranean Programme of the Robert Schuman Centre for Advanced Studies at the European University Institute (March 2004)

49. Ibid.

50. 'Freedom and justice for the farmers of Sarando: Call for solidarity', The Arabic Network for Human Rights Information (June 2008)

51. The Land Center for Human Rights drew a direct link between Law 96 and the rise in the number of Egyptians trying to escape Egypt's borders. 'Immigrants will find a million ways to reach their destination because they are desperate,' reported the organization – El-Mahdi and Marfleet in *Egypt: Moment of Change*, p. 8

52. Hanieh, *Lineages of Revolt*, p. 35

53. James V. Grimaldi and Robert O'Harrow Jr, 'In Egypt, corruption cases had an American root', *Washington Post* (19 October 2011)

54. El-Naggar in *Egypt: Moment of Change*, p. 44

55. Ibid., p. 43

56. Ibid., p. 49

57. Alexander and Bassiouny, *Bread, Freedom, Social Justice*, pp. 52–3

58. El-Naggar and Joel Beinin in *Egypt: Moment of Change*, pp. 49, 76

59. El-Naggar in ibid., p. 42

60. Alexander and Bassiouny, *Bread, Freedom, Social Justice*, p. 53

61. 'Egypt: The arithmetic of revolution', Gallup (April 2011)

62. Jonathan Wright, 'Poverty grows in Egypt despite rapid growth – U. N.', Reuters (17 October 2007)

63. Alaa Al-Aswany, *On the State of Egypt: What Caused the Revolution* (Canongate, 2011), p. 14

64. Osman, *Egypt on the Brink*, p. 11

65. 'EGYPT: Nearly a third of children malnourished – report', IRIN (5 November 2009)

66. 'Arab Republic of Egypt – 2010 Article IV Consultation Mission, Concluding Statement', IMF (16 February 2010)

67. Mitchell, *Rule of Experts*, pp. 280, 292–3

68. Marfleet in *Egypt: Moment of Change*, p. 22

69. El-Naggar in ibid., pp. 45–6

70. John Sfakianakis, 'The whales of the Nile: Networks, businessmen, and bureaucrats during the era of privatization in Egypt', in Steven Heydemann (ed.), *Networks of Privilege in the Middle East: The Politics of Economic Reform Revisited* (Palgrave Macmillan, 2004), p. 88

71. Robert E. Green, 'The ABCs of privatization: A case study of Al Ahram Beverages Company in Egypt', *Lights: The Messa Quarterly*, Vol. 1, Issue 1 (Autumn 2011)

72. Dieter Weiss and Ulrich Wurzel, *The Economics and Politics of Transition to an Open Market Economy: Egypt* (OECD Publishing, 1998), pp. 129–30

73. Maha Abdelrahman, *Egypt's Long Revolution: Protest Movements and Uprisings* (Routledge, 2014), p. 13
74. Thomas Easton, 'Emerging market oasis', *Forbes* (22 March 1999)
75. Grimaldi and O'Harrow Jr, 'In Egypt, corruption cases had an American root'
76. Abdelrahman, *Egypt's Long Revolution*, p. 10
77. Marfleet and El-Naggar in *Egypt: Moment of Change*, pp. 17, 48
78. The only real improvements to the Egyptian economy during the early structural adjustment era came from a $15 billion write-off of US debt interest by Washington as a result of Egypt's decision to support the first Gulf War, and a rise in rents derived from public resources like the Suez Canal, neither of which can realistically be attributed to neo-liberal reforms – Mitchell, *Rule of Experts*, pp. 276–7
79. Ibid., p. 282
80. Marfleet in *Egypt: Moment of Change*, p. 18
81. Marfleet and El-Naggar in ibid., pp. 17, 49
82. All examples from Mitchell, *Rule of Experts*, pp. 285–6
83. Ibid., p. 286
84. Sfakianakis, 'Whales of the Nile'
85. 'Ferry survivors describe ordeal', *BBC News* (4 February 2006)
86. Belal Fadl, 'The senile state: A close reading (Part 1)', Mada Masr (13 December 2014)
87. Ibid.
88. Ingy Hassieb and Diana Maher, 'Souq El-Gomaa fire leaves residents feeling helpless', *Daily News Egypt* (24 June 2010)
89. Ibid.
90. Jason Hickel, 'Neoliberal Egypt: The hijacked revolution', Al Jazeera (29 March 2012)
91. Anne Alexander in *Egypt: Moment of Change*, p. 146
92. Mandelson founded Global Counsel, a strategic advice service, in 2010 and continues to chair the company. Mandelson and Global Counsel have gone to extraordinary lengths to keep the identity of clients secret, but are known to have worked with powerful members of the Russian oligarchy, including many individuals closely connected to President Putin – Guy Adams, 'Putin and the Prince of Darkness: Revealed: The web of links between Peter Mandelson's shadowy global consultancy firm and the billionaire power brokers of Putin's Russia', *Daily Mail* (26 July 2014)
93. Lord Mandelson of Foy and Hartlepool, 'Military must give reformers free rein', *Financial Times* (2 February 2011)

2. PALACE GHOSTS AND DESERT DREAMS

1. Quotes taken from interviews conducted as part of the *Model Citizens* project, produced by Wouter Osterholt and Elke Uitentuis at the Townhouse Gallery, Cairo (2008–9): http://www.wouterosterholt. com/model-citizens/model-citizens

2. David Sims, *Understanding Cairo: The Logic of a City Out of Control* (AUC Press, 2010), p. 10

3. Ibid., p. 75

4. Ibid.

5. By 2011, more than a dozen close associates of Mubarak, nearly all of them NDP members (including former housing minister Ahmed Al-Maghrabi and former tourism minister Zoheir Garana) were charged in court with involvement in corrupt land sales. Both claimed they were acting on orders from Mubarak himself – Emad Mekay, 'Corruption: Post-Mubarak Egypt probes public land contracts', *IPS News* (30 March 2011); Gamal Essam El-Din, 'Ex-ministers face trial', *Al-Ahram Weekly* (24–30 March 2011)

6. John Argaman, 'Cairo: The myth of a city on the verge of explosion', *Jadaliyya* (11 February 2014)

7. 'Egypt in dire need of push for low-income mortgages' Mada Masr (3 March 2014)

8. Sims, *Understanding Cairo*, p. 206

9. Some estimates put the population of the tomb districts as high as five million, and the imagery of cemeteries being invaded by squatters has become a powerful trope in both domestic and foreign depictions of the city. But although there certainly are a considerable group of Cairenes living in among the tombs, Galila el-Kadi (cited in ibid., p. 22) has shown that the media hype has vastly exaggerated their numbers. According to her field research, most of those described as 'tomb dwellers' actually live in ordinary apartment blocks in the cemetery districts; of the estimated 13,000 actually living in the grave complexes, about half are private tomb guards and their families, suggesting that tomb squatters probably number less than 7,000.

10. Bradley Hope, 'The Mubarak family's assets', *The National* (23 October 2012)

11. Cited in Nada Tarbush, 'Cairo 2050: Urban dream or modernist delusion', *Journal of International Affairs*, Vol. 65, Issue 2 (Spring/ Summer 2012), p. 181

12. Cited in Sims, *Understanding Cairo*, p. 15
13. Gamal Nkrumah, 'Living on the edge', *Al-Ahram Weekly* (11–17 September 2008)
14. Saad Eddin Ibrahim, *Egypt, Islam and Democracy: Twelve Critical Essays* (AUC Press, 1995), cited by W. J. Dorman in Diane Singerman (ed.), *Cairo Contested: Governance, Urban Space and Global Modernity* (AUC Press, 2009), p. 272
15. Salah el-Din Hafez in *al-Ahram* (December 1992), cited in Singerman, *Cairo Contested*, p. 119
16. Nabil 'Umar in *al-Ahram* (December 1992), ibid., p. 120
17. *Al-Sha'b* (December 1992), ibid., p. 119
18. Nabil 'Umar in *al-Ahram* (December 1992), ibid., p. 120
19. *Akhir sa'a* (April 1993), ibid., p. 120
20. Oliver Wainwright, 'Is Beirut's glitzy downtown redevelopment all that it seems?', *Guardian* (22 January 2015)
21. David Sims, 'The Arab housing paradox', *Cairo Review of Global Affairs* (24 November 2013)
22. Sims, *Understanding Cairo*, p. 100
23. See Agnès Deboulet's study of informality in Fustat, *Cairo Contested*
24. Leïla Vignal and Eric Denis in Diane Singerman and Paul Amar (eds.), *Cairo Cosmopolitan: Politics, Culture and Urban Space in the New Globalized Middle East* (AUC Press, 2006), p. 142
25. Asef Bayat, Life as Politics: How Ordinary People Change the Middle East (Stanford University Press, 2010), pp. 176–81
26. Sims, *Understanding Cairo*, p. 92
27. Dorman in *Cairo Contested*, pp. 276–7
28. Deboulet in ibid., p. 223
29. Dorman in ibid., p. 282
30. Deboulet in ibid., p. 226
31. John Hall, 'Meet Mansa Musa I of Mali – the richest human being in all history', *Independent* (16 October 2012)
32. All examples from the excellent Max Rodenbeck, *Cairo: The City Victorious* (AUC Press, 1999)
33. Nicholas Hamilton and Meredith Hutchinson, 'The contested road to Khufu: Why the proposed new road wouldn't solve any of the problems it claims to', Cairo from Below (16 January 2012): http://cairofrombelow.org/2012/01/16/the-contested-road-to-khufu-why-the-proposed-newroad-wouldnt-solve-any-of-the-problems-it-claims-to/
34. ' "We are not dirt": Forced Evictions in Egypt's Informal Settlements', Amnesty International (2011)

35. Ursula Lindsey, 'Neglected, mismanaged Cairo is also resourceful and forbearing', *The National* (6 May 2011)

36. Saul Kelly, *The Hunt for Zerzura: The Lost Oasis and the Desert War* (John Murray, 2002), pp. 12–13

37. With thanks to Professor John Baines, Oxford University, and Cassandra Vivian, who writes in more detail on this subject in *The Western Desert of Egypt: An Explorer's Handbook* (AUC Press, 2008).

38. For more on the feasibility studies, or absence of them, see Emma Deputy, 'Designed to deceive: President Hosni Mubarak's Toshka Project' (MA thesis, University of Texas, 2011)

39. Niveen Wahish, 'Toshka turns millennial green', *Al-Ahram Weekly* (27 August 1998)

40. 'Awards', Abdel-Tawwab Youssef: http://ayoussef.org/award_en.html

41. Deputy, *Designed to Deceive*

42. Andre Fecteau, 'On Toshka New Valley's mega-failure', *Egypt Independent* (26 April 2012)

43. Ibid.

44. Deputy, *Designed to Deceive*

45. Timothy Mitchell, *Rule of Experts: Egypt, Techno-Politics, Modernity* (University of California Press, 2002), pp. 273–4

46. Wahish, 'Toshka turns millennial green'

47. Mitchell, *Rule of Experts*, pp. 273–4

48. Marica Merry Baker, 'Mubarak: Toshka Project opens way toward "new civilization" in Egypt', *Executive Intelligence Review*, Vol. 24, Issue 51 (19 December 1997)

3. 'I LOVE TO SINGA'

1. Video at YouTube: https://www.youtube.com/watch?v=ytR7-wToQqw

2. Mohamed Elshahed, 'Pageantry, Military Myths, and Egypt's "Daddy Complex"', *Jadaliyya* (24 April 2012)

3. Mona El-Ghobashy, 'Egyptian Politics Upended', MER Online (20 August 2012)

4. 'Selmeyyah: Jamal Mahjoub interviews Ahdaf Soueif', *Guernica* (15 March 2011)

5. Alaa Al-Aswany, *On the State of Egypt: What Caused the Revolution* (Canongate, 2011), p. 119

6. For more on Umm Kulthum's legendary status, see Max Rodenbeck, *Cairo: The City Victorious* (AUC Press, 1999), p. 329

7. Tarek Osman, *Egypt on the Brink* (Yale University Press, 2011), p. 8

8. Rod Norland, 'Saudis and the last Egyptian belly dancer', *Newsweek* (31 May 2008); Jack Shenker, 'Egypt: Hyatt and dry – Saudi hotel owner takes the fizz out of Cairo's tourist allure', *Guardian* (21 July 2008)

9. Author interview with Mohamed Elshahed

10. Rodenbeck, *Cairo: The City Victorious,* p. 218

11. Hadeel Al-Shalchi, 'Van Gogh painting stolen from museum in Egypt', Associated Press (22 August 2010)

12. Author interview with Mohamed Elshahed

13. Maria Golia, *Cairo: City of Sand* (Reaktion Books, 2004), p. 126

14. Alexander Dziadosz, 'Bulldozers overhaul Luxor, city of pashas and pharaohs', Reuters (1 April 2010)

15. Caroline Williams in Diane Singerman and Paul Amar (eds.), *Cairo Cosmopolitan: Politics, Culture and Urban Space in the New Globalized Middle East* (AUC Press, 2006), p. 270

16. Nezar AlSayyad, *Cairo: Histories of a City* (Harvard University Press, 2013), p. 278

17. Adel Iskandar, *Egypt in Flux: Essays on an Unfinished Revolution* (AUC Press, 2013), p. 31

18. 'Zahi Hawass Collection', Art Zulu website (page now deleted)

19. Ali Abdel Mohsen, 'Egypt's museums: From Egyptian Museum to "torture chamber"', *Egypt Independent* (20 April 2011)

20. Mohamed Elshahed, 'The case against the Grand Egyptian Museum', *Jadaliyya* (16 July 2011)

21. Jack Shenker, 'Egypt's man from the past who insists he has a future', *Guardian* (19 May 2011)

22. Zeinobia, 'A shameful royal moment', *Egyptian Chronicles* (11 November 2009): http://egyptianchronicles.blogspot.co.uk/2009/11/shameful-royal-moment.html

23. Iskandar, *Egypt in Flux*, p. 80

24. Ibid.

25. It also led to errant conclusions being drawn about youth apathy in Egypt. A 2010 'Survey of Young People in Egypt' reported both civic engagement and political participation on the part of youth to be 'very weak' – a stark contrast to the intensity of youth activism in the run-up to 2011, particularly following the death of Khaled Said. For more, see Mariz Tadros, *IDS Bulletin*, Vol. 43, Issue 1 (January 2012), p. 5

26. Jack Shenker, 'Discontent in Egypt's heart', *Guardian* (2 June 2009)

27. Ibid.

28. Ted Swedenburg in Jeannie Sowers and Chris Toensing (eds.), *The Journey to Tahrir: Revolution, Protest and Social Change in Egypt* (Verso, 2012), p. 285

29. Richard Poplak, 'Heavy metal Cairo', *Daily Maverick* (8 February 2011)

30. John Daniszewski, 'Tales of teen Satanism have Egypt inflamed', *Los Angeles Times* (10 February 1997)

31. Jack Shenker, 'Egypt's emos, the latest hate figures', *Guardian* (6 May 2009)

32. Ibid.

33. Zeinobia, 'Egyptian Emos', *Egyptian Chronicles* (12 March 2009): http://egyptianchronicles.blogspot.com/2009/03/egyptian-emos.html

34. Asef Bayat, *Life as Politics: How Ordinary People Change the Middle East* (Stanford University Press, 2010), p. 154

35. From the film *Children of the Revolution,* directed by May Abdalla and produced by Inigo Gilmore (2012)

36. Jack Shenker and Julian Borger, 'Egypt's day of rumour and expectation ends in anger and confusion', *Guardian* (11 February 2011)

37. Video at YouTube: http://www.youtube.com/watch?v=SgjlgMdsEuk

38. Farha Ghannam, *Live and Die Like a Man: Gender Dynamics in Urban Egypt* (Stanford University Press, 2013), p. 1

39. Norma Claire Moruzzi, 'Gender and the revolutions: Critique interrupted', *Middle East Report,* Issue 268 (Autumn 2013)

40. Melissa Spatz, 'Huda Shaarawi', *Postcolonial Studies @ Emory* (May 2012): https://scholarblogs.emory.edu/postcolonialstudies/2014/06/12/shaarawi-huda/

41. Cynthia Nelson, *Doria Shafik: Egyptian Feminist – A Woman Apart* (AUC Press, 1996)

42. The ideas here are strongly inspired by the writings of Sara Salem, which can be found at the website Neo-colonialism and its Discontents (http://neocolonialthoughts.wordpress.com/). Of particularly relevance is her insightful discussion of sociologist Nadia Fadil's perspectives on Amin – Sara Salem, 'The emergence of the "Muslim woman question" in Egypt', Neo-colonialism and its Discontents (11 June 2013): http://neocolonialthoughts.wordpress.com/2013/06/11/the-emergence-of-the-muslim-woman-question-in-egypt/

43. Leila Ahmed, *Women and Gender in Islam: Historical Roots of a Modern Debate* (Yale University Press, 1992), p. 157

44. Nergis Mazid, 'Western mimicry or cultural hybridity: Deconstructing Qasim Amin's "Colonized Voice"', *The American Journal of Islamic Social Sciences,* Vol. 19, Issue 4 (Autumn 2002)

45. Moruzzi, 'Gender and the revolutions'

46. Mervat Hatem, 'Gender and revolution in Egypt', *Middle East Report,* Issue 261 (Winter 2011)

47. Ghada Abdel Aal, *'Ayiza Atgawwiz* ['I Want to Get Married'] (Shorouk, 2008)

48. Hanan Kholoussy, 'The fiction (and non-fiction) of Egypt's marriage crisis', MER Online (December 2010)

49. Dena Rashed, 'Legally yours', *Al-Ahram Weekly* (1–7 June 2006)

50. Neil Macfarquhar, 'Paternity suit against TV star scandalizes Egyptians', *New York Times* (26 January 2005)

51. Ibid.

52. Jack Shenker, 'Sex and the civil servant', *Guardian* (30 October 2008)

53. Noha El-Hennawy, 'Babylon & Beyond blog', *Los Angeles Times* (10 July 2008)

54. Kholoussy, 'The fiction (and non-fiction) of Egypt's marriage crisis'

55. The use of thugs was particularly prevalent during protests against a constitutional referendum held in May 2005, which opposition activists claimed was a way of giving legal cover to the Mubarak dictatorship. At a rally near Saad Zaghoul, a neighbourhood just south of central Cairo, Human Rights Watch quoted an eyewitness detailing the *baltagiyya* tactics: 'The police would let a bunch of them cross into the Kifaya group, where they would single out one person to pull out to their side, all the while beating that person,' claimed the eyewitness. 'They'd repeat that. It was almost choreographed, someone would say "attack" and then say "stop". It was brutal but it was not chaotic.' – 'Egypt: Calls for reform met with brutality', Human Rights Watch (25 May 2005)

56. Paul Amar, *The Security Archipelago: Human-Security States, Sexuality Politics, and the End of Neoliberalism* (Duke University Press, 2013), p. 308

57. Ibid., p. 309

58. Vickie Langohr, 'This is our square: Fighting sexual assault at Cairo protests', *Middle East Report,* Issue 268 (Autumn 2013). Although Egypt's public prosecutor refused to pursue any legal redress against the assailants, human rights lawyers successfully pushed the case through to the African Commission on Human and People's Rights,

which ruled that Egypt was in violation of international law. The Commission's verdict concluded: 'It is clear that the sexual assaults against the victims ... were acts of gender-based violence perpetrated by state actors, and non-state actors under the control of state actors, that went unpunished. The violations were designed to silence women who were participating in the demonstration and deter their activism in the political affairs of the Respondent State [Egypt] which in turn failed in its inescapable responsibility to take action against the perpetrators.' Full judgement available at: http://eipr.org/ sites/default/files/pressreleases/pdf/text_of_the_afriocan_commission_ decisionenglish.pdf

59. Testimony collected by the el-Nadim Center and cited in Amar, *The Security Archipelago,* p. 309

60. Sandmonkey, 'The Eid sexual harassment incident', *Rantings of a Sandmonkey* (30 October 2006): http://www.sandmonkey.org/2006/ 10/30/the-eid-sexual-harassment-incident/

61. Amar, *The Security Archipelago,* pp. 314–15

62. Khaled Diab, 'Egyptian men behaving badly', *Guardian* (3 September 2008)

63. El-Hennawy, 'Babylon & Beyond blog'

64. Jack Shenker, 'Women in Egypt get hi-tech aid to beat sexual harassment', *Guardian* (19 September 2010); Jack Shenker, 'Tackling sexual harassment in Egypt', *Guardian* (21 September 2010)

65. Sharon Otterman, 'In Cairo, a groping case ends in a prison sentence', *New York Times* (23 October 2008)

66. Amar, *The Security Archipelago,* pp. 312–13

67. Surveys indicate that 83 per cent of Egyptian women have experienced some form of sexual harassment – Magdi Abdelhadi, 'Egypt's sexual harassment "cancer"', *BBC News* (18 July 2008). In 2013, the UN released a report quoting an even higher (and more plausible) figure, suggesting 99.3 per cent of Egyptian women have experienced harassment – Basil El-Dabh, '99.3% of Egyptian women experienced sexual harassment: report', *Daily News Egypt* (28 April 2013)

68. Shenker, 'Tackling sexual harassment in Egypt'

69. Amar, *The Security Archipelago,* p. 319

70. Reem Leila, 'Unsafe streets', *Al-Ahram Weekly* (9–15 October 2008)

71. Ursula Lindsey, 'Veil your lollipop', *The Arabist* (25 June 2008): http:// arabist.net/blog/2008/6/25/veil-your-lollipop.html

72. Al-Aswany, *On the State of Egypt,* p. 73

4. THE COLONEL'S REVENGE

1. Charles Royle, *The Egyptian Campaigns 1882–1899* (Hurst and Blackett, 1900), p. 69
2. Sean Lyngaas, 'Ahmad Urabi: Delegate of the people – social mobilization in Egypt on the eve of colonial rule', *Al Nakhlah* (The Fletcher School Online Journal for issues related to Southwest Asia and Islamic Civilization) (Spring 2011)
3. Royle, *The Egyptian Campaigns,* p. 109
4. Ibid., p. 111
5. Ibid., p. 108
6. With thanks to Khaled Fahmi
7. 'Records of the strike in Egypt under Ramses III, *c.* 1155 BC', *Libcom* (26 February 2007)
8. Zachary Lockman, 'British policy toward Egyptian labour activism', *International Journal of Middle East Studies,* Vol. 20, Issue 3 (August 1998), p. 267
9. Zachary Lockman, (ed.) *Workers and Working Classes in the Middle East: Struggles, Histories, Historiographies* (SUNY Press, 1994), p. 89
10. Cited by John Chalcraft, *The Striking Cabbies of Cairo and Other Stories: Crafts and Guilds in Egypt, 1863–1914* (SUNY Press, 2004), pp. 175–6
11. Joel Beinin, 'Labor, capital and the state in Nasserist Egypt, 1952–61', *International Journal of Middle East Studies,* Vol. 21, Issue 1 (February 1989), cited in Anne Alexander and Mostafa Bassiouny, *Bread, Freedom, Social Justice* (Zed Books, 2014), p. 44
12. Joel Beinin in Rabab El-Mahdi and Philip Marfleet (eds.), *Egypt: Moment of Change* (AUC Press, 2009), pp. 68–9
13. Egyptian workers also deployed a range of mechanisms to wage 'quiet resistance' from inside the factory floor. For more, see Samer S. Shehata, *Shop Floor Culture and Politics in Egypt* (AUC Press, 2010)
14. Beinin in *Egypt: Moment of Change,* pp. 70–71
15. Ibid., p. 72
16. 'Egyptians cancel food-price rise after riots In an industrial town', *New York Times* (2 October 1994)
17. Rabab El-Mahdi, 'Labour protests in Egypt: Causes and meanings', *Review of African Political Economy,* Vol. 38, Issue 129 (2011), pp. 390–11
18. Alexander and Bassiouny, *Bread, Freedom, Social Justice,* p. 76

19. Ibid., p. 82
20. Ibid., p. 85
21. Ibid.
22. El-Mahdi, 'Labour protests in Egypt,' p. 396
23. Ibid., p. 397
24. Joe Stork, 'Egypt's factory privatization campaign turns deadly', *Middle East Report,* Issue 192 (January–February 1995)
25. From the film *The Factory,* directed by Cristina Bocchialini and Ayman El Gazwy (2012)
26. Ibid.
27. Ibid.
28. Khaled Ali in *IDS Bulletin,* Vol. 43, Issue 1 (January 2012), p. 18
29. Fazia Rady, 'Twice as dead', *Al-Ahram Weekly* (7–13 July 2005)
30. Beinin in *Egypt: Moment of Change,* pp. 79–80
31. Alexander and Bassiouny, *Bread, Freedom, Social Justice,* p. 119
32. Posted by Karim al-Buhayri, founder of the most popular Egyptian labour protests blog, *Egyworkers* (http://egyworkers.blogspot.co.uk/), and cited by Beinin in *Egypt: Moment of Change,* p. 84
33. Beinin in *Egypt: Moment of Change,* p. 84
34. Adam Hanieh, *Lineages of Revolt: Issues of Contemporary Capitalism in the Middle East* (Haymarket Books, 2013), p. 58
35. In 2004, the World Bank called upon Egypt (along with Tunisia and Morocco) to 'lower labour costs, increase productivity, and improve access to cheap inputs' to boost the textile industry's competitiveness, even though labour costs in the sector, inclusive of all social security, were already as low or even lower as they were in Egypt's Asian 'rivals' – ibid., pp. 58–60
36. Ibid., p. 60
37. Ali in *IDS Bulletin,* p. 19
38. Beinin in *Egypt: Moment of Change,* p. 83
39. Joel Beinin, quoted in Jack Shenker, 'Egypt's state circus joins growing unrest', *Guardian* (18 April 2009)
40. Ali in *IDS Bulletin,* p. 19
41. Alexander and Bassiouny, *Bread, Freedom, Social Justice,* p. 115
42. Hossam el-Hamalawy, 'Ghazl Shebeen, Kafr el-Dawwar strikes ... VICTORY!', 3arabawy (10 February 2007): http://arabawy.org/585/
43. Mostafa Bassiouny and Omar Said, 'A new workers' movement: The strike wave of 2007', *International Socialism,* Issue 118 (March 2008)
44. Alexander and Bassiouny, *Bread, Freedom, Social Justice,* p. 116

45. El-Mahdi, 'Labour protests in Egypt', p. 398
46. Jack Shenker, 'Egypt's state circus joins growing unrest'
47. Ibid.
48. Gamal Amin, *Whatever Else Happened to the Egyptians?* (AUC Press, 2004), pp. 146–7
49. Ibid., p. 149
50. Ibid., p. 150
51. Jean Lachapelle, 'Lessons from Egypt's tax collectors', *Middle East Report,* Issue 264 (Autumn 2012)
52. For more on the property tax collectors' strike, see Alexander and Bassiouny, *Bread, Freedom, Social Justice,* pp. 161–72
53. Ibid., p. 164
54. Ibid., p. 165
55. Ibid., p. 167
56. Kamal Abu Eita, quoted in ibid., p. 167
57. Alexander and Bassiouny, *Bread, Freedom, Social Justice,* p. 120
58. Bocchialini and el-Gazwy, *The Factory*
59. Lesley Wroughton, 'Egypt finance minister wins key IMF policy post', Reuters (6 October 2008)

5. 'WHO TOLD YOU WE WERE WEAK?'

1. The original recipe is set out in a medieval Andalusian cookbook, and available online: http://www.medievalcookery.com/search/display. html?anony:445:SPKNRT
2. Jennifer Bell in Diane Singerman (ed.), *Cairo Contested: Governance, Urban Space and Global Modernity* (AUC Press, 2009, p. 360
3. Ibid.
4. The land ownership claims are complicated by the fact that much of Qursaya's landmass has been created by residents themselves; in Mohamed Abla's words, 'there are few documents because the land didn't exist before.' Despite this, the right of residents to remain on Qursaya has been repeatedly confirmed by the courts. Officially Qursaya is designated a 'natural protectorate' under a long-standing prime ministerial decree, which acknowledges the agricultural activities taking place on the island. In addition a ruling from the Court of Administrative Justice in 2008 stated that the government was obliged to 'renew residents' leases on the island and uphold the usufruct rights of the island residents, as they have a legal right to live on the island and farm it' – a decision reconfirmed by the Supreme Administrative

Court in 2010. More details at 'Against the backdrop of a land dispute on Qursaya Island . . .', EIPR (25 November 2012): http://eipr.org/en/pressrelease/2012/11/25/1551

5. Jonathan Wright, 'Egyptian army weighs in on disputed Nile island', Reuters (12 December 2007)

6. 'Egypt: State of the Environment Report 2008', *Egyptian Environmental Affairs Agency* (September 2009)

7. Jack Shenker, 'Nile Delta: "We are going underwater. The sea will conquer our lands"', *Guardian* (21 August 2009)

8. Ibid.

9. Ibid.

10. Ibid.

11. Bell in *Cairo Contested*, pp. 354–9

12. Hoda Baraka, 'Egypt's lakes: "a truly tragic environmental tale"', *Egypt Independent* (11 February 2012)

13. Shenker, 'Nile Delta: "We are going underwater. The sea will conquer our lands"'

14. 'Sectoral Survey 2: The Production and Processing of Egyptian Livestock, Poultry and Fish Products', USAID Report (1982)

15. 'RDI Policy Brief Issue 19 – Fisheries Development in Egypt: Policy Barriers and Recommendations', USAID Report (October 1999)

16. Ray Bush and Amal Sabri in Jeannie Sowers and Chris Toensing (eds.), *The Journey to Tahrir: Revolution, Protest and Social Change in Egypt* (Verso, 2012), p. 246

17. Matt Bradley, 'How Somali pirates became Egyptian fishermen's catch of the day', *The National* (27 August 2009)

18. Adam Hanieh, *Lineages of Revolt: Issues of Contemporary Capitalism in the Middle East* (Haymarket Books, 2013), p. 68

19. Khaled Ali in *IDS Bulletin*, Vol. 43, Issue 1 (January 2012), p. 21

20. Ibid.

21. Ibid.

22. Philip Marfleet in Rabab El-Mahdi and Philip Marfleet (eds.), *Egypt: Moment of Change* (AUC Press, 2009), p. 17

23. This tale comes from the late fourteenth century Sunni cleric and historian al-Maqrizi, as recounted by Max Rodenbeck, *Cairo: The City Victorious* (AUC Press, 1999), pp. 79–80

6. ENOUGH

1. Interview with Hossam El-Hamalawy
2. Ibid.
3. The committee raised the equivalent of $400,000 in donations, and collected a remarkable 100,000 signatures on a petition calling on Mubarak's regime to sever diplomatic ties with Israel – Rabab El-Mahdi in Rabab El-Mahdi and Philip Marfleet (eds.), *Egypt: Moment of Change* (AUC Press, 2009), p. 94
4. Ibid., p. 95
5. Manar Shourbagy, 'The Egyptian movement for change – Kefaya: redefining politics in Egypt', *Public Culture*, Vol. 19, Issue 1 (Winter 2007)
6. Maha Abdelrahman, *Egypt's Long Revolution: Protest Movements and Uprisings* (Routledge, 2014), p. 38
7. El-Mahdi in *Egypt: Moment of Change*, p. 90
8. 'Downtown showdown', *Al-Ahram Weekly* (4–10 August 2005)
9. 'President Bush, Egyptian President Mubarak meet with reporters', The White House (President George W. Bush Archives) (12 April 2004)
10. Martin Asser, 'Mubarak's quarter of a century', *BBC News* (13 October 2006)
11. Baheyya, 'Debunking the myth that won't die', *Baheyya: Egypt Analysis and Whimsy* (9 June 2005): http://baheyya.blogspot.co.uk/2005/06/debunking-myth-that-wont-die.html
12. 'Egypt café owner describes police beating death', *Gulf News* (13 June 2010)
13. Alaa Al-Aswany, *On the State of Egypt: What Caused the Revolution* (Canongate, 2011), p. 24
14. Aida Seif El-Dawla in *Egypt: Moment of Change*, pp. 122, 129
15. Amro Ali, 'Saeeds of revolution: De-mythologizing Khaled Saeed', *Jadaliyya* (5 June 2012)
16. Ibid.
17. Emma Deputy, 'Propaganda and popular uprisings: The case of Egypt under Hosni Mubarak' – paper presented at the Middle Eastern Studies Association Annual Meeting (December 2011)
18. Jack Shenker, 'Egypt's discredited elections blighted by shadow of police violence', *Observer* (28 November 2010)
19. Mohsen Abdel Razeq, 'Minister: Egyptians burning themselves won't spark revolution', *Egypt Independent* (19 January 2011)

20. For a fascinating insight into the politics behind rival interpretations of the poem, see Elliott Colla, 'The people want', *Middle East Report*, Issue 263 (Summer 2012) and M. Lynx Qualey, 'The politics of translating al-Shabbi's "If the People Choose to Live One Day"', *Arabic Literature (in English)* (22 January 2011): http://arablit.org/2011/01/22/the-politics-of-translating-al-shabbis-if-the-people-choose-to-live-one-day/

7. 'THE STREETS ARE OURS'

1. Jack Shenker, 'Bloody and bruised: the journalist caught in Egypt unrest', *Guardian* (27 January 2011)
2. Patrick Kingsley, 'How did 37 prisoners come to die at Cairo prison Abu Zaabal?', *Guardian* (22 February 2014)
3. James Glanz and John Markoff, 'Egypt leaders found "off" switch for internet', *New York Times* (15 February 2011)
4. Nezar Al Sayyad, 'A history of Tahrir Square', *Midan Masr*
5. Sara Elkamel, 'Mohamed Abla: on art and change', *Ahram Online* (21 February 2011)
6. Anne Alexander and Mostafa Bassiouny, *Bread, Freedom, Social Justice* (Zed Books, 2014), pp. 197–8
7. Peter Beaumont and Jack Shenker, 'Egypt's protesters refuse to leave the streets until Mubarak steps down', *Guardian* (1 February 2011)
8. Hani Shukrallah, 'A people's history of the Egyptian revolution (1)', *Ahram Online* (4 September 2013)
9. Jack Shenker, 'Egyptian cameraman at the heart of the Tahrir Square clashes', *Guardian* (2 December 2011)
10. Sami Aboudi, 'Saudi king expresses support for Mubarak', Reuters (29 January 2011)
11. Chris McGreal, 'Tony Blair: Mubarak is "immensely courageous and a force for good"', *Guardian* (2 February 2011)
12. Blair claims to have later provided a donation equal to the cost of staying in the villa, paid to an *'unnamed charity'* of Hosni Mubarak's choice – Michael Clarke, 'Blair accused over his family's free Egyptian holiday', *Daily Mail* (5 April 2002)
13. Jack Shenker, 'Egypt protests: government to meet key opposition figures', *Guardian* (5 February 2011)

8. THE OLD WAYS AND THE NEW

1. Rasha Abdulla, 'I'm 18, in prison, pending investigation', *Mada Masr* (16 July 2014)
2. Video at YouTube: https://www.youtube.com/watch?v=F2i8HVnKtls
3. Sarah Carr, 'Informal settlement dwellers evicted, despite housing promises', *Egypt Independent* (31 July 2011)
4. 'Warnings and reassurances for Egyptian protesters in SCAF press conference', *Ahram Online* (12 July 2011)
5. Video at YouTube: https://www.youtube.com/watch?v=EtQsMPk6hiQ
6. Heba Morayef, 'Torture and imprisonment of Egypt protesters still rife, says human rights activist', *Guardian* (20 May 2011)
7. Maha Abdelrahman, *Egypt's Long Revolution: Protest Movements and Uprisings* (Routledge, 2014), p. 82
8. John Chalcraft, 'Horizontalism in the Egyptian revolutionary process', *Middle East Report*, Issue 262 (Spring 2012)
9. Interview with Khaled Fahmy
10. Mona El-Ghobashy, 'Egyptian politics upended', MER Online (20 August 2012)
11. Grif Witte, Mary Beth Sheridan and Karen DeYoung, 'In Egypt, Muslim Brotherhood reverses course, agrees to talks on transition', *Washington Post* (6 February 2011)
12. Abdelrahman, *Egypt's Long Revolution*, pp. 76–9
13. Gilbert Achcar, *The People Want: A Radical Exploration of the Arab Uprising* (Saqi, 2013), p. 255
14. Quoted in ibid., p. 258
15. Video at YouTube: https://www.youtube.com/watch?v=Fr2-VlldcuE
16. Achcar, *The People Want*, pp. 272–4
17. Osman El Sharnoubi, 'Is torture on the rise under President Mohamed Morsi?', *Ahram Online* (21 February 2013)
18. Nawara Negm, 'That's not the way to do things', *Al-Tahrir* (1 February 2013) – English translation published at *The Arabist* (6 April 2013): http://arabist.net/blog/2013/2/6/in-translation-a-president-who-does-not-know-how-to-address.html
19. Baheyya, 'Death knell for an old political style', *Baheyya: Egypt Analysis and Whimsy* (8 December 2012): http://baheyya.blogspot.co.uk/2012/12/death-knell-for-an-old-political-style.html
20. Omar Robert Hamilton, 'Selective memories', Mada Masr (10 July 2013)
21. Jack Shenker, 'Egypt elections: "My vote will make a difference"', *Guardian* (29 November 2011)

22. Lizzy Davies and Jo Adetunji, 'Middle East live', *Guardian* (2 September 2011)

23. Jack Shenker, 'Fury over advert claiming Egypt revolution as Vodafone's', *Guardian* (3 June 2011)

24. Mona El-Ghobashy, 'Politics by other means', *Boston Review* (1 November 2011)

25. Fareed Zakaria, 'A region at war with its history', *Fareed Zakariu* (6 April 2012): http://fareedzakaria.com/2012/04/06/a-region-at-war-with-its-history/

26. Hussein Ibish, 'Was the Arab Spring worth it?', *Foreign Policy* (18 June 2012); Jack Cafferty, 'Was the Arab Spring worth it?', CNN (12 September 2012)

27. Ursula Lindsey, 'In Cairo', *London Review of Books* (15 February 2013)

28. Sameh Naguib, 'Part I: From the end of the revolutionary wave to preparing for a new revolution', Global Revsoc.me (2 July 2014): https://global.revsoc.me/2014/07/part-1-from-the-end-of-the-revolutionary-wave-to-preparing-for-a-new-revolution/

29. Charles Tilly, 'The analysis of a counter-revolution', *History and Theory*, Vol. 3, Issue 1 (1963), pp. 30–58

30. Haifaa G. Khalafallah, 'Taking sides in Egypt's troubled revolution: but which?', *Open Democracy* (8 May 2014)

31. Jack Shenker, 'Beyond the voice of battle', Mada Masr (19 August 2013)

32. Laura Dean, 'Egypt's factions are already twisting Wednesday's massacre', *New Republic* (15 August 2013)

33. 'All According to Plan: The Rab'a Massacre and Mass Killings of Protesters in Egypt, Human Rights Watch (2014)

34. 'Escape from hell – A Rabaa medic's testimony of bloody massacre', Ikhwanweb (16 August 2013)

35. Jack Shenker, 'Beyond the voice of battle', Mada Masr (19 August 2013)

36. Yasmin El-Rifae, 'Dispatches', Cairo, again (17 August 2013): https://cairoagain.wordpress.com/2013/08/17/dispatches/

37. Omar Robert Hamilton, 'Everything was possible', Mada Masr (17 August 2013)

38. Alaa Abdel Fattah, 'A letter from Alaa', *Open Democracy* (24 January 2014)

39. Laura Dean, 'The Cairo diary: days of cold tea and rotting lemons', Lawfare (3 February 2014)

40. ' "The walls of the cell were smeared with blood" – Third Anniversary of Egypt's Uprising Marred by Police Brutality', Amnesty International (4 February 2014)

41. Patrick Kingsley, 'Tony Blair backs Egypt's government and criticises Brotherhood', *Guardian* (30 January 2014)

42. 'Sisi's resignation speech in full', Al Jazeera (26 March 2014)

43. Khaled Fahmy, 'The threat to Egypt's mighty state', *Ahram Online* (25 August 2013)

44. Ibid.

45. Belal Fadl, 'Egypt: The nation of snitches makes a comeback', Mada Masr (9 November 2014)

46. Erin Cunningham and Abigail Hauslohner, 'Egyptian TV airs arrest of Al Jazeera reporters', *Washington Post* (3 February 2014)

47. Erin Cunningham, 'Egypt's latest terror suspect: The popular felt-and-yarn puppet Abla Fahita', *Washington Post* (2 January 2014)

48. 'TV host: 'Police rape case is a ploy to target the interior ministry', Mada Masr (17 January 2015)

49. 'Egypt's military leaders unveil devices they claim can detect and cure Aids', *Guardian* (28 February 2014)

50. Sheila Carapico, 'You can watch the circus from your couch', MER Online (6 May 2014)

51. Anne Alexander and Mostafa Bassiouny, *Bread, Freedom, Social Justice* (Zed Books, 2014), p. 320

52. Video at YouTube: https://www.youtube.com/watch?v=i1BUTwSWZ6c

9. SHEEP MANURE AND CARAMEL

1. Bassem Abo Alabass, ' "I am the noblest businessman on Earth": Egypt's tycoon Abul-Einein', *Ahram Online* (18 July 2012)

2. 'Jobless Egyptian man saved after threatening suicide with son', *Ahram Online* (10 March 2013)

3. Adam Hanieh, *Lineages of Revolt: Issues of Contemporary Capitalism in the Middle East* (Haymarket Books, 2013)

4. From the film *Children of the Revolution*, directed by May Abdalla and produced by Inigo Gilmore (2012)

5. For more on *fi'awi* rhetoric, see Hesham Sallam, 'Striking back at Egyptian workers', *Jadaliyya* (16 June 2011). Sallam's essay on the political use of the term remains one of the most important explications of competing economic narratives surrounding the revolution that I've come across.

6. Examples from Sallam's essay, ibid.

7. Shana Marshall and Joshua Stacher, 'Egypt's generals and transnational capital', *Middle East Report*, Issue 262 (Spring 2012)

8. Source details not provided to protect activist's identity.

9. Kyle Kim, 'Here are the top 10 American corporations profiting from Egypt's military', *Global Post* (16 August 2013)

10. Source details not provided to protect activist's identity.

11. Patrick Werr, 'Egypt's new finance minister Hazem el-Beblawi', Reuters (17 July 2011)

12. 'Transmission,' *Kharafi National Magazine*, Issue 28 (May 2011)

13. Marshall and Stacher, 'Egypt's generals and transnational capital'

14. Ali Abdel Mohsen, 'Thursday's papers', *Egypt Independent* (15 March 2012)

15. 'Rights groups condemn Petrojet worker arrests', *Egypt Independent* (8 June 2011)

16. Sameh Naguib in Rabab El-Mahdi and Philip Marfleet (eds.), *Egypt: Moment of Change* (AUC Press, 2009), p. 108

17. Ibid.

18. Ibid., p. 109

19. Maha Abdelrahman, *Egypt's Long Revolution: Protest Movements and Uprisings* (Routledge, 2014), p. 129

20. Naguib in *Egypt: Moment of Change*, p. 116 and Wael Gamal, 'QIZ: Egyptian jeans under the patronage of the Muslim Brotherhood', *Ahram Online* (19 January 2013)

21. Marwa Awad, 'Egypt Brotherhood businessman: manufacturing is key', Reuters (28 October 2011)

22. 'Jail for former Egyptian trade minister', Al Jazeera (25 June 2011)

23. Lamia Nabil, 'Egyptian government attempts to woo former regime businessmen', *Daily News Egypt* (24 February 2013)

24. David J. Lynch, 'Egypt wants its business tycoons to return', Bloomberg (21 February 2013)

25. 'Hassan Malik organizes international conference to support Egypt's economy through business', Ikhwanweb (27 February 2012)

26. Suzy Hansen, 'The economic vision of Egypt's Muslim Brotherhood millionaires', Bloomberg (19 April 2012)

27. Andrew Torchia, 'Mideast money – rising Arab Islamist parties woo private sector', Reuters (23 November 2011)

28. 'OBG talks to Hassan Malek, founder and chairman, Egyptian Business Development Association', *The Report: Egypt 2012* Oxford Business Group (2012)

29. Sameh Elbarqy, quoted in Hansen, 'The economic vision of Egypt's Muslim Brotherhood millionaires'

30. David D. Kirkpatrick, 'Keeper of Islamic flame rises as Egypt's new decisive voice', *New York Times* (12 March 2012)

31. Gilbert Achcar, *The People Want: A Radical Exploration of the Arab Uprising* (Saqi, 2013), p. 280

32. 'Court orders 3 privatized companies returned to state', *Egypt Independent* (21 September 2011)

33. Marwa Hussein, 'Pining for the public sector: Egypt workers tell of privatisation woes', *Ahram Online* (6 October 2011)

34. In 2004, the Brotherhood stated that QIZs were a disaster for Egypt, claiming they failed to create meaningful new jobs, boost exports or protect the domestic textiles sector from collapse (all arguments that had been made by the regime in defence of QIZs). Overall, concluded the Brotherhood, QIZs constituted 'a serious threat to national security' because they represented 'the first economic and industrial agreement with the Zionist enemy'. Subsequent independent reports suggest that the Brotherhood of 2004 was right about the economic flaws of the QIZ model – Gamal, 'QIZ: Egyptian jeans under the patronage of the Muslim Brotherhood'

35. Ahmed A. Namatalla and Abdel Latif Wahba, 'Qandil says Egypt to sell Sukuk after new law is approved', Bloomberg (9 September 2012)

36. Ian Hartshorn, 'Labor unions under attack in Morsi's Egypt', *Muftah* (30 November 2012)

37. 'Egypt: Independent unions, revolutionary activists slam conscription of rail strikers', MENA Solidarity Network (10 April 2013): http://menasolidaritynetwork.com/2013/04/10/egypt-independent-union-federation-condemns-conscriptio/ (statement edited for clarity)

38. Joel Beinin, 'Workers, trade unions and Egypt's political future', *MER Online* (18 January 2013)

39. The forcible enlisting of strikers into the armed forces was a shocking move and prompted a huge backlash, including several solidarity protests and legal complaints. The order was later rescinded under popular pressure. More details can be found in Jano Charbel, 'State backs down on forcing striking train drivers into army', *Egypt Independent* (11 April 2013)

40. Binyamin Appelbaum, 'World Bank and I. M.F. discuss inequality in Middle East', *New York Times* (14 April 2011)

41. 'Deauville partnership with Arab countries in transition', US Department of State (2012)

42. Karen Pfeifer, 'Rebels, reformers and empire', *Middle East Report*, Issue 274 (Spring 2015)

43. 'Omar Effendi: Summary of Proposed Investment', International Finance Corporation (World Bank Group) (2007)

44. Michael Termini, 'Egypt privatization and the sordid tale of World Bank managing director Mahmoud Mohieldin', Government Accountability Project (10 August 2011)

45. 'The great Middle East Beanfeast – How "development" Banks Are Using Public-Private Partnerships to Carve up the Arab Spring Countries' Counter Balance (2013)

46. Borzou Daraghi, 'EFG-Hermes linked to Egypt graft claims', *Financial Times* (30 May 2012)

47. 'The Great Middle East Beanfeast', Counter Balance

48. This funding was sometimes in the form of equity investments, sometimes as financial credit lines – ibid.

49. Ibid.

50. 'Financial Sector Reform Programme (FRSP-1) Egypt – Programme Completion Report', African Development Bank (December 2012) (programme funding details in Annexe 1)

51. 'Egypt: Finance Contracts Signed 2000–2011', European Investment Bank

52. Nicholas Watt and Robert Booth, 'David Cameron's Cairo visit overshadowed by defence tour', *Guardian* (21 February 2011)

53. Nicholas Watt, 'David Cameron arrives in Egypt to meet military rulers', *Guardian* (21 February 2011)

54. 'Remarks by the President on the Middle East and North Africa', The White House (19 May 2011)

55. Nadim Kawach, 'Arab economic reforms to take time', *Emirates 24/7* (19 May 2011)

56. Hernando de Soto, 'The free market secret of the Arab revolutions', *Financial Times* (8 November 2011)

57. Adam Hanieh, 'Egypt's "orderly transition"?', *International Socialist Review*, Issue 78 (July 2011)

58. Video at YouTube: http://www.youtube.com/watch?v=Wd7jR4obhH8

59. Sophia Jones, 'Here's what $230 million in US aid bought Egypt's military since the revolution', *Global Post* (25 November 2013)

60. Charles Levinson, 'Muslim Brotherhood looks West in bid to revive Egyptian economy', *Wall Street Journal* (17 February 2012)

61. David D. Kirkpatrick, 'Keeper of Islamic flame rises as Egypt's new decisive voice', *New York Times* (12 March 2012)

62. Nicholas Timmins and Chris Giles, 'Private finance costs taxpayer £20bn', *Financial Times* (7 August 2011)

63. 'Neoliberal shock therapy kills: The case of Russia and Eastern Europe after 1989', *Progress or Collapse* (26 March 2012)

64. Patrick Hamm, Lawrence P. King and David Stuckler, 'Mass privatization, state capacity, and economic growth in post communist countries', *American Sociological Review*, Issue 77 (April 2012), pp. 295–324

65. Naomi Klein, *The Shock Doctrine: The Rise of Disaster Capitalism* (Penguin, 2008), p. 171

66. 'Who we monitor: European Bank for Reconstruction and Development', Bankwatch

67. Neil Buckley, 'EBRD delivers stark warning to eastern Europe on wealth gap', *Financial Times* (20 November 2013)

68. 'Egypt's Request for Country of Operations Status – Technical Assessment', European Bank for Reconstruction and Development (27 September 2011)

69. 'Egypt: Country Assessment', European Bank for Reconstruction and Development (31 October 2012)

70. 'La FEMIP lance un ambitieux programme d'assistance technique pour favoriser le recours aux PPP dans les pays partenaires méditerranéens', European Investment Bank. (8 February 2011)

71. 'OPIC Factsheet Egypt – OPIC Support for Private Sector Investment in Egypt', OPIC (2011)

72. 'Egypt – agribusiness linkages global development alliance', ACDI/VOCA

73. 'ACDI/VOCA hosts conference on boosting agricultural investment in Upper Egypt', ACDI/VOCA (3 October 2013)

74. Eighty-five per cent of this external debt (as of 2011) was public or publicly guaranteed (i.e. taken on by the Mubarak government). More details at Adam Hanieh, 'Egypt's "orderly transition"?', *International Socialist Review*, Issue 78 (July 2011)

75. 'Life and Debt: Global Studies of Debt and Resistance – Case Study Four: Egypt', Jubilee Debt Campaign (October 2013)

76. Hanieh, 'Egypt's "orderly transition"?'

77. Hadley Gamble, 'Egypt's foreign minister: Invest, invest, invest!' CNBC (9 December 2013)

78. Mohammed Mossallem, 'The Illusion Dispelled: Egypt's Economic Crisis', EIPR (2013)

79. 'Gov't celebrates completion of Suez Canal popular funding scheme', Mada Masr (17 September 2014)

80. Video at YouTube: http://www.youtube.com/watch?v=KJIW4LX8Tus

81. Video at YouTube: http://www.youtube.com/watch?v=iMDjl9a4rUc

82. Ahmed Feteha and Bassem Abo Alabass, 'Mubarak-linked CEO banned from travel after ceramics workers stage demo', *Ahram Online* (6 July 2012)

83. 'Egypt security forces teargas Cleopatra Ceramics labour protest in Suez', *Ahram Online* (17 July 2012)

84. Video at YouTube: https://www.youtube.com/watch?v=iMDji9a4rUc

85. Joel Beinin, 'Workers, trade unions and Egypt's political future', *MER Online* (18 January 2013)

86. Ahmed Aboulenein, 'Labour strikes and protests double under Morsi', *Daily News Egypt* (28 April 2013)

87. 'Annual Report Brief on Labor Movement in Egypt', El-Mahrousa Center for Socioeconomic Development (2014)

88. 'Cairo metro workers suspend strike following victory', *Ahram Online* (14 November 2012)

89. Video at YouTube: https://www.youtube.com/watch?v=XX15KZJ-3WE For more on the Torah factory strike, see Yassin Gaber, 'The spirit of Tahrir lives on in Egypt's factories', *Ahram Online* (26 February 2011)

90. Video at YouTube: http://www.youtube.com/watch?v=txhyJMdAxBI

91. Video at YouTube: http://www.youtube.com/watch?v=vMShsRIKBTQ

92. Jano Charbel, 'Egyptian experiments in workers' self-management', *she212*: http://she212.blogspot.co.uk/2009/08/egyptian-experiments-in-workers-self.html

93. 'Egypt: Workers from Kouta Steel send solidarity to Greece', MENA Solidarity Network (20 February 2013): http://menasolidaritynetwork.com/2013/02/20/egypt-workers-from-kouta-steel-send-solidarity-to-greece/

94. Anne Alexander, 'The growing social soul of Egypt's democratic revolution', *International Socialism*, Issue 131 (June 2011). With thanks to Anne for writing about Manshiyet el-Bakri Hospital and bringing the story to my attention.

95. Interview with Abdel Abou Ela

96. Joel Beinin, 'Egyptian workers after June 30', *MER Online* (23 August 2013)

97. 'Egypt: Trade union rights campaigners condemn police torture of workers', MENA Solidarity Network (17 September 2014): http://menasolidaritynetwork.com/2014/09/24/egypt-trade-union-rights-campaigners-condemn-police-torture-of-workers

98. Tom Dale, 'What a Sisi presidency in Egypt would look like', *Global Post* (26 March 2014)

99. Rana Allam, ' "Catastrophic" it is!', *Daily News Egypt* (5 July 2014)

100. Edmund Bower, 'Egypt's billionaires 80% richer than before the revolution', Mada Masr (5 May 2015)

101. Ibid.

102. Dale, 'What a Sisi presidency in Egypt would look like'

103. 'Egypt draft law bars third-party challenges to contracts – source', Reuters (24 February 2014); Miriam Ross, 'TTIP is an affront to democracy', *New Internationalist* (11 July 2014)

104. Tom Rollins and Does Vandousselaere, 'New investment law leaves the door wide open for corruption', Mada Masr (22 March 2014)

105. 'What was pledged at Egypt's investment conference?', EgyptSource – Atlantic Council (16 March 2015)

106. 'ECESR: Foreign direct investment alone won't cure Egypt's economic woes', Mada Masr (22 February 2015)

107. Ben Flanagan, 'Egypt close to revealing plan for its "new" New Cairo capital', *The National* (25 February 2015)

108. Patrick Kingsley and Manu Abdo, 'Thousands of Egyptians evicted without compensation for Suez project', *Guardian* (3 September 2014); Isabel Esterman, 'A reality check on the New Suez Canal', Mada Masr (3 August 2015)

109. Hanieh, *Lineages of Revolt*, pp. 138–9

110. Abigail Hauslohner, 'Egypt's military expands its control of the country's economy', *Washington Post* (16 March 2014)

111. 'Armed Forces to donate LE1 bn to Sisi's fundraising drive', Mada Masr (26 June 2014)

112. 'New military company established with wide mandate', Mada Masr (23 May 2015)

113. Mian Ridge, 'Egypt's al-Sisi: So far so good, say economists', *Financial Times* (16 September 2014)

114. 'Egypt: Steadfast reforms key for economic stability, jobs, growth', *IMF Survey Magazine* (11 February 2015)

115. Patrick Kingsley, 'Egyptian army runs Cairo buses amid ongoing strikes', *Guardian* (27 February 2014)

116. 'Egypt: "Do not let the army fool you" – independent union leader speaks out', MENA Solidarity Network (26 July 2013): http://menasolidarity network.com/2013/07/26/egypt-do-not-let-the-army-fool-you-independent-union-leader-speaks-out/

10. 'NOW WE MAKE OUR DREAMS
REAL IN THE DAYTIME'

1. Mohamed M. Megahed, 'Feasibility of nuclear power and desalination on El-Dabaa site', *Desalination*, Vol. 246, Issue 2 (September 2009), pp. 238–56
2. Jeff Hecht, 'Mediterranean's "horror" tsunami may strike again', *New Scientist* (15 March 2008)
3. 'Prosecution reviews charges against Mubarak of burying nuclear waste', *Ahram Online* (10 November 2012)
4. 'Parliament committee says armed forces responsible for securing Dabaa nuclear site', *Egypt Independent* (21 February 2012)
5. 'Nuclear power authority warns against encroachment on Dabaa site', *Egypt Independent* (30 July 2012)
6. Jano Charbel, 'Egypt's nuclear dream, or nuclear nightmare?', *Egypt Independent* (15 July 2012)
7. 'Dabaa nuclear project awaits Parliament', *Egypt Independent* (13 January 2013)
8. '3,000 Bedouins attack Egyptian reactor site', *World Tribune* (17 February 2012)
9. Charbel, 'Egypt's nuclear dream, or nuclear nightmare?'
10. Megan Detrie, 'In Dabaa, the fight to halt nuclear power continues', *Egypt Independent* (20 November 2012)
11. Tamsin Carlisle, 'Agrium stays the course in Egypt', *The National* (2 October 2008); Sherif Elmusa and Jeannie Sowers, 'Damietta mobilizes for its environment', MER Online (21 October 2009)
12. Zeinobia, 'Damietta crisis: More than the eye can see !! "2" ', *Egyptian Chronicles* (14 November 2011): http://egyptianchronicles.blogspot.co.uk/2011/11/damietta-crisis-more-than-eye-can-see-2.html
13. Interviews conducted in Damietta
14. Clayton Fisher, 'Egypt's lost power', Al-Jazeera English (2014)
15. Nadine Ibrahim, 'New Giza power plant threatens Abu Ghaleb farming village', *Egypt Independent* (21 November 2012)
16. Louise Sarant, 'Egypt's biggest refinery about to get bigger', Mada Masr (25 July 2013)
17. Mika Minio-Paluello, 'Winning against the odds – How an Egyptian community stopped BP in its tracks', *Platform* (25 June 2013)
18. Steven Viney, 'Is fracking responsible for the flooding of an Upper Egyptian village?', *Egypt Independent* (29 January 2013)

19. Dina Zayed and Jeannie Sowers, 'The campaign against coal in Egypt', *Middle East Report*, Issue 271 (Summer 2014)

20. 'Cabinet approves draft law aimed at opening electricity sector', Mada Masr (18 February 2015); 'Petroleum ministry moves to liberalize gas sector', Mada Masr (25 February 2015); 'Egypt reaches deal to rent second gas import terminal', Mada Mars (3 August 2015)

21. Abulkasim al-Jaberi, 'Once again, Qursaya residents fight for their land', *Egypt Independent* (19 November 2011)

22. Nada El-Kouny, 'Egyptian Delta village declares "Independence" after decades of neglect', *Ahram Online* (1 October 2012)

23. Video at YouTube: https://www.youtube.com/watch?v=O8pZUznaLrc

24. Ahmed Morsy, 'Breakaway town folks', *Al-Ahram Weekly* (4–10 October 2012)

25. Isabel Esterman, 'Putin visit awakens nuclear energy ambitions', Mada Masr (9 March 2015)

26. Nada Arafat, 'Stolen waters, stolen livelihoods', Mada Masr (18 March 2015)

11. WRITING WALLS

1. Okka and Ortega (also known as '8%') – lyrics quoted in *Electro Chaabi*, the film directed by Hind Meddeb (2013)

2. DJ Figo – lyrics quoted in *Electro Chaabi*

3. Okka, Ortega and Weza – lyrics quoted in *Electro Chaabi*

4. DJ Figo and Alaa Fifty – lyrics quoted in *Electro Chaabi*

5. Samia Mehrez, *Egypt's Culture Wars: Politics and Practice* (AUC Press, 2010), p. 73

6. Richard N. Verdery, 'The publications of the Bulaq Press under Muhammad 'Ali of Egypt', *Journal of the American Oriental Society*, Vol. 91, Issue 1 (1971)

7. Mehrez, *Egypt's Culture Wars*, p. 124

8. Ibid., p. 6

9. Rania Khallad, 'Change, not reform', *Al-Ahram Weekly* (11–17 August 2005)

10. Sabry Hafez, 'The new Egyptian novel', *New Left Review*, Issue 64 (July–August 2010)

11. Dalia Chams, 'Writing to escape the chaos', *Passages – The Cultural Magazine of Pro Helvetia*, Vol. 58, Issue 1 (2012)

12. Ahdaf Soueif, 'In times of crisis, fiction has to take a back seat', *Guardian* (17 August 2012)

13. Elliot Colla, 'Revolution bookshelf: Blacklist', *Jadaliyya* (12 August 2013)
14. Elliot Colla, 'Revolution bookshelf: Revolution is my name', *Jadaliyya* (3 July 2013)
15. Ibid.
16. Charles Tripp, *The Power and the People: Paths of Resistance in the Middle East* (CUP, 2013)
17. Bruce Ferguson, 'Art of protest', *News – AUC* (3 October 2012)
18. Interview with Samia Mehrez
19. Nina Grønlykke Mollerup and Sherief Gaber, *Making Media Public: On Revolutionary Street Screenings in Egypt* (2015)
20. Andeel, 'You just got mahraganed', Mada Masr (22 September 2013)
21. Mona Prince, 'Freedom, freedom, come, embrace us', *Cairo Review of Global Affairs*, Issue 6 (Summer 2012)
22. Quoted in *Electro Chaabi*
23. Jace Clayton, 'Cairo: Something new', *The Fader*, Issue 82 (October 2012)
24. Quoted in *Electro Chaabi*
25. Andeel, 'You just got mahraganed'
26. Part of the 'Coloring Thru Corruption' project. For more details see Thoraia Abou Bakr, 'Operation-ColoringThruCorruption', *Daily News Egypt* (21 February 2013)
27. Jack Shenker, 'Egypt's uprising brings DIY spirit out on to the streets', *Guardian* (19 May 2011)
28. Andeel, ' "Take it" back please, Ramy Essam' Mada Masr (8 February 2015)
29. Ursula Lindsey, 'Art in Egypt's revolutionary square', *MER Online* (January 2012)
30. Ashraf El-Sherif, 'The ultras' politics of fun confront tyranny', *Egypt Independent* (3 February 2012)
31. Ilka Eickhof, 'Graffiti, capital and deciding what's inappropriate', Mada Masr (7 April 2015)
32. Ahmed El Shamsy, 'Sisi, Nasser, & the great Egyptian novel', *Muftah* (15 October 2013)
33. Elliot Colla, 'Revolution on ice', *Jadaliyya* (6 January 2014)
34. 'Sisi asks media to focus on dangers to national security', Mada Masr (10 August 2014)
35. 'Egypt chief editors pledge support for state institutions', *Ahram Online* (26 October 2014)

36. Nour Youssef, 'How Egyptian media has become a mouthpiece for the military state', *Guardian* (25 June 2015)
37. 'Syria, Iraq, Egypt most deadly nations for journalists', Committee to Protect Journalists (30 December 2013)
38. Andy Young, 'The writing on the wall: Graffiti, poetry, and protest in Egypt', *Los Angeles Review of Books* (3 March 2013)
39. Khaled Fahmy, 'The production of knowledge', *Egypt Independent* (6 March 2012)
40. Judy Barsalou, 'Recalling the past: The battle over history, collective memory and memorialization in Egypt', *Jadaliyya* (22 June 2012)
41. Interview with Mohamed ElShahed
42. 'Egypt: Video shows police shot woman at protest', Human Rights Watch (1 February 2015)
43. Lucy Thornton and Anthony Bond, 'Shaima al-Sabbagh: Heartbreaking picture shows moments of panic after leading Egyptian female protester dies after being "shot by police" ', *Daily Mirror* (25 January 2015)
44. David D. Kirkpatrick, 'Egyptian official says protester, Shaimaa el-Sabbagh, died in shooting because she was too thin', *New York Times* (22 March 2015)

12. BODY PAINT

1. Amira Elmasry, 'The state's moral authority', Mada Masr (13 April 2015)
2. Quote from the National Center for Pedagogic and Developmental Research, which is affiliated to the ministry of education.
3. 'Statement of HE Ambassador Amr Abul Atta, Permanent Representative of the Arab Republic of Egypt, to the United Nations in New York before the General Assembly Plenary meeting in Observance of the Twentieth Anniversary of the International Year of the Family', Egyptian Ministry of Foreign Affairs (3 December 2014)
4. Ibrahim El-Houdaiby, 'Islamism now', *Cairo Review of Global Affairs*, Issue 6 (Summer 2012)
5. Dalia Rabie, 'Dostour stumbles on its path to democracy', *Egypt Independent* (11 April 2013)
6. The precise number of Copts in Egypt is highly disputed, and official records vary. For more on the debate, see Abdel Rahman Youssef, 'Egyptian Copts: It's all in the number', *Al-Akhbar English* (30 September 2012)

7. Paul Sedra, 'Reconstituting the Coptic community amidst revolution', *Middle East Report*, Issue 265 (Winter 2012)

8. Mariz Tadros, *Copts at the Crossroads* (AUC Press, 2013), p. 13

9. Jack Shenker, 'Egypt's Coptic Christians struggle against institutionalised prejudice', *Guardian* (23 December 2012)

10. Azer, 'The prior Coptic revolution'

11. Sherif Azer, 'The prior Coptic revolution', Mada Masr (7 January 2015)

12. Yasmine Fathi, 'Egypt's Mina Danial: The untold story of a revolutionary', *Ahram Online* (9 October 2012)

13. Sherief Gaber, 'Maspero and memory', Mada Masr (9 October 2013)

14. Wael Eskander, 'No apologies, simply blindness', *Notes from the Underground* (24 March 2014): http://blog.notesfromtheunderground.net/2014/03/no-apologies-simply-blindness.html

15. Joseph Fahim, 'Egypt's Copts may soon regret supporting Sisi', *Al-Monitor* (4 July 2014)

16. Mariz Tadros, 'Copts under Mursi', *Middle East Report*, Issue 267 (Summer 2013)

17. Sarah Carr, 'none of your business', *Egypt Independent* (16 April 2013)

18. Samira Ibrahim's sexual assault by army officers, referred to by the military as a 'virginity test', was a deeply traumatizing experience and one that she understandably finds it very difficult to retell. When we arranged to meet, I agreed not to ask her about the specifics of her experience in the military prison; instead she asked me to take quotes regarding the 'virginity test' from her only public interview that goes into graphic detail on the subject. It is a video recorded by *Tahrir Diaries* and available online at YouTube (https://www.youtube.com/watch?v=c29CAXR14Is). Ibrahim's testimony regarding the military prison is taken from the video; all other quotes are from our meeting in January 2014.

19. 'Egypt: Military pledges to stop forced 'virginity tests', Amnesty International (27 June 2011)

20. 'Egypt: Abdul Fattah al-Sisi profile', *BBC News* (16 May 2014)

21. Khaled Fahmy, 'Samira's honor, the army's shame', *Egypt Independent* (23 March 2012)

22. Mai Shams El-Din, 'Activists testify in virginity tests case, verdict expected March 11', *Daily News Egypt* (26 February 2012)

23. Ethar Shalaby, 'Morsi announces initiative to support women's rights', *Daily News Egypt* (24 March 2013)

24. Iman Ismail, 'Your daughter is a wife of the future – how should you prepare her?!', Ikhwan Online (3 January 2007) – English translation published at mbinenglish (23 April 2013): https://mbinenglish.wordpress.com/2013/04/23/your-daughter-is-a-wife-of-the-future-how-should-you-prepare-her/

25. Yasmine Nagaty, 'Women face same barriers in Morsi's Egypt', Al-Monitor (17 March 2013)

26. Mariz Tadros, 'Mutilating bodies: The Muslim Brotherhood's gift to Egyptian women', Open Democracy (24 May 2012)

27. 'The Supreme Guide: Christians and women are forbidden from being President of the Republic pursuant to jurisprudential preference', Ikhwan Online (6 November 2007) – English translation published at mbinenglish (10 April 2013): https://mbinenglish.wordpress.com/2013/04/10/the-supreme-guide-christians-and-women-are-forbidden-from-being-president-of-the-republic-pursuant-to-jurisprudential-preference/

28. 'Muslim Brotherhood statement denouncing UN women declaration for violating sharia principles', Ihkwanweb (14 March 2013)

29. Bel Trew, 'Unkindest cut: 13-year-old's death shines spotlight on rise of FGM in Egypt', Evening Standard (13 June 2013)

30. Tadros, 'Mutilating bodies'. As Tadros rightly argues, FGM 'is an issue that necessitates vigorous resistance. While it is true that FGM is a hyper-sensitive issue partly because Western feminists' and policy-makers' engagement with the issue in the 1980s and 1990s reeked of Orientalism and racism. It is also true that FGM cannot be privileged as a social justice issue when unemployment, deprivation, poverty, security, political repression are very acute. However, local activists have developed contextually sensitive approaches to eliciting social change and champion an agenda to preserve and protect women's bodily integrity. The FGM issue is one tangible manifestation of the reconfiguration of power relations between men and women, state and society in Egypt.'

31. Mayy El Sheikh and David D. Kirkpatrick, 'Egypt's Everywoman finds her place is in the presidential palace', New York Times (27 June 2012)

32. Zainab Magdy, 'Undressing Um Ahmad: Egyptian women between the bikini and the burquaa', Open Democracy (30 July 2012)

33. 'Women "hit worst" by austerity measures', Poverty and Social Exclusion in the United Kingdom (2012): http://www.poverty.ac.uk/report-gender-tax-benefits-government-cuts-government-policy/women-%E2%80%98hit-worst%E2%80%99-austerity-measures

34. Michael Collins Dunn, 'Anatomy of a hoax and media credulity: The "Egypt Necrophilia Law" story', Middle East Institute (27 April 2012): http://mideasti.blogspot.co.uk/2012/04/anatomy-of-hoax-and-media-credulity.html

35. For a particularly toe-curling example of this, pre-revolution, see Karin Badt, 'Sex with Egyptian women (according to Mike)', *Huffington Post* (19 October 2010). For an excellent critique of Badt's piece, see Sara Salem, 'The orientalizing effects of "Sex with Egyptian women (according to Mike)"', *Muftah* (23 January 2013) and Sarah Carr, 'Gigolow', *Inanities* (14 April 2010): http://inanities.org/2010/04/gigolow/

36. Yasmine Fathi, 'The circle of hell: Inside Tahrir's mob sexual assault epidemic', *Ahram Online* (21 February 2013)

37. Sonia Dridi, 'I was gang raped in Cairo's Tahrir Square', *Australian Women's Weekly* (2 July 2013)

38. 'Testimonies on the recent sexual assaults on Tahrir Square vicinity', Nazra for Feminist Studies (13 June 2012)

39. Vickie Langohr, 'This is our square: Fighting sexual assault at Cairo protests', *Middle East Report*, Issue 268 (Autumn 2013)

40. Ibid.

41. Mariam Kirollos, 'Sexual violence in Egypt: Myths and realities', *Jadaliyya* (16 July 2013)

42. Langohr, 'This is our square: Fighting sexual assault at Cairo protests'

43. Susan Kroll and Marian Smith, 'Women violated in the cradle of Egypt's revolution, activists say', *NBC News* (23 March 2013)

44. Mariz Tadros, 'Politically motivated sexual assault and the law in violent transitions: A case study from Egypt' in Evidence Report No. 8, IDS (June 2013), p. 18

45. Rana Muhammad Taha, 'Shura Council members blame women for harassment', *Daily News Egypt* (11 February 2013)

46. Sarah Carr, 'Sexual assault and the state: A history of violence', Mada Masr (7 July 2014)

47. 'Continued militarization: Increased violence against women human rights defenders during dispersal of cabinet sit-in . . .', Nazra for Feminist Studies (18 December 2011)

48. 'Egypt: Token reforms fail to end scourge of pervasive violence against women', Amnesty International (21 January 2015)

49. Aaron Ross, 'Harassment of women may be getting more violent, but activists are fighting back', *Egypt Independent* (27 September 2012)

50. Langohr, 'This is our square Fighting sexual assault at Cairo protests'. For more on domestic violence, see Diana Eltahawy, 'Egypt: Time to address violence against women in all its forms', Amnesty International (6 June 2013)

51. Wiam El-Tamami, 'To willingly enter the circles, the square', *Jadaliyya* (30 July 2013)

52. Dalia Rabie, 'Five takes on female cops fighting harassment on Cairo's streets', Mada Masr (26 July 2015)

53. Sarah El Masry, 'The proliferation of women initiatives', *Daily News Egypt* (28 November 2012)

54. Bret Stephens, 'Islam's improbable reformer', *Wall Street Journal* (20 March 2015)

55. Rami Galal, 'Egypt's religious book burning backfires', *Al-Monitor* (22 April 2015)

56. Joe Williams, 'Egypt: Gay foreigners can be banned from entry or deported', *Pink News* (15 April 2015)

57. 'Journalists Syndicate chairman calls for reporting journalists inciting against army, police', *Egypt Independent* (2 February 2015)

58. Menan Khater, 'Religious Endowments Ministry to form anti-atheism awareness groups', *Daily News Egypt* (15 April 2015)

59. Maha Abdelrahman, 'Report thy neighbour: Policing Sisi's Egypt', Open Democracy (23 February 2015); 'Surveillance cameras to be installed nationwide', Mada Masr (6 May 2015)

60. J. Lester Feder and Maged Atef, 'Egyptian doctors think this torturous exam can detect "chronic homosexuals"', BuzzFeed (16 February 2015)

61. Ibid.

62. Sarah Carr, 'Of moral panics and state security', Mada Masr (25 November 2013)

63. Bel Trew, 'Egypt's growing gay-rights movement', *Daily Beast* (21 May 2013)

64. Scott Long, 'New arrests for "homosexuality" in Egypt', *A Paper Bird* (14 October 2013): http://paper-bird.net/2013/10/14/new-arrests-for-homosexuality-in-egypt-the-leaden-dream/

65. Scott Long, 'Dozens arrested for "perversion" in a huge raid in Cairo', *A Paper Bird* (8 December 2014): http://paper-bird.net/2014/12/08/dozens-arrested-cairo/

66. Pesha Magid, 'On being transgender in Egypt', Mada Masr (4 June 2015)

67. Heba Afify, 'Lessons in morality from Egyptian media', Mada Masr (16 May 2015)

68. Amr Abdelatty, 'Are Egypt's women really better off under Sisi?', *Al-Monitor* (6 March 2015)
69. Nicola Pratt, 'Gendered paradoxes of Egypt's transition', Open Democracy (2 February 2015)
70. Mervat Hatem, 'Gender and revolution in Egypt', *Middle East Report*, Issue 261 (Winter 2011)
71. Shereen El Feki, 'Is the Egyptian state using sexual torture against women?', *Guardian* (18 May 2015)
72. Dalia Rabie, 'Sisi and his women', Mada Masr (25 May 2014)
73. Fahmy, 'Samira's honor, the army's shame'

EPILOGUE: JOURNEYS

1. Egypt the Future (official website of the Egypt Economic Development Conference): http://www.egyptthefuture.com/
2. Jack Shenker, 'Sharm el-Sheikh rumbles with grand promises of the international elite', *Guardian* (15 March 2015)
3. Allison Corkery and Heba Khalil, 'Nothing new on the Nile', *Foreign Policy* (12 March 2015)
4. Brian Rohan and Sarah El Deeb, 'Egypt basks in world support at investor conference', Associated Press (15 March 2015)
5. Ibid.
6. Elias Groll, 'Egypt to investors: Autocratic government means we're safe for business', *Foreign Policy* (22 January 2015)
7. 'Egypt: Rash of deaths in custody', Human Rights Watch (21 January 2015)
8. Image of blocked webpage available on Twitter feed of Erin Cunningham (@erinncunningham): https://twitter.com/erinmcunningham/status/577025877218877440 (15 March 2015)
9. Shenker, 'Sharm el-Sheikh rumbles with grand promises of the international elite'
10. Well over a thousand death sentences for Islamists have been handed down since July 2013, but some were later commuted to life in prison. For more, see Patrick Kingsley, 'Egypt carries out first death sentence after mass trials of Morsi supporters', *Guardian* (7 March 2015)
11. Information collated from relevant organization websites – Richard Attias & Associates (http://www.richardattiasassociates.com/en/home) and Global Counsel (http://www.global-counsel.co.uk/) – and Jason Lewis, 'Lord Mandelson courted Mubarak's dying regime', Telegraph (17 December 2011)

12. Tamim Elyan, 'Egypt hires Lazard to help project planning for investor summit', Bloomberg (17 November 2014); Seumas Milne, 'Tony Blair to advise Egypt president Sisi on economic reform', *Guardian* (2 July 2014)

13. Jim Pickard, 'Lord Mandelson adds BP to Global Counsel's elite client list', *Financial Times* (13 January 2014)

14. Wil Crisp, 'BP optimistic about Egyptian stability', MEED (14 March 2015)

15. Melanie Newman, 'PR uncovered: Top lobbyists boast of how they influence the PM', The Bureau of Investigative Journalism (5 December 2011)

16. Rachel Oldroyd, 'PCC rejects Bell Pottinger's complaint against Bureau investigation', The Bureau of Investigative Journalism (26 July 2012)

17. Osama Diab, 'Egypt hires PR to revamp its image', *Worldpress* (21 October 2010)

18. Newman, 'PR uncovered: Top lobbyists boast of how they influence the PM'

19. Melanie Newman, 'PR uncovered: Lifting the travel ban on a dictator', The Bureau of Investigative Journalism (5 December 2011); Lord Bell's plan to improve image of dictatorship', Charter 97 (13 December 2012)

20. 'Country Brand Index 2014–15', FutureBrand

21. Melissa Aronczyk, *Branding the Nation: The Global Business of National Identity* (OUP USA, 2013)

22. Video at YouTube: http://www.youtube.com/watch?v=hSsuPBUxn3Y

23. Andeel, 'Egypt is close, and it's got women in it', Mada Masr (2 March 2015)

24. Amro Ali, 'Egypt's long walk to despotism', Tahrir Institute for Middle East Policy (21 January 2015)

25. Ibid.

26. 'Egypt's Sisi says protests not priority under current circumstances', *Ahram Online* (20 January 2015)

27. Examples from the Egyptian ministry of interior's Facebook page (https://www.facebook.com/MoiEgy); '32 small political parties heed Sisi's call for unified electoral list', *Ahram Online* (1 June 2015)

28. Farah Montasser, 'The martyrs obelisk', *Ahram Online* (27 January 2012)

29. Jack Shenker, 'Band of outsiders', *The National* (7 November 2008)

30. Video at YouTube: https://www.youtube.com/watch?v=wh8nwXugNgs; **Details of BP operations on relevant pages of the BP website: BP**

in **Azerbaijan** (http://www.bp.com/en/global/corporate/about-bp/bp-worldwide/bp-in-azerbaijan.html), BP in Algeria (http://www.bp.com/en/global/corporate/about-bp/bp-worldwide/bp-in-algeria.html), **BP in Angola** (http://www.bp.com/en/global/corporate/about-bp/bp-worldwide/bp-in-angola.html); **Mary Carson et al, 'Colombian takes BP to court in UK over alleged complicity in kidnap and torture'**, Guardian (**22 May 2015**)

31. Clayton Swisher, 'Egypt's lost power', Al Jazeera English (2014)
32. Video at You Tube: https://www.youtube.com/watch?v=wh8nwXugNgs
33. Mika Minio-Paluello, 'Winning against the odds – How an Egyptian community stopped BP in its tracks', *Platform* (25 June 2013)
34. Felicity Lawrence and Harry Davies, 'Revealed: BP's close ties with the UK government', *Guardian* (20 May 2015)
35. Georg Menz, 'Neoliberalism, privatisation and the outsourcing of migration management: A five country comparison', *Competition and Change,* Vol. 15, Issue 2 (2011) pp. 116–35
36. War on Want 'G4S: Securing Profits, Globalising Injustice', War on Want (June 2014)
37. Adam Lusher, 'Jimmy Mubenga death: G4S guards "ignored deportee's cries" before he died on airliner', *Independent* (4 November 2014)
38. Matthew Taylor and Robert Booth, 'G4S guards found not guilty of manslaughter of Jimmy Mubenga', *Guardian* (16 December 2014)
39. Robert Booth, 'Jimmy Mubenga: Judge refused to allow jury to hear about guards' racist texts', *Guardian* (17 December 2014)
40. Clare Sambrook, 'Man, 84, dies handcuffed in hospital: UK border control by the GEO Group', Open Democracy (16 January 2014)
41. Eric Allison, 'Man, 84, dies at immigration detention centre', *Guardian* (19 February 2013)
42. Phil Miller, 'Investigating Mitie, the market leader in UK immigration detention', *Guardian* (4 September 2014)
43. '"Care & Custody": Mitie's detention centre contracts', Corporate Watch (1 September 2014)
44. 'Preliminary announcement of results for the year ended 31 March 2015', Mitie Group PLC 'We are Mitie: Annual Report and Accounts 2014', Mitie Group PLC
45. 'Serco surrender flagship detention centre to Mitie', Corporate Watch (12 February 2014)
46. '"It's gonna break": Life in UK's biggest detention centre', Corporate Watch (4 March 2015)

47. Ibid.
48. *'The State of Detention: Immigration Detention in the UK in 2014'* Detention Action (2014)
49. Acromas Holdings Limited is the parent company of Saga, the holidays division of which runs several tours to Egypt – see http://travel. saga.co.uk/destinations/africa/egypt.aspx for more details. CVC, one of the private equity companies that owns Acromas, worked on a bid for the Middle Eastern fast-food franchising operation Americana, currently owned by the Kharafi Group, in 2014 – see David French, 'KKR/CVC pick advisers in race for Kuwait's Americana – sources', Reuters (18 November 2014) for more details. The Kharafi Group makes several mentions of its relationship with the Egyptian military in *Transmission* (Kharafi National Magazine), Issue 28 (May 2011)
50. 'Capita gets contract to find 174,000 illegal immigrants', *BBC News* (18 September 2012)
51. 'Tier 1 (Investor) visa guide', UK Government website
52. 'Capita boss quits over Blair loan', *BBC News* (23 March 2006); 'Serco', NHS For Sale? http://www.nhsforsale.info/private-providers/ private-provider-profiles-2/serco.html
53. 'Public sector outsourcing: The political connections', *Channel 4 News* (29 August 2012); 'Geo Group', Influence Explorer: http:// influenceexplorer.com/organization/geo-group/7dfa33488aad4908ac 1c75336c20db05
54. David Leigh et al, 'Fugitives, aides and bagmen: HSBC's "politically exposed" clients', *Guardian* (12 February 2015)
55. Isabel Esterman, 'Q&A with military expert Robert Springborg on US aid to Egypt', Mada Masr (2 April 2015)
56. Benoît Bréville and Martine Bulard, 'The injustice industry', *Le Monde diplomatique* (June 2014)
57. 'Speeches & Transcripts: World Bank Managing Director Sri Mulyani Indrawati at the Egypt Economic Development Conference', World Bank (13 March 2015)
58. Randa Ali et al, 'Egypt garners pledges of financial and political support on 1st day of Sharm conference', *Ahram Online* (13 March 2015)
59. Adam Hanieh, *Lineages of Revolt: Issues of Contemporary Capitalism in the Middle East* (Haymarket Books, 2013), p. 176
60. Patrick Kingsley, 'A new New Cairo: Egypt plans £30bn purpose-built capital in desert', *Guardian* (16 March 2015)
61. 'Mubarak-era tycoons sponsor canal opening ceremony', Mada Masr (6 August 2015)

62. Jano Charbel, 'What Sisi didn't say about labor conditions in constructing the New Suez Canal', Mada Masr (7 August 2015)

63. Mahmoud Elassal, 'Egyptian footballers vow support for Abou-Treika after asset confiscation', *Ahram Online* (8 May 2015); Patrick Kingsley, 'Egyptian satirist Bassem Youssef winds up TV show due to safety fears', *Guardian* (2 June 2014)

64. 'Former Al-Zamalek player fired over criticism of Al-Sisi', *Daily News Egypt* (4 July 2015)

65. Abdullah al-Sinnawi, 'Normalization with the past', *Al-Shorouk* (6 May 2015) – English translation published at *The Arabist* (13 May 2015): http://arabist.net/blog/2015/5/13/in-translation

66. 'Lawyers call for strike across Egypt's courts to protest police brutality', Mada Masr (4 June 2015)

67. Amira Howeidy, 'Matariyya, Egypt's new theater of dissent', *MER Online* (4 June 2015)

68. Ibid.

69. 'Egypt releases schoolchildren arrested for Morsi protest', *Ahram Online* (1 October 2013); 'Egypt: Schoolboy detained, as supports ex-president: Khaled Mohamed Bakara', Amnesty International (12 December 2013)

70. Richard Spencer, 'Egypt unites against jailing of female "terrorists"', *Telegraph* (2 December 2013)

Acknowledgements

A vast number of people made this book possible. Friends provided inspiration, criticism, time and sanity, without which I would never have had the stamina to complete it. There are far too many to allow me to thank each and every one of them by name, but I hope they all know that I am endlessly grateful for their support. If the book deserves any credit then it is due to them; the missteps and mistakes are all my own.

I owe a particular debt to Amy Horton, to all of my family, to colleagues at the *Guardian* and colleagues in Egypt – especially the journalists and editors of Mada Masr, whose courageous reporting enables the rest of us to do our jobs – as well as to everyone quoted in the book who so generously shared their stories with me. Karim Mehdat Ennarah, Simon Hanna, Ayman Farag, Amira Ahmed, Sarah Sigarny, Elisabeth Jaquette, Ben Du Preez, Josh Rogers, Anne Alexander and Jason Larkin gave me everything, as did the amazing publishing team of Karolina Sutton, Casiana Ionita, Helen Conford and Bela Cunha.

Earlier in the book I mentioned the difficulties of trying to write about revolution (and counter-revolution) when one is wrapped up in the middle of it. Whenever I found that challenge overwhelming and got lost, the people above helped me find a way out.

A final *shukran*: Abdel Abo Ela, Abdel Rahman Hussein, Ahmed Awadalla, Ahmed el-Droubi, Ahmed Ghamrawi, Ahmed Salah, Aida Seif el-Dawla, Amir Matar, Amr Adly, Cressida Trew, H. A. Hellyer, Hady Kamar, Heba Morayef, Hossam Bahgat, Hossam el-Hamalawy, Jano Charbel, Josh Leffler, Khaled Fahmy, Khalid Abdallah, Lina Attalah, Lobna Darwish, Louis Lewarne, Mariam Kirollos, Max

Strasser, Miral al-Tahawy, Mohamed Effat, Mohamed El Dahshan, Mostafa Bassiouny, Mozn Hassan, Omar Robert Hamilton, Osama Diab, Patrick Kingsley, Philip Rizk, Rob Lewis, Salma Said, Sarah Carr, Sarah Hawas, Shereen Zaky, Sherief Gaber, Sherif Abdel Kouddous, Tamer Mowafy, Tarek Shalaby, Timothy Kaldas, Wael Eskander, Yasmine Moataz, Yassin Gaber and Dora.

Index

[Text to come]

INDEX

INDEX

INDEX